T0235619

Lecture Notes in Computer Science 12134

Founding Editors

Gerhard Goos
Karlsruhe Institute of Technology, Karlsruhe, Germany
Juris Hartmanis
Cornell University, Ithaca, NY, USA

Editorial Board Members

Elisa Bertino
Purdue University, West Lafayette, IN, USA
Wen Gao
Peking University, Beijing, China
Bernhard Steffen
TU Dortmund University, Dortmund, Germany
Gerhard Woeginger
RWTH Aachen, Aachen, Germany
Moti Yung
Columbia University, New York, NY, USA

More information about this series at http://www.springer.com/series/7408

Simon Bliudze · Laura Bocchi (Eds.)

Coordination Models and Languages

22nd IFIP WG 6.1 International Conference, COORDINATION 2020
Held as Part of the 15th International Federated Conference
on Distributed Computing Techniques, DisCoTec 2020
Valletta, Malta, June 15–19, 2020
Proceedings

 Springer

Editors
Simon Bliudze (iD)
Project-team SPIRALS
Inria Lille – Nord Europe
Villeneuve d'Ascq, France

Laura Bocchi (iD)
School of Computing
University of Kent
Canterbury, UK

ISSN 0302-9743   ISSN 1611-3349   (electronic)
Lecture Notes in Computer Science
ISBN 978-3-030-50028-3   ISBN 978-3-030-50029-0   (eBook)
https://doi.org/10.1007/978-3-030-50029-0

LNCS Sublibrary: SL2 – Programming and Software Engineering

© IFIP International Federation for Information Processing 2020
This work is subject to copyright. All rights are reserved by the Publisher, whether the whole or part of the material is concerned, specifically the rights of translation, reprinting, reuse of illustrations, recitation, broadcasting, reproduction on microfilms or in any other physical way, and transmission or information storage and retrieval, electronic adaptation, computer software, or by similar or dissimilar methodology now known or hereafter developed.
The use of general descriptive names, registered names, trademarks, service marks, etc. in this publication does not imply, even in the absence of a specific statement, that such names are exempt from the relevant protective laws and regulations and therefore free for general use.
The publisher, the authors and the editors are safe to assume that the advice and information in this book are believed to be true and accurate at the date of publication. Neither the publisher nor the authors or the editors give a warranty, express or implied, with respect to the material contained herein or for any errors or omissions that may have been made. The publisher remains neutral with regard to jurisdictional claims in published maps and institutional affiliations.

This Springer imprint is published by the registered company Springer Nature Switzerland AG
The registered company address is: Gewerbestrasse 11, 6330 Cham, Switzerland

Foreword

The 15th International Federated Conference on Distributed Computing Techniques (DisCoTec 2020) took place during June 15–19, 2020. It was organized by the Department of Computer Science at the University of Malta, but was held online due to the abnormal circumstances worldwide affecting physical travel.

The DisCoTec series is one of the major events sponsored by the International Federation for Information Processing (IFIP). It comprises three conferences:

- The IFIP WG6.1 22nd International Conference on Coordination Models and Languages (COORDINATION 2020)
- The IFIP WG6.1 20th International Conference on Distributed Applications and Interoperable Systems (DAIS 2020)
- The IFIP WG6.1 40th International Conference on Formal Techniques for Distributed Objects, Components and Systems (FORTE 2020)

Together, these conferences cover a broad spectrum of distributed computing subjects, ranging from theoretical foundations and formal description techniques to systems research issues. As is customary, the event also included several plenary sessions in addition to the individual sessions of each conference, that gathered attendants from the three conferences. These included joint invited speaker sessions and a joint session for the best papers from the respective three conferences.

Associated with the federated event, two satellite events took place:

- The 13th International Workshop on Interaction and Concurrency Experience (ICE 2020)
- The First International Workshop on Foundations of Consensus and Distributed Ledgers (FOCODILE 2020)

I would like to thank the Program Committee chairs of the different events for their help and cooperation during the preparation of the conference, and the Steering Committee and Advisory Boards of DisCoTec and their conferences for their guidance and support. The organization of DisCoTec 2020 was only possible thanks to the dedicated work of the Organizing Committee, including Davide Basile and Francisco "Kiko" Fernández Reyes (publicity chairs), Antonis Achilleos, Duncan Paul Attard, and Ornela Dardha (workshop chairs), Lucienne Bugeja (logistics and finances), as well as all the students and colleagues who volunteered their time to help. Finally, I would like to thank IFIP WG6.1 for sponsoring this event, Springer's *Lecture Notes in Computer Science* team for their support and sponsorship, EasyChair for providing the reviewing framework, and the University of Malta for providing the support and infrastructure to host the event.

June 2020   Adrian Francalanza

Preface

This volume contains the papers presented at COORDINATION 2020, the 22nd International Conference on Coordination Models and Languages, organized online by the University of Malta in Valletta during June 15–19, 2020, as part the federated DisCoTec conference.

The COORDINATION conference provides a well-established forum for the growing community of researchers interested in coordination models and languages, architectures, verification, and implementation techniques necessary to cope with the complexity induced by the demands of today's software development. COORDINATION 2020 had two dedicated sessions for special topics: Microservices (in collaboration with the Microservices Community) and Techniques to reason about interacting digital contracts.

For the second year in a row, COORDINATION called for tool papers describing experience reports, technological artefacts, and innovative prototypes, as well as educational tools in the scope of the research topics of the conference. Tool papers were selected according to the combination of an extended abstract and a short video demonstration, after which full papers were produced to be included in these proceedings following a light-weight review. In addition, seeking to further reinforce the practical applicability aspects of the COORDINATION community research, we have explicitly included among the topics of interest the industry-led efforts in coordination and industrial case studies.

The Program Committee of COORDINATION 2020 comprised 27 researchers from 13 countries. We received 21 full paper submissions, 4 short paper submissions, and 5 tool paper submissions. Each paper was evaluated by at least three reviewers and this process was supplemented by an in-depth discussion phase during which the merits of all the papers were considered. The contributions published in this volume were selected according to their quality, originality, clarity, and relevance. The final program comprised 12 full papers, 6 short papers, and 4 tool papers. The program also included two invited tutorials and one invited talk. The invited talk was given by Peter Kriens from aQute and the OSGi Alliance. A short abstract of this talk is included in this volume under the title "Formal Specifications to Increase Understanding."

We are grateful to all authors who have submitted their work, to the members of the Program Committees and their sub-reviewers for their help in evaluating the papers, and to all the participants for their interest in the conference. We would particularly like to express our gratitude to Hugo Torres Vieira and Omar Inverso, the chairs of the Tool Track, to Stephanie Balzer and Anastasia Mavridou, the organizers of the special topic on digital contracts, and Ivan Lanese and Alberto Lluch Lafuente, the organizers of the special topic on microservices. Their strong involvement was a key enabling factor for the preparation of the conference. Furthermore, we wish to thank the Steering Committee of COORDINATION and the Steering Board of DisCoTec for their support.

DisCoTec 2020 – the federated conference whereof COORDINATION is part – took place during the Covid-19 pandemics with many countries having imposed travel restrictions and some of the participants being in lock-down. The decision to maintain the dates and hold the conference online imposed radical changes in the required infrastructure. In the name of all COORDINATION participants, we thank the Organizing Committee chaired by Adrian Francalanza for having quickly and efficiently adapted to the new circumstances and allowing the conference to proceed smoothly despite the inherent difficulties of holding it online. Personal thanks go to Kiko Fernández-Reyes and Davide Basile for their help with the conference publicity and running the website.

Simon Bliudze thanks the Hauts-de-France region for the financial support provided in the framework of the *Soutiens aux Talents de la Recherche Scientifique* program.

Finally, we would like to thank the International Federation for Information Processing (IFIP) WG6.1 for the financial support, to Springer Nature for their sponsorship and personally Anna Kramer for the support during the production phase of the proceedings, EasyChair for the paper collection, reviewing, and proceedings preparation environment, the University of Malta for providing the infrastructure, and the Microservices Community for the additional publicity they provided.

May 2020   Simon Bliudze
                                                                         Laura Bocchi

Organization

Program Committee Chairs

Simon Bliudze   Inria Lille - Nord Europe, France
Laura Bocchi   University of Kent, UK

Steering Committee

Gul Agha   University of Illinois at Urbana Champaign, USA
Farhad Arbab   CWI and Leiden University, The Netherlands
Wolfgang De Meuter   Vrije Universiteit Brussels, Belgium
Rocco De Nicola   IMT - School for Advanced Studies, Italy
Giovanna di   Université de Genève, Switzerland
   Marzo Serugendo
Tom Holvoet   KU Leuven, Belgium
Jean-Marie Jacquet   University of Namur, Belgium
Christine Julien   The University of Texas at Austin, USA
Eva Kühn   Vienna University of Technology, Austria
Alberto Lluch Lafuente   Technical University of Denmark, Denmark
Michele Loreti   University of Camerino, Italy
Mieke Massink   ISTI CNR, Italy
Jose Proença   University of Minho, Portugal
Rosario Pugliese   Università di Firenze, Italy
Hanne Riis Nielson   DTU, Denmark
Marjan Sirjani   Reykjavik University, Iceland
Carolyn Talcott   SRI International, USA
Emilio Tuosto   University of Leicester, UK, and Gran Sasso Science
     Institute, Italy
Vasco T. Vasconcelos   University of Lisbon, Portugal
Mirko Viroli   University of Bologna, Italy
Gianluigi Zavattaro (Chair)   University of Bologna, Italy

Program Committee

Stephanie Balzer   CMU, USA
Chiara Bodei   Università di Pisa, Italy
Marius Bozga   Université Grenoble Alpes, France
Roberto Bruni   Università di Pisa, Italy
Ornela Dardha   University of Glasgow, UK
Fatemeh Ghassemi   University of Tehran, Iran
Roberto Guanciale   KTH, Sweden
Ludovic Henrio   CNRS, France

Omar Inverso	Gran Sasso Science Institute, Italy
Jean-Marie Jacquet	University of Namur, Belgium
Eva Kühn	Vienna University of Technology, Austria
Ivan Lanese	University of Bologna, Italy
Alberto Lluch Lafuente	Technical University of Denmark, Denmark
Michele Loreti	University of Camerino, Italy
Anastasia Mavridou	NASA Ames Research Center, USA
Mieke Massink	ISTI CNR, Italy
Hernán Melgratti	Universidad de Buenos Aires, Argentina
Claudio Antares Mezzina	Università degli Studi di Urbino, Italy
Rumyana Neykova	Brunel University London, UK
Luca Padovani	Università di Torino, Italy
Kirstin Peters	TU Darmstadt, Germany
Danilo Pianini	University of Bologna, Italy
Rene Rydhof Hansen	Aalborg University, Denmark
Gwen Salaün	Université Grenoble Alpes, France
Meng Sun	Peking University, China
Hugo Torres Vieira	C4 - Universidade da Beira Interior, Portugal
Emilio Tuosto	University of Leicester, UK, and Gran Sasso Science Institute, Italy

Tool Track Chairs

| Omar Inverso | Gran Sasso Science Institute, Italy |
| Hugo Torres Vieira | C4 - Universidade da Beira Interior, Portugal |

Special Session Organizers

Microservices:

| Ivan Lanese | University of Bologna, Italy |
| Alberto Lluch Lafuente | Technical University of Denmark, Denmark |

Techniques to reason about interacting digital contracts:

| Stephanie Balzer | CMU, USA |
| Anastasia Mavridou | NASA Ames Research Center, USA |

Additional Reviewers

Giorgio Audrito
Claudia Chirita
Giovanni Ciatto
Stefan Crass
Ankush Das
Gerson Joskowicz
Ajay Krishna
Alexander Kurz
Diego Latella

Yuteng Lu
Stefano Mariani
Agustín Eloy Martinez Suñé
Zeynab Sabahi Kaviani
Larisa Safina
Martina Sengstschmid
Catia Trubiani
Xiyue Zhang

Sponsors

Région
Hauts-de-France

Formal Specifications to Increase Understanding (Invited Talk)

Peter Kriens

aQute and OSGi Alliance
peter.kriens@aqute.biz

Abstract. I've been active in the Alloy (MIT, Daniel Jackson) community for the last few years. Alloy is an interactive formal specification tool using SAT and SMT to find counterexamples. However, despite my enthusiasm, I am also quite frustrated with how the focus is on the least interesting aspects for me: 'proving' the correctness of a specification. It is for me the least interesting because it requires the spec to be correct, which is very hard. However, even harder, it requires the implementation to follow the spec exactly. The people involved in this area seem to leave these all-important aspects as a detail for the practitioners. Instead, they focus on the more and more esoteric things like beating the combinatorial explosion in the proving aspects. I think 'something' like Alloy could be eminently useful if it is used to define the semantics of APIs. Today, we define those semantics in comments or, worse, some external Word document. Formally defining service APIs seems a low hanging fruit that would boost development productivity significantly. As a developer you spend most of your time trying to understand the domain and testing (the tool could generate test case data). Using the service API as an anchor point of such a tool would make it modular, allowing larger specifications that could still be proven. This presentation will explore how such a tool could look like.

Contents

Tutorials

CHOReVOLUTION: Hands-On In-Service Training for Choreography-Based Systems

Marco Autili⬤, Amleto Di Salle⬤, Claudio Pompilio$^{(\boxtimes)}$⬤, and Massimo Tivoli⬤

University of L'Aquila, L'Aquila, Italy
{marco.autili,amleto.disalle,claudio.pompilio,massimo.tivoli}@univaq.it

Abstract. CHOReVOLUTION is a platform for the tool-assisted development and execution of scalable applications that leverage the distributed collaboration of services specified through service choreographies. It offers an Integrated Development and Runtime Environment (IDRE) comprising a wizard-aided development environment, a system monitoring console, and a back-end for managing the deployment and execution of the system on the cloud. In this tutorial paper, we describe the platform and demonstrate its step-by-step application to an industrial use case in the domain of Smart Mobility & Tourism.
(Demo Video: youtu.be/ae2jI9SYsvg)
(GitHub: https://github.com/chorevolution/CHOReVOLUTION-IDRE)

Keywords: Service choreographies · Automated synthesis · Distributed computing · Distributed coordination · Adaptation

1 Introduction

The Future Internet [15] is now a reality that reflects the changing scale of the Internet. The expanding network infrastructure is supporting the today's trend toward the fruitful cooperation of different business domains through the interorganizational composition of a virtually infinite number of software services[1]. This vision is embodied by reuse-based service-oriented systems, in which services play a central role as effective means to achieve interoperability among different parties of a business process, and new systems can be built by reusing and composing existing services.

Service choreographies are a form of decentralized composition that model the external interaction of the participant services by specifying peer-to-peer message exchanges from a global perspective. When third-party (possibly black-box) services are to be composed, obtaining the distributed coordination logic

---

[1] http://www.fiware4industry.com.

© IFIP International Federation for Information Processing 2020
Published by Springer Nature Switzerland AG 2020
S. Bliudze and L. Bocchi (Eds.): COORDINATION 2020, LNCS 12134, pp. 3–19, 2020.
https://doi.org/10.1007/978-3-030-50029-0_1

required to enforce the realizability of the specified choreography is non-trivial and error prone. Automatic support is then needed [1,3].

The CHOReVOLUTION H2020 EU project[2] develops a platform for the generation and execution of scalable distributed applications that leverage the distributed collaboration of services and things by means of service choreographies. In particular, it realizes an Integrated Development and Runtime Environment (IDRE) that comprises a wizard-aided development environment, a system monitoring console, and a back-end for managing the deployment and execution of the system on the cloud.

The CHOReVOLUTION IDRE makes the realization of choreography-based smart applications easier by sparing developers from writing code that goes beyond the realization of the internal business logic related to the provisioning of the single system functionalities, as taken in isolation. That is, the distributed coordination logic, which is needed to realize the global collaboration prescribed by the choreography specification, is automatically synthesized by the IDRE, without requiring any specific attention by developers for what concerns coordination aspects. Furthermore, developers can also more easily reuse existing consumers/providers services. These aspects have been appreciated by the industrial partners in that the approach permits to develop distributed applications according to their daily development practices.

The IDRE is open-source and free software, available under Apache license. The binaries and the source code of version 2.2.0 can be downloaded at the following URL https://github.com/chorevolution/CHOReVOLUTION-IDRE/ releases. Documentation[3] is also available.

The paper is organized as follows. Section 2 briefly introduces the problem solved by the CHOReVOLUTION IDRE together with a brief discussion on related work. Section 3 describes the overall approach supported by CHOReVOLUTION, and Sect. 4 describes the actual development process supported by IDRE. Section 5 gives an overview of the main components constituting the IDRE. Section 6 presents the IDRE at work on an industrial use case in the Smart Mobility and Tourism domain, and Sect. 7 concludes the paper.

2   Problem Statement and Related Works

Choreographies model peer-to-peer communication by defining a multiparty protocol that, when put in place by the cooperating participants, allows reaching the overall choreography goal in a fully distributed way. In this sense, choreographies differ significantly from other forms of service composition such as orchestrations, where all participants (but the orchestrator) play the passive role of receiving requests by the orchestrator only.

So far, choreographies have been solely used for design purposes, simply because there was no technological support for enabling a smooth transition from choreography design to execution. In the literature, many approaches have

---

[2] http://www.chorevolution.eu.
[3] https://github.com/chorevolution/CHOReVOLUTION-IDRE/wiki/User-Guide.

been proposed to deal with the foundational problems of checking choreography realizability, analyzing repairability of the choreography specification, verifying conformance, and enforcing realizability [4, 8, 10, 11, 14, 18, 19]. These approaches provide researchers with formal means to address fundamental aspects of choreographies. They are based on different interpretations of the choreography interaction semantics, concerning both the subset of considered choreography constructs, and the used formal notations.

The need for practical approaches to the realization of choreographies was recognized in the OMG's BPMN 2.0[4] standard, which introduces dedicated *Choreography Diagrams*, a practical notation for specifying choreographies that, following the pioneering BPMN process and collaboration diagrams, is amenable to be automatically treated and transformed into actual code. BPMN2 choreography diagrams focus on specifying the message exchanges among the participants from a global point of view. A participant role models the expected behavior (i.e., the expected interaction protocol) that a concrete service should be able to perform to play the considered role.

When considering choreography-based systems, the following two problems are usually taken into account: (i) *realizability check* – checks whether the choreography can be realized by implementing each participant so as it conforms to the played role; and (ii) *conformance check* – checks whether the set of services satisfies the choreography specification. In the literature, many approaches have been proposed to address these problems, e.g., [8, 9, 11, 13, 16, 17, 19–21].

However, to put choreographies into practice, we must consider realizing them by reusing third-party services. This leads to a further problem: the *automatic realizability enforcement* problem. It can be informally phrased as follows.

> Problem statement: *given a choreography specification and a set of existing services, externally* **coordinate** *and* **adapt** *their interaction so to fulfill the collaboration prescribed by the choreography specification.*

By taking as input a BPMN2 Choreography Diagram, and by exploiting a service inventory where existing services are published in order to be reused for choreography realization purposes, a set of software artefacts are automatically generated in order to implement the adaptation and distributed coordination logic prescribed by the choreography specification. These artefacts adapt and coordinate the interaction among the services – selected as suitable choreography participants – in order to ensure that their distributed cooperation runs by performing the flows specified in the BPMN2 Choreography Diagram only, hence preventing both interface and interoperability mismatches (application- and middleware-level adaptation) and the execution of possible flows violating the specification (correct coordination). Furthermore, when needed, specific security policies can be enforced on the participants interaction so to make the choreography secure. These policies concern correct inter-process authentication and authorization. The generated artefacts are:

---

[4] http://www.omg.org/spec/BPMN/2.0.2/.

- **Binding Components (BCs)** serve to ensure middleware-level interoperability among the possibly heterogenous services involved in the choreography. For instance, a BC can be generated in order to make a SOAP web service able to communicate with a REST service.
- When needed, **Security Filters (SFs)** secure the communication among involved services by enforcing specified security policies.
- Abstract services defined in the choreography specification characterizes the expected interface of the choreography participants. When using the IDRE to implement the specified choreography participants, concrete services (possibly black-box) are selected from a service inventory and reused. Thus, a concrete service has to match the interface of the participants it has to realize. Here, **Adapters (As)** come into place. That is, if needed, an Adapter is used to adapt the interface of a concrete service in order to match the one of the abstract service it implements.
- **Coordination Delegates (CDs)** supervise the interaction among the involved participants in order to enforce the service coordination logic prescribed by the choreography specification in a fully-distributed way. In other words, CDs act as distributed controllers. That is, they ensure that the distributed interaction among the reused concrete services will run according to the execution flows described by the choreography specification, hence preventing distributed interactions that could violate the specification.

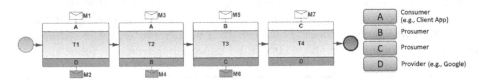

Fig. 1. BPMN2 choreography diagram example

For those readers new to choreographies, Fig. 1 shows a simple example of a BPMN2 Choreography Diagram. Choreography diagrams define the way business participants coordinate their interactions. The focus is on the exchange of messages among the involved participants. A choreography diagram models a distributed process specifying activity flows where each activity represents a message exchange between two participants. Graphically, a choreography task is denoted by a rounded-corner box. The two bands, one at the top and one at the bottom, represent the participants involved in the interaction captured by the task. A white band is used for the participant initiating the task that sends the initiating message to the receiving participant in the dark band that can optionally send back the return message.

The choreography in Fig. 1 involves four participants, A, B, C, and D, for the execution of four sequential tasks, T1, T2, T3 and T4. Specifically, A sends the message M1 to D, enabling it for the execution of T1. After that, D replies to A by sending the message M2. At this point, A sends M3 to B that, after the execution of T2, replies M4 to A and sends M5 to C. Only when M5 is received by C, it executes T3, replies M6 to B and sends M7 to D. Finally, D executes T4 and the choreography ends.

By analyzing the choreography, we can distinguish three different types of participants: *consumer*, *provider*, and *prosumer* (i.e., both consumer and provider). For instance, considering a reuse-based development scenario in which existing services are published in a suitable service inventory, the consumer participant A might be played by an existing Client App; the provider participant D by an existing Web Service, e.g., Google Maps; B and C might be two prosumers that have to be developed from scratch in order to realize the choreography.

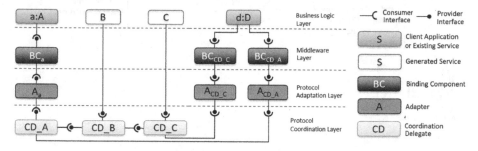

Fig. 2. Choreography architectural style (a sample instance of)

Figure 2 shows architecture of the system that realizes the choreography specified in Fig. 1, and that is automatically generated by the IDRE. The top-most layer contains the services representing the business logic. In particular, a:A denotes that the role of the consumer participant A is played by a, the Client App in our example; d:D denotes that the role of the provider participant D is played by d, an existing provider service to be reused, whereas, concerning the participants B and C, we do not make use of the notation x:X simply to indicate that they are not existing prosumer services and thus they can be either implemented from scratch or partially reused (for the provider part). Then, the second layer contains the BCs to cope with possibly needed middleware-level protocol adaptation, e.g., REST versus SOAP adaptation. It is worth mentioning that SOAP is the default interaction paradigm for the underlying layers. Finally, the last two layers include the Adapter and CD artefacts for adaptation and coordination purposes, respectively. Note that Fig. 2 shows the case in which the participants B and C are implemented from scratch, and hence BCs together with As are not needed.

The generated artefacts are not always required; rather, it depends on the specified choreography and the characteristics of the existing services (e.g., application-level interaction protocols, interface specifications, middleware-level interaction paradigms) that have been selected to instantiate the roles of the choreography participants. For instance, for this illustrative example, no security policy is specified and, hence, no SF is generated.

3   CHOReVOLUTION Approach

This section describes the CHOReVOLUTION approach for realizing service choreographies by possibly reusing existing services. The approach distinguishes two main phases: "From idea to model" and "From model to runtime".

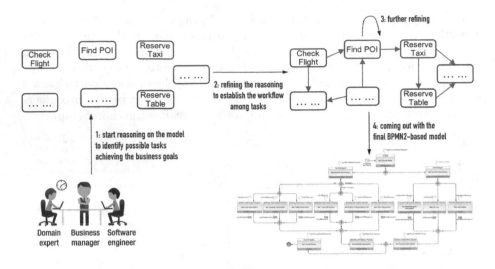

Fig. 3. From idea to model

From Idea to Model. As shown in Fig. 3, system modelers seat together and cooperate to set what are the business goals of the system they have in mind. For instance, a possible goal might be: assisting travelers from arrival, to staying, to departure. For that purpose, system modelers identify the tasks and the participants that will perform them so as to achieve the goal, e.g., reserving a taxi from the local company, purchasing digital tickets at the train station, performing transactions through services based on near field communication in a shop (step 1). Once business tasks have been identified, system modelers specify how the involved participants must collaborate as admissible flows of the identified tasks, hence producing an high-level specification of the system to be (steps 2 and 3). Note that the definition of the high-level specification is not covered by the CHOReVOLUTION approach. Thus, system modelers can use the notation they are more comfortable with. After the complete workflow among tasks has been established, the high-level specification is concretized into a BPMN2 Choreography Diagram (step 4), which, as introduced above, represents the choreography model the IDRE requires to start with in order to realize the specified system.

From Model to Runtime. As shown in Fig. 4, starting from the choreography diagram, the developer interacts with the IDRE in order to generate the code of the needed Binding Components, Adapters and Coordination Delegates, that are used to correctly implement the specified choreography. As already introduced, a service inventory is also accounted for. It contains services published by providers that, for instance, have identified business opportunities in the domain of interest. Providers can be transportation companies, airport retailers, local municipalities, etc., which can be reused in the resulting choreographed system. By exploiting the Enactment Engine provided by the IDRE, the pro-

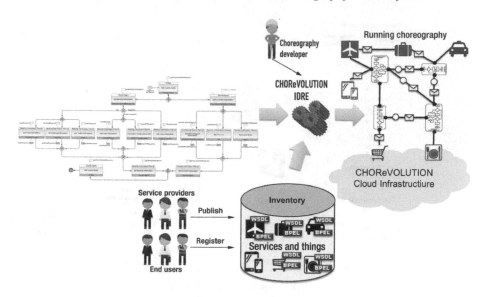

Fig. 4. From model to runtime

duced software artefacts are deployed over the Cloud infrastructure, the resulting choreography is enacted and executed.

4 CHOReVOLUTION Development Process

The CHOReVOLUTION development process consists of a set of core *code generation phases* (see Fig. 5) that takes as input a choreography specification and automatically generates the set of additional software entities previously mentioned. When interposed among the services, these software entities "proxify" the participant services to externally coordinate and adapt their business-level interaction, as well as to bridge the gap of their middleware-level communication paradigms and enforce security constraints.

Validation. This activity validates the correctness of the choreography specification against the constraints imposed by the BPMN2 standard specification. The goal is to check practical constraints concerning both choreography realizability and its enforceability.

Choreography Projection. Taking as input the BPMN2 Choreography Diagram and the related Messages XML schema, this activity automatically extracts all the choreography participants and applies a model-to-model (M2M) transformation to derive the related Participant Models, one for each participant. A participant model is itself a BPMN2 Choreography Diagram. It contains only the choreography flows that involve the considered participant. The generated participant models will be then taken as input by the Coordination Delegate (CD) Generation activity.

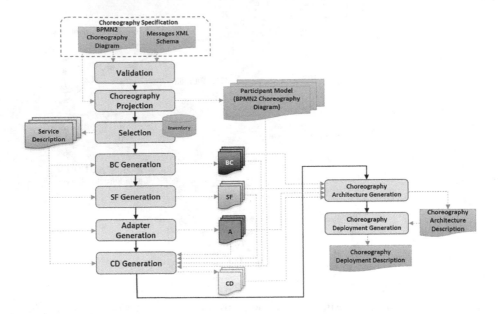

Fig. 5. CHOReVOLUTION development process

Selection. This activity is about querying the Service Inventory in order to select concrete services that can play the roles of the choreography participants. Once the right services have been selected, the related description models will be used to generate the Binding Components (BCs), Adapters (As), and Coordination Delegates (CDs).

BC Generation. BCs are generated when the middleware-level interaction paradigm of a selected service is different from SOAP[5], which is used by the CDs as the middleware-level interaction paradigm.

SF Generation. SFs are generated for those (selected) services having security policies associated. SFs filter the services interactions according to the specified security requirements.

Adapter Generation. When needed, adapters allow to bridge the gap between the interfaces and interaction protocols of the selected services and the ones of the (respective) participant roles they have to play, as obtained via projection. In other words, adapters solve possible interoperability issues due to operation names mismatches and I/O data mapping mismatches (see [6,22]).

CD Generation. CDs are in charge of coordinating the interactions among the selected services so as to fulfill the global collaboration prescribed by the choreography specification, in a fully distributed way (see [2,3,5,7]).

Choreography Architecture Generation. Considering the selected services and the generated BCs, As, and CDs, an architectural description is automatically generated, and a graphic representation of the choreographed system is

---

[5] http://www.w3.org/TR/soap/.

provided, where all the system's architectural elements and their interdependencies are represented.

Choreography Deployment Generation. The last activity of the development process concerns the generation of the Choreography Deployment Description (called `ChorSpec`) out of the Choreography Architecture model. The deployment description will be used for deploying and enacting the realized choreography.

5   CHOReVOLUTION IDRE

As depicted in Fig. 6, the CHOReVOLUTION IDRE is layered into: a front–end layer (1), a back–end layer (2), and a cloud layer (3).

The Front-end layer (1) consists of two components: a development studio and a web console.

The **CHOReVOLUTION Studio** is an Eclipse-based IDE that allows for (i) designing a BPMN2 Choreography Diagrams; (ii) defining all the details required to instrument the interaction among the services involved in the choreography (e.g., service signatures, identity attributes and roles); (iii) wizarding the code generation phases.

The **CHOReVOLUTION Console** is a web application based on Apache Syncope[6]. It allows to (i) configure, administer, and trigger actions on running services and choreographies; (ii) monitor the execution of a choreography with respect to relevant parameters, such as execution time of choreography tasks, number of messages exchanged, end-to-end deadlines, etc.

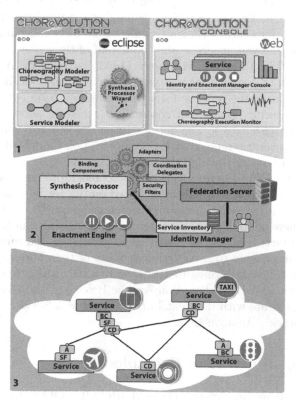

Fig. 6. CHOReVOLUTION IDRE overview

---

[6] https://syncope.apache.org/.

The Back-end layer (2) consists of the following components.

The **Synthesis Processor** is realized by a set of REST services that implement the model transformations to generate BCs, SFs, CDs, As, the architecture, and the deployment descriptor, as described in previous sections.

The **Enactment Engine (EE)** is a REST API that extends the Apache Brooklyn project[7]. It automatically deploys the choreography according to its deployment description by using the Cloud Layer. The EE also interacts with the Identity Manager to include into the deployment description the actual deployment and runtime details. Then, once a choreography is deployed and running, the EE listens for command requests from the Identity Manager for runtime choreography control. It is worth noticing that, although choreography monitoring and control is performed by centralized IDRE components (e.g., EE and IdM), the realization and running of the choreography is fully distributed into the various artefacts generated by the Synthesis Processor.

The **Federation Server** handles the runtime authentication and authorization for services that uses different security mechanism at the protocol level by storing various credentials on behalf of the caller.

The **Identity Manager (IdM)** is based on Apache Syncope project also. It is responsible for managing users and services. In particular, the IdM is able to query the services for supported application contexts and played roles; force a specific application context for a certain service (put in "maintenance" or disable/enable). The Service Inventory is a sub-component of the IdM. It acts as a central repository for the description models of the services and things that can be used during the synthesis process.

The Cloud layer (3) executes choreography instances on a cloud infrastructure and adapts their execution based on the actual application context.

At execution time, for each choreography, in the CHOReVOLUTION cloud, there are (i) a set of choreography instances at different execution states; (ii) a set of virtual machines executing a custom-tailored mix of services and middleware components to serve different parts of the choreography. Virtual Machines are installed and configured with services according to selectable policies. Due to the fact that EE is based on Apache Brooklyn, the CHOReVOLUTION IDRE can integrate with different Infrastructure as a Service (IaaS) platforms (e.g., Open Stack[8], Amazon EC2[9]).

6   Illustrative Example

This section describes the CHOReVOLUTION IDRE at work on a Smart Mobility and Tourism (SMT) use case. Figure 7 shows the specified BMPN2 choreography diagram. The SMT choreography is used to realize a Collaborative Travel Agent System (CTAS) through the cooperation of several content and service providers, organizations and authorities. It involves a mobile application as an

---

[7] https://brooklyn.apache.org/.

[8] https://www.openstack.org/.

[9] https://aws.amazon.com.

"Electronic Touristic Guide" that exploits CTAS to provide both smart mobility and touristic information.

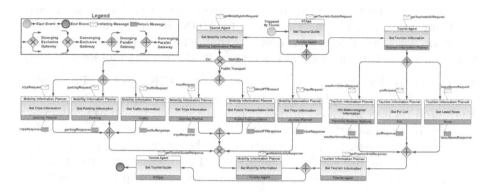

Fig. 7. Smart mobility and tourism choreography

The choreography starts with the mobile application STApp detecting the current position of the user, and asking for which type of point of interest to visit and which type of transport mode to use. From this information, Tourist Agent initiates two parallel flows in order to retrieve the information required by the "Electronic Touristic Guide" (see the parallel branch with two outgoing arrows after the choreography task Get Tourist Guide). In particular, in the left-most branch of the choreography, Mobility Information Planner is in charge of the retrieval of smart mobility information according to the selected transport mode (see the conditional branching), while in the right-most branch, Tourism Information Planner is responsible for gathering touristic information. After that, the two parallel flows are joined together to produce the data needed for the "Electronic Touristic Guide" (see the merging branch with two incoming arrows in the bottom side of the choreography). Finally, the guide is shown to the user by means of STApp.

In the remainder of this section, the application of the IDRE to the SMT use case is discussed by distinguishing the actions performed by the two possible types of users: service providers and choreography developers. A user guide to replicate the example can be found at https://github.com/chorevolution/CHOReVOLUTION-IDRE/wiki/User-Guide.

Service Provider. A service provider uses the IDRE to publish the description models of the services into the Service Inventory. The IDRE allows to deal with heterogeneous services. It provides a uniform description for any service, given by means of the Generic Interface Description Language (GIDL) [12] or the WSDL[10] in case of SOAP services. GIDL supports interface description for any kind of possible services (e.g., REST services). As introduced above, the published

---

[10] https://www.w3.org/TR/wsdl20-primer/.

services are selected in order to play the participants roles of a choreography. Then, the next phases will use the services' models to generate BCs, SFs, CDs, and As.

Referring to the SMT example, the service provider has to create a Service/Thing project inside the CHOReVOLUTION Studio by using a GIDL description for the following services: `Journey Planner`, `Parking`, `Traffic`, `Public Transportation`, `Personal Weather Stations`, `Poi` and `News`.

Choreography Developer. A developer uses the CHOReVOLUTION Studio to model a choreography and to realize it. The developer has to create a CHOReVOLUTION Synthesis project. Then, she models the BPMN2 choreography diagram by using the Eclipse BPMN2 choreography modeler[11] embedded in the Studio. Afterwards, the developer starts the synthesis process. The first two activities of the process (i.e., Validation and Choreography Projection) do not require any user interaction. The other activities are supported by suitable wizards, as discussed in the following.

Binding Component Generation

ⓘ The BC generation activity concerns the generation of the Binding Components. BCs are generated when the interaction paradigm of a selected service (or thing) is different from SOAP, which is the default interaction paradigm.

Non SOAP Provider participants:

Participant	Service ID	Service Name	Service Location	Interface Description Type
Journey Planner	68dfafc2-f8b0-4e33-9faf-c2f8b0ee3346	JourneyPlanner	http://ge-srv.e-mixer.com/Rest/Jou...	GIDL
Parking	6e5f0c55-d389-48c1-9f0c-55d38948c1bc	Parking	http://srvwebri.softeco.it/t-cube/Re...	GIDL
Traffic	8510f31c-1bfb-41a9-90f3-1c1bfb51a9bd	Traffic	http://cho-noauth-srv.e-mixer.com/...	GIDL
Public Transportation	df53e511-e353-4d41-93e5-11e3533d41c1	PublicTransportation	http://cho-noauth-srv.e-mixer.com/...	GIDL
Personal Weather Stations	ed999c52-f506-4b4b-999c-52f506cb4bee	Personal Weather Stations	http://cho-srv.e-mixer.com/service...	GIDL
Poi	7d39107b-862e-4978-b910-7b862e497815	Poi	http://srvwebri.softeco.it/t-cube/Re...	GIDL
News	51340ccf-95c5-47b8-b40c-cf95c577b8c2	News	http://srvwebri.softeco.it/t-cube/Re...	GIDL

Interaction paradigm of the Client participant: [REST ◌]

Fig. 8. BC generation activity

- *Selection.* For each participant, the developer selects the corresponding concrete service, as published into the Service Inventory. For instance, for the SMT choreography, the above seven mentioned services.
- *BC Generation.* Figure 8 shows the wizard that is used to configure the BCs generator for those selected services that do not rely on SOAP. Considering the SMT example, all the selected services are REST services. Thus, in Fig. 8, they are all listed in the wizard together with their GIDL description.
- *SF Generation.* None of the services for the SMT choreography defines security policies. Therefore, the SF Generation step is skipped.
- *Adapter Generation.* We recall that some mismatches can arise due to possible heterogeneities between the interfaces of the abstract services in the specification and the ones of the concrete services selected from the inventory (e.g., operation names mismatches and I/O data mapping mismatches).

---

[11] https://www.eclipse.org/bpmn2-modeler/.

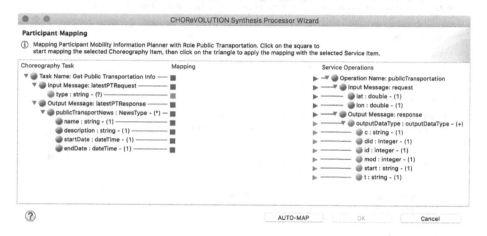

Participant to Service Adapter Generation

⊗ Please create all the Adapter(s) before proceeding.

Participant(s) that needs to be mapped with Service(s):

Initiating Participant	Task Name	Receiving Participant	Receiving Participant Service	Service Location	Adapter Model
Mobility Information Planner					
	Get Trips Information	Journey Planner	JourneyPlanner	http://ge-srv.e-mixer.com/Rest/...	...
	Get Parking Information	Parking	Parking	http://srvwebri.softeco.it/t-cube...	...
	Get Traffic Information	Traffic	Traffic	http://cho-noauth-srv.e-mixer.c...	...
	Get Public Transportation Info	Public Transportation	PublicTransportation	http://cho-noauth-srv.e-mixer.c...	...
Tourism Information Planner					
	Get Meteorological Information	Personal Weather Stations	PersonalWeatherStations	http://cho-srv.e-mixer.com/servi...	...
	Get Poi List	Poi	Poi	http://srvwebri.softeco.it/t-cube...	...
	Get Latest News	News	News	http://srvwebri.softeco.it/t-cube...	...

Fig. 9. Adapter generation activity

CHOReVOLUTION Synthesis Processor Wizard

Participant Mapping

ⓘ Mapping Participant Mobility Information Planner with Role Public Transportation. Click on the square to start mapping the selected Choreography Item, then click on the triangle to apply the mapping with the selected Service Item.

Choreography Task   Mapping   Service Operations

▼ ⬤ Task Name: Get Public Transportation Info — ■   ▶ —▼ ⬤ Operation Name: publicTransportation
 ▼ ⬤ Input Message: latestPTRequest ————— ■   ▶ ——▼ ⬤ Input Message: request
  ⬤ type : string - (?) ————————— ■   ▶ ——— ⬤ lat : double - (1)
 ▼ ⬤ Output Message: latestPTResponse ———— ■   ▶ ——— ⬤ lon : double - (1)
  ▼ ⬤ publicTransportNews : NewsType - (*) — ■   ▶ —▼ ⬤ Output Message: response
   ⬤ name : string - (1) ————————— ■   ▶ ——▼ ⬤ outputDataType : outputDataType - (+)
   ⬤ description : string - (1) ——————— ■   ▶ ——— ⬤ c : string - (1)
   ⬤ startDate : dateTime - (1) ————— ■   ▶ ——— ⬤ did : integer - (1)
   ⬤ endDate : dateTime - (1) ————— ■   ▶ ——— ⬤ id : integer - (1)
                                                        ▶ ——— ⬤ mod : integer - (1)
                                                        ▶ ——— ⬤ start : string - (1)
                                                        ▶ ——— ⬤ t : string - (1)

? 　　　　　　　　　　AUTO-MAP　　　　OK　　　　Cancel

Fig. 10. Adapter mapping

Regarding the SMT choreography, all the selected services exhibit some mismatches with respect to the corresponding choreography participants. The Adapter Generation wizard asks the developer for specifing the needed adaptation logic. In particular, the wizard shows all the choreography tasks that require adaptation, they are grouped by their initiating participant, see the leftmost column in Fig. 9. By clicking on the button labeled with "..." a new dialog window is opened, as shown in Fig. 10.

At this stage, the developer can map task messages to service operations messages. The elements identified with the red shapes are mandatory to be mapped, whereas those in orange are optional. In order to ease the mapping definition, the wizards provides a "AUTO-MAP" functionality to automatically generate the mappings by performing a syntactic binding to be refined afterwards.

–CD Generation. The last step of the wizard concerns the Coordination Delegates generation (Fig. 11).

If needed, the developer can specify "causality" correlations between different choreography tasks. Two tasks are correlated when they respectively represent an asynchronous request (the first task) and the subsequent callback (the second task). This also means that the initiating (resp., receiving) participant of the first task must be the receiving (resp., initiating) one of the second task. Considering the SMT choreography, the mobile application starts the choreography by sending the user preferences (current position, type of transport mode to use, etc.) and finally it gets back all the information needed to show an "Electronic Touristic Guide" to the user. Thus, the developer has to specify a correlation between the task Get Tourist Guide and the task Set Tourist Guide.

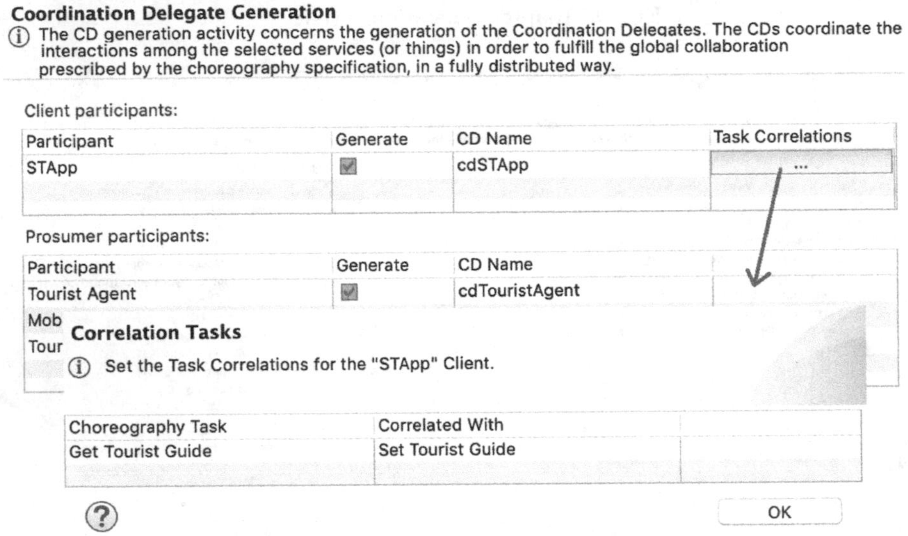

Coordination Delegate Generation
ⓘ The CD generation activity concerns the generation of the Coordination Delegates. The CDs coordinate the interactions among the selected services (or things) in order to fulfill the global collaboration prescribed by the choreography specification, in a fully distributed way.

Client participants:

Participant	Generate	CD Name	Task Correlations
STApp	☑	cdSTApp	...

Prosumer participants:

Participant	Generate	CD Name	
Tourist Agent	☑	cdTouristAgent	

Mob
Tour **Correlation Tasks**
ⓘ Set the Task Correlations for the "STApp" Client.

Choreography Task	Correlated With	
Get Tourist Guide	Set Tourist Guide	

Ⓐ   OK

Fig. 11. CD generation activity

By clicking on the Finish button, all the software artefacts (BCs, SFs, ADs, CDs) are generated. In addition, for each participant that acts as both an initiating participant in some task and a receiving participant in a different task (i.e., Tourist Agent, Mobility Information Planner, and Tourism Information Planner), the skeleton code of its business logic is generated to be then completed by the developer. This is the construction logic for the messages sent by the participant.

Figure 12 shows the code completed by the developer for building the message getMobilityInfoResponse (see local variable result). The implemented logic starts with the retrieval of the message tripsResponse sent by Journey Planner within the task Get Trips Information (line 297). The content of this message is used to set the trip information of getMobilityInfoResponse (line 298). Then getMobilityInfoRequest sent by Tourist Agent is retrieved (lines 300–301). Based on the transportation mean chosen by the user, which is contained in the transportMode element of the message, different data can be used to construct the response message getMobilityInfoResponse.

```
Ji MobilityInformationPlannerServiceImpl.java ⊠
 292    @Override
 293    public GetMobilityInfoResponse createGetMobilityInfoResponse(
 294           ChoreographyInstanceMessages choreographyInstanceMessages, String choreographyTaskName,
 295           String receiverParticipantName) {
 296       GetMobilityInfoResponse result = new GetMobilityInfoResponse();
 297       TripsResponse tripsResponse = (TripsResponse) choreographyInstanceMessages
 298              .getMessageSentFromParticipant("tripsResponse", "Journey Planner", "Get Trips Information");
 299       result.setTrip(tripsResponse);
 300       GetMobilityInfoRequest getMobilityInfoRequest = (GetMobilityInfoRequest) choreographyInstanceMessages
 301              .getMessageSentFromParticipant("GetMobilityInfoRequest", "Tourist Agent","Get Mobility Information");
 302       if(getMobilityInfoRequest.getTransportMode().equals(Modes.CAR)) {
 303          ParkingResponse parkingResponse = (ParkingResponse) choreographyInstanceMessages
 304                 .getMessageSentFromParticipant("parkingResponse", "Parking", "Get Parking Information");
 305          result.getParkings().addAll(parkingResponse.getParkings());
 306          TrafficResponse trafficResponse = (TrafficResponse) choreographyInstanceMessages
 307                 .getMessageSentFromParticipant("trafficResponse", "Traffic", "Get Traffic Information");
 308          result.getTrafficInfos().addAll(trafficResponse.getTrafficInfos());
 309       }
 310       if(getMobilityInfoRequest.getTransportMode().equals(Modes.PUBLIC_TRANSPORT)) {
 311          LatestPTResponse latestResponse = (LatestPTResponse) choreographyInstanceMessages
 312                 .getMessageSentFromParticipant("latestPTResponse", "Public Transportation",
 313                    "Get Public Transportation Info");
 314          result.getPublicTransportInfo().addAll(latestResponse.getPublicTransportNews());
 315       }
 316       return result;
 317    }
```

Fig. 12. Prosumer business logic implementation

Choreography Architecture Generation - Finally, considering the selected services and the generated BCs, SFs, ADs, and CDs, an architectural description is automatically generated in both a textual and a graphical form.

7 Conclusion

This paper has presented the CHOReVOLUTION IDRE, an integrated platform for developing, deploying, executing and monitoring choreography-based distributed applications.

In this tutorial paper, an industrial use case, in the Smart Mobility and Tourism domain, has been used to show the CHOReVOLUTION IDRE at work. The industrial partners that provided us with the use case have experienced with its modeling and automatic development and enactment, by using the IDRE. While interacting with the IDRE software development facilities and wizards discussed in this paper, the involved industrial partners experienced a significant time decrease with respect to realizing the use case by exploiting their daily development approaches. Their feedbacks on that indicate that the CHOReVOLUTION IDRE has a great potential in developing choreography-based applications and the use case got a full benefit from it.

More pilots and development cases will allow to consolidate the technical maturity of the product and pose the basis for a commercial validation.

Acknowledgments. Supported by: (i) EU H2020 Programme grant no. 644178 (CHOReVOLUTION - Automated Synthesis of Dynamic and Secured Choreographies for the Future Internet), (ii) the Ministry of Economy and Finance, Cipe resolution n. 135/2012 (INCIPICT), and (iii) the SISMA national PRIN project (contract no. 201752ENYB).

References

1. Autili, M., Inverardi, P., Tivoli, M.: Automated synthesis of service choreographies. IEEE Softw. **32**(1), 50–57 (2015). https://doi.org/10.1109/MS.2014.131
2. Autili, M., Inverardi, P., Perucci, A., Tivoli, M.: Synthesis of distributed and adaptable coordinators to enable choreography evolution. In: de Lemos, R., Garlan, D., Ghezzi, C., Giese, H. (eds.) Software Engineering for Self-Adaptive Systems III. Assurances. LNCS, vol. 9640, pp. 282–306. Springer, Cham (2017). https://doi.org/10.1007/978-3-319-74183-3_10
3. Autili, M., Inverardi, P., Tivoli, M.: Choreography realizability enforcement through the automatic synthesis of distributed coordination delegates. Sci. Comput. Program. **160**, 3–29 (2018). https://doi.org/10.1016/j.scico.2017.10.010
4. Autili, M., Di Ruscio, D., Di Salle, A., Inverardi, P., Tivoli, M.: A model-based synthesis process for choreography realizability enforcement. In: Cortellessa, V., Varró, D. (eds.) FASE 2013. LNCS, vol. 7793, pp. 37–52. Springer, Heidelberg (2013). https://doi.org/10.1007/978-3-642-37057-1_4
5. Autili, M., Ruscio, D.D., Salle, A.D., Perucci, A.: Choreosynt: enforcing choreography realizability in the future internet. In: Proceedings of the 22nd ACM SIGSOFT International Symposium on Foundations of Software Engineering, (FSE-22), Hong Kong, China, 16–22 November 2014, pp. 723–726 (2014). https://doi.org/10.1145/2635868.2661667
6. Autili, M., Salle, A.D., Gallo, F., Pompilio, C., Tivoli, M.: Model-driven adaptation of service choreographies. In: Proceedings of the 33rd Annual ACM Symposium on Applied Computing, SAC 2018, pp. 1441–1450 (2018). https://doi.org/10.1145/3167132.3167287
7. Autili, M., Salle, A.D., Gallo, F., Pompilio, C., Tivoli, M.: On the model-driven synthesis of evolvable service choreographies. In: 12th European Conference on Software Architecture: Companion Proceedings, ECSA, pp. 20:1–20:6 (2018). https://doi.org/10.1145/3241403.3241425
8. Basu, S., Bultan, T.: Choreography conformance via synchronizability. In: Proceedings of the 20th International Conference on World Wide Web, WWW 2011, Hyderabad, India, March 28–April 1 2011, pp. 795–804 (2011). https://doi.org/10.1145/1963405.1963516
9. Basu, S., Bultan, T.: Automatic verification of interactions in asynchronous systems with unbounded buffers. In: ACM/IEEE International Conference on Automated Software Engineering, ASE 2014, Vasteras, Sweden - 15–19 September 2014, pp. 743–754 (2014). https://doi.org/10.1145/2642937.2643016
10. Basu, S., Bultan, T.: Automated choreography repair. In: Stevens, P., Wąsowski, A. (eds.) FASE 2016. LNCS, vol. 9633, pp. 13–30. Springer, Heidelberg (2016). https://doi.org/10.1007/978-3-662-49665-7_2
11. Basu, S., Bultan, T., Ouederni, M.: Deciding choreography realizability. In: Proceedings of the 39th ACM SIGPLAN-SIGACT Symposium on Principles of Programming Languages, POPL 2012, Philadelphia, Pennsylvania, USA, 22–28 January, pp. 191–202 (2012). https://doi.org/10.1145/2103656.2103680
12. Bouloukakis, G.: Enabling emergent mobile systems in the IoT: from middleware-layer communication interoperability to associated QoS analysis. Ph.D. thesis, Inria, Paris, France (2017)
13. Calvanese, D., De Giacomo, G., Lenzerini, M., Mecella, M., Patrizi, F.: Automatic service composition and synthesis: the Roman model. IEEE Data Eng. Bull. **31**(3), 18–22 (2008)

14. Carbone, M., Montesi, F.: Deadlock-freedom-by-design: multiparty asynchronous global programming. In: Proceedings of 40th Symposium on Principles of Programming Languages, pp. 263–274 (2013). https://doi.org/10.1145/2429069.2429101
15. European Commission: Digital agenda for Europe - Future Internet Research and Experimentation (FIRE) initiative (2017). https://ec.europa.eu/digital-single-market/en/future-internet-research-and-experimentation
16. Gössler, G., Salaün, G.: Realizability of choreographies for services interacting asynchronously. In: Arbab, F., Ölveczky, P.C. (eds.) FACS 2011. LNCS, vol. 7253, pp. 151–167. Springer, Heidelberg (2012). https://doi.org/10.1007/978-3-642-35743-5_10
17. Güdemann, M., Poizat, P., Salaün, G., Ye, L.: Verchor: a framework for the design and verification of choreographies. IEEE Trans. Serv. Comput. 9(4), 647–660 (2016). https://doi.org/10.1109/TSC.2015.2413401
18. Lanese, I., Montesi, F., Zavattaro, G.: The evolution of Jolie: from orchestrations to adaptable choreographies. In: De Nicola, R., Hennicker, R. (eds.) Software, Services, and Systems. LNCS, vol. 8950, pp. 506–521. Springer, Cham (2015). https://doi.org/10.1007/978-3-319-15545-6_29
19. Poizat, P., Salaün, G.: Checking the realizability of BPMN 2.0 choreographies. In: Proceedings of the ACM Symposium on Applied Computing, SAC 2012, Riva, Trento, Italy, 26–30 March 2012, pp. 1927–1934 (2012). https://doi.org/10.1145/2245276.2232095
20. Salaün, G.: Generation of service wrapper protocols from choreography specifications. In: Sixth IEEE International Conference on Software Engineering and Formal Methods, SEFM 2008, Cape Town, South Africa, 10–14 November 2008, pp. 313–322 (2008). https://doi.org/10.1109/SEFM.2008.42
21. Salaün, G., Bultan, T., Roohi, N.: Realizability of choreographies using process algebra encodings. IEEE Trans. Serv. Comput. 5(3), 290–304 (2012). https://doi.org/10.1007/978-3-642-00255-7_12
22. Di Salle, A., Gallo, F., Perucci, A.: Towards adapting choreography-based service compositions through enterprise integration patterns. In: Bianculli, D., Calinescu, R., Rumpe, B. (eds.) SEFM 2015. LNCS, vol. 9509, pp. 240–252. Springer, Heidelberg (2015). https://doi.org/10.1007/978-3-662-49224-6_20

Choreographic Development
of Message-Passing Applications
A Tutorial

Alex Coto[1]([⊠]) [iD], Roberto Guanciale[2] [iD], and Emilio Tuosto[1] [iD]

[1] Gran Sasso Science Institute, L'Aquila, Italy
{alex.coto,emilio.tuosto}@gssi.it
[2] KTH, Stockholm, Sweden
robertog@kth.se

Abstract. Choreographic development envisages distributed coordination as determined by interactions that allow peer components to harmoniously realise a given task. Unlike in orchestration-based coordination, there is no special component directing the execution. Recently, choreographic approaches have become popular in industrial contexts where reliability and scalability are crucial factors. This tutorial reviews some recent ideas to harness choreographic development of message-passing software. The key features of the approach are showcased within Chor-Gram, a toolchain which allows software architects to identify defects of message-passing applications at early stages of development.

1 Introduction

Choreographic approaches advocate model-driven engineering (MDE) based on two different *views* of distributed applications. A **global view** specifies the interactions among the various distributed components (aka *participants*) while a **local view** models each component of the system.

This tutorial illustrates how global and local views enable both top-down and bottom-up engineering of message-passing applications. This interplay can be described by the following diagram:

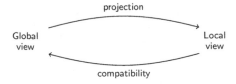

In the top-down engineering approach, designers provide the global view which can then be "projected" to obtain local views. Developers can independently

Research partly supported by the EU H2020 RISE programme under the Marie Skłodowska-Curie grant agreement No. 778233 and by the MIUR project PRIN 2017FTXR7S "IT-MaTTerS" (Methods and Tools for Trustworthy Smart Systems).

© IFIP International Federation for Information Processing 2020
Published by Springer Nature Switzerland AG 2020
S. Bliudze and L. Bocchi (Eds.): COORDINATION 2020, LNCS 12134, pp. 20–36, 2020.
https://doi.org/10.1007/978-3-030-50029-0_2

realise components and test their "compliance" with the corresponding local view. In the bottom-up approach, one can extract the local view from existing components, check for their compatibility, and generate a global view. Besides documenting the composition and enhancing program comprehension, global views yield an abstract model that can be used to evolve the system.

Choreographic development of message-passing applications offers, among others, the following advantages:

- Global views are amenable to being expressed using visual languages understandable to lay stakeholders (akin to BPMN [11] or UML diagrams [21], message-sequence charts [17], etc.).
- Local views can be algorithmically projected from global specifications. Also, projected local views:
  - come with correctness guarantees when global views satisfy sufficient conditions (*well-formedness*) for communication soundness,
  - are typically executable models that can be developed independently.
- The execution model of local views is close to several programming languages and environments like Golang, Erlang, Elixir, Akka, or JMS.

Model-driven approaches provide some support, but require care: models may be incomplete or have subtle issues that can lead to misbehaviour such as deadlocks or message loss.

Structure of the Paper. Section 2 surveys the models used in the tutorial. Section 3 shows how the top-down approach works in a simple scenario. Section 4 highlights some of the problems that a "bad design" may cause. Section 5 discusses how to analyse and fix design errors. Section 6 demonstrates the support that choreographic development may provide when amendments are necessary. Section 7 shows choreographic bottom-up engineering. Section 8 draws some conclusions.

2   Our Models

A global view can be represented in terms of a distributed workflow (e.g., BPMN [11] diagrams) or as specifications (similar to UML sequence diagrams or message-sequence charts). We survey the formal models that we use to represent global and local views of choreographies. This is an informal presentation; the referred literature yields the technical details.

Hereafter, we assume two disjoint sets: *participants* and *messages*, respectively ranged over by A, B, etc. and by m.

2.1   Partially Ordered Multisets

Pomsets [24] model concurrency in terms of partial orders of multisets of events. Pomsets provide a general model of concurrency; for instance message-sequence charts are a particular class of pomsets. We use pomsets of communication events as defined in [25] (which also provide a formal overview of pomsets).

Roughly speaking, we consider pomsets as directed-acyclic graphs where nodes are labelled by communication actions and edges capture causality among communications. A simple example illustrates this. The following diagram

$$
r_{(1)} = \begin{bmatrix} \text{A B!int} \longrightarrow \text{A B?int} \\ \downarrow \qquad\qquad \downarrow \\ \text{A B!bool} \longrightarrow \text{A B?bool} \end{bmatrix}
\tag{1}
$$

represents a pomset $r_{(1)}$ capturing the causality relations among the communication events between participants A and B; in (1), horizontal arrows establish the causality relations induced by the interactions of participants, while vertical arrows order the communications events of each participant (marked with background colours for the sake of illustration). More precisely, A sends to B a message of type int and one of type bool; the two leftmost nodes are indeed the output events labelled with A B!int and A B!bool while the rightmost nodes are the corresponding input events A B?int and A B?bool. Moreover, the edges establish that the each output event *precedes* the corresponding input event (the horizontal edges in (1)) and that the events involving integers precede those involving booleans. Intuitively, $r_{(1)}$ models process A that first sends a int and then a bool message to B, which on turn receives the messages in the sending order.

To represent alternative executions we simply take collections of pomsets. For instance, the set made of the following two pomsets

$$
\begin{bmatrix} \text{A B!int} \longrightarrow \text{A B?int} \\ \downarrow \qquad\qquad \downarrow \\ \text{A B!int} \longrightarrow \text{A B?int} \end{bmatrix}
\qquad
\begin{bmatrix} \text{A B!bool} \longrightarrow \text{A B?bool} \\ \downarrow \qquad\qquad \downarrow \\ \text{A B!bool} \longrightarrow \text{A B?bool} \end{bmatrix}
\tag{2}
$$

represents a system where A sends B either two int or two bool messages.

We remark that events involving the same participants are not ordered unless explicitly stated by the pomset. For instance, if we remove the rightmost vertical edge imposing an order of the input events from the pomset (1) then the messages sent by A can be received in any order by B.

2.2   A Workflow Model

The global view of a choreography can be suitably specified as workflows. We use *global choreographies* [12,25] (g-choreographies for short), a structured version of *global graphs* [8,20]. This model is appealing as it has a syntactic and diagrammatic presentation amenable of a formal semantics in terms of pomsets.

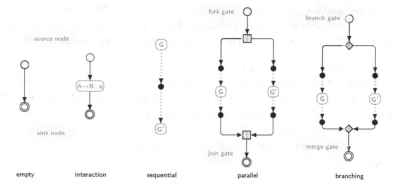

Fig. 1. A visual presentation of g-choreographies

The syntax of g-choreographies is given by the following grammar:

$$G ::= (o)$$ empty

| A→B: m   interaction

| G; G   sequential

| G | G   fork

| sel {G + ··· + G}   choice

Productions are given according to the decreasing order of precedence of connectives. Curly brackets can modify precedence. Iterative g-choreographies are omitted since they are not used in this tutorial. The grammar of data types is left implicit; in examples we will assume that m ranges over basic types such as int, bool, string, etc.

The empty g-choreography (o) yields no interactions; trailing occurrences of (o) may be omitted. An interaction A→B: m represents the exchange of a message of type m between A and B, provided that A ≠ B. We remark that data values are abstracted away: the payload m in A→B: m is not a value and should rather be thought of as (the name of) a data type. G-choreographies can be composed sequentially or in parallel (G; G′ and G | G′). A (non-deterministic) choice sel $\{G_1 + \cdots + G_n\}$ specifies the possibility to continue according to either of the g-choreographies $G_1, \ldots, G_n$.

The syntax of g-choreographies can be visually depicted as in Fig. 1. A global graph G is represented as a rooted graph with a single "enter" and "exit" nodes, respectively called *source* (graphically ○) and *sink* (graphically ◎). Special nodes, dubbed *gates*, are used for branch and fork points (respectively depicted as ◇ and ▢). Each fork or branch gate in our visual notation will have a corresponding join and merge "closing" gate.

The semantics of a global graph is a family of pomsets; each pomset in the family partially orders the communication events on a particular "trace" of g-choreography. For instance, the semantics $[\![(o)]\!]$ is simply the set $\{\epsilon\}$ containing the empty pomset ϵ while for interactions we have

$$[\![A{\rightarrow}B\colon m]\!] = \left\{ [\, A\,B!m \longrightarrow A\,B?m \,] \right\}$$

namely, the semantics of an interaction is a pomset where the output event precedes the input event. The semantics of the other operations is basically obtained by composing the semantics of sub g-choreographies. More precisely,

- for a choice we have $[\![G + G']\!] = [\![G]\!] \cup [\![G']\!]$;
- the semantics of the parallel composition $G \mid G'$ is essentially built by taking the set of the disjoint union of each pomset in $[\![G]\!]$ with each one in $[\![G']\!]$;
- the semantics of the sequential composition $[\![G; G']\!]$ is the set of the disjoint union of each pomset in $[\![G]\!]$ with each one in $[\![G']\!]$ and adding causal relations from events in $[\![G]\!]$ to those in $[\![G']\!]$ if they are executed by the same participant (i.e., making the former precede the latter).

3   When All Goes Fine

We use a simple yet representative application to highlight a top-down choreographic approach to the design and prototyping of message-passing applications.

A server S allows client C to convert strings into a date format and vice versa (we assume a basic data type dateFmt to represent formats). Both C and S use a logger service L to record their requests and responses respectively; for this, data types reqLog and resLog are used.

We first consider a couple of solutions that straightforwardly model the scenario above. Take the global specification

```
sel {
  {C → L: logReq  | C → S: dateFmt};    .. date2string & logging
     S → L: logRes;
     S → C: string
  +
  {C → L: logReq  | C → S: string};     .. string2date & logging
     S → L: logRes;
     S → C: dateFmt
}
```

Despite its simplicity, it is not immediate that the g-choreography above is sound. To illustrate this, consider that

- the first interaction between the client C and the server allows S to determine which service is requested (convert a date to a string or vice versa),
- the logger behaves uniformly through the choice (since it first receives the log message of a request and then the one of a response).

Notice that, although L is oblivious of the choice, its behaviour cannot be syntactically factored out without violating some dependencies among communications.

A variant of the above g-choreography is

```
sel {
  {C → L: logReq  | C → S: dateFmt};
     sel {
```

```
        S → L:  logRes
        +                        .. S may send less informative logs
        S → L:  basicLog
      };
      S → C:  string
  +
  {C → L:  logReq  |  C → S:  string};
      S → L:  logRes;
      S → C:  dateFmt
  }
```

where, once a request to transform a date into a string is made, S may decide to log the response either fully or send L less information with `basicLog`. Note that C is now unaware of this choice between S and L while L can discern the initial choice made by C.

Once the soundness of a g-choreography is attained, local behaviours can be automatically projected either to local specifications or to executable code. For instance, ChorGram can generate *communicating finite-state machines* [6] that specify the behaviour of each component of the system as well as executable Erlang code implementing the communication pattern of the g-choreography. Notably, this approach is an instance of a *correctness-by-design* principle: the projected behaviour is *communication sound* in the sense that it does not exhibit misbehaviour such as deadlocks or loss of messages (provided that the communication infrastructure does not fail).

4   Designing Problems

Models featuring distributed workflows (such as BPMN or the g-choreographies adopted here) may introduce inconsistency related to distributed choices. In scenario-based models, the designer may overlook cases that may lead to run-time errors. This is illustrated with the following examples.

Consider the protocol specified by the following two pomsets

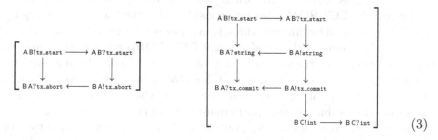

$$\tag{3}$$

Participant A starts a transaction with B by sending message `tx_start` and then engages in a distributed choice where either B aborts the transaction immediately, or it send a string with A and commits the transaction before sending an integer with C. This specification leaves C uncertain about whether the integer from B is going to be sent or not. Hence C could locally decide to

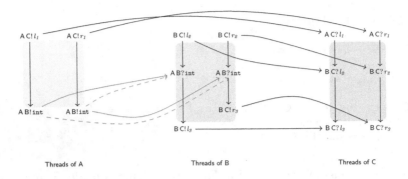

Fig. 2. Inter-participant closure

(a) terminate immediately and not receive the integer from B or

(b) to wait for the integer, even if B opted to abort the transaction.

Relying on the pomset semantics of g-choreographies, in [25] we defined *termination awareness* in order to avoid reaching run-time configurations where non-terminating participants unnecessarily lock resources once the coordination is completed. This condition requires that in no accepting configuration the participants of interest have input transitions. More precisely, a set of pomsets R violates the terminating condition for participant A if there are two pomsets r and r' in R such that an execution trace of A in r is a prefix of an execution trace of A in r' and the difference between the two traces starts with an input. Basically, the designer can specify which participants should be aware of the termination of the choreography. Note that, depending on the application requirements, termination awareness may be important for B, but not for C; in the example above for instance, the termination of C is not crucial if it is not locking resources or if it is immaterial that such resources are left locked.

In [25], besides the terminating condition above, we identified two other pomset-based conditions dubbed **CC2-POM** and **CC3-POM** to check realisability of global specifications. We briefly describe those *closure* conditions.

Intuitively, **CC2-POM** takes into consideration the executions emerging from "confusion" caused by different threads in a pomset (such as the one in (4)). For a given set of pomsets R, the satisfaction of **CC2-POM** ensures that if an execution trace t cannot be distinguished by any of the participants from a valid trace of R then t is a trace of R. To check **CC2-POM**, one needs to compute a closure set of pomsets out of R; the closure set yields the pomsets characterising the execution traces due to inter-participants' concurrency. This closure generates all "acceptable" matches between output and input events entailed by a pomset capturing the behaviour of a participant. We borrow and adapt Fig. 2 from [25] to give an intuition of this construction. The participants A, B, and C there have each two threads, the "left" and the "right" thread; those are identified by sorts l_i and r_i which are meta-variables on sorts immaterial here (with the only assumption that $l_i \neq r_i$ for each $i \in \{1, 2, 3\}$). The bottom-most solid edges from the threads of A to those of B represent the causality relations specified in the original design. The closure of the original design however yields also the execution with the causality relations given by the bottom-most dashed edges.

The condition **CC3-POM** accounts for implied executions that may break distributed choices. It is similar to **CC2-POM** barred that the closure set is built by checking all the prefixes of the traces of the pomsets.

We remark that our framework focuses on the identification of communication problems that are data-oblivious. For this reason the implementations of some specifications may exhibit unintended interactions even if they satisfy the verification conditions. Consider the following example:

$$\begin{bmatrix} \begin{array}{cc} AB!int \longrightarrow AB?int & AB!string \longrightarrow AB?string \\ \downarrow & \downarrow & \downarrow & \downarrow \\ AB!bool \longrightarrow AB?bool & AB!bool \longrightarrow AB?bool \end{array} \end{bmatrix} \qquad (4)$$

which specifies two concurrent threads[1] whereby A (threads with green background) and B (threads with orange background) exchange two boolean values after exchanging an integer and a string. In an asynchronous setting, the boolean values may "swap", namely the one sent by the thread which sent the integer is received by the thread which received the string, and vice-versa. Notice that this does not yield communication problems, but may violate the dependencies among data induced by the causal dependencies specified in the pomset.

To sum up, we address termination awareness, thread confusion (**CC2**), and undetermined choices (**CC3**). The violation of termination awareness could lead to participants oblivious of the termination of the protocol, the violation of **CC2** could make messages to be consumed by a unintended threads of a participant, **CC3** could lead to participants to follow one branch of a choice while other participants are executing another branch.

5   When Something Goes Wrong

We now consider some examples where development is not as straightforward as in the examples of Sect. 3. More precisely, we consider scenarios where the closure properties **CC2-POM** or **CC3-POM** may be violated, or termination awareness does not hold for some participants. For the analysis we rely on PomCho, part of the ChorGram tool chain that supports choreographic development through the models discussed in Sect. 2.

Let us start with the following (erroneous) g-choreography giving another variant of the protocol in Sect. 3 where a less informative log message is sent when C requests to transform a date in a string and a more informative one otherwise:

---

[1] Note the bracketing here: enclosing the two groups of events in different brackets would correspond to specifying a choice between the pomsets.

```
sel {
   {C → L: logReq | C → S: dateFmt};
      L → S: basicLog;                        .. oops
      S → C: string
   +
   {C → L: logReq | C → S: string};
      S → L: logRes;
      S → C: dateFmt
}
```

The attentive reader may have noticed a problem: the exchange of basicLog should go the other way around. This intentional mistake is instrumental to illustrate the analysis of the g-choreography above, summarised by the screenshots in Fig. 3. Before doing so, we briefly digress about the GUI. After loading, ChorGram computes the g-choreography to analyse as shown in the left-most screenshot in Fig. 3. The other screenshot presents a counterexample of the violation of termination awareness once such analysis is executed. Note that the hierarchical menu in the left pane is dynamically expanded to include clickable references to the results of the operations. The right-hand side pane of the second screenshot, represents the pomset of the first branch of the previous g-choreography. This pomset is a counterexample showing the violation of **CC3-POM** (as shown on the hierarchical menu). The events performed by each participant are grouped with a box to make the pomset clearer to the user.

Let us return to our analysis. The screenshots in Fig. 3 show that while the closure properties are satisfied, termination awareness is violated for L. By inspecting the pomset in the top-right screenshot we can notice that the logging information in the two branches wrongly goes from L to S (instead of going the other way around). This is immediately evident from the projection on L reported in the bottom-most screenshot of Fig. 3; notice that state 1 is a mixed-choice state, namely that it has both input and output outgoing transitions.

Swapping the sender and the receiver in the introduced interaction solves all the issues (which results in ChorGram displaying empty lists of counterexamples). One could argue that this is such a blunt glitch that one could spot it immediately and without the use of tools. While this might be true for simple examples like this one, these mishaps might not be as obvious in larger designs.

The next variant of our protocol exhibits a subtle problem. Consider

```
sel {
   {C → L: logReq | C → S: dateFmt};
      S → L: basicLog;
      S → L: logReqExt;
      S → C: string
   +
   {C → L: logReq | C → S: string};
      S → L: logReqExt;
      S → L: basicLog;
      S → C: dateFmt
}
```

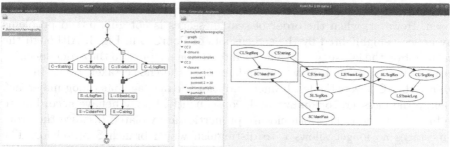

The left-hand pane allows the user to select the model onto which to apply the next operation; results are displayed in the pane on the right-hand side.

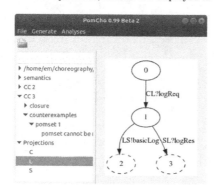

A possible way of representing local views is by *communicating finite-state machines* [6] which basically are finite-state automata where transitions are labelled by communication actions. A projection function of ChorGram can generate CFSMs of participants from a g-choreography as illustrated for L here.

Fig. 3. Violation of termination awareness and projection on L

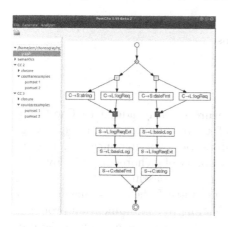

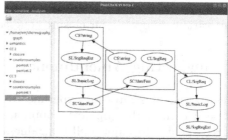

The output of `logReqExt` precedes the one of `basicLog` (implying that S opted for the left-most branch of the g-choreography). However, the corresponding input events of L are in the opposite order (making L follow the right-most branch).

Fig. 4. Problems with non-FIFO asynchrony

The analysis must take into account the semantics of communication. In particular, asynchronous communications require care. In fact, if the messages are buffered and accessed according to a FIFO discipline, in the above g-choreography the message `basicLog` is before (resp. after) the message `logResExt` in the buffer from S to L when the first (resp. second) branch is chosen. However, when the order of sent messages is not guaranteed problems may arise, as highlighted by the screenshots of PomCho in Fig. 4. Although the screenshot on the left suggests that the interactions happen in the order specified in the g-choreography, L may "misunderstand" the choice taken by C. In fact, suppose that C selects the left branch and that the message `basicLog` may reach L before the message `logResExt` and, consequently, L may behave according to the branch on the right. Both closure properties are violated because the order of messages no longer allows L to distinguish which branch S opted for. The pomset depicted in the screenshot on the right shows possible executions where the order of outputs is not preserved.

The above problem can be fixed by letting L acknowledge the first message from the server S, namely

```
sel {
  {C → L:  logReq  |  C → S:  dateFmt};
      S → L:  basicLog;
      L → S:  ack;                            .. L acknowledges S
      S → L:  logReqExt;
      S → C:  string
  +
  {C → L:  logReq  |  C → S:  string};
      S → L:  logReqExt;
      L → S:  ack;                            .. L acknowledges S
      S → L:  basicLog;
      S → C:  dateFmt
}
```

This variant enjoys all our closure conditions.

6   Suggesting Amendments

This section illustrates an experimental feature recently added to ChorGram. As seen earlier, the top-down approach of choreographic design requires g-choreographies to enjoy well-formedness properties. For instance, the closure properties surveyed in Sect. 4 ensure the realisability of g-choreographies by components coordinating through asynchronous message-passing.

Attaining well-formedness requires some ingenuity. In fact, designers can easily overlook problems and introduce defects leading to communication problems such as those in the scenarios of Sect. 5. When this happens, as seen in the previous examples, ChorGram identifies counterexamples that highlight defects. It may therefore be helpful to have advice on how to possibly fix problems.

Possible amendments are suggested by ChorGram as a g-choreography, determined out of the initial one and the counterexample identified in the analysis. We demonstrate this by considering a further variation of the application used in Sect. 5. The following g-choreography models a protocol where a less informative log message is sent when C requests to transform a date into a string:

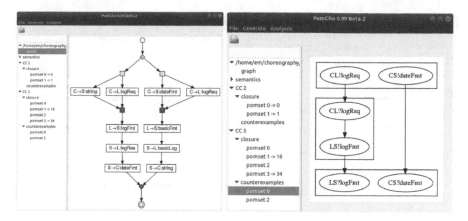

Fig. 5. An unexpected execution

```
sel {
    {C → L: logReq | C → S: dateFmt};
       L → S: basicFmt;
       S → L: basicLog;
       S → C: string
    +
    {C → L: logReq | C → S: string};
       L → S: logFmt;
       S → L: logRes;
       S → C: dateFmt
}
```

Notice that L informs S about the format of the log. The analysis in Fig. 5 shows that, while **CC2-POM** is satisfied (since no counterexample exists), **CC3-POM** is however violated due to an unsound choice. In fact, the screenshot on the right of Fig. 5 represents the pomset missing from the semantics of the global model. In this counterexample, S gets stuck after receiving the two parallel inputs from C and L. Here, the problem arises because L cannot identify which message should be sent to S, since L receives the same message in both branches. Accordingly, L is not informed about the branch selected by C. This problem is evident in the screenshots of Fig. 6, which report the projection of L, the g-choreography corresponding to the counterexample, and a model consisting of a suggested amendment. This model maps the counterexample back to the initial g-choreography. This is attained by computing the "minimal" transformation required on the original design to match the counterexample. More precisely, ChorGram applies an edit-distance algorithm to the (part of the) original design to be changed so that it corresponds to the counterexample. The algorithm can be tuned up by setting a *cost* to edit operations.

The edit operations are

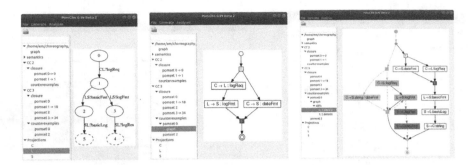

Fig. 6. A possible amendment (Color figure online)

- node insertion/deletion
- edge insertion/deletion
- modifications to sender/receivers/payload of interactions.

Pictorially, nodes and edges in green represent unchanged elements, those in blue represent additions to make, and those in dashed gray represent elements to be deleted. For instance, the amendment in Fig. 6 suggests to preserve the right-most branch and change the left-most branch by removing the nodes and edges in gray, adding the blue edges, and modifying the payload of the communication from C to S (from `string` to `dateFmt`).

Note that the suggested amendments are computed without "interpreting" the g-choreography and therefore they may not be meaningful. The designer still needs to vet and approve them. As said, this is an experimental feature added to ChorGram, and we plan to investigate how to improve it. For instance, an interesting development could be to identify how to assign costs depending on the applications at hand. In fact, in some cases it may not be reasonable to apply some of the operations above. This can be improved upon by properly assigning costs (undesired operations should have a higher cost than admissible ones).

7   Going Bottom-Up

We now consider how choreographies can support bottom-up engineering. There are two key motivations for which this support is appealing. Firstly, the validation of composition of distributed components. For instance, service-oriented architectures such as micro-services envisage software development as the composition of publicly available services. One would like to validate that such compositions communicate as expected. Secondly, software evolution possibly compromises the communication soundness of an application.

In the rest of the section, such a scenario is used to show the kind of support offered by choreographies in bottom-up engineering. To this purpose we look at a possible evolution of the last g-choreography in Sect. 5: Suppose that the developers want to deploy a new version of the logger service L that requires

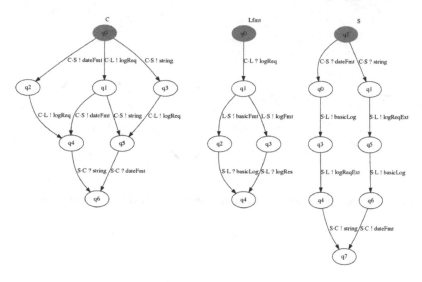

Fig. 7. The system with the evolved L

specific formats for the log information sent by the server S. Therefore, developers implement a new version of L, say Lfmt, that behaves according to the CFSM in Fig. 7. (Note that the CFSMs of C and S do not change.) After the request of the client, the new logger informs S of the format (transitions q1→q2 and q1→q3 of Lfmt). The server reacts accordingly with transitions from its initial state.

It is worth remarking that what usually happens is that the code implementing L evolves without modifying the corresponding models (if any). After a new version of a component is released, one could extract[2] a model like the CFSM on the left to describe its behaviour. This is what we assume in this scenario.

Figure 7 yields a problematic system: The bottom-up analysis of ChorGram (done before deploying Lfmt) flags the problem with the message:

```
Branching representability: [Bp "C" "q4", Bp "C" "q5", Bp "C" "q6",
Bp "L" "q1",Bp "L" "q2",Bp "L" "q3",Bp "L" "q4",
Bp "S" "q0",Bp "S" "q1",Bp "S" "q3",Bp "S" "q4",
Bp "S" "q5",Bp "S" "q6",Bp "S" "q7"]
```

which we now decipher. This message basically reports the CFSMs whose transitions are not reflected in their parallel composition due to some branching.

For instance, in our model, Bp"S" "q0" states that some transitions expected from state q0 of the server S cannot be fired in a configuration of the systems where the local state of S is q0; in fact, in configuration q4 of the system, the local machine of S is in state q0, which has the transition S L!basicLog (not reflected in the system).

---

[2] This operation can be done either by *inferring* the model from the code (if possible) or by *learning* it by observing the behaviour of the new version of the component.

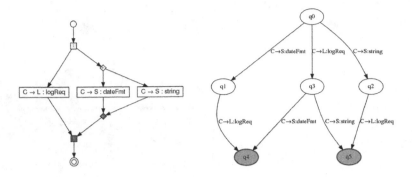

Fig. 8. G-choreography and transition system determined by bottom-up analysis

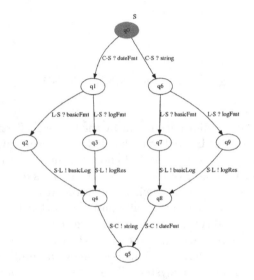

Fig. 9. An amended S

This analysis can be conducted in a more user-friendly way by inspecting the models in Fig. 8, also provided by ChorGram.

The g-choreography contains the "sound" interactions only. In fact, the transition system in Fig. 8 highlights two configurations, q4 and q5, that violate the branching property. This is due to the fact that S is not aware of the choice taken in the local state q1 of the CFSM Lfmt in Fig. 7. This problem can be solved by modifying S, as illustrated in the CFSM of Fig. 9.

8   Concluding Remarks

Tool support for analyzing realisability of global specifications is necessary to enable model-driven development of choreographies. Indeed, as observed in [1], a source of problems is that there could be some specifications that are impossible to implement using the local views in a given communication model. Several works addressed the realisability of scenario-based global models, like *message-sequence charts* (MSCs) [2,9,14–16,22,23].

A mechanism to statically detect realisability in MSCs is proposed in [4]. The notions of non-local choices and of termination considered in [4] are less permissive than our verification conditions since intra-participant concurrency is not allowed and termination awareness is not enforced. Closure conditions for realisability have been initially proposed in [1] to study realisability of MSC and have been extended in [13] to handle sets of pomsets (the latter were reviewed in Sect. 2). This extension yields more general results and more efficient analyses, since it enables multi-threaded participants and does not require to explicitly compute all possible executions (which can be large due to the number of possible interleaving of concurrent threads) of the global model.

In the context of choreographies, the integration of ChorGram features in the CHOReVOLUTION platform [3] is of particular interest to us. In fact, CHOReVOLUTION is a rather sophisticated platform for the top-down development featuring many important aspects complementary to the functionalities of ChorGram (e.g., low-level binding of components, or security aspects).

Other possible integrations are with tools based on behavioural types [19]. The tools proposed in this context (see [10] for a survey) are typically based on theories defining constraints aimed to guarantee the soundness of the projections of global specifications (as e.g., in [5,7,18]). A peculiarity of ChorGram is that it can provide some feedback to support model-driven engineering of applications. This is not usually the case in other contexts based on behavioural types where, for instance, behavioural type checkers do not provide feedback.

Acknowledgments. We warmly thank Simon Bliudze for his helpful comments which allowed us to improve the presentation of this paper.

References

1. Alur, R., Etessami, K., Yannakakis, M.: Inference of message sequence charts. IEEE Trans. Softw. Eng. **29**(7), 623–633 (2003)
2. Alur, R., Holzmann, G.J., Peled, D.: An analyzer for message sequence charts. In: Margaria, T., Steffen, B. (eds.) TACAS 1996. LNCS, vol. 1055, pp. 35–48. Springer, Heidelberg (1996). https://doi.org/10.1007/3-540-61042-1_37
3. Autili, M., Di Salle, A., Gallo, F., Pompilio, C., Tivoli, M.: CHOReVOLUTION: automating the realization of highly–collaborative distributed applications. In: Riis Nielson, H., Tuosto, E. (eds.) COORDINATION 2019. LNCS, vol. 11533, pp. 92–108. Springer, Cham (2019). https://doi.org/10.1007/978-3-030-22397-7_6
4. Ben-Abdallah, H., Leue, S.: Syntactic detection of process divergence and non-local choice in message sequence charts. In: Brinksma, E. (ed.) TACAS 1997. LNCS, vol. 1217, pp. 259–274. Springer, Heidelberg (1997). https://doi.org/10.1007/BFb0035393
5. Bocchi, L., Melgratti, H., Tuosto, E.: Resolving non-determinism in choreographies. In: Shao, Z. (ed.) ESOP 2014. LNCS, vol. 8410, pp. 493–512. Springer, Heidelberg (2014). https://doi.org/10.1007/978-3-642-54833-8_26

6. Brand, D., Zafiropulo, P.: On communicating finite-state machines. J. ACM **30**(2), 323–342 (1983)
7. Carbone, M., Honda, K., Yoshida, N.: A calculus of global interaction based on session types. Electron. Notes Theor. Comput. Sci. **171**(3), 127–151 (2007)
8. Deniélou, P.-M., Yoshida, N.: Multiparty session types meet communicating automata. In: Seidl, H. (ed.) ESOP 2012. LNCS, vol. 7211, pp. 194–213. Springer, Heidelberg (2012). https://doi.org/10.1007/978-3-642-28869-2_10
9. Gaudin, E., Brunel, E.: Property verification with MSC. In: Khendek, F., Toeroe, M., Gherbi, A., Reed, R. (eds.) SDL 2013. LNCS, vol. 7916, pp. 19–35. Springer, Heidelberg (2013). https://doi.org/10.1007/978-3-642-38911-5_2
10. Gay, S., Ravara, A. (eds.): Behavioural Types: From Theory to Tools. Automation, Control and Robotics. River, Gistrup (2009)
11. Object Management Group: Business Process Model and Notation (2011). http://www.bpmn.org
12. Guanciale, R., Tuosto, E.: An abstract semantics of the global view of choreographies. In: Interaction and Concurrency Experience, pp. 67–82 (2016)
13. Guanciale, R., Tuosto, E.: Realisability of pomsets. J. Log. Algebr. Methods Program. **108**, 69–89 (2019)
14. Gunter, E.L., Muscholl, A., Peled, D.A.: Compositional message sequence charts. In: Margaria, T., Yi, W. (eds.) TACAS 2001. LNCS, vol. 2031, pp. 496–511. Springer, Heidelberg (2001). https://doi.org/10.1007/3-540-45319-9_34
15. Gunter, E.L., Muscholl, A., Peled, D.: Compositional message sequence charts. Int. J. Softw. Tools Technol. Transfer **5**(1), 78–89 (2002). https://doi.org/10.1007/s10009-002-0085-2
16. Harel, D., Marelly, R.: Come, Let's Play: Scenario-Based Programming Using LSCs and the Play-Engine. Springer, Heidelberg (2003). https://doi.org/10.1007/978-3-642-19029-2
17. Harel, D., Thiagarajan, P.: Message sequence charts. In: Lavagno, L., Martin, G., Selic, B. (eds.) UML for Real, pp. 77–105. Springer, Boston (2003). https://doi.org/10.1007/0-306-48738-1_4
18. Honda, K., Yoshida, N., Carbone, M.: Multiparty asynchronous session types. J. ACM **63**(1), 9:1–9:67 (2016). Extended version of a paper presented at POPL08
19. Hüttel, H., et al.: Foundations of session types and behavioural contracts. ACM Comput. Surv. **49**(1), 3:1–3:36 (2016)
20. Lange, J., Tuosto, E., Yoshida, N.: From communicating machines to graphical choreographies. In: SIGPLAN-SIGACT Symposium on Principles of Programming Languages, pp. 221–232 (2015)
21. Micskei, Z., Waeselynck, H.: UML 2.0 sequence diagrams' semantics. Technical report, LAAS (2008)
22. Formal description techniques (FDT) - Message Sequence Chart (MSC). Recommendation ITU-T Z.120 (2011). http://www.itu.int/rec/T-REC-Z.120-201102-I/en
23. Muscholl, A., Peled, D.: Deciding properties of message sequence charts. In: Leue, S., Systä, T.J. (eds.) Scenarios: Models, Transformations and Tools. LNCS, vol. 3466, pp. 43–65. Springer, Heidelberg (2005). https://doi.org/10.1007/11495628_3
24. Pratt, V.: Modeling concurrency with partial orders. Int. J. Parallel Prog. **15**(1), 33–71 (1986)
25. Tuosto, E., Guanciale, R.: Semantics of global view of choreographies. J. Log. Algebr. Methods Program. **95**, 17–40 (2018)

Coordination Languages

ARx: Reactive Programming
for Synchronous Connectors

José Proença[1](✉) and Guillermina Cledou[2](✉)

[1] CISTER, ISEP, Porto, Portugal
pro@isep.ipp.pt
[2] HASLab/INESC TEC, Universidade do Minho, Braga, Portugal
mgc@inesctec.pt

Abstract. Reactive programming (RP) languages and Synchronous Coordination (SC) languages share the goal of orchestrating the execution of computational tasks, by imposing dependencies on their execution order and controlling how they share data. RP is often implemented as libraries for existing programming languages, lifting operations over values to operations over streams of values, and providing efficient solutions to manage how updates to such streams trigger reactions, i.e., the execution of dependent tasks. SC is often implemented as a standalone formalism to specify existing component-based architectures, used to analyse, verify, transform, or generate code. These two approaches target different audiences, and it is non-trivial to combine the programming style of RP with the expressive power of synchronous languages.

This paper proposes a lightweight programming language to describe component-based Architectures for Reactive systems, dubbed *ARx*, which blends concepts from RP and SC, mainly inspired to the Reo coordination language and its composition operation, and with tailored constructs for reactive programs such as the ones found in ReScala. ARx is enriched with a type system and with algebraic data types, and has a reactive semantics inspired in RP. We provide typical examples from both the RP and SC literature, illustrate how these can be captured by the proposed language, and describe a web-based prototype tool to edit, parse, and type check programs, and to animate their semantics.

1   Introduction

This paper combines ideas from *reactive programming languages* and from *synchronous coordination languages* into a new reactive language that both enriches the expressiveness of typical reactive programs and facilitates the usage of typical synchronous coordination languages.

Reactive programming languages, such as Yampa [14], ReScala [11], and Angular[1], address how to lift traditional functions from concrete data values to

---

[1] https://angular.io/.

© IFIP International Federation for Information Processing 2020
Published by Springer Nature Switzerland AG 2020
S. Bliudze and L. Bocchi (Eds.): COORDINATION 2020, LNCS 12134, pp. 39–56, 2020.
https://doi.org/10.1007/978-3-030-50029-0_3

streams of values. These face challenges such as triggering reactions when these streams are updated, while avoiding glitches in a concurrent setting (temporarily inconsistent results), distinguishing between continuous streams (always available) and discrete streams (publishing values at specific points in time), and avoiding the callback hell [15] resulting from abusing the observable patterns that masks interactions that are not explicit in the software architecture.

Synchronous coordination languages, such as Reo [2], Signal Flow Graphs [7], or Linda [9], address how to impose constraints over the interactions between software objects or components, restricting the order in which the interactions can occur, and where data should flow to. These face challenges such as how to balance the expressivity of the language—capturing, e.g., real-time [16], data predicates [18], and probabilities [3]—with the development of tools to implement, simulate, or verify these programs.

Both programs in Reactive Programming (RP) and Synchronous Coordination (SC) provide an architecture to reason about streams: how to receive incoming streams and produce new outgoing ones. They provide mechanisms to: (1) calculate values from continuous or discrete data streams, and (2) constraint the scheduling of parallel tasks. RP is typically more pragmatic, focused on extending existing languages with constructs that manage operations over streams, while making the programmer less aware of the stream concept. SC is typically more fundamental, focused on providing a declarative software layer that does not address data computation, but describes instead constraints over interactions that can be formally analysed and used to generate code.

This paper provides a blend of both worlds, by proposing a language—ARx—with a syntactic structure based on *reactive programs*, and with a semantics that captures the synchronisation aspects of *synchronous coordination programs*. This paper starts by providing a better context overview of reactive and synchronous programs (Sect. 2). It then introduces the toolset supporting ARx in Sect. 3, available both to use as a web-service[2] or to download and run locally. The rest of the paper formalises the ARx language, without providing correctness results and focusing on the tools. It presents the core features of ARx in Sect. 4, introducing an intermediate language to give semantics to ARx of so-called stream-builders and providing a compositional encoding of ARx into stream-builders. Two extensions to ARx are then presented. The first consists of algebraic data types, in Sect. 5, making the data values more concrete. The second, in Sect. 6, enriches the syntax of ARx and of stream-builders, and introduces new rules to the operational semantics, to support the notion of reactivity.

2   Overview over Reactive and Synchronous Programs

This section selects a few representative examples of reactive programs and of synchronous coordinators. It uses a graphical notation to describe these programs, partially borrowed from Drechsler et al. [11], and explains the core challenges addressed by both approaches.

---

[2] http://arcatools.org/#arx.

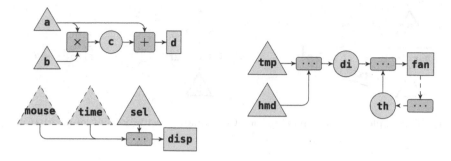

Fig. 1. Example of typical Reactive Programs.

Reactive Programs. Figure 1 includes 3 examples of reactive programs:

(top-left) A simple arithmetic computation, used by Bainomugisha et al. [5], with the program "$c = a \times b; d = a + c$" using reactive variables.

(right) A controller of a fan switch for embedded systems, used by Sakurai et al. [19], with the program "$di = 0.81 \times tmp + 0.01 \times hmd \times (0.99 \times tmp - 14.3) + 46.3$; $fan = di >= th$; $th = 75 + $ if $fan@last$ then -0.5 else 0.5".

(bottom-left) A GUI manager that selects which information to display, either from the continuous stream of mouse coordinates, or from the continuous stream of current time, with the program '$disp = $ if sel then _mouse_ else _time_".

Consider the arithmetic computation example. It has 4 (reactive) variables, a, b, c, d, and the sources (depicted as triangles) may *fire* a new value. Firing a new value triggers computations connected by arrows; e.g., if b fires 5, the ⊠ operation will try to recompute a new product, and will update c, which in turn will *fire* its new value. So-called *glitches* can occur, for example, if a fires a value, and ⊞ is calculated with the old value of c (before ⊠ updates its value). Different techniques exist to avoid glitches, by either enforcing a scheduling of the tasks, or, in a distributed setting, by including extra information on the messages used to detect missing dependencies. Languages that support reactive programming often include operations to fire a variable (e.g., `a.set("abc")` in ReScala), to react to a variable update (e.g., `d.observe(println)` in ReScala), to ask for a value to be updated and read (e.g., `d.now` in ReScala), and to read or update a value without triggering computations. Hence the effort is in managing the execution of a set of tasks, while buffering intermediate results, and propagate updates triggered by new data.

Consider now the fan controller. It includes a loop with dashed arrows, capturing the variable $fan@last$, i.e., the previous value of fan. This is a solution to handle loops, which are either forbidden or troublesome in RP. Consequently, the system must know the initial value of fan using a dedicated annotation.

Finally, consider the GUI example. This includes dashed triangles, which denote continuous streams of data (often refer to as *behaviour* in functional RP, as opposed to *signal*). This means that updates to the mouse coordinates or

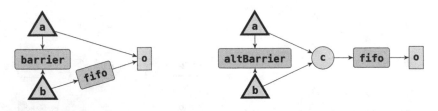

Fig. 2. Example of typical Synchronous Coordinators: variations of an alternator.

to the time passing do not trigger a computation. Here *sel* can fire a boolean that will trigger data to flow from either *mouse* or *time* to *disp*. Furthermore, the computation may not depend on all of its inputs, as opposed to the other operations seen so far. Hence, the composing operation depends, at each phase, on either *mouse* or *time*, and not on both.

Synchronous Coordinators. Synchronous coordinators provide a finer control over the scheduling restrictions of each of the stream updates, as illustrated in the two examples of Fig. 2. These represent different coordinators that have two inputs, a and b, and alternate their values to an output stream o. In RP a similar behaviour could be captured by "$o = if(aLast)$ then b else a ; $aLast =$ not($aLast@last$)". Using a synchronous coordinator, one can exploit synchrony and better control the communication protocol.

The coordinators of Fig. 2 use the blocks `fifo`, `barrier`, and `altBarrier`, and may connect streams directly. Unlike RP, these connections are *synchronous*, meaning that all streams involved in an operation must occur atomically. E.g., each stream can fire a single message only if the connected block or stream is ready to fire, which in turn can only happen if all their outputs are ready to fire. In the left coordinator, the top a can output a message only if it can send it to both o and the `barrier`. This `barrier` blocks a or b unless both a and b can fire atomically. The `fifo` can buffer at most one value, blocking incoming messages when full. The left coordinator receives each data message from both a and b, sending the message from a to c atomically and buffering the value from b; later the buffered message is sent to c, and only then streams a and b can fire again. The right coordinator uses a `altBarrier` that alternates between blocking a and blocking b, and it buffers the value temporarily to avoid o from having to synchronise with a or b.

Remarks. In SC data streams can fire only once, and do not store this value unless it is explicit in the coordinator. In RP, when a stream fires a value, this value is stored for later reuse – either by the sender or by the computing tasks, depending on the implementation engine. Also, the notion of synchronisation, describing sets of operations that occur atomically, is not common in RP, since RP targets efficient implementations of tasks that run independently.

The term *reactive* has also been applied in the context of *reactive systems* and *functional reactive systems*. The former addresses systems that react to incoming stimuli and are responsive, resilient, elastic and message driven, described

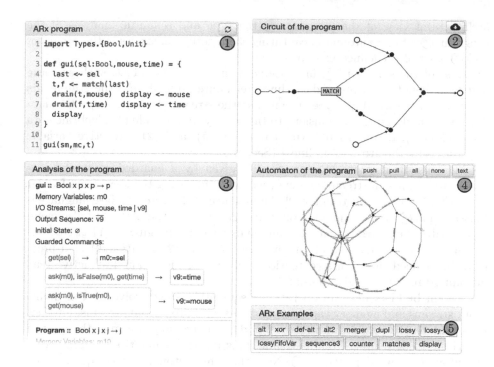

Fig. 3. Screenshot of the widgets in the online tool for ARx programs.

in the *Reactive Manifesto* [1]. The latter is a specific take on reactive programming based on functions over streams that distinguish (continuous) behaviour from (discrete) events [12]. Early work on synchronous languages for (real-time) reactive systems has been focused on safety-critical reactive control system, and includes synchronous programming and (synchronous) dataflow programming [5]. Similarly to synchronous coordination, synchronous languages such as Esterel [6] and StateCharts [13], assume that reactions are atomic and take no time, simplifying programs and allowing their representation as finite state machines which can be later translated into sequential programs.

3 ARx Toolset

We implemented an open-source web-based prototype tool to edit, parse, and type check ARx programs, and to animate their semantics.[3] These tools are developed in Scala, which is compiled to JavaScript using ScalaJS.[4] This section starts by giving a quick overview on how to use the tools, using as running example a version of the GUI manager from Fig. 1 in ARx. The toolset includes several widgets, depicted in Fig. 3: ① the editor to specify the program, ② the

---

[3] http://arcatools.org/#arx.

[4] https://www.scala-js.org.

architectural view of the program, ③ the type and semantic analysis of the program, ④ a finite automaton capturing the reactive semantics of the program, and ⑤ a set of predefined examples.

Most of the syntax in ① in introduced in Sect. 4. Variables, such as `mouse` and `time`, denote streams of data; line breaks are ignored; and the statements "`display←mouse display←time`" mean that the stream `display` merges the data from `mouse` and `display`. Extensions to the core syntax include (1) algebraic data types (Sect. 5), deconstructed with `match` (line 5), and (2) a reactive variable introduced by the arrow `⤳` in line 4 (Sect. 6).

The semantics of an ARx program is given by a guarded command language, which we call stream builders (Sect. 4.2), following the ideas from Dokter and Arbab's stream constraints [10]. An instance of this intermediate language is illustrated in ③, and includes not only stream variables from ARx, but also memory variables (e.g., `m0`). Guarded commands include the guards (1) `get(mouse)` to denote a destructive read from the `mouse` stream, (2) `isFalse(m0)` as a predicate introduced in our first extension, and `ask(m0)` is a non-destructive read introduced in our second extension.

Stream builders have an operational semantics: they evolve by consuming input streams and memory variables, and by writing to output streams. Furthermore, the reactive extension in Sect. 6 adds an extra step to signal the interest in writing-to or reading-from a stream. This reactive semantics is animated in an automata view, depicted in ④. Note that this automata grows quickly, but it is usually unnecessary, as the stream builders act as a compact and symbolic representation of the automata.

4   Core ARx

4.1   ARx: Syntax

A program is a statement, according to the syntax in Fig. 4. Expressions are either *terms t*, or names of so-called *stream builders bn* parameterised by a sequence of variables $\overline{x}$. In turn, terms can be *stream variables x*, *data values d*, or *function* names parameterised by variables $\overline{x}$.

So far we leave open the notions of *stream builders* and *functions*. Stream builders will be introduced in Sect. 4.2, and will give semantics to ARx programs. Functions are assumed to be deterministic and total with an interpretation $\mathcal{I}$ that maps closed terms to values; in Sect. 5 we will restrict to constructors of user-defined algebraic data types, as in our prototype implementation.

Regarding the remaining constructions, a *statement* is either an assignment *a*, a stream expression *e*, a builder definition *d*, or a parallel composition of statements *s s*. An *assignment* assigns a stream expression *e* to a non-empty sequence of stream variables $\overline{x}$. A builder definition **def** introduces a name *bn* associated to a new stream builder of a given block of statements *s*.

Examples. The examples below assume the existence of stream builders `fifo` and `barrier`,[5] and the function `ifThenElse` with some interpretation. Consider

---

[5] `barrier` is known as `drain` in our tools.

Statement $s ::= a \mid e \mid d \mid s\,s$	**Stream Expression** $e ::= t \mid bn(\overline{x})$	
Assignment $a ::= \overline{x} \leftarrow e$	**Term** $t ::= x \mid d \mid fn(\overline{x})$	
	Builder Definition $d ::= \mathbf{def}\ bn(\overline{x}) = \{s\}$	

Fig. 4. ARx' basic syntax, where bn ranges over names of stream builders, fn ranges over names of functions, and x over stream variables.

the `alternator` definition, capturing the program from the left of Fig. 2. This has two input streams as parameters: `a` and `b`, which must fire together because of the `barrier`. Their values are redirected to `c`: the one from `a` flows atomically, and the one from `b` is buffered until a follow-up step. The stream `c` is the only output of the definition block.

```
def alternator(a,b) = {        def gui(sel,mouse,time) = {
    barrier(a,b)   c←a             display ←
    c←fifo(b)      c                   ifThenElse(sel,mouse,time)
}                              }
```

Stream builders are typed, indicating the data types that populate the each input and output stream. Our implementation uses a type-inference engine that unifies matching streams and uses type variables. In our example from Fig. 3, the inferred type of the `gui` builder is $\mathsf{Bool} \times \mathsf{p} \times \mathsf{p} \rightarrow \mathsf{p}$, meaning that its first argument has type `Bool`, and all other ports must have the same type `p`. The type system also imposes all input stream variables inside **def** clauses to be parameters. We leave the type rules out of the scope of this paper, which focuses on the tools and on the semantics of ARx.

4.2   Stream Builders: Syntax

Programs in ARx express functions from streams to streams, and describe the (non-strict) order between consuming and producing values. ARx's semantics is given by stream builders, defined below, which are closely inspired on Dokter and Arbab's stream constraints [10].

Definition 1 (Stream builder). *A stream builder sb follows the grammar:*

$$
\begin{array}{rll}
sb ::= & \overline{upd} \wedge [\overline{gc}] & \text{(stream builder)} \\
gc ::= & \overline{guard} \rightarrow \overline{upd} & \text{(guarded command)} \\
guard ::= & \mathsf{get}(v) \mid \mathsf{und}(v) \mid t & \text{(guard)} \\
upd ::= & v := t & \text{(update)}
\end{array}
$$

where v is a variable name, t is a term, and $\overline{x}$ is a sequence of elements from x.

Each variable v can represent an *input stream* or an *output stream* (or both), as in ARx, or *internal memory*. Terms t are the same as in ARx, but with variables also over the internal memory, and we write $\mathsf{fv}(t)$ to denote the set variables in t. Let s be a variable pointing to a stream and m a memory variable. Intuitively, a guard $\mathsf{get}(s)$ means that the head of s, denoted by $s(0)$, is ready to be read; a guard $\mathsf{get}(m)$ means that the memory variable m is defined; and a guard $\mathsf{und}(x)$ means that x has no value yet or is undefined.

A stream builder consists of an initial update that initialises memory variables and a set of guarded commands of the form $g \to u$ that specify a set of non-deterministic rules, such that the update u can be executed whenever guard g holds. When **executing** an update from a guarded command with a guard that succeeds, each $s := t$ sets $s(0)$ to the value obtained from t, each $m := t$ sets m to be the value from t; every stream s with $\mathsf{get}(s)$ in the guard is updated to s' (the head of s is consumed), and every memory m with $\mathsf{get}(m)$ in the guard—and not set in the update—becomes undefined. As a side-remark, these constructions get, und, and $v := t$ are analogue to the operations *get*, *nask*, and *tell*, respectively, over shared tuple-spaces in Linda-like languages, well studied in the literature in that context [8].

We further restrict which streams can be used in updates and guards based on whether they are input streams I—that can be read—or output streams O—that can be built. This is formalised by the notion of well-definedness below. Intuitively, in addition to the previous restrictions, the initial updates can be only over memory variables and use terms with no variables, i.e., memory variables can only be initialized with data values rather than streams; and for every guarded command, undefined variables cannot be "gotten", both guards and terms in updates can only use defined memory and input stream variables, and assignments in guarded commands cannot have cycles (which can occur since input and output stream variables may intersect). We use the following notation: given a stream builder sb, we write $sb.I$, $sb.O$, and $sb.M$ to denote its input streams, output streams, and memory variables; and we write $\mathsf{get}(\overline{v})$ (and analogously for und) to denote a set of occurrences of $\mathsf{get}(v)$, for every $v \in \overline{v}$.

Definition 2 (Well-defined stream builder). *Let sb be the stream builder:*

$$\overline{v_{init} := t_{init}} \wedge [\mathsf{get}(\overline{v_{get}}), \mathsf{und}(\overline{v_{und}}), \overline{t_{guard}} \to \overline{v_{out} := t_{out}}, \ldots].$$

We say sb is well-defined *if $\overline{v_{init}} \subseteq sb.M$ and $\mathsf{fv}(t_{init}) = \emptyset$, and if for every guarded command, the following conditions are met:*

$$\overline{v_{get}} \cap \overline{v_{und}} = \emptyset \qquad \overline{v_{get}} \cup \overline{v_{und}} \subseteq sb.I \cup sb.M \qquad \overline{v_{out}} \subseteq sb.O \cup sb.M$$

$$\mathsf{fv}(t_{guard}) \subseteq \overline{v_{get}} \qquad \mathsf{fv}(\overline{t_{out}}) \times \overline{v_{out}} \text{ is acyclic} \qquad \mathsf{fv}(t_{out}) \subseteq \overline{v_{get}}$$

Examples. We omit the initial updates of a stream builder when empty, and write $\mathtt{builder}\langle v_1, v_2, \ldots \rangle = \overline{upd} \wedge \overline{gc}$ in the examples below to define a stream builder $\mathtt{builder}$ as $\overline{upd} \wedge \overline{gc}$ over variables $\{v_1, v_2, \ldots\}$, using the convention that i

denotes an input stream, o denotes an output stream, and m denotes a memory.

$$sb_{add}\langle i_1, i_2, o \rangle = [\mathsf{get}(i_1), \mathsf{get}(i_2) \rightarrow o := i_1 + i_2]$$
$$sb_{xor}\langle i, o_1, o_2 \rangle = [\mathsf{get}(i) \rightarrow o_1 := in \; , \; \mathsf{get}(i) \rightarrow o_2 := in]$$
$$sb_{fifo}\langle i, o, m \rangle = [\mathsf{get}(i), \mathsf{und}(m) \rightarrow m := i \; , \; \mathsf{get}(m) \rightarrow o := m]$$
$$sb_{fifoFull42}\langle i, o, m \rangle = m := 42 \wedge sb_{fifo}\langle i, o, m \rangle$$
$$sb_{barrier}\langle i_1, i_2 \rangle = [\mathsf{get}(i_1), \mathsf{get}(i_2) \rightarrow \emptyset]$$
$$sb_{alternator}\langle i_1, i_2, o, m \rangle = \begin{bmatrix} \mathsf{get}(i_1), \mathsf{get}(i_2), \mathsf{und}(m) \rightarrow o := i_1, m := i_2 \\ \mathsf{get}(m) \rightarrow o := m \end{bmatrix}$$

Informally, the sb_{add} stream builder receives values from two streams and outputs their sum. At each round, it atomically collects a value from each input stream and produces a new output value. In sb_{xor} there are two non-deterministic options at each round: to send data to one output stream or to a second output stream. In sb_{fifo} the two options are disjoint: if m is undefined only the left rule can be triggered, and if m is defined only the right rule can be triggered, effectively buffering a value when m is undefined, and sending m when m is defined (becoming undefined again). The formal behaviour is described below. Later in the paper, we will present a composition operator for stream builders, allowing $sb_{alternator}$ to be built out of simpler builders.

4.3   Stream Builders: Operational Semantics

Consider a stream builder $sb = \overline{init} \wedge \overline{gc}$ with an interpretation $\mathcal{I}$ of closed terms as data values. The semantics of sb is given by a rewriting rule over the state of a stream builder. This state consists of a map σ_m that assigns memory variables to their data values, and is initially set to $\langle \overline{init} \rangle$. We use the following notation: $t[\sigma]$ captures the substitution on t of σ, $\mathsf{dom}(\sigma)$ is the domain of σ, $\sigma - X$ is the map σ excluding the keys in X, $\sigma_1 \cup \sigma_2$ is the map σ_1 extended with σ_2, updating existing entries, and $\mathsf{gets}(g)$ returns the variables within get constructs in the guard g. We use σ_i and σ_o to represents the current mapping from (the first element of) input and output stream variables to data values, respectively.

Definition 3 (Guard satisfaction). *Given a guard g and the current state of a system, given by σ_m and σ_i, the satisfaction of g, denoted $\sigma_m, \sigma_i \models g$, is defined as follows.*

$$\sigma_m, \sigma_i \models \mathsf{get}(\overline{v}) \text{ if } \overline{v} \subseteq \mathsf{dom}(\sigma_m) \cup \mathsf{dom}(\sigma_i) \qquad \sigma_m, \sigma_i \models t \text{ if } \mathcal{I}(t[\sigma_m][\sigma_i]) = true$$
$$\sigma_m, \sigma_i \models \mathsf{und}(\overline{v}) \text{ if } \overline{v} \cap \sigma_m = \emptyset \qquad \sigma_m, \sigma_i \models \overline{g} \text{ if } \forall_{g_i \in \overline{g}} \cdot \sigma_m, \sigma_i \models g_i$$

Definition 4 (Operational semantics). *The semantics of a stream builder $sb = \overline{init} \wedge \overline{gc}$ is given by the rule below, with an initial configuration $\langle \overline{init} \rangle$.*

$$\frac{\begin{array}{ll} (g \rightarrow u) \in \overline{gc} & \sigma_o = \{ v \mapsto d \mid (v := t) \in u, \ v \in sb.O, d = \mathcal{I}(t[\sigma_m][\sigma_i]) \} \\ \sigma_m, \sigma_i \models g & \sigma'_m = \{ v \mapsto d \mid (v := t) \in u, \ v \in sb.M, d = \mathcal{I}(t[\sigma_m][\sigma_i]) \} \end{array}}{\langle \sigma_m \rangle \xrightarrow{\sigma_i, \sigma_o} \langle (\sigma_m - \mathsf{gets}(g)) \cup \sigma'_m \rangle}$$

Intuitively, $\langle \sigma \rangle \xrightarrow{\sigma_i,\sigma_o} \langle \sigma' \rangle$ means that, for every variable i and data value d such that $\sigma(i) = d$, the state evolves by reading the value d from the head of the stream i, and by adding a value to each stream $o \in \mathsf{dom}(\sigma_o)$, given by $\sigma_o(o)$. The internal state is captured by σ_m that stores values of memory variables in $sb.M$, which is updated based on σ_i. Furthermore, the system can only evolve by executing an *active* guarded command. Intuitively, a guarded command is active if the current state of memory (σ_m) and input stream (σ_i) variables satisfy the guard g, such that: each term guard has an interpretation that evaluates to *true*; all required input stream variables coincide with the set of defined input stream variables; all required memory variables are contained in the defined memory variables; and all required undefined memory variables are indeed undefined. For example, the following are valid runs of the stream builders of Sect. 4.2.

$$sb_{alternator} : \quad \langle \emptyset \rangle \xrightarrow{\{in_1 \mapsto 5, in_2 \mapsto 8\}, \{out_1 \mapsto 5\}} \langle m \mapsto 8 \rangle \xrightarrow{\emptyset, \{out \mapsto 8\}} \langle \emptyset \rangle$$

$$sb_{add} : \quad \langle \emptyset \rangle \xrightarrow{\{in_1 \mapsto 3, in_2 \mapsto 2\}, \{out \mapsto 3+2\}} \langle \emptyset \rangle \xrightarrow{\{in_1 \mapsto 2, in_2 \mapsto 7\}, \{out \mapsto 2+7\}} \langle \emptyset \rangle$$

4.4 Composing Stream Builders

The composition of two stream builders yields a new stream builder that merges their initial update and their guarded commands, under some restrictions. I.e., the memory variables must be disjoint, some guarded commands can be included, and some pairs of guarded commands from each stream builder can be combined. This is formalised below in Definitions 5 and 6 after introducing some preliminary concepts. In the following we use the following auxiliary functions: $out(gc)$ returns the output streams assigned in the RHS of gc, $in(gc)$ returns the input streams inside **get** statements of gc, and $vars(gc)$ returns $out(gc) \cup in(gc)$.

The composition of stream builders follows the same principles as the composition of, e.g., constraint automata (CA) [4]. But unlike CA and most Reo semantics, it supports explicit many-to-many composition. I.e., a builder with an input stream i can be composed with another builder with the same input stream i, preventing individual guarded commands from each builder to use i without involving the other stream builder. Similarly, a builder with an output stream o can be combined with another one with the same output stream o, although only one builder can write to o at a time. A builder with an input stream x can be composed with another with an output stream with the same name x, making x both an input and an output in further compositions. The composition rules were carefully designed to keep the composition commutative and associative, which we do not prove in this paper.

We introducing the following auxiliary predicates used in the composition, using gc_i to range over guarded commands and I_1 to range over stream variables (meant to be from the same stream builder as gc_1).

$$matchedOuts(I_1, gc_1, gc_2) \quad \equiv \quad I_1 \cap out(gc_2) \subseteq in(gc_1)$$
$$matchedIns(I_1, gc_1, gc_2) \quad \equiv \quad I_1 \cap in(gc_2) \subseteq vars(gc_1)$$
$$exclusiveOut(gc_1, gc_2) \quad \equiv \quad out(gc_1) \cap out(gc_2) = \emptyset$$
$$noSync(I_1, gc_2) \quad \equiv \quad I_1 \cap vars(gc_2) = \emptyset$$

The predicate $matchedOuts(I_1, gc_1, gc_2)$ means that any input stream in I_1 that is an output of gc_2 must be read by gc_1, i.e., must be an input stream used by gc_1. Its dual $matchedIns(I_1, gc_1, gc_2)$ is not symmetric: it means that any input stream in I_1 that is an input gc_2 must either be written-to or read-by gc_1. This reflects the fact that input streams replicate data, and that input streams may also be output streams that could be used to synchronise. The predicate $exclusiveOut(gc_1, gc_2)$ states that gc_1 and gc_2 do not share output streams, reflecting the fact that only one rule can write to a stream at a time. The last predicate $noSync(I_1, gc_2)$ states that gc_2 will not affect any of the input streams in I_1. Intuitively this means that gc_2 may read-from or write-to streams from another builder sb_1 if they can also be written by sb_1, but not if they are read by sb_1.

The composition of guarded commands and of stream builders is defined below, based on these predicates.

Definition 5 (Composition of guarded commands $(gc_1 \bowtie gc_2)$). *For $i \in \{1,2\}$, let $gc_i = get(\overline{v_{gi}}), und(\overline{v_{ui}}), \overline{t_{gi}} \to \overline{v_{oi} := t_{oi}}$ be two guarded commands. Their composition yields $gc_1 \bowtie gc_2$ defined below.*

$$get((\overline{v_{g1}} \cup \overline{v_{g2}}) - (\overline{v_{o1}} \cup \overline{v_{o2}})), und(\overline{v_{u1}} \cup \overline{v_{u2}}), \overline{t_{g1}} \cup \overline{t_{g2}} \to \overline{v_{o1} := t_{o1}} \cup \overline{v_{o2} := t_{o2}}$$

Definition 6 (Composition of stream builders $(sb_1 \bowtie sb_2)$). *For $i \in \{1,2\}$, let $sb_i = \overline{init_i} \wedge \overline{[gc_i]}$ be two stream builders. Their composition yields $sb = sb_1 \bowtie sb_2 = (\overline{init_1} \cup \overline{init_2}) \wedge [gcs]$, where $sb.O = sb_1.O \cup sb_2.O$, $sb.I = sb_1.I \cup sb_2.I$, $sb.M = sb_1.M \cup sb_2.M$, and gcs is given by the smallest set of guarded commands that obeys the rules below, which are not exclusive.*

$$\text{(COM1)} \frac{\begin{array}{c} gc \in \overline{gc_1} \\ noSync(sb_2.I, gc) \end{array}}{gc}$$

$$\text{(COM2)} \frac{\begin{array}{c} gc \in \overline{gc_2} \\ noSync(sb_1.I, gc) \end{array}}{gc}$$

$$\text{(COM3)} \frac{\begin{array}{c} \forall i, j \in \{1,2\}, i \neq j : \quad gc_i \in \overline{gc_i} \\ matchedOuts(sb_i.I, gc_i, gc_j) \\ matchedIns(sb_i.I, gc_i, gc_j) \\ exclusiveOut(gc_i, gc_j) \end{array}}{gc_1 \bowtie gc_2}$$

Intuitively, any guarded command can go alone, unless it must synchronise on shared streams. Any two guarded commands can go together if their synchronization is well-defined and do not perform behaviour that must be an exclusive choice. Observe that the composition of two well-defined stream builders (c.f. Definition 2) may not produce a well-defined stream builder (e.g. cyclic assignments), in which case we say that the stream builders are incompatible and cannot be composed.

Example. The sequential composition of two `fifo` builders is presented below, annotated with the rule name that produced it. The $\mathsf{get}(b)$ guard was dropped during composition (Definition 5), but included here to help understanding. The last two guarded commands, in gray, denote scenarios where the middle stream b remains open for synchronization. These are needed to make the composition operator associative, but can be discarded when hiding the internal streams like b. This is not explained here, but is implemented in our prototype tool. Following a similar reasoning, the stream builder $sb_{alternator}$ can be produced by composing the stream builders $sb_{barrier}\langle a, b\rangle$, $sb_{fifo}\langle b, c, m\rangle$, and $sb_{sync}\langle a, c\rangle$, which has no internal streams.

$$sb_{fifo}\langle a, b, m_1\rangle \bowtie sb_{fifo}\langle b, c, m_2\rangle =$$

$$\begin{bmatrix}
\mathsf{get}(a), \mathsf{und}(m_1) \rightarrow m_1 := a & (\textsc{Com1}) \\
\mathsf{get}(b), \mathsf{get}(m_1), \mathsf{und}(m_2) \rightarrow b := m_1 , m_2 := b & (\textsc{Com3}) \\
\mathsf{get}(a), \mathsf{und}(m_1), \mathsf{get}(m_2) \rightarrow m_1 := a , c := m_2 & (\textsc{Com3}) \\
\mathsf{get}(m_2) \rightarrow c := m_2 & (\textsc{Com2}) \\
\mathsf{get}(a), \mathsf{und}(m_1), \mathsf{get}(b), \mathsf{und}(m_2) \rightarrow m_1 := a, m_2 := b & (\textsc{Com3}) \\
\mathsf{get}(b), \mathsf{und}(m_2) \rightarrow m_2 := b & (\textsc{Com2})
\end{bmatrix}$$

4.5   ARx's Semantics: Encoding into Stream Builders

$$[\![bn(\overline{x})]\!]_\Gamma = \left(sb\left[\overline{x}/\overline{x_I}, \overline{y}/\overline{x_O}, \overline{z}/\overline{rest}\right], \overline{y}\right) \quad \begin{cases} \Gamma(bn) = (sb, \overline{x_I}, \overline{x_O}) \\ \overline{rest} = \mathsf{fv}(sb) - \overline{x_I} - \overline{x_O} \\ \text{for some fresh } \overline{y}, \overline{z} \end{cases}$$

$$[\![t]\!]_\Gamma = \left(\left[\overline{\mathsf{get}(\mathsf{fv}(t))} \rightarrow o := t\right], o\right) \quad \begin{cases} \text{for some fresh } o \\ I = \mathsf{fv}(t), O = \{o\}, M = \emptyset \end{cases}$$

$$[\![x]\!]_\Gamma = ([\mathsf{get}(x) \rightarrow o := x], o) \quad \begin{cases} \text{for some fresh } o \\ I = \{x\}, O = \{o\}, M = \emptyset \end{cases}$$

$$[\![\overline{x} \leftarrow e]\!]_\Gamma = (sb[\overline{x}/\overline{x_O}], \emptyset) \quad \{ [\![e]\!]_\Gamma = (sb, \overline{x_O})$$

$$[\![s_1\ s_2]\!]_\Gamma = (sb_1 \bowtie sb_2, \overline{x_O} \cdot \overline{y_O}) \quad \begin{cases} [\![s_1]\!]_\Gamma = (sb_1, \overline{x_O}) \\ [\![s_2]\!]_\Gamma = (sb_2, \overline{y_O}) \end{cases}$$

$$\left[\!\!\left[\begin{matrix}\mathbf{def}\ bn(\overline{x}) = \{s_1\} \\ s_2\end{matrix}\right]\!\!\right]_\Gamma = [\![s_2]\!]_{\Gamma[bn \mapsto (sb, \overline{x}, \overline{x_O})]} \quad \{ [\![s_1]\!]_\Gamma = (sb, \overline{x_O})$$

Fig. 5. Semantics: encoding of statements of ARx as a stream builder.

A statement in ARx can be encoded as a single stream builder under a context Γ of existing stream builders. More precisely, Γ maps names of stream builders bn to triples $(sb, \overline{x_I}, \overline{x_O})$ of a stream builder sb, a sequence of variables for input streams $\overline{x_I}$ of sb, and a sequence of variables for output streams $\overline{x_O}$. Given a statement s and a context Γ, we define the encoding of s as $[\![s]\!]_\Gamma$, defined in Fig. 5. Evaluating $[\![s]\!]_\Gamma$ results in a pair $(sb, \overline{x_O})$ containing the encoded stream buffer and a sequence of variables. This sequence captures the output stream variables of sb. In the encoding definition we write $[x/y]$ to mean that y substitutes x. Our implementation further applies a simplification of guarded commands in the **def** clause, by hiding output streams not in $\overline{x_O}$ and guarded commands that consume streams that are both input and output; but we do omit this process in this paper.

The composition exemplified in Sect. 4.4, regarding the alternator, is used when calculating the encoding of "barrier(a,b) c←fifo(b) c←a" below, where $\Gamma = \{\mathtt{fifo} \mapsto (sb_{fifo}\langle i, o\rangle, i, o), \mathtt{barrier} \mapsto (sb_{barrier}\langle i_1, i_2\rangle, i_1 \cdot i_2, \emptyset)\}$.

$$[\![\mathtt{barrier(a,b)}]\!]_\Gamma = ([\mathsf{get}(a), \mathsf{get}(b) \to \emptyset], \emptyset) \tag{sb_1}$$

$$[\![\mathtt{fifo(b)}]\!]_\Gamma = ([\mathsf{get}(b), \mathsf{und}(y_1) \to y_1 := b, \mathsf{get}(y_1) \to y_2 := y_1], y_2)$$

$$[\![\mathtt{c{\leftarrow}fifo(b)}]\!]_\Gamma = ([\mathsf{get}(b), \mathsf{und}(y_1) \to y_1 := b, \mathsf{get}(y_1) \to c := y_1], \emptyset) \tag{sb_2}$$

$$[\![\mathtt{c{\leftarrow}a}]\!]_\Gamma = ([\mathsf{get}(a) \to c := a], c) \tag{sb_3}$$

$$\left[\!\!\left[\begin{array}{l} \mathtt{barrier(a,b)} \\ \mathtt{c{\leftarrow}fifo(b)} \\ \mathtt{c{\leftarrow}a} \end{array} \right]\!\!\right]_\Gamma = (sb_1 \bowtie sb_2 \bowtie sb_3, \emptyset) = (sb_{alternator}\langle a, b, c, y_1\rangle, \emptyset)$$

5   Extension I: Algebraic Data Types

This section extends our language of stream builders with constructs for algebraic data types, allowing types to influence the semantics. The grammar, presented in Fig. 6, extends the grammar from Fig. 4 with declarations of Algebraic Data Types (ADTs), **build** and **match** primitive stream builders, and type annotations for builder definitions. For simplicity, we use the following notation: we omit $\overline{X}$, $\langle \overline{X}\rangle$, and $(\overline{X})$ when $\overline{X}$ is empty; we write **build**, **match**, and $bn(x)$ instead of **build**$\langle\alpha\rangle$, **match**$\langle\alpha\rangle$, and $bn(x : \alpha)$, respectively, when α is a type variable not used anywhere else; and we omit the output type $\overline{\mathcal{T}}$ in builder definitions to denote a sequence of fresh type variables, whose dimension is determined during type-checking (when unifying types).

Program	$P ::= \overline{\mathcal{D}}\ s$	New Data Type	$\mathcal{D} ::= \mathbf{data}\ D\langle\overline{\alpha}\rangle = Q(\overline{\mathcal{T}})\ \big|\ Q(\overline{\mathcal{T}})$
Data Type	$\mathcal{T} ::= \alpha \mid D\langle\overline{\mathcal{T}}\rangle$	Stream Expression	$e ::= \cdots \mid \mathbf{build}\langle\mathcal{T}\rangle(\overline{x}) \mid \mathbf{match}\langle\mathcal{T}\rangle(\overline{x})$
Data Term	$t ::= Q(\overline{x})$	Builder Definition	$d ::= \mathbf{def}\ bn(\overline{x : \mathcal{T}}) : \overline{\mathcal{T}} = \{s\}$

Fig. 6. Syntax: extending the syntax from Fig. 4 with ADTs, where α ranges over type variables, D over type names, and Q over data constructors.

A program starts by a list of definitions of algebraic data types, such as the ones below, which we will assume to be included in the header of all programs.

$$\textbf{data Unit} = \textsf{U} \qquad\qquad \textbf{data Nat} \quad = \textsf{Zero} \mid \textsf{Succ(Nat)}$$
$$\textbf{data Bool} = \textsf{True} \mid \textsf{False} \qquad \textbf{data List}\langle\alpha\rangle = \textsf{Nil} \mid \textsf{Cons}(\alpha, \textsf{List}\langle\alpha\rangle)$$

These ADTs are interpreted as the smallest fix-point of the underlying functor, i.e., they describe finite terms using the constructors for data types. All constructors Q must have at least one argument, but we write Q without arguments to denote either $Q(\textsf{Unit})$ or $Q(\textsf{U})$. Each definition of an ADT **data** $D\langle\overline{\mathcal{T}}\rangle = Q_1(\overline{g}) \mid \ldots \mid Q_n(\overline{g})$, e.g., **data** $\textsf{List}\langle\alpha\rangle = \textsf{Nil} \mid \textsf{Cons}(\alpha, \textsf{List}\langle\alpha\rangle)$, introduces:

- *Term constructors* Q_i to build new terms, e.g. $\textsf{Nil}$ and $\textsf{Cons}(\textsf{True}, \textsf{Nil})$;
- *Term inspectors* $isQ_i(x)$ that check if x was built with Q_i, e.g. $is\textsf{Nil}$ and $is\textsf{Cons}$ return $\textsf{True}$ only if their argument has shape $\textsf{Nil}$ or $\textsf{Cons}$, respectively;
- *Term projections* $getQ_{i,j}$ that given a term built with Q_i return the j-th argument, e.g. $get\textsf{Cons}_2(\textsf{Cons}(\textsf{True}, \textsf{Cons}(\textsf{False}, \textsf{Nil}))) = \textsf{Cons}(\textsf{False}, \textsf{Nil})$;

$$[\![\textbf{match}\langle D\langle\overline{\mathcal{T}}\rangle\rangle]\!] =$$
$$\left(\begin{bmatrix} \textbf{get}(in), isQ_1(in) \;\rightarrow\; out_{1,1} := getQ_{1,1}(in), \ldots, out_{1,k_1} := getQ_{1,k_1}(in) \\ \cdots \\ \textbf{get}(in), isQ_n(in) \;\rightarrow\; out_{n,1} := getQ_{n,1}(in), \ldots, out_{n,k_n} := getQ_{n,k_n}(in) \end{bmatrix}, \\ out_{1,1} \cdots out_{1,k_1} \cdots out_{n,1} \cdots out_{n,k_n} \right)$$

$$[\![\textbf{build}\langle D\langle\overline{\mathcal{T}}\rangle\rangle]\!] =$$
$$\left(\begin{bmatrix} \textbf{get}(in_{1,1}), \ldots, \textbf{get}(in_{1,k_1}) \;\rightarrow\; out := Q_1(in_{1,1}, \ldots, in_{1,k_1}) \\ \cdots \\ \textbf{get}(in_{n,1}), \ldots, \textbf{get}(in_{n,k_n}) \;\rightarrow\; out := Q_n(in_{n,1}, \ldots, in_{n,k_n}) \end{bmatrix}, out \right)$$

Fig. 7. Semantics of match and build, considering that D is defined as **data** $D\langle\overline{\mathcal{T}}\rangle = Q_1(g_{1,1}, \ldots, g_{1,k_1}) \mid \ldots \mid Q_n(g_{n,1}, \ldots, g_{n,k_n})$.

Given these new constructs the new semantic encodings is presented in Fig. 7. For example, $[\![\textbf{match}\langle\textsf{List}\langle\alpha\rangle\rangle]\!]$ yields the builder below, and $[\![\textbf{match}\langle\alpha\rangle]\!]$ is undefined unless the type-inference can instantiate α with a concrete ADT.

$$\begin{bmatrix} \textbf{get}(in), is\textsf{Nil}(in) \;\;\rightarrow\; out_{1,1} := get\textsf{Nil}_1(in); \\ \textbf{get}(in), is\textsf{Cons}(in) \;\;\rightarrow\; out_{2,1} := get\textsf{Cons}_1(in), out_{2,2} := get\textsf{Cons}_2(in) \end{bmatrix}$$

6   Extension II: Reactive Semantics

In reactive languages, produced data is typically kept in memory, possibly triggering consumers when it is initially produced. In this section we provide a finer control about who can trigger the computation, and a notion of memory that is read without being consumed. This will allow us to have memory variables that trigger computations, and others that do not.

In the semantics of stream builders we add a notion of *active* variables, whereas a guarded command can only be selected if one of its variables is active, and adapt the operational semantics accordingly. We also introduce a new element to the guards: $\mathsf{ask}(v)$, that represents a non-destructive read.

Syntax: asking for data The extension for our language updates the grammar for assignments:

$$\text{Assignment} \qquad\qquad a ::= \overline{x} \leftarrow e \mid \overline{x} \leftarrow\!\!\!\leftsquigarrow e$$

whose squiggly arrow is interpreted as a creation of a reactive variable: the values from e are buffered before being used by $\overline{x}$, and this values can be read (non-destructively) when needed using the new guard ask. This is formalised below.

$$[\![\overline{x} \leftsquigarrow e]\!]_\Gamma = [\![(\overline{y} \leftarrow e)\ (\overline{x} \leftsquigarrow \overline{y})]\!]_\Gamma \qquad \text{for some fresh } \overline{y}$$
$$[\![x \leftsquigarrow y]\!]_\Gamma = \big([\mathsf{ask}(m) \rightarrow x := m \ , \ \mathsf{get}(y) \rightarrow m := y] \ , \ \emptyset\big)$$

Observe that "$\mathsf{get}(m) \rightarrow x := m, m := m$" is very similar to "$\mathsf{ask}(m) \rightarrow x := m$". The former consumes the variable m and defines it with its old value, and the latter reads m without consuming it. This subtle difference has an impact in our updated semantics, defined below, by marking assigned variables as *"active"*. In the first case m becomes active, allowing guarded commands that use m to be fired in a follow up step. In the second case m will become inactive, and guarded commands using m with no other active variables will not be allowed to fire.

Semantics: Active/Passive Variables. The reactive semantics for a stream builder $sb = \overline{init} \wedge \overline{gc}$ is given by the rules below. The state is extended with two sets of so-called *active* input and output variables, with initial state $\langle \overline{init}, \emptyset, \emptyset \rangle$. A system can evolve in two ways: (1) by evolving the program as before, consuming and producing data over variables, or (2) by an update to the context that becomes ready to write to (push) or read from (pull) a stream. Below we write "out(u)" to return the assigned variables in u (c.f. Sect. 4.4), "in(g)" to return the variables of g within get and ask constructs, and $\langle \sigma \rangle \xrightarrow{x}_{g,u} \langle \sigma' \rangle$ to denote the step from state σ to σ' by x when selecting the guarded command $g \rightarrow u$.

$$\frac{\begin{array}{l}(g \rightarrow u) \in \overline{gc} \quad \langle \sigma_m \rangle \xrightarrow{\sigma_i, \sigma_o}_{g,u} \langle \sigma'_m \rangle \\ (\mathsf{in}(g) \cap A_i \neq \emptyset) \vee (\mathsf{out}(u) \cap A_o \neq \emptyset) \\ A'_i = (A_i - \mathsf{in}(g)) \cup (\mathsf{out}(u) \cap sb.M) \\ A'_o = A_o - \mathsf{out}(u)\end{array}}{\langle \sigma_m, A_i, A_o \rangle \xrightarrow{\sigma_i, \sigma_o} \langle \sigma'_m, A'_i, A'_o \rangle} \qquad \frac{\langle \sigma_m \rangle \nrightarrow \langle \sigma'_m \rangle \quad x \in sb.I}{\langle \sigma_m, A_i, A_o \rangle \xrightarrow{\mathsf{push}(x)} \langle \sigma'_m, A_i \cup \{x\}, A_o \rangle}$$

$$\frac{\langle \sigma_m \rangle \nrightarrow \langle \sigma'_m \rangle \quad x \in sb.O}{\langle \sigma_m, A_i, A_o \rangle \xrightarrow{\mathsf{pull}(x)} \langle \sigma'_m, A_i, A_o \cup \{x\} \rangle}$$

The previous semantic rules must be accommodated to take the ask constructor into account. This is done by redefining the *guard satisfaction* definition in Sect. 4.3 to incorporate a new rule, presented below, and *vars* in Sect. 4.4 to include also the ask variables.

$$\sigma_m, \sigma_i \models \mathsf{ask}(\overline{v}) \qquad\qquad \overline{v} \subseteq \mathsf{dom}(\sigma_m)$$

Example: ADT and Reactivity. We illustrate the encoding and semantics of reactive stream builders using the GUI manager example (Fig. 1 and Fig. 3). The equality below depicts the adapted system following the ARx syntax (left) and its semantics (right).

$$
\begin{bmatrix}
\text{last} \leftsquigarrow \text{sel} \\
\text{t,f} \leftarrow \text{match(last)} \\
\text{barrier(t,mouse)} \\
\text{barrier(f,time)} \\
\text{display} \leftarrow \text{mouse} \\
\text{display} \leftarrow \text{time} \\
\text{display}
\end{bmatrix}
=
\begin{bmatrix}
\text{get(sel)} & \rightarrow & m := \text{sel} \\
\text{get(mouse),} & & \text{last} := m, \\
\text{get(last),get(t),} & \rightarrow & \text{t} := getTrue_1(\text{last}), \\
\text{ask}(m), isTrue(m) & & \text{display} := \text{mouse} \\
\text{get(time),} & & \text{last} := m, \\
\text{get(last),get(f),} & \rightarrow & \text{f} := getFalse_1(\text{last}), \\
\text{ask}(m), isFalse(m) & & \text{display} := \text{time}
\end{bmatrix}
$$

This encoding also returns the sequence of output streams, which in this case is display. The stream builder is further simplified by our toolset by removing intermediate stream variables last, t, and f from the updates, as depicted in the screenshot of Fig. 3-③.

The following transitions are valid runs of this program.

$$\langle \emptyset, \emptyset, \emptyset \rangle \xrightarrow{\text{pull(display)}} \langle \emptyset, \emptyset, \{\text{display}\} \rangle$$

$$\xrightarrow{\text{push(sel)}} \langle \emptyset, \{\text{sel}\}, \{\text{display}\} \rangle$$

$$\xrightarrow{\text{sel} \mapsto \text{True}} \langle \{m \mapsto \text{True}\}, \{m\}, \{\text{display}\} \rangle$$

$$\xrightarrow{\text{mouse} \mapsto (2,3); \text{display} \mapsto (2,3)} \langle \{m \mapsto \text{True}\}, \emptyset, \emptyset \rangle$$

$$\xrightarrow{\text{pull(display)}} \langle \{m \mapsto \text{True}\}, \emptyset, \{\text{display}\} \rangle$$

$$\xrightarrow{\text{mouse} \mapsto (5,8); \text{display} \mapsto (5,8)} \langle \{m \mapsto \text{True}\}, \emptyset, \emptyset \rangle$$

7   Conclusions

We proposed *ARx*, a lightweight programming language to specify component-based architecture for reactive systems, blending principles from reactive programming and synchronous coordination languages. *ARx* supports algebraic data types and is equipped with a type checking engine (not introduced here) to check if streams are well-composed based on the data being streamed.

Programs are encoded into *stream builders*, which provide a formal and compositional semantics to build programs out of simpler ones. A stream builder specifies the initial state of a program and a set of guarded commands which describe the steps (commands) that the program can perform provided some conditions (guards)—over the internal state and the inputs received from the environment—are satisfied.

We built an online tool to specify, type check, and analyse the semantics of ARx programs, and visualize both the architectural view of the program and its operational reactive semantics.

Future work plans include the *verification* of properties, the addition of new *semantic extensions*, and the development of *code generators*. These properties could be specified using hierarchical dynamic logic and verified with model checkers such as mCRL2, following [17], or could address the possibility of infinite loops caused by priorities of push and pulls from the environment. The semantic extensions could target, e.g., notions of variability, probability, time, and quality of service.

Acknowledgment. This work was partially supported by National Funds through FCT/MCTES (Portuguese Foundation for Science and Technology), within the CISTER Research Unit (UIDB/04234/2020); by the Norte Portugal Regional Operational Programme (NORTE 2020) under the Portugal 2020 Partnership Agreement, through the European Regional Development Fund (ERDF) and also by national funds through the FCT, within project NORTE-01-0145-FEDER-028550 (REASSURE); and by the Operational Competitiveness Programme and Internationalization (COMPETE 2020) under the PT2020 Partnership Agreement, through the European Regional Development Fund (ERDF), and by national funds through the FCT, within projects POCI-01-0145-FEDER-029946 (DaVinci) and POCI-01-0145-FEDER-029119 (PReFECT).

References

1. The reactive manifesto v2.0 (2014). https://www.reactivemanifesto.org
2. Arbab, F.: Reo: a channel-based coordination model for component composition. Math. Struct. Comput. Sci. **14**(3), 329–366 (2004)
3. Baier, C.: Probabilistic models for Reo connector circuits. J. Univ. Comput. Sci. **11**(10), 1718–1748 (2005)
4. Baier, C., Sirjani, M., Arbab, F., Rutten, J.J.M.M.: Modeling component connectors in Reo by constraint automata. Sci. Comput. Program. **61**(2), 75–113 (2006)
5. Bainomugisha, E., Carreton, A.L., Cutsem, T.V., Mostinckx, S., De Meuter, W.: A survey on reactive programming. ACM Comput. Surv. **45**(4), 52:1–52:34 (2013)
6. Berry, G.: The foundations of Esterel. In: Plotkin, G.D., Stirling, C., Tofte, M. (eds.) Proof, Language, and Interaction, pp. 425–454. The MIT Press (2000)
7. Bonchi, F., Sobocinski, P., Zanasi, F.: Full abstraction for signal flow graphs. In: Proceedings of the 42nd Annual Symposium on Principles of Programming Languages, POPL 2015, pp. 515–526. ACM, New York (2015)
8. Brogi, A., Jacquet, J.-M.: On the expressiveness of coordination via shared dataspaces. Sci. Comput. Program. **46**(1–2), 71–98 (2003)
9. Cridlig, R., Goubault, E.: Semantics and analysis of linda-based languages. In: Cousot, P., Falaschi, M., Filé, G., Rauzy, A. (eds.) WSA 1993. LNCS, vol. 724, pp. 72–86. Springer, Heidelberg (1993). https://doi.org/10.1007/3-540-57264-3_30
10. Dokter, K., Arbab, F.: Rule-based form for stream constraints. In: Di Marzo Serugendo, G., Loreti, M. (eds.) COORDINATION 2018. LNCS, vol. 10852, pp. 142–161. Springer, Cham (2018). https://doi.org/10.1007/978-3-319-92408-3_6

11. Drechsler, J., Salvaneschi, G., Mogk, R., Mezini, M.: Distributed REScala: an update algorithm for distributed reactive programming. In: Black, A.P., Millstein, T.D. (eds) Proceedings of the 2014 ACM International Conference on Object Oriented Programming Systems Languages & Applications, OOPSLA 2014, Part of SPLASH 2014, Portland, OR, USA, 20–24 October 2014, pp. 361–376. ACM (2014)

12. Elliott, C., Hudak, P.: Functional reactive animation. In: International Conference on Functional Programming (1997)

13. Harel, D.: Statecharts: a visual formalism for complex systems. Sci. Comput. Program. **8**(3), 231–274 (1987)

14. Hudak, P., Courtney, A., Nilsson, H., Peterson, J.: Arrows, robots, and functional reactive programming. In: Jeuring, J., Jones, S.L.P. (eds.) AFP 2002. LNCS, vol. 2638, pp. 159–187. Springer, Heidelberg (2003). https://doi.org/10.1007/978-3-540-44833-4_6

15. Maier, I., Rompf, T., Odersky, M.: Deprecating the observer pattern, p. 18 (2010)

16. Meng, S., Arbab, F.: On resource-sensitive timed component connectors. In: Bonsangue, M.M., Johnsen, E.B. (eds.) FMOODS 2007. LNCS, vol. 4468, pp. 301–316. Springer, Heidelberg (2007). https://doi.org/10.1007/978-3-540-72952-5_19

17. Hojjat, H., Massink, M. (eds.): FSEN 2019. LNCS, vol. 11761. Springer, Cham (2019). https://doi.org/10.1007/978-3-030-31517-7

18. Proença, J., Clarke, D.: Interactive interaction constraints. In: De Nicola, R., Julien, C. (eds.) COORDINATION 2013. LNCS, vol. 7890, pp. 211–225. Springer, Heidelberg (2013). https://doi.org/10.1007/978-3-642-38493-6_15

19. Sakurai, Y., Watanabe, T.: Towards a statically scheduled parallel execution of an FRP language for embedded systems. In: Proceedings of the 6th ACM SIGPLAN International Workshop on Reactive and Event-Based Languages and Systems, REBLS 2019, pp. 11–20. Association for Computing Machinery, New York (2019)

Towards Energy-, Time- and Security-Aware Multi-core Coordination

Julius Roeder[1], Benjamin Rouxel[1], Sebastian Altmeyer[2],
and Clemens Grelck[1(✉)]

[1] University of Amsterdam, Science Park 904, 1098XH Amsterdam, Netherlands
{j.roeder,b.rouxel,c.grelck}@uva.nl
[2] University of Augsburg, Universitätsstr. 2, 86159 Augsburg, Germany
altmeyer@informatik.uni-augsburg.de

Abstract. Coordination is a well established computing paradigm with a plethora of languages, abstractions and approaches. Yet, we are not aware of any adoption of the principle of coordination in the broad domain of cyber-physical systems, where non-functional properties, such as execution/response time, energy consumption and security are as crucial as functional correctness.

We propose a coordination approach, including a functional coordination language and its associated tool flow, that considers time, energy and security as first-class citizens in application design and development. We primarily target cyber-physical systems running on off-the-shelf heterogeneous multi-core platforms. We illustrate our approach by means of a real-world use case, an unmanned aerial vehicle for autonomous reconnaissance mission, which we develop in close collaboration with industry.

Keywords: Cyber-physical systems · Non-functional properties · Real-time · Energy · Security

1 Introduction

Cyber-physical systems (CPS) deeply intertwine software with physical components, such as sensors and actuators that impact the physical world. Broadly speaking the software controls the actuators of a physical system based on input from the sensors and specified policies. Our world is full of cyber-physical systems, ranging from washing machines to airplanes. Designing secure, safe and correct cyber-physical systems requires a tremendous amount of verification, validation and certification.

A common characteristic of cyber-physical systems is that non-functional properties of the software, such as time, energy and security, are as important for correct behaviour as purely functional correctness. Actuators must react on

---

This work is supported and partly funded by the European Union Horizon-2020 research and innovation programme under grant agreement No. 779882 (TeamPlay).

© IFIP International Federation for Information Processing 2020
Published by Springer Nature Switzerland AG 2020
S. Bliudze and L. Bocchi (Eds.): COORDINATION 2020, LNCS 12134, pp. 57–74, 2020.
https://doi.org/10.1007/978-3-030-50029-0_4

sensor input within a certain time limit, or the reaction might in the worst case become useless. In addition to general environmental concerns, energy consumption of computing devices becomes crucial in battery-powered cyber-physical systems. Security concerns are paramount in many cyber-physical systems due to their potentially harmful impact on the real world. However, more security typically requires more computing effort. More computing effort takes more time and consumes more energy. Thus, time, energy and security are connected in the triangle of non-functional properties.

The multi-core revolution has meanwhile also reached the domain of cyber-physical systems. A typical example is the ARM big. LITTLE CPU architecture that features four energy-efficient Cortex A7 cores and four energy-hungry, but computationally more powerful, Cortex A15 cores. Many platforms complement this heterogeneous CPU architecture with an on-chip GPU. Such architectures create previously unknown degrees of freedom regarding the internal organisation of an application: what to compute where and when. This induces a global optimisation problem, for instance minimising energy consumption, under budget constraints, for instance in terms of time and security.

We propose the domain-specific functional coordination language TeamPlay and the associated tool chain that consider the aforementioned non-functional properties as first-class citizens in the application design and development process. Our tool chain compiles coordination code to a final executable linked with separately compiled component implementations. We combine a range of analysis and scheduling techniques for the user to choose from like in a tool box. The generated code either implements a static (offline) schedule or a dynamic (online) schedule. With static/offline scheduling all placements and activation times are pre-computed; with dynamic/online scheduling certain decisions are postponed until runtime.

Both options are driven by application-specific global objectives. The most common objective is to minimise energy consumption while meeting both time and security constraints. A variation of the theme would be to maximise security while meeting time and energy constraints. Less popular, but possible in principle, would be the third combination: minimising time under energy and security constraints.

Both offline and online scheduling share the concept of making conscious and application-specific decisions as to what compute where and when. Our work distinguishes itself from, say, operating system level scheduling by the clear insight into both the inner workings of an application and into the available computing resources.

The specific contribution of this paper lies in the design of the energy-, time- and security-aware coordination language and the overall approach. Due to space limitations we can only sketch out the various elements of our tool chain and must refer the interested reader to future publications to some degree.

The remainder of the paper is organised as follows: In Sect. 2 we explain our view on coordination followed by a detailed account of our (domain-specific) coordination language in Sect. 3. In Sect. 4 we illustrate our approach by means of a real-world use-case, and in Sect. 5 we sketch out our tool chain implementation. We discuss related work in Sect. 6 and conclude in Sect. 7.

2   Coordination Model

The term *coordination* goes back to the seminal work of Gelernter and Carriero [13] and their coordination language Linda. Coordination languages can be classified as either *endogenous* or *exogenous* [5]. Endogenous approaches provide coordination primitives within application code. The original work on Linda falls into this category. Exogenous approaches fully separate the concerns of coordination programming and application programming

We pursue an exogenous approach and foster the separation of concerns between intrinsic component behaviour and extrinsic component interaction. The notion of a component is the bridging point between low-level functionality implementation and high-level application design.

2.1   Components

We illustrate our component model in Fig. 1. Following the keyword `component` we have a unique component name that serves the dual purpose of identifying a certain application functionality and of locating the corresponding implementation in the object code.

A component interacts with the outside world via component-specific numbers of typed and named input ports and output ports. As the Kleene star in Fig. 1 suggests, a component may have zero input ports or zero output ports. A component without input ports is called a *source component*; a component without output ports is called a *sink component*. Source components and sink components

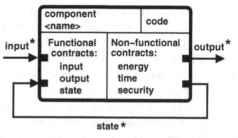

Fig. 1. Illustration of component model

form the quintessential interfaces between the physical world and the cyber-world representing sensors and actuators in the broadest sense. We adopt the firing rule of Petri-nets, i.e. a component is activated as soon as data (tokens) are available on each of its input ports.

Technically, a component implementation is a function adhering to the C calling and linking conventions [21]. Name and signature of this function can be derived from the component specification in a defined way. This function may call other functions using the regular C calling convention. The execution of a component (function), including execution of all subsidiary regular functions, must be free of side-effects. In other words, input tokens must map to output tokens in a purely functional way. Exceptions are source and sink components that are supposed to control sensors and actuators, respectively.

2.2   Stateful Components

Our components are conceptually stateless. However, some sort of state is very common in cyber-physical systems. We model such state in a functionally transparent way as illustrated in Fig. 1, namely by so-called state ports that are short-circuited from output to input. In analogy to input ports and output ports, a component may well have no state ports. We call such a component a (practically) *stateless* component.

Our approach to state is not dissimilar from main-stream purely functional languages, such as Haskell or Clean. They are by no means free of state either, for the simple reason that many real-world problems and phenomena are stateful. However, purely functional languages apply suitable techniques to make any state fully explicit, be it monads [28] in Haskell or uniqueness types [1] in Clean. Making state explicit is key to properly deal with state and state changes in a declarative way. In contrast, the quintessential problem of impure functional and even more so imperative languages is that state is potentially scattered all over the place. And even where this is not the case in practice, proving this property is hardly possible.

2.3   ETS-aware Components

We are particularly interested in the non-functional properties of code execution. Hence, any component not only comes with functional contracts, as sketched out before, but additionally with non-functional contracts concerning energy, time and security (and potentially more in the future).

These three non-functional properties are inherently different in nature. Execution time and energy consumption can be measured, depend on a concrete execution machinery and vary between different hardware scenarios. In contrast, security, more precisely algorithmic security, depends on the concrete implementation of a component, for example using different levels of encryption, etc. However, different security levels almost inevitably incur different computational demands and, thus, are likely to expose different runtime behaviour in terms of time and energy consumption as well.

Knowledge about non-functional properties of components is at the heart of our approach. It is this information that drives our scheduling and mapping decisions to solve the given optimisation problem (e.g. minimising energy consumption) under constraints (e.g. execution deadlines and minimum security requirements).

2.4   Multi-version Components

As illustrated in Fig. 2, a component may have multiple versions with identical functional behaviour, but with different implementations and, thus, different energy, time and (possibly) security contracts. Multi-version components add another degree of freedom to the scheduling and mapping problem that we address: selecting the best fitting variant of a component under given optimisation objectives and constraints.

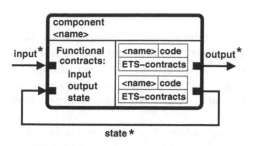

Fig. 2. Multi-version component with individual energy, time and security contracts

Take as an example our reconnaissance drone use case, that we will explore in more detail in Sect. 4. A drone could adapt its security protocol for communication with the base station in accordance with changing mission state: low security while taking off or landing, medium security while navigating to/from mission area, high security during mission. Continuous adaptation of security levels results in less computing and, thus, in energy savings that could be exploited for longer flight times.

Our solution is to provide different versions of the same component (similar to [24]) and to select the best version regarding mission state and objectives based on the scheduling strategy. For the time being, we only support off-line version selection, but scenarios with online version control, as sketched out above, are on our agenda.

2.5 Component Interplay

Components are connected via FIFO channels to exchange data, as illustrated in Fig. 3. Depending on application requirements, components may start computing at statically determined time slots (when all input data is guaranteed to be present) or may be activated dynamically by the presence of all required input data. Components may produce output data on all or on selected output ports.

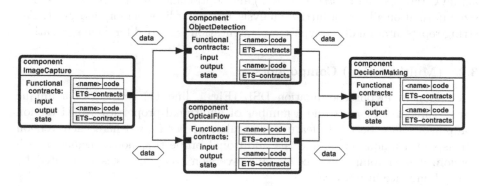

Fig. 3. Illustration of data-driven component interplay via FIFO channels

3   Coordination Language

Our coordination language focuses on the design of arbitrary synchronous data-flow-oriented applications. It describes a graph structure where vertices are components (*actors*, *tasks*) while edges represent dependencies between components. A dependency/edge defines a data exchange between a source and a sink through a FIFO channel. Such a data item, called *token*, can have different types, from primitive types to more elaborate structures.

Similar to periodic task models [18] a data-flow graph instance is called an *iteration*. A *job* is a component instance inside an iteration. As usual we require graphs to be acyclic (i.e. DAGs). The DAG iteratively executes until the end of time (or platform shutdown). The job execution order follows the (aforementioned) constraint that job i must finish before job i+1. However, iteration j+1 can start before the completion of iteration j as long as dependencies are satisfied. This allows us to exploit job parallelism, e.g. pipelining [26].

Figure 4 presents the grammar of our coordination language written in pseudo-Xtext style. In the following we describe each production rule in more detail.

3.1   Program Header

Rule *Application* (Fig. 4, line 1) describes the root element of our application. It is composed of the application name, a deadline and a period. All times refer to one iteration of the graph; they can be given in, for instance, hours, milliseconds, hertz or clock cycles.

Rule *Datatype* (Fig. 4, line 9) declares the data types used throughout the coordination specification. One data type declaration consists of the type's name, followed by a string representation of its implementation in user code (i.e. the actual C type like *int* or *struct FooBar*) and, optionally, by the size in bytes. The size information allows for further analysis, e.g. regarding memory footprint. The string representation of the type's implementation is needed for code generation.

3.2   (Multi-version) Components

A component in our coordination DSL (Fig. 4, line 11) consists of a unique name, three sets of *ports* and a number of additional properties. Multi-version components (see Sect. 2.4) feature a number of *versions*, where each version consists of a unique name and the additional properties, now specific to each version. The simplified syntax for single-version components is motivated by their abundance in practice.

Ports represent the interface of a component. The *inports* specify the data items (or tokens) consumed by a component while the *outports* specify the data items (or tokens) that a component (potentially) produces. The third set of ports, introduced by the keyword `state`, are both input ports and output ports at the same time, where the output ports are short-circuited to the corresponding input ports, as explained in Sect. 2.2.

```
1   Application: 'app' ID '{'
2                  'deadline' TIME
3                  'period' TIME
4                  'datatypes' '{' Datatype+ '}'
5                  'components' '{' Component+ '}'
6                  'edges' '{' Edge+ '}'
7                '}';
8
9   Datatype: '(' ID ',' STRING (',' UINT)?;
10
11  Component: ID '{'
12              ('inports' ':' '[' Port* ']')?
13              ('outports' ':' '[' Port* ']')?
14              ('state' ':' '[' Port* ']')?
15              (Properties | Version+)
16            '}';
17
18  Port: '(' ID (',' INT)? ',' DatatypeRef ')';
19
20  Properties: ('deadline' TIME)?
21              ('period' TIME)?
22              ('arch' STRING)*
23              ('security' UINT)?
24
25  Version: 'version' ID '{' Properties '}';
26
27  Edge:  SimpleEdge | BroadcastEdge | DataOrEdge
28         | SchedOrEdge | EnvOrEdge;
29
30  SimpleEdge: OutPort '->' InPort;
31
32  BroadcastEdge: OutPort '->' InPort ('&' InPort)+;
33
34  DataOrEdge: OutPort '->' InPort
35              ('|' OutPort '->' InPort)+;
36
37  SchedOrEdge: OutPort '->' InPort ('|' InPort)+;
38
39  EnvOrEdge: OutPort '->' InPort 'where' STRING
40            ('|' InPort 'where' STRING)+;
41
42  OutPort: CompRef ('.' OutPortRef)?
43
44  InPort: CompRef ('.' InPortRef)?
```

Fig. 4. Coordination language pseudo-Xtext grammar

A port specification includes a unique name, the token multiplicity and a data type identifier. Token multiplicities are optional and default to one. They allow components to consume a fixed number of tokens on an input port at once, to produce a fixed number of tokens on an output port at once or to keep multiple tokens of the same type as internal (pseudo) state. The firing rule for components is amended accordingly and requires (at least) the right number of tokens on each input port. Typing ports is useful to perform static type checking and to guarantee that tokens produced by one component are expected by a subsequent component connected by an edge. To start with we require type equality, but we intend to introduce some form of subtyping at a later stage,

Our three non-functional properties behave differently. While the security level is an algorithmic property of a component (version), energy and time critically depend on the execution platform. Therefore, we encode the (application-specific) security (level) as an integer number in the code, but not energy and time information. We keep the coordination code platform-independent and obtain energy and time information from a separate data base (to be elaborated on in Sect. 5).

3.3 Dependencies

Dependencies (or *edges*) represent the flow of tokens in the graph. Their specification is crucial for the overall expressiveness of the coordination language. We support a number of constructions to connect output ports to input ports (Fig. 4, line 27). In the following we illustrate each such construction with both a graphical sketch and the corresponding textual representation.

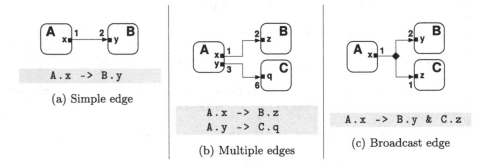

Fig. 5. Various edge construction examples

Figure 5a presents a simple edge between the output port x of component A and the input port y of component B. In our example the output port has a multiplicity of one token while the input port has a multiplicity of two tokens. We show token multiplicities in Fig. 5a for illustration only. In the coordination program token multiplicities are part of the port specification (Fig. 4, line 18), not the edge specification (line 30). Coming back to the example of Fig. 5a, component A produces one output token per activation, but component B only becomes activated once (at least) two tokens are available on its input port. Thus, component A must fire twice before component B becomes activated.

Figure 5b shows an extension of the previous dependency construction where component A produces a total of four tokens: one on port x and three on port y. Component B expects two tokens on input port z while sink component C expects a total of six tokens on input port q. These examples can be extended to fairly complex dependency graphs.

Figure 5c shows a so-called *broadcast edge* between a source component A producing one token and two sink components B and C consuming two tokens and one token, respectively (corresponding to Fig. 4, line 32). This form of component dependency duplicates the token produced on the output port of the source component and sends it to the corresponding input ports of all sink components. Token multiplicities work in the very same way as before: any tokens produced by a source component go to each sink component, but sink components only become activated as soon as the necessary number of tokens accumulate on their input ports. A broadcast edge does not copy the data associated with a token, only the token itself. Hence, components B and C in the above example will operate on the same data and, thus, are restricted to read access.

Components with a single input port or a single output port are very common. In these cases port names in edge specifications can be omitted, as they are not needed for disambiguation.

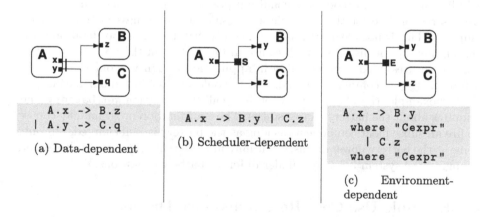

(a) Data-dependent

```
A.x -> B.z
| A.y -> C.q
```

(b) Scheduler-dependent

```
A.x -> B.y | C.z
```

(c)   Environment-dependent

```
A.x -> B.y
where "Cexpr"
| C.z
where "Cexpr"
```

Fig. 6. Data-, scheduler- and environment-dependent edges

Figure 6a illustrates a data-driven conditional dependency (corresponding to Fig. 4, line 34). In this case, component B and component C are dependent on component A, but only one is allowed to actually execute depending on which output port component A makes use of. If at the end of the execution of A a token is present on port x then component B is fired; if a token is present on port y then component C is fired. If no tokens are present on either port at the end of the execution of A then neither B nor C are fired. This enables a powerful mechanism that can be used in control programs where the presence of a stimulus enables part of the application. For example, in a face recognition system an initial component in a processing pipeline could detect if there are any person on an image. If so, the image is forwarded to the subsequent face recognition sub-algorithms; otherwise, it is discarded.

Figure 6b allows conditional dependencies driven by the scheduler (corresponding to Fig. 4, line 37. Similar to the previous case, component B and component C depend on component A, but only one is allowed to actually execute depending on a decision by the scheduler. For example, if the time budget requested by component B is lower than that requested by component C, the scheduler can choose to fire component B instead of C. Such a decision could be motivated by the need to avoid a deadline miss at the expense of some loss of accuracy.

Figure 6c allows conditional dependencies driven by the user (corresponding to Fig. 4, line 39). In this case components B and C again depend on component A, but this time the dependency is guarded by a condition. If the condition evaluates to true then the token is sent to the corresponding route. There is no particular evaluation order for conditions, and tokens are simultaneously sent to all sink components whose guards evaluate to true. Like in the case of the broadcast edge all fired components receive the very same input data. If no guard returns *true*, the token is discarded.

The guards come in the form of strings as inline C code. The code generator will literally place this code into condition positions in the generated code. The user is responsible for the syntactic and semantic correctness of these C code snippets. This is not ideal with respect to static validation of coordination code, but similar to, for instance, the if-clause in OpenMP. On the positive side, this feature ensures maximum flexibility in application design without the need for a fully-fledged C compiler frontend, which would be far beyond our means.

For example, the *Cexpr* could contain a call to a function `get_battery` that enquires about the battery charge status. The coordination program may choose to fire all subsequent components as long as the battery is well charged, but only some as the battery power drains. Or, it may fire different components altogether, changing the system behaviour under different battery conditions.

4   Example Use Case Reconnaissance Drone

We illustrate our coordination approach by means of a use case that we develop jointly with our project partners University of Southern Denmark and Sky-Watch A/S [25]. Fixed-wing drones can stay several hours in the air, making them ideal equipment for surveillance and reconnaissance missions. In addition to the flight control system keeping the drone up in the air, our drone is equipped with a camera and a payload computing system. Since fixed-wing drones are highly energy-efficient, computing on the payload system does have a noticeable impact on overall energy consumption and, thus, on mission length. We illustrate our coordination approach in Fig. 7; the corresponding coordination code is shown in Fig. 8. We re-use the original application building blocks developed and used by Sky-Watch A/S.

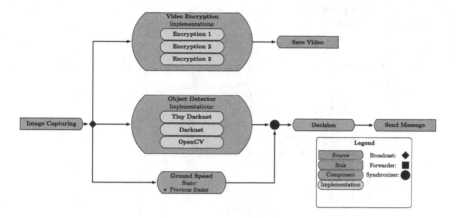

Fig. 7. Reconnaissance drone use case coordination model

The drone's camera system takes pictures in predefined intervals. Our *Image-Capture* component represents this interface to the physical world. Global period and deadline specifications correspond to the capture frequency of the camera. The non-standard data types declared in the `datatypes` section of the coordination program are adopted from the original application code. We use the C types in string form for code generation and require that corresponding C type definitions are made available to the backend C compiler via header files.

Images are broadcast to three subsequent components. The *VideoEncryption* component encrypts the images of the video stream and forwards the encrypted images to follow-up component *SaveVideo* that stores the video in persistent memory for post-mission analysis and archival. Video encryption comes with three different security levels. For simplicity we just call them *Encryption1*, *Encryption2* and *Encryption3*. Different encryption levels could be used, for instance, for different mission environments, from friendly to hostile.

The drone also performs on-board analyses of the images taken. These are represented by our components *ObjectDetector* and *GroundSpeed*. Object detection can choose between three algorithms with different accuracy, time and energy properties: Darknet[1], Tiny Darknet[2], OpenCV. The ground speed estimator works by comparing two subsequent images from the video stream. This is the only stateful component in our model. The results of object detection and ground speed estimation are synchronised and fed into the follow-up component

---

[1] https://pjreddie.com/darknet/.
[2] https://pjreddie.com/darknet/tiny-darknet/.

```
app drone {
  deadline 50Hz
  period 50Hz
  datatypes {
    (frame, "jpegFrame*")
    (num, "uint32_t")
    (enc, "encryptedData*")
    (string, "char*")
  }
  components {
    ImageCapture { outports [ (out, frame) ] }
    Encryption {
      inports [ (in, frame) ]
      outports [ (out, enc) ]
      version Encryption1 {security 4}
      version Encryption2 {security 6}
      version Encryption3 {security 9}
    }
    ObjectDetector {
      inports [ (in, frame) ]
      outports [ (obj, num) (frame, frame) ]
      version TinyDarknet {arch "cpu/big"}
      version Darknet {arch "cpugpu"}
      version OpenCV {arch "cpugpu"}
    }
    GroundSpeed {
      inports [ (in, frame) ]
      outports [ (speed, num) ]
      state [ (s, frame) ]
    }
    Decision {
      inports [(obj, num) (frame, frame) (speed, num)]
      outports [ (msg, string) ]
    }
    SaveVideo { inports [ (in, enc) ] }
    SendMessage {  inports [ (msg, string) ] }
  } edges {
    ImageCapture -> Encryption & ObjectDetector & GroundSpeed
    Encryption -> SaveVideo
    ObjectDetector.obj -> Decision.obj
    ObjectDetector.frame -> Decision.frame
    GroundSpeed -> Decision.speed
    Decision -> SendMessage
} }
```

Fig. 8. Coordination program for drone use case

Decision that combines all information and decides whether or not to notify the base station about a potentially relevant object detected.

Transmission of the message is modelled by the sink component *SendMessage*, where the action returns to the physical world. To implement dynamic adaptation to dynamically changing mission phases, as sketched out in Sect. 2.4, we would need multiple versions of this component with different security levels as well. However, we leave dynamic adaptation to future work for now.

As Fig. 8 demonstrates, our coordination language allows users to specify non-trivial cyber-physical applications in a concise and comprehensible way. The entire wiring of components only takes a few lines of code. Our approach facilitates playing with implementation variations and, thus, enables system engineers to explore the consequences of design choices on non-functional properties at an early stage. Note that all ports in our example have a token multiplicity of one, and we consistently make use of default ports where components only feature a single input port or a single output port.

5   Coordination Tool Chain

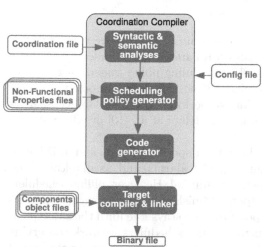

Fig. 9. Coordination workflow

Figure 9 illustrates our coordination tool chain; its four main inputs are:

1. the *coordination program*, as described in Sect. 3;
2. *timing and energy information per component*: provided by timing/energy harvesting tools such as AbsInt aiT [12] for a specific architecture;
3. *object files*: provided by a C-compiler such as WCC [10], containing binary code for each component (version).
4. a *config file* with configuration information, e.g. target hardware, security-level mission specifications, compiler passes to apply, etc.

For syntactic and semantic analysis, we use the parser generator ANTLR to derive a C++ parser from an Xtext grammar specification that is very similar to the one shown in Fig. 4. This implementation choice provides us with a graphical editor plug-in for the Eclipse IDE for free[3]. The resulting parser validates the syntax and creates an abstract syntax tree (AST), on which we validate a number of semantic rules:

---

[3] https://www.eclipse.org/Xtext/.

- ports refer to well defined data types;
- edges connect existing components;
- edges connect output ports with input ports;
- versions target available architectures.

Type checking entails validating that output and input ports connected by an edge use equivalent types. Using standard graph terminology this can be formalised as

$$\forall src, sink \in E : src_{type} = sink_{type} \tag{1}$$

Deadlock checking in our context entails static detection of stable token consumption/production rates. Formally, the number of tokens produced by a component (vertex) must coincide with the sum of tokens expected by all successor components:

$$\forall v \in V : v_{prod} = \sum_{p \in V_{succ}} p_{cons} \tag{2}$$

Likewise, the number of tokens consumed by a component must match the sum of tokens produced by all predecessor components:

$$\forall v \in V : v_{cons} = \sum_{p \in v_{pred}} p_{prod} \tag{3}$$

The second block of our coordination tool chain in Fig. 9 is the *scheduling policy generator*, which depends on configuration parameters provided by the user. In the case of static offline scheduling, the scheduling policy generator generates a schedule table with locations and release times for each component [22,23]. In the case of dynamic online scheduling it performs a schedulability analysis for which we have adapted the techniques of Melani et al. [19] or, alternatively, those of Casini et al. [8].

Offline and online schedulers both have their specific benefits and drawbacks: offline schedulers are easy to implement (e.g. with alarms) and, as all release times are decided a-priori, scheduling overhead is minimal. However, offline schedulers are not work-conserving. Should a component finish quicker than suggested by its worst-case execution time, the corresponding core stays idle until the subsequent release time of some component. In contrast, online schedulers are work-conserving and, thus, more efficient in practice. However, this efficiency comes at the cost of higher runtime overhead and implementation difficulty since we need a mechanism that decides at runtime which component to execute next.

Whether to opt for offline or online scheduling depends on the application scenario at hand. Our tool chain merely facilitates users to make this choice. For offline scheduling we provide both an ILP-based solution [22] and a heuristic for larger use cases, where the solving an ILP proves to be too time-consuming.

Code generation is the final step in our tool flow. For the coordination part of an application, we generate C-code that manages components and their interaction through threads and processes according to the configured scheduling policy, including releasing, synchronisation, and communication of components.

In a final step the generated C-code is compiled by a platform-specific C compiler and linked with the likewise compiled component implementations into an executable binary, ready to be deployed to the platform of choice.

We successfully applied our tool chain to the drone use-case presented in Sect. 4. At the time of writing we are able to generate a static schedule (both ILP- and heuristics-based) that optimises the overall energy consumption while meeting all time and security constraints. Our project partner Sky-Watch A/S successfully tested this code on an actually flying drone. We are still in the process of evaluating the outcome of these experiments compared to the original hand-coded software of Sky-Watch A/S. We envision in the very near future to have our code generator ready to produce dynamically scheduled applications.

6   Related Work

Coordination is a well established computing paradigm with a plethora of languages, abstractions and approaches, surveyed in [9]. Yet, we are neither aware of any adoption of the principle in the broader domain of mission-critical cyber-physical systems, nor are we aware of energy-, time- or security-aware approaches to coordination similar to our approach.

In the area of exogenous coordination languages we mention the work on Reo [4]. The objective of Reo is in the modelling and formal property verification of coordination protocols. Reo has a graphical syntax, in which every Reo program is a labeled directed hypergraph. Reo further has a (or rather many) formal semantics [17]. Compared to our work, Reo is a much more theoretical approach to exogenous coordination, whereas our objective lies in the creation of a practical (and pragmatic) DSL to create executable energy-, time- and security-aware programs running on concrete machinery.

Another example of an exogenous coordination language is S-Net [14], from which we draw inspiration and experience for our proposed design. However, S-Net merely addresses the functional aspects of coordination programming and has left out any non-functional requirements, not to mention energy, time and security, in particular.

A notable exception in the otherwise fairly uncharted territory of resource-aware (functional) languages is Hume [16]. Hume was specifically designed with real-time systems in mind, and, thus, guarantees on time (and space) consumption are key. However, the main motivation behind Hume was to explore how far high-level functional programming features, such as automatic memory management, higher-order functions, polymorphism, recursion, etc can be supported while still providing accurate real-time guarantees.

Bondavalli et al. [7] present a simple in-the-large programming language to describe the structure of a graph-based application. However, they only model what we call components and simple edges, whereas their simple language neither accounts for multi-version components nor for complex communication structures, not to mention any notion of non-functional properties.

A term related to coordination is *algorithmic skeletons*. Merely as examples we mention FastFlow [2] and Musket [20]. Again, all work in this area that we are aware of in one way or another focuses on the trade-off between programming efficiency and execution performance, whereas our focus is on energy, time and security as non-functional properties.

Lustre [6,15] was designed to program reactive system, such as automatic control and monitoring systems. In contrast to general-purpose programming language, Lustre models the flow of data. The idea is to represent actions done on data at each time tick, like in an electronic circuit. The tick can be extended to represent periods and release times for tasks, but still an action is required to describe outputs for each tick (like reusing the last produced data).

Lustre is synchronous which seems necessary for time-sensitive applications. However, Lustre does not decouple the program source code from its structure. The flow of data is extracted by the compiler through data dependencies of variables. We aim at expressing the flow of data with a much simpler and more explicit approach. We also act at a higher level by focusing on the interaction of components considered as black boxes.

In [3] Lustre is extended by meta-operators to integrate a complete model-based design tool from a high-level Simulink model to a low-level implementation. Still, this extension, called Lustre++, does not separate the design of the program structure from actual feature implementation and remains at a too low level to only represent application structure as we intend to do.

The StreamIT [27] language also describes graph-based streaming applications, but it is restricted to fork-join graphs while we need to support arbitrary graphs, possibly with multiple sources and/or sinks.

The Architecture Analysis & Design Language (AADL) [11] targets real-time system design. It provides formal modeling concepts for the description and analysis of application architectures in terms of distinct components and their interactions. AADL supports early prediction and analysis with respect to performance, schedulability and reliability.

7   Conclusion

We propose the TeamPlay coordination language and component technology for the high-level design and development of cyber-physical systems. Our coordination DSL allows users to specify non-trivial streaming applications in a few lines of code while treating crucial non-functional properties such energy, time and security as first-class citizens throughout the application design process.

We describe a complete tool flow from syntactic and semantic validation of coordination programs to code generation for typical off-the-shelf heterogeneous multi-core hardware for cyber-physical systems. Our tool flow includes a variety of offline and online scheduling and mapping techniques that form a tool box, from which the user can choose the most appropriate combination with respect to application needs.

We apply our approach to a real-world use case: a mission-critical reconnaissance drone. We demonstrate the merits of our approach in terms of specification conciseness. An initial version of our tool chain is functional, and we have run preliminary experiments on an actually flying drone. However, the outcome of these experiments is still under analysis and beyond the scope of this paper.

Our work continues in multiple directions. We currently work on a number of further application use cases, among others a car park monitoring system, a satellite communication system and a camera pill application from the medical domain. Further experience with these additional use cases will most likely motivate us to refine the design of our coordination DSL.

Implementation-wise we plan to extend and refine the various scheduling and mapping options. Our code generator currently expects a Linux-like environment with a certain level of operating system support. This is a realistic assumption for many cyber-physical systems, but others run in more bare-metal environments, e.g. where the form factor requires minimal computing hardware. Our more long-term vision is to adapt our coordination technology for safety-critical applications that must be secured against component failure or cyber attacks.

References

1. Achten, P., Plasmeijer, M.: The ins and outs of Clean I/O. J. Funct. Program. **5**(1), 81–110 (1995)
2. Aldinucci, M., Danelutto, M., Kilpatrick, P., Torquati, M.: Fastflow: high-level and efficient streaming on multicore. In: Programming Multi-core and Many-core Computing Systems. Wiley (2017)
3. Alras, M., Caspi, P., Girault, A., Raymond, P.: Model-based design of embedded control systems by means of a synchronous intermediate model. In: International Conference on Embedded Software and Systems, pp. 3–10. IEEE (2009)
4. Arbab, F.: Reo: a channel-based coordination model for component composition. Math. Struct. Comput. Sci. **14**(3), 329–366 (2004)
5. Arbab, F.: Composition of interacting computations. In: Goldin, D., Smolka, S., Wegner, P. (eds.) Interactive Computation, pp. 277–321. Springer, Heidelberg (2006). https://doi.org/10.1007/3-540-34874-3_12
6. Benveniste, A., Caspi, P., Edwards, S.A., Halbwachs, N., Le Guernic, P., De Simone, R.: The synchronous languages 12 years later. Proc. IEEE **91**(1), 64–83 (2003)
7. Bondavalli, A., Strigini, L., Simoncini, L.: Dataflow-like languages for real-time systems: issues of computational models and notation. In: 11th Symposium on Reliable Distributed Systems (SRDS 1992), pp. 214–221. IEEE (1992)
8. Casini, D., Biondi, A., Nelissen, G., Buttazzo, G.: Partitioned fixed-priority scheduling of parallel tasks without preemptions. In: 2018 IEEE Real-Time Systems Symposium (RTSS 2018), pp. 421–433. IEEE (2018)
9. Ciatto, G., Mariani, S., Louvel, M., Omicini, A., Zambonelli, F.: Twenty years of coordination technologies: state-of-the-art and perspectives. In: Di Marzo Serugendo, G., Loreti, M. (eds.) (COORDINATION'18). LNCS, vol. 10852, pp. 51–80. Springer, Heidelberg (2018). https://doi.org/10.1007/978-3-319-92408-3_3
10. Falk, H., Lokuciejewski, P., Theiling, H.: Design of a WCET-aware C compiler. In: 2006 IEEE/ACM/IFIP Workshop on Embedded Systems for Real Time Multimedia (ESTIMedia 2006), pp. 121–126. IEEE (2006)
11. Feiler, P.H., Gluch, D.P., Hudak, J.J.: The architecture analysis and design language (AADL): an introduction. Technical report, Carnegie-Mellon University, Pittsburgh, USA, Software Engineering Institute (2006)

12. Ferdinand, C., Heckmann, R.: aiT: worst-case execution time prediction by static program analysis. In: Jacquart, R. (ed.) Building the Information Society. IIFIP, vol. 156, pp. 377–383. Springer, Boston (2004). https://doi.org/10.1007/978-1-4020-8157-6_29
13. Gelernter, D., Carriero, N.: Coordination languages and their significance. Commun. ACM **35**(2), 97–107 (1992)
14. Grelck, C., Scholz, S.B., Shafarenko, A.: Asynchronous stream processing with S-Net. Int. J. Parallel Prog. **38**(1), 38–67 (2010). https://doi.org/10.1007/s10766-009-0121-x
15. Halbwachs, N., Caspi, P., Raymond, P., Pilaud, D.: The synchronous data flow programming language LUSTRE. Proc. IEEE **79**(9), 1305–1320 (1991)
16. Hammond, K., Michaelson, G.: Hume: a domain-specific language for real-time embedded systems. In: Pfenning, F., Smaragdakis, Y. (eds.) GPCE 2003. LNCS, vol. 2830, pp. 37–56. Springer, Heidelberg (2003). https://doi.org/10.1007/978-3-540-39815-8_3
17. Jongmans, S.S., Arbab, F.: Overview of thirty semantic formalisms for Reo. Sci. Ann. Comput. Sci. **22**(1), 201–251 (2012)
18. Liu, C.L., Layland, J.W.: Scheduling algorithms for multiprogramming in a hard-real-time environment. J. ACM (JACM) **20**(1), 46–61 (1973)
19. Melani, A., Bertogna, M., Bonifaci, V., Marchetti-Spaccamela, A., Buttazzo, G.C.: Response-time analysis of conditional dag tasks in multiprocessor systems. In: 27th Euromicro Conference on Real-Time Systems (RTS 2015), pp. 211–221. IEEE (2015)
20. Rieger, C., Wrede, F., Kuchen, H.: Musket: A domain-specific language for high-level parallel programming with algorithmic skeletons. In: 34th ACM Symposium on Applied Computing (SAC 2019), pp. 1534–1543. ACM, New York (2019)
21. Ritchie, D.M., Kernighan, B.W., Lesk, M.E.: The C Programming Language. Prentice Hall, Englewood Cliffs (1988)
22. Roeder, J., Rouxel, B., Altmeyer, S., Grelck, C.: Interdependent multi-version scheduling in heterogeneous energy-aware embedded systems. In: 13th Junior Researcher Workshop on Real-Time Computing (JRWRTC 2019) of the 27th International Conference on Real-Time Networks and Systems (RTNS 2019) (2019)
23. Rouxel, B., Skalistis, S., Derrien, S., Puaut, I.: Hiding communication delays in contention-free execution for SPM-based multi-core architectures. In: 31st Euromicro Conference on Real-Time Systems (ECRTS 2019) (2019)
24. Rusu, C., Melhem, R., Mossé, D.: Multi-version scheduling in rechargeable energy-aware real-time systems. J. Embed. Comput. **1**(2), 271–283 (2005)
25. Seewald, A., Schultz, U.P., Roeder, J., Rouxel, B., Grelck, C.: Component-based computation-energy modeling for embedded systems. In: Proceedings Companion of the 2019 ACM SIGPLAN International Conference on Systems, Programming, Languages, and Applications: Software for Humanity. SPLASH Companion 2019. ACM, New York (2019)
26. Tendulkar, P., Poplavko, P., Galanommatis, I., Maler, O.: Many-core scheduling of data parallel applications using SMT solvers. In: 17th Euromicro Conference on Digital System Design (DSD 2014), pp. 615–622. IEEE (2014)
27. Thies, W., Karczmarek, M., Amarasinghe, S.: StreamIt: a language for streaming applications. In: Horspool, R.N. (ed.) CC 2002. LNCS, vol. 2304, pp. 179–196. Springer, Heidelberg (2002). https://doi.org/10.1007/3-540-45937-5_14
28. Wadler, P.: The Essence of Functional Programming. In: 19th ACM Symposium on Principles of Programming Languages (POPL 1992), pp. 1–14. ACM Press (1992)

Message-Based Communication

Team Automata@Work: On Safe Communication

Maurice H. ter Beek[1][(✉)] ⓘ, Rolf Hennicker[2], and Jetty Kleijn[3] ⓘ

[1] ISTI–CNR, Pisa, Italy
`maurice.terbeek@isti.cnr.it`
[2] Ludwig-Maximilians-Universität München, Munich, Germany
`hennicker@ifi.lmu.de`
[3] LIACS, Leiden University, Leiden, The Netherlands
`h.c.m.kleijn@liacs.leidenuniv.nl`

Abstract. We study requirements for safe communication in systems of reactive components in which components communicate via synchronised execution of common actions. These systems are modelled in the framework of team automata in which any number of components can participate—as a sender or as a receiver—in the execution of a communication action. Moreover, there is no fixed synchronisation policy as these policies in general depend on the application. In this short paper, we reconsider the concept of safe communication in terms of reception and responsiveness requirements, originally defined for synchronisation policies determined by a synchronisation type. Illustrated by a motivating example, we propose three extensions. First, compliance, i.e. satisfaction of communication requirements, does not have to be immediate. Second, the synchronisation type (and hence the communication requirements) no longer has to be uniform, but can be specified per action. Third, we introduce final states to be able to distinguish between possible and guaranteed executions of actions.

1 Introduction

For the correct functioning of systems built from reactive components which collaborate by message exchange, it is important to exclude communication failures during execution, like message loss or indefinite waiting for input. This requires a thorough understanding of their synchronisation policies [5,8,11,17,18] to establish compatibility of communicating components [1,3,4,9,10,12,15]. Compatibility in multi-component systems was studied in [12] for services and in [10] for team automata, in both cases with the assumption that systems are full synchronous products of their components. Thus global states are Cartesian products of local states and all system transitions that represent the execution of an action leading from one global state to a next global state, involve all and only those component automata that have that action. A main reason to focus first on this kind of systems is that synchronous product automata are known for

© IFIP International Federation for Information Processing 2020
Published by Springer Nature Switzerland AG 2020
S. Bliudze and L. Bocchi (Eds.): COORDINATION 2020, LNCS 12134, pp. 77–85, 2020.
https://doi.org/10.1007/978-3-030-50029-0_5

their appealing compositionality and modularity properties [6,7,14,16,18] and are thus easier to analyse.

Team automata, introduced in [2,5,13], represent a useful model to specify different forms of intended behaviour of reactive systems and they were shown to form a suitable formal framework for lifting the concept of compatibility to a multi-component setting. Explorations on generalising compatibility notions from full synchronous products to arbitrary synchronisation policies in the framework of team automata can be found in [3,4].

In [3], synchronisation types are used to classify synchronisation policies that can be realised in team automata. A synchronisation type is a pair (snd, rcv) that specifies the ranges for the number of senders and the number of receivers taking part in the transitions (communications) of the team automaton. A synchronisation type thus defines the transitions of the team automaton (its synchronisation policy). On the other hand, if at a given global state an appropriate number of components are ready to send (receive) an action, there is the requirement of synchronisation with a suitable number of other components that will receive (send, respectively) that action. Thus for output actions, requirements for reception at a given global state can be formulated. Conversely, locally enabled input actions give rise to responsiveness requirements. In [3], we have introduced a formal notation for expressing communication requirements and we have shown how such requirements can automatically be generated from a given synchronisation type. A team automaton is said to be compliant with a given set of communication requirements if in each reachable state of the team the requirements are met (the communication is safe).

Contribution. In this paper, we discuss, by means of an informal example, situations that can be seen as an impediment to this approach, in the sense that the application of the communication requirements appears to be too restrictive. As a solution, we propose the following three extensions to the idea of safe communication.

Compliance: the notion of compliance is made less restrictive by allowing *intermediate transitions by other components* before a particular communication requirement is fulfilled.
Actions: we propose an individual assignment of synchronisation types to communication actions to fine tune the number of participating sending and receiving components *per action.*
States: it may be the case that (local) enabledness of an action indicates only readiness for communication and not so much that communication is required; to make this distinction between possible and required communication explicit, we propose to add *final states* to components.

Outline. The paper starts with a brief summary of the principal notions of team automata, followed by a discussion of communication safety and compliance that is illustrated by an example from [3]. We point out some issues not covered by the original definition of communication requirements, based on which we formulate extensions to make compliance a more liberal concept still following our intuition.

2 Team Automata

In the team automata framework, a *system* $S = \{ \mathcal{A}_i \mid i \in \{1, \ldots, n\}\}$ consists of a (finite) set of reactive components modelled by component automata $\mathcal{A}_i$. Each component automaton has its own set of—local—states (with distinguished initial states), an alphabet of actions that are either input or output (not both)[1] to that component, and a labelled transition relation. The alphabet of actions of S consists of all actions of the $\mathcal{A}_i$. An action is called *communicating* (in S) if it occurs in some automata of S as an output action and in some (other) automata of S as an input action. The state space of S is the Cartesian product of the state spaces of all $\mathcal{A}_i$, i.e. global states are tuples $\bar{q} = (q_1, \ldots, q_n)$ with local states q_i. The initial states of S are those global states that have only initial states as their local states. The possible transitions from one global state to another are described by labelled *system transitions*. The label of a system transition from $\bar{q}$ to $\bar{p}$ is an action a from the alphabet of S such that, for all i, whenever $q_i \neq p_i$, component $\mathcal{A}_i$ has an a-labelled transition from q_i to p_i. Thus any number of components in which a is *locally enabled* at q_i can participate simultaneously in a system transition from $\bar{q}$. An a-labelled transition in which both a component of which a is an output action (a *sender*) and one which has a as an input action (a *receiver*) participate, is a *communication* (via a).

One of the strengths of the team automata approach is that no a priori restrictions are imposed on system transitions. In general, it depends on the application which transitions from the set of all possible system transitions are relevant. Formally, a *synchronisation policy* is a subset δ of the system transitions of S. Such policy δ determines a *team automaton* $\mathcal{T}$ over S which has as its state space the set of all global states of S that are reachable by δ from the initial states of S.

In [3], *synchronisation types* are proposed to specify synchronisation policies for team automata. A synchronisation type (*snd, rcv*) determines ranges for the number of senders and the number of receivers that may take part in communications. For instance, if *snd* $= [k, l]$ (with $0 \leq k \leq l$) and *rcv* $= [m, n]$ (with $0 \leq m \leq n$) then at least k and at most l senders and at least m and at most n receivers are allowed. The synchronisation policy δ generated by (*snd, rcv*), consists of all system transitions that satisfy this constraint. While k, m are always natural numbers, the delimiters l, n can also be given as $*$ which indicates that no upper limit is imposed. Important synchronisation types are, eg., $([1,1], [1,1])$ which expresses binary communication, and $([1,1], [1,*])$ for multicast communication in which exactly one component outputs a communicating action while arbitrarily many (but at least one) components input that action.[2]

---

[1] For simplicity of presentation, we do not consider internal actions here.

[2] In [3], we have also introduced notations for (strong and weak) broadcast communication and for full synchronisation, amongst others, which are not used here.

3   On Safe Communication

The idea underlying a communication-safe team automaton is that, in every (reachable) global state, whenever a communicating action is enabled (according to the prevailing synchronisation policy) at some of the local states of its components, these components can execute this action from these local states as a communication of the team.

As an example, let us consider a team automaton T with synchronisation type $([1,1],[1,*])$. Then, to guarantee that at a global state $\bar{q} = (q_1,\ldots,q_n)$, output action a of component A_i, which is locally enabled at q_i, can be received by at least one other component, one would impose a *receptiveness requirement*, written as $\mathrm{rcp}(i,a)@\bar{q}$. If T is compliant with (satisfies) this requirement, it is guaranteed that a can be executed by T at $\bar{q}$. Note that in case A_i could also execute another output action b at state q_i, also subject to the receptiveness requirement, the two requirements would be combined through a conjunction, denoted by $\mathrm{rcp}((i,a) \wedge (i,b))@\bar{q}$. The reason for this is that components control their output actions and execution of either of them should lead to a reception.

For input actions one could require responsiveness with the intuition that enabled inputs should be served by appropriate outputs. Unlike output actions, however, input actions are controlled by the environment. Guaranteeing that for a choice of enabled inputs, one of them is provided by an output of the environment suffices for the progress of a component waiting for a signal from its environment. Hence, if component A_j enables input actions a and b in its local state q_j, then the *responsiveness requirements*, denoted by $\mathrm{rsp}(j,a)@\bar{q}$ and $\mathrm{rsp}(j,b)@\bar{q}$, respectively, would be combined with a disjunction as $\mathrm{rsp}((j,a) \vee (j,b))@\bar{q}$.

In general, a team automaton T over a system S is called *communication-safe* if it is compliant with all communication requirements (at all states of T) derived from its synchronisation type. We refer to [3] for the formal definition of compliance and the general procedure for deriving communication requirements.

Motivating Example
Consider a distributed chat system where buddies can interact once registered. There are three types of components: clients, servers, and arbiters; see Fig. 1, where input actions are annotated by ? and output actions by !. Initial states are marked with an incoming arrowhead. A server controls new entries into the chat as well as exits from the chat (actions *join* and *leave*, respectively). It also coordinates the main activities in the chat. The overall messaging protocol assumes registered clients to communicate messages to servers (action *msg*) which, upon arbiter approval (action *grant*), send the received messages to clients in the chat (action *fwdmsg*).

The chat system S considered here consists of two clients, one server, and one arbiter. The team automaton T_{chat} over S is defined by the synchronisation type $([1,1],[1,*])$, as the reception of forwarded messages may involve more than one component. Also in [3], this synchronisation type was applied. The states of T_{chat} are tuples (q_1,q_2,q_3,q_4) in which the first and second entries are client states, the third entry is a server state, and the fourth state is an arbiter state.

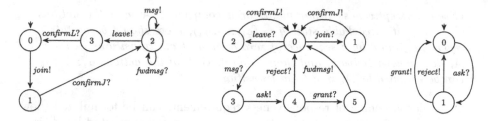

Fig. 1. [from left to right] Component automata for clients, servers, arbiters

An example of a receptiveness requirement, for all (reachable) states of $\mathcal{T}_{chat}$ with the server being in state 5, would be the following:

$$\mathbf{rcp}(Server, fwdmsg)@(q_1, q_2, 5, q_4)$$

$\mathcal{T}_{chat}$ is compliant with this requirement since one of the clients locally enables *fwdmsg*. This is because, whenever the server is in state 5, at least one of the clients is in its state 2 (and the arbiter must be in state 0).

An example of a responsiveness requirement would be the following:

$$\mathbf{rsp}((Server, join) \vee (Server, leave) \vee (Server, msg))@(q_1, q_2, 0, q_4)$$

$\mathcal{T}_{chat}$ is compliant with this requirement too, since whenever the server is in state 0 then each of the clients is in state 0 or in state 2. Hence there is always a client in a state that enables one of the required outputs for communication with the server (*join* in state 0 and *msg* or *leave* in state 2).

Extending Communication Safety

Using this example to illustrate our motivations, we will now introduce three useful extensions of the concept of communication-safety discussed so far.

Compliance: Intermediate Communications.

First consider state $(2, 0, 5, 0)$ of $\mathcal{T}_{chat}$, where the second client locally enables the execution of its output action *join*. According to the synchronisation type that defines $\mathcal{T}_{chat}$, the output action *join* can be executed from local state 0 with the receptiveness requirement at this state being as follows:

$$\mathbf{rcp}(Client_2, join)@(2, 0, 5, 0)$$

$\mathcal{T}_{chat}$ is not compliant with this requirement. Output action *join* of the second client has to be received as input by at least one of the other components. The only component with *join* as an input action is the server, but *join* is not enabled at its local state 5. The server can however transit from state 5 to state 0 (by a communication with the first client) after which it is ready to execute *join* in a communication with the second client. Hence, we propose a generalisation of the compliance notion along the following lines:

> Given a receptiveness requirement for a component $\mathcal{A}_i$ and the actions $a_1, \ldots, a_k$ at a reachable state $\overline{q} = (q_1, \ldots, q_n)$, there should be a state $\overline{p}$ reachable from $\overline{q}$ by a sequence of zero or more team transitions in which $\mathcal{A}_i$ does not participate, and then, from $\overline{p}$, each of the actions $a_1, \ldots, a_k$ can be executed by $\mathcal{A}_i$ in a team transition.

A similar loosening of responsiveness requirements can be formulated (now requiring that at least one of the actions $a_1, \ldots, a_n$ can be executed by $\mathcal{A}_i$ in a team transition from $\overline{p}$).

Actions: Individual Synchronisation Types. Next, consider again the state $(2, 0, 5, 0)$ of $\mathcal{T}_{chat}$, but now with the following receptiveness requirement:

$$\mathbf{rcp}((\mathit{Client}_1, \mathit{leave}) \wedge (\mathit{Client}_1, \mathit{msg}))@(2, 0, 5, 0)$$

This requirement expresses that the first client in state 2 can (internally) decide to execute either its output action *leave* or its output action *msg*, and for each, there should be at least one other component be ready (possibly after some team transitions not involving the first client, as discussed above) to execute this action as an input action. The server, that is in state 5, has only its output action *fwdmsg* locally enabled. Hence, by the synchronisation type $([1, 1], [1, *])$ of $\mathcal{T}_{chat}$, this requires a communication with a client. That client has to be the second client, which however currently is in state 0 with only output action *join* locally enabled. Consequently, the team automaton does not satisfy the receptiveness requirement of the first client at $(2, 0, 5, 0)$.

If, instead, we would have $([1, 1], [0, *])$ as a synchronisation type for the chat system, then the server would be allowed to move to state 0 by executing its output action *fwdmsg* on its own (rather than in a communication) after which the server would be ready to accept inputs as required. Thus it would be allowed that not every occurrence of *fwdmsg* will be received. However, $([1, 1], [0, *])$ is not an acceptable synchronisation type for other actions (like *join*, *leave*, etc). Indeed, a client performing a *join* action without acceptance by the server should not be permitted. Therefore, we propose to no longer require a uniform synchronisation type for all actions of the system, but rather to assign synchronisation types individually for each single action. In our example, this leads to the following action synchronisation types:

$$\mathbf{stype}(\mathit{join}) = \ldots = \mathbf{stype}(\mathit{reject}) = ([1, 1], [1, 1])$$
$$\mathbf{stype}(\mathit{fwdmsg}) = ([1, 1], [0, *])$$

With this assignment we would also solve another issue with a chatting system which was also mentioned in [3]: Assume that, in order to increase robustness, we were to extend the system and let it consist of two servers and, as before, two clients and the arbiter. In case we would use the synchronisation type $([1, 1], [0, *])$ (or $([1, 1], [1, *])$) for the whole system, a client may send a message to two servers, who both forward the message (upon approval from the arbiter). The assignment of synchronisation types per action would solve the problem of duplicate message forwarding, because we can now assign to the action msg the synchronisation type $([1, 1], [1, 1])$.

Hence, as exemplified above, the idea is to introduce the syntactic concept of a *synchronisation type specification*. Such a specification is a mapping stype, which assigns to each communicating action a of the system a synchronisation type $\text{stype}(a) = (snd, rcv)$ that determines ranges for the number of senders and receivers that may take part in a synchronisation (communication) on the action a. Each synchronisation type specification stype over a system $\mathcal{S}$ generates a unique team automaton $\mathcal{T}(\text{stype})$ over $\mathcal{S}$ with a synchronisation policy that comprises all system transitions that—if labelled by a communicating action a—satisfy the synchronisation type $\text{stype}(a)$. It remains to establish what this allows us to say about the communication safety of $\mathcal{T}(\text{stype})$. Communication safety concerns receptiveness and responsiveness. Therefore, the systematic derivation of receptiveness and responsiveness requirements for a team automaton from a given uniform synchronisation type as developed in [3] has to be generalised by deriving receptiveness and responsiveness requirements individually per action.

States: Final States. Finally, assume that the behaviour of a client terminates after leaving the chat. In that case, input action $confirmL$ would lead from state 3 to a new state 4. When all clients have terminated, the following responsiveness requirement of the server (in its state 0) could not be satisfied anymore:

$$\text{rsp}((\mathcal{S}erver, join) \vee (\mathcal{S}erver, leave) \vee (\mathcal{S}erver, msg))@(4, 4, 0, 0)$$

This is, however, not a problem if the input actions $join$, $leave$, and msg are seen as no more than services offered by the server: whether or not these services are called is irrelevant, clients are free to use or not to use a service. On the other hand, in its local state 4 the server definitely wants to get a response, *reject* or *grant*, from the arbiter. Hence, we need formal means to discriminate the quality of the two server states 0 and 4. Our idea is to declare some states of a component automaton as final states. Similarly to automata theory, where final states are accepting states which, nevertheless, may have outgoing transitions, in our framework a final state would be a state where execution can stop but may also continue.

In the example, state 0 of the server would be declared as final with the consequence that the server is no longer required to continue, i.e. there is no responsiveness requirement that one of its inputs $join$, $leave$, or msg must be served. (Still, the server offers these actions as input and thus can satisfy reception requirements from clients.) On the other hand, state 4 of the server should not be final because the server intends to proceed from this state. It is expecting a response from the arbiter which can be formalised, e.g., by the following responsiveness requirement:

$$\text{rsp}((\mathcal{S}erver, reject) \vee (\mathcal{S}erver, grant))@(2, 0, 4, 1)$$

This requirement is indeed fulfilled.

Of course, also the symmetric case has to be considered, i.e. what does the combination of final and non-final states with outputs mean. As an example, consider state 1 of the arbiter with the two outgoing transitions for the output of *grant* and *reject*, respectively. If this state were a final state, then this would mean that the arbiter may internally decide to stop here. Then the above responsiveness requirement of the server would not be satisfied anymore. Therefore, this state should definitely be a non-final state. Now consider state 0 of a client. If this were a final state, then a client might decide to never join a chat. This is not a problem if the server is not expecting any client to join, i.e. if the server's state 0 is declared to be final as discussed above.

Outlook. In summary, the addition of final states to component automata has significant consequences for the derivation of communication requirements and for our compliance notions, which must be adjusted accordingly. This is an important next step of our work. Another issue concerns the modelling of open systems and the composition of open team automata. We are specifically interested in investigating conditions under which communication safety of team automata is preserved by composition. This should eventually lead to a methodology for the modelling and analysis of large distributed systems with a significant communication behaviour.

Acknowledgements. The work of the first author was partially supported by the MIUR PRIN 2017FTXR7S project IT MaTTerS (Methods and Tools for Trustworthy Smart Systems). We thank the reviewers for their useful comments.

References

1. Bauer, S.S., Mayer, P., Schroeder, A., Hennicker, R.: On weak modal compatibility, refinement, and the MIO workbench. In: Esparza, J., Majumdar, R. (eds.) TACAS 2010. LNCS, vol. 6015, pp. 175–189. Springer, Heidelberg (2010). https://doi.org/10.1007/978-3-642-12002-2_15
2. ter Beek, M.H.: Team automata: a formal approach to the modeling of collaboration between system components. Ph.D. thesis, Leiden University (2003). http://hdl.handle.net/1887/29570
3. ter Beek, M.H., Carmona, J., Hennicker, R., Kleijn, J.: Communication requirements for team automata. In: Jacquet, J.-M., Massink, M. (eds.) COORDINATION 2017. LNCS, vol. 10319, pp. 256–277. Springer, Cham (2017). https://doi.org/10.1007/978-3-319-59746-1_14
4. ter Beek, M.H., Carmona, J., Kleijn, J.: Conditions for compatibility of components. In: Margaria, T., Steffen, B. (eds.) ISoLA 2016. LNCS, vol. 9952, pp. 784–805. Springer, Cham (2016). https://doi.org/10.1007/978-3-319-47166-2_55
5. ter Beek, M.H., Ellis, C.A., Kleijn, J., Rozenberg, G.: Synchronizations in team automata for groupware systems. Comput. Sup. Coop. Work **12**(1), 21–69 (2003). https://doi.org/10.1023/A:1022407907596
6. ter Beek, M.H., Kleijn, J.: Team automata satisfying compositionality. In: Araki, K., Gnesi, S., Mandrioli, D. (eds.) FME 2003. LNCS, vol. 2805, pp. 381–400. Springer, Heidelberg (2003). https://doi.org/10.1007/978-3-540-45236-2_22

7. ter Beek, M.H., Kleijn, J.: Modularity for teams of I/O automata. Inf. Process. Lett. **95**(5), 487–495 (2005). https://doi.org/10.1016/j.ipl.2005.05.012

8. Brim, L., Cerná, I., Vareková, P., Zimmerova, B.: Component-interaction automata as a verification-oriented component-based system specification. ACM Softw. Eng. Notes **31**(2) (2006). https://doi.org/10.1145/1118537.1123063

9. Carmona, J., Cortadella, J.: Input/Output compatibility of reactive systems. In: Aagaard, M.D., O'Leary, J.W. (eds.) FMCAD 2002. LNCS, vol. 2517, pp. 360–377. Springer, Heidelberg (2002). https://doi.org/10.1007/3-540-36126-X_22

10. Carmona, J., Kleijn, J.: Compatibility in a multi-component environment. Theor. Comput. Sci. **484**, 1–15 (2013). https://doi.org/10.1016/j.tcs.2013.03.006

11. de Alfaro, L., Henzinger, T.A.: Interface automata. In: ESEC/FSE 2001, pp. 109–120. ACM (2001). https://doi.org/10.1145/503209.503226

12. Durán, F., Ouederni, M., Salaün, G.: A generic framework for n-protocol compatibility checking. Sci. Comput. Program. **77**(7–8), 870–886 (2012). https://doi.org/10.1016/j.scico.2011.03.009

13. Ellis, C.A.: Team automata for groupware systems. In: GROUP 1997, pp. 415–424. ACM (1997). https://doi.org/10.1145/266838.267363

14. Gössler, G., Sifakis, J.: Composition for component-based modeling. Sci. Comput. Program. **55**, 161–183 (2005). https://doi.org/10.1016/j.scico.2004.05.014

15. Hennicker, R., Bidoit, M.: Compatibility properties of synchronously and asynchronously communicating components. Log. Methods Comput. Sci. **14**(1), 1–31 (2018). https://doi.org/10.23638/LMCS-14(1:1)2018

16. Jonsson, B.: Compositional specification and verification of distributed systems. ACM Trans. Program. Lang. Syst. **16**(2), 259–303 (1994). https://doi.org/10.1145/174662.174665

17. Larsen, K.G., Nyman, U., Wąsowski, A.: Modal I/O automata for interface and product line theories. In: De Nicola, R. (ed.) ESOP 2007. LNCS, vol. 4421, pp. 64–79. Springer, Heidelberg (2007). https://doi.org/10.1007/978-3-540-71316-6_6

18. Lynch, N.A., Tuttle, M.R.: An introduction to input/output automata. CWI Q. **2**(3), 219–246 (1989). https://ir.cwi.nl/pub/18164

Choreography Automata

Franco Barbanera[1]([✉]), Ivan Lanese[2], and Emilio Tuosto[3,4]

[1] Department of Mathematics and Computer Science, University of Catania,
Catania, Italy
barba@dmi.unict.it
[2] Focus Team, University of Bologna/INRIA, Bologna, Italy
ivan.lanese@gmail.com
[3] Gran Sasso Science Institute, L'Aquila, Italy
emilio.tuosto@gssi.it
[4] University of Leicester, Leicester, UK

Abstract. Automata models are well-established in many areas of computer science and are supported by a wealth of theoretical results including a wide range of algorithms and techniques to specify and analyse systems. We introduce *choreography automata* for the choreographic modelling of communicating systems. The projection of a choreography automaton yields a system of *communicating finite-state machines*. We consider both the standard asynchronous semantics of communicating systems and a synchronous variant of it. For both, the projections of well-formed automata are proved to be live as well as lock- and deadlock-free.

1 Introduction

Choreographies are gaining momentum in the design and implementation of distributed applications also in the ICT industrial sector. This is witnessed by the effort of defining standards for specification languages such as WS-CDL [31] or BPMN [40] as well as the recognition of choreographies as suitable approaches to describe modern architectures such as microservices [2,12]. Choreographic approaches to the modelling, analysis, and programming of message-passing applications abound. For instance, in [5,34] abstract models have been applied to verify and debug BPMN specifications. Also, behavioural types have been proposed as suitable formalisations of choreographies [29] and for the analysis of properties such as liveness or deadlock freedom (e.g., [20,45] and the survey [30]

Research partly supported by the EU H2020 RISE programme under the Marie Skłodowska-Curie grant agreement No. 778233, by the MIUR project PRIN 2017FTXR7S "IT-MaTTerS" (Methods and Tools for Trustworthy Smart Systems). and by the Piano Triennale Ricerca - UNICT 2016–19. The first and second authors have also been partially supported by INdAM as members of GNCS (Grup po Nazionale per il Calcolo Scientifico). The authors thanks the reviewers for their helpful comments and also M. Dezani for her support.

© IFIP International Federation for Information Processing 2020
Published by Springer Nature Switzerland AG 2020
S. Bliudze and L. Bocchi (Eds.): COORDINATION 2020, LNCS 12134, pp. 86–106, 2020.
https://doi.org/10.1007/978-3-030-50029-0_6

to mention but few), while other approaches have considered syntax-free models [48]. At a programming level, choreographic programming has been explored in [35,39].

A distinguished trait of choreographies is the coexistence of two distinct but related views of a distributed system: the *global* and the *local* views. The former is an abstraction that yields a *holistic* description of the system. A global view indeed describes the coordination necessary among the various components of the system "altogether". In contrast, the local views specify the behaviour of the single components in "isolation".

In this paper we revisit the use of finite state automata to formally specify (and analyse) global views of message-passing systems, following an intuition similar to conversation protocols (CP) [16,26,27], a formalism where choreographies for asynchronous systems are described by means of Büchi automata. Our model, dubbed choreography automata (c-automata, for short), differs from CP in spite of the similarities in the syntax adopted for the choreographies. In particular, conversation protocols and c-automata differ both in their semantics and in the underlying communication models. Moreover, unlike for CPs, our conditions for realisability do not require any communication properties, rather they imply several communication properties. This is further discussed in Sect. 6. The transitions of c-automata are labelled with *interactions*. As in most approaches, an interaction A→B: m states that *participant* A sends message m to participant B, which in turn receives it. For instance, consider the c-automaton

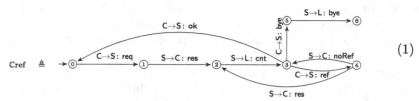

$$(1)$$

used to illustrate our model and as our working example through the paper. The c-automaton Cref specifies the coordination among participants C, S, and L whereby a request req from client C is served by server S which replies with a message (of type) res and logs some meta-information cnt on a service L (e.g., for billing purposes). Client C may acknowledge a response of S (*i*) with an ok message to restart the protocol, or (*ii*) by requiring a refinement of the response with a ref message, or else (*iii*) by ending the protocol with a bye message which S forwards to L. In the second case, S sends C either a noRef message if no refinement is possible or another res (with the corresponding cnt to L).

Note that Cref has nested as well as entangled loops. The support for entangled loops is a distinguishing and expressive feature of automata-based models, not present in many existing models of choreographies or multiparty session types (MST), and that we shall discuss in Sect. 6.

We argue that c-automata provide a number of benefits. An advantage of c-automata is that finite state automata are well-known structures used both in theoretical and applied computer science. For instance, the c-automaton

Cref above can be easily understood by practitioners while retaining rigour. Another advantage is that c-automata are *syntax-independent*; they do not rely on complex linguistic constructs (such as the process algebraic constructs usually adopted in behavioural types). More crucially, we can re-use well-known results of the theory of automata and formal languages (e.g., we use determinisation and trace equivalence) as well as related algorithms. We discuss these advantages more extensively in Sect. 6.

Choreographies enable a so called top-down approach whereby local views can be *projected* from the global view. Projections are expected to reflect the global specification without spoiling communication soundness (e.g., deadlock freedom, liveness, etc.). These results do not hold in general. In fact, global views abstract away from "low level" peculiarities and projections may exhibit unintended behaviour.

The *realisability* of a global specification is a natural question to ask:

Can global views such as Cref be realised by distributed components C, S, and L coordinating with each other without intermediaries?

The answer to such question (obviously) depends on the communication infrastructure the distributed components use for the coordination. In fact, global views in general *abstractly* specify the coordination disregarding several details. For instance, the c-automaton Cref in (1) is oblivious of the communication infrastructure used by the participants to coordinate with each other. Are the communications among C, S, and L synchronous or asynchronous? In the latter case, are messages received in their sending order? How is the sequencing reflected at the local level? For instance, should the messages that C sends from state 3 in (1) be sent after L receives the message cnt from S?

Tackling the realisability of global views is not a trivial endeavour. For instance, the recent analysis done in [45] highlights glitches in several projection operations of behavioural types. Also, some decidability results on the realisability of CPs [9], the only other automata-based choreographic setting that we are aware of, have been recently proved erroneous [24].

One would also like to understand whether the distributed components realising a choreography enjoy nice communication properties, e.g., will a component ready to engage in a communication eventually progress? Will a message sent by a participant eventually be received? We will consider such problems, showing that a set of conditions we define on c-automata do guarantee the choreography both to be realisable and to enjoy a number of relevant communication properties such as liveness and deadlock freedom.

Contributions and Structure. After a preliminary section (Sect. 2) recalling the main notions we deal with in the paper, in Sect. 3 we formalise c-automata and their projections. We adopt *communicating systems* [13] (reviewed in Sect. 2) for the local views of choreographies.

We consider both the case of synchronous and asynchronous communications for the local views. The projection from c-automata to communicating systems is defined in Sect. 3 while in Sect. 4 we define the class of *well-formed* c-automata for the synchronous case. There we show that, on well-formed c-automata, our notion of projection is correct (cf. Theorem 4.14) and guarantees liveness, lock- and deadlock-freedom in the synchronous semantics (cf. Theorem 4.15). In Sect. 5 we generalise the above results to the case of asynchronous communications (cf. Theorems 5.6 and 5.7). Concluding remarks, related and future work are discussed in Sect. 6. Additional material and complete proofs can be found in [7].

Some interesting technical points are worth noticing. Firstly, most of our con- structions and results rely on basic notions of formal languages and automata theory. This greatly simplifies the presentation and the proofs. The generali- sation from synchronous to asynchronous communications requires only a mild strengthening of our notion of well-formedness and no changes to c-automata or their projection. These are further advantages of the use of finite-state automata.

2   Preliminaries

A *Labelled Transition System* (LTS) is a tuple $A = \langle \mathbb{S}, s_0, \mathcal{L}, \rightarrow \rangle$ where

- $\mathbb{S}$ is a set of states (ranged over by $s, q, \ldots$) and $s_0 \in \mathbb{S}$ is the *initial state*;
- $\mathcal{L}$ is a finite set of labels (ranged over by $l, \lambda, \ldots$);
- $\rightarrow \subseteq \mathbb{S} \times (\mathcal{L} \cup \{\varepsilon\}) \times \mathbb{S}$ is a set of transitions where $\varepsilon \notin \mathcal{L}$ is a distinguished label.

We define a Finite-State Automaton (FSA) as an LTS where $\mathbb{S}$ is finite. We use the usual notation $s_1 \xrightarrow{\lambda} s_2$ for the transition $(s_1, \lambda, s_2) \in \rightarrow$, and $s_1 \rightarrow s_2$ when there exists λ such that $s_1 \xrightarrow{\lambda} s_2$, as well as $\rightarrow^*$ for the reflexive and transitive closure of $\rightarrow$. The set of *reachable states* of A is $\mathcal{R}(A) = \{s \mid s_0 \rightarrow^* s\}$.

Remark 2.1. Our definition of FSA omits the set of *accepting* states since we consider only FSAs where each state is accepting (which is the normal case in LTSs). We discuss this point further at the end of the paper.   ◇

We recall standard notions on LTSs.

Definition 2.2 (Traces and Trace equivalence). *A run of an LTS $A = \langle \mathbb{S}, s_0, \mathcal{L}, \rightarrow \rangle$ is a (possibly empty) finite or infinite sequence of consecutive tran- sitions starting at s_0. The* trace *(or word) w of a run $(s_{i-1} \xrightarrow{\lambda_{i-1}} s_i)_{1 \leq i \leq n}$ of A is the concatenation of the labels of the run (assume $n = \infty$ if the run is infi- nite), namely $w = \lambda_0 \cdot \lambda_1 \cdots \lambda_n$; label ε, as usual, denotes the identity element of concatenation; if the run is empty then $w = \varepsilon$.*

The language $\mathfrak{L}(A)$ *of A is the set of the traces of the runs of A. Two LTSs A and B are* trace equivalent *iff $\mathfrak{L}(A) = \mathfrak{L}(B)$. Also, A accepts w if $w \in \mathfrak{L}(A)$, A accepts w from s if $w \in \mathfrak{L}(\langle \mathbb{S}, s, \mathcal{L}, \rightarrow \rangle)$, and an s-run (resp. s-trace) of A is a run (resp. trace) of $\langle \mathbb{S}, s, \mathcal{L}, \rightarrow \rangle$.*

The notion of language in the definition above includes infinite words; this extends the standard notion of language accepted by an FSA. In particular, we consider an infinite word to be accepted by an FSA if each of its prefixes is accepted in the standard way. This is equivalent to look at an FSA both as a standard FSA and as a Büchi automaton where all the states are final.

Definition 2.3 (Deterministic LTSs). *An LTS* $A = \langle \mathbb{S}, s_0, \mathcal{L}, \rightarrow \rangle$ *is deterministic if*

– *it is ε-free, i.e. there is no transition of the form $q \xrightarrow{\varepsilon} q'$, and*
– *whenever $q \xrightarrow{\lambda} q_1$ and $q \xrightarrow{\lambda} q_2$ then $q_1 = q_2$.*

We denote the determinisation of A (i.e. the translation of a nondeterministic LTS/FSA to a deterministic one) as $\det(A)$[1].

We adopt communicating finite-state machines (CFSMs) [13] to model the local behaviour of systems of distributed components. The following definitions are borrowed from [13] and adapted to our context.

Let $\mathfrak{P}$ be a set of *participants* (or *roles*, ranged over by A, B, etc.) and $\mathcal{M}$ a set of *messages* (ranged over by m, n, etc.). We take $\mathfrak{P}$ and $\mathcal{M}$ disjoint.

Definition 2.4 (Communicating system). *A* communicating finite-state machine *(CFSM) is an FSA on the set*

$$\mathcal{L}_{act} = \{A\,B!m, A\,B?m \mid A, B \in \mathfrak{P}, m \in \mathcal{M}\}$$

of actions. *The* subject *of an output (resp. input) action* $A\,B!m$ *(resp.* $A\,B?m$*) is A (resp. B). A CFSM is A-*local *if all its transitions have subject A.*

A (communicating) system *is a map* $S = (M_A)_{A \in \mathcal{P}}$ *assigning an A-local CFSM M_A to each participant $A \in \mathcal{P}$ such that $\mathcal{P} \subseteq \mathfrak{P}$ is finite and any participant occurring in a transition of M_A is in $\mathcal{P}$.*

Note that CFSMs may contain ε-transitions. However, projection (see Definition 3.3 below) yields ε-free CFSMs.

Besides being a well-known and widely adopted model, CFSMs are equipped with both synchronous and asynchronous semantics. This enables a uniform treatment of both communication models. The use of CFMSs is also helpful to compare c-automata with other models which are projected on CFSMs as well, such as global graphs [37] and some versions of global types [23].

The synchronous semantics of communicating systems is an LTS where labels are *interactions*:

$$\mathcal{L}_{int} = \{A{\rightarrow}B\colon m \mid A \neq B \in \mathfrak{P} \text{ and } m \in \mathcal{M}\}$$

Definition 2.5 (Synchronous semantics). *Let* $S = (M_A)_{A \in \mathcal{P}}$ *be a communicating system where* $M_A = \langle \mathbb{S}_A, q_{0A}, \mathcal{L}_{act}, \rightarrow_A \rangle$ *for each participant $A \in \mathcal{P}$. A synchronous configuration of S is a map* $s = (q_A)_{A \in \mathcal{P}}$ *assigning a local state $q_A \in \mathbb{S}_A$ to each $A \in \mathcal{P}$. We denote q_A by $s(A)$ and may denote s by $\vec{q}$.*

The synchronous semantics *of S is the transition system* $[\![S]\!]^s = \langle \mathbb{S}, \vec{q}_0, \mathcal{L}_{int}, \rightarrow \rangle$ *defined as follows*

– $\mathbb{S}$ *is the set of synchronous configurations of S, as defined above, and* $\vec{q}_0 = (q_{0A})_{A \in \mathcal{P}} \in \mathbb{S}$ *is the initial configuration*
– $\vec{q}_1 \xrightarrow{A{\rightarrow}B\colon m} \vec{q}_2$ *if*

---

[1] The result of $\det(A)$ may actually depend on the chosen algorithm, but that is irrelevant for our results.

1. $\vec{q_1}(A) \xrightarrow{AB!m}_A \vec{q_2}(A)$ and $\vec{q_1}(B) \xrightarrow{AB?m}_B \vec{q_2}(B)$, and
2. for all $C \neq A, B$, $\vec{q_1}(C) = \vec{q_2}(C)$.

In this case, we say that $\vec{q_1}(A) \xrightarrow{AB!m}_A \vec{q_2}(A)$ and $\vec{q_1}(B) \xrightarrow{AB?m}_B \vec{q_2}(B)$ are component transitions of $\vec{q_1} \xrightarrow{A \to B:\, m} \vec{q_2}$.

- $\vec{q_1} \xrightarrow{\varepsilon} \vec{q_2}$ if $\vec{q_1}(A) \xrightarrow{\varepsilon}_A \vec{q_2}(A)$, and for all $B \neq A$, $\vec{q_1}(B) = \vec{q_2}(B)$.

Note that ε-transitions in the semantics of a communicating system are induced by those of the constituent CFSMs. Also, $[\![S]\!]^s$ is finite; in fact, it is in general a non-deterministic automaton on the alphabet $\mathcal{L}_{\text{int}}$.

As one would expect, the notion of synchronous semantics is invariant under language equivalence of CFSMs.

Proposition 2.6. *Let* $S = (M_A)_{A \in \mathcal{P}}$ *and* $S' = (M'_A)_{A \in \mathcal{P}}$ *be two communicating systems. If* $\mathcal{L}(M_A) = \mathcal{L}(M'_A)$ *for all* $A \in \mathcal{P}$ *then* $\mathcal{L}([\![S]\!]^s) = \mathcal{L}([\![S']\!]^s)$.

The asynchronous semantics of systems is defined in terms of transition systems which keep track of both the state of each machine and the content of unbounded FIFO queues b_{AB} which are associated to each channel $(A, B) \in \mathcal{C}$, where $\mathcal{C} = \mathcal{P} \times \mathcal{P} \setminus \{(A, A) \mid A \in \mathcal{P}\}$. The queue b_{AB} is where M_A puts the messages to M_B and from which M_B consumes the messages from M_A. To avoid cumbersome parenthesis, we write $A B \in \mathcal{C}$ for $(A, B) \in \mathcal{C}$.

Definition 2.7 (Asynchronous semantics). *Let* $S = (M_A)_{A \in \mathcal{P}}$ *be a communicating system where* $M_A = \langle S_A, q_{0A}, \mathcal{L}_{act}, \to_A \rangle$ *for each participant* $A \in \mathcal{P}$. *An asynchronous configuration of* S *is a pair* $s = \langle \vec{q}\,;\, \vec{b} \rangle$ *where* $\vec{q} = (q_A)_{A \in \mathcal{P}}$ *with* $q_A \in Q_A$ *and* $\vec{b} = (b_{AB})_{AB \in \mathcal{C}}$ *with* $b_{AB} \in \mathcal{M}^*$; *we write* $s(A)$ *for* $\vec{q}(A)$ *and denote by* ε *the empty queue. The* asynchronous semantics *of* S *is the transition system* $[\![S]\!]^a = \langle \mathbb{S}, s_0, \mathcal{L}_{act}, \to \rangle$ *defined as follows*

- $\mathbb{S}$ *is the set of asynchronous configurations of* S *and* $s_0 = \langle \vec{q_0}\,;\, \vec{b} \rangle$ *is the* initial configuration *where* $\vec{q_0} = (q_{0A})_{A \in \mathcal{P}}$ *and all the queues are empty.*
- $s \xrightarrow{l} s'$ *if* $s = \langle \vec{q}\,;\, \vec{b} \rangle$, $s' = \langle \vec{q'}\,;\, \vec{b'} \rangle$ *and either (1) or (2) below holds:*

1. $l = A B!m$ *and* $s(A) \xrightarrow{l}_A s'(A)$ *and* 2. $l = A B?m$ *and* $s(B) \xrightarrow{l}_B s'(B)$ *and*

   a. $s(C)' = s(C) \;\forall C \neq A \in \mathcal{P}$ *and*   a. $s'(C) = s(C) \;\forall C \neq B \in \mathcal{P}$ *and*
   b. $b'_{AB} = b_{AB}.m$ *and*   b. $b_{AB} = m.b'_{AB}$ *and*
   c. $b'_{CD} = b_{CD}$ *for all* $CD \in \mathcal{C}, CD \neq AB$ c. $b'_{CD} = b_{CD}$ *for all* $CD \in \mathcal{C}, CD \neq AB$

   In the first (resp. second) case we say that $s(A) \xrightarrow{AB!m}_A s'(A)$ *(resp.* $s(B) \xrightarrow{AB?m}_B s'(B)$) *is a* component transition *of* $s \xrightarrow{A \to B:\, m} s'$.

- $\langle \vec{q}\,;\, \vec{b} \rangle \xrightarrow{\varepsilon} \langle \vec{q'}\,;\, \vec{b'} \rangle$ *if* $\vec{q}(A) \xrightarrow{\varepsilon} \vec{q'}(A)$ *for some* $A \in \mathcal{P}$ *and for all* $B \neq A$, $\vec{q}(B) = \vec{q'}(B)$, *and* $\vec{b} = \vec{b'}$.

State q_A keeps track of the state of the machine M_A and buffer b_{AB} keeps track of the messages sent from A to B (and not yet received by B). In a transition $s \xrightarrow{AB!m} s'$, participant A adds message m in the queue of the channel $A B$ and symmetrically, in a transition $s \xrightarrow{AB?m} s'$, participant B consumes message m from the top of the queue of the channel $A B$. In both cases, any machine or queue not involved in the transition is left unchanged.

The asynchronous semantics is also invariant under equivalence of CFSMs.

Proposition 2.8. *Let* $S = (M_A)_{A \in \mathcal{P}}$ *and* $S' = (M'_A)_{A \in \mathcal{P}}$ *be two communicating systems. If* $\mathfrak{L}(M_A) = \mathfrak{L}(M'_A)$ *for all* $A \in \mathcal{P}$ *then* $\mathfrak{L}([\![S]\!]^a) = \mathfrak{L}([\![S']\!]^a)$.

For both the synchronous and the asynchronous semantics we restrict the attention to *fair runs*. An infinite run is fair if each transition which is continuously enabled is taken in a finite number of steps. A finite run is always fair.

We are interested in standard properties of communicating systems which we now recall. Definitions are alike in the synchronous and asynchronous semantics, hence, to avoid repetitions, below $[\![\text{-}]\!]$ stands for $[\![\text{-}]\!]^s$ or $[\![\text{-}]\!]^a$.

Definition 2.9 (Communication properties). *Let* $S = (M_A)_{A \in \mathcal{P}}$ *be a communicating system.*

  i) **Liveness:** S *is* live *if for each configuration* $s \in \mathcal{R}([\![S]\!])$ *and each* $A \in \mathcal{P}$ *with outgoing transitions from* $s(A)$ *in* M_A *there exists a run of* $[\![S]\!]$ *from* s *including a transition of* A *as a component transition.*
  ii) **Lock freedom:** *A configuration* $s \in \mathcal{R}([\![S]\!])$ *is a* lock *if*
    – there is $A \in \mathcal{P}$ *with an outgoing transition* t *from* $s(A)$ *in* M_A *and*
    – there exists a run of $[\![S]\!]$ *starting from* s, *maximal w.r.t. prefix order, and containing no transition* t' *involving* A.
  System S *is* lock-free *if for each* $s \in \mathcal{R}([\![S]\!])$, s *is not a lock.*
  iii) **Deadlock freedom:** *A configuration* $s \in \mathcal{R}([\![S]\!])$ *is a* deadlock *if*
    – s has no outgoing transitions in $[\![S]\!]$ *and*
    – there exists $A \in \mathcal{P}$ *such that* $s(A)$ *has an outgoing transition in* M_A.
  System S *is* deadlock-free *if for each* $s \in \mathcal{R}([\![S]\!])$, s *is not a deadlock.*

Liveness, as in [41], establishes the progress of communicating systems we are interested in. Lock freedom casts in our framework the idea that, similarly to [32,33], certain communications happen, whereas deadlock freedom extends the definition of deadlock in [19] to a setting which can be synchronous or asynchronous (as done also in [37,48]).

3   Choreography Automata

We introduce *choreography automata* (c-automata) as an expressive and flexible model of global specifications, following the styles of conversation protocols [27], choreographies [14,31,40], global graphs [48] and multiparty session types [17, 28,30]. As customary in choreographic frameworks, we show how to project c-automata on local specifications. As anticipated, our projection yields a system of CFSMs formalising the local behaviour of the participants of a choreography.

C-automata (ranged over by $\mathbb{CA}$, $\mathbb{CB}$, etc.) are FSAs with labels in $\mathcal{L}_{int}$.

Definition 3.1 (Choreography automata). *A* choreography automaton *(c-automaton) is an FSA on the alphabet* $\mathcal{L}_{int}$. *Elements of* $\mathcal{L}^*_{int}$ *are* choreography words, *subsets of* $\mathcal{L}^*_{int}$ *are* choreography languages.

Remark 3.2. Definition 3.1 admits non-deterministic c-automata. This does not increase the expressiveness of our framework. In fact, (i) the notions that we use for our results rely on traces and (ii) our projection operation (cf. Definition 3.3) is insensitive to non-determinism (cf. Proposition 3.6). Non-deterministic specifications are however desirable since they are easier to attain for the designer.   ◇

Given a c-automaton, our projection operation builds the corresponding communicating system consisting of the set of projections of the c-automaton on each participant, each projection yelding a CFSM. Hereafter, $\mathcal{P} \subseteq \mathfrak{P}$ is the set of participants of c-automata; note that $\mathcal{P}$ is necessarily finite.

Definition 3.3 (Automata Projection). *The* projection on A *of a transition* $t = q \xrightarrow{\lambda} q'$ *of a c-automaton, written* $t\!\downarrow_{\mathsf{A}}$ *is defined by:*

$$t\!\downarrow_{\mathsf{A}} = \begin{cases} q \xrightarrow{\mathsf{A\,C!m}} q' & \text{if } \lambda = \mathsf{B}{\to}\mathsf{C}\colon \mathsf{m} \quad \text{and} \quad \mathsf{B} = \mathsf{A} \\ q \xrightarrow{\mathsf{B\,A?m}} q' & \text{if } \lambda = \mathsf{B}{\to}\mathsf{C}\colon \mathsf{m} \quad \text{and} \quad \mathsf{C} = \mathsf{A} \\ q \xrightarrow{\varepsilon} q' & \text{otherwise} \end{cases}$$

The projection *of a c-automaton* $\mathbb{CA} = \langle \mathbb{S}, q_0, \mathcal{L}_{int}, \to \rangle$ *on a participant* $\mathsf{A} \in \mathcal{P}$, *denoted* $\mathbb{CA}\!\downarrow_{\mathsf{A}}$, *is obtained by determinising and minimising up-to-language equivalence the* intermediate *automaton*
$$A_{\mathsf{A}} = \langle \mathbb{S}, q_0, \mathcal{L}_{act} \cup \{\varepsilon\}, \{(q \xrightarrow{\lambda} q')\!\downarrow_{\mathsf{A}} \mid q \xrightarrow{\lambda} q'\}\rangle$$
The projection of $\mathbb{CA}$, *written* $\mathbf{CA}\!\downarrow$, *is the communicating system* $(\mathbb{CA}\!\downarrow_{\mathsf{A}})_{\mathsf{A} \in \mathcal{P}}$. *The projection function trivially extends to choreography words and languages.*

The projection defined above, apart for determinisation and minimisation, is essentially homomorphic, as most of the projections in the literature. Other approaches such as [25,43] add hidden communications to be able to deal with larger classes of choreographies. We prefer the former approach for its simplicity. Hidden communications can however be added directly at the choreographic level as proposed in [36].

It is a simple observation that the projection on A of $\mathbb{CA}$ is A-local, deterministic and hence ε-free. Thanks to the properties of determinisation and minimisation (as, e.g., in the partition refinement algorithm [42]), the states of $\mathbb{CA}\!\downarrow_{\mathsf{A}}$ are sets of states of $\mathbb{CA}$.

Example 3.4 (Projections of $\mathbb{C}ref$). The projections of our working example are

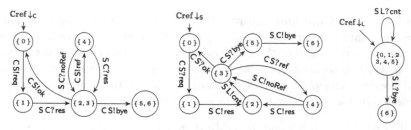

For instance, $\mathbb{C}ref\!\downarrow_C$ is obtained by determinising (minimisation is the identity in this case) the following intermediate automaton obtained as described in Definition 3.3.

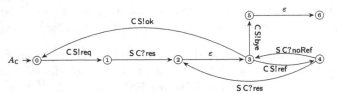

The following proposition relates the language of the projection with the language of the original automaton.

Proposition 3.5. *For all c-automata* $\mathbb{C}A$ *and* $A \in \mathcal{P}$, $\mathcal{L}(\mathbb{C}A\!\downarrow_A) = \mathcal{L}(\mathbb{C}A)\!\downarrow_A$.

The projection operation is well-behaved with respect to trace equivalence.

Proposition 3.6. *If* $\mathbb{C}A$ *and* $\mathbb{C}A'$ *are trace-equivalent c-automata then* $\mathbb{C}A\!\downarrow_A$ *and* $\mathbb{C}A'\!\downarrow_A$ *are isomorphic for each participant* $A \in \mathcal{P}$.

4   Well-Formed Choreography Automata

To ensure that the communicating system obtained by projection of a c-automaton is well-behaved, some conditions are necessary. Since the conditions depend on the used communication infrastructure, we consider first synchronous communication, leaving to Sect. 5 the case of asynchronous communication.

Definition 4.1 (Concurrent transitions). *Let* $\mathbb{C}A = \langle \mathbb{S}, q_0, \mathcal{L}, \rightarrow \rangle$. *Two transitions* $q \xrightarrow{l_1} q_1$ *and* $q \xrightarrow{l_2} q_2$ *are concurrent iff there is a state* $q' \in \mathbb{S}$ *and transitions* $q_1 \xrightarrow{l_2} q'$ *and* $q_2 \xrightarrow{l_1} q'$.

Well-branchedness (cf. Definition 4.6) is a key notion which intuitively states that each participant is aware of the choices made in the choreography when its behaviour depends on those choices. The awareness of choice is checked on *spans*, namely pairs of runs that may constitute alternative branches of choices. Spans are formalised building on the notion of *candidate branch* which, in turn, is defined in terms of *pre-candidate branch*.

Definition 4.2 (Candidate q-branch). *Let* q *be a state of a c-automaton* $\mathbb{C}A$. *A pre-candidate q-branch of* $\mathbb{C}A$ *is a q-run of* $\mathbb{C}A$ *such that each cycle has at most one occurrence within the whole run (i.e. any subsequence of the form* $q \rightarrow \dots \rightarrow q$, *where* q *occurs only at the beginning and at the end of the subsequence, is not present more than once in the run). A candidate q-branch is a maximal pre-candidate q-branch with respect to prefix order.*

We often refer to a (pre-)candidate q-branch simply as "(pre-)candidate of q". Due to the condition about cycles in Definition 4.2, the following holds trivially.

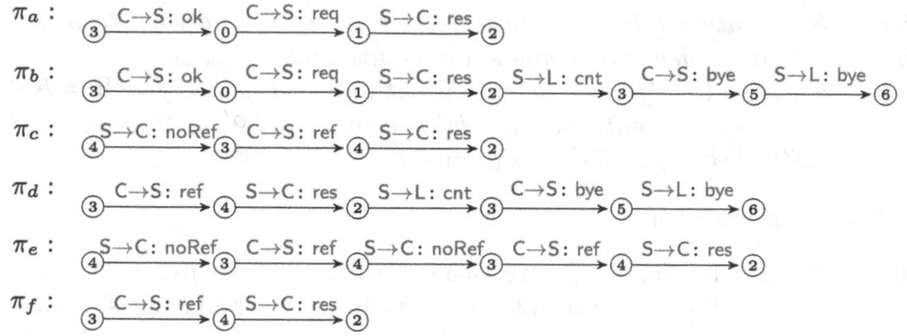

π_a :   ③ $\xrightarrow{\text{C→S: ok}}$ ⓪ $\xrightarrow{\text{C→S: req}}$ ① $\xrightarrow{\text{S→C: res}}$ ②

π_b :   ③ $\xrightarrow{\text{C→S: ok}}$ ⓪ $\xrightarrow{\text{C→S: req}}$ ① $\xrightarrow{\text{S→C: res}}$ ② $\xrightarrow{\text{S→L: cnt}}$ ③ $\xrightarrow{\text{C→S: bye}}$ ⑤ $\xrightarrow{\text{S→L: bye}}$ ⑥

π_c :   ④ $\xrightarrow{\text{S→C: noRef}}$ ③ $\xrightarrow{\text{C→S: ref}}$ ④ $\xrightarrow{\text{S→C: res}}$ ②

π_d :   ③ $\xrightarrow{\text{C→S: ref}}$ ④ $\xrightarrow{\text{S→C: res}}$ ② $\xrightarrow{\text{S→L: cnt}}$ ③ $\xrightarrow{\text{C→S: bye}}$ ⑤ $\xrightarrow{\text{S→L: bye}}$ ⑥

π_e :   ④ $\xrightarrow{\text{S→C: noRef}}$ ③ $\xrightarrow{\text{C→S: ref}}$ ④ $\xrightarrow{\text{S→C: noRef}}$ ③ $\xrightarrow{\text{C→S: ref}}$ ④ $\xrightarrow{\text{S→C: res}}$ ②

π_f :   ③ $\xrightarrow{\text{C→S: ref}}$ ④ $\xrightarrow{\text{S→C: res}}$ ②

Fig. 1. Runs of $\mathbb{C}$ref.

Fact 1. *Given a state q of a c-automaton $\mathbb{C}A$, the set of its pre-candidates is finite, and so is, a fortiori, that of its candidates.*

Example 4.3 ((Pre-)candidate branches in $\mathbb{C}$ref). The sequences in Fig. 1 are runs of the c-automaton of our working example. They are all pre-candidates of either 3 or 4, but run π_e, which is not a pre-candidate of 4 since the cycle 4–3–4 occurs twice. Runs π_b and π_d are also candidates of 3, being maximal pre-candidates with respect to prefix order. ◇

Definition 4.4 (q-span). *Given a state q of a c-automaton $\mathbb{C}A$, a pair (σ, σ') of pre-candidate q-branches of $\mathbb{C}A$ is a q-span if σ and σ' are*

- *either cofinal, with no common node but q and the last one;*
- *or candidate q-branches with no common node but q;*
- *or a candidate q-branch and a loop on q with no other common nodes.*

A participant $\mathsf{A} \in \mathcal{P}$ chooses at a q-span (σ, σ') if the first transition of both σ and σ' has A as sender.

Example 4.5 (Spans of $\mathbb{C}$ref). The states with spans of our working example are 3 and 4. A span from 3 is (π_a, π_f), where π_a and π_f are as in Fig. 1. Indeed, π_a and π_f are cofinal (in 2) pre-candidates of 3 with no common states but 3 and 2. Participant C chooses at (π_a, π_f). The pair (π_b, π_d), instead, is not a span from 3, since π_b and π_d are maximal, but share other nodes than 3. ◇

Intuitively, a choice is well-branched when the participants other than the one opting for alternative runs either behave uniformly in each branch, or can ascertain which branch has been chosen from the messages they receive.

Definition 4.6 (Well-branchedness). *A c-automaton $\mathbb{C}A$ is well-branched if for each state q in $\det(\mathbb{C}A)$ and $\mathsf{A} \in \mathcal{P}$ sender in a transition from q, all of the following conditions must hold:*

(1) all transitions from q involving A, have sender A;

(2) for each transition t from q whose sender is not A and each transition t' from q whose sender is A, t and t' are concurrent;

(3) for each q-span (σ, σ') where A chooses at and each participant $\mathsf{B} \neq \mathsf{A} \in \mathcal{P}$, the first pair of different labels on the runs $\sigma\downarrow_{\mathsf{B}}$ and $\sigma'\downarrow_{\mathsf{B}}$ (if any) is of the form $(\mathsf{C}\,\mathsf{B}?\mathsf{m}, \mathsf{D}\,\mathsf{B}?\mathsf{n})$ with $\mathsf{C} \neq \mathsf{D}$ or $\mathsf{m} \neq \mathsf{n}$.

We dub A a selector at q.

In the above definition loops are taken into account in item (3) since the notion of span is defined in terms of candidate branch. The latter is a maximal run where cycles can be considered at most once, as shown in Example 4.3.

In case of a nondeterministic c-automaton, the conditions of Definition 4.6 are checked after the c-automaton has been determinised. In fact, recalling Remark 3.2, we consider properties of languages of c-automata, and determinisation, as well as minimisation, of FSA preserve languages. Also, both operations preserve the system resulting from projection (cf. Proposition 3.6). (Observe that here we exploit classical results of automata theory.) Also, by Fact 1 and the obvious decidability of the conditions of Definitions 4.4 and 4.6 we get

Fact 2. *Well-branchedness is a decidable property.*

Example 4.7 (Well-branchedness of $\mathbb{C}$ref). All the states of $\mathbb{C}$ref satisfy the conditions of Definition 4.6; the only non-trivial cases are states 3 and 4. Condition (1) holds for C, which is the selector of the choice at 3, and for S, which is the selector of the choice at 4; condition (2) holds vacuously, and condition (3) holds for both S and L in all the spans from 3 and from 4. For instance, in the span (π_a, π_f) from 3, described in Example 4.5, the first actions of S on π_a and π_f are the inputs from C which have different messages, whereas, for what concerns L, the condition holds vacuously. As a matter of fact, since π_a and π_f are cofinal in 2, the well-branchedness conditions on state 2 do guarantee L to behave properly afterwards, independently on whether π_a or π_f have been followed before.   ◇

Condition (2), vacuously true in our working example, is needed when multiple participants act as sender in the same state: this ensures that the only possibility is that actions of different participants are concurrent so that possible choices at a state are not affected by independent behaviour.

We add a further condition to rule out c-automata having consecutive transitions involving disjoint participants and not actually concurrent.

Definition 4.8 (Well-sequencedness). *A c-automaton $\mathbb{C}A$ is well-sequenced if for each two consecutive transitions $q \xrightarrow{\mathsf{A}\to\mathsf{B}:\,\mathsf{m}} q' \xrightarrow{\mathsf{C}\to\mathsf{D}:\,\mathsf{n}} q''$ either*

- *they share a participant, that is $\{\mathsf{A}, \mathsf{B}\} \cap \{\mathsf{C}, \mathsf{D}\} \neq \emptyset$, or*
- *they are concurrent, i.e. there is q''' such that $q \xrightarrow{\mathsf{C}\to\mathsf{D}:\,\mathsf{n}} q''' \xrightarrow{\mathsf{A}\to\mathsf{B}:\,\mathsf{m}} q''$.*

Notice that, by finiteness of the transition relation of c-automata, we get

Fact 3. *Well-sequencedness is a decidable property.*

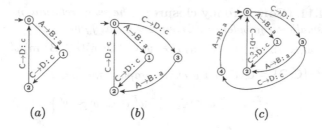

(a)   (b)   (c)

Fig. 2. Failure of well-sequencedness completion.

Notation. For the sake of readability, a well-sequenced c-automaton can be represented by omitting, for each diamond, two of its consecutive transitions. We call such representation *compact*. Notice that, given a compact representation, it is always possible to recover the original c-automaton. So far and hereafter we assume that all c-automata are compactly represented.

Example 4.9 (Well-sequencedness of $\mathbb{C}$*ref).* It is not difficult to check that $\mathbb{C}$ref is well-sequenced because the first condition of Definition 4.8 holds for any pair of consecutive transitions in $\mathbb{C}$ref.   ◇

Well-sequencedness is necessary to establish a precise correspondence between the language of a c-automaton and of its projection (cf. Theorem 4.14 and the discussion following it).

Remark 4.10. We show that not all c-automata can be "completed" to well-sequenced ones. Consider the c-automaton of Fig. 2(a), which is not well-sequenced because of the transitions from state 0 to state 1 and from state 1 to 2. By "completing the diamond" for such transitions (i.e., by adding the new state 3 and the transitions $0 \xrightarrow{\mathsf{C} \to \mathsf{D} : \mathsf{c}} 3$ and $3 \xrightarrow{\mathsf{A} \to \mathsf{B} : \mathsf{a}} 2$) we obtain the c-automaton of Fig. 2(b). This is still not well sequenced, because of the transitions $3 \xrightarrow{\mathsf{A} \to \mathsf{B} : \mathsf{a}} 2$ and $2 \xrightarrow{\mathsf{C} \to \mathsf{D} : \mathsf{c}} 0$. So we try to make it well-sequenced by completing the diamond once again and obtain the c-automaton of Fig. 2(c). The resulting c-automaton is still not well-sequenced, because of the transitions $4 \xrightarrow{\mathsf{A} \to \mathsf{B} : \mathsf{a}} 0$ and $0 \xrightarrow{\mathsf{C} \to \mathsf{D} : \mathsf{c}} 3$. Again a vain attempt, because of the transitions $5 \xrightarrow{\mathsf{A} \to \mathsf{B} : \mathsf{a}} 3$ and $3 \xrightarrow{\mathsf{C} \to \mathsf{D} : \mathsf{c}} 4$. It is immediate to check that we could go on indefinitely.

It is impossible to complete the initial c-automaton since the intended completed automaton should generate a non-regular language (since it should generate strings with a number of $\mathsf{C} \to \mathsf{D} : \mathsf{c}$ interactions which is, roughly, double of the number of $\mathsf{A} \to \mathsf{B} : \mathsf{a}$ interactions). It would hence be interesting to know whether, in case the expected completed interaction language of a c-automaton is regular and prefix-closed, it is possible to generate it also by means of a well-sequenced c-automaton. It would be also interesting to establish a condition on cycles (if any) that guarantees the effectiveness of the completion of a c-automaton. We leave these questions for future work.   ◇

We show a closure property of the languages of well-sequenced c-automata.

Definition 4.11 (Concurrency closure). *The* swap *relation on choreography words is the smallest equivalence relation* _ $\sim$ _ *satisfying*

$$w(A \rightarrow B\colon m)(C \rightarrow D\colon n)w' \sim w(C \rightarrow D\colon n)(A \rightarrow B\colon m)w'$$

where $\{A, B\} \cap \{C, D\} = \emptyset$. *Given a choreography language* $\mathcal{L}$

$$close(\mathcal{L}) = \{\, w \in \mathcal{L}_{int} \mid \exists w' \in \mathcal{L}.\ w \sim w' \,\}$$

is the concurrency closure *of* $\mathcal{L}$.

The above relation is reminiscent of the *swapping* relation introduced in [18], with similar aims.

Proposition 4.12. *Let* $\mathbb{C}A$ *be a well-sequenced c-automaton. Then* $\mathcal{L}(\mathbb{C}A)$ *is concurrency closed, i.e.* $\mathcal{L}(\mathbb{C}A) = close(\mathcal{L}(\mathbb{C}A))$.

Notice that the converse of the above proposition does not hold in general. In fact, consider the following c-automaton

we can check that $\mathcal{L}(\mathbb{C}A) = close(\mathcal{L}(\mathbb{C}A))$ but $\mathbb{C}A$ is not well-sequenced.

The notion of well-formedness below sums up the requirements needed in order for a c-automaton to be projected to a well-behaved communicating system.

Definition 4.13 (Well-formedness). *A c-automaton is* well-formed *if it is both well-branched and well-sequenced.*

The next result in Theorem 4.14 establishes that the language of a well-formed c-automaton coincides with the language of the communicating system obtained by projection. This provides a correctness criterion for our projection operation.

Theorem 4.14. $\mathcal{L}(\mathbb{C}A) = \mathcal{L}(\llbracket \mathbb{C}A {\downarrow} \rrbracket^s)$ *for any well-formed c-automaton* $\mathbb{C}A$.

Notice that well-formedness is a necessary condition for the theorem above. It is in fact easy to check that

$$(C \rightarrow D\colon m)(A \rightarrow B\colon n) \in \mathcal{L}(\llbracket \mathbb{C}A {\downarrow} \rrbracket^s) \quad \text{and} \quad (C \rightarrow D\colon m)(A \rightarrow B\colon n) \notin \mathcal{L}(\mathbb{C}A)$$

when $\mathbb{C}A$ is one of the c-automata (a), (b) or (c) of Fig. 3. In particular, (a) is not well-sequenced whereas (b) and (c) are not well-branched: for (b), item (2) of well-branchedness (Definition 4.6) does not hold; (c) instead violates item (3).

We can now show that the projections of well-formed choreography automata enjoy the communication properties of Definition 2.9.

Theorem 4.15. *Given a well-formed c-automaton* $\mathbb{C}A$, *its projection* $(\mathbb{C}A {\downarrow}_A)_{A \in \mathcal{P}}$ *is live, lock-free, and deadlock-free with respect to the synchronous semantics.*

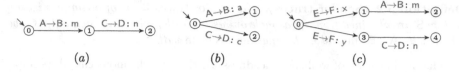

Fig. 3. Well-formedness is necessary for Theorem 4.14.

5 Asynchronous Communications

We now transfer the results of the previous sections to the asynchronous semantics of communicating systems (Definition 2.7). Remarkably, the semantics does
not affect the definition of c-automata (and of projections) since it is independent
of the communication model. Hence, any result depending only on the definition
of c-automata still holds. Well-sequencedness instead needs updating.

Definition 5.1 (Asynchronous well-sequencedness). *A c-automaton is
asynchronously well-sequenced if for each two consecutive transitions*
$q \xrightarrow{A \to B:\, m} q' \xrightarrow{C \to D:\, n} q''$ *either*

- *the sender of the second transition occurs in the first one, that is* $C \in \{A, B\}$,
- *or they are concurrent, i.e. there is* q''' *such that* $q \xrightarrow{C \to D:\, n} q''' \xrightarrow{A \to B:\, m} q''$.

Asynchronous well-sequencedness (Definition 4.8) implies the synchronous
one. Indeed, asynchronous well-sequencedness requires either two transitions to
be concurrent or that the sender of the second transition occurs in the first one.
The latter condition is weaker than having disjoint participants as required in
the synchronous case.

Note that our working example is well-sequenced but not asynchronously
well-sequenced (because e.g., of transitions $2 \xrightarrow{S \to L:\, cnt} 3 \xrightarrow{C \to S:\, bye} 5$). Thus, we
now consider it as the *compact* representation of the actual c-automaton accord-
ing to Notation on page 12.

Unlike well-sequencedness, the notion of well-branchedness has not to be
changed in case asynchronous communications are considered. So, in the asynchronous setting, we define *asynchronous well-formedness* as the conjunction of
asynchronous well-sequencedness (Definition 5.1) and well-branchedness (Definition 4.6).

The correspondence result between the semantics of a c-automaton and of its
projection requires to decide which actions to observe on the projection. Indeed,
in a c-automaton, each interaction is seen as an atomic event, while in the
asynchronous semantics of communicating systems each interaction corresponds
to two events: a sending event and a receiving event. We opt to observe sending
events only because (internal) choices are determined by sending events. This
decision also plays well with the notion of well-branchedness, where most of the
conditions concern sender participants. Other possible options are discussed in
[35], in a process algebraic setting. This idea is formalised by *sender traces*.

Definition 5.2 (Sender traces). *The* sender traces $\mathfrak{L}^!(S)$ *of a communicating system* S *are obtained from its asynchronous traces by replacing each output label* A B!m *with* A→B: m *and each input label* A B?m *with* ε.

The modification of well-sequencedness for the asynchronous case does imply that we need to "update" the definition of concurrency closure as well.

Definition 5.3 (Asynchronous concurrency closure). *The* asynchronous swap *relation on choreography words is the smallest pre-order* _ ≤ _ *satisfying*

$$w(A{\to}B\colon m)(C{\to}D\colon n)w' \leq w(C{\to}D\colon n)(A{\to}B\colon m)w' \qquad \textit{where } C \notin \{A, B\}.$$

The downward closure of a choreography language $\mathcal{L}$ *with respect to* _ ≤ _

$$close_a(\mathcal{L}) = \{ w \in \mathcal{L}_{int} \mid \exists w' \in \mathcal{L}.\ w \leq w' \}$$

is the asynchronous concurrency closure *of* $\mathcal{L}$.

The condition for asynchronous concurrency closure is weaker than the one in the synchronous case. This is due to the fact that sender-traces must be closed under asynchronous concurrency (cf. Lemma 5.4 below), so to guarantee that the traces of an automaton do coincide with the sender-traces of its projection (Theorem 5.6 below). We discuss such a necessity with an example after Theorem 5.6.

Lemma 5.4. *Let* $\mathbb{C}A$ *be a c-automaton. Then* $\mathfrak{L}^!(\llbracket \mathbb{C}A{\downarrow} \rrbracket^a) = close_a(\mathfrak{L}^!(\llbracket \mathbb{C}A{\downarrow} \rrbracket^a))$.

We now proceed to prove the correctness of projection for asynchronous systems. We will reduce it to the corresponding result for synchronous systems (Theorem 4.14). This is done by showing that all asynchronous runs are pairable (see below), that is they can be put in a suitable normal form which directly corresponds to a synchronous run. Notably, such a result is false for c-automata which are not asynchronously well-formed.

Definition 5.5 (Pairable runs). *Let* $\mathbb{C}A$ *be a c-automaton. A run* σ *in* $\llbracket \mathbb{C}A{\downarrow} \rrbracket^a$ *is paired into a run* σ' *in* $\llbracket \mathbb{C}A{\downarrow} \rrbracket^a$ *iff they are coinitial, produce the same sender trace, and each output* A B!m *in* σ' *is immediately followed by the corresponding input* A B?m. *A run* σ *is* pairable *if it is paired into a run* σ'.

Theorem 5.6. *Let* $\mathbb{C}A$ *be an asynchronously well-formed c-automaton.*

$$\mathfrak{L}^!(\llbracket \mathbb{C}A{\downarrow} \rrbracket^a) = \mathfrak{L}(\mathbb{C}A)$$

Similarly to Theorem 4.14, asynchronous well-formedness is a necessary condition for Theorem 5.6. Examples (*b*) and (*c*) of Fig. 3 work the same also for the asynchronous case, since we do not changed the definition of well-branchedness. We changed instead the definition of well-sequencedness to a stricter version and the c-automaton (*a*) of Fig. 3 is hence not enough to show the necessity of asynchronous well-sequencedness; this can however be easily done using the following c-automaton which is well-sequenced but not asynchronouly well-sequenced.

$$\mathbb{C}A \rightarrow \underset{0}{\circ} \xrightarrow{A \rightarrow B:\ m} \underset{1}{\circ} \xrightarrow{C \rightarrow B:\ m} \underset{2}{\circ}$$

Since outputs of asynchronous CFSMs can always be fired, there is a run of the projected system beginning with $C\,B!m$ and producing the sender trace $(C \rightarrow B:\ m)(A \rightarrow B:\ m) \in \mathfrak{L}^i(\llbracket\mathbb{C}A\rrbracket^a)$ which trivially does not belong to $\mathfrak{L}(\mathbb{C}A)$ because the interactions cannot be swapped (cf. Definition 5.3).

The communication properties for projected systems can also be obtained.

Theorem 5.7. *Given an asynchronous well-formed c-automaton* $\mathbb{C}A$, *its projection* $(\mathbb{C}A\!\downarrow_A)_{A\in\mathcal{P}}$ *is live, lock-free, and deadlock-free with respect to the asynchronous semantics.*

6   Conclusion, Related Work and Future Work

We introduced a model of choreographies based on FSAs whose transitions are labelled by interactions. We showed relevant results both for a synchronous and an asynchronous underlying communication infrastructure. We established a correspondence between the language of an automaton and the one of its projection, as well as proofs of liveness, lock, and deadlock freedom for the latter.

The adoption of an automata-based model brings in two main benefits. Firstly, the constructions that we provided are based on set-theoretic notions and are *syntax-independent*. This contrasts with syntax-driven models (such as behavioural type systems [30]) where expressiveness may be limited and definitions may be more complex due to syntactic reasons. E.g., the example in Sect. 1 cannot be modelled in many behavioural type systems since entangled loops cannot be represented using a recursion operator. Secondly, we can re-use well-known results of the theory of automata (e.g., we used notions of trace equivalence and determinisation) and related tools.

Related Work. Automata-based models for specifying the local behaviour of distributed components are commonplace in the literature (see e.g., [13,21]). Less so is for the global specifications of choreographies: to the best of our knowledge, the conversation protocols (CP) in [9,26,27] (and references therein) are the only such model in the literature. The realisability of CP has been first studied in [27]; this is indeed the work closest to ours. Conversation protocols are non-deterministic Büchi automata whose labels resemble our interactions (barred the fact that, contrarily to our formalism, in [27] the sender and the receiver of each message are determined by its content). Our c-automata are basically finite-state automata where infinite words can be taken into account by looking at them as Büchi automata where all states are actually final. It is not immediate to provide a detailed comparison between conversation protocols and c-automata because their semantics and underlying communication models differ. As for the communication model, conversation protocols are realised in a subclass of CFSMs (cf. Section 5 of [27]), whereas we consider the unrestricted model of CFSMs, as well as a synchronous version of it. Concerning the semantics, Definition 4 (item 3(b)) of [27] restricts the runs to those where all messages in queues are eventually consumed, that is they require by definition a form of liveness. Instead, one of our goals is to identify conditions that guarantee relevant liveness properties. We prove them in Theorem 5.7, and in Proposition D.1 in [7] we prove the exact property assumed in [27]. The realisability conditions of conversation protocols are *lossless join*, *synchronous compatibility*, and *autonomy*. Those conditions cannot easily be compared with well-formedness, due to the differences in the models and in the semantics. Furthermore, the style of the conditions is very different, and it also induces very different proof strategies in many cases. In particular,

- our well-sequencedness is checked on pairs of consecutive transitions and well-branchedness on pairs of coinitial paths;
- lossless join is a global property, that is a condition on the automaton consisting of the product of the languages of the local projections;
- synchronous compatibility is defined in terms of pairs of traces in the projection but verified with an algorithm that checks a global property of an automata construction, and the same holds for autonomy.

Thus, while the conditions capture similar intuitions, a detailed comparison is very hard. When restricting to the common part of the two models, well-branchedness implies autonomy while the opposite does not hold. Indeed, by well-branchedness the selector is output-ready (according to the terminology in [27]), while any other participant either behaves uniformly in each branch (and is thus either input-ready or output-ready or termination-ready) or it is made aware of the choice by distinct inputs (that is it is input-ready). In all the cases autonomy is satisfied. In the other direction, a choice between traces $(A{\rightarrow}B\colon l)(B{\rightarrow}C\colon n)(C{\rightarrow}D\colon w)$ and $(A{\rightarrow}B\colon r)(B{\rightarrow}C\colon n)(C{\rightarrow}D\colon z)$ satisfies autonomy but not well-branchedness.

As for lossless join, we do not assume it. Actually, it is equivalent to one of our results, namely the correctness of the projection in the synchronous case (Theorem 4.14). Such a result is also used in the asynchronous case (Theorem 5.6), which is proved by reduction to the synchronous one via paired runs. We leave a detailed comparison of the two sets of constraints, in a common setting, for future work. Later works on CP (see, e.g., [9]) changed the approach and relied on model checking to show realisability instead of well-formedness conditions. Unfortunately, some of their main decidability results were flawed [24].

Conditions similar to well-branchedness and well-sequencedness do naturally arise in investigations related to choreographies and their realisability. A unique sender driving a choice is a condition present in several multiparty session types formalisms ([28] and [20] to cite just a couple of them), global graphs formalisms [48], choreography languages in general (for instance see the notion of *dominant role* in [44]). Conditions related to item (3) of Definition 4.6 can also be found in multiparty session types formalisms [46] or in conversation protocols, as discussed above. Also, notions close to well-sequencedness turn out to arise quite naturally in "well-behaved" choreographies (see for instance the notion of *well-informedness* of [15] in the context of collaboration diagrams).

Similarly to what discussed in Remark 4.10, some approaches propose techniques to fix choreographies which are not well-behaved. This issue is considered in some multiparty session types [10,11], in algebraic and automata-based frameworks for choreographies [8,36] as well as in the choreographic middleware ChoreOS [3,4]. While they consider different conditions than ours, trying to adapt their approaches to our setting is an interesting item for future work.

As said, most approaches are not based on automata. For instance, [22,35,44] use algebraic operators to build larger choreographies from smaller ones, and give conditions on such operations ensuring that the resulting choreography is "well-behaved". This technique is not applicable in our case, since, like most works on automata, we do not consider an algebra to build automata.

While the main aim of c-automata is to provide a choreography model based on FSAs, we remark here that it is rather expressive and complements existing models of choreographies or multiparty session types (MST). In particular, the expressive power of c-automata is not comparable with the one of the MST in [45], which subsumes most systems in the literature. More precisely, the c-automaton Cref in Sect. 1 cannot be syntactically written in [45] due to the two entangled loops. That example cannot be expressed in global graphs [48] either, again due to the intersecting loops. We note that the infinite unfolding of the c-automaton is regular and therefore it would fit in the session type system considered in [47]. However, this type system has not been conceived for choreographies (it is a binary session type system) and does not allow non-determinism.

On the other side, examples such as [45, Example 2, Fig. 4] cannot be written in our model (since we expect the same roles to occur in branches which are coinitial, branches inside loops require that all participants in a loop are notified when the loop ends). We conjecture that a refinement of well-branchedness is possible to address this limitation. Global graphs are another model of global specifications. Their advantage is that they feature parallel composition, which c-automata lack. We note however that one could use the classical product of automata on c-automata to model parallel composition in the case where the two branches have disjoint sets of participants (as typically assumed in MST with parallel composition). Mapping global graphs without parallel composition into c-automata is trivial. The same considerations apply to choreography languages where possible behaviours are defined by a suitable process algebra with parallel composition such as [14,35].

Future Work. One of the main motivations to develop a choreography model based on automata was to lift the compositional mechanism discovered in [6] on CFSMs to global specifications, in such a way that composition of global specifications preserves well-formedness. This is the problem we are currently addressing.

An interesting future development is also to adopt Büchi automata as c-automata. This extension is technically straightforward (just add accepting states to Definition 3.1 and define ω-languages accordingly), but it probably impacts greatly the underlying theory. An interesting yet not trivial effort is the identification of well-formedness conditions on this generalised class of c-automata that guarantee a precise correspondence with the ω-languages of the projections.

The interplay between FSAs and formal languages could lead to a theory of projection of choreographies based on languages instead of automata. For instance, one could try to characterise the languages accepted by well-formed c-automata, similarly to what done in [1,38,48]. In those approaches global specifications are rendered as partial orders and the distributed realisability is characterised in terms of closure properties of languages.

A final direction for future work concerns the implementation of tool support for the approach. We are currently working in this direction. A very preliminary and partial implementation by Simone Orlando and Ivan Lanese is available at https://github.com/simoneorlando/Corinne.

References

1. Alur, R., Etessami, K., Yannakakis, M.: Inference of message sequence charts. IEEE Trans. Softw. Eng. **29**(7), 623–633 (2003)
2. Ariola, W., Dunlop, C.: Testing in the API Economy. Top 5 Myths. https://api2cart.com/api-technology/api-testing-myths-infographic/
3. Autili, M., Inverardi, P., Tivoli, M.: Choreography realizability enforcement through the automatic synthesis of distributed coordination delegates. Sci. Comput. Program. **160**, 3–29 (2018)
4. Autili, M., Di Ruscio, D., Di Salle, A., Perucci, A.: CHOReOSynt: enforcing choreography realizability in the future internet. In: Cheung, S.-C., Orso, A., Storey, M.-A.D. (eds.) Proceedings of the 22nd ACM SIGSOFT International Symposium on Foundations of Software Engineering (FSE-22), Hong Kong, China, 16–22 November 2014, pp. 723–726. ACM (2014)
5. Autili, M., Di Salle, A., Gallo, F., Pompilio, C., Tivoli, M.: CHOReVOLUTION: automating the realization of highly–collaborative distributed applications. In: Riis Nielson, H., Tuosto, E. (eds.) COORDINATION 2019. LNCS, vol. 11533, pp. 92–108. Springer, Cham (2019). https://doi.org/10.1007/978-3-030-22397-7_6
6. Barbanera, F., De'Liguoro, U., Hennicker, R.: Connecting open systems of communicating finite state machines. J. Log. Algebraic Methods Program. **109**, 100476 (2019)
7. Barbanera, F., Lanese, I., Tuosto, E.: Choreography automata, April 2020. http://www.cs.unibo.it/~lanese/choreography_automata.pdf. Full version
8. Basu, S., Bultan, T.: Automated choreography repair. In: Stevens, P., Wąsowski, A. (eds.) FASE 2016. LNCS, vol. 9633, pp. 13–30. Springer, Heidelberg (2016). https://doi.org/10.1007/978-3-662-49665-7_2
9. Basu, S., Bultan, T., Ouederni, M.: Deciding choreography realizability. In: Proceedings of the 39th ACM SIGPLAN-SIGACT Symposium on Principles of Programming Languages, POPL 2012, Philadelphia, Pennsylvania, USA, 22–28 January 2012, pp. 191–202 (2012)
10. Bocchi, L., Lange, J., Tuosto, E.: Amending contracts for choreographies. In: ICE, volume 59 of EPTCS, pp. 111–129 (2011)
11. Bocchi, L., Lange, J., Tuosto, E.: Three algorithms and a methodology for amending contracts for choreographies. Sci. Ann. Comput. Sci. **22**(1), 61–104 (2012)

12. Bonér, J.: Reactive Microsystems - The Evolution of Microservices at Scale. O'Reilly, Sebastopol (2018)
13. Brand, D., Zafiropulo, P.: On communicating finite-state machines. J. ACM **30**(2), 323–342 (1983)
14. Bravetti, M., Zavattaro, G.: Towards a unifying theory for choreography conformance and contract compliance. In: Lumpe, M., Vanderperren, W. (eds.) SC 2007. LNCS, vol. 4829, pp. 34–50. Springer, Heidelberg (2007). https://doi.org/10.1007/978-3-540-77351-1_4
15. Bultan, T., Xiang, F.: Specification of realizable service conversations using collaboration diagrams. Serv. Oriented Comput. Appl. **2**(1), 27–39 (2008). https://doi.org/10.1007/s11761-008-0022-7
16. Bultan, T., Fu, X., Hull, R., Su, J.: Conversation specification: a new approach to design and analysis of e-service composition. In: Hencsey, G., White, B., Chen, Y.-F.R., Kovács, L., Lawrence, S. (eds.) Proceedings of the Twelfth International World Wide Web Conference, WWW 2003, Budapest, Hungary, 20–24 May 2003, pp. 403–410. ACM (2003)
17. Carbone, M., Honda, K., Yoshida, N.: Structured communication-centred programming for web services. In: De Nicola, R. (ed.) ESOP 2007. LNCS, vol. 4421, pp. 2–17. Springer, Heidelberg (2007). https://doi.org/10.1007/978-3-540-71316-6_2
18. Carbone, M., Montesi, F.: Deadlock-freedom-by-design: multiparty asynchronous global programming. In: Giacobazzi, R., Cousot, R. (eds.) POPL, pp. 263–274. ACM (2013)
19. Cécé, G., Finkel, A.: Verification of programs with half-duplex communication. I&C **202**(2), 166–190 (2005)
20. Coppo, M., Dezani-Ciancaglini, M., Yoshida, N., Padovani, L.: Global progress for dynamically interleaved multiparty sessions. Math. Struct. Comput. Sci. **26**(2), 238–302 (2016)
21. de Alfaro, L., Henzinger, T.A.: Interface automata. In: Proceedings of the 8th European Software Engineering Conference Held Jointly with 9th ACM SIGSOFT International Symposium on Foundations of Software Engineering 2001, Vienna, Austria, 10–14 September 2001, pp. 109–120 (2001)
22. Deniélou, P.-M., Yoshida, N.: Dynamic multirole session types. In: Ball, T., Sagiv, M. (eds.) POPL, pp. 435–446. ACM (2011)
23. Deniélou, P.-M., Yoshida, N.: Multiparty session types meet communicating automata. In: Seidl, H. (ed.) ESOP 2012. LNCS, vol. 7211, pp. 194–213. Springer, Heidelberg (2012). https://doi.org/10.1007/978-3-642-28869-2_10
24. Finkel, A., Lozes, E.: Synchronizability of communicating finite state machines is not decidable. In: ICALP, pp. 122:1–122:14 (2017)
25. Francalanza, A., Mezzina, C.A., Tuosto, E.: Reversible choreographies via monitoring in Erlang. In: Bonomi, S., Rivière, E. (eds.) DAIS 2018. LNCS, vol. 10853, pp. 75–92. Springer, Cham (2018). https://doi.org/10.1007/978-3-319-93767-0_6
26. Fu, X., Bultan, T., Su, J.: Conversation protocols: a formalism for specification and verification of reactive electronic services. In: Ibarra, O.H., Dang, Z. (eds.) CIAA 2003. LNCS, vol. 2759, pp. 188–200. Springer, Heidelberg (2003). https://doi.org/10.1007/3-540-45089-0_18
27. Xiang, F., Bultan, T., Jianwen, S.: Conversation protocols: a formalism for specification and verification of reactive electronic services. Theor. Comput. Sci. **328**(1–2), 19–37 (2004)
28. Honda, K., Yoshida, N., Carbone, M.: Multiparty asynchronous session types. In: Necula, G.C., Wadler, P. (eds.) POPL, pp. 273–284. ACM Press (2008)

29. Honda, K., Yoshida, N., Carbone, M.: Multiparty asynchronous session types. J. ACM **63**(1), 9:1–9:67 (2016). Extended version of a paper presented at POPL08
30. Hüttel, H., et al.: Foundations of session types and behavioural contracts. ACM Comput. Surv. **49**(1), 3:1–3:36 (2016)
31. Kavantzas, N., Burdett, D., Ritzinger, G., Fletcher, T., Lafon, Y., Barreto, C.: Web services choreography description language version 1.0. Technical report, W3C (2005). http://www.w3.org/TR/ws-cdl-10/
32. Kobayashi, N.: A partially deadlock-free typed process calculus. ACM TOPLAS **20**(2), 436–482 (1998)
33. Kobayashi, N.: Type-based information flow analysis for the pi-calculus. Acta Informatica **42**(4–5), 291–347 (2005)
34. Krishna, A., Poizat, P., Salaün, G.: Checking business process evolution. Sci. Comput. Program. **170**, 1–26 (2019)
35. Lanese, I., Guidi, C., Montesi, F., Zavattaro, G.: Bridging the gap between interaction- and process-oriented choreographies. In: Software Engineering and Formal Methods, SEFM 2008, pp. 323–332 (2008)
36. Lanese, I., Montesi, F., Zavattaro, G.: Amending choreographies. In: Ravara, A., Silva, J. (eds.) WWV, volume 123 of EPTCS, pp. 34–48 (2013)
37. Lange, J., Tuosto, E., Yoshida, N.: From communicating machines to graphical choreographies. In: Rajamani, S.K., Walker, D. (eds.) POPL, pp. 221–232. ACM (2015)
38. Lohrey, M.: Safe realizability of high-level message sequence charts*. In: Brim, L., Křetínský, M., Kučera, A., Jančar, P. (eds.) CONCUR 2002. LNCS, vol. 2421, pp. 177–192. Springer, Heidelberg (2002). https://doi.org/10.1007/3-540-45694-5_13
39. Montesi, F.: Choreographic programming. Ph.D. thesis, University of Copenhagen (2013)
40. OMG. Business Process Model and Notation (BPMN), Version 2.0, January 2011. https://www.omg.org/spec/BPMN
41. Padovani, L., Vasconcelos, V.T., Vieira, H.T.: Typing liveness in multiparty communicating systems. In: Kühn, E., Pugliese, R. (eds.) COORDINATION 2014. LNCS, vol. 8459, pp. 147–162. Springer, Heidelberg (2014). https://doi.org/10.1007/978-3-662-43376-8_10
42. Paige, R., Tarjan, R.: Three partition refinement algorithms. SIAM J. Comput. **16**(6), 973–989 (1987)
43. Dalla Preda, M., Gabbrielli, M., Giallorenzo, S., Lanese, I., Mauro, J.: Dynamic choreographies: theory and implementation. Log. Methods Comput. Sci. **13**(2), 1–57 (2017)
44. Qiu, Z., Zhao, X., Cai, C., Yang, H.: Towards the theoretical foundation of choreography. In: Williamson, C.L., Zurko, M.E., Patel-Schneider, P.F., Shenoy, P.J. (eds.) Proceedings of the 16th International Conference on World Wide Web, WWW 2007, Banff, Alberta, Canada, 8–12 May 2007, pp. 973–982. ACM (2007)
45. Scalas, A., Yoshida, N.: Less is more: multiparty session types revisited. PACMPL **3**(POPL), 30:1–30:29 (2019)
46. Severi, P., Dezani-Ciancaglini, M.: Observational equivalence for multiparty sessions. Fundamenta Informaticae **170**, 267–305 (2019)
47. Severi, P., Padovani, L., Tuosto, E., Dezani-Ciancaglini, M.: On sessions and infinite data. Log. Methods Comput. Sci. **13**(2), 1–39 (2017)
48. Tuosto, E., Guanciale, R.: Semantics of global view of choreographies. J. Log. Algebraic Methods Program. **95**, 17–40 (2018)

A Choreography-Driven Approach to APIs: The OpenDXL Case Study

Leonardo Frittelli[1], Facundo Maldonado[1], Hernán Melgratti[2(✉)],
and Emilio Tuosto[3,4]

[1] McAfee Cordoba, Córdoba, Argentina
{leonardo_frittelli,Facundo_Maldonado}@mcafee.com
[2] ICC - Universidad de Buenos Aires - Conicet, Buenos Aires, Argentina
hmelgra@dc.uba.ar
[3] Gran Sasso Science Institute, L'Aquila, Italy
emilio.tuosto@gssi.it
[4] University of Leicester, Leicester, UK

Abstract. We propose a model-driven approach based on formal data-driven choreographies to model message-passing applications. We apply our approach to the *threat intelligence exchange* (TIE) services provided by McAfee through the OpenDXL industrial platform. We advocate a chain of model transformations that (i) devises a visual presentation of communication protocols, (ii) formalises a global specification from the visual presentation that captures the data flow among services, (iii) enables the automatic derivation of specifications for the single components, and (iv) enables the analysis of software implementations.

1 Introduction

We propose a methodology for the modelling and analysis of (part of) OpenDXL, a distributed platform that embraces the principles of the *API-economy* [10,17]. In this context applications are services built by composing APIs and made available through the publication of their own APIs. In fact, the APIs of OpenDXL are paramount for enabling the openness of the platform, its growth in terms of services (currently the platform offers hundreds of different services), and its trustworthiness. The overall goal of OpenDXL is to provide a shared platform for the distributed coordination of security-related operations. A key aspect of the platform is to foster public APIs available to stakeholders for the provision or consumption of cyber-security services.

Research partly supported by the EU H2020 RISE programme under the Marie Skłodowska-Curie grant agreement No. 778233, by UBACyT projects 20020170100544BA and 20020170100086BA, PIP project 11220130100148CO, and by MIUR project PRIN 2017FTXR7S *IT MATTERS* (Methods and Tools for Trustworthy Smart Systems).

© IFIP International Federation for Information Processing 2020
Published by Springer Nature Switzerland AG 2020
S. Bliudze and L. Bocchi (Eds.): COORDINATION 2020, LNCS 12134, pp. 107–124, 2020.
https://doi.org/10.1007/978-3-030-50029-0_7

A well-known issue in API-based development is that APIs interoperability heavily depends on the (quality of) documentation: "An API is useless unless you document it" [29]. Proper documentation of APIs is still a problem. The current practice is to provide informal or semi-formal documentation that makes it difficult to validate software obtained by API composition, to establish their properties, and to maintain and evolve applications [2]. The OpenDXL platform is no exception. The APIs of the platform is mostly described in plain English.

We advocate a more systematic approach that, turning informal documentation of APIs in precise models, enables the application of formal methods to develop and analysis services. We focus on *threat intelligence exchange* (TIE) [23], one of the OpenDXL APIs for the coordination of activities such as assessment of security-related digital documents or reaction to indicators flagging suspicious behaviour or data. The API of TIE is part of OpenDXL and it has been designed to enable the coordination of distributed security-related activities. More precisely, TIE APIs support the management of crucial cyber-security information about assets (digital or not) of medium-size to big organisations.

Components for TIE developed by third-party stakeholders sometimes exhibit unexpected behaviour due to the ambiguity of the documentation of communication protocols. In fact, TIE relies on an event-notification communication infrastructure to cope with the high number of components and the volume of the communication. This asynchronous communication mechanism requires the realisation of a specific communication protocol (an application-level protocol) for the various components of the architecture to properly coordinate with each other. To address these issues, we propose a more rigorous approach to the development and documentation of the APIs. We adopt a recent behavioural type system [5] to give a precise model of some TIE services. Besides the resolution of ambiguities in the API documentation, our model enables some static and run-time verification of TIE services. We will discuss how these models could be used to check that the communication pattern of components is the expected one. Also, we will show how our behavioural types can be used to automatically verify logs of executions that may flag occurrences of unexpected behaviour.

Summary of the Contributions. Our overall contribution is a methodology for the design, rigorous documentation, and analysis message-passing applications. We firstly introduce our methodology and describe the model-transformations it entails. An original aspect of our approach is the combination of two models conceived to tackle different facets of message-passing applications. More precisely we rely on *global choreographies* (g-choreographies, for short; see e.g., [13,32] and references therein) to specify the communication pattern of a message-passing system and on *klaimographies* [5] to capture the data-flow and the execution model of our application domain.

We aim to show how a model-driven approach can be conducive of a fruitful collaboration between academics and practitioners. We draw some considerations about this in Sect. 6. Our approach consists of the following steps:

1. Device a graphical model G representing the coordination among the components of the application; for this we use *global choreographies* (cf. Sect. 2.1).

2. Transform G into behavioural types formalising the protocol into a behavioural type K representing the global behaviour of the application; for this we use *klaimographies* (cf. Sect. 2.2).
3. Transform K into specifications of each component of the application; for this we project K on *local types* (cf. Sect. 4).
4. Transform the local types into state machines from which to derive monitors to check for possible deviations from expected behaviour and verify implementations of components (cf. Sect. 5).

Although, g-choreographies are crucial to settle a common ground between academics and practitioners, they do not capture the data-flow and the execution model of OpenDXL. To cope with this drawback we formalise TIE with *klaimographies*, a data-driven model of choreographies.

Structure of the Paper. An overview of the TIE and an informal account of our behavioural types system is given in Sect. 2.1 (we refer the reader to [5] for the full details). The behavioural types of TIE are reported in Sect. 3; there we clarify that our model falls in the setting of "top-down" choreographic approaches. This amounts to say that we first give global specification that formally captures the main aspects of the communication protocol of all TIE from a holistic point of view. Then, in Sect. 4 we discuss how to automatically derive (by *projection*) the local behaviour of each component of TIE. We consider a few real scenarios in Sect. 5 and draw some conclusions in Sect. 6.

2   Preliminaries

We survey the two main ingredients of this paper, OpenDXL and klaimographies. We focus on the part of OpenDXL relevant to our case study and only give an informal account of klaimographies (see [5] for details).

2.1   An Informal Account of OpenDXL

The Open Data Exchange Layer (OpenDXL, https://www.opendxl.com/) is an open-source initiative aiming to support the exchange of timely and accurate cyber-security information in order to foster the dynamic adaptation of interconnected services to security threats. OpenDXL is part of the McAfee Security Innovation Initiative [22], a consortium of about hundred ICT companies including HP, IBM, and Panasonic.

A main goal of OpenDXL is to provide a shared platform to enable the distributed coordination of security-related operations. This goal is supported by the *threat intelligence exchange* (TIE) reputation APIs [23] designed to enable the coordination of activities involving

- the assessment of the security threats of an environment (configuration files, certificates, unsigned or unknown files, etc.);
- the prioritisation of analysis steps (focusing on malicious or unknown files);

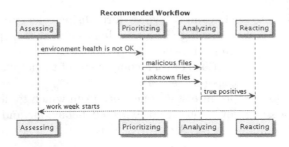

Fig. 1. Documenting TIE [23]

- the customisation of security queries based on reputation-based data (such as product or company names);
- the reaction to suspicious indicators.

A key aspect of OpenDXL lays in its service-oriented nature. Providers use the APIs to offer various services such as reporting services, firewalls, security analytics, etc. Consumers of these APIs (typically companies or large institutions) can either use existing services, or combine them to develop their own functionalities. The basic communication infrastructure features an event-notification architecture whereby participants subscribe to topics of interests to generate events or query services. Such topics are also used to broadcast security information of general interest. The main components of OpenDXL are clients (C), servers (S), and brokers (B). The latter mediate interactions among clients and servers in order to guarantee service availability. Brokers interact with each other to dynamically assign servers to clients when default servers are unavailable.

The high-level workflow of the TIE APIs is specified by the sequence diagram in Fig. 1 (borrowed from [23]). Together with other informal documentation, the diagram guides the implementation of new components or the composition of services available in the platform. For instance, the documentation describing how clients can set the reputation of a file specifies that a client "must have permission to send messages to the `/mcafee/service/tie/reputation/set` topic".

2.2   Data-Driven Global Types

Unlike "standard" behavioural types, klaimographies model data flows in a communication model not based on point-to-point interactions. Interactions in a klaimography happen through *tuple spaces* in the style of Linda-like languages [12]. Instead of relying on primitives for sending and receiving messages over a channel, here there are primitives for inserting a tuple on a tuple space, for reading (without consuming) a tuple from a tuple space, or for retrieving a tuple from a tuple space. We call these interactions data-driven, as the coordination is based on (the type of) the exchanged tuples and the *roles* played by components. In fact, the communication model uses pattern matching to establish when a message from a sender may be accessed by a receiver. Crucially, klaimographies also feature *multi-roles*, namely roles that may be enacted by an arbitrary number of instances. Let us discuss these points with a simple example:

$$K = C \rightarrow S : (\texttt{bool} \cdot \texttt{int}) @ \ell . S \rightarrow C : (\texttt{int} \cdot \texttt{str}) @ \ell$$

The klaimography K specifies the communication protocol between (arbitrarily many) clients C and (arbitrarily many) servers S. More precisely, each client makes a request to a server by inserting a tuple consisting of a boolean and an integer at the tuple space ℓ, as indicated by the prefix $C \rightarrow S : (\texttt{bool} \cdot \texttt{int}) @ \ell$. A server consumes the request and generates a response to be consumed by a client, as specified by $S \rightarrow C : (\texttt{int} \cdot \texttt{str}) @ \ell$. Remarkably, K does not prescribe that the particular client and server involved in the first interaction are also the ones involved in the second interaction; K above establishes instead that every client starts by producing a tuple to be consumed by a server and then consumes a tuple generated by a server (also K stipulates that servers behave dually). As a consequence, the participants in K cannot correlate messages in different interactions. This can be achieved by using binders, e.g.,

$$K' = C \rightarrow S : (\texttt{bool} \cdot \nu x : \texttt{int}) @ \ell . S \rightarrow C : (x : \texttt{int} \cdot \texttt{str}) @ \ell$$

The first interaction in K' introduces a new name x for the integer value exchanged in the first message. The use of x in the second interaction constraints the instances of S and C to share a tuple whose integer expression matches the integer shared in the first interaction. Consequently, the two messages in the protocol are correlated by the integer values in the two messages.

Tuple spaces may simulate other communication paradigms such as multicast or event-notification. For instance, a tuple space ℓ can be thought of as a topic; messages can be produced, read and consumed only by those roles that know such topic. Binders can also be used to ensure the creation of new topics. Consider the klaimography below:

$$K'' = C \rightarrow S : (\texttt{bool} \cdot \texttt{int} \cdot \nu \ell' : \texttt{loc}) @ \ell . S \rightarrow C : (\texttt{int} \cdot \texttt{str}) @ \ell'$$

K'' is similar to K but for the fact that each client communicates to the server a new tuple space ℓ' known only to the particular client and server that communicate in the first interaction; the second interaction takes place by producing and consuming messages on such new tuple space.

Broadcast can be achieved by producing persistent messages, e.g.,

$$K''' = C \rightarrow S : (\texttt{bool} \cdot \texttt{int}) @ \ell . S ! \texttt{int} \cdot \texttt{str} @ r$$

where $S ! \texttt{int} \cdot \texttt{str} @ r$ states that servers insert their responses at locality r. The absence of round brackets around the tuple expresses that such tuple is read-only (i.e., they cannot be removed from the tuple space); the absence of a receiver expresses that any role can read the tuple; consequently, the generated tuple can be read by any role "knowing" the locality r.

Additionally, klaimographies provide operators for sequential composition ($\prec$), choices ($+$) and recursion ($\mu_\rho X.K$), illustrated in the following section.

3   Klaimographies for OpenDXL

The first problem we had to face in the modelling of the protocol was to find a common ground between academic and industrial partners. This is important in order to have enough confidence that the produced formalisation faithfully represent the protocol. To attain this we gave a first approximation of the protocol as the g-choreography in Fig. 2 which we now describe. A client C and a server S engage in a protocol where C may (repeatedly) either (i) send S meta-data regarding some file x or (ii) request the analysis of a file x. A server S reacts to a request from a client in four possible ways depending on the information S may need to further acquire from the requesting client. In the protocol these alternatives are encoded with a message $Res_{bb'}(x)$ where b and b' are two boolean flags; the first boolean is set to true when the server needs meta-data related to the file x while b' is set to true if more context information about the file is necessary. The client reacts to this request from the sever as appropriate. For instance, if C receives the message $Res_{tt}(x)$ then it has to send both meta-data and context information, while only the latter are sent if $Res_{ft}(x)$ is received. Before iterating back, the server may publish a new report[1]; this is modelled by the activity K_{NR} which we leave unspecified. This activity consists of a possible emission of a new report about file x that the server S may decide to multi-cast to clients (not just to clients currently engaging with the server).

We remark that the g-choreography in Fig. 2 represents the interactions between clients and servers and has been introduced as a first step in the formalisation of the protocol to pave the way for its algebraic definition as klaimographies. Firstly, a graphical representation played a central rôle when validating protocol interactions with industrial partners. Secondly, the graph was used as a blueprint for the formalisation. Hence, we invite the reader to follow such graph as the formal definitions unroll.

In the OpenDXL platform several clients and servers may interact by exchanging messages. The interaction in TIE is always triggered by a client which, as seen in Sect. 2.1, iteratively decides to either send some metadata on a file or request for the reputation of a specific file. This can be defined as follows

$$K_{TIE} \triangleq \mu_C \ X.K_{BODY} \prec X \tag{1}$$

where $\mu_C \ X.K_{BODY} \prec X$ is the recursive type to express iterative behaviour; it indicates that role C is the one controlling the iteration. Namely, C decides whether to repeat the execution of the body K_{BODY} or to end it. The sequential composition $K_{BODY} \prec X$ is just syntax to express that, after the execution of K_{BODY}, the iteration restarts.

Notation. *We write $\_ \triangleq \_$ as "macros" so that occurrences of the left-hand side of the equation are verbatim replaced for its right-hand side.*

The body of the iteration in (1), defined as

$$K_{BODY} \triangleq (K_{MD}(x, \ell) + K_{REQ}(x, \ell)) \prec K_{NR}(x) \tag{2}$$

---

[1] The server is actually multi-threaded and could issue new reports about files other than x at any time; for simplicity, we do not model this aspect.

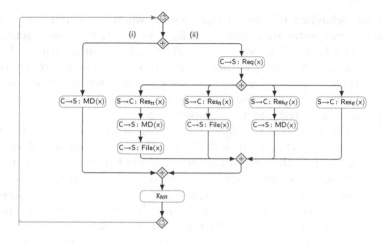

Fig. 2. A g-choreography for TIE APIs

specifies that each iteration consists of a choice between $K_{MD}(x, \ell)$ and $K_{REQ}(x, \ell)$ followed by $K_{NR}(x)$:

- The branch $K_{MD}(x, \ell)$ accounts for the case in which a client sends new metadata to a server.
- The branch $K_{REQ}(x, \ell)$ describes the interaction for the case in which the client sends a reputation request.
- The continuation $K_{NR}(x)$ describes the decision of the server of emitting a reputation report.

Notation. *In accordance with the previous notation,* x *and* ℓ *above are just meta-identifiers for the same syntactic identifier across equations.*

Let b be a globally known location representing the public name on which a client sends requests to a server. The branches of the body are defined as:

$$K_{MD}(x, \ell) \triangleq C \rightarrow S : (MD \cdot \nu x : Dgt \cdot \nu \ell : loc) @ b$$

$$K_{REQ}(x, \ell) \triangleq C \rightarrow S : (Req \cdot \nu x : Dgt \cdot \nu \ell : loc) @ b . K_{INFO}(x, \ell) \tag{3}$$

In both cases the first interaction takes place on the tuple space b.

In $K_{MD}(x, \ell)$, the client simply sends a tuple $MD \cdot \nu x : Dgt \cdot \nu \ell : loc$ made of three fields. The first field has sort MD which is a tag for messages carrying metadata. The second field is a *named* sort $\nu x : Dgt$, where (i) the sort Dgt (after digest) types values that are hash codes of files and (ii) the identifier x is introduced to establish the correlation that will be used in the following interactions. This mechanism enables the tracking of data dependencies among interactions. Finally, the third field is another named sort $\ell : loc$; basically, the client communicates also the name ℓ of a new tuple space, to be used in the subsequent communications. For instance, the continuation type

$$K_{NR}(x) \triangleq \quad S!Report \cdot x : Dgt @ b' + \mathbf{0}$$

describes the behaviour of a server that decides whether to emit a new report about the received metadata or not. Type $K_{NR}(x)$ consists of a non-deterministic choice between a branch $S!Report \cdot x : Dgt @ b'$ and the empty type 0. The former specifies that the server publishes a new report for the file by emitting a (persistent) tuple of type $Report \cdot x : Dgt$ on a publicly known[2] tuple space b'. Note that the use of x constraints the new report produced by server S to be related to a file digest communicated earlier to S.

The interaction prefixes $C \rightarrow S : (...) @ \ell$ are quite different than the prefix $S!Report \cdot x : Dgt @ \ell$. This is a remarkable peculiarity of klaimographies that is quite useful to model TIE. Firstly, the former kind of prefix describes an interaction between two roles: clients are supposed to produce messages of some sort for servers. Instead, the behavioural type $S!Report \cdot x : Dgt @ \ell$ only prescribes the expected communication from a single role, the server. This allows *any* role to access the tuple types generated by this kind of prefixes.

Another important aspect is the other syntactic difference: the messages in round brackets are produced to be consumed, while the ones not surrounded by brackets are persistent and can only be read; moreover, the message can be read by any role able to access the tuple space ℓ. For instance, requests of clients are eventually handled by a server, while any role can read, but not remove, reports.

Let us now return to the comment on the other branch in (2). In the klaimography $K_{REQ}(x, \ell)$, a client sends a request for the reputation of a file by sending a message whose tag is of type Req. In that message, the client sends the digest Dgt that identifies the file and, analogously to $K_{MD}(x, \ell)$, a fresh locality ℓ; the correlation x and the locality ℓ are used in the subsequent interactions, which are described by $K_{INFO}(x, \ell)$ below.

$$\begin{aligned}
K_{INFO}(x, \ell) \triangleq \quad & S \rightarrow C : (Res_{tt} \cdot x : Dgt) @ \ell . K_{TT}(x, \ell) \\
+ \; & S \rightarrow C : (Res_{tf} \cdot x : Dgt) @ \ell . K_{TF}(x, \ell) \\
+ \; & S \rightarrow C : (Res_{ft} \cdot x : Dgt) @ \ell . K_{FT}(x, \ell) \\
+ \; & S \rightarrow C : (Res_{ff} \cdot x : Dgt) @ \ell
\end{aligned}$$

This klaimography corresponds to the inner-most choice of the graph in Sect. 2.1; it prescribes the possible responses that the server may send to the client. We start commenting on the last branch. If the server does not require further information, it simply informs the client that the interaction for that request concludes. The remaining branches of $K_{INFO}(x, \ell)$ model the cases in which the server requests both the metadata and the file (first branch), just the metadata (second branch) or just the file (third branch). When both metadata and file are requested, then the protocol continues as follows

$$K_{TT}(x, \ell) \triangleq \quad C \rightarrow S : (MD \cdot x : Dgt) @ \ell . C \rightarrow S : (File \cdot x : Dgt) @ \ell$$

---

[2] Here we simplify the actual implementation where the topic used to publish the report is related to the file used in the request.

And, when the server asks for either the metadata or the file, then

$$K_{\mathrm{TF}}(x, \ell) \triangleq \quad C \rightarrow S : (MD \cdot x : Dgt) @ \ell$$
$$K_{\mathrm{FT}}(x, \ell) \triangleq \quad C \rightarrow S : (File \cdot x : Dgt) @ \ell$$

which is in accordance with the g-choreography in Sect. 2.1.

4   Projections

As commonplace in choreographic approaches, the description of the expected behaviour of each participant in a protocol can be obtained by *projection*. In our case, this is an operation that takes a klaimography and a role and generates a description, dubbed *local* type, of the flow of messages sent and received by that participant. Local types are meant to give an abstract specification of the processes implementing the roles of the klaimography. We write the projection of a klaimography K for the role ρ as $K \downarrow_\rho$. Note that the projection operation is completely automatic; given a klaimography the behaviour of each component is algorithmically derived. We omit here the formal definition of $K \downarrow_\rho$, which can be found at [5], and illustrate its application to K_{TIE} in (1).

We consider $K_{\mathrm{TIE}} \downarrow_C$ first. The projection operation is defined by induction on the syntax of the klaimography; hence we focus on the constituent parts of K_{TIE}. Consider the branch $K_{\mathrm{MD}}(x, \ell)$, which is defined in (3) as the interaction $C \rightarrow S : (MD \cdot \nu x : Dgt \cdot \nu \ell : loc) @ b$. The projection of this interaction on the client role just consists of the behaviour that generates a message of type $MD \cdot \nu x : Dgt \cdot \nu \ell : loc$ on the locality b; formally, this is written

$$K_{\mathrm{MD}}(x, \ell) \downarrow_C = (MD \cdot \nu x : Dgt \cdot \nu \ell : loc)!b$$

Note (a) the use of the round brackets to represent message consumption, and (b) the projection is oblivious of the intended receiver (the server). In fact, the behavioural type system of klaimographies ensures that if the actual components abide by the klaimographies given in Sect. 3, then only components enacting the role of the server will access those kind of tuples.

The projection for $K_{\mathrm{REQ}}(x, \ell)$ (and all its constituents) is analogous:

$$K_{\mathrm{REQ}}(x, \ell) \downarrow_C = (Req \cdot \nu x : Dgt \cdot \nu \ell : loc)!b . K_{\mathrm{INFO}}(x, \ell) \downarrow_C$$

$$
\begin{aligned}
K_{\mathrm{INFO}}(x, \ell) \downarrow_C = \quad & (Res_{tt} \cdot x : Dgt)?\ell . K_{\mathrm{TT}}(x, \ell) \downarrow_C \\
& + (Res_{tf} \cdot x : Dgt)?\ell . K_{\mathrm{TF}}(x, \ell) \downarrow_C \\
& + (Res_{ft} \cdot x : Dgt)?\ell . K_{\mathrm{FT}}(x, \ell) \downarrow_C \\
& + (Res_{ff} \cdot x : Dgt)?\ell
\end{aligned}
$$

$$K_{\mathrm{TT}}(x, \ell) \downarrow_C = (MD \cdot x : Dgt)!\ell . (File \cdot x : Dgt)!\ell$$

$$K_{\mathrm{TF}}(x, \ell) \downarrow_C = (MD \cdot x : Dgt)!\ell$$

$$K_{\mathrm{FT}}(x, \ell) \downarrow_C = (File \cdot x : Dgt)!\ell$$

Observe that the projection for K_{INFO} is a choice in which C expects (and consumes) one of the four possible messages produced by the server at locality ℓ.

Finally, the projection of $K_{\text{NR}}(x)$ is

$$K_{\text{NR}}(x) \downharpoonleft_C = \text{Report} \cdot x : \text{Dgt}?b' + \mathbf{0}$$

Differently from the projection of interactions in which the client consumes the messages, the first branch of the above projection just reads the message at the locality ℓ. Note the difference between $(t)?\ell$ (consumption) and $t?\ell$ (read), which reflects the usage of round bracket discussed in Sect. 3.

Projection works homomorphically on choices and sequential composition, hence the projection of K_{BODY} in (2) we have

$$K_{\text{BODY}} \downharpoonleft_C = (K_{\text{MD}}(x, \ell) \downharpoonleft_C + K_{\text{REQ}}(x, \ell) \downharpoonleft_C) \prec K_{\text{NR}}(x) \downharpoonleft_C$$

We now give the projection of K_{TIE}, which is a recursive klaimography. Then,

$$K_{\text{TIE}} \downharpoonleft_C = \big(\mu X(b).\langle \text{stop}\rangle! b.\mathbf{0} + \langle \nu y : \text{loc}\rangle! b . K_{\text{BODY}} \downharpoonleft_C \prec X\langle y\rangle\big)\langle b\rangle \qquad (4)$$

The projection of a recursive klaimography is also a recursive local type. However, the projection introduces auxiliary interactions to coordinate the execution of the loop. Since C is the role that coordinates the recursion in K_{TIE}, in the projection C starts its body by communicating its decision to terminate or to continue. Namely, the body of $K_{\text{TIE}} \downharpoonleft_C$ has two branches, $\langle \text{stop}\rangle! b$ communicates the termination of the recursion, while the other starting with $\langle \nu y : \text{loc}\rangle! b$ iterates (and distributes a fresh localities for the next iteration).

Note that recursive variables X in the local types are parameterised variables $X(b)$ and $X\langle b\rangle$. In general, a klaimography $\mu_\rho X.K$ is projected as a recursive local type $(\mu X(\widetilde{x}).L)\langle \widetilde{\ell}\rangle$ where the formal parameters $\widetilde{x}$ stand for the locations used for coordination and $\widetilde{\ell}$ are the initial values, in this case, b. The projection for the behaviour of the server is obtained analogously.

5   Types at Work

Like data types, behavioural types can be regarded as specifications of the intended behaviour of a system. As such they can check that the components implementing the protocol abide by their specifications. Customarily, approaches to behavioural types focus on static enforcement [9, 15, 16], i.e., the source code implementing a role is type-checked against its local type and the soundness of the type checking algorithm ensures that well-typed code behaves as prescribed by its type. Also the dynamic enforcement of protocols based on local types has been addressed in the literature [3, 11, 27]. In most cases, monitors dynamically check that the messages exchanged by the components comply with the protocol. Deviations from the expected behaviour are singled out and offending components are blamed.

```
2019-03-27T15:59:49, 649, clientA, server1, Req, file1
2019-03-27T15:59:49, 649, server1, clientA, Res, 1, 0, file1
2019-03-27T15:59:50, 649, clientA, server1, MD, file1
2019-03-27T15:59:50, 340, clientC, server1, Req, file2
2019-03-27T15:59:50, 340, server1, clientC, Res, 1, 1, file2
2019-03-27T15:59:50, 699, clientD, server1, MD, file2
2019-03-27T15:59:50, 340, clientC, server1, File, file2
2019-03-27T15:59:51, 021, clientE, server1, Req, file3
2019-03-27T15:59:51, 021, server1, clientE, Res, 0, 0, file3
2019-03-27T15:59:51, 370, clientF, server1, MD, file3
2019-03-27T15:59:51, 721, server1, broadcast, Report, file3
...
```

Fig. 3. A simplified snippet of a real (anonymised) log

In this work we explore the usage of local types for the off-line monitoring of role implementations. In particular, we use projections to check that the different implementations of the multirole C in TIE follow the protocol. We take advantage of the fact that the communication infrastructure of TIE keeps a log with the communication messages generated by the different roles.

In Fig. 3 we show an anonymised (and simplified) version of a few entries of a real log. Each entry corresponds to an interaction between a client and a server and it consists of a record of comma-separated fields which we now describe:

- the first field is a global timestamp used to order the entries chronologically;
- the second field is the *locality*, which is encoded by a three-digits number;
- the third and fourth fields are the identity of the *sender* and of the *receiver* respectively (for obvious reasons, the real identities have been obfuscated; Fig. 3 uses symbolic names clientA, server1, etc.);
- the remaining fields are the payloads of the message, which varies depending on the type of the message.

The type of each message is identified by a tag: Req, MD, and File have analogous meaning to the ones used in the specification of the protocol in Sects. 3 and 4. The sorts such as Res_{tf} used in our specification are rendered in the implementation with a payload consisting of three parts: the tag Res and two binary digits; used to encode the subscript (with 1 representing true and 0 representing false); for instance, the subscript tf above is encoded as the pair 1, 0. We use $file_i$ to represent the different digests transmitted over the messages.

The first entry in the log of Fig. 3 is generated by the interaction

$$C \rightarrow S : (\mathsf{Req} \cdot \nu x : \mathsf{Dgt} \cdot \nu \ell : \mathsf{loc}) @ \, \mathtt{b}$$

executed by $K_{\mathrm{REQ}}(x, \ell)$, where the instance clientA of the role C sends to the instance server1 of S a request for a reputation report about the file file1. The second entry in the log corresponds to the selection of the branch

$$S \rightarrow C : (\mathsf{Res}_{tf} \cdot x : \mathsf{Dgt}) @ \, \ell . K_{\mathrm{TF}}(x, \ell)$$

in $K_{\mathrm{INFO}}(x, \ell)$ in which the server asks the client for the metadata of the file; the messages in which the client sends the metadata can be seen in the third line

```
@startuml left to right direction
[*] --> S0
S0 --> S0: 'MD'@l @Dgt
S0 --> S1: 'Req'@l
S1 --> S2: ('Res', '1', '1')@l -> @Dgt
S1 --> S3: ('Res', '0', '1')@l -> @Dgt
S1 --> S4: ('Res', '1', '0')@l -> @Dgt
S1 --> S0: ('Res', '0', '0')@l
S2 --> S3: 'MD'@l -> @Dgt
S3 --> S0: 'File'@f
S4 --> S0: 'MD'@l

@enduml
```

Fig. 4. $K_{DXL} \downharpoonright_C$ as UML diagram (textual representation)

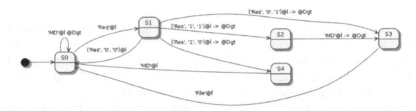

Fig. 5. $K_{DXL} \downharpoonright_C$ as UML diagram (graphical representation)

of the log. Obviously, the interactions among different instances need not to be consecutive, as it is the case for the entries at locality 340 which are on the lines 4, 5 and 7. Observe also that the last entry in Fig. 3 has broadcast as its receiver. This message corresponds to the publication of a reputation report by the server, which is defined in $K_{NR}(x)$ as Report $\cdot$ x : Dgt?ℓ.

We have implemented in Python an off-line monitor that takes a log and a local type in input and checks whether the log faithfully follows behaviour described by the local type. Local types are turned into a textual representation of finite state automata that can be depicted as UML state machines. For instance, the local type $K_{TIE} \downharpoonright_C$ is defined as shown in Fig. 4, which can be graphically represented as shown in Fig. 5.

These representations are obtained by "massaging" the projections defined in Sect. 4. The main difference between the UML representation and the local type (besides the obvious syntactic changes) is that the former does not contain the messages for coordinating the recursion in (4) (i.e., stop and $\nu y : loc$); those have been omitted because not explicitly exchanged by the components. As a consequence, we assume that the client continues the loop if it keeps sending messages and it finishes silently otherwise. Another simplification for the sake of the presentation is the omission of $K_{NR}(x) \downharpoonright_C$, essentially because the observable behaviour of the client is unaffected if it reads or not a report. In fact, the log is not informative enough to discriminate on the choice made by the client.

Once such simplifications are in place, (4) can be easily matched with the graphical representation in Fig. 5. The state S0 represents $K_{TIE} \downharpoonright_C$. The self-loop stands for the selection of the branch $K_{MD}(x, \ell) \downharpoonright_C$, i.e., the client sends a message containing metadata, and then restart the loop. The transition from S0 to S1 represents instead the choice of the branch $K_{\text{REQ}}(x, \ell) \downarrow_C$, i.e., the client request of a reputation report. The remaining states are in one-to-one correspondence with the following projections defined in the previous section: S1 stands for $K_{\text{INFO}}(x, \ell) \downarrow_C$, S2 for $K_{\text{TT}}(x, \ell) \downarrow_C$, S3 for $K_{\text{FT}}(x, \ell) \downarrow_C$, and S4 for $K_{\text{TF}}(x, \ell) \downarrow_C$. All the transitions are decorated with the associated messages sent or received by a client. Note also that S1, S3 and S4 have transitions to the state S0 meaning that execution of the body the is completed and that the body can be restarted.

With this implementation we have detected a few deviations from the expected behaviour. In particular, some clients exhibit the following violations:

- files are sent for analysis without a prior request,
- requests for further information from the server are not honoured.

The first violation is detected by the presence of an entry of the log with a message tagged `File` without a previous message from the server with tag Res_{tt} or Res_{ft}. The second violation is due to the absence of an entry related to a given hash used by the server for asking further information.

Our implementation can also check other properties. For example, TIE clients should guarantee a so-called "time-window" property which requires that

"a request for the analysis of the same file from a client must not happen before a given amount of time elapsed from the previous request from the client for the same file."

This property (as well as others) can be checked by monitor derived from the local types as done in the examples above.

6 Conclusions, Related and Future Work

Summary. We reported on a collaboration between industrial and academic partners which applied formal methods to address a key problem affecting APIs-based software. More precisely, the problem that informal specifications of the behaviour of services may lead to errors in message-passing applications. For instance, third-party clients of TIE services exhibit anomalous when interacting with the services developed at McAfee. To overcome this problem, TIE services are engineered with a rather defensive approach to anticipate anomalous interactions. Unintended behaviours are reported to third-parties after a "post-mortem" analysis of execution logs.

We devised a model-driven approach to model and validate message-passing software. We applied the methodology in the context of the OpenDXL platform, an initiative of a consortium of industries conceived for the development of cyber-security functionalities. The platform provides an API to allow developers to access and combine the functionalities of a service-oriented architecture. In this context we applied the methodology to the *threat intelligence exchange* (TIE) service provided by McAfee Cordoba for the assessment of security threats, prioritisation of analysis steps, reputation-based data queries.

Related Work. The use of behavioural types for the specification and analysis of message-passing application is widespread (see [16] for a survey). Semantics of behavioural types (operational or denotational) abstract the behaviour of systems and enables the use of formal methods and tools to check their properties.

Our proposal hinges on a form of choreographies in the vein of global type systems [15], which formally capture the design of WSCDL [18]. In fact, the specification of a global view is the starting step of our methodology and the use of a projection operation to (automatically) derive local views is a paramount step in the model-transformation chain described in Sect. 1. The literature offers several variants of choreographic models [4,6,8,14,30,32] (to mention but a few). A common treat of those models is that they are grounded on point-to-point communication in traditional settings (such as the use of the actor model [1] or π-calculus [25,26,31]). A distinguished feature of OpenDXL is that it relies on event-notification mechanisms. This is the main motivation for the adoption of *klaimographies* [5]. In fact, unlike other choreographic approaches, klaimographies advocate a peculiar interpretation of interactions. More precisely, interactions A$\rightarrow$B: m are generally interpreted as *"an instance* of A and *an instance* of B exchange message m". The interpretation of A$\rightarrow$B: m drastically changes in klaimographies and becomes *"any instance* of A generates the message m expected to be handled by *any instance* of B". This interpretation is the cornerstone for a faithful modelling of OpenDXL.

Lesson Learned. Although we are at an early stage of the collaboration, we can draw some conclusions.

A first point worth remarking is about the **effectiveness** of our methodology. On the one hand, the academic partners were oblivious of several current practices (such as the continuous defensive patching TIE servers). On the other hand, the industrial partners acquired some notions about behavioural specifications during the participation of a school [24] organised by the academic partners as well as presented the OpenDXL platforms at the school. The methodology was applied immediately after the school and the bulk of modelling and analysis of TIE was concluded in about 3-persons month. In the chain of model transformations of our methodology, steps (1) and (4) were paramount for practitioners to apply this methodology: the use of visual, intuitive, yet formal models enabled a fruitful collaboration among stakeholders. In fact, g-choreographies were key to tune up the model and to identify the main aspects of the intended communication protocol as well as to ease the collaboration between practitioners and academics. Basically, g-choreographies gave a first intuitive presentation capturing the essential interactions of TIE. This has been instrumental for an effectual collaboration. Once the g-choreography expressing the intended behaviour has been identified, the academic partners have devised the klaimographies formalising the expected behaviour. The identification of the corresponding klaimographies allowed us to automatically derive local specifications (step (iii)) and use them as precise blue-prints of components as well as to automatically derive monitors (step (iv)). Remarkably, the transformation from local types to state machines was suggested by our industrial partners who saw it as a more streamlined way of sharing the specifications among practitioners (including those outside McAfee). At this stage we do not have data to measure the impact of the enhanced documentation on the quality of the software produced.

This experience also highlights the importance of **non-deterministic abstractions** and of **visual tools** in practice. We argue that these elements are paramount for collaborations that could be beneficial to both academics and practitioners. In fact, behavioural types (as many formal methods) may not be easy for practitioners to handle. To tackle this issue we opted for models offering a visual and intuitive presentations of the formal models used in the specifications. The specification in terms of g-choreographies and klaimographies was attained in few days of man-power involving academics and practitioners. This hints that our model-driven methodology can significantly reduce the steepness of the learning curve that formal methods often require.

The problem of informal behavioural specification is ubiquitous in API-based software. The approach we followed aimed at some **generality**: instead of devising ad-hoc formal methods for the OpenDXL case study, we decided to apply existing frameworks. In fact, both g-choreographies and klaimographies had been developed before and independently of this collaboration. The methodology proposed here assumes only that components communicate through generative coordination mechanisms [12]. As noted by one of the reviewers, "tuple-semantics are well-suited not only for this use case but for the modern age of IoT, where event-based middlewares are becoming the norm."

A final note on the connection with other formal methods. Behavioural specifications offer also support to "bottom-up" engineering (see, e.g., [19,21]). This would require to infer the behaviour to analyse from logs and, as noted by another reviewer, one could spare "to model the whole behaviour [...] and focus on specific components." We concur that our methodology can be complemented by such technique (and this is indeed one of the goals within the BehAPI project). Also, one may wonder if the methodology can be combined with model checking. This is indeed the case since our models feature operation semantics amenable to be model checked. A drawback of model checking is that practitioners would find it hard to express the properties to check. Instead the top-down approach allowed them to express such conditions in terms of state machines.

Future Work. Global graphs have been key to facilitate the collaboration between academics and industrial partners for the former can use g-choreographies precisely (since they come with a precise semantics) and the latter can use the visual and intuitive presentation of g-choreographies. It is in the scope of future work to use the formal framework of g-choreographies. In fact, we can use g-choreographies to verify liveness properties of the communication protocols, or to generate executable template code to be refined by practitioners. We plan to extend **ChorGram** [20], a tool based on g-choreographies, to support the methodology. For instance, projection operations from global to local views are a key feature of our choreographic framework. Here, we have manually given klaimographies and their projections. This can be automatised by algorithmically transforming g-choreographies into klaimographies. Another possibility is to exploit **ChorGram** to generate code; for instance, **ChorGram** can map g-choreographies to (executable) Erlang code. These sort of functionalities are highly appealing to industrial stakeholders due (a) to the "correct-by-construction" principle they support and (b) to the fact that each release of TIE services requires the realisation of in-house clients for many different languages and platforms. For instance, OpenDXL needs to develop several version of each component for different execution environments. Also, TIE clients have to be implemented in different programming languages or for operating systems; this could be done by devising each software component by projection from a global view. Having tools that generate template code for implementing the communication protocol of each component would speed up the development process and reduce the time of testing (which would not need to focus on communications which would be correct-by-construction). In order to attain this, it could be useful to "dress up" g-choreographies with existing industrial standards that practitioners may find more familiar (and may be more appealing). An interesting candidate for this endeavour is BPMN [28] since its coordination mechanisms are very close to those of g-choreographies. In fact, BPMN is becoming popular in industry and it has recently gained the attention of the scientific community which is proposing formal semantics of its constructs. For instance, the formal semantics in [7] could be conducive of a formal mapping from BPMN to g-choreographies or global types. In this way practitioners may specify global views within a context without spoiling the rigour of our methodology.

For simplicity in this paper we abstracted away from some aspects of TIE. The extension of our approach to the complete protocol is not conceptually complex, but it is scope for future work. This will include the analysis to further properties expected of TIE components and that can be checked from the logs. Following our methodology, we plan to devise monitors for the run-time verification of those properties as well.

A final remark is about other advantages of behavioural types that we can exploit in the future. For instance, one goal is to device tools for checking the compliance of components to the TIE protocol. This can be achieved by type-checking components against their projections.

Acknowledgments. We thank the anonymous reviewers for their many insightful comments and suggestions.

References

1. Agha, G.: Actors: A Model of Concurrent Computation in Distributed Systems. MIT Press, Cambridge (1986)
2. Ariola, W., Dunlop, C.: Testing in the API Economy. Top 5 Myths. https://alm.parasoft.com/api-testing-myths
3. Bocchi, L., Chen, T.-C., Demangeon, R., Honda, K., Yoshida, N.: Monitoring networks through multiparty session types. In: Beyer, D., Boreale, M. (eds.) FMOODS/FORTE -2013. LNCS, vol. 7892, pp. 50–65. Springer, Heidelberg (2013). https://doi.org/10.1007/978-3-642-38592-6_5

4. Bravetti, M., Zavattaro, G.: Contract compliance and choreography conformance in the presence of message queues. In: Bruni, R., Wolf, K. (eds.) WS-FM 2008. LNCS, vol. 5387, pp. 37–54. Springer, Heidelberg (2009). https://doi.org/10.1007/978-3-642-01364-5_3

5. Bruni, R., Corradini, A., Gadducci, F., Melgratti, H., Montanari, U., Tuosto, E.: Data-driven choreographies à la Klaim. In: Boreale, M., Corradini, F., Loreti, M., Pugliese, R. (eds.) Models, Languages, and Tools for Concurrent and Distributed Programming. LNCS, vol. 11665, pp. 170–190. Springer, Cham (2019). https://doi.org/10.1007/978-3-030-21485-2_11

6. Busi, N., Gorrieri, R., Guidi, C., Lucchi, R., Zavattaro, G.: Choreography and orchestration conformance for system design. In: Ciancarini, P., Wiklicky, H. (eds.) COORDINATION 2006. LNCS, vol. 4038, pp. 63–81. Springer, Heidelberg (2006). https://doi.org/10.1007/11767954_5

7. Corradini, F., Morichetta, A., Re, B., Tiezzi, F.: Walking through the semantics of exclusive and event-based gateways in BPMN choreographies. In: Alvim, M.S., Chatzikokolakis, K., Olarte, C., Valencia, F. (eds.) The Art of Modelling Computational Systems: A Journey from Logic and Concurrency to Security and Privacy. LNCS, vol. 11760, pp. 163–181. Springer, Cham (2019). https://doi.org/10.1007/978-3-030-31175-9_10

8. Dalla Preda, M., Gabbrielli, M., Giallorenzo, S., Lanese, I., Mauro, J.: Dynamic choreographies. In: Holvoet, T., Viroli, M. (eds.) COORDINATION 2015. LNCS, vol. 9037, pp. 67–82. Springer, Cham (2015). https://doi.org/10.1007/978-3-319-19282-6_5

9. Dezani-Ciancaglini, M., de'Liguoro, U.: Sessions and session types: an overview. In: Laneve, C., Su, J. (eds.) WS-FM 2009. LNCS, vol. 6194, pp. 1–28. Springer, Heidelberg (2010). https://doi.org/10.1007/978-3-642-14458-5_1

10. Doerrfeld, B., Wood, C., Anthony, A., Sandoval, K., Lauret, A.: The API Economy - Disruption and the Business of APIs. Nodic APIs (nordicapis.com), May 2016. http://nordicapis.com/ebook-release-api-economy-disruption-business-apis

11. Francalanza, A., Mezzina, C.A., Tuosto, E.: Reversible choreographies via monitoring in Erlang. In: Bonomi, S., Rivière, E. (eds.) DAIS 2018. LNCS, vol. 10853, pp. 75–92. Springer, Cham (2018). https://doi.org/10.1007/978-3-319-93767-0_6

12. Gelernter, D.: Generative communication in Linda. ACM Trans. Program. Lang. Syst. **7**(1), 80–112 (1985)

13. Guanciale, R., Tuosto, E.: Realisability of Pomsets via communicating automata. In: Proceedings 9th Interaction and Concurrency Experience, ICE 2016, Heraklion, Greece, 8–9 June 2016 (2018)

14. Guanciale, R., Tuosto, E.: Realisability of Pomsets via communicating automata. J. Logic Algebraic Methods Program. (2019, to appear). Accepted for Publication

15. Honda, K., Yoshida, N., Carbone, M.: Multiparty asynchronous session types. J. ACM 63(1), 9:1–9:67 (2016). Extended version of a paper presented at POPL08

16. Hüttel, H., et al.: Foundations of session types and behavioural contracts. ACM Comput. Surv. **49**(1), 3:1–3:36 (2016)

17. The API-Economy. http://ibm.com/apieconom

18. Kavantzas, N., Burdett, D., Ritzinger, G., Fletcher, T., Lafon, Y.: http://www.w3.org/TR/2004/WD-ws-cdl-10-20041217. Working Draft 17 December 2004

19. Lange, J., Tuosto, E.: Synthesising choreographies from local session types. In: Koutny, M., Ulidowski, I. (eds.) CONCUR 2012. LNCS, vol. 7454, pp. 225–239. Springer, Heidelberg (2012). https://doi.org/10.1007/978-3-642-32940-1_17

20. Lange, J., Tuosto, E.: ChorGram: tool support for choreographic development (2015). https://bitbucket.org/emlio_tuosto/chorgram/wiki/Home

21. Lange, J., Tuosto, E., Yoshida, N.: From communicating machines to graphical choreographies. In: POPL 2015, pp. 221–232 (2015)
22. McAfee. Mcafee Security Innovation Alliance. https://www.mcafee.com/enterprise/en-us/partners/security-innovation-alliance.html
23. McAfee. Threat intelligence exchange recommended workflow. https://kc.mcafee.com/corporate/index?page=content&id=KB86307
24. Melgratti, H.C., Tuosto, E.: Summer School on Behavioural Approaches for API-Economy with Applications, 8–12 July 2019. https://www.um.edu.mt/projects/behapi/leicester-summer-school-behavioural-approaches-for-api-economy-with-applications
25. Milner, R.: Communicating and Mobile Systems: the π-Calculus. Cambridge University Press, Cambridge (1999)
26. Milner, R., Parrow, J., Walker, D.: A calculus of mobile processes, I and II. Inf. Comput. **100**(1), 41–77 (1992)
27. Neykova, R., Bocchi, L., Yoshida, N.: Timed runtime monitoring for multiparty conversations. Formal Aspects Comput. **29**(5), 877–910 (2017). https://doi.org/10.1007/s00165-017-0420-8
28. Object Management Group. Business Process Model and Notation. http://www.bpmn.org
29. Orenstein, D.: Application Programming Interface. Computer World, January 2000. http://www.computerworld.com/article/2593623/app-development/application-programming-interface.html
30. Qiu, Z., Zhao, X., Cai, C., Yang, H.: Towards the theoretical foundation of choreography. In: Proceedings of the 16th International Conference on World Wide Web, WWW 2007, pp. 973–982 (2007)
31. Sangiorgi, D., Walker, D.: The π-Calculus: A Theory of Mobile Processes. Cambridge University Press, Cambridge (2002)
32. Tuosto, E., Guanciale, R.: Semantics of global view of choreographies. J. Log. Algebraic Methods Program. **95**, 17–40 (2018)

Communications: Types and Implementations

Implementing Multiparty Session Types in Rust

Nicolas Lagaillardie[1]([✉])(iD), Rumyana Neykova[2]([✉])(iD),
and Nobuko Yoshida[1]([✉])(iD)

[1] Imperial College London, London, UK
{n.lagaillardie19,n.yoshida}@imperial.ac.uk
[2] Brunel University London, London, UK
rumyana.neykova@brunel.ac.uk

Abstract. Multiparty Session Types (MPST) is a typing discipline for distributed protocols, which ensures communication safety and deadlock-freedom for more than two participants. This paper reports on our research project, implementing multiparty session types in Rust. Current Rust implementations of session types are limited to binary (two-party communications). We extend an existing library for binary session types to MPST. We have implemented a simplified Amazon Prime Video Streaming protocol using our library for both shared and distributed communication transports.

1 Introduction

In the last decade, the software industry has seen a shift towards programming languages that promote the coordination of concurrent and/or distributed software components through the exchange of messages over *communication channels*. Languages with native message-passing primitives (e.g., Go, Elixir and Rust) are becoming increasingly popular. In particular, Rust has been named the most loved programming language in the annual Stack Overflow survey for four consecutive years (2016–19)[1].

The advantage of message-passing concurrency is well-understood: it allows cheap horizontal scalability at a time when technology providers have to adapt and scale their tools and applications to various devices and platforms. Message-passing based software, however, is as vulnerable to errors as other concurrent programming techniques [16]. Much academic research has been done to develop rigorous theoretical frameworks for verification of message-passing programs. One such framework is *multiparty session types* (MPST) [5] – a type-based discipline that ensures that concurrent and distributed systems are *safe by design*. It guarantees that message-passing processes following a predefined communication protocol, are free from communication errors and deadlocks.

---

[1] https://insights.stackoverflow.com/survey/2019.

© IFIP International Federation for Information Processing 2020
Published by Springer Nature Switzerland AG 2020
S. Bliudze and L. Bocchi (Eds.): COORDINATION 2020, LNCS 12134, pp. 127–136, 2020.
https://doi.org/10.1007/978-3-030-50029-0_8

Rust is a particularly appealing language for the practical embedding of session types. Its *affine type system* allows for static typing of linear resources – an essential requirement for the safety of session type systems. Rust combines efficiency with message-passing abstractions, thread and memory safety [15], and has been used for the implementation of large-scale concurrent applications such as the Mozilla browser, Firefox, and the Facebook blockchain platform, Libra. Despite the interest in the Rust community for verification techniques handling multiple communicating processes[2], the existing Rust implementations [8,9] are limited to *binary* (two-party) session types.

In this short paper, we present our design and implementation for multi-party session types in Rust. Our design follows a state-of-the-art encoding of multiparty into binary session types [13]. We generate local types in Rust, utilising the Scribble toolchain [12,18]. Our library for MPST programming in Rust, `mpst-rust`, is implemented as a thin wrapper over an existing binary session types library [9]. Differently from other MPST implementations that check the linear usage of channels at runtime (e.g. [6,13]), we rely on the Rust affine type system to type-check MPST programs. In addition, since we generate the local types from a readable global specification, errors caused by an affine (and not linear) usage of channels, a well-known limitation of the previous libraries [8,9], are easily avoided.

This paper is organised as follows: Sect. 2 gives an overview of our framework with a usecase; Sect. 3 shows our implementation and discusses the advantages of our approach; and Sect. 4 concludes with related and future work. Our library is available from https://github.com/NicolasLagaillardie/mpst_rust_github.

2   From Binary to Multiparty Sessions in Rust

Framework Overview: MPST in Rust. Our design resembles the top-down methodology of multiparty session types, as illustrated in Fig. 1. It follows three main steps [5,17]. First, a *global type*, also called a *global protocol*, is defined as a shared contract between communicating endpoint processes. A global protocol is then *projected* to each endpoint process, resulting in a *local type*. A local type involves only the interactions specific to a given endpoint. Finally, each endpoint process is type-checked against its projected local type.

The specific parts of our framework that distinguish it from other state-of-the-art MPST works are highlighted in *red*, which corresponds to our new library for MPST programming in Rust, `mpst-rust`. It is realised as a thin wrapper on top of an existing Rust library for validation of binary (2-party-only) session types. Developers use the MPST primitives provided by `mpst-rust` to implement endpoint programs. Also, our framework allows the types for each communication primitive to be either (1) generated from the Scribble toolchain; or (2) written by the developers. The Scribble toolchain [18] provides facilities for writing, verifying and projecting global protocols. Our framework guarantees

---

[2] https://users.rust-lang.org/t/anybody-working-on-multiparty-session-types-for-rust/10610.

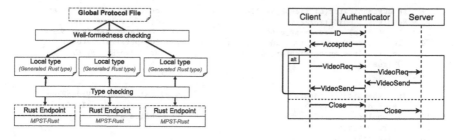

Fig. 1. MPST Workflow (left) and Amazon Prime Video usecase (right)

that processes implemented using `mpst-rust` primitives with Scribble-generated types are free from deadlocks, reception errors, and protocol deviations. Next, we explain, via an example, how the framework of MPST can be applied to Rust.

Example: Amazon Prime Video Streaming. The Amazon Prime Video streaming service is a usecase which can take full advantage of multiparty session types. Each streaming application connects to servers, and possibly other devices, to access services, and follows some specific protocol. To present our design, we use a simplified version of the protocol, illustrated in the diagram in Fig. 1 (right). The diagram should be read from top to bottom. The protocol involves three services – an `Authenticator` service, a `Server` and a `Client`. At first, `Client` connects to `Authenticator` by providing an identifying id. If the id is accepted, the session continues with a choice on `Client` to either request a video or end the session. The first branch is, *a priori*, the main service provided by Amazon Prime Video. `Client` cannot directly request videos from `Server`, and has to go through `Authenticator` instead. On the diagram, the choice is denoted as the frame `alt` and the choices are separated with the horizontal dotted line. The protocol is recursive, and `Client` can request new videos as many times as needed. The arrow going back on `Client` side in Fig. 1 represents this recursive behaviour. To end the session, `Client` first sends `Close` message to `Authenticator`, which then subsequently sends a `Close` message to `Server`.

Implementing the Authenticator role Using `mpst-rust`. Due to space limitations, we only show the implementation of the `Authenticator` role (hereafter role A), the implementations of the other roles (role B for the `Server` and role C for the `Client`) are similar. The Rust code for role A using the `mpst-rust` library is given in Fig. 2 (left). It closely follows the local protocol in Fig. 2 (right), that is projected from the global protocol by the Scribble toolchain. First, line 1 declares a function `authenticator` that is parametric in a multiparty channel s of type `VideoP_A`. The type `VideoP_A` specifies which operations are allowed on s. This type can either be written by the developer, or generated by Scribble (cf. Listing 1).

On line 3, A receives an identifying id from C. The function `recv_mpst_a_to_c`, provided by `mpst-rust` library returns the received value (the id) and the new multiparty channel, to be used in subsequent communications. Line 3 rebinds

```
1   fn authenticator(s: VideoP_A<i32>)->        local protocol VideoP at A(
2   Result<(), Box<Error>> {                     role B, role C)
3     let (id, s) = recv_mpst_a_to_c(s)?;         { Declare(int) from C;
4     let s = send_mpst_a_to_c(id + 1, s);        Accept(string) to C;
5     let result = authenticator_recurs(s)?;      do VideoPRec(B, C);
6     Ok(result)
7   }                                            }
8
9   fn authenticator_recurs(                     local protocol VideoPRec
10    s: VideoPRec_A<i32>)                        at A(role B, role C){
11  -> Result<(), Box<Error>> {                   choice at C {
12  offer_mpst_a_to_c!(s,
13  ChoiceA::Video(
14    SessionMpst{ch_ab, ch_ac, q})
15  => {                                           VideoRequest(
16    let s = SessionMpst{ch_ab,ch_ac, q}           string) from C;
17    let (req, s) = recv_mpst_a_to_c(s)?;         VideoRequest(
18    let s = send_mpst_a_to_b(req, s);             string) to B;
19    let (v, s) = recv_mpst_a_to_b(s)?;           SendVideo(Video) from B;
20    let s = send_mpst_a_to_c(v, s);             SendVideo(Video) to C;
21    authenticator_recurs(s)},                   do VideoPRec(B, C);
22  ChoiceA::End(SessionMpst{ch_ab, ch_ac, q})   } or {
23  => {
24    let s = SessionMpst{ch_ab, ch_ac, q};        Close() from C;
25    close_mpst(s)?;                             Close() to B, C;
26    Ok(())})?;...}                              }}
```

Fig. 2. Rust implementation of role A (left) and its local Scribble protocol (right)

the multiparty channel s with the new channel that is returned. Then, on line 4, we send back the answer to C, by utilising another mpst-rust communication primitive, send_mpst_a_to_c. The variable s is rebound again to the newly returned multiparty channel. Note that although the name of the function, send_mpst_a_to_c, suggests a binary communication, the function operates on a multiparty channel s. Our implementation follows the encoding, presented in [13], which encodes a multiparty channel as an indexed tuple of binary channels. Internally, send_mpst_a_to_c extracts from s the binary channel established between A and C and uses it for sending.

Lines 9–26 proceeds by implementing the recursive part of the protocol. The implementation of authenticator_recurs realises an internal choice – A can either receive a VideoRequest or a Close. This behaviour is realised by the mpst-rust macro offer_mpst_a_to_c! (line 12), which is applied to a multiparty channel s of a sum type between ChoiceA::Video and ChoiceA::End. The behaviour of each branch in the protocol is implemented as an anonymous function. For example, code in lines 13–21 supplies an anonymous function that implements the behaviour when C sends a VideoRequest, while lines 22–26 handle the Close request. Finally, close_mpst(s) closes all binary channels stored inside s. The types of the multiparty channel, as well as the generic types in the declaration of the mpst-rust communication functions, enable compile-time detection of protocol violations, such as swapping line 3 and line 4, using another communication primitive or using the wrong payload type.

```
1   /// Binary session types for A and C
2   type InitA<N> = Recv<N, Send<N,
3     RecvChoice<N>>>;
4   type RecvChoice<N> =
5     Recv<ChoiceA<N>, End>;
6   type AtoCVideo<N> =
7     Recv<N, Send<N, RecvChoice<N>>
8   type AtoCClose = End;
9
10
11  /// Binary session types for A and B
12  type AtoBVideo<N> =
13    Send<N, Recv<N, End>>;
14  type AtoBClose = End;
15
16  /// Declare usage order of channels
17  type QueueAInit = RoleAtoC<RoleAtoC<
18    RoleAtoC<RoleEnd>>>;
19  type QueueAChoice = RoleAtoC<RoleEnd>;
```

```
20  /// Declare usage order of channels
21  type QueueAVideo =
22    RoleAtoC<RoleAtoB<RoleAtoB<
23    RoleAtoC<RoleAtoC<RoleEnd>>>>>;
24  type QueueAClose = RoleEnd;
25
26  /// Declare MPST
27  type VideoP_A<N> = SessionMpst<End,
28    InitA<N>, QueueAInit>;
29
30  type VideoPRec_A<N> = SessionMpst<
31    End, RecvChoice<N>, QueueAChoice>;
32
33  enum ChoiceA<N> {
34    Video(SessionMpst<AtoBVideo<N>,
35    AtoCVideo<N>, QueueAVideo>),
36    End(SessionMpst<AtoBClose,
37    AtoCClose, QueueAClose>)
38  }
```

Listing 1. Local Rust types for role A

Typing the Authenticator Role. The types for the Authenticator role, used in Fig. 2 (left), are given in Listing 1. These types can be either written by the developer or generated from a global protocol, written in Scribble. Reception error safety is ensured since the underlying mpst-rust library checks *statically* that all pairs of binary types are dual to each other. Deadlock-freedom is ensured only if types are generated from Scribble since this guarantees that types are projected from a well-formed global protocol.

Next, we explain a type declaration for the Authenticator role. Lines 27–37 specify the three SessionMpst types which correspond to the types of the session channels used in Fig. 2 (left) – types VideoP_A (line 1), Video_PRec_A (line 9), and the types used inside the offer construct – ChoiceA::Video (line 13), and ChoiceA::End (line 22).

In the encoding of [13], which underpins mpst-rust, a multiparty channel is represented as an indexed tuple of binary channels. This is reflected in the implementation of SessionMpst, which is parameterised on the required binary session types. For example, the VideoP_A<N> takes as a parameter the binary types between A and C, and between A and B. At the beginning of the protocol (lines 1–7 in Fig. 2 (left)) B and A do not interact, hence the binary type for B is End. The type InitA<N> (line 2 in Listing 1) specifies the behaviour between A and C, notably that A first receives a message, then it sends a message, and later it continues as the type RecvChoice<N>. The binary session types between A and B, and between A and C are given in lines 12–14 and lines 2–9 respectively; we use the primitives declared in the existing binary session types library [9]. The generic parameter N refers to a trait such as i32.

The third parameter for VideoP_A<N> (line 27) is a queue-like data structure, QueueAInit (line 17), that codifies the order of usage of each binary channel inside a multiparty session channel. This is needed to preserve the causality, imposed by the global protocol. The queues for the other SessionMpst types are given in lines 21–24. For instance, the queue for the ChoiceA:Video branch of the protocol is `QueueAVideo`. Note that, according to the protocol, A first has to receive a `VideoRequest` message from C, and then it has to forward that message to B Hence, swapping of lines 17 and 18 from Fig. 2 is a protocol violation error. We can detect such violations since the queue for the type `ChoiceA::Video`, `QueueAVideo` (line 21), is specified as `RoleAtoC<RoleAtoB ...>`, which codifies that first the channel for C and then the channel for B should be used. Note that none of the defined queues is recursive. Recursion is implicitly specified on binary types, while each queue is related to a `SessionMpst` type.

Distributed Execution Environment. The default transport of `mpst-rust` is the built-in Rust communication channels (crossbeam_channel). Also, to test our example in a more realistic distributed environment, we have also connected each process through MQTT (MQ Telemetry Transport) [7]. MQTT is a messaging middleware for exchanging messages between devices, predominantly used in IoT networks. At the start of the protocol, each process connects to a public MQTT channel, and a session is established. Therefore, we have mapped binary channels to MQTT sockets, in addition to the built-in Rust channels.

3 Design and Implementation of `mpst-rust`

Multiparty Channels as an Ordered Tuple of Binary Channels. The main idea of the design of our framework is that a multiparty session can be realised with two ingredients: (1) a list of separate binary sessions (one session for each pair of participants) and (2) a queue that imposes the ordering between the binary channels. Listing 2 (lines 2–3) shows the implementation of a multiparty channel in a 3-party protocol. The `SessionMpst` structure holds two fields, `session1` and `session2`, that are of a binary session type. For an illustration purpose, we show only the implementation of a multiparty channel for three processes. The same approach can be generalised, using our code generation tool, to any number of communicating processes. For example, in case of a protocol with four roles, each multiparty session will have four fields – a field for the binary session between each pair of participants and a field for the queue.

The order of usage of the binary channels of a `SessionMpst` object is stored inside the `queue` field. For instance, the behaviour that role A has to communicate first with role B, then with a role C, and then the session ends can be specified using a queue of type `RoleAtoB<RoleAtoC<RoleEnd>>`. Note that all queue types, such as `RoleAtoB`, `RoleAtoC`, are generated.

MPST Communication Primitives as Wrappers of Binary Channels. As explained in Sect. 2, programming with `mpst-rust` relies on communication primitives, such as `send_mpst_a_to_b`, that have the sender and receiver roles baked into their name. To ensure that the binary channels are used as specified by the global protocol, each communication function is parametric on a generic quadruple type `<T, S1, S2, R>` where T is a payload type, S1 and S2 are binary session types and R is a type for a queue (MPST-queue type) that imposes the order in which the binary sessions inside a multiparty session must be used.

```
1    // Basic structure for MPST
2    pub struct SessionMpst< S1: Session, S2: Session, R: Role> {
3      pub session1: S1, pub session2: S, pub queue: R }

4    // Implementation of a communication function from the mpst-rust library
5    pub fn send_mpst_a_to_b<T, S1, S2, R>(x: T,
6      s: SessionMpst<Send<T, S1>, S2, RoleAtoB<R>>,) -> SessionMpst<S1, S2, R>
7      where T: ..., S1: Session, S2: Session, R: Role,
8      { let new_session = send(x, s.session1);
9        let new_queue = next_a_to_b(s.queue); ... }

9    /// Offer a choice at A from C wrapped in an 'enum'
10   #[macro_export]
11   macro_rules! offer_mpst_a_to_c {($session ... => {
12       let (l, s) = recv_mpst_a_to_c($session)?; // receive a label l
13       cancel(s); // cancel the existing binary channels on s
14       match l { pat_i=>invoke...} // Call the associated function
15           // with a new SessionMpst
16   }
17
18   #[macro_export]
19   macro_rules! choose_mpst_c_to_all(s ...) {
20       ...// test for the choice condition ...and get the label l
21       let s = send_mpst_c_to_a(s, l); // send the label to A
22       let s = send_mpst_c_to_b(s, l), // send the label to B
23       cancel(s); // cancel the existing binary channels on s
24       // return new SessionMpst channel
25       ...
26   }
```

Listing 2. MPST Rust communication primitives

Listing 2 (lines 5–9) shows the implementation for `send_mpst_a_to_b()`. As clear from the type parameters, the client of the function should supply a MPST-queue type `RoleAtoB<R>`. The binary session type `S1` should be encapsulated in a `Send<T, S1>`. The body of the function sends the message of type `T` on the binary channel stored in the first field, `session1` (corresponding to the binary session with role `B`), of the multiparty session `s`. Since the communication is on a binary channel, we reuse the binary `send` primitive from [9].

External and internal choices are implemented as macros that require an argument of type `SessionMpst`. The implementation of `offer_mpst_a_to_c` is given in lines 11–14. In essence, a choice is implemented as a broadcast from one role to the others. In our usecase, the active role that makes the choice is C. Hence, the macro `offer_mpst_a_to_c` explicitly performs a receive (`recv_mpst_a_-to_c(s)`) on the session channel `s`. The received value is pattern matched and passed to any of the functions given as arguments to `offer_mpst_a_to_c`. Similarly, `choose_mpst_c_to_all` in lines 19–26 is a macro that performs a select operation. The active role C sends the selected label to all roles in the protocol. In our particular example, C sends the selected label l to A and B.

Discussions. Our implementation, although intuitive, does not resolve the inherent conflict between Rust, which is *affine*, and session types, which are *linear*. The implementation suffers from the same drawback as [9]. However, the MPST methodology is a step forward in terms of usability. Differently than the Rust local types which can get convoluted, the syntax of global protocols is user-friendly and readable. Developers can use the global protocol as guidance, and hence avoid errors such as prematurely ending of a session. Moreover, as observed in Kokke's library [9], most of the errors are caused by misuse of methods and functions. Since we are code-generating the local types, the chance of misspelling is significantly reduced. Another viable option for our framework is to take the *bottom-up* approach: to check directly whether a set of manually-written Rust local types satisfy *safety/liveness* properties by a model checker [14] or the *multiparty compatibility* (a property which guarantees deadlock-freedom of communicating automata, which are equivalent to local session types) [2,11].

4   Related and Future Work

The Rust library in [8] implements binary session types, following [4]. It checks at compile-time that the behaviours of two endpoint processes are *dual*, i.e the processes are compatible. The library in [9], based on the EGV calculus by Fowler *et al.* [3], provides constructs for writing and checking binary session types, and additionally supports exception handling constructs. We build on top of the library in [9] since it offers several improvements in comparison to [8]. Most importantly, the treatment of closing a channel prematurely in [8] may lead to memory leaks. Both libraries suffer from a well-known limitation of binary session types[3]. Notably, since deadlock-freedom is ensured only inside a session, a Rust endpoint process, that communicates with more than one other process, is prone to deadlocks and communication errors. Our framework solves that limitation by expanding the scope of a session to multiple participants.

Our proposed design follows the methodology given by [6], which generates Java communicating APIs from Scribble. This, and other multiparty session types implementations, exploit the equivalence between local session types and communicating automata to generate session types APIs for mainstream programming languages (e.g., Java [6,10], Go [1], F# [13]). Each state from state automata is implemented as a class, or in the case of [10], as a type state. To ensure safety, state automata have to be derived from the same global specification. All of the works in this category use the Scribble toolchain to generate the state classes from a global specification and detect linearity violations *at runtime*. This paper proposes the generation of protocol-specific APIs, which promotes type checking of protocols *at compile-time*. This is done by projecting the endpoints' state space in those protocols to groups of channel types in the desired language. In the future, we plan to implement the bottom-up approach, in addition to the top-down approach outlined in this paper, as to compare their productivity and scalability.

Acknowledgement. The work has been partially supported by the following funding schemes VeTSS, EPSRC EP/K011715/1, EP/K034413/1, EP/L00058X/1, EP/N027833/1, EP/N028201/1, EP/T006544/1 and, EP/T014709/1.

---

[3] https://github.com/Munksgaard/session-types/issues/62.

References

1. Castro, D., Hu, R., Jongmans, S.S., Ng, N., Yoshida, N.: Distributed programming using role parametric session types in Go. In: 46th ACM SIGPLAN Symposium on Principles of Programming Languages, vol. 3, pp. 29:1–29:30. ACM (2019)
2. Deniélou, P.-M., Yoshida, N.: Multiparty compatibility in communicating automata: characterisation and synthesis of global session types. In: Fomin, F.V., Freivalds, R., Kwiatkowska, M., Peleg, D. (eds.) ICALP 2013. LNCS, vol. 7966, pp. 174–186. Springer, Heidelberg (2013). https://doi.org/10.1007/978-3-642-39212-2_18
3. Fowler, S., Lindley, S., Morris, J.G., Decova, S.: Exceptional asynchronous session types: session types without tiers. Proc. ACM Program. Lang. **3**(POPL), 28:1–28:29 (2019). https://doi.org/10.1145/3290341
4. Honda, K., Vasconcelos, V.T., Kubo, M.: Language primitives and type discipline for structured communication-based programming. In: Hankin, C. (ed.) ESOP 1998. LNCS, vol. 1381, pp. 122–138. Springer, Heidelberg (1998). https://doi.org/10.1007/BFb0053567
5. Honda, K., Yoshida, N., Carbone, M.: Multiparty asynchronous session types. POPL **43**(1), 273–284 (2008)
6. Hu, R., Yoshida, N.: Hybrid session verification through endpoint API generation. In: Stevens, P., Wąsowski, A. (eds.) FASE 2016. LNCS, vol. 9633, pp. 401–418. Springer, Heidelberg (2016). https://doi.org/10.1007/978-3-662-49665-7_24
7. Hunkeler, U., Truong, H.L., Stanford-Clark, A.: MQTT-S-a publish/subscribe protocol for wireless sensor networks. In: 2008 3rd International Conference on Communication Systems Software and Middleware and Workshops, COMSWARE 2008, pp. 791–798. IEEE (2008)
8. Jespersen, T.B.L., Munksgaard, P., Larsen, K.F.: Session types for Rust. In: Proceedings of the 11th ACM SIGPLAN Workshop on Generic Programming, pp. 13–22. ACM (2015). https://doi.org/10.1145/2808098.2808100
9. Kokke, W.: Rusty variation: deadlock-free sessions with failure in Rust. In: Proceedings 12th Interaction and Concurrency Experience, ICE 2019, Copenhagen, Denmark, 20–21 June 2019, pp. 48–60 (2019). https://doi.org/10.4204/EPTCS.304.4
10. Kouzapas, D., Dardha, O., Perera, R., Gay, S.J.: Typechecking protocols with Mungo and StMungo. In: PPDP, pp. 146–159 (2016). https://doi.org/10.1145/2967973.2968595
11. Lange, J., Yoshida, N.: Verifying asynchronous interactions via communicating session automata. In: Dillig, I., Tasiran, S. (eds.) CAV 2019. LNCS, vol. 11561, pp. 97–117. Springer, Cham (2019). https://doi.org/10.1007/978-3-030-25540-4_6
12. Jespersen, T.B.L., Munksgaard, P., Larsen, K.F.: Session types for Rust. In: Proceedings of the 11th ACM SIGPLAN Workshop on Generic Programming, pp. 13–22. Association for Computing Machinery, New York (2015). https://doi.org/10.1145/2808098.2808100. ISBN 9781450338103
13. Scalas, A., Dardha, O., Hu, R., Yoshida, N.: A linear decomposition of multiparty sessions for safe distributed programming. In: 31st European Conference on Object-Oriented Programming. LIPIcs, vol. 74, pp. 24:1–24:31. Schloss Dagstuhl (2017)
14. Scalas, A., Yoshida, N.: Less is more: multiparty session types revisited. In: 46th ACM SIGPLAN Symposium on Principles of Programming Languages, vol. 3, pp. 30:1–30:29. ACM (2019)

15. Klabnik, S., Nichols, C.: The Rust Programming Language. 1.35.0 edn. (2019). https://doc.rust-lang.org/1.35.0/book/. Contributions from the Rust Community
16. Tu, T., Liu, X., Song, L., Zhang, Y.: Understanding real-world concurrency bugs in Go. In: ASPLOS, pp. 865–878. ACM (2019)
17. Yoshida, N., Gheri, L.: A very gentle introduction to multiparty session types. In: Hung, D.V., D'Souza, M. (eds.) ICDCIT 2020. LNCS, vol. 11969, pp. 73–93. Springer, Cham (2020). https://doi.org/10.1007/978-3-030-36987-3_5
18. Yoshida, N., Hu, R., Neykova, R., Ng, N.: The scribble protocol language. In: Abadi, M., Lluch Lafuente, A. (eds.) TGC 2013. LNCS, vol. 8358, pp. 22–41. Springer, Cham (2014). https://doi.org/10.1007/978-3-319-05119-2_3

GoPi: Compiling Linear and Static Channels in Go

Marco Giunti$^{(\boxtimes)}$

NOVA LINCS, NOVA School of Science and Technology, Lisbon, Portugal
marco.giunti@gmail.com

Abstract. We identify two important features to enhance the design of communication protocols specified in the pi-calculus, that are linear and static channels, and present a compiler, named *GoPi*, that maps high level specifications into executable *Go* programs. Channels declared as linear are deadlock-free, while the scope of static channels, which are bound by a *hide* declaration, does not enlarge at runtime; this is enforced statically by means of type inference, while specifications do not include annotations. Well-behaved processes are transformed into Go code that supports non-deterministic synchronizations and race-freedom. We sketch two main examples involving protection against message forwarding, and forward secrecy, and discuss the features of the tool, and the generated code. We argue that GoPi can support academic activities involving process algebras and formal models, which range from the analysis and testing of concurrent processes for research purposes to teaching formal languages and concurrent systems.

1 Introduction

Concurrent programming is nowadays pervasive to most software development processes. However, it poses hard challenges to the developers, which must envisage and try to solve without automatic support undesired behaviours like security breaches, deadlocks, races, often leading to bugs of substantial impact [11,22]. Automated techniques and tools are thus needed to analyse and ensure secure and correct concurrent code. Formal methods have been advocated as an effective tool to analyse and deploy secure communicating programs and protocols [10]. Process calculi, in particular, allow to study prototype analysis techniques that could be embedded into next generation compilers for distributed languages, and to investigate high-level security abstractions that can be effectively deployed into lower-level languages, thus providing for *APIs* for secure process interaction (e.g., [2,5]).

This work is partially supported by the EU Horizon 2020 research and innovation programme under the MSCA RISE grant agreement N° 77823 (BehAPI), and by Fundacão para a Ciência e a Tecnologia, Ministério da Ciência, Tecnologia e Ensino Superior, via project PTDC/CCI-COM/32166/2017 (DeDuCe). Tool available at: https://github.com/marcogiunti/gopi. Demo video available at: https://sites.fct.unl.pt/gopi.

© IFIP International Federation for Information Processing 2020
Published by Springer Nature Switzerland AG 2020
S. Bliudze and L. Bocchi (Eds.): COORDINATION 2020, LNCS 12134, pp. 137–152, 2020.
https://doi.org/10.1007/978-3-030-50029-0_9

let $Alice = priv?(c).c!$helloAlice in
let $Bob = priv?(c).c!$helloBob.$pub!priv$ in
let $Carl = pub?(p).p?(c).c!$helloCarl in
let $Board = *chat?($message$).$print :: message$ in
let $Setup = *priv!chat$ in
let $Chat = [$**hide** $chat][Board \mid ($**new** $priv)(Setup \mid Alice \mid Bob) \mid Carl]$ in $Chat$

Fig. 1. Suspicious specification of a secret chat in the *LSpi* language

This paper presents a contribution towards this direction by introducing a fully-automated tool, named GoPi [1], that allows to analyse and run communication protocols specified in a variant of the pi calculus featuring linear channels that must be used exactly once for input and once for output, and static channels that are never extruded. Well-behaved high-level processes are mapped into executable Go programs communicating through message-passing: rather than enforcing the channels' constraints at the target language level, GoPi performs a static analysis of the specification and only generates executable Go code that at runtime preserves the specified invariants. The analysis is based on type inference, while the specification language does not include type decorations. GoPi supports further non-trivial features, which include a contextual analysis of static channels, and deadlock detection on linear channels, at the source language level, and non-deterministic synchronizations, and race-freedom, at the target language level.

The aim is twofold:

- to provide for an automated static analysis of processes described in a variant of the linear pi-calculus without relying on annotations;
- to make available a message-passing runtime system for well-behaved pi-calculus processes featuring static channels that are never extruded.

1.1 Message Forwarding Protection

To illustrate our approach, we consider the case when we want to study the design of a messaging application supporting secret chats[1] featuring *message forwarding protection*. To this aim, we analyse an instance of a secret chat that involves three users, and describe the protocol as follows: "*Alice, Bob*, and *Carl* share a *hidden chat* channel with *static* scope including the users, the board, and a setup process that distributes the channel to the users, where the scope of the channel should never be enlarged". The static scope invariant offers protection against message forwarding, and only processes that are included in the scope of the channel in the specification will be able to ever use the channel at runtime.

---

[1] https://www.viber.com/blog/2017-03-13/share-extra-confidently-secret-chats.

Figure 1 presents a formal specification of the protocol in a variant of the pi-calculus featuring secret channels. The program is based on message-passing and builds around three main channels: the hidden channel *chat*, the distribution channel *priv*, and a public channel *pub*. Base channels are noted in typewriter. We use !, ?, . , *, and | to indicate output, input, sequence, loop and parallel execution constructors, respectively; channels are created with the new and hide constructors by indicating their scope with parentheses (new) and squares (hide). The print imperative construct allows to print channels. In order to be safe, the program in Fig. 1 should preserve the static scope invariant, that is: *the scope of the hidden channel must not be enlarged at runtime*. The specification is suspicious since Carl, who is left out of the distribution process, is invited to the chat by receiving the private channel *priv* from the open channel *pub*, perhaps because of a bad design choice.

By running GoPi, we verify that, when considered in isolation, the program in Fig. 1 is safe: intuitively, this holds since all processes receiving the hidden channel are included in its static scope (the squares). However, the protocol is flagged as *contextually unsafe*: the reason is that there exists a process that, once put in parallel with the *Chat* process, can break the static scope invariant by receiving the hidden channel. That is, because of non-determinism, the private channel *priv* can be received by a parallel process that is listening on the open channel *pub*, rather than by Carl, thus allowing a process outside the squares to receive the hidden channel *chat*. To fix to the program in Fig. 1 we can resort to *linear channels* that must be used exactly once for input and once for output. By declaring *pub* as linear, written as $\langle pub \rangle$, the protocol $SafeChat \triangleq \langle pub \rangle Chat$ gains protection from parallel (typed) processes, which are assumed to do not break linearity, and in turn contextual safety, as established by GoPi.

The static analysis is relevant since, in general, detecting if a program may extrude a secret channel by code inspection can be hard, because of channel mobility, and of the arbitrary length of the attack sequence. To see that, take $P \triangleq (\textbf{new}\, a_1, \ldots, a_n)([\text{hide}\, c][a_n!c] \mid a_1!a_2 \mid \cdots \mid a_{n-1}!a_n \mid pub!a_1)$, for some $n > 1$: the secret channel c is sent over a restricted channel a_n, which in turn is sent over a restricted channel a_{n-1}, and so on, while the error is that the first channel in the chain, a_1, is sent over a public channel *pub*, allowing processes running in parallel with P to receive the hidden channel from a_n.

1.2   Related Work

We briefly discuss work related to the design of the specification language, and to runtime systems for process calculi and Go as a target language.

Language Design. Secret channels have been studied by the author at the language [16] and type [15] level; this work integrates those results by presenting a compiler based on a novel type inference algorithm. The paper [16] presents a variant of the pi-calculus introducing a further operator, *hide*, that allows to declare channels that can be passed over channels, but cannot be extruded, and studies its behavioural properties. The static scope mechanism is embedded in the operational semantics of the language, where a dynamic check ensures that the context cannot receive channels protected by *hide*. In subsequent work [15], the mechanism is shifted to the level of types by means of a declarative system that enforces the static scope invariant in a standard pi-calculus. These mechanisms, complemented with linear type qualifiers (cf., [14,18]) and deadlock detection (cf., [17]), are the core of the static analysis performed by the GoPi tool.

Static channels and boundaries in process calculi have been investigated since the origins of this research area [28], and more recently in, e.g., [6,7,26]. The work in [6] has similarities with our approach and introduces a pi-calculus featuring a group creation operator, and a typing system that disallows channels to be sent outside of the group. Programmers must declare which is the group type of the payload: the typing system rules out processes of the form $Q \triangleq (\mathsf{new}\, p\colon U)(P \mid (\mathsf{new}\, G)((\mathsf{new}\, x\colon G[])(p!x)))$ since the type U of channel p cannot mention the secret type G, which is local. In contrast, we do not rely on type decorations and accept process Q whenever x is hidden and P does not allow to extrude x, e.g., P does not input on p or distribute p. From the point of view of the language design, we share some similarity with the ideas behind the boxed pi-calculus [26]. A box in [26] acts as wrapper where we can confine untrusted processes; communication among the box and the context is subject to a fine-grained control that prevents the untrusted process to interfere with the protocol. Our *hide* construct is based on the symmetric principle: a process is trusted whenever contexts cannot interfere with the process' protocol, that is contexts cannot enlarge the scope of the hidden channels of the process.

Runtime System. To the best of our knowledge, most interpreters for distributed calculi do not rely on channel-based mechanisms at the target language level; such implementations, pioneered by [25,27,29] for the pi-calculus, are commonly based on simulating non-determinism and concurrency by process interleaving. Previous attempts to develop calculi-inspired languages with native support for channel-over-channel passing include *JoCaml* [12], where mobility is now discontinued [23].

Recently, a behavioural static analysis of Go programs based on multiparty session types (*MPST*, [19]) has been presented in [20,21]. The approach followed in that line of work consists in analysing existing Go programs to ensure stronger properties at compile-time, e.g., deadlock-freedom. None of those works, however, support channel-over-channel passing. Castro et al. [8] introduced a framework to translate distributed MPST written in the *Scribble* protocol language into a Go API; safety in API's clients is enforced at runtime by generating linearity exceptions. Differently, we obtain safety of Go programs statically by means of type inference of pi-calculus channels.

Structure of the Paper

Section 2 presents the specification language and the notion of error, and sketches few examples. The next two sections introduce the two main parts of the GoPi compiler: the static analyser, presented in Sect. 3, and the Go code generator, presented in Sect. 4. We conclude in Sect. 5 by envisioning possible usage scenarios of GoPi, and by discussing limitations and future work.

2   The LSpi Specification Language

This section introduces the syntax of the language processed by the GoPi compiler. We consider communication channels, or variables, $a, \ldots, z$, and processes generated by the grammar:

$$P, Q ::= x!v.P \mid x?(y).P \mid (P \mid Q) \mid \mathbf{0} \mid [\mathbf{hide}\, x][P] \mid (\mathbf{new}\, x)(P) \mid {*}P \mid$$
$$\langle a, \ldots, x \rangle P \mid \mathbf{let}\ X = P \ \mathbf{in}\ Q \mid X \mid \mathbf{print} :: v$$

Most operators are standard for message passing languages, with some exceptions. We have primitives for sending and receiving channels and continuing as P, noted as $x!v.P$ and $x?(y).P$, respectively, for parallel composition, noted $P \mid Q$, for inert processes, noted $\mathbf{0}$, for channel creation, noted $(\mathbf{new}\, x)(P)$, for process variables, noted X, and for assigning processes to process variables, noted $\mathbf{let}\ X = P \ \mathbf{in}\ Q$. The hide operator is the main feature of the language and shall be interpreted as follows: $[\mathbf{hide}\, c][P]$ declares that the fresh channel c should be confined into the (fixed) square brackets *even* when process P interacts with other processes. In the pi-calculus jargon, this is better summarized by the sentence: "scope extrusion of channel c is disallowed ". The other crucial feature is the linear channel declaration $\langle a, \ldots, x \rangle P$, which declares that each of the channels $a, \ldots, x$ must be used exactly once for input and once for output. Loops are programmed with the construct ${*}P$, which executes P forever. The construct $\mathbf{print} :: v$ supplies an imperative command to observe the channel v.

We assume the usual notions of free and bound variables and process variables, which we deem pairwise distinct by following the Barendregt convention, and let x be bound in $[\mathbf{hide}\, x][P]$, $(\mathbf{new}\, x)(P)$, and $a?(x).P$, and be free otherwise, and X be bound in $\mathbf{let}\ X = P \ \mathbf{in}\ Q$, and free otherwise. The process $\mathbf{let}\ X = P \ \mathbf{in}\ Q$ is acyclic whenever X is not free in P, and P, Q are acyclic; the remaining cases are homomorphic. We only consider acyclic processes not containing free process variables. We will often avoid training nils, use the _ variable wildcard, and refer to channels not used in input or output as to base values, and write them in typewriter style, when convenient.

2.1   Runtime and Errors

GoPi allows to run LSpi processes by mapping well-behaved processes into executable Go programs. At a more abstract level, the semantics of the language is provided by translating LSpi processes into standard (typed) pi-calculus processes: intuitively, the hide construct is mapped into a restriction and has standard semantics (cf., [15]), while linear annotations are separated from processes and used in the static analysis. For instance, the specification

$[\text{hide}\,c][a!c] \mid a?(x).P$ declares that c should be confined in the squares, while at runtime P can receive the restricted channel c: therefore this process is unsound and should be rejected at compile-time.

LSpi programs can contain three kind of errors, all detected by the GoPi compiler:

(A) channels declared as hidden that can be received by processes outside the static scope of the channels;
(B) channels declared as linear that are not used exactly once for input and once for output;
(C) channels declared as linear that at runtime give rise to deadlocks.

Examples. Process *Chat* in Fig. 1 does not contain errors. In contrast, process *Chat* $\mid P$, where $P \triangleq pub?(x_{priv}).x_{priv}?(x_{chat}).Q$, is an error of kind A: there is a sequence of reductions which leads to the instantiation of the variable x_{chat} in Q with the hidden channel *chat*, that is the channel *chat* can be received by a process outside its static scope. Because of that, GoPi flags *Chat* as contextually unsafe. Process *SafeChat* $\triangleq \langle pub \rangle$ *Chat* does not contain errors, and is contextually safe, as we will see in Sect. 3: intuitively, this holds since process P above is no longer a valid (typed) opponent, because channel *pub* is linear and cannot be accessed by the context.

To see an example of an error of kind B, take process $\langle priv \rangle$ *Chat*, where channel *priv* is declared as linear. The linear invariant does not hold, because channel *priv* is used three times in input, by Alice, Bob and Carl (through delegation), respectively, and an unbound number of times in output, by process *Setup*.

Typical errors of kind C are processes containing self-deadlocks, which arise when a linear input (output) prefixes a continuation containing the matching output (input), and processes containing mutual deadlocks. The variant of process *Chat* below, where an *ack* is sent after sending channel *priv* over channel *pub*, and where channels *ack* and *pub* are linear, contains a mutual deadlock:

$\cdots$ let $Bob = priv?(c).c!\texttt{helloBob}.pub!priv.ack!\texttt{ok}$ in

let $Carl = ack?(x).confirm!x.pub?(p).p?(c).c!\texttt{helloCarl}$ in $\cdots$ in

let $ChatAck = \langle ack, pub \rangle$ *Chat* in *ChatAck*   (1)

At runtime the continuation of process *Bob* will be stuck on the output on the linear channel *pub*, which can be only unblocked by *Carl*, because *pub* is linear and must be used exactly once for input and once for input. Since *Carl*, in turn, is blocked on the linear channel *ack*, the process will deadlock.

An interesting example of security error is process *FSA* below, which abstracts a forward secrecy attack. Process *FSA* distributes a secret channel c on a private channel a, sends a password on c, and afterwards releases channel c on a public channel *pub*:

$$FSA \triangleq (\texttt{new}\,a)([\text{hide}\,c][a!c.c!\texttt{pwd} \mid a?(x).x?(\_).pub!x]) \mid pub?(z).Q \quad (2)$$

```
;; DATATYPES
(declare-datatypes () ((Scope static dynamic)))
(declare-datatypes () ((ChanType top
 (channel (scope Scope)(payload ChanType)(id Int)(i Int)(o Int)(ord Int)))))
```

Fig. 2. LSpi types in the SMT-LIB language

By considering that a hide is mapped into a new at runtime, process *FSA* might be interpreted as secure, because the context cannot observe the exchange over the restricted channel c, and in turn cannot retrieve the password. However, preserving the invisibility of restricted communications when pi-calculus processes are deployed in open, untrusted networks is problematic, exactly because of scope extrusion (cf., [3]), and eventually leads to complex solutions based on cryptographic protocols relying on trusted authorities (cf., [5]). For these reasons, we advocate that processes relying on dynamic scope restriction for security should be rejected (cf., [15,16]). In fact, process *FSA* contains an error of kind A, because at runtime the secret channel c can be received by a process outside the squares, that is c can be received from *pub*.

The forward secrecy attack hints on how to use secret channels to develop more secure programs: *whenever a secret is sent over an hidden channel of an error-free process, the secret will be unknown outside the static scope of the hide declaration.* Process *FSecret* is one of such secure programs, where we note that the distribution channel a can occur in processes outside the scope of the hide:

$$FSecret \triangleq (\text{new } a)(\text{new } b)(([\text{hide } c][a!c.c!\text{pwd} \mid a?(x).x?(\_)] \mid b!a \mid b?(\_)))$$

3 Static Analyser

The static analyser is based on the type inference of LSpi channels and is implemented as an automatically generated constraint system written in the *SMT-LIB* language [4], and decided through the *Z3* theorem prover [24]. Notably, the constraint system does not make use of quantifiers.

Figure 2 presents the syntax of the type of LSpi channels, named *ChanType*: base values are represented by the *top* constructor, while channels are built with the *channel* constructor receiving six arguments, where the last three (integer) constructors are for linearity. Type inference of a process P relies on a set of *allowed* identifiers (cf., *id*), which are the type identifiers that each input process is allowed to receive. Roughly, the static scope analysis is based on this technique.

To illustrate, consider the encoding[2] of the forward secrecy attack *FSA* in (2); the input on a is allowed to receive both (dynamic) channels tagged with 0 and the static channel identified by id_c, while the input on *pub* can only receive channels tagged with 0:

$$(\text{new } a: \text{dyn}@0)((\text{new } c: \text{stat}@id_c)a!c.c!\text{pwd} \mid a?(x).x?(\_).\text{pub}!x)) \mid \text{pub}?(z).Q$$

---

[2] The main rationale is that a new is mapped into a new with a dynamic type tagged with 0, while a hide is mapped into a new with a static type tagged with a positive identifier.

The corresponding SMT-LIB assertions generated by GoPi enforce the invariants for a and pub through their payload, where the randomly generated identifier that instantiates id_c is 345:

```
(assert (! (= (id c) 345) :named A5))
(assert (! (= c (payload a)) :named A12))
(assert (! (and (= (payload a) x) (or (= (id x) 0) (= (id x) 345)):named A23))
(assert (! (= x (payload pub)) :named A46))
(assert (! (and (= (payload pub) z) (= (id z) 0)) :named A48))
```

These assertions make the model *UNSAT*, as expected, because by transitivity we obtain $345 = 0$: that is, the variable z bound by the input prefix on channel pub should have id equal to 0, while it has the id of the static (hidden) channel.

3.1   Contextual Safety

Contextual safety is analysed by resorting to auto-generated catalysers (cf., [9]) of order n, that are processes that can both inject and receive channels, on which they inject and receive channels, and so on, with depth n. Catalysers are put in parallel with the process in order to collect the process' global constraints, as if the process was immersed in an arbitrary (typed) context. The contexts under consideration are those that respect the linearity invariants of the process: that is, we generate catalysers from the unrestricted free variables of the process.

To see an example of catalyser, consider process *Chat* in Fig. 1, where we note that the only unrestricted free variable of *Chat* is pub. The catalyser below is generated by following the structure of *Chat* and by matching each input (output) on pub with an output (input) on pub with depth three, which is the maximum order of *Chat*, where f is a randomly generated channel distinct from any channel in the free and bound variables of *Chat*:

$$Cat \triangleq pub?(x).(x?(y).y?(z) \mid \mathbf{0}) \mid pub!f.(f?(x).x?(y) \mid f?(x).(x?(y).y?(z) \mid \mathbf{0}))$$

Process *Chat* is contextually unsafe because *Chat* | *Cat* contains an error: the hidden channel *chat* at runtime can be received by process *Cat*, which is outside the static scope of the channel (cf., Sect. 2). This is established by GoPi via the generation of the SMT-LIB assertions of *Chat* | *Cat*, and by discovering that the model is UNSAT; we omit the core assertions, which are similar to those of the forward secrecy attack.

As a further example, consider *SafeChat* $\triangleq \langle pub \rangle$ *Chat*. Given that the set of the unrestricted free variables of *SafeChat* is empty, we generate an inert catalyser (cf., $\mathbf{0}$), and in turn obtain that *SafeChat* is contextually safe because the SMT-LIB model generated from *SafeChat* | $\mathbf{0}$ is *SAT*, that is the parallel composition is error-free.

3.2   Linearity Analysis

To enforce linearity, we use the input, output, and order integer constructors, noted i, o, and ord, respectively, of the type *ChanType* in Fig. 2. Input (output) fields contain the number of times that the input (output) capability is used for a variable of the given type. Order fields are manipulated by the solver to find an ordering among linear channels.

The linearity analysis is performed by mapping the actual usage of channels into assertions of the constraint system. While analysing processes and generating the corresponding assertions for type reconstruction, we build a usage table that maps channels x to entries of the form (n_i, n_o, ls), where n_i, n_o are integers tracking the usage of x in input and output, respectively, and ls is a list containing the channels where x has been sent. At the end of the process analysis, the contents of the table are transformed into assertions and added to the constraint system.

The SMT-LIB assertions below are an excerpt of the model generated from process *ChatAck* in (1):

```
(assert (! (=> (isLinear ack) (< (ord pub) (ord ack))) :named A67))
(assert (! (=> (isLinear pub) (< (ord ack) (ord pub))) :named A96))
(assert (! (isLinear ack) :named A111))
(assert (! (isLinear pub) :named A112))
(assert (! (=> (isLinear ack) (and (= (o ack) 1) (= (o ack) (+ 1 0 ))))
 :named A113))
(assert (! (=> (isLinear ack) (and (= (i ack) 1) (= (i ack) (+ 1 0 ))))
 :named A114))
(assert (! (=> (isLinear pub) (and (= (o pub) 1) (= (o pub) (+ 1 0 ))))
 :named A137))
(assert (! (=> (isLinear pub) (and (= (i pub) 1) (= (i pub) (+ 1 0 ))))
 :named A138))
```

Assertions A111 and A112 come from the linear declaration $\langle ack, pub \rangle$ in (1). Assertions A113, A114, A137, and A138 are generated from the usage table, where, for each conjunction, the first entry is the expected value, and the second entry is the actual value. The assertions are satisfiable: that is, each i/o capability of channel *ack*, and of channel *pub*, respectively, is used exactly once in (1). The model is UNSAT because the conclusions in the assertions A67 and A96 state that the order of *pub* is smaller than the order of *ack*, and vice-versa. We note that the unsatisfiability of the model prevents the mutual deadlock inside *ChatAck* (cf., Sect. 2).

4   Go Code Generation

Given a well-behaved LSpi process, and the type of its channels, GoPi generates executable Go code that is based on the channels' types. Channel types in Go have the following syntax[3], where ElementType is any type:

```
ChannelType = ("chan" | "chan" "<-" | "<-" "chan") ElementType .
```

We map types in Fig. 2 to types of the form above by ignoring all fields but the *payload*, and by mapping the *top* type to **string**.

The generation of code implementing LSpi processes is not straightforward: while the target language features concurrent goroutines (cf., go f(a ,..., z)) that are a natural candidate to represent high-level parallel processes, the whole application's design must be carefully pondered.

---

[3] https://golang.org/ref/spec.

```
1  var pub chan chan chan base
2  //Chat process
3  func(){
4    chat := make(chan base) ; ...
5    func(){ ...
6      priv := make(chan chan base); ...
7      go func(){ ... ; pub ← priv}() //Bob
8    }()
9    go func(){ p := ←pub; fmt.Print("Retrieved:", p); ... }(); //Carl
10  }()
11  //Parallel process
12  go func(){ a := make(chan chan base) ; pub ← a}()
```

Fig. 3. Naive implementation of the *Chat* protocol in Go

As a first attempt, we could map input and output constructs of LSpi directly into receive and send primitives of Go, respectively. To illustrate, take the parallel execution of process *Chat* in Fig. 1 with a process sending a fresh channel a over the public channel *pub*, that is process $Chat_{ND} \triangleq Chat \mid (\text{new } a)(pub!a)$, where the subscript stands for non-deterministic, since *Carl* can receive *priv* from *Bob*, or a from the parallel process, non-deterministically. Process $Chat_{ND}$ would be mapped into Go code of the form outlined in Fig. 3, where we list the parts that are related to the communication over channel *pub*. The scope of channel *chat* is grouped by the function call in lines 3–10, while the scope of channel *priv* is grouped by the function call in lines 5–8. The listed processes that are executed concurrently are *Bob* (line 7), *Carl* (line 9), and the parallel process (line 12).

While appealingly simple, the implementation in Fig. 3 has at least two main drawbacks:

- in the vast majority of cases, i.e., $\sim 90\%$, p is bound to *priv*, while the probability should be 50%, being receiving *priv* from *pub* equally probable to receiving a from *pub*;
- channels have no name associated, making difficult the interpretation of the output of the program, e.g., "*Retrieved: 0xc000022060*".

4.1   Channel Servers

The envisioned solution consists in using channel servers that take care of input and output requests of clients, while internally managing both non-deterministic synchronizations, and the naming of channels. The access to channel servers is regulated by an API for communication, implemented as methods of a *type environment* infrastructure; the structure, represented by the *typeEnv* typed collection in Fig. 4, aggregates channel servers by their order.

Servers are equipped with dynamic arrays, referred as *queues*, that collect the values concurrently sent on the channel by output clients, and act as a bridge between input and output clients: input clients send requests to the server and receive values sent by output clients and stored in the queue. Non-determinism is simulated through a randomization of queues, and can be pushed forward by

```
1  type base string
2  type basePair struct{
3      ch base
4      replych chan bool
5  }
6  type queueBase [] basePair ;
7  type chan0 chan base
8  type chan0Pair struct{
9      ch chan0
10     replych chan bool
11 }
12 type queueChan0 [] chan0Pair ;
13 type chan1 chan chan0 ; ...
14 type typeEnv struct{
15     ord struct{ ... }
16     ord0 struct{
17        toStr map[chan0]string //marshalling
18        fromStr map[string]chan0 //unmarshalling
19        queue map[chan0]queueBase
20        dequeue map[chan0]func() //instantiated at registration
21        mux sync.Mutex
22     }
23     ord1 struct{
24        toStr map[chan1]string //marshalling
25        fromStr map[string]chan1 //unmarshalling
26        queue map[chan1]queueChan0
27        dequeue map[chan1]func() //instantiated at registration
28        mux sync.Mutex
29     } ; ...
```

Fig. 4. Type of channel servers

tuning the timeouts in retrieving messages[4]. A *mutex* regulating the access to queue and dequeue operations prevents data races; this is verified with Go's race detector.

Server Registration. A channel server of order $n \geq 0$ is registered by instantiating the entries of ord_n in the (unique) variable Γ of type *typeEnv* (cf., Fig. 4). The procedure to register a channel server of order zero for the name "a", where, by convention, zero is the order of channels conveying base values, consists of five major steps:

1. create a fresh channel c of type *chan0*;
2. acquire the lock (cf., line 21)
3. **defer** the unlock
4. insert the mappings between "a" and c (cf., lines 17, 18)
5. insert the mapping from c to a function (cf., line 20) that retrieves values from *Gamma.ord0.queue[c]* (cf., line 19).

4.2 Clients' Access to Servers

The channels servers are accessed by clients by means of methods of the variable Γ of type *typeEnv*. The signatures below list the most relevant operations.

---

[4] Non-zero dequeue timeouts are optional, and discouraged for non-academic purposes.

```
1 //Methods of typeEnv accessed by clients
2 func (t *typeEnv) register(name string, nameType string) error
3 func (t *typeEnv) dequeue(input value) error
4 func (t *typeEnv) queue(output value, payload value,
5                        replyCh chan bool) error
6 func (t *typeEnv) nameOf(c value) string
```

The *register* method is invoked by clients in correspondence of a new or of a hide declaration, where the second parameter is the order of the declared channel. The *dequeue* method is called by input clients, where *value* is an **interface** implemented by channels and base values. The *queue* method is invoked by output clients, where the third parameter will be instantiated by a (fresh) ack channel, to enforce synchronous communications. The *nameOf* method is called by print clients in order to print the string associated to a channel reference.

4.3   Working Example

Figure 5 contains the code generated by GoPi for the *Chat* process (cf., Fig. 1), where we only list the code of clients, being the code of servers invariant. The outer function call generates channel *chat* and closes its scope. In the body of the call, we have the parallel execution of *Board* (lines 5–20), of (new *priv*)(*Setup* | *Alice* | *Bob*) (lines 21–51), and of *Carl* (lines 52–62). Generation of fresh channels is implemented by a mechanism that uses randomly generated keys, and a counter protected by a mutex, for loops (cf., lines 7, 9, 27, 29).

The code implementing *Board* invokes the *dequeue* method of Γ (line 10), which triggers the selection of a message m from the queue of channel *chat* and the dispatch of m over *chat*. Subsequently, the message is retrieved from *chat* and printed, where the code in lines 13–17 implements the polymorphic **print** construct of LSpi. The sending on channel *done* (line 19) is discussed below.

The code for *Setup* continuously uses the *queue* method of Γ to send *chat* over *priv* (cf., lines 28–33); to enforce synchrony, the write request includes a reply boolean channel that will be unblocked by the server once *priv* is retrieved in the queue (cf., lines 30, 32).

The code for *Bob* sends three requests to Γ: one *dequeue*, to retrieve a channel from *priv* (line 39), one *queue*, to send the string *helloBob* over the channel retrieved from *priv* (line 42), and one *queue*, to send *priv* over *pub* (line 45). Before the exit, a boolean ack is sent over channel *done* (line 47), to signal that the thread ended. The ack is received by the loop in line 63, which allows the program to wait for the termination of all threads until a given timeout, to increase the chances to retrieve messages from queues. This mechanism is followed by all threads, regardless of loops.

Finally, the code for *Carl* sends three requests to Γ: one *dequeue*, to retrieve a channel from *pub* (line 54), one *dequeue*, to retrieve a channel c from the channel retrieved from *pub* (line 56), and one *queue*, to send the string *helloCarl* over c (line 59).

```
1   var Gamma typeEnv ; ...
2   func(){
3     Gamma.register("chat"+ string(counter.Value(key)), "0")
4     chat := Gamma.chanOf("chat"+ string(counter.Value(key))).(chan0)
5     //Board
6     go func() {
7       key := RandStringRunes(32)
8       for{
9         counter.Inc(key)
10        Gamma.dequeue(chat)
11        message := ← chat
12        var v value = message
13        switch v.(type){
14          case base: fmt.Printf("Print %v\n",message)
15          default: fmt.Printf("Print %v with address %v\n",
16                          Gamma.nameOf(message), message)
17        }
18      }
19      done ← true
20    }()
21    go func() {
22      func() {
23        Gamma.register("priv"+ string(counter.Value(key)), "1")
24        priv := Gamma.chanOf("priv"+ string(counter.Value(key))).(chan1)
25        //Setup
26        go func() {
27          key := RandStringRunes(32)
28          for{
29            counter.Inc(key)
30            privReply0 := make(chan bool)
31            Gamma.queue(priv, chat, privReply0)
32            _ =← privReply0
33          }
34          done ← true
35        }()
36        //Alice ...
37        //Bob
38        go func() {
39          Gamma.dequeue(priv)
40          ch2 := ← priv
41          ch2Reply2 := make(chan bool)
42          Gamma.queue(ch2, helloBob, ch2Reply2)
43          _ =← ch2Reply2
44          pubReply3 := make(chan bool)
45          Gamma.queue(pub, priv, pubReply3)
46          _ =← pubReply3
47          done ← true
48        }()
49      }()
50      done ← true
51    }()
52    //Carl
53    go func() {
54      Gamma.dequeue(pub)
55      ch3 := ← pub
56      Gamma.dequeue(ch3)
57      c := ← ch3
58      cReply4 := make(chan bool)
59      Gamma.queue(c, helloCarl, cReply4)
60      _ =← cReply4
61      done ← true
62    }()
63    for { ←done }
64  }()
```

Fig. 5. GoPi's implementation of the *Chat* process

5 Discussion

GoPi's main aim is to support academic activities involving process algebras and formal models, which range from the analysis and testing of concurrent processes for research purposes to teaching formal languages and concurrent systems.

In this context, we have done some tests[5] with encouraging results, e.g, GoPi decided the safety of a complex variant of the secret chat protocol of Sect. 1 involving a communication of order seven and more than thirty programming constructs in 0.2 s, producing 600 constraints and a Go file of 1Kloc (cf., [1]). On the Go's side, we ran the code generated from a LSpi process continuously creating, sending and printing fresh channels for one day, without encountering exceptions. With António Ravara, we plan to use GoPi in the course Modelling and Validating Concurrent Systems of the Integrated Master in Computer Engineering, New University of Lisbon, 2020/21.

5.1 Limitations

The current architecture of GoPi does not allow to separate the static analysis from the generation of the Go code, and in turn to generate code based on type annotations provided by different tools. Another limitation is that modifications of the Go code made by the programmer are lost when the specification is changed, since GoPi does not support annotations of the specification with Go snippets. We also note that the static analysis is not compositional, since to determine whether a process is safe, we perform a contextual analysis.

The information reported in case of failure of the analysis is not parsed into an human-readable format; this limits the usability of the tool.

At the language level, one current limitation is that delegation of partial capabilities of linear channels is rejected, because of issues related to the detection of deadlocks (cf., [17]). Another limitation, which is common in the context of behavioural type systems (cf., [13]), is that deadlocks are detected on linear channels, while unrestricted channels, interpreted as open ports, can give rise to runtime locks caused by decoupled input and output communications.

5.2 Future Work

GoPi aims at being an open and live project developing and maintaining a compiler for a language with built-in support for mobility, security, resource-awareness, and deadlock-resolution. In that direction, most limitations outlined above need to be overcome.

The separation of the static analysis and of the generation of Go code, and the readability of the output of the static analysis, appear as the most urgent issues. We believe that both features could be supported in the next release of GoPi, while the presentation of the results of the static analysis could (at least) state a list of channels, and the kind or error encountered (cf., Sect. 2).

---

[5] Testing machine: MacBook 2 GHz i5 8 GB 1867 MHz LPDDR3.

Supporting partial delegation of linear capabilities is another feature that we are keen to support in future releases, while the static analysis may be more involved, because of deadlock detection.

Acknowledgements. The author would like to warmly thank the anonymous reviewers for their competent comments and constructive criticism on a previous draft of the paper, and for providing insightful suggestions in the preparation of this paper.

References

1. The GoPi Compiler. https://github.com/marcogiunti/gopi. https://sites.fct.unl.pt/gopi
2. 4th Workshop on Principles of Secure Compilation. POPL (2020). https://popl20.sigplan.org/home/prisc-2020
3. Abadi, M.: Protection in programming-language translations. In: Larsen, K.G., Skyum, S., Winskel, G. (eds.) ICALP 1998. LNCS, vol. 1443, pp. 868–883. Springer, Berlin, Heidelberg (1998). https://doi.org/10.1007/BFb0055109
4. Barrett, C., Fontaine, P., Tinelli, C.: The SMT-LIB Standard: Version 2.6. Technical report, Department of Computer Science, The University of Iowa (2017)
5. Bugliesi, M., Giunti, M.: Secure implementations of typed channel abstractions. In: POPL, pp. 251–262. ACM (2007)
6. Cardelli, L., Ghelli, G., Gordon, A.D.: Secrecy and group creation. Inf. Comput. **196**(2), 127–155 (2005). https://doi.org/10.1016/j.ic.2004.08.003
7. Castagna, G., Vitek, J., Nardelli, F.Z.: The seal calculus. Inf. Comput. **201**(1), 1–54 (2005). https://doi.org/10.1016/j.ic.2004.11.005
8. Castro, D., Hu, R., Jongmans, S., Ng, N., Yoshida, N.: Distributed programming using role-parametric session types in Go: statically-typed endpoint APIs for dynamically-instantiated communication structures. PACMPL **3**(POPL), 29:1–29:30 (2019). https://doi.org/10.1145/3290342
9. Coppo, M., Dezani-Ciancaglini, M., Yoshida, N., Padovani, L.: Global progress for dynamically interleaved multiparty sessions. Math. Struct. Comput. Sci. **26**(2), 238–302 (2016)
10. Cortier, V., Kremer, S. (eds.): Formal Models and Techniques for Analyzing Security Protocols, Cryptology and Information Security, vol. 5. IOS Press, Amsterdam (2011)
11. Fonseca, P., Li, C., Singhal, V., Rodrigues, R.: A study of the internal and external effects of concurrency bugs. In: DSN, pp. 221–230. IEEE Computer Society (2010). https://doi.org/10.1109/DSN.2010.5544315
12. Fournet, C., Le Fessant, F., Maranget, L., Schmitt, A.: JoCaml: a language for concurrent distributed and mobile programming. In: Jeuring, J., Jones, S.L.P. (eds.) AFP 2002. LNCS, vol. 2638, pp. 129–158. Springer, Berlin, Heidelberg (2003). https://doi.org/10.1007/978-3-540-44833-4_5
13. Gay, S., Ravara, A. (eds.): Behavioural Types: From Theory to Tools. River Publishers (2017). https://doi.org/0.13052/rp-9788793519817
14. Giunti, M.: Algorithmic type checking for a pi-calculus with name matching and session types. J. Logic Algebraic Program. **82**(8), 263–281 (2013). https://doi.org/10.1016/j.jlap.2013.05.003
15. Giunti, M.: Static semantics of secret channel abstractions. In: Bernsmed, K., Fischer-Hübner, S. (eds.) NordSec 2014. LNCS, vol. 8788, pp. 165–180. Springer, Cham (2014). https://doi.org/10.1007/978-3-319-11599-3_10

16. Giunti, M., Palamidessi, C., Valencia, F.D.: Hide and new in the pi-calculus. In: EXPRESS/SOS. EPTCS, vol. 89, pp. 65–79 (2012)
17. Giunti, M., Ravara, A.: Towards static deadlock resolution in the π-calculus. In: Abadi, M., Lluch Lafuente, A. (eds.) TGC 2013. LNCS, vol. 8358, pp. 136–155. Springer, Cham (2014). https://doi.org/10.1007/978-3-319-05119-2_9
18. Giunti, M., Vasconcelos, V.T.: Linearity, session types and the pi calculus. Math. Struct. Comput. Sci. **26**(2), 206–237 (2016). https://doi.org/10.1017/S0960129514000176
19. Honda, K., Yoshida, N., Carbone, M.: Multiparty asynchronous session types. J. ACM **63**(1), 9:1–9:67 (2016)
20. Lange, J., Ng, N., Toninho, B., Yoshida, N.: Fencing off Go: liveness and safety for channel-based programming. In: POPL, pp. 748–761. ACM (2017)
21. Lange, J., Ng, N., Toninho, B., Yoshida, N.: A static verification framework for message passing in Go using behavioural types. In: ICSE, pp. 1137–1148. ACM (2018). https://doi.org/10.1145/3180155.3180157
22. Lu, S., Park, S., Seo, E., Zhou, Y.: Learning from mistakes: a comprehensive study on real world concurrency bug characteristics. In: ASPLOS, pp. 329–339. ACM (2008). https://doi.org/10.1145/1346281.1346323
23. Mandel, L., Maranget, L.: The JoCaml Language, Release 4.01, 14 March 2014. http://jocaml.inria.fr/doc
24. de Moura, L., Bjørner, N.: Z3: an efficient SMT solver. In: Ramakrishnan, C.R., Rehof, J. (eds.) TACAS 2008. LNCS, vol. 4963, pp. 337–340. Springer, Berlin, Heidelberg (2008). https://doi.org/10.1007/978-3-540-78800-3_24
25. Pierce, B.C., Turner, D.N.: Pict: a programming language based on the pi-calculus. In: Proof, Language, and Interaction, Essays in Honour of Robin Milner, pp. 455–494. The MIT Press (2000)
26. Sewell, P., Vitek, J.: Secure composition of untrusted code: box pi, wrappers, and causality. J. Comput. Secur. **11**(2), 135–188 (2003)
27. Sewell, P., Wojciechowski, P.T., Unyapoth, A.: Nomadic Pict: programming languages, communication infrastructure overlays, and semantics for mobile computation. ACM Trans. Program. Lang. Syst. **32**(4), 12:1–12:63 (2010). https://doi.org/10.1145/1734206.1734209
28. Thomsen, B.: Plain CHOCS: a second generation calculus for higher order processes. Acta Inf. **30**(1), 1–59 (1993). https://doi.org/10.1007/BF01200262
29. Turner, D.N.: The polymorphic pi-calculus: theory and implementation. Ph.D. thesis, University of Edinburgh (1995)

SFJ: An Implementation of Semantic Featherweight Java

Artem Usov and Ornela Dardha$^{(\boxtimes)}$ (iD)

School of Computing Science, University of Glasgow, Glasgow, UK
2296905U@student.gla.ac.uk, ornela.dardha@glasgow.ac.uk

Abstract. There are two approaches to defining subtyping relations:
the *syntactic* and the *semantic* approach. In semantic subtyping, one
defines a model of the language and an interpretation of types as subsets
of this model. Subtyping is defined as inclusion of subsets denoting types.

An orthogonal subtyping question, typical of object-oriented languages, is the *nominal* versus the *structural* subtyping. Dardha *et al.*
[11,12] defined boolean types and semantic subtyping for Featherweight
Java (FJ) and integrated both nominal and structural subtyping, thus
exploiting the benefits of both approaches. However, these benefits were
illustrated only at a theoretical level, but not exploited practically.

We present SFJ—Semantic Featherweight Java, an implementation
of FJ which features boolean types, semantic subtyping and integrates
nominal as well as structural subtyping. The benefits of SFJ, illustrated
in the paper and the accompanying video (with audio/subtitles) [27],
show how static type-checking of boolean types and semantic subtyping gives higher guarantees of program correctness, more flexibility and
compactness of program writing.

Keywords: Nominal subtyping · Structural subtyping · Semantic
Featherweight Java · Object-oriented languages · Boolean types · Type
theory

1 Introduction

There are two approaches to defining subtyping relations: the *syntactic* and the
semantic approach. Syntactic subtyping [20] is more mainstream in programming
languages and is defined by means of a set of formal deductive subtyping rules.
Semantic subtyping [1,10] is more recent and less known: one defines a formal
model of the language and an interpretation of types as subsets of this model.
Then, subtyping is defined as set inclusion of subsets denoting types.

Supported by the UK EPSRC grant EP/K034413/1, "From Data Types to Session
Types: A Basis for Concurrency and Distribution" (ABCD), and by the EU HORI-
ZON 2020 MSCA RISE project 778233 "Behavioural Application Program Interfaces"
(BehAPI).

© IFIP International Federation for Information Processing 2020
Published by Springer Nature Switzerland AG 2020
S. Bliudze and L. Bocchi (Eds.): COORDINATION 2020, LNCS 12134, pp. 153–168, 2020.
https://doi.org/10.1007/978-3-030-50029-0_10

Orthogonally, for object-oriented languages there are two approaches to defining subtyping relations: the *nominal* and the *structural* approach [21,22]. Nominal subtyping is based on declarations by the developer and is *name*-based: "*A* is a subtype of *B* if and only if it is declared to be so, that is if the class *A* extends (or implements) the class (or interface) *B*". Structural subtyping instead is based on the *structure* of a class, its fields and methods: "a class *A* is a subtype of a class *B* if and only if the fields and methods of *A* are a superset of the fields and methods of *B*, and their types in *A* are subtypes of the types in *B*". For example, the set of inhabitants of a class *Student* is smaller than the set of inhabitants of a class *Person*, as each Student is a Person, but not the other way around. However, the set of fields and methods of *Student* is a superset of that of *Person*. Hence, *Student* is a structural subtype of *Person*, even if it is not declared so.

Dardha *et al.* [11,12] define boolean types—based on set-theoretic operations such as **and**, **not**, **or**—and semantic subtyping for *Featherweight Java* (FJ) [17]. This approach allows for the integration of both nominal and structural subtyping in FJ, bringing in higher guarantees of program correctness, flexibility and compactness in program writing. Unfortunately, these benefits were only presented at a theoretical level and not exploited practically, due to the lack of an implementation of the language, its types and type system.

In this paper, we present SFJ—*Semantic Featherweight Java* Sect. 3, an implementation of FJ with boolean types and semantic subtyping. In SFJ the developer has a larger and more expressive set of types, by using boolean connectives **and**, **not**, **or**, with the expected set-theoretic interpretation. On the other hand, this added expressivity does not add complexity. Rather the opposite is true, as the developer has an easier, more compact and elegant way of programming. SFJ integrates both structural and nominal subtyping, and the developer can choose which one to use. Finally, as discussed in Dardha *et al.* [12, Sect. 8.4], thanks to semantic subtyping, we can easily encode in SFJ standard programming constructs and features of the full Java language, such as lists, or overloading classes via multimethods [5], which are missing in FJ, thus making SFJ a more complete language closer to Java.

Example 1 (Polygons). This will be our running example both in the paper and in the tool video [27] to illustrate the benefits of boolean types and semantic subtyping developed by Dardha *et al.* [11,12] and implemented as SFJ.

Consider the set of polygons, such as triangles, squares and rhombuses given by a class hierarchy. We want to define a method *diagonal* that takes a polygon and returns the length of its longest diagonal. This method makes sense only if the polygon passed to it has at least four sides, hence triangles are excluded. In Java this could be implemented in the following ways:

```
class Polygon {...}
class Triangle extends Polygon {...}
class Other_Polygons extends Polygon {
    double diagonal(Other_Polygons shape) {...}

            ...

}
class Square extends Other_Polygons {...}
class Rhombus extends Other_Polygons {...}
```

Or by means of an interface *Diagonal*:

```
public interface Diagonal {
    double diagonal(Polygon shape);
}
class Polygon {...}
class Triangle extends Polygon {...}
class Square extends Polygon  implements Diagonal {...}
class Rhombus extends Polygon  implements Diagonal {...}
            // other polygons ...
```

Now, suppose our class hierarchy is such that *Polygon* is the parent class and all other geometric figures extend *Polygon*, which is how one would naturally define the set of polygons. Suppose the class hierarchy is given and is part of legacy code, which cannot be changed. Then again, a natural way to implement this in Java is by defining the method *diagonal* in the class *Polygon* and using an **instanceof**, for example, inside a **try-catch** construct. Then, an exception would be thrown at run time, if the argument passed to the method is a triangle.

We propose a more elegant solution, by combining boolean types and semantic subtyping, where only static type-checking is required and we implement this in SFJ [27]: it is enough to define a method *diagonal* that has an argument of type *Polygon* **and not** *Triangle*, thus allowing the type-checker to check at compile time the restrictions on types:

```
class Polygon {...}
class Triangle extends Polygon {...}
class Square extends Polygon {...}
class Rhombus extends Polygon {...}

            ...

class Diagonal {

            ...

    double diagonal((Polygon and not Triangle) shape){...}
}
```

We can now call *diagonal* on an argument of type *Polygon*: if the polygon is **not** a *Triangle*, then the method computes and returns the length of its longest diagonal; otherwise, there will be a type error at compile time.

Structure of the Paper: In Sect. 2 we present the types and terms of the SFJ language. In Sect. 3 we present the design and implementation of SFJ; we discuss our two main algorithms, Algorithm 1 in Sect. 3.1 which checks the validity of type definitions, and Algorithm 2 in Sect. 3.2 which generates the semantic subtyping relation. Further, we discuss typing of SFJ in Sect. 3.3; nominal vs. structural subtyping in Sect. 3.5; method types in Sect. 3.6; and code generation in Sect. 3.7. We discuss related work and conclude the paper in Sect. 4.

2   Background

The technical developments behind semantic subtyping and its properties are complex, however, they are completely transparent to the programmer. The framework is detailed and proved correct in the relevant work by Dardha *et al.* [11,12], and SFJ builds on that framework.

In this section we will briefly detail the types and terms of SFJ.

2.1   Types

The syntax of types τ is defined by the following grammar:

$$
\begin{array}{lll}
\tau ::= \alpha \mid \mu & & \textit{Types} \\
\alpha ::= \mathbf{0} \mid \mathbb{B} \mid \widetilde{[l : \tau]} \mid \alpha \textbf{ and } \alpha \mid \textbf{not } \alpha & & \textit{Field types (α-types)} \\
\mu ::= \alpha \rightarrow \alpha \mid \mu \textbf{ and } \mu \mid \textbf{not } \mu & & \textit{Method types (μ-types)}
\end{array}
$$

The α-types are used to type fields and the μ-types are used to type methods. Type $\mathbf{0}$ is the empty type. Type $\mathbb{B}$ denotes the *basic* types, such as integers, booleans, etc. Record types $[\widetilde{l : \tau}]$, where $\widetilde{l}$ is a sequence of disjoint labels, are used to type objects. Arrow types $\alpha \rightarrow \alpha$ are used to type methods.

The boolean connectives **and** and **not** in the α-types and μ-types have their expected set-theoretic meanings. We let $\alpha \setminus \alpha'$ denote α **and** (**not** α'), and α **or** α' denote **not**(**not** α **and** (**not** α')).

2.2   Terms

The syntax of terms is defined by the following grammar and is based on the standard syntax of terms in FJ [17]:

Class declaration	$L ::= \textbf{class } C \textbf{ extends } C \ \{\widetilde{\alpha\,a};\ K;\ \widetilde{M} \ \}$
Constructor	$K ::= C \ (\widetilde{\alpha\,x}) \ \{ \ \textbf{super}(\widetilde{x});\ \widetilde{\textbf{this}.a = \widetilde{x};} \ \}$
Method declaration	$M ::= \alpha \ m \ (\alpha \ x) \ \{ \ \textbf{return } e; \ \}$
Expressions	$e ::= x \mid c \mid e.a \mid e.m(e) \mid \textbf{new } C(\widetilde{e})$

We assume an infinite set of names, with some special names: *Object* denotes the root class, **this** denotes the current object and **super** denotes the parent object. We let $A, B, \ldots$ range over classes; $a, b, \ldots$ over fields; $m, n, \ldots$ over methods and $x, y, z, \ldots$ over variables.

A program $(\tilde{L}, e)$ is a pair of a sequence of class declarations $\tilde{L}$, giving rise to a class hierarchy as specified by the inheritance relation, and an expression e to be evaluated. A class declaration L specifies the name of the class, the name of the parent class it extends, its typed fields, the constructor K and its method declarations M. The constructor K initialises the fields of the object by assigning values to the fields inherited by the super-class and to the fields declared in the current **this** class. A method declaration M specifies the signature of the method, namely the return type, the method name and the formal parameter as well as the body of the method. Notice that in our theoretical development we use unary methods, without loss of generality: tuples of arguments can be modelled by an object that instantiates a "special" class containing as fields all the needed arguments. Expressions e include variables, constants, field access, method call and object creation.

Following FJ [17], we rule out ill-formed programs, such as declaring a constructor named B within a class named A, or multiple fields or methods having the same name, or fields having the same type as the class they are defined in.

3   The SFJ Language

3.1   On Valid Type Definitions

Since we want to use types τ to program in SFJ, we restrict them to *finite trees* whose leaves are basic types $\mathbb{B}$ Sect. 2.2 with no cycles. For example, a recursive type $\alpha = [a : \alpha]$ denotes an infinite program tree **new** $C(\textbf{new } C(\cdots))$, hence we rule it out as it is not inhabitable. Similarly, the types $\alpha = [b : \beta]$, $\beta = [a = \alpha]$ create a cycle and thus would not be inhabitable. Notice that these types can be defined and inhabited in Java by assigning *null* to all fields in a class, however they are not useful in practice.

SFJ is implemented using ANTLR [24]. We start by defining the grammar of the language in Extended Backus-Naur Form (EBNF), following Sect. 2.1 and by running ANTLR, we can automatically generate a parser for SFJ and extend it in order to implement the required checks for our types and type system.

Running the parser on an SFJ program returns an abstract syntax tree (AST) of that program. When visiting the AST, we check if the program is well-formed, following the intuition at the end of Sect. 2. We mark any classes containing only fields typed with basic types as *resolved*, otherwise we mark them as *unresolved*. Using this information, Algorithm 1 checks if the type definitions in a program are valid, namely if they are finite trees whose leaves are basic types with no cycles. The algorithm returns *True* only if all the types in the SFJ program are resolved, otherwise it returns *False*, meaning there is at least one type definition which is invalid and contains a cycle.

Algorithm 1: Validity Check for Type Definitions

Input   : *classes*, the set of classes in an SFJ program marked *resolved*, if their fields contain only basic types, *unresolved* otherwise.

Output : *True* if all classes are valid type definitions, *False* otherwise.

```
 1 begin
 2 │   do
 3 │   │   resolutionOccured ⟵ False
 4 │   │   for class that is unresolved in classes do
 5 │   │   │   resolved ⟵ True
 6 │   │   │   for field in class that contains a class type do
 7 │   │   │   │   if type of field is unresolved then
 8 │   │   │   │   │   resolved ⟵ False
 9 │   │   │   │   end
10 │   │   │   end
11 │   │   │
12 │   │   │   if resolved = True then
13 │   │   │   │   class ⟵ resolved
14 │   │   │   │   resolutionOccured ⟵ True
15 │   │   │   end
16 │   │   end
17 │   while resolutionOccured = True
18 │
19 │   if not all classes are resolved then
20 │   │   return False
21 │   else
22 │   │   return True
23 │   end
24 end
```

3.2   Building Semantic Subtyping for SFJ

If Algorithm 1 returns *True*, meaning all type definitions in a program are valid, we can then build the semantic subtyping. Leveraging the interpretation of types as sets of values to define semantic subtyping for FJ [11,12], in SFJ we keep track of the semantic subtyping relation by defining a map from a type to the set of its subtypes, satisfying the property that the set of values of a subtype is included in the set of values of the type.

Algorithm 2: Semantic Subtyping for SFJ—*generateRelation*

Input   : *classes*, the set of classes in an SFJ program.
               relation, the mapping of types to the set of subtypes, initially Map 3.1.

```
 1  begin
 2  │   Function generateRelation(classes: List<Class>):
 3  │   │   unprocessed : List < Class > ⟵ []
 4  │   │   for class in classes do
 5  │   │   │   if addClass(class) = False then
 6  │   │   │   │   unprocessed.add(class)
 7  │   │   │   end
 8  │   │   end
 9  │   │   if untyped ≠ [] then
10  │   │   │   generateRelation(unprocessed)
11  │   │   end
12  │   end
13  │
    │   /* algorithm continued on next page... */
```

We start with basic types and let *Universe* be a supertype of all types. The full mapping for basic types is defined in Map 3.1.

$$
\begin{aligned}
Double &= \{Double, Float, Int, Short, Byte\} \quad Float = \{Float, Short, Byte\} \\
Long &= \{Long, Int, Short, Byte\} \qquad\qquad\quad Int = \{Int, Short, Byte\} \\
Short &= \{Short, Byte\} \qquad\qquad\qquad\qquad\quad Byte = \{Byte\} \\
Boolean &= \{Boolean\} \qquad\qquad\qquad\qquad\quad\; Void = \{Void\} \\
Universe &= \{Double, Float, Long, Int, \\
&\qquad Short, Byte, Boolean, Void\}
\end{aligned}
$$

$$(3.1)$$

Note that *Int* is not a subtype of *Float* as a 32-bit *float* cannot represent the whole set of 32-bit *integer* values accurately and therefore *Int* is not fully set-contained in *Float*, however this is not the case for *Int* and *Double*. Similarly, *Long* is not a subtype of *Double*.

Algorithm 2 builds the semantic subtyping relation for all class types of an SFJ program by calling the function *generateRelation*. Given that classes are valid type definitions by Algorithm 1, we are guaranteed that Algorithm 2 will terminate.

The semantic subtyping generated by Algorithm 2 is a preorder: it is reflexive and transitive. This is also illustrated by Map 3.1.

Some comments on Algorithm 2 follow. In function *generateRelation* we iterate over the set of classes in an SFJ program. If the class currently being processed contains types in its fields or methods not present in the subtyping relation (lines 5 and 30, 42 in the continuation of the algorithm in the next page), then we add the current class to the list of *unprocessed* classes (line 6) so we can process its fields and methods first and the class itself later after having all required

---

Algorithm 2: Semantic Subtyping for SFJ—*addClass* and *checkSuperSet*

```
     /* ...algorithm continued from previous page */
13
14   Function addClass(class: Class) → boolean:
15       for existing class type in relation do
16           if checkSuperSet(class, existingClass) = False then
17               return False
18           end
19           checkSuperSet(existingClass, class)
20       end
21       relation[class].add(class)
22       relation[Universe].add(class)
23       return True
24   end
25
26   Function checkSuperSet(class: Class, other: Class) → boolean:
27       flag ⟵ True
28       for field in class do
29           if field contains type not in relation then
30               return False
31           end
32           if other does not contain field then
33               flag ⟵ False
34           else
35               if other.field.types does not fully contain field.types then
36                   flag ⟵ False
37               end
38           end
39       end
40       for method in class do
41           if method contains type not in relation then
42               return False
43           end
44           if other does not contain method then
45               flag ⟵ False
46           else
47               if other.method.types does not fully contain method.types then
48                   flag ⟵ False
49               end
50           end
51       end
52       if flag = True then
53           relation[other].add
54       end
55   end
56 end
```

type information. The set of unprocessed classes will then be inspected again in a recursive call (line 10).

The next two functions of the algorithm, *addClass* and *checkSuperSet* given in the next page, check subtyping for the current *class* being processed and update *relation*, which is a mapping from a type to its subtypes and originally only consists of entries from Map 3.1. In function *addClass(class)* we check if the type *class* is a subtype of an existing type in *relation* (lines 15–18), as well as the opposite, meaning if *class* is a supertype of an existing type in *relation* (line 19). In order to do so *checkSuperSet* checks all fields (lines 28–39) and all methods (lines 40–51) in *class* and compares them with an *existingClass* in *relation*. If a subtyping relation is established, then it is added to *relation* (line 53). Finally, upon returning from *checkSuperSet*, we also add *class* to its own relation (line 21) to satisfy reflexivity and to *Universe* (line 22), which is a supertype of all types.

It is worth noticing that the subtyping algorithm finds all nominal and structural subtypes of a given type. This is due to the fact that all pairs of types are inspected. Recall from Sect. 1 that nominal subtyping is name-based and given by the class hierarchy defined by the programmer, whereas structural subtyping is structure-based and given by the set-inclusion of fields and methods. In particular, structural subtyping is contra-variant with respect to this set-inclusion. Algorithm 2 finds all structural subtypes of a given class because it checks that its fields and methods are a superset of existing types in *relation*. For example, all classes are structural subtypes of type *empty* = []. On the other hand, it also finds all nominal subtypes because a class inherits all fields and methods of its superclass and as such its fields and methods are a superset of its superclass. This means that checking for structural subtyping is enough because nominal subtyping will be captured due to inheritance of fields and methods.

Finally, a note on complexity. The complexity of Algorithm 1 is $\mathcal{O}(n)$, and the complexity of Algorithm 2 is $\mathcal{O}(n^2)$, with n being the size of the input. The reason for a quadratic complexity of Algorithm 2 is due to the symmetric check of structural subtyping between a *class* and an *existingClass* in *relation*. Notice that if we were to only work with nominal subtyping, then we would only require traversing the class hierarchy once, which gives an $\mathcal{O}(n)$ complexity.

3.3 Type System for SFJ

The type system for the SFJ language, given in Sect. 2.2, is based on the type system by Dardha *et al.* [11,12] where the formal typing rules and soundness properties are detailed. As these formal developments are beyond the scope of this paper, we discuss typing for SFJ only informally.

A program $(\tilde{L}, e)$ is well typed if both $\tilde{L}$ and e are well typed. Class declaration L and method declaration M are well typed if all their components are well typed. Let us move onto expressions E. Field access $e.a$, method call $e.m(e)$ and object creation **new** $C(\tilde{e})$ are typed in the same way as in Java: we inspect the type of the field and the type of the method and its arguments to determine the type of the field access and method call, respectively. The type of an object creation is determined by the type of its class. Regarding constants, in order to respect the set-theoretic interpretation of types as sets of values, we type constants with the most restrictive type, i.e., the type representing the smallest set of values containing the value itself. For example, the type system would assign to the value 42 the type **byte**, which is the smallest in the sequence **byte, short, int** (see Map 3.1 for details).

Finally, the subtyping relation generated by Algorithm 2 is used in the type system for the SFJ language via a subsumption typing rule:

$$\frac{\Gamma \vdash e : \alpha_1 \qquad \alpha_1 \leq \alpha_2}{\Gamma \vdash e : \alpha_2}$$

We read this typing rule as follows: if an expression e is of type α_1 under a typing context Γ (details of a typing context are irrelevant here) and type α is a subtype $\leq$ of α_2, then expression e can be typed with α_2.

3.4 Polygons: Continued

Let us illustrate the semantic subtyping algorithm on our *Polygons* given in Example 1. Algorithm 2 generates the subtyping relation given in Map 3.2, together with the subtyping relation for basic types, omitted here and defined in Map 3.1. Notice that the mapping for *Universe* is extended with the new types for polygons.

$$
\begin{aligned}
Polygon &= \{Polygon, Triangle, Square, Rhombus\} \quad Triangle = \{Triangle\}\\
Square &= \{Square\} \qquad\qquad\qquad\qquad\qquad\quad Rhombus = \{Rhombus\}\\
Universe &= \{Double, Float, Long, Int, Short, Byte \quad Diagonal = \{Diagonal\}\\
&\qquad Boolean, Void, Polygon, Square\\
&\qquad Square, Rhombus, Diagonal\}
\end{aligned}
$$

$$(3.2)$$

Recall the method *diagonal* in class *Diagonal*, with signature

double *diagonal*((*Polygon* **and not** *Triangle*) *shape*)

The result of the set operation on its parameter type gives the following set of polygons:

Polygon **and not** *Triangle* = {*Polygon, Square, Rhombus*}

In order to define the **not** *Triangle* type we need the *Universe* type so that we can define it as $Universe \setminus Triangle$. Then, the **and** connective is the intersection of sets of *Polygon* with **not** *Triangle*.

If we write in our SFJ program the following expression:

(**new** *Diagonal*()).*diagonal*(**new** *Square*())

the argument **new** *Square*() of the *diagonal* method is of type *Square*, by the type system in Sect. 3.3 and *Square* is contained in the set of the parameter type of the method, so this expression will successfully type-checks.

However, if we write the following SFJ expression:

$$(\mathbf{new}\ Diagonal()).diagonal(\mathbf{new}\ Triangle())$$

Type $Triangle$ is not contained in $\{Polygon, Square, Rhombus\}$, therefore this expression will not type-check and will return a type error at compile time.

This is further illustrated in the accompanying video of this paper [27].

3.5   Nominal vs. Structural Subtyping

In this section we will comment on pros and cons of nominal vs. structural subtyping.

Structural subtyping allows for more flexibility in defining this relation and the user does not need to explicitly definite it, as would do with nominal subtyping. However, for this flexibility we might need to pay in meaning. For example, consider the following two structurally equivalent classes, hence record types $coordinate = [x : int, y : int, z : int]$ and $colour = [x : int, y : int, z : int]$. While they can be used interchangeably in a type system using structural subtyping, their "meaning" is different and we might want to prohibit it, because intuitively speaking we do not want to use a $colour$ where a $coordinate$ is expected.

On the other hand, while nominal subtyping can avoid the above problem, it can introduce others and in particular, a developer can define an overridden method to perform the opposite logic to what the super class is expecting, as illustrated by the following classes in Java:

```
class A extends Object {          class B extends A {
        ...                              ...
    int n;                           int length(){ return −n; }
    int length(){ return n; }    }
}
```

Both approaches have their pros and cons, and they leave an expectation on the developer to use the logic behind subtyping correctly when writing code. The integration of both subtyping approaches in SFJ gives the developer the freedom to choose the most suitable subtyping relation to use for a given task.

3.6   Methods in SFJ

On Multimethods. Since FJ is a core language, some features of the full Java are removed, such as overloading methods. In our framework, by leveraging the expressivity of boolean connectives and semantic subtyping, we are able to restore overloading, among other features [12, §8.4]. We can thus model *multimethods*, [5], which according to the authors is *"very clean and easy to understand [...] it would be the best solution for a brand new language"*. As an example, taken from Dardha *et al.* [11,12], consider the following class declarations:

```
class A extends Object {            class B extends A {
    int length (string s){ ... }        int length (int n){ ... }
}                                   }
```

Method *length* has type **string** → **int** in class A. However, because class B extends class A, *length* has type (**string** → **int**) **and** (**int** → **int**) in class B, which can be simplified to (**string or int**) → **int**.

Method Types. Let us illustrate the method types given in Sect. 2.1 via an alternative implementation of the class *Diagonal* at the end of Example 1.

```
class Diagonal {
        ...
    double diagonal((diagonal : void → double) shape)
                { return  shape.diagonal(); }
}
```

We define the type of the (outside) *diagonal* method as accepting any type and its subtypes implementing the (inside) *diagonal* method with type signature **void** to **double**.

In order to type check an argument passed to the (outside) *diagonal* method, at compile time we build a collection of types $\{type_1, type_2, \ldots\}$ which are class types where the (inside) *diagonal* method is defined. As such, we iterate over the list of *classes* in an SFJ program (as we did in Algorithm 2) to check for the required method. The resulting collection of types is the union of all classes where *diagonal* is defined together with their subtypes ($[\![type_1]\!] \cup [\![type_2]\!] \cup \ldots$), where each $[\![type_i]\!]$ denotes a mapping of $type_i$ to the set of its subtypes, similar to Map 3.2.

However, calculating this collection of types for each method of every class would be computationally inefficient and most importantly unnecessary as only few methods would in turn be used as method types. Therefore we only compute them on demand during type-checking when we come across such a type.

We can therefore use method types to statically include or exclude a portion of our class hierarchy. However, unlike with interfaces as in Example 1, the values that can be accepted by a method type do not have to be related to each other in any way in the class hierarchy. This indeed is useful if we are dealing with legacy code as we can still accept all classes where *diagonal* is defined, without having to go back and add interface implementations.

3.7   Code Generation

SFJ only includes the typechecking component of the language. In this section, we provide a sketch of the code generation algorithm, which is work in progress.

Given the similarity of SFJ to Java, our approach is to translate an SFJ program into Java bytecode and then run it on the Java Virtual Machine (JVM) [19]. This is a standard approach also used by other object-oriented languages, for example, Kotlin[1].

The main challenge in translating SFJ into bytecode is translating types using boolean connectives. For example, a field f_1 of type **int or bool**, will be translated as two Java fields, one of type **int** and one of type **bool**, and only one of the two types will be inhabited by a value. In order to achieve this, we first analyse our program and reduce the boolean types by keeping only the alternatives which actually get used in the program. For example, if the field of type **int or bool** only ever gets initialised with a boolean value, we can reduce it and make it a field of a single type **bool**. After this reduction phase, we then consider the remaining types which use boolean connectives and could not be reduced. On the example above, consider again field f_1 of type **int or bool**. This will be translated as two fields **int**_f_1 and **bool**_f_1 with the corresponding types. In order to initialise these fields, we use the constructor overloading capabilities of the JVM to generate an overloaded version for each alternative type. In each constructor, only the field that matches the type of the parameter is initialised with all other fields set to *null*. To access the field of an object, we generate code that checks each alternative of the field if it is non-null and includes the rest of the code generation for the expression for each branch. At run time, only one branch will be true, and this is the branch of generated code which will be executed.

For methods, we also use the overloading capabilities of the JVM to define an overloaded method for each type in the expanded method parameter, all with the same method body. Depending on which alternative the argument inhabits at run time, a different method will be dispatched to. Like methods with boolean types, we similarly implement methods with method types, as we discussed in Sect. 3.6, by defining an overloaded alternative for each type that implements the specified method. This concludes the code generation phase for all expressions in SFJ given in Sect. 2.2.

4 Related Work and Conclusion

Semantic subtyping goes back to more than two decades ago [1,10]. Hosoya and Pierce [14–16] define XDuce, an XML-oriented language designed specifically to transform XML documents in other XML documents satisfying certain properties. Frisch *et al.* [13] extend XDuce by introducing less XML specific types such as records, boolean connectives and arrow types, and implement it as CDuce. Their work is similar to ours in that our class-based semantic type system is a combination of the CDuce record types with arrow types. Castagna *et al.* define $\mathbb{C}\pi$ [7], a variant of the asynchronous π-calculus, where channel types are augmented with boolean connectives; semantic subtyping for ML-like languages [8] and semantic subtyping in a gradual typing framework [6]. Ancona

---
[1] https://kotlinlang.org/

and Lagorio [3] define subtyping for infinite types by using union and object type constructors, where types are interpreted as sets of values of the language. Bonsangue *et al.* [4] study a coalgebraic approach to coinductive types and define a set-theoretic interpretation of coinductive types with union types. Pearce [26] defines semantic subtyping for rewriting rules in the Whiley Rewrite Language and for a flow-typing calculus [25].

Regarding implementations of semantic subtyping, to the best of our knowledge, there are only a few works in the literature. Muehlboeck and Tate [23] define a syntactic framework with boolean connectives which has been implemented in the Ceylon programming language [18]. Ancona and Corradi [2] define semantic subtyping for an imperative object-oriented language with mutable fields. In our framework we are considering only the functional fragment of Java, which is FJ, and as a result the semantic subtyping framework is simpler. The authors also propose a prototype implementation of their subtyping algorithm. Chaudhuri *et al.* [9] present the design and implementation of FLOW, which is a type checker for JavaScript. They use boolean connectives **and**, **not**, **or** for their predicates, however they do not define semantic subtyping for their language.

In this paper we presented the design and implementation of SFJ—Semantic Featherweight Java, an extension of Featherweight Java featuring boolean types, semantic subtyping, and integrating both nominal and structural subtyping. Due to the expressivity of semantic subtyping, in SFJ we are able to restore standard Java constructs and features for example, lists and overloading meathods, which were not present in FJ, thus making SFJ a more complete language. We presented Algorithm 1 on validity of type definitions and Algorithm 2 on semantic subtyping, which finds all nominal and structural subtypes for all types in an SFJ program. We also described typing of terms in SFJ, which follows that of Java and builds upon relevant work [11,12]. As future work, we aim to finalise the code generation phase, which is sketched in Sect. 3.7.

References

1. Aiken, A., Wimmers, E.L.: Type inclusion constraints and type inference. In: Proceedings of the Conference on Functional Programming Languages and Computer Architecture, FPCA, pp. 31–41. ACM, New York (1993). https://doi.org/10.1145/165180.165188
2. Ancona, D., Corradi, A.: Semantic subtyping for imperative object-oriented languages. In: Visser, E., Smaragdakis, Y. (eds.) Proceedings of the International Conference on Object-Oriented Programming, Systems, Languages, and Applications, OOPSLA, pp. 568–587. ACM (2016). https://doi.org/10.1145/2983990.2983992
3. Ancona, D., Lagorio, G.: Coinductive subtyping for abstract compilation of object-oriented languages into horn formulas. In: Proceedings of the Symposium on Games, Automata, Logic, and Formal Verification, GANDALF, EPTCS, vol. 25, pp. 214–230 (2010). https://doi.org/10.4204/EPTCS.25.20
4. Bonsangue, M., Rot, J., Ancona, D., de Boer, F., Rutten, J.: A coalgebraic foundation for coinductive union types. In: Esparza, J., Fraigniaud, P., Husfeldt, T., Koutsoupias, E. (eds.) ICALP 2014. LNCS, vol. 8573, pp. 62–73. Springer, Heidelberg (2014). https://doi.org/10.1007/978-3-662-43951-7_6

5. Boyland, J., Castagna, G.: Parasitic methods: an implementation of multi-methods for Java. In: Proceedings of the Conference on Object-Oriented Programming Systems, Languages & Applications OOPSLA, pp. 66–76. ACM (1997). https://doi.org/10.1145/263698.263721

6. Castagna, G., Lanvin, V.: Gradual typing with union and intersection types. Proc. ACM Program. Lang. 1(ICFP), 41:1–41:28 (2017). https://doi.org/10.1145/3110285

7. Castagna, G., Nicola, R.D., Varacca, D.: Semantic subtyping for the pi-calculus. Theor. Comput. Sci. 398(1–3), 217–242 (2008). https://doi.org/10.1016/j.tcs.2008.01.049

8. Castagna, G., Petrucciani, T., Nguyen, K.: Set-theoretic types for polymorphic variants. In: Garrigue, J., Keller, G., Sumii, E. (eds.) Proceedings of the International Conference on Functional Programming, ICFP, pp. 378–391. ACM (2016). https://doi.org/10.1145/2951913.2951928

9. Chaudhuri, A., Vekris, P., Goldman, S., Roch, M., Levi, G.: Fast and precise type checking for Javascript. In: Proceedings of the International Conference on Object-Oriented Programming, Systems, Languages, and Applications, OOPSLA, vol. 1, pp. 481–4830 (2017). https://doi.org/10.1145/3133872

10. Damm, F.M.: Subtyping with union types, intersection types and recursive types. In: Hagiya, M., Mitchell, J.C. (eds.) TACS 1994. LNCS, vol. 789, pp. 687–706. Springer, Heidelberg (1994). https://doi.org/10.1007/3-540-57887-0_121

11. Dardha, O., Gorla, D., Varacca, D.: Semantic subtyping for objects and classes. In: Beyer, D., Boreale, M. (eds.) FMOODS/FORTE -2013. LNCS, vol. 7892, pp. 66–82. Springer, Heidelberg (2013). https://doi.org/10.1007/978-3-642-38592-6_6

12. Dardha, O., Gorla, D., Varacca, D.: Semantic subtyping for objects and classes. Comput. J. 60(5), 636–656 (2017). https://doi.org/10.1093/comjnl/bxw080

13. Frisch, A., Castagna, G., Benzaken, V.: Semantic subtyping: dealing set-theoretically with function, union, intersection, and negation types. J. ACM 55(4), 1–64 (2008). https://doi.org/10.1145/1391289.1391293

14. Hosoya, H., Pierce, B.C.: Regular expression pattern matching for XML. SIGPLAN Not. 36(3), 67–80 (2001). https://doi.org/10.1145/373243.360209

15. Hosoya, H., Pierce, B.C.: XDuce: a statically typed XML processing language. ACM Trans. Internet Technol. 3(2), 117–148 (2003). https://doi.org/10.1145/767193.767195

16. Hosoya, H., Vouillon, J., Pierce, B.C.: Regular expression types for XML. ACM Trans. Program. Lang. Syst. 27(1), 46–90 (2005). https://doi.org/10.1145/1053468.1053470

17. Igarashi, A., Pierce, B.C., Wadler, P.: Featherweight Java: a minimal core calculus for Java and GJ. ACM Trans. Program. Lang. Syst. 23(3), 396–450 (2001). https://doi.org/10.1145/503502.503505

18. King, G.: The Ceylon Language Specification, Version 1.3 (2016). https://ceylon-lang.org/documentation/1.3/spec/

19. Lindholm, T., Yellin, F., Bracha, G., Buckley, A.: Java Virtual Machine Specification, Java SE 7 Edition: Java Virt Mach Spec Java_3. Addison-Wesley (2013)

20. Liskov, B.H., Wing, J.M.: A behavioral notion of subtyping. ACM Trans. Program. Lang. Syst. 16(6), 1811–1841 (1994). https://doi.org/10.1145/197320.197383

21. Malayeri, D., Aldrich, J.: Integrating nominal and structural subtyping. In: Vitek, J. (ed.) ECOOP 2008. LNCS, vol. 5142, pp. 260–284. Springer, Heidelberg (2008). https://doi.org/10.1007/978-3-540-70592-5_12

22. Malayeri, D., Aldrich, J.: Is structural subtyping useful? An empirical study. In: Castagna, G. (ed.) ESOP 2009. LNCS, vol. 5502, pp. 95–111. Springer, Heidelberg (2009). https://doi.org/10.1007/978-3-642-00590-9_8

23. Muehlboeck, F., Tate, R.: Empowering union and intersection types with integrated subtyping. Proc. Conf. Object-Oriented Program. Syst. Lang. Appl. OOPSLA **2**, 1–29 (2018). https://doi.org/10.1145/3276482

24. Parr, T.: The Definitive ANTLR 4 Reference. Pragmatic Bookshelf (2013)

25. Pearce, D.J.: Sound and complete flow typing with unions, intersections and negations. In: Giacobazzi, R., Berdine, J., Mastroeni, I. (eds.) VMCAI 2013. LNCS, vol. 7737, pp. 335–354. Springer, Heidelberg (2013). https://doi.org/10.1007/978-3-642-35873-9_21

26. Pearce, D.J.: On declarative rewriting for sound and complete union, intersection and negation types. J. Comput. Lang. **50**, 84–101 (2019). https://doi.org/10.1016/j.jvlc.2018.10.004

27. Usov, A., Dardha, O.: SFJ: An implementation of Semantic Featherweight Java, On YouTube and on Dardha's website (2020). https://youtu.be/oTFIjm0A2O8, http://www.dcs.gla.ac.uk/~ornela/publications/SFJ.mp4

Service-Oriented Computing

Event-Based Customization
of Multi-tenant SaaS Using Microservices

Espen Tønnessen Nordli[1], Phu H. Nguyen[2]([⊠]) [iD], Franck Chauvel[2],
and Hui Song[2]

[1] University of Oslo, Oslo, Norway
espentno@ifi.uio.no
[2] SINTEF, Oslo, Norway
{phu.nguyen,franck.chauvel,hui.song}@sintef.no

Abstract. Popular enterprise software such as ERP, CRM is now being made available on the Cloud in the multi-tenant Software as a Service (SaaS) model. The added values come from the ability of vendors to enable customer-specific business advantage for every different tenant who uses the same main enterprise software product. Software vendors need novel customization solutions for Cloud-based multi-tenant SaaS. In this paper, we present an event-based approach in a non-intrusive customization framework that can enable customization for multi-tenant SaaS and address the problem of too many API calls to the main software product. The experimental results on Microsoft's eShopOnContainers show that our approach can empower an event bus with the ability to customize the flow of processing events, and integrate with tenant-specific microservices for customization. We have shown how our approach makes sure of tenant-isolation, which is crucial in practice for SaaS vendors. This direction can also reduce the number of API calls to the main software product, even when every tenant has different customization services.

Keywords: Microservices · Architecture · Event-based · Cloud · SaaS · Customization · IoT · Edge · Security

1 Introduction

Most businesses and public services rely on enterprise software such as enterprise resource planning (ERP) or customer relationship management (CRM), to name a few. Because every company has its unique organization, processes and culture, no off-the-shelf software directly fits. Companies eventually *customize* these software systems to meet their specific requirements. For simple

---

The research leading to these results has received funding from the European Commission's H2020 Programme under the grant agreement number 780351 (ENACT), and from the Research Council of Norway under the grant agreement numbers 296651 (ASAM) and 256594 (Cirrus).

© IFIP International Federation for Information Processing 2020
Published by Springer Nature Switzerland AG 2020
S. Bliudze and L. Bocchi (Eds.): COORDINATION 2020, LNCS 12134, pp. 171–180, 2020.
https://doi.org/10.1007/978-3-030-50029-0_11

scenarios, software vendors predict where and how their software products may be customized, and provide their customers with application programming interfaces (API), extension points or configuration choices. However, there are always customers whose requirements overstep the embedded customization capacity. These customers need the vendors to provide mechanisms for performing *deep customization*, that goes beyond the vendors' prediction.

Deep customization may affect any parts of a software product, including the user interface (UI), the business logic (BL), the database schemas (DB) or any combination thereof. When a software product used to be deployed on the customers' premises, each customer naturally ran its own customized version, in full isolation. Nowadays, software vendors are migrating their software products to the Cloud. In the Cloud-based multi-tenant software-as-a-service (SaaS) model, however, every customer must run the same code base (main product), which cannot be directly modified for one customer without affecting other customers. Software vendors desperately need novel deep customization solutions for the Cloud-based multi-tenant SaaS model.

More recently, leveraging the microservices architecture [1,6,14] for enabling deep customization of multi-tenant SaaS is a very promising direction as presented in [8–12]. These microservices-based customization approaches vary in how they balance *isolation* and *assimilation*. Isolation guarantees tenant-specific customization only affects that one single tenant, whereas assimilation guarantees that customization capability can alter anything in the main software product. Intrusive microservices [9,10,12] provide tight assimilation at the cost of security (tenant isolation), whereas the non-intrusive approach called MiSC-Cloud [7,8,11] trades assimilation for higher security. MiSC-Cloud orchestrates customization using microservices via API gateways.

In this paper, we present an event-based non-intrusive deep customization approach for multi-tenant SaaS using microservices as part of the MiSC-Cloud framework [8]. The event-based approach, in combination with the synchronous way of customization in [8], shows how the MiSC-Cloud framework can coordinate the execution of the BL components (microservices) of the main product as well as the customization microservices of tenants to obtain the desired customization effects in the multi-tenant context.

The remainder of this paper is structured as follows: Sect. 2 defines deep customization. Then, Sect. 3 presents the event-based customization approach with key techniques. In Sect. 4, we show a proof-of-concept for the proposed approach by applying it on a reference application for microservice architecture by Microsoft . Section 5 discusses related work. Finally, we provide in Sect. 6 our conclusions and possible future research directions.

2   Deep Customization

By contrast with other customization means such as settings, scripting languages or API, deep customization demands that one can possibly make *any* change to the system, as one can do with direct access to the source code. Changes can, therefore, affect the user interface (UI), the business logic (BL), the database schema (DB), or any combination thereof. Deep customization turns out difficult in multi-tenant SaaS environments, where all tenants originally run the same code (UI, BL and DB). Tenant-specific customization must affect only one single tenant. This work focuses on the customization of BL, especially based on events. In this way, customization microservices communicate with the main product, either in a synchronous way by requesting data and waiting for the response (RPC-like), or in an asynchronous way, by publishing and subscribing to events (pub/sub). The customization of UI and DB can be found in [8–12].

3   Event-Based Customization Approach

In this section, we first present the main components for enabling event-based customization of multi-tenant SaaS in Sect. 3.1. Then, Sect. 3.2 details how the event-based customization approach works. In Sect. 3.3, we discuss how the event-based customization fulfils the requirements of tenant isolation.

3.1   Main Components for Enabling Event-Based Customization

Among the five main components of the `MiSC-Cloud` framework as presented in [7,8], we focus on presenting the `Tenant Manager` and the Event Bus as the key parts of the event-based customization approach. The `API gateways`, `IAM Service`, and `WebMVC Customizer` are the same as we described in [8].

The `Tenant Manager` is a service that manages the registration of customization microservices including the events registered for customization for different tenants. The service has a simple database that stores all the tenants that are using the application, all the different events that exist in the main product and finally all the customization microservices that exist for tenants and specific events. Additionally, it stores an endpoint for each customization that is used for halting the flow of events to be discussed further in the next section.

The `Event Bus` is key to enable event-based customization. Therefore, the prerequisite for enabling event-based customization is that the main product already has (part of) its logic flow orchestrated via events. If the main product already has an `Event Bus`, such an `Event Bus` can be extended to enable event-based customization. If the main product does not have an `Event Bus`, a new one can be introduced as presented in [8]. It is important to note that a software product can be re-engineered to enable event-based logic orchestration at the back-end via an `Event Bus`. Different migration approaches from monolithic to microservices architecture already show some patterns and practices to migrate from synchronous calls into event-based communication between microservices [4,13]. Moreover, software vendors can also create user or system events within their software product to allow authorized event-based integration with external systems (of their customers). This event-based integration is similar to the traditional way of offering a rich REST API for synchronous integration, e.g., using traditional GET-PUT-POST statements.

3.2   Event-Based Customization Flow

A customization microservice can subscribe to an event that is published to the Event Bus when something notable happens, such as when another microservice (of the main product or another tenant-specific customization) updates a business entity. When a microservice receives an event, it can update its business entities, which might lead to the publishing of more events. We design the event bus as a multi-tenant interface with the tenant-specific APIs needed to subscribe and unsubscribe to events and to publish events.

The flow of processing events in the original `Event Bus` implementation must be changed for customization purposes. Before publishing events to the consumers, it checks with the `Tenant Manager` for any customization that has been registered for any event and tenant (see Fig. 1). If an event is not customized, then the event is processed in the standard fashion. In the case that an event is customized, the event is sent to the endpoint that is part of the response from the `Tenant Manager`. At this point, the tenant's microservice is responsible for storing the event until the required customization has been achieved. Then, the tenant's microservice can republish the event to the Event Bus, along with a flag that instructs the `Event Bus` to not check for customization again, to avoid an infinite loop.

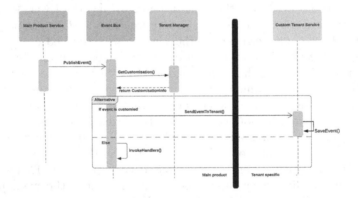

Fig. 1. Event-based customization flow.

In some cases, customization microservices would require some execution context from the main product that does not exist in the events that they receive. To obtain such context, customization microservices can make authorized synchronous calls to the APIs of the main product as presented in [8]. In fact, events often contain enough execution context for customization microservices to execute customization scenarios. This means that only a few special customization scenarios would require such synchronous calls from customization microservices to the API of the main product. Combining the synchronous and asynchronous ways of customization can offer a more complete non-intrusive customization approach for multi-tenant SaaS. However, we recommend the use of event-based customization for as many customization scenarios as possible to reduce the traffic of API calls to the main product, which often leads to performance bottleneck when there are many customized tenants with unpredictable loads.

3.3 Tenant-Isolation and Tenant-Specific Event-Handlers

The Event Bus implementation and architecture in the main product must ensure that tenant isolation is still preserved. Instead of having one connection to a single event bus, there must be multiple connections, one per tenant. One example of such an event bus implementation is based on RabbitMQ that can make use of virtual hosts[1]. This way allows us to have a logical separation per tenant, and the permission can easily be set so that each tenant is only allowed to interact with its own virtual host.

4 Proof-of-Concept and Evaluation

In this section, we show a proof of concept of our approach for enabling deep customization of the eShopOnContainers by extending the Event Bus in the application. The .NET Microservices Sample Reference Application eShopOn-Containers[2] has been chosen for a couple of reasons. First, eShopOnContainers has a clear separation between the user interface and the business logic of the application as a prerequisite of the MiSC-Cloud framework. Secondly, the application follows the microservices architecture, and as such, has loose coupling as compared to a monolithic application. Finally, the collaboration between the microservices that the application as a whole is made up of is done using events and a publish/subscribe system.

An Event Bus implementation must be associated with the authentication and authorization mechanisms of the IAM service for multi-tenant SaaS-based on Open ID Connect or OAuth 2.0. As an implementation of RabbitMQ already exists in the eShopOnContainers, we have extended it to enable event-based customization.

Let us consider the original eShopOnContainers in the GitHub repository as the main product being customized. We show how our event-based customization approach can enable different customization scenarios for two tenants as the representatives of multi-tenant context[3]. The first use case in Sect. 4.1 adds new logic to the main flow of the ordering process, without altering any of the existing functionality. The second use case in Sect. 4.2 requires a modification of the existing logic of the ordering process by halting the flow of the order.

---

[1] https://www.rabbitmq.com/vhosts.html.

[2] https://github.com/dotnet-architecture/eShopOnContainers.

[3] https://github.com/Espent1004/eShopOnContainersCustomised.

4.1 Tenant A's Customization of the Ordering Process

The original ordering process is straightforward. After having logged in, a customer can add items in the shopping cart and then create an order with card payment and shipping address. What happens at the back-end is that the `Basket` service of the `eShopOnContainers` publishes a `UserCheckoutAcceptedIntegrationEvent`, which is consumed by the `Ordering` service to create and process the order, e.g., generating `OrderSubmittedIntegrationEvent`. `Tenant A` wants to change the original ordering process of `eShopOnContainers` to incorporate the shipping information from external (third-party) systems. This means that after the `Basket` service has published a `UserCheckoutAcceptedIntegrationEvent`, the `Ordering` service validates the order request before creating an order and an `OrderSubmittedIntegrationEvent` to trigger this customization. Here, we demonstrate the customization of Tenant A using the asynchronous way. The synchronous way of customization has been presented in [8].

The asynchronous way of customization has been used for the customization scenario in which the user has checked out (`UserCheckoutAcceptedIntegrationEvent`), and the corresponding order has been made (`OrderSubmittedIntegrationEvent`). The customization microservice `Shipping` of Tenant A intercepts the `OrderSubmittedIntegrationEvent` and queries an external system for an estimated time for delivery. This information is then stored in the microservice's database, which can then be retrieved whenever the `My Orders` page is displayed. The customization result can be seen in Fig. 2. The parts in red, e.g., `SHIPPING DATE`, are the customized content, which are only available for the users of Tenant A. What happens in the background is that we have added a new `Event Handler` that consumes the `OrderSubmittedIntegrationEvent`. Whenever this event is published by the main product to the event bus of Tenant A, the `Event Handler` consumes the event and calls the customization microservice `Shipping`, which is responsible for calculating the shipping information by integrating with an external system.

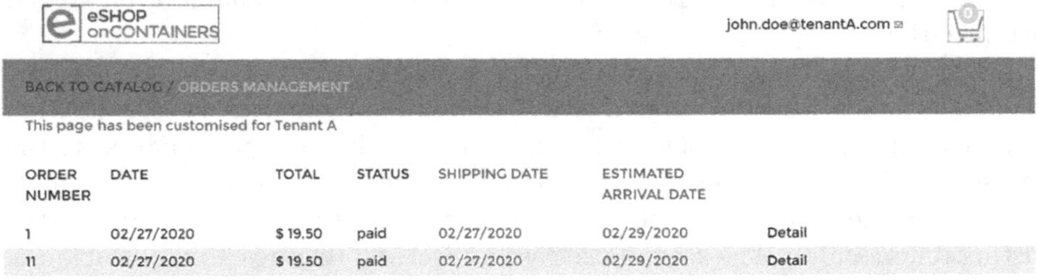
eSHOP onCONTAINERS
john.doe@tenantA.com
BACK TO CATALOG / ORDERS MANAGEMENT
This page has been customised for Tenant A
ORDER NUMBER
DATE
TOTAL
STATUS
SHIPPING DATE
ESTIMATED ARRIVAL DATE
1
02/27/2020
$ 19.50
paid
02/27/2020
02/29/2020
Detail
11
02/27/2020
$ 19.50
paid
02/27/2020
02/29/2020
Detail

Fig. 2. Customization of Tenant A: An estimated time for delivery.

4.2 Tenant B's Customization of the Ordering Process

Tenant B wants to customize the ordering process with some additional steps to mark all the items with RFID. Before the order status is set to confirmed, all the order lines in the order should be scanned. Further, the order status should only be set to confirmed when all the items in the order have been scanned.

The second use case requires that the status of the order is not set to confirmed until all the items in the order have been scanned. To ensure this, we need to halt the flow of the application by capturing the `OrderStatus-ChangedToAwaitingValidationIntegrationEvent`. This is done by registering this event for the specific tenant in the `Tenant Manager`, as well as the endpoint that we want the event to be sent to. Figure 3 shows the customization flow triggered by the `OrderStatusChangedToAwaitingValidationIntegrationEvent`. This event is then stored in the database of the microservice for this customization until the `RFIDTagScannedIntegrationEvent` is published by the `TenantARFIDService`.

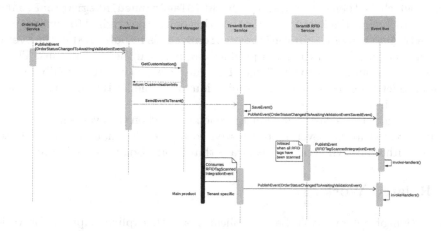

Fig. 3. Customization of Tenant B: The customization flow around the OrderStatus-ChangedToAwaitingValidationIntegrationEvent.

The customization scenario depicted in Fig. 3 starts when the `Ordering` service publishes the `OrderStatusChangedToAwaitingValidationIntegration-Event`. Next, the `Event Bus` implementation checks for any customization for this event by querying the `Tenant Manager`. As Tenant B has customized this event, the `Event Bus` sends the event to the endpoint specified in the response from the `Tenant Manager` rather than publishing to the RabbitMQ instance. At this point, the tenant has control of the event and can save it to the local database of Tenant B's `Event Service` before publishing `OrderStatusChangedToAwaitingValidationEventSavedEvent` to the

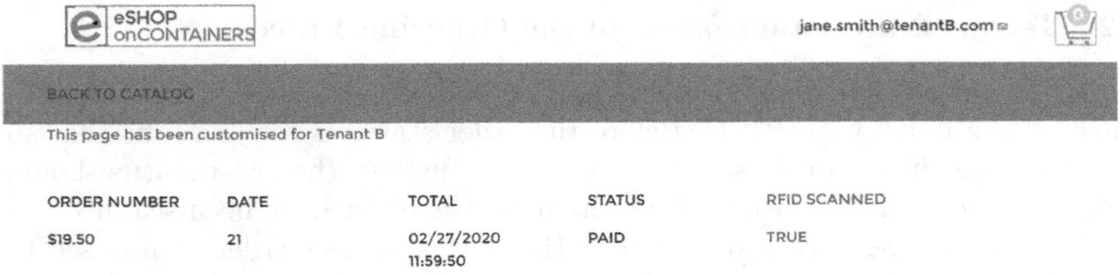

Fig. 4. Customization of Tenant B: After all the RFID tags have been scanned.

Event Bus. The `OrderStatusChangedToAwaitingValidationEventSavedEv-entHandler` in Tenant B's `RFID Service` consumes this event, and stores the necessary data in its database.

The next step of the use case is triggered whenever the endpoint in Tenant B's `RFID Service` is used to indicate that all the order lines have been scanned. The use of this endpoint also triggers `RFIDTagScannedIntegration-Event`, which is then consumed by the `RFIDTagScannedIntegrationEvent-Handler` in Tenant B's `Event Service`. At this point, the original `OrderStatus-ChangedToAwaitingValidationIntegrationEvent` is re-published to the `Event Bus`, and the handlers in the main product can perform their operations. Then, the event is re-published to the `Event Bus`, and it is processed normally by the main product. The result of the customization, after the RFID tags are scanned can be seen in Fig. 4.

The asynchronous customization approach is based on the events in the application. Because all the events are isolated so that each tenant is only able to interact with their own events. This means that tenant isolation is still preserved.

5   Related Work

The notion of customizable SaaS applications with explicit support for variability management has been proposed and explored extensively [3]. There are many technical approaches addressing these complexities, such as design patterns, dependency injection (DI), software product lines (SPL), or API. While these approaches help predefining customization at design time, they do not have sufficient support for the complex and unanticipated behavioural coordination between the custom code and the main product at runtime.

The majority of SaaS customization approaches focus on a high-level modification of the service composition. Mietzner and Leymann [5] present a customization approach based on the automatic transformation from a variability model to BPEL process. Here customization is a re-composition of services provided by vendors. Tsai and Sun [15] follow the same assumption but propose multiple layers of compositions. All the composite services are customizable until reaching atomic services, which are assumed to be provided by the vendors.

Middleware techniques can also support the customization of SaaS. Guo et al. [2] discuss, in a high abstraction level, a middleware-based framework for the development and operation of customization, and highlighted the key challenges. Walraven et al. [16] implemented such a customization, enabling middleware using Dependency Injection. The dependency injection way for customization allows the custom code developers to introduce arbitrary coordination behaviour with the main product, and thus achieve a strong expression power. However, it also brings tight coupling between the custom code and the main product. Operating the custom code as an external microservice eases performance isolation, misbehaviour of the custom code only fails the underlying container, and the main product only perceives a network error, which does not affect other tenants. Besides, external microservices ease management: scaling independently resource-consuming customization and eventually billing tenants accordingly.

6   Conclusions

In this paper, we have presented an event-based customization approach that is part of our non-intrusive customization framework for multi-tenant SaaS. This asynchronous way of customization means that customization microservices can have event-based communication with the main product BL components for customization purposes. Using event-based communication between customization microservices and the main product BL components is important not only for the microservices architecture but also for non-intrusive deep customization capability. Enabling customization both synchronously and asynchronously provides a more flexible way of coordinating the customization logic between the BL components (microservices) of the main product and the customization microservices of tenants to obtain the desired customization effects in the multi-tenant context. Our event-based customization approach makes sure of tenant-isolation, which is crucial in practice for SaaS vendors. This approach can also help reducing the number of API calls that may lead to performance bottleneck when there are many customized tenants with unpredictable loads. We planned to collaborate with two SaaS vendors and their customer companies for an empirical study. Enabling event-based customization is also a way to prepare for offloading custom code to the Edge devices. The event bus could be open to events from microservices on Edge devices and maybe even to "things" in the IoT context.

References

1. Dragoni, N., et al.: Microservices: yesterday, today, and tomorrow. Present and Ulterior Software Engineering, pp. 195–216. Springer, Cham (2017). https://doi.org/10.1007/978-3-319-67425-4_12
2. Guo, C.J., Sun, W., Huang, Y., Wang, Z.H., Gao, B.: A framework for native multi-tenancy application development and management. In: The 9th IEEE International Conference on E-Commerce Technology and the 4th IEEE International Conference on Enterprise Computing, E-Commerce, and E-Services, 2007, CEC/EEE 2007. pp. 551–558. IEEE (2007)

3. Kabbedijk, J., Bezemer, C.P., Jansen, S., Zaidman, A.: Defining multi-tenancy: a systematic mapping study on the academic and the industrial perspective. J. Syst. Softw. **100**, 139–148 (2015)
4. Mazzara, M., Dragoni, N., Bucchiarone, A., Giaretta, A., Larsen, S.T., Dustdar, S.: Microservices: migration of a mission critical system. IEEE Trans. Serv. Comput. 1 (2018). https://doi.org/10.1109/TSC.2018.2889087
5. Mietzner, R., Leymann, F.: Generation of BPEL customization processes for SaaS applications from variability descriptors. In: IEEE International Conference on Services Computing, 2008, SCC 2008, vol. 2, pp. 359–366. IEEE (2008)
6. Newman, S.: Building Microservices: Designing Fine-Grained Systems. O'Reilly Media Inc., Sebastopol (2015)
7. Nguyen, P.H., Song, H., Chauvel, F., Levin, E.: Towards customizing multi-tenant cloud applications using non-intrusive microservices. In: The 2nd International Conference on Microservices, Dortmund (2019)
8. Nguyen, P.H., Song, H., Chauvel, F., Muller, R., Boyar, S., Levin, E.: Using microservices for non-intrusive customization of multi-tenant SaaS. In: Proceedings of the 2019 27th ACM Joint Meeting on European Software Engineering Conference and Symposium on the Foundations of Software Engineering, ESEC/FSE 2019, pp. 905–915. Association for Computing Machinery, New York (2019). https://doi.org/ 10.1145/3338906.3340452
9. Song, H., Chauvel, F., Nguyen, P.H.: Using microservices to customize multi-tenant software-as-a-service. Microservices, pp. 299–331. Springer, Cham (2020). https:// doi.org/10.1007/978-3-030-31646-4_12
10. Song, H., Chauvel, F., Solberg, A.: Deep customization of multi-tenant SaaS using intrusive microservices. In: Proceedings of the 40th International Conference on Software Engineering: New Ideas and Emerging Results, ICSE-NIER 2018, pp. 97–100. ACM, New York (2018). https://doi.org/10.1145/3183399.3183407
11. Song, H., Nguyen, P.H., Chauvel, F.: Using microservices to customize multi-tenant SaaS: from intrusive to non-intrusive. In: Cruz-Filipe, L., Giallorenzo, S., Montesi, F., Peressotti, M., Rademacher, F., Sachweh, S. (eds.) Joint Post-proceedings of the First and Second International Conference on Microservices (Microservices 2017/2019). OpenAccess Series in Informatics (OASIcs), vol. 78, pp. 1:1–1:18. Schloss Dagstuhl-Leibniz-Zentrum fuer Informatik, Dagstuhl, Germany (2020). https://doi.org/10.4230/OASIcs.Microservices.2017-2019.1, https://drops. dagstuhl.de/opus/volltexte/2020/11823
12. Song, H., Nguyen, P.H., Chauvel, F., Glattetre, J., Schjerpen, T.: Customizing multi-tenant SaaS by microservices: a reference architecture. In: 2019 IEEE 26th International Conference on Web Services (2019)
13. Taibi, D., Auer, F., Lenarduzzi, V., Felderer, M.: From monolithic systems to microservices: an assessment framework. arXiv preprint arXiv:1909.08933 (2019)
14. Thönes, J.: Microservices. IEEE Softw. **32**(1), 116–116 (2015). https://doi.org/10. 1109/MS.2015.11
15. Tsai, W., Sun, X.: SaaS multi-tenant application customization. In: 2013 IEEE Seventh International Symposium on Service-Oriented System Engineering, pp. 1–12, March 2013. https://doi.org/10.1109/SOSE.2013.44
16. Walraven, S., Truyen, E., Joosen, W.: A middleware layer for flexible and cost-efficient multi-tenant applications. In: Kon, F., Kermarrec, A.-M. (eds.) Middleware 2011. LNCS, vol. 7049, pp. 370–389. Springer, Heidelberg (2011). https:// doi.org/10.1007/978-3-642-25821-3_19

Quality of Service Ranking
by Quantifying Partial Compliance
of Requirements

Agustín Eloy Martinez Suñé[1]($\boxtimes$) (ID) and Carlos Gustavo Lopez Pombo[1,2] (ID)

[1] Departamento de Computación, Universidad de Buenos Aires,
Buenos Aires, Argentina
{aemartinez,clpombo}@dc.uba.edu.ar
[2] Instituto de Investigación en Ciencias de la Computación (ICC), CONICET–UBA,
Buenos Aires, Argentina

Abstract. While there is not much discussion on the importance of formally describing and analysing quantitative requirements in the process
of software construction; in the paradigm of API-based software systems
it could be vital. Quantitative attributes can be thought as attributes
determining the *Quality of Service* – QoS provided by a software component published as a service. In this sense, they play a determinant role in
classifying software artifacts according to specific needs stated as requirements. In previous works we presented an efficient, and fully automatic,
analysis technique for establishing *Service Level Agreements* – SLA. Such
a proposal relays on describing QoS contracts as convex specifications,
and compliance checking is performed by the application of an analysis
algorithm based on state of the art techniques used in hybrid system
verification. Such a technique succeeds in offering a procedure for determining SLA but fails in the more realistic scenario where, potentially,
no service fully satisfies the requirements. In this scenario the running
application may still prefer to invoke the service that offers the best
chances of successfully executing with values for QoS attributes meeting
the requirements satisfactorily.

In this work we propose and implement a metric for automatically
quantifying partial satisfaction of QoS requirements, leading to a way of
ranking services according to such notion of partial compliance.

1 Introduction

Distributed software resulting from paradigms such as *Service-Oriented Computing (SOC)* or the API's economy is based on the idea of constructing software artifacts by composing services provided by third parties and registered in

Research partly supported by the European Unions Horizon 2020 research and innova-
tion programme under the Marie Sklodowska-Curie grant agreement No 778233. Carlos
G. Lopez Pombo's research is supported by Universidad de Buenos Aires through grant
UBACyT 20020170100544BA, and Consejo Nacional de Investigaciones Científicas y
Técnicas through grant PIP 11220130100148CO.

© IFIP International Federation for Information Processing 2020
Published by Springer Nature Switzerland AG 2020
S. Bliudze and L. Bocchi (Eds.): COORDINATION 2020, LNCS 12134, pp. 181–189, 2020.
https://doi.org/10.1007/978-3-030-50029-0_12

repositories. This envisages a generation of applications which, at run-time, are transparently reconfigured by the intervention of a dedicated middleware with the capability to bind a running application that has certain requirements to a service capable of fulfilling them, subject to the negotiation of a *Service Level Agreement* – SLA; in this way, services can collectively fulfill certain business goals [4].

Requirements can be formalised as contracts between software components, and satisfaction of such contracts is usually dealt with by checking whether a judgment of the form $Pr \vdash Rq$ holds or not, where Pr is the provision contract and Rq is the requirements contract. In the literature, functional requirements have been identified as those describing what the system has to do, while non-functional ones are assumed to characterise how the system develops the behaviour described by the functional ones.

In this work we focus on *Quantitative requirements* as a proper subclass of non-functional requirements of a software system. From our perspective, quantitative requirements formalise the admissible values of specific attributes that can be interpreted over a metric space [2]. Such attributes are referred to as *Quantitative attributes*. For practical reasons, the real numbers constitute a good candidate over which these can be interpreted, formalised and analysed.

In this sense, quantitative requirements might be used to characterise the *Quality of Service* – QoS provided by a software component available as service. While services may have the same functional behaviour, they might differ on their non-functional one (for example, a service may offer low-speed computation at a very low cost while another, functionally equivalent one, might be faster but more onerous); a motivation shared with other works like [14]. Therefore, quantitative requirements might be considered as a way to classify functionally equivalent services by their QoS.

In [12] we presented an efficient, and fully automatic, analysis procedure for checking a judgment of the shape $Pr \vdash Rq$ where Pr is the provision contract and Rq is the requirements contract, thus serving the purpose of establishing SLA. Such an approach guarantees the selection of a service satisfying the requirements of the executing application but it does not provide any insight when there is no service whose provision contract is fully compliant with the requirement contract. A geometrical interpretation of the judgment $Pr \vdash Rq$ expresses that all the satisfying values of real attributes of Pr also satisfy Rq. Thus, a negative answer just means that there is at least one value satisfying Pr and not satisfying Rq pushing the application to abort its execution because there is no possible SLA on the required QoS.

In this paper we propose an automatic procedure[1] for evaluating partial compliance of QoS contracts by estimating what we call the *inclusion ratio*: the intersection of the set of satisfying values of the provision and requirement contracts interpreted relative to the size of the set of values satisfying the provision contract. This metric leads to a natural way of ranking services. While the problem of raking services according to their QoS has been studied and different

---

[1] A demonstration video of the tool can be found on http://bit.do/QoS-Rank.

approaches to tackle the problem have been proposed, in general, these are based on monitoring run-time behavior of specific attributes [1,9] or by socially sharing the users' opinion [11,15] but, to the best of our knowledge, there is none focussing on QoS ranking where the QoS is formally specified and SLA is guaranteed through an automated procedure.

2 Formalisation and Analysis of Quantitative Attributes

The selection of a service requires establishing an SLA, part of which is the QoS agreement. Given a formal QoS requirement contract Rq; a service that declares a formal QoS provision contract Pr will be a good candidate only if $Pr \implies Rq$ holds. In [12] we adopted *monotone Satisfiability Modulo Convex (SMC) formulae* [13] as specification language and proposed a method to check QoS compliance. *SMC formulae* are defined as quantifier-free formulae in conjunctive normal form, with atomic propositions ranging over a subset of the propositional variables and convex constraints[2]. Then, given two SMC formulas Pr and Rq, the proposed method to check whether $Pr \vdash Rq$ holds or not is done by determining if the formula $Pr \wedge \neg Rq$ is not satisfiable.

Such a procedure does not provide any hint on what to do when no service registered in the repository fully satisfies the requirements. That is, no QoS provision contract satisfies the QoS requirements contract.

A different way of formalising QoS contracts is as a set of real values satisfying the specification. Next we present this alternative formalisation of quantitative non-functional requirements. Throughout the rest of the paper, letters $\mathcal{I}$, $\mathcal{J}$ and $\mathcal{K}$ will be used to denote index sets.

Definition 1. *Let $\mathcal{X}$ be a set of real variables. We define a QoS specification on quantitative attributes $\mathcal{X}$ to be $\langle \mathcal{X}, \alpha \rangle$, with α being a formula with shape $\bigvee_{i \in \mathcal{I}} \mathrm{P}_i$. Each P_i is a convex polytope expressed as $\bigwedge_{k \in \mathcal{K}_i} f_{i,k}(\overrightarrow{x}) \mathcal{R} 0$, where $\mathcal{R} \in \{<, \leq\}$ such that each $f_{i,k}(\overrightarrow{x}) \mathcal{R} 0$ is a convex constraint. The set of QoS specifications over the set of quantitative attributes $\mathcal{X}$ will be referred to as $QoS\_spec(\mathcal{X})$.*

Let $\langle \mathcal{X}, \alpha \rangle \in QoS\_spec(\mathcal{X})$. We define a valuation for α as $v : \mathcal{X} \rightarrow \mathbb{R}$. Satisfaction is a relation $\models \subseteq [\mathcal{X} \rightarrow \mathbb{R}] \times QoS\_spec(\mathcal{X})$ defined as $\overrightarrow{x} \models \alpha$ if and only if there exists $i \in \mathcal{I}$, such that for all $k \in \mathcal{K}_i$, $f_{i,k}(\overrightarrow{x}) \mathcal{R} 0$. The set of values satisfying α is defined as $\llbracket \alpha \rrbracket = \left\{ \overrightarrow{x} \mid \overrightarrow{x} \models \alpha \right\}$.

Essentially, the set of admissible values of the quantitative attributes $\mathcal{X}$ in a *QoS_spec* is characterised by a set of convex polytopes over $\mathcal{X}$. Notice that, under some reasonable assumptions, *SMC formulae* can be translated to specifications in $QoS\_spec(\mathcal{X})$ by simply iterating the satisfying valuations of the boolean abstraction of the formulae, and collecting the polytopes determined by the positive literals.

---

[2] The interested reader will find the formal definition in [13].

A specification like this can capture many quantitative aspects of a software system. For example, the formulae below show a specification of an API-based software application requiring a service to be paid exclusively for the time it is used. Consider as relevant quantitative attributes *a) perSec*: the cost per second of the session, and *b) maxWait*: the maximum waiting time. Then, such attributes can be formalised by a QoS specification $\langle \langle \mathcal{X} \rangle, \alpha \rangle$ where $\mathcal{X} = \{perSec, maxWait\}$. To characterise a service that is more expensive when it is faster a possible α would be the disjunction of the following formulae:

$$0 < maxWait \le 100 \wedge 0.1 \le perSec < 0.3,$$
$$100 < maxWait \le 1000 \wedge 0.0 \le perSec \le 0.1$$

A geometrical interpretation of the formula $Pr \implies Rq$ leads to the possibility of measuring different degrees of partial compliance, which range between total compliance (all values allowed by Pr are accepted by Rq) and no compliance at all (no value allowed by Pr is accepted by Rq).

Based on the previous definitions, proving the formula $Pr \vdash Rq$ is to check whether $[\![Pr]\!] \subseteq [\![Rq]\!]$. We propose to compute the volume of the intersection between $[\![Pr]\!]$ and $[\![Rq]\!]$ relative to the volume of $[\![Pr]\!]$, referred to as *inclusion ratio*. This indicator quantifies what is the percentage of the QoS values allowed by the provision contract that is actually accepted by the requirements contract. For us, this indicator serves the purpose of quantifying the partial compliance of Rq by Pr; therefore, functionally compliant services can be chosen from a ranking built by using inclusion ratio as the ordering criterion.

2.1   On the Complexity of the Volume Computation

In the literature, the volume of a polytope is invariably defined in terms of the sum of the volumes of a certain decomposition of such polytope into a family of convex ones [6]. Fortunately, Definition 1 assists us by already expressing the set of values in a QoS contract as the union of the sets of values of each member of a family of convex polytopes, expressed as $Pr = \bigvee_{i \in \mathcal{I}} P_i$ and $Rq = \bigvee_{j \in \mathcal{J}} R_j$. As neither family is guaranteed to be a partition, volumes must be computed following the *Principle of inclusion-exclusion* [10, Chap. 4]. Then, the inclusion ratio is calculated as follows:

First: Compute the volume (denoted as #) of intersection between Pr and Rq:

$$\# \left(\bigcup_{i \in \mathcal{I}} [\![P_i]\!] \cap \bigcup_{j \in \mathcal{J}} [\![R_j]\!] \right) = \sum_{\emptyset \neq \mathcal{K} \subseteq \mathcal{I} \times \mathcal{J}} (-1)^{|\mathcal{K}|-1} \# \left(\bigcap_{(i,j) \in \mathcal{K}} ([\![P_i]\!] \cap [\![R_j]\!]) \right) \quad (1)$$

Second: Compute the volume of P:

$$\# \left(\bigcup_{i \in \mathcal{I}} [\![P_i]\!] \right) = \sum_{\emptyset \neq \mathcal{K} \subseteq \mathcal{I}} (-1)^{|\mathcal{K}|-1} \# \left(\bigcap_{k \in \mathcal{K}} [\![P_k]\!] \right) \quad (2)$$

Third: Compute the inclusion ratio of Pr in Rq as: $\frac{\#([\![Pr]\!] \cap [\![Rq]\!])}{\#([\![Pr]\!])}$.

In the late 80's Dyer et al. [3] and Khachiyan [8] proved the complexity of computing the volume of a convex polytope to be **#P-Hard**. The first estimation algorithm was presented by Kannan et al. in [7]. Later in [5], an estimation algorithm based on the *Multiphase Monte-Carlo algorithm* is proposed and the authors show that it can efficiently handle instances of dozens of dimensions with high accuracy. The complexity is shown to be $O^*(m \cdot n^3)$, where n is the dimensions, m is the number of constraints, and the Soft-O notation (O^*) omits logarithmic factors. The estimation method tool is distributed under the name `PolyVest`.

The implementation of the algorithm presented above for computing the inclusion ratio requires $2^{|\mathcal{I}| \cdot |\mathcal{J}|} + 2^{|\mathcal{I}|}$ invocations to the function computing the volume of a convex polytope. Such complexity forces us to consider a further dimension of approximation in order to make the calculation of the inclusion ratio viable in practice. In the next section we study the appropriateness of considering only some of the intersections involved in the calculation as an estimation of the volume.

3 Experimental Results

Our first research question is related to the complexity of the exact computation of the volume of a polytope $\mathcal{P}$. For the sake of understanding the limits imposed by such complexity, the research question will be stated in terms of a single polytope decomposed as a family of convex polytopes.

RQ1: How does the complexity of $\# \left(\bigcup_{i \in \mathcal{I}} \mathcal{P}_i \right)$ impacts in practice?

From our experiments[3] it is possible to identify the exponential nature of the computation and that the majority of cases could not be completed within the time budget, hence the method cannot be applied to more realistic case-studies. The applicability of the technique, therefore, rests on the possibility of computing a good and efficient approximation of the volume operator. A natural way of doing this is by considering only a limited number of terms of the sum in Eq. 1. The next proposition formalises the intuition that subsequent partial sums represent an upper, and a lower, bound for the exact value of the volume.

Proposition 1. *Let* $P = \{P_i\}_{i \in \mathcal{I}}$ *and* $0 < n < |\mathcal{I}|$, *with* $n \equiv 0 \pmod 2$ *then*

$$\sum_{\substack{\emptyset \neq \mathcal{K} \subseteq \mathcal{I} \\ 0 < |\mathcal{K}| \leq n}} (-1)^{|\mathcal{K}|-1} \# \left(\bigcap_{k \in \mathcal{K}} [\![P_k]\!] \right) \leq \#(P) \leq \sum_{\substack{\emptyset \neq \mathcal{K} \subseteq \mathcal{I} \\ 0 < |\mathcal{K}| \leq n+1}} (-1)^{|\mathcal{K}|-1} \# \left(\bigcap_{k \in \mathcal{K}} [\![P_k]\!] \right) .$$

Computing an approximation of a magnitude requires the introduction of a metric for measuring the effectiveness of such estimation. As usual, the relative error between the magnitude x and an approximate value x_0 is defined to be $\frac{|x_0 - x|}{|x|}$.

---

[3] Synthetic case-studies were generated automatically consisting of families of 5–11 convex polytopes over 10–35 quantitative attributes. For each case the procedure was run over 20 different instances, with a 1 h time budget.

The next proposition provides upper bounds for the relative error that do not depend on the exact value v of the volume but on two consecutive approximations: $\{v_{k-1}, v_k\}$ or $\{v_k, v_{k+1}\}$.

Proposition 2. *Let* $v, v_{k-1}, v_k, v_{k+1} \in \mathbb{R}$, *then:*

- *if* $0 < v_{k-1} < v < v_k$, *then* $\frac{v_k - v}{v} \leq \frac{v_k - v_{k-1}}{v_{k-1}}$ *(denoted ρ_k),*
- *if* $v_k > v > v_{k+1} > 0$, *then* $\frac{v_k - v}{v} \leq \frac{v_k - v_{k+1}}{v_{k+1}}$ *(denoted σ_k)*
- *if* $v_{k-1} \geq v_{k+1} > 0$, *then* $\rho_k \geq \sigma_k$.

Using these bounds, and considering Proposition 1, we can design an algorithm for computing the approximate volume of a polytope, by computing successive approximations until the desired value for the relative error is guaranteed. Notice that if we require a relative error equal to 0, the complexity of the algorithm is still $O(2^n)$, but when the bound is big enough to let the algorithm converge in the second approximation, the complexity drops to $O(n^2)$. Our second research question analises the practical impact of approximating the volume of a polytope using these bounds.

RQ2: How do the partial sums of the terms in the sum of Eq. 1 converge to the value $\# \left(\bigcup_{i \in \mathcal{I}} \mathcal{P}_i \right)$ with 1% and 5% tolerance?

Results[4] show that the number of successive approximations needed for a calculation with an error within 1% tolerance is between 2 and 5, while for an error within 5% tolerance is between 2 and 3. In both scenarios the estimated computation greatly outperformed the exact one, being able to compute the mayority of cases within the time budget.

A natural follow-up from these results is to explore the scalability of the procedure for volume estimation. Table 1 show the maximum size of the family of polytopes whose approximate volume can be computed in one hour, considering relative errors with bounds set to 1% and 5%. *Size* denotes the number of polytopes in the family and *App* the number of successive approximations needed in each case.

As we mentioned in Sect. 2, efficiently computing the volume of these types of polytopes is just a means for quantifying partial compliance of QoS contracts.

RQ3: how does the performance gain obtained by approximating the volume impacts the computation of the inclusion ratio?

Our results[5] show that as the size of the contracts increases the efficiency gain between 0%, 1% and 5% tolerance is dramatically better. There are cases where the approximate volume computation is performed in 4% of the time required by the exact volume computation, and several cases for which the exact inclusion ratio fails to be computed within the 10 h time budget but becomes feasible when a bound for the relative error is introduced.

---

[4] The experiment was conducted over the same dataset as for **RQ1**.

[5] Case studies were generated following the same guidelines as for **RQ2**. A time budget of 10 h is considered.

Table 1. Upper limit for computation of approximated volume.

	Number of quantitative attributes								
	10			15			20		
	Size	App.	Time	Size	App.	Time	Size	App.	Time
1%	11	4.95	1452.42	15	3	3067.82	22	2	3320.67
5%	15	3.72	1857.42	24.92	2	1218.55	22	2	3320.67

	Number of quantitative attributes				
	25			30	
	Size	App.	Time	Size	App.	Time
1%	14	2	3481.29	9	2	3120.49
5%	14	2	3481.29	9	2	3120.49

Inclusion ratio provides a way of ranking services according to partial satisfaction. Thus, it is worth knowing how an approximate computation of the volume propagates the relative error to the computation of the inclusion ratio. In the end, this will impact the actual selection of a service candidate. The next proposition establishes lower and upper bounds for the distance between approximate inclusion ratio and exact inclusion ratio.

Proposition 3. *Given two volume approximations v_k, w_k, where the exact volumes are v, k, respectively. Let e be the bound for the relative error (i.e., $\frac{|v-v_k|}{|v|} \le e$ and $\frac{|w-w_k|}{|w|} \le e$) then:*

1. $(1-e) \cdot v \le v_k \le (1+e) \cdot v$ *(respectively $(1-e) \cdot w \le w_k \le (1+e) \cdot w$), and*
2. $\frac{(1-e) \cdot v}{(1+e) \cdot w} \le \frac{v_k}{w_k} \le \frac{(1+e) \cdot v}{(1-e) \cdot w}$ *(equivalently $\frac{1-e}{1+e} \cdot \frac{v}{w} \le \frac{v_k}{w_k} \le \frac{1+e}{1-e} \cdot \frac{v}{w}$).*

Consider, as an example, the bounds obtained from Proposition 3 for the approximate inclusion ratio, when approximate volumes are computed with relative error bound to be smaller than 5% and 1%, as we did in the previous experiments. Let eir be the exact inclusion ratio, $ir5$ the inclusion ratio computed with a relative error below 5% and $ir1$ the inclusion ratio computed with a relative error below 1%; then, we obtain that $0.905 \cdot eir \approx \frac{0.95}{1.05} \cdot eir \le ir5 \le \frac{1.05}{0.95} \cdot eir \approx 1.105 \cdot eir$ and $0.98 \cdot eir \approx \frac{0.99}{1.01} \cdot eir \le ir1 \le \frac{1.01}{0.99} \cdot eir \approx 1.02 \cdot eir$, respectively.

Our final research question focuses on effectively ranking different provision contracts using the inclusion ratio as a metric for quantifying partial satisfaction.

RQ4: What is the impact of the proposed approximation in the construction of a ranking of a set of services?

For this experiment we performed 3 examples of ranking 20 provision contracts by partial satisfaction of a single requirements contract. The datasets were synthetically generated following the guidelines used for generating the case-studies used in **RQ3**. Each ranking correspond to a different size of the families of polytopes as follows: a) $|Pr| = 2$, $|Rq| = 4$, b) $|Pr| = 3$, $|Rq| = 3$, c) $|Pr| = 4$, $|Rq| = 2$.

For each dataset we performed the ranking order using the exact inclusion ratio, and also using 1% and 5% bounds for the relative error. The results of the experiment show that in all of the examples the ranking obtained by using the exact volume computation is preserved when resorting to approximate volume computations.

4   Conclusions and Further Work

We extended previous work where we proposed a formalisation of QoS contract as convex specifications [13]. Under a geometrical interpretation, a contract can be seen as a family of convex polytopes characterising the admissible values for the quantitative attributes and a judgement of the shape $Pr \vdash Rq$ as polytope inclusion. From this perspective, we proposed a way of QoS ranking services by quantifying the volume of the intersection between $[\![Pr]\!]$ and $[\![Rq]\!]$, under the name *inclusion ratio*. Since this indicator quantifies the percentage of values allowed by the provision contract that are actually accepted by the requirement contract we sustain that it serves the purpose of quantifying partial compliance. The exponential nature of computing the volume of a family of convex polytopes forced us to propose a volume approximation technique based on imposing an upper bound to the relative error.

We evaluated the performance of the approximated volume computation against the exact volume computation, the scalability of the approximate volume computation and the performance of computing the inclusion ratio with respect to the exact computation. Finally, we showed examples of the impact of approximate inclusion ratio in ranking services by comparing the ideal ranking, obtained by resorting to the exact inclusion ratio, and the one obtained by resorting to approximate inclusion ratio, for different bounds to the relative error.

This technique for evaluating partial satisfaction of QoS contracts triggers what we believe is one of the most important questions regarding the automation of service broking. Under partial satisfaction of QoS contracts, we would like to establish preferences among different quantitative attributes of the different candidates. For example, if we consider two services with the same inclusion ratio, a low budget application would like to express it's preference for cheaper services, even at the cost of degraded performance, over a more expensive and efficient one. This problem will be addressed in the near future aiming at a more realistic view of an automatic procedure for checking QoS compliance for determining SLA in a service-based architecture.

References

1. Al-Masri, E., Mahmood, Q.H.: QoS-based discovery and ranking of web services. In: Guo, K. (ed.) Proceedings of 16th International Conference on Computer Communications and Networks, IEEE ICCCN 2007, pp. 529–534. IEEE Computer Society, August 2007

2. Bryant, V.: Metric Spaces: Iteration and Application. Mathematical Systems Theory. Cambridge University Press, Cambridge (1985)
3. Dyer, M.E., Frieze, A.M.: On the complexity of computing the volume of a polyhedron. SIAM J. **17**(5), 967–974 (1988)
4. Fiadeiro, J.L., Lopes, A., Bocchi, L.: An abstract model of service discovery and binding. Formal Aspects Comput. **23**(4), 433–463 (2011). https://doi.org/10.1007/s00165-010-0166-z
5. Ge, C., Ma, F.: A fast and practical method to estimate volumes of convex polytopes. In: Wang, J., Yap, C. (eds.) FAW 2015. LNCS, vol. 9130, pp. 52–65. Springer, Cham (2015). https://doi.org/10.1007/978-3-319-19647-3_6
6. Gritzmann, P., Klee, V.: On the complexity of some basic problems in computational convexity. In: Bisztriczky, T., McMullen, P., Schneider, R., Weiss, A.I. (eds.) Polytopes: Abstract, Convex and Computational. ASIC, vol. 440, pp. 373–466. Springer, Dordrecht (1994). https://doi.org/10.1007/978-94-011-0924-6_17
7. Kannan, R., Lovász, L., Simonovits, M.: Random walks and an $o^*(n^5)$ volume algorithm for convex bodies. Random Struct. Algorithms **11**(1), 1–50 (1991)
8. Khachiyan, L.G.: The problem of calculating the volume of a polyhedron is enumerably hard. Russ. Math. Surv. **44**(3), 199–200 (1989)
9. Liu, Y., Ngu, A.H., Zeng, L.: QoS computation and policing in dynamic web service selection. In: Feldman, S.I., Uretsky, M., Najork, M., Wills, C.E. (eds.) Proceedings of 13th International Conference on World Wide Web - WWW 2004, pp. 66–73. ACM Press, May 2004
10. Liu, Z.: Introduction to Combinatorial Mathematics. McGraw-Hill Book Company, New York City (1968)
11. Mao, C., Chen, J., Towey, D., Chen, J., Xie, X.: Search-based QoS ranking prediction for web services in cloud environments. Future Gener. Comput. Syst. **50**, 111–126 (2015)
12. Martinez Suñé, A.E., Lopez Pombo, C.G.: Automatic quality-of-service evaluation in service-oriented computing. In: Riis Nielson, H., Tuosto, E. (eds.) COORDINATION 2019. LNCS, vol. 11533, pp. 221–236. Springer, Cham (2019). https://doi.org/10.1007/978-3-030-22397-7_13
13. Shoukry, Y., Nuzzo, P., Sangiovanni-Vincentelli, A.L., Seshia, S.A., Pappas, G.J., Tabuada, P.: SMC: satisfiability modulo convex optimization. In: Proceedings of the 20th International Conference on Hybrid Systems: Computation and Control, pp. 19–28. ACM Press, New York (2017)
14. Strunk, A.: QoS-aware service composition: a survey. In: Brogi, A., Pautasso, C., Papadopoulos, G.A. (eds.) Proceedings of 8th IEEE European Conference on Web Services, ECOWS 2010, pp. 67–74. IEEE Computer Society, December 2010
15. Zheng, Z., Wu, X., Zhang, Y., Lyu, M.R., Wang, J.: QoS ranking prediction for cloud services. IEEE Trans. Parallel Distrib. Syst. **24**(6), 1–50 (2013)

Large-Scale Decentralised Systems

Time-Fluid Field-Based Coordination

Danilo Pianini[1]([envelope])[iD], Stefano Mariani[2][iD], Mirko Viroli[1][iD],
and Franco Zambonelli[2][iD]

[1] ALMA MATER STUDIORUM—Università Bologna, Cesena, Italy
{danilo.pianini,mirko.viroli}@unibo.it
[2] Università di Modena e Reggio Emilia, Reggio Emilia, Italy
{stefano.mariani,franco.zambonelli}@unimore.it

Abstract. Emerging application scenarios, such as cyber-physical systems (CPSs), the Internet of Things (IoT), and edge computing, call for coordination approaches addressing openness, self-adaptation, heterogeneity, and deployment agnosticism. Field-based coordination is one such approach, promoting the idea of programming system coordination declaratively from a global perspective, in terms of functional manipulation and evolution in "space and time" of distributed data structures, called *fields*. More specifically, regarding time, in field-based coordination it is assumed that local activities in each device, called *computational rounds*, are regulated by a fixed clock, typically, a fair and unsynchronized distributed scheduler. In this work, we challenge this assumption, and propose an alternative approach where the round execution scheduling is naturally programmed along with the usual coordination specification, namely, in terms of a *field of causal relations* dictating what is the notion of causality (why and when a round has to be locally scheduled) and how it should change across time and space. This abstraction over the traditional view on global time allows us to express what we call "time-fluid" coordination, where causality can be finely tuned to select the event triggers to react to, up to to achieve improved balance between performance (system reactivity) and cost (usage of computational resources). We propose an implementation in the aggregate computing framework, and evaluate via simulation on a case study.

Keywords: Aggregate computing · Fluidware · IoT · Internet of Things · Edge computing · Causality · Time · Reactive

1 Introduction

Emerging application scenarios, such as the Internet of Things (IoT), cyber-physical systems (CPSs), and edge computing, call for software design approaches addressing openness, heterogeneity, self-adaptation, and deployment agnosticism [19]. To effectively address this issue, researchers strive to define increasingly higher-level concepts, reducing the "abstraction gap" with the problems at hand, e.g., by designing new languages and paradigms. In the context

© IFIP International Federation for Information Processing 2020
Published by Springer Nature Switzerland AG 2020
S. Bliudze and L. Bocchi (Eds.): COORDINATION 2020, LNCS 12134, pp. 193–210, 2020.
https://doi.org/10.1007/978-3-030-50029-0_13

of coordination models and languages, field-based coordination is one such approach [3,5,21,23,37,40]. In spite of its many variants and implementations, field-based coordination roots in the idea of programming system coordination declaratively and from a global perspective, in terms of distributed data structures called (computational) *fields*, which span the entire deployment in space (each device holds a value) and time (each device continuously produces such values).

Regarding time, which is the focus of this paper, field-based coordination typically abstracts from it in two ways: *(i)* when a specific notion of local time is needed, this is accessed through a sensor as for any other environmental variable; and *(ii)* a specification is actually interpreted as a small computation chunk to be carried on in *computation rounds*. In each round a device: *(i)* sleeps for some time; *(ii)* gathers information about state of computation in previous round, messages received by neighbors while sleeping, and contextual information (i.e. sensor readings); and *(iii)* uses such data to evaluate the coordination specification, storing the state information in memory, producing a value output, and sending relevant information to neighbors. So far, field-based coordination approaches considered computational rounds as being regulated by an externally imposed, fixed distributed clock: typically, a fair and unsynchronized distributed scheduler. This assumption however, has a number of consequences and limitations, both philosophical and pragmatic, which this paper aims to address.

Under a philosophical point of view, it follows a pre-relativity view of time that meets general human perception, i.e., where time is absolute and independent of the actual dynamics of events. This hardly fits with more modern views connecting time with a deeper concept of *causality* [22], as being only meaningful relative to the existence of events as in *relational* interpretations of space-time [30], or even being a mere derived concept introduced by our cognition [29]—as in Loop Quantum Gravity [31]. Under a practical point of view, consequences on field-based coordination are mixed. The key practical advantage is simplicity. First, the designer must abstract from time, leaving the scheduling issue to the underlying platform. Second, the platform itself can simply impose local schedulers statically, using fixed frequencies that at most depend on the device computational power or energetic requirements. Third, the execution in proactive rounds allows a device to discard messages received few rounds before the current one, thus considering non-proactive senders to have abandoned the neighborhood, and simply modeling the state of communication by maintaining the most recent message received from each neighbor.

However, there is a price to pay for such a simple approach. The first is that "stability" of the computation, namely, situations in which the field will not change after a round execution, is ignored. As a consequence, sometimes "unnecessary" computations are performed, consuming resources (both energy and bandwidth capacity), and thus reducing the *efficiency* of the system. Symmetrically, there is a potential *responsiveness* issue: some computations may require to be executed more quickly under some circumstances. For instance, consider a crowd monitoring and steering system for urban mass events as the one exemplified in [7]: in case the measured density of people gets dangerous, a more frequent evaluation of the steering advice field is likely to provide more precise and timely advices. Similar considerations apply for example to the area of landslide monitoring [28], where long intervals of immobility are interspersed by sudden slope movements: sensors sampling rate can and should be low most of the time, but it needs to get promptly increased on slope changes. This generally suggests a key unexpressed potential for field-based computation: the general ability to provide improved balance between performance (system reactivity) and cost (usage of computational resources). For instance, the crowd monitoring and landslide monitoring systems should ideally slow down (possibly, halt entirely) the evaluation in case of sparse crowd density or of absence of surface movements, respectively. And they should start being more and more responsive with growing crowd densities or in case of landslide activation.

The general idea that round execution distribution can actually dynamically depend on the outcome of computation itself, can be captured in field-based coordination by modeling time by a *causality field*, namely, a field programmable along with (and hence intertwined with) the usual coordination specification, dictating (at each point in space-time) what are the triggers whose occurrence should correspond to the execution of computation rounds. Programming causality along with coordination leads us to a notion of *time-fluid coordination*, where it is possible to flexibly control the balance between performance and cost of system execution. Accordingly, in this work we discuss a causality-driven interpretation of field-based coordination, proposing an integration with the field calculus [3] with the goal of evaluating a model for time-fluid, field-based coordination. In practice, we assume computations are not driven by time-based rounds, but by *perceivable local event triggers* provided by the platform (hardware/-software stack) executing the aggregate program, such as messages received, change in sensor values, and time passing by. The aggregate program specification itself, then, may affect scheduling of subsequent computations through policies (expressed in the same language) based on such triggers.

The contribution of this work can be summarized under three points of view. First, the proposed model enriches the *coordination abstraction* of field-based coordination with the possibility to explicitly and possibly reactively program the scheduling of the coordination actions; second, it enables a *functional description of causality and observability*, since manipulation of the interaction frequency among single components of the coordinated system reflects in changes in how causal events are perceived, and actions are taken in response to event triggers; third, the most immediate *practical implication* of a time-fluid coordination when compared to a traditional time-driven approach is improved efficiency, intended as improved responsiveness with the same resource cost.

The remainder of this work is as follows: Sect. 2 frames this work with respect to the existing literature on topic; Sect. 3 introduces the proposed time-fluid model and discusses its implications; Sect. 4 presents a prototype implementation in the framework of aggregate computing, showing examples and evaluating the potential practical implications via simulation finally, Sect. 5 discusses future directions and concludes the work.

2   Background and Related Work

Time and synchronization have always been key issues in the area of distributed and pervasive computing systems. In general, in distributed systems, the absence of a globally shared physical clock among nodes makes it impossible to rely on absolute notions of time. Logical clocks are hence used instead [17], realizing a sort of causally-driven notion of time, in which the "passing time" of a distributed computation (that is, the ticks of logical clocks) directly expresses causal relations between distributed events. As a consequence, any observation of a distributed computation that respects such causal relations, independently of the relative speeds of processes, is a consistent one [4]. Our proposal absorbs these foundational lessons, and brings them forward to consider the strict relations between the spatial dimension and the temporal dimension that situated aggregate computations have to account for.

In the area of sensor networks, acquiring a (as accurate as possible) globally shared notion of time is of fundamental importance [33], to properly capture snapshots of the distributed phenomena under observation. However, global synchronization also serves energy saving purposes. In fact, when not monitoring or not communicating, the nodes of the network should go to sleep to avoid energy waste, but this implies that to exchange monitoring information with each other they must periodically wake-up in a synchronized way. In most of existing proposals, though, this is done in awakening and communicating rounds of fixed duration, which makes it impossible to adapt to the actual dynamics of the phenomena under observation. Several proposals exist for adaptive synchronization in wireless sensor networks [1,13,16], dynamically changing the sampling frequency (and hence frequency of communication rounds) so as to adapt to the dynamics of the observed phenomena. For instance, in the case of crowd monitoring systems, it is likely that people (e.g, during an event) stay nearly immobile for most of the time, then suddenly start moving (e.g., at the end of the event). Similarly, in the area of landslide monitoring, the situation of a slope is stable for most of the time, with periodic occurrences of (sometimes very fast) slope movements. In these cases, waking up the nodes of the network periodically would not make any sense and would waste a lot of energy. Nodes should rather sleep most of the time, and wake up only upon detectable slope movements.

Such adaptive sampling approaches challenge the underlying notion of time, but they tend to focus on the temporal dimension only (i.e., adapting to the dynamics of a phenomena as locally perceived by the nodes). Our approach goes further, by making it possible to adapt in time and space as well: not only how fast a phenomenon changes in time, but how fast it propagates and induces causal effects in space. For instance, in the case of landslide monitoring or crowd monitoring, adapting to the dynamics of local perceived movements to the overall propagation speed of such movements across the monitored area.

Besides sensor networks, the issue of adaptive sampling has recently landed in the broader area of IoT systems and applications [35], again with the primary goal of optimizing energy consumption of devices while not losing relevant phenomena under observation. However, unlike what promoted in sensor networks, such optimizations typically take place in a centralized (cloud) [34] or semi-decentralized (fog) way [18], which again disregards spatial issues and the strict space-time relations of phenomena.

Since coordination models and languages typical address a crosscutting concern of distributed systems, they are historically concerned with the notion of time in a variety of ways. For instance, time is addressed in space-based coordination since Javaspaces [12], and corresponding foundational calculi for time-based Linda [6,20]: the general idea is to equip tuples and query operations with timeouts, which can be interpreted either in terms of global or local clocks. The problem of abstracting the notion of time became crucial when coordination models started addressing self-adaptive systems, and hence openness and reactivity. In [25], it is suggested that a tuple may eventually fade, with a rate that depends on a usefulness concepts measuring how many new operations are related to such tuple. In the biochemical tuple-space model [38], tuples have a time-dynamic "concentration" driven by stochastic coordination rules embedded in the data-space.

Field-based coordination emerged as a coordination paradigm for self-adaptive systems focusing more on "space" rather than "time", in works such as TOTA [24], field calculus [3,37], and fixpoint-based computational fields [21]. However, the need for dealing with time is a deep consequence of dealing with space, since propagation in space necessarily impacts "evolution". These approaches tend to abstract from the scheduling dynamics of local field evolution, in various ways. In TOTA, the update model for distributed "fields of tuples" is an asynchronous event-based one: anytime a change in network connectivity is detected by a node, the TOTA middleware provides for triggering an update of the distributed field structures so as to immediately reflect the new situation. In the field calculus and aggregate computing [5] as already mentioned, an external, proactive clock is typically used. In [21] this issue is mostly neglected since the focus is on the "eventual behavior", namely the stabilized configuration of a field, as in [36]. For all these models, scheduling of updates is always transparent to the application/programming level, so the application designer cannot intervene on coordination so as to possible optimize communication, energy expenses, and reactivity.

3   Time-Fluid Field-Based Coordination

In this section, we introduce a model for time-fluid field-based coordination. The core idea of our proposed approach is to leverage the field-based coordination itself for maintaining a *causality field* that drives the dynamics of computation of the application-level fields. Our discussion is in principle applicable to any field-based coordination framework, however, for the sake of clarity, we here focus on the field calculus [3].

3.1   A Time-Fluid Model

Considering a field calculus program **P**, each of its rounds can be though of as consuming: *i)* a set of valid messages received from neighbors, $M \in \mathcal{M}$; and *ii)* some contextual information $S \in \mathcal{S}$, usually obtained via so-called sensors. The platform or middleware in charge of executing field calculus programs has to decide when to launch the next evaluation round of **P**, also providing valid values for $\mathcal{M}$ and $\mathcal{S}$. Note that in general the platform could execute many programs concurrently.

In order to support causality-driven coordination, we first require the platform to be able to reactively respond to *local event triggers*, each representing some kind of change in the values of $\mathcal{M}$ or $\mathcal{S}$—e.g., "a new message is arrived", "a given sensor provides a new value", or "1 second is passed". We denote by $\mathcal{T}$ the set of all possible local event triggers the platform can manage.

Then, we propose to associate to every field calculus program **P** a guard policy **G** (policy in short), which itself denotes a field computation—and can hence be written with a program expressed in the same language of **P**, as will be detailed in next section. Most specifically, whenever evaluated across space and time, the field computation of a policy can be locally modeled as a function

$$f_G \colon (\mathcal{S}, \mathcal{M}) \to (\{0,1\}, \mathcal{P}(\mathcal{T}))$$

where $\mathcal{P}(\mathcal{T})$ denotes the powerset of $\mathcal{T}$. Namely, a policy has the same input of any field computation, but specifically returns a pair of Boolean $b \in \{0,1\}$ and a set of event triggers $T_c \subseteq \mathcal{T}$. T_c is essentially the *set of "causes"*: **G** will get evaluated next time by the platform only when a new event trigger is detected that belongs to T_c. Then, such an evaluation produces the second output b: when this is true (value 1) it means that the program **P** associated to the policy must be evaluated as soon as possible. On system bootstrap, every policy gets evaluated for the first time.

In the proposed framework, hence, computations are caused by a field of event triggers (the *causality field*) computed by a policy, which is used to *i)* decide whether to run the actual application round immediately, and *ii)* decide which event triggers will cause a re-evaluation of the policy itself. This mechanism thus introduces a sort of guard mediating between the evolution of the *causality field* and the actual execution of application rounds, allowing for fine control over the actual temporal dynamics, as exemplified in Sect. 4.2.

Crucially, the ability to sense context (namely, the contents of $\mathcal{S}$) and to express event triggers (namely, the possible contents of $\mathcal{T}$) has a large impact on the expressivity of the proposed model. For the remainder of this work, we will assume the platform or middleware hosting a field computation to provide the following set of features, which we deem reasonable for any such platform—this is for the sake of practical expressiveness, since even a small set of event triggers could be of benefit. First, $\mathcal{T}$ must include changes to any value of $\mathcal{S}$; this allows the computation to be reactive to changes in the device perception, or, symmetrically speaking, makes such changes the *cause* of the computation. Second, timers can be easily modeled as special Boolean sensors flipping their value from `false` to `true`; making the classic time-driven approach a special case of the proposed framework. Third, which specific event trigger caused the last computation should be available in S, accessible through the appropriate sensor. Fourth, the most recent result of any field computation **P** that should affect the policy must be available in S; this is crucial for field computations to depend on each other, or, in other words, for a field computation to be the cause of another, possibly more intensive field computation. For instance, consider the crowd sensing and steering application mentioned in Sect. 1 to be decomposed in two sub-field computations: the former, lightweight, computing the local crowd density under a policy triggering the computation anytime a presence sensor counts a different number of people in the monitored area; the latter, resource intensive, computing a crowd steering field guiding people out of the over-crowded areas, whose policy can leverage the value of the density field to raise the evaluation frequency when the situation gets potentially dangerous. Fifth, the conclusion of a round of any field program is a valid source of event triggers, namely, T also contains a Boolean indicating whether a field program of interest completed its round.

3.2   Consequences

Programming *the* Space-Time and Propagating Causality. As soon as we let the application affect its own execution policy, we are effectively programming *the* time (instead of *in* time, as is typically done in field-based coordination): evaluating the field computation at different frequencies would actually amount at modulating the perception of time from the application standpoint. For instance, sensors' values may be sampled more often or more sparsely, affecting the perception that the application has of its operating environment along the time scale. In turn, as stemming from the distributed nature of the communicating system at hand, such an adaptation along time would immediately cause adaptation across space too, by affecting the communication rate of devices, hence the rate at which events and information spread across the network. It is worth emphasizing that this a consequence of embracing a notion of time founded on causality. In fact, as we are aware of computational models adaptive to the time fabric, as mentioned in Sect. 2, we are not aware of any model allowing *programming* the perception of time at the application level.

Adapting to Causality. Being able to program the space-time fabric as described above necessarily requires the capability of being *aware* of the space-time fabric in the first place. When the notion of space-time is crafted upon the notion of causality between events, such a form of awareness translates to awareness of the *dynamics of causal relations* among events. Under this perspective, the application is no longer adapting to the passage of time and the extent of space, but to the temporal and spatial distribution of causal relations among events. In other words, the application is able to "chase" events not only as they travel across time and space, but also as their "traveling speed" changes. For instance, whenever in a given region of space some event happens more frequently, devices operating in the same area may compute more frequently as well, increasing the rate of communications among devices in that region, thus leading to an overall better recognition of the quickening dynamics of the phenomenon under observation.

Controlling Situatedness. The ability to control both the above mentioned capabilities at the application level enables unprecedented fine control over the *degree of situatedness* exhibited by the overall system, along two dimensions: the ability to decide the granularity at which event triggers should be perceived; and the ability to decide how to adapt to changes in events dynamics. In modern distributed and pervasive systems the ability to quickly react to changes in environment dynamics are of paramount importance [32]. For instance, in the mentioned case of landslide monitoring, as anomalies in measurement increase in frequency, intensity, and geographical coverage, the monitoring application should match the pace of the accelerating dynamics.

Co-causal Field Computation. On the practical side, associating field computations to programmable scheduling policies brings both advantages and risks (as most extensions to expressiveness do). One important gain in *expressiveness* is the ability to let field computation affect the scheduling policy of other field computations, as in the example of crowd steering or landslide monitoring: the denser some regions get, the faster will the steering field be computed; the more intense vibrations of the ground get, the more frequently monitoring is performed. On the other hand, this opens the door to *circular dependencies* among fields computations and the scheduling policies, which can possibly lead to *deadlocks* or *livelocks*. Therefore, it is good practice for time-fluid field coordination systems that at least one field computation depends solely on local event triggers, and that dependencies among diverse field computations are carefully crafted and possibly enriched with local control.

Pure Reactivity and Its Limitations. Technically, replacing a scheduler guided by a fixed clock with one triggering computations as consequence of events, turns the system from time-driven to *event-driven*. In principle, this makes the system *purely reactive*: the system is idle unless some event trigger happens. Depending on the application at hand, this may be a blessing or a curse: since pro-activity is lost, the system is chained to the dynamics of event triggers, and cannot act on its own will. Of course, it is easy to overcome such a limitation: assuming a clock is available in the pool of event triggers makes pro-activity a particular case of reactivity, where the tick of the clock dictates the granularity. Furthermore, since policies allow the specification of a set of event triggers causing re-evaluation, the designer can always design a "fall-back" plan relying on expiration of a timer: for instance, it's possible (and reasonable) to express a policy such as "trigger as soon as ϵ happens, or timer τ expires, whichever comes first".

4 Time-Fluid Aggregate Computing

The proposed model has been prototypically reified within the framework of aggregate computing [5]. In particular, we leveraged the Alchemist Simulator [26]'s pre-existing support for the Protelis programming language [27] and the Scafi Scala DSL [39], and we produced a modified prototype platform supporting the definition of policies using the same aggregate programming language used for the actual software specification. The framework has been open sourced and publicly released, and it has been exercised in a paradigmatic experiment.

In this section we first briefly provide details about the Protelis programming language, which we use to showcase the expressive power of the proposed system by examples, then we present an experiment showing how the time-fluid architecture may allow for improved precision as well as reduced resource use.

4.1 A Short Protelis Primer

This Protelis language primer is intended as a quick reference for understanding the subsequent examples. Entering the language details is out of the scope of this work, only the set of features used in this paper will be introduced. Protelis is a purely functional, higher-order, interpreted, and dynamically typed aggregate programming language interoperable with Java.

Programs are written in modules, and are composed of any number of function definitions and of an optional main script. `module some:namespace` creates a new module whose fully qualified name is `some:namespace`. Modules' functions can be imported locally using the `import` keyword followed by the fully qualified module name. The same keyword can be used to import Java members, with `org` `.protelis.Builtins`, `java.lang.Math`, and `java.lang.Double` being pre-imported. Similarly to other dynamic languages such as Ruby and Python, in Protelis top level code outside any function is considered to be the main script.

`def f(a, b) { code }` defines a new function named `f` with two arguments `a` and `b`, which executes all the expressions in `code` upon invocation, returning the value of the last one. In case the function has a single expression, a shorter, Scala/Kotlin style syntax is allowed: `def f(a, b) = expression`.

The `rep (v <- initial) { code }` expression enables stateful computation by associating `v` with either the previous result of the `rep` evaluation, or with the value of the `initial` expression, The `code` block is then evaluated, and its result is returned (and used as value for `v` in the subsequent round).

The `if(condition) {then} else {otherwise}` expression requires `condition` to evaluate to a boolean value; if such value is `true` the `then` block is evaluated and the value of its last expression returned, while if the value of `condition` is `false` the `otherwise` code block gets executed, and the value of its last expression returned. Notably, `rep` expressions that find themselves in a non-evaluated branch lose their previously computed state, hence restarting the state computation from the initial value. This behavior is peculiar of the field calculus semantics, where the branching construct is lifted to a distributed operator with the meaning of domain segmentation [3].

The `let v = expression` statement adds a variable named `v` to the local name space, associating its value to the value of the `expression` evaluation. Square brackets delimit tuple literals: `[]` evaluates to an empty tuple, `[1, 2,"foo"]` to a tuple of three elements with two numbers and a string. Methods can be invoked with the same syntax of Java: `obj.method(a, b)` tries to invoke method `member` on the result of evaluation of expression `obj`, passing the results of the evaluation of expressions `a` and `b` as arguments. Special keywords `self` and `env` allow access to contextual information. `self` exposes sensors via direct method call (typically leveraged for system access), while `env` allows dynamic access to sensors by name (hence supporting more dynamic contexts).

Anonymous functions are written with a syntax reminiscent of Kotlin and Groovy: `{ a, b, -> code }` evaluates to an anonymous function with two parameters and `code` as body. Protelis also shares with Kotlin the *trailing lambda convention*: if the last parameter of a function call is an anonymous function, then it can be placed outside the parentheses. If the anonymous function is the only argument to that call, the parentheses can be omitted entirely. The following calls are in fact equivalent:

```
1 [1, 2].map({ a -> a + 1 }) // returns [2, 3]
2 [1, 2].map() { a -> a + 1 } // returns [2, 3]
3 [1, 2].map { a -> a + 1 } // returns [2, 3]
```

4.2 Examples

In this section we exemplify how the proposed approach allows for a single field-based coordination language to be used for expressing both **P** and **G**. In the following discussion, event triggers provided by the platform (i.e., members of $\mathcal{T}$), will be highlighted in green. In our first example, we show a policy recreating the round-based, classic execution model, thus demonstrating how this approach supersedes the previous. Consider the following Protelis functions, which detect changes in a value:

```
1 def updated(current, condition) = rep(old <- current) {
2   if (condition(current, old)) { current } else { old }
3 } == current
4 def changed(current) = updated(current){cur, old -> cur!=old}
```

where `current` is the current value of the signal being tracked, and `condition` is a function comparing the current with the previously memorized value and returning `true` if the new value should replace the old one. Function `changed` is the simplest use of `update`, returning true whenever the input signal `current` changes. In the showcased code, the second argument to `updated` is provided using the trailing lambda syntax (see Sect. 4.1). They can be leveraged for writing a policy sensitive to platform timeouts. For instance, in the following code, we write a policy that gets re-evaluated every second (we only return `TIMER(1)` of all the possible event triggers in $\mathcal{T}$), and whose associated program runs if at least one second passed since the last round.

```
1 import platform.EventType.TIMER
2 [updated(self.getCurrentTime()) { now, last -> now-last >1 },
3    [TIMER(1)]]
```

On the opposite side of the spectrum of possible policies is a purely reactive execution: the local field computation is performed only if there is a change in the value of any available sensors (SENSOR(".*")); if a message with new information is received (MESSAGE_RECEIVED); or if a message is discarded from the neighbor knowledge base (MESSAGE_TIMEOUT), for instance because the sender of the original message is no longer available:

```
1 import platform.EventType.*
2 let reason = env.get("platform.event")
3 [reason == MESSAGE_TIMEOUT || reason == SENSOR(".*") // Regex
4    || changed(env.get("platform.neighborstate")),
5 [MESSAGE_RECEIVED, MESSAGE_TIMEOUT, SENSOR(".*")]]
```

Finally, we articulate a case in which the result of an aggregate computation is the cause for another computation to get triggered. Consider the crowd steering system mentioned in Sect. 1: we would like to update the crowd steering field only when there is a noticeable change in the perceived density of the surroundings. To do so, we first write a Protelis program leveraging the SCR pattern [8] to partition space in regions 300 meters wide and compute the average crowd density within them. Functions S (network partitioning at desired distance), summarize (aggregation of data over a spanning tree and partition-wide broadcast of the result), and distanceTo (computation of distance) come from the Protelis-lang library shipped with Protelis [11].

```
1 module io:github:steering:density
2 import ...
3 let distToLeader = distanceTo(S(300)) // network partitioning
4 // sum of all the perceived people
5 let count=summarize(distToLeader,env.get("people_count"),sum)
6 // computes an upper bound to the radius
7 let radius = summarize(distToLeader, distToLeader, max)
8 count/(2*PI*radius)//approximate crowd density as people/area
```

Its execution policy could be, for instance, reactive to updates from neighbors and to changes in a "people counting sensor", reifying the number of people perceived by this device (e.g. via a camera).

```
1  import  platform . EventType .∗
2  let  reason  =  env . get ("platform . event")
3  [reason  ==  MESSAGE_TIMEOUT  ||  reason  ==  MESSAGE_RECEIVED  ||
4  changed ( env . get ("people_count")) ,  [SENSOR("people_count")]]
```

Now that density computation is in place, the platform reifies its final result as
a local sensor, which can in turn be used to drive the steering field computation
with a policy such as:

```
1  import  ...
2  let  density  =  "io : github : steering : density"
3  [changed ( exponentialBackOff ( env . get ( density ) ,0.1 )) { cur , old −>
4    abs ( cur  −  old ) > 0.5
5  },  [SENSOR( density )]]
```

in which a low pass filter `exponentialBackOff` avoids to get the program running in case of spikes (e.g. due to the density computation re-stabilization). Note
that access to the density computation is realized by accessing a sensor with the
same name of the `module` containing the density evaluation program, thus reifying
a causal chain between field computations.

4.3 Experiment

We exercise our prototype by simulating a distance computation over a network
of situated devices. We consider a 40×40 irregular grid of devices, each located
randomly in a disc centered on the corresponding position of a regular grid; and
a single mobile node positioned to the top left of the network, free to move at a
constant speed v from left to right. Once the mobile device leaves the network,
exiting to the right side, another identical one enters the network from the left
hand side. Mobile devices and the leftmost device at bottom are "sources", and
the goal for each device is to estimate the distance to the closest source.

Computing distance from a source without a central coordinator in arbitrary networks is a representative application of aggregate computing, for which
several implementations exist [36]. In this work, since the goal is exploring the
behavior of the platform rather than the efficiency of the algorithm, we use an
adaptive Bellman-Ford [9], even though it's known not to be the most efficient
implementation for the task at hand [2]. We choose to compute the distance
from a source (a gradient) as our reference algorithm as it is one of the most
common building block over which other, more elaborate forms of coordination

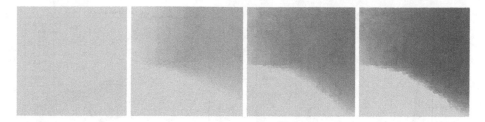

Fig. 1. Heat-map representation of executed rounds with time. Each device is depicted as a point located on its actual coordinates, time progresses from left to right. Devices start (left) with no round executed (yellow) and, with the simulation progression (left to right), execute rounds, changing their color to red. Devices closer to the static source (on the bottom left of the scenario) execute fewer rounds than those closer to the moving source, hence saving resources. (Color figure online)

get built [10,36]. We expect that an improvement in performance on this simple algorithm may lead to a cascading effect on the plethora [11] of algorithms based on it, hence our choice as a candidate for this experiment.

We let devices compute the same aggregate program with diverse policies. The baseline for assessing our proposal is the *classic* approach to aggregate computing: time-driven, unsynchronized, and fair scheduling of rounds set at 1 Hz. We compare the classic approach with time fluid versions whose policy is: *run if a new message is received or an old message timed out, and the last round was at least f^{-1} seconds ago*. The latter clause sets an upper bound to the number of event triggers a device can react to, preventing well-known limit situations such as the "raising value problem" for the adaptive Bellman-Ford [2] algorithm used in this work. We run several versions of the reactive algorithm, with diverse values for f; and we also vary $\|v\|$. For each combination of f and $\|v\|$, we perform 100 simulations with different random seeds, which also alter the irregular grid shape. We measure the overall number of executed rounds, which is a proxy metric for resource consumption (both network and energy), and the root mean square error of each device. The simulation has been implemented in Alchemist [26], writing the aggregate programs in Protelis [27]. Data has been processed with Xarray [14], and charts have been produced via matplotlib [15]. For the sake of reproducibility, the whole experiment has been automated, documented, and open sourced[1].

Intuitively, devices situated closer to the static source than to the trajectory of mobile sources should be able to execute less often. Figure 1 confirms such intuition: there is a clear border separating devices always closer to the static source, which execute much less often, from those that at times are instead closer to the mobile source. Figure 2 shows the precision of the computation for diverse values of $\|v\|$ and f, compared to the baseline. The performance of baseline is equivalent with the performance of the time-fluid version with

---

[1] https://github.com/DanySK/Experiment-2020-Coordination-Time-Fluid-AC.

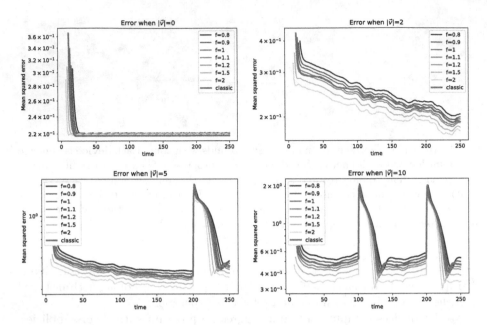

Fig. 2. Root mean squared error for diverse v. When the network is entirely static (top left), after a short stabilization time the network converges to a very low error. Errors is lower with higher f values. The performance with $f = 1$ is equivalent with the performance of the baseline. When $\|v\| \geq 5$, there is enough time for the mobile device to leave the system and for a new one to join, creating a spike in error and requiring a re-stabilization.

$f = 1$ Hz. Higher values of f decrease the error, and lower values moderately increase it. Figure 3 depicts the cost to be paid for the algorithm execution. The causal version of the computation has a large advantage when there is nothing to recompute: if the mobile device is stands still, and the gradient value does not need to be recomputed, the computation is fundamentally halted. When $\|v\| \neq 0$, the resource consumption grows; however, compared to the classic version, we can sustain $f = 1.5$ Hz with the same resource consumption. Considering that the performance of the classic version gets matched with $f = 1$ Hz, and cost gets equalized at $f = 1.5$ Hz, when 1Hz $< f < 1.5$Hz we achieve *both* better performance and lower cost. In conclusion, the time-fluid version provides a higher performance/cost ratio.

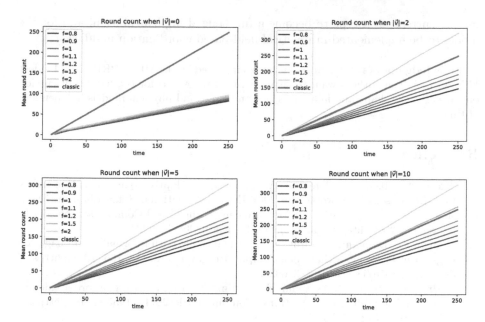

Fig. 3. Root mean squared error for diverse $\|v\|$. When the network is entirely static (top left), raising f has a minimal impact on the overall cost of execution, as the network stabilizes and recomputes only in case of time outs. In dynamic cases, instead, higher f values come with a cost to pay. However, in the proposed experiment, the cost for the baseline algorithm matches the cost of the time fluid version with $f = 1.5\,\mathrm{Hz}$, which in turn has lower error (as shown in Fig. 2).

5   Conclusion and Future Work

In this work we introduced a different concept of time for field-based coordination systems. Inspired by causal models of space-time in physics, we introduce the concept of *field of causality* for field computations, intertwining the usual coordination specification with its own actual evaluation schedule. We introduce a model that allows expressing the field of causality with the coordination language itself, and discuss the impact of its application. A model prototype is then implemented in the Alchemist simulation platform, supporting the execution of the aggregate computing field-based coordination languages Protelis, demonstrating the feasibility of the approach. Finally, the prototype is exercised in a paradigmatic experiment, highlighting the practical relevance of the approach by showing how it can improve efficiency—intended as precision in field evaluation over resource consumption.

Future work will be devoted to provide more in-depth insights by evaluating the impact of the approach in realistic setups, both in terms of scenarios (e.g. using real world data) and evaluation precision (e.g. by leveraging network simulators such as Omnet++ or NS3). Moreover, further work is required both for the current prototype to become a full fledged implementation, and for the model to be implemented in practical field-based coordination middlewares.

Acknowledgements. This work has been supported by the MIUR PRIN 2017 Project "Fluidware". The authors want to thank dr. Lorenzo Monti for the fruitful discussion on causality, the shape and fabric of space and time, and physical models independent of time.

References

1. Ageev, A., Macii, D., Flammini, A.: Towards an adaptive synchronization policy for wireless sensor networks. In: 2008 IEEE International Symposium on Precision Clock Synchronization for Measurement, Control and Communication. IEEE, September 2008. https://doi.org/10.1109/ispcs.2008.4659224
2. Audrito, G., Damiani, F., Viroli, M.: Optimal single-path information propagation in gradient-based algorithms. Sci. Comput. Program. **166**, 146–166 (2018). https://doi.org/10.1016/j.scico.2018.06.002
3. Audrito, G., Viroli, M., Damiani, F., Pianini, D., Beal, J.: A higher-order calculus of computational fields. ACM Trans. Comput. Logic **20**(1), 1–55 (2019). https://doi.org/10.1145/3285956
4. Babaoğlu, O., Marzullo, K.: Consistent Global States of Distributed Systems: Fundamental Concepts and Mechanisms, pp. 55–96. ACM Press/Addison-Wesley Publishing Co., New York/Boston (1993)
5. Beal, J., Pianini, D., Viroli, M.: Aggregate programming for the Internet of Things. IEEE Comput. **48**(9), 22–30 (2015). https://doi.org/10.1109/MC.2015.261
6. Busi, N., Gorrieri, R., Zavattaro, G.: Process calculi for coordination: from Linda to JavaSpaces. In: Rus, T. (ed.) AMAST 2000. LNCS, vol. 1816, pp. 198–212. Springer, Heidelberg (2000). https://doi.org/10.1007/3-540-45499-3_16
7. Casadei, R., Fortino, G., Pianini, D., Russo, W., Savaglio, C., Viroli, M.: Modelling and simulation of opportunistic IoT services with aggregate computing. Future Gener. Comput. Syst. **91**, 252–262 (2018). https://doi.org/10.1016/j.future.2018.09.005
8. Casadei, R., Pianini, D., Viroli, M., Natali, A.: Self-organising coordination regions: a pattern for edge computing. In: Riis Nielson, H., Tuosto, E. (eds.) COORDINATION 2019. LNCS, vol. 11533, pp. 182–199. Springer, Cham (2019). https://doi.org/10.1007/978-3-030-22397-7_11
9. Dasgupta, S., Beal, J.: A Lyapunov analysis for the robust stability of an adaptive Bellman-Ford algorithm. In: 55th IEEE Conference on Decision and Control, CDC 2016, Las Vegas, 12–14 December 2016, pp. 7282–7287 (2016). https://doi.org/10.1109/CDC.2016.7799393
10. Fernandez-Marquez, J.L., Serugendo, G.D.M., Montagna, S., Viroli, M., Arcos, J.L.: Description and composition of bio-inspired design patterns: a complete overview. Nat. Comput. **12**(1), 43–67 (2013). https://doi.org/10.1007/s11047-012-9324-y
11. Francia, M., Pianini, D., Beal, J., Viroli, M.: Towards a foundational API for resilient distributed systems design. In: 2nd IEEE International Workshops on Foundations and Applications of Self* Systems, FAS*W@SASO/ICCAC 2017, Tucson, AZ, USA, 18–22 September 2017, pp. 27–32 (2017). https://doi.org/10.1109/FAS-W.2017.116

12. Freeman, E., Hupfer, S., Arnold, K.: JavaSpaces: Principles, Patterns, and Practice. Addison-Wesley, Boston (1999)
13. Ho, Y., Huang, Y., Chu, H., Chen, L.: Adaptive sensing scheme using naive Bayes classification for environment monitoring with drone. IJDSN **14**(1), 1550147718756036 (2018). https://doi.org/10.1177/1550147718756036
14. Hoyer, S., Hamman, J.: Xarray: N-D labeled arrays and datasets in Python. J. Open Res. Softw. 5(1) (2017). https://doi.org/10.5334/jors.148
15. Hunter, J.D.: Matplotlib: a 2D graphics environment. Comput. Sci. Eng. **9**(3), 90–95 (2007). https://doi.org/10.1109/MCSE.2007.55
16. Kho, J., Rogers, A., Jennings, N.R.: Decentralized control of adaptive sampling in wireless sensor networks. TOSN **5**(3), 19:1–19:35 (2009). https://doi.org/10.1145/1525856.1525857
17. Lamport, L.: Time, clocks, and the ordering of events in a distributed system. Commun. ACM **21**(7), 558–565 (1978). https://doi.org/10.1145/359545.359563
18. Lee, J., Yoon, G., Choi, H.: Monitoring of IoT data for reducing network traffic. In: Tenth International Conference on Ubiquitous and Future Networks, ICUFN 2018, Prague, Czech Republic, 3–6 July 2018, pp. 395–397 (2018). https://doi.org/10.1109/ICUFN.2018.8436601
19. de Lemos, R., et al.: Software engineering for self-adaptive systems: research challenges in the provision of assurances. In: de Lemos, R., Garlan, D., Ghezzi, C., Giese, H. (eds.) Software Engineering for Self-Adaptive Systems III. Assurances. LNCS, vol. 9640, pp. 3–30. Springer, Cham (2017). https://doi.org/10.1007/978-3-319-74183-3_1
20. Linden, I., Jacquet, J.: On the expressiveness of timed coordination via shared dataspaces. Electron. Notes Theor. Comput. Sci. **180**(2), 71–89 (2007). https://doi.org/10.1016/j.entcs.2006.10.047
21. Lluch-Lafuente, A., Loreti, M., Montanari, U.: Asynchronous distributed execution of fixpoint-based computational fields. Log. Methods Comput. Sci. **13**(1) (2017). https://doi.org/10.23638/LMCS-13(1:13)2017
22. Lobo, F.S.: Nature of time and causality in physics. In: Psychology of Time, pp. 395–422. Emerald Group Publishing Limited, Bingley (2008)
23. Mamei, M., Zambonelli, F.: Field-Based Coordination For Pervasive Multiagent Systems. Springer Series on Agent Technology. Springer, Heidelberg (2006). https://doi.org/10.1007/3-540-27969-5
24. Mamei, M., Zambonelli, F.: Programming pervasive and mobile computing applications: the TOTA approach. ACM Trans. Softw. Eng. Methodol. **18**(4), 15:1–15:56 (2009). https://doi.org/10.1145/1538942.1538945
25. Menezes, R., Wood, A.: The fading concept in tuple-space systems. In: Haddad, H. (ed.) Proceedings of the 2006 ACM Symposium on Applied Computing (SAC), Dijon, France, 23–27 April 2006, pp. 440–444. ACM (2006). https://doi.org/10.1145/1141277.1141379
26. Pianini, D., Montagna, S., Viroli, M.: Chemical-oriented simulation of computational systems with Alchemist. J. Simul. **7**(3), 202–215 (2013). https://doi.org/10.1057/jos.2012.27
27. Pianini, D., Viroli, M., Beal, J.: Protelis: practical aggregate programming. In: Proceedings of the 30th Annual ACM Symposium on Applied Computing, Salamanca, Spain, 13–17 April 2015, pp. 1846–1853 (2015). https://doi.org/10.1145/2695664.2695913
28. Rosi, A., et al.: Landslide monitoring with sensor networks: experiences and lessons learnt from a real-world deployment. IJSNet **10**(3), 111–122 (2011). https://doi.org/10.1504/IJSNET.2011.042195

29. Rovelli, C.: Quantum mechanics without time: a model. Phys. Rev. D **42**(8), 2638–2646 (1990). https://doi.org/10.1103/physrevd.42.2638
30. Rovelli, C.: Relational quantum mechanics. Int. J. Theor. Phys. **35**(8), 1637–1678 (1996). https://doi.org/10.1007/bf02302261
31. Rovelli, C.: Loop quantum gravity. Living Rev. Relativ. **1**(1) (1998). https://doi.org/10.12942/lrr-1998-1
32. Schuster, D., Rosi, A., Mamei, M., Springer, T., Endler, M., Zambonelli, F.: Pervasive social context: taxonomy and survey. ACM TIST **4**(3), 46:1–46:22 (2013)
33. Sundararaman, B., Buy, U., Kshemkalyani, A.D.: Clock synchronization for wireless sensor networks: a survey. Ad Hoc Netw. **3**(3), 281–323 (2005). https://doi.org/10.1016/j.adhoc.2005.01.002
34. Traub, J., Breß, S., Rabl, T., Katsifodimos, A., Markl, V.: Optimized on-demand data streaming from sensor nodes. In: Proceedings of the 2017 Symposium on Cloud Computing, SoCC 2017, Santa Clara, CA, USA, 24–27 September 2017, pp. 586–597 (2017). https://doi.org/10.1145/3127479.3131621
35. Trihinas, D., Pallis, G., Dikaiakos, M.: Low-cost adaptive monitoring techniques for the Internet of Things. IEEE Trans. Serv. Comput. 1 (2018). https://doi.org/10.1109/tsc.2018.2808956
36. Viroli, M., Audrito, G., Beal, J., Damiani, F., Pianini, D.: Engineering resilient collective adaptive systems by self-stabilisation. ACM Trans. Model. Comput. Simul. **28**(2), 1–28 (2018). https://doi.org/10.1145/3177774
37. Viroli, M., Beal, J., Damiani, F., Audrito, G., Casadei, R., Pianini, D.: From field-based coordination to aggregate computing. In: Di Marzo Serugendo, G., Loreti, M. (eds.) Coordination Models and Languages. COORDINATION 2018. LNCS, vol 10852, pp. 252–279. Springer, Cham (2018). https://doi.org/10.1007/978-3-319-92408-3_12
38. Viroli, M., Casadei, M.: Biochemical tuple spaces for self-organising coordination. In: Field, J., Vasconcelos, V.T. (eds.) COORDINATION 2009. LNCS, vol. 5521, pp. 143–162. Springer, Heidelberg (2009). https://doi.org/10.1007/978-3-642-02053-7_8
39. Viroli, M., Casadei, R., Pianini, D.: Simulating large-scale aggregate MASs with Alchemist and Scala. In: Proceedings of the 2016 Federated Conference on Computer Science and Information Systems, FedCSIS 2016, Gdańsk, Poland, 11–14 September 2016, pp. 1495–1504 (2016). https://doi.org/10.15439/2016F407
40. Viroli, M., Pianini, D., Beal, J.: Linda in space-time: an adaptive coordination model for mobile ad-hoc environments. In: Sirjani, M. (ed.) COORDINATION 2012. LNCS, vol. 7274, pp. 212–229. Springer, Heidelberg (2012). https://doi.org/10.1007/978-3-642-30829-1_15

Resilient Distributed Collection Through Information Speed Thresholds

Giorgio Audrito[1]($\boxtimes$)(iD), Sergio Bergamini[1], Ferruccio Damiani[1](iD),
and Mirko Viroli[2](iD)

[1] Dipartimento di Informatica, University of Torino, Torino, Italy
{giorgio.audrito,ferruccio.damiani}@unito.it,
sergio.bergamini@edu.unito.it
[2] Alma Mater Studiorum–Università di Bologna, Cesena, Italy
mirko.viroli@unibo.it

Abstract. One of the key coordination problems in physically-deployed distributed systems, such as mobile robots, wireless sensor networks, and IoT systems in general, is to provide notions of "distributed sensing" achieved by the strict, continuous cooperation and interaction among individual devices. An archetypal operation of distributed sensing is data summarisation over a region of space, by which several higher-level problems can be addressed: counting items, measuring space, averaging environmental values, and so on. A typical coordination strategy to perform data summarisation in a peer-to-peer scenario, where devices can communicate only with a neighbourhood, is to progressively accumulate information towards one or more collector devices, though this typically exhibits problems of reactivity and fragility, especially in scenarios featuring high mobility. In this paper, we propose coordination strategies for data summarisation involving both idempotent and arithmetic aggregation operators, with the idea of controlling the minimum information propagation speed, so as to improve the reactivity to input changes. Given suitable assumptions on the network model, and under the restriction of no data loss, these algorithms achieve optimal reactivity. By empirical evaluation via simulation, accounting for various sources of volatility, and comparing to other existing implementations of data summarisation algorithms, we show that our algorithms are able to retain adequate accuracy even in high-variability scenarios where all other algorithms are significantly diverging from correct estimations.

Keywords: Data aggregation · Adaptive algorithm · Aggregate programming · Computational field · Gradient

1 Introduction

Nowadays physical environments are more and more filled with heterogeneous connected devices (intelligent and mobile, such as smartphones, drones, robots).

© IFIP International Federation for Information Processing 2020
Published by Springer Nature Switzerland AG 2020
S. Bliudze and L. Bocchi (Eds.): COORDINATION 2020, LNCS 12134, pp. 211–229, 2020.
https://doi.org/10.1007/978-3-030-50029-0_14

These contexts increasingly call for new mechanisms of collective adaptation, ultimately supporting a view of environments as acting as true *pervasive computing fabric*, where sensing, actuation and computation are naturally seen as inherently resilient and distributed across physical space [16]. In this paper we are concerned with the design of a self-adaptive coordination strategy able to realise *distributed sensing* concerning physical properties of the environment or virtual/digital characteristic of the computational one. By the strict cooperation and interaction of dynamic sets of mobile entities situated in physical proximity, distributed sensing can generally support forms of complex situation recognition [18], better monitoring of physical environment [16], and observation (and then control) of teams of agents [33]. In the context of coordination models and languages, field-based coordination [23, 31, 32] has been recently proposed as framework to program increasingly complex self-organising coordination strategies for such scenarios.

A paradigmatic coordination operation of distributed sensing is data summarisation performed on devices filling a region of space: it is a key component on top of which one can then realise other operations such as counting, integration, averaging, maximisation, and the like. In fact, data summarisation corresponds to the *reduce* phase of the MapReduce paradigm [19] ported into a "spatial" context of agents spread in a physical environment and communicating by proximity, and has close analogues designed for wireless sensor networks [29]. Data summarisation can be solved by an algorithm of *distributed collection*, where information propagates towards one or more collector devices, and combine *enroute* until reaching a unique value, i.e, the result of collection. This component of self-organising behaviour (sometimes named the "C" building block, in short [30]), is one of the most basic and widely used components of collective adaptive systems (CASs). Seen in terms of field-based coordination, collection is essentially a distributed coordination algorithm that computes a specific case of "computational field" [3, 11], namely, a data structure distributed across space such that each device holds only the local value—which, in the case of collection represents a partial result of counting in a whole sub-region. This "brick" can be applied to a variety of different contexts, as it can be instantiated for values of any data type with an associative and commutative aggregation operator.

However, implementing C can be very tricky, especially in mobile and faulty environments (i.e., with changes in the network of computational devices), which are the norm in several emerging application contexts, including airborne sensing by drones [15], crowd management by people smartphones [14], and vehicular networks [25]: existing implementations based on heuristic reasoning (single-path and multi-path [5, 30]) tend to be very fragile in practice.

In this paper we present two new algorithms for effectively and efficiently carrying on the computation of the C building block, based on a theoretical approach backed up by simulation results, which is able to achieve adequate accuracy in highly volatile scenarios. In the algorithm for idempotent aggregation (e.g. set union, maximum), as for existing multi-path collection algorithms, data chunks flow through agents through many possible links of the underlying proximity network. Which links to use are selected by imposing differentiated thresholds on minimum information propagation speed, threshold which in turn are set to the highest value ensuring that data is not discarded by all neighbours (under suitable assumptions on the network configuration). Instead, in the algorithm for arithmetic aggregation (e.g. sum, product), data chunks flow through a single outgoing link selected to ensure the maximum information propagation speed in the worst-case scenario. In both arithmetic and idempotent aggregation, the algorithms chosen are designed to maximise the worst-case information propagation speed under the given assumptions. Notice that which of the two algorithms applies depends only on the problem at hand and not on the runtime setup of a network. Thus, a system designer can decide which of the two algorithms are to be exploited depending on the properties of the aggregation operator only, and there is no overlap: arithmetic operators are never idempotent.

We validate the performance of the algorithms in archetypal situations, taking into account agent mobility and discontinuities in network configuration, as well as network size and density. Ultimately, by accounting for various sources of volatility, using different state-of-the-art distance estimations, and comparing to other existing implementations of aggregation algorithms, we show that these algorithms are able to retain acceptable precision even in high-variability scenarios where all other algorithms are significantly diverging from correct estimations.

The work of this paper is arguably a significant step in the context of engineering CASs. In general, the proposed coordination algorithm can be used as a solid component for engineering collection services in highly distributed and mobile systems. On the other hand, in the specific context of field-based coordination and aggregate computing framework [14], these algorithms provide an implementation for the fundamental "C block" as advocated in [30], coupling that of "G block" as of [6], and together forming a set of combinators effectively supporting construction of higher-level, self-stabilising coordination strategies in mobile distributed systems, such as e.g. the SCR pattern proposed in [17].

The remainder of this paper is organised as follows. Section 2 presents the state-of-the-art in data summarisation techniques and necessary backgrounds. Section 3 presents the algorithms together with the assumptions that ensure achieving optimal reactivity. Section 4 compares these algorithms with the state-of-the-art in archetypal scenarios particularly hard for summarising algorithms. Finally, Sect. 5 concludes with directions of future research.

2   Background and Related Work

2.1   Computational Model

In aggregate programming [14], a distributed network consists of mobile devices, capable to perform asynchronous computations and interacting by exchanging messages. Every device performs periodically the same sequence of operations, with an usually steady rate T: collection of received messages, computation, and

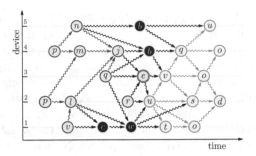

Fig. 1. Representation of an event structure, together with literal values depending on events. Past events of event e (circled blue) are depicted in red, future events in green, concurrent events in black. (Color figure online)

transmission of messages. The instants and places when and where devices start their computation are called *events* ϵ, and constitute basic element modelling the system evolution. Every event is a spatio-temporal point, happening on a device $\delta(\epsilon)$ at a certain moment in time $t(\epsilon)$ and position in space $p(\epsilon)$. The values manipulated by an aggregate program are distributed in space and evolve in time, and can thus be represented as functions of events $v(\epsilon)$. Furthermore, events are structured by the message-passing relation among them.

Definition 1 (neighbour). *An event ϵ' is a* neighbour *of an event ϵ, denoted as $\epsilon' \rightsquigarrow \epsilon$, if a message sent by ϵ' was the last from $\delta(\epsilon')$ able to reach $\delta(\epsilon)$ before ϵ occurred (and has not been discarded as obsolete since).*

Note that, in an actual asynchronous distributed system, a device could fire more frequently than another, hence multiple messages from a "fast" device could reach a "slow" target before it can fire a new round: the above definition will allow us to focus only on the latter received one. Similarly, no messages from a "slow" device could reach a "fast" target during a round, and the above definition allows to retain messages from such a slow device across rounds, increasing the computation stability. Details on when messages are persisted or discarded are not given in the definition, leaving them as a choice during system design.

The neighbouring relation on events forms a direct acyclic graph (DAG), since it is time-driven and anti-symmetric (unlike spatial-only neighbouring which is usually symmetric). The transitive closure of this relation defines the *causality* partial order $\leq$, so that $\epsilon' \leq \epsilon$ iff there exists a sequence of events $\epsilon' \rightsquigarrow \ldots \rightsquigarrow \epsilon$ connecting ϵ' to ϵ. The causality relation defines which events constitute the past, future or are concurrent to any given event. A set of events with a neighbouring and causality relation is also called *event structure*[1] (represented in Fig. 1), and

---

[1] Event structures for Petri Nets are used to model a spectrum of *possible evolutions* of a system, hence include also an *incompatibility* relation, discriminating between alternate future histories and modelling non-deterministic choice. However, following [21], we use event structures to model a "timeless" *unitary history* of events, thus avoiding the need for an incompatibility relation.

provides a basis to formally define the behaviour of a distributed system. In the remainder of this paper, we shall use the following quantities and primitives:

- the radius R within which communication succeeds;[2]
- the device $\delta(\epsilon)$ and time $t(\epsilon)$ in which event ϵ takes place;
- the time difference (lag) between neighbour events $\text{lag}(\epsilon', \epsilon) = t(\epsilon) - t(\epsilon')$;[3]
- the measured distance between neighbour events $\text{dist}(\epsilon', \epsilon)$, possibly affected by errors.

The latter can be obtained in three main different ways, depending on the time to which the two positions p' and p involved refer to: *(i)* in GPS-based systems, p' is the position measured in $t(\epsilon')$ and p is the position measured in $t(\epsilon)$; *(ii)* if distance is sensed at message receipt, both positions refer to $t(\epsilon')$; *(iii)* if distance can be sensed in every moment, then both positions may refer to $t(\epsilon)$.

Throughout the description of algorithms we will use the notation $X(\epsilon)$ to represent a distributed value X depending on *events*, while $X_{\epsilon'}(\epsilon)$ will symbolize a value depending on *neighbouring relationships* $\epsilon' \rightsquigarrow \epsilon$, that is, a quantity computed in ϵ with respect to a neighbour event ϵ'.

2.2 Self-stabilising Building Blocks

Recent works promoted an approach to engineer complex field-based coordination algorithms by combination of basic building blocks [30], capturing key mechanisms of self-organisation such as spreading (block "G"), collection (block "C"), time evolution (block "T"), leader election and partitioning (block "S"), measuring centrality [7] and so on. For instance, self-organising coordination regions can be developed by a S-G-C-G composition [17].

The most basic and versatile building block is called *gradient* (G block), which provides distance estimation, creating a spanning tree and performing broadcast operations. In particular, the *potential field* $P(\epsilon)$ of distances from a source is a crucial input of every data aggregation routine (C block), providing means to guide the direction of aggregation. Accurately computing distances in a distributed and volatile scenario is a demanding task, which can be tackled in different ways depending on the context. In spite of variations, the general framework is that of gradient-based *field computations* [23,24], where local estimates from the source are repetitively shared with neighbours and combined with proximity estimates of mutual distance.

If no proximity sensors are available, the harsh *hop-count* measure can be improved through statistical tools [22], obtaining continuous and adaptive distance estimates. Furthermore, even when a proximity sensor is available, reactivity to input changes and network variability may be impaired by the *rising value problem*[4]—simply, reaction to changes causing increase of distance is very

---

[2] In reality, the communication range of a node is very irregular. As suggested by Zhou et al. [35], such an irregular radius can be bounded, justifying the usage of a fixed quantity.

[3] Note that this quantity can be computed with reasonable accuracy even in absence of a global clock [10].

[4] Also known as the *count to infinity* problem in routing algorithms.

low [9]. Several solutions have been proposed to tackle this problem. Following recent reviews of distance estimation algorithms [6,9] three solutions are shown to always outperform basic algorithms: FLEX [12], BIS [8], and ULT [6].

FLEX is an algorithm aimed at maximising stability of values while containing the error within predictable bounds, which also addresses the rising value problem by introducing a metric distortion. BIS, instead, exploits time information in order to solve the rising value problem obtaining optimal single-path reactivity to input changes, without concerns on value stability. ULT develops on BIS by adding a stale values detector running at (faster) multi-path speed, while addressing value stability with the addition of filters and dampers. Being obtained by the integration of different methods, ULT is tuned by a large number of parameters, and can range to being almost identical to BIS (when filters and dampers are disabled) to being closer to FLEX (when dampers are active).

2.3   Distributed Data Collection

Data collection (also called aggregation) is a key component of distributed algorithms. It has been tacked in different ways depending on the application context (like, e.g., wireless sensor networks [26,29], high-performance computing [19] and spatial computing [13]). Notably, all of these different approaches rely on the same basic mechanisms. In data collection, distributed values are combined together through an aggregation operator $\oplus$ that enjoys the following properties:

1. *commutativity*: $u \oplus v = v \oplus u$;
2. *associativity*: $u \oplus (v \oplus w) = (u \oplus v) \oplus w$.

Provided that the above properties hold, the aggregation $\bigoplus C$ of the elements of a multi-set C is well-defined (the order in which the individual elements are aggregated is immaterial). Some common aggregation operators are the idempotent operators maximum and minimum, and the arithmetic operators addition and multiplication. Scenarios with intrinsic communication errors and input volatility (like, e.g., wireless sensor networks and spatial computing) require to consider a further property:

3. *continuity*: the effect on the aggregation of a certain percentage p of errors tends to zero as p tends to zero.

This property holds for the idempotent and arithmetic aggregation operators cited above, however, it does not hold for other operations like, e.g., modular sum: the modular addition of a single spurious element can fully disrupt the outcome of the aggregation of an arbitrary big collection of elements.

In the context of an environment with proximity-based interactions, given a commutative and associative operator, a data aggregation algorithm asynchronously combines input values $x(\epsilon)$ from different devices into a single value in a selected device called *source* (or *collector*). The algorithm manages the flow of data towards the source to avoid multiple aggregation of the same values.

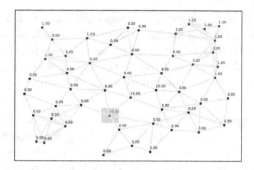

Fig. 2. A collection field in a p2p scenario that, by using single-path aggregation, counts the number of blue agents and collects the result in the red agent. Each agent holds a partial result of counting, based on how many "single-path flows" from blue agents to red agent cross it. Connections are bidirectional, and aggregation flows from smaller to greater values. (Color figure online)

This twofold prerequisite, of *acyclic* flows *directed* towards the source, is met by relying on a given *potential field* $P(\epsilon)$, approximating a certain measure of distance from the selected source. As long as information flows descending the potential field, cyclic dependencies are prevented and eventual reaching of the source is guaranteed. For each event ϵ, potential descent is enforced by splitting the set of neighbours events $E_\epsilon = \{\epsilon' \mid \epsilon' \rightsquigarrow \epsilon\}$ according to their potential value into the two disjoint sets:

$$E_\epsilon^- = \{\epsilon' \in E_\epsilon \mid P_{\epsilon'}(\epsilon) < P(\epsilon)\} \qquad \text{and} \qquad E_\epsilon^+ = \{\epsilon' \in E_\epsilon \mid P_{\epsilon'}(\epsilon) > P(\epsilon)\}.$$

Thus, values can be received only from E_ϵ^+ and must be sent only to E_ϵ^-. Three main algorithms implementing the collection block have been proposed so far: *single-path*, *multi-path* and *weighted multi-path*, all scaling to arbitrarily large systems as they require constant computational resources per node.

Single-Path Aggregation. The single-path algorithm C_{sp} ensures that information flows through a forest in the network, by sending the whole partial aggregate $C_{\mathrm{sp}}(\epsilon)$ computed during event ϵ to the single neighbour $m(\epsilon) = \epsilon'$ with minimum potential $P_{\epsilon'}$ among all neighbour events in E_ϵ. This is accomplished by repeatedly applying the following rule:

$$C_{\mathrm{sp}}(\epsilon) = x(\epsilon) \oplus \bigoplus_{\epsilon' \in E_\epsilon^+ \wedge \, \delta(m(\epsilon'))=\delta(\epsilon)} C_{\mathrm{sp}}(\epsilon') \tag{1}$$

Equation 1 computes the partial aggregate in ϵ by combining together the local input value $x(\epsilon)$ and the partial aggregates from direct predecessors ϵ' with higher potential for which $\delta(\epsilon)$ is the selected device $\delta(m(\epsilon'))$. A screenshot of this algorithm after convergence is reached is shown in Fig. 2.

Since data flows descending the potential as fast as possible, single-path aggregation attains optimal reactivity to input changes in static environments.

However, in mutable environments, the message from ϵ to $m(\epsilon)$ may be lost, disrupting communication and pruning the entire branch of the forest rooted in ϵ. This phenomenon translates into poor performances, provided that values far from the source contribute significantly to the aggregation (e.g., non-zero values for summation, high values for minimisation, and so on).

Multi-path Aggregation. The multi-path algorithm C_{mp} allows information to flow through every path compatible with the given potential field. In order to avoid double counting, it is thus necessary to divide the partial aggregate of an event ϵ equally among *every* event ϵ' with lower potential, by iteratively applying the following rule:

$$C_{\mathrm{mp}}(\epsilon) = x(\epsilon) \oplus \bigoplus_{\epsilon' \in E_\epsilon^+} \{C_{\mathrm{mp}}(\epsilon') \oslash N(\epsilon')\} \tag{2}$$

where $N(\epsilon) = |E_\epsilon^-|$ and $\oslash$ is a binary operator such that $v \oslash n$ means "dividing by n", i. e., an element that aggregated with itself n times produces the original value v. Since information needs to be "divisible" for $\oslash$ to exist, two categories of aggregation operators are supported:

1. *arithmetic operations*, e.g., point-wise sum and multiplication of vectors $v \in \mathbb{R}^n$ of real numbers (for which $\oslash$ is respectively division and root extraction);
2. *idempotent operations*, e.g., computation of maximum and minimum among values v in a partially ordered set (for which $\oslash$ is the identity function).

Thus, theoretically, multi-path has a narrower scope than single-path. However, the vast majority of practically occurring (continuous) aggregation operators can be typically recast to be either arithmetic or idempotent. In particular, idempotent operations have been used to emulate several different aggregations through statistical tools: distinct count, sum, uniform sampling, selection of most frequent values [26], and order statistics [34].

Since data flows through every possible path, it is unlikely for devices to be excluded from the aggregation, thus preventing data loss. On the other hand, the reactivity to input changes of multi-path aggregation is particularly poor. In fact, even in static environments, values flow through every possible path including the *longest* path, forcing reaction to changes to be delayed until all paths have been exploited (in particular for idempotent operations), and resulting in a reaction speed inversely proportional to the device density. In mutable environments, the problem is further exacerbated by the creation of *information loops*, which occur when two or more moving devices of similar potential invert their relative potential order in consecutive rounds, causing information from a device δ to come back to the same device, slowing down even further the reaction speed of the algorithm, and inducing exponential overestimations in the arithmetic case.

Weighted Multi-path Aggregation. Recent works [4,5] develop on the multi-path algorithm, by allowing partial aggregates to be divided unequally among neighbours. Weights corresponding to neighbours are calculated in order to penalise devices that are likely to lose their "receiving" status, a situation that can happen in two cases:

1. if the "receiving" device is too close to the edge of proximity of the "sending" device, so that it might step outside of it in the immediate future breaking the connection;
2. if the potential of the "receiving" device is too close to the potential of the "sending" device, so that their relative role of sender/receiver might be switched in the immediate future, possibly creating an "information loop" between the two devices.

Both situations are addressed by a weight function $w_{\epsilon'}(\epsilon) = d(\epsilon', \epsilon) \cdot p(\epsilon', \epsilon)$, measuring how much of the information from ϵ should be sent to a neighbour $\delta(\epsilon')$ as the product of the two corresponding factors $d(\epsilon', \epsilon) = R - \mathrm{dist}(\epsilon', \epsilon)$ and $p(\epsilon', \epsilon) = |P(\epsilon) - P(\epsilon')|$, where R is the communication radius and $\mathrm{dist}(\epsilon', \epsilon)$ the distance measured between the events. Since these weights do not sum up to any particular value, they need to be normalised by the factor $N(\epsilon) = \sum_{\epsilon' \in E_\epsilon^-} w_{\epsilon'}(\epsilon)$, obtaining normalised weights $w_{\epsilon'}(\epsilon)/N(\epsilon')$. The partial aggregates accumulated by devices can then be calculated as in C_{mp} (see 2) with the addition of weights, by iteratively applying the following rule:

$$C_{\mathrm{wmp}}(\epsilon) = x(\epsilon) \oplus \bigoplus_{\epsilon' \in E_\epsilon^+} \left\{ C_{\mathrm{wmp}}(\epsilon') \otimes \frac{w_{\delta(\epsilon)}(\epsilon')}{N(\epsilon')} \right\} \tag{3}$$

where $\otimes$ is a binary operator such that $v \otimes k$ "extracts" a certain percentage k of a local value v.[5] In particular, if $\oplus$ is arithmetic (addition) then $\otimes$ is multiplication, whereas if $\oplus$ is idempotent then $\otimes$ is a threshold function regulating which links should be exploited for transmission and which should be ignored.

This algorithm has been shown to significantly outperform both the single-path and multi-path strategies, however, it is based on heuristics hence cannot provide correctness guarantees: in fact, it produces exponentially growing peaks of error for arithmetic aggregations in scenarios with high mobility [5].

3   Collection by Lossless Information Speed Thresholds

In this section, we present the *Lossless Information Speed Thresholds* collection algorithm (C_{list}). It maximises information speed under the general assumptions presented in Sect. 2.1 and the additional assumptions on the network model given in Sect. 3.1, with respect to the algorithms satisfying the constraints given in Sect. 3.2.

---

[5] We also used the notation $w_\delta(\epsilon')$ as alias of $w_{\epsilon''}(\epsilon')$ where $\delta(\epsilon'') = \delta$.

3.1 Network Model Assumptions

As for the other summarisation algorithms, we assume a potential field $P(\epsilon)$ to be available as input in each event. Given an event ϵ, we denote as ϵ_{next} the following event on the same device, so that $\epsilon \rightsquigarrow \epsilon_{next}$ and $\delta(\epsilon) = \delta(\epsilon_{next})$. In order for C_{list} to be computed, we need a minimal degree of forecasting values in next events ϵ_{next}, as stated by the following assumptions.

- *Sure connection.* For each event ϵ and neighbour ϵ', there is a Boolean value surelyConnected$_{\epsilon'}(\epsilon)$ which is true iff ϵ is sure that its messages will be received by the next event ϵ'_{next} on $\delta(\epsilon')$, and is true for at least one neighbour event ϵ'. Such value can be computed using an upper bound on distance dist(ϵ', ϵ) together with a lower bound on connection radius R and possibly an upper bound V on device movement speed, as in the following:

$$\text{maxDistNow}(\epsilon', \epsilon) = \text{dist}(\epsilon', \epsilon) + kV \, \text{lag}(\epsilon', \epsilon) \tag{4}$$

$$\text{surelyConnected}_{\epsilon'}(\epsilon) \Leftrightarrow \text{maxDistNow}(\epsilon', \epsilon) \leq R \tag{5}$$

  where k is 0 if dist refers to $t(\epsilon)$, 1 if it refers to both $t(\epsilon')$ and $t(\epsilon)$ (GPS-based), 2 if it refers to $t(\epsilon')$ (see Sect. 2.1).
- *Scheduled time.* For each event ϵ, we assume that an upper bound $t^u(\epsilon)$ to $t(\epsilon_{next})$ is known. Notice that this is easily satisfied with high accuracy, as activations need to be scheduled and do not happen randomly.
- *Potential evolution.* For each event ϵ, we assume that an upper bound $P^u(\epsilon)$ to $P(\epsilon_{next})$ is known. For instance, given the upper bound V on device movement speed, we may set $P^u(\epsilon) = P(\epsilon) + V \cdot (t^u(\epsilon) - t(\epsilon))$. This bound may need to be corrected for the error on potential computations, and could be significantly improved if the movement direction is known.

3.2 Algorithmic Constraints

Under the previous assumptions, we focus on collection algorithms satisfying the following constraints.

- *Lossless.* A collection algorithm is *lossless* if it ensures that the input value $x(\epsilon)$ in any event participates in the outcome $C(\epsilon')$ of the algorithm for at least one event ϵ' on the collection source (that is, such that $P(\epsilon') = 0$).
- *Scalable.* We say that a distributed algorithm is *scalable* if it uses $O(1)$ message size and $O(N)$ computation time and space in every event ϵ, where N is the number of neighbours $N = |E_\epsilon|$.

3.3   Idempotent Aggregation

In the idempotent case data duplication is not an issue, and thus data loss can be easily avoided by resorting to a multi-path algorithm. However, as we will see in Sect. 4.1, plain multi-path is slow in recovering to the point of being effectively equivalent to a gossip algorithm [20]. We thus propose an algorithm that adopts intermediate strategy (as in previous heuristic-based attempts [4,5]), which transmits data on a selected set of links, maximising the *speed of information flow v* (measured as units of potential descended over time) under the assumptions on the network model illustrated in Sect. 3.1. In fact, by discarding for every starting event ϵ the longer paths towards the source and preserving the shortest ones, we ensure that old information is quickly discarded, thus allowing the algorithm to promptly adjust to input changes.

Notice that it is not possible for a *scalable* algorithm to select paths for their overall information speed v, since partial results would not be locally computable in intermediate events. Given the candidate values i reaching a same event with a potential descended of ΔP_i and a time elapsed of Δt_i, we need to select a constant-sized subset of them, without knowing the additional time Δt needed to reach the source, and thus the overall speed that each candidate may achieve. Thus, we indirectly select paths by imposing speed constraints in *each one* of their edges.

Given a potential field $P(\epsilon)$ of distances from the source, we compute a *threshold speed* $\theta(\epsilon)$ for each event ϵ, so that a message $\epsilon \rightsquigarrow \epsilon'$ is discarded iff:

$$v(\epsilon, \epsilon') = \frac{P(\epsilon) - P(\epsilon')}{t(\epsilon') - t(\epsilon)} < \theta(\epsilon) \tag{6}$$

that is, the information from ϵ to ϵ' is descending the potential at a speed lower than the threshold $\theta(\epsilon)$ computed in ϵ. We allow these thresholds to depend on the event, as a fixed global threshold can easily induce loss of data for large parts of the network. Furthermore, we compute these thresholds as the maximal (in order to prune the most paths possible) granting that at least one neighbour will not discard the message (*lossless* algorithm).

In order to compute these thresholds efficiently and effectively, we base on the network model assumptions in Sect. 3.1. For each event ϵ, we need to prevent at least one of the neighbour events $\epsilon' \rightsquigarrow \epsilon$ for which surelyConnected$_{\epsilon'}(\epsilon)$ is true from discarding the message. We then use $P^u(\cdot)$ and $t^u(\cdot)$ to predict a lower bound on the speed of the information flowing from ϵ to ϵ'_{next}:

$$v(\epsilon, \epsilon'_{\text{next}}) = \frac{P(\epsilon) - P(\epsilon'_{\text{next}})}{t(\epsilon'_{\text{next}}) - t(\epsilon)} \geq \frac{P(\epsilon) - P^u(\epsilon')}{t^u(\epsilon') - t(\epsilon)} = v_{\epsilon'}^{\text{wst}}(\epsilon) \tag{7}$$

Thus, the maximum threshold ensuring no data loss is the following:[6]

$$\theta(\epsilon) = \max\left\{ v_{\epsilon'}^{\text{wst}}(\epsilon) : \text{ surelyConnected}_{\epsilon'}(\epsilon) = \top \right\} \tag{8}$$

---

[6] If no neighbour satisfies surelyConnected$_{\epsilon'}(\epsilon)$, the no-data-loss requirement is not satisfiable and the threshold is set to $-\infty$, thus falling back to a gossip algorithm.

The partial aggregates accumulated by devices can then be calculated by iteratively applying the following rule:

$$C_{\text{list}}(\epsilon) = x(\epsilon) \oplus \bigoplus_{\epsilon' \in E_\epsilon} \left\{ C_{\text{list}}(\epsilon') : \ v(\epsilon', \epsilon) = \frac{P(\epsilon) - P(\epsilon')}{t(\epsilon) - t(\epsilon')} \geq \theta(\epsilon') \right\} \qquad (9)$$

The algorithm C_{list}, globally defined by Eqs. (7) to (9), computes the partial aggregate associated with event ϵ by combining together the local value $x(\epsilon)$ and the partial aggregates from direct predecessors ϵ' for which the true information speed $v(\epsilon', \epsilon)$ was above the threshold computed in the previous events $\theta(\epsilon')$. Although every event computes the threshold by maximising the expected future information speed, and thus choosing a neighbour that theoretically guarantees the best speed, C_{list} is not a single-path algorithm: messages $\epsilon \rightsquigarrow \epsilon'_{\text{next}}$ can flow at speed greater than the estimated $v_{\epsilon'}^{\text{wst}}(\epsilon)$ (defined in Eq. (7)) and thus pass the threshold even though the threshold was not designed for them.

According to the above explanation, the following property holds.

Property 1 (C_{list} local optimality among lossless collection algorithms). Let $\theta(\epsilon)$ be such that using information available in an event ϵ it is possible to guarantee a lowest speed of information exiting ϵ of at least $\theta(\epsilon)$ without data loss. Then the lowest speed of information exiting ϵ for C_{list} is at least $\theta(\epsilon)$.

3.4 Arithmetic Aggregation

In the arithmetic case, the situation is made more challenging by the necessity of avoiding data duplication, which can in this case lead to exponentially increasing overestimates. In order to avoid it, we modify C_{list} to become a purely single-path algorithm,[7] although the main structure remains the same. Based on Eqs. (6) to (8), we choose a selected neighbour $m(\epsilon)$ maximising $v_{m(\epsilon)}^{\text{wst}}(\epsilon)$:[8]

$$m(\epsilon) \in \left\{ \epsilon' \in E_\epsilon : \ \text{surelyConnected}_{\epsilon'}(\epsilon) = \top \ \wedge \ v_{\epsilon'}^{\text{wst}}(\epsilon) = \theta(\epsilon) \right\} \qquad (10)$$

Partial aggregates can then be accumulated as in C_{sp} (see 1):

$$C_{\text{list}}(\epsilon) = x(\epsilon) \oplus \bigoplus_{\epsilon' \in E_\epsilon \wedge \delta(m(\epsilon')) = \delta(\epsilon)} C_{\text{list}}(\epsilon') \qquad (11)$$

Thus, the C_{list} algorithm for arithmetic aggregation computes partial aggregates by combining together the local value $x(\epsilon)$ and the partial aggregates from direct predecessors ϵ' for which $\delta(\epsilon)$ was the selected device $\delta(m(\epsilon'))$.

---

[7] We also need to guarantee that a message from an event ϵ is not able to reach more than one event on a same device, that is, messages are not retained across rounds.

[8] If no neighbour satisfies surelyConnected$_{\epsilon'}(\epsilon)$, the no-data-loss requirement is not satisfiable and we select the neighbour $m(\epsilon)$ minimising the probability of data loss.

4   Experimental Evaluation

We compared the new algorithm against reference single-path, multi-path and weighted multi-path implementations (*sp* [30], *mp* [30], *wmp* [5]). The algorithms were implemented in Protelis [28], which is an implementation of the *field calculus* [11] universal language for field-based computations [3]. In particular, the implementation uses the recently proposed *share* operator [2].

The potential estimates guiding aggregation were computed using the state-of-the-art algorithm BIS introduced in [8] (see Sect. 2.2) ensuring theoretically optimal recovery speed. We also tested the usage of an exponential back-off filter to stabilise the collection results: however, we report in the following graphs only its usage for *list* on arithmetic aggregation, since it was the only case where it had a positive effect. For both the idempotent and arithmetic case, the same archetypal scenarios were selected according to the guidelines developed in [9]. The scenarios consisted of a variable number of devices with almost identical computation rate (1% systematic and accidental error) and unit disc communication model, randomly distributed in a circular area with a source device on the right end of the circle at simulation start, then discontinuously moved to the left end. Devices were moving at constant speed through randomly selected waypoints within the area. The scenarios were tested varying the three fundamental characteristics of such a network (all normalised in order to abstract from a specific communication radius or computation rate):

Hop diameter: the diameter of the circular area where devices are randomly displaced, measured as the number of communication radiuses (hops) contained. Values from 2 to 16 were considered (with a step of 1), using 10 when evaluating the other characteristics.
Neighbourhood size: the average number of devices in a communication radius area. Values from 5 to 40 were considered (with a step of 2.5), using 25 when evaluating the other characteristics.
Device speed: the movement speed of devices, measured as a percentage of the communication radius area covered during one computation round. Values from 0 to 50% were considered (with a step of 2.5%), using 25% when evaluating the other characteristics.

For each of the resulting 49 different scenarios, 10 runs with different random seeds were performed, averaging the results.[9] The default values (10 hops, 25 neighbours, 25% speed) were chosen after a broader search in the parameter space, as they were good representatives of the behaviour for most considered parameter values. The simulations were obtained with Alchemist as simulator [27] and the supercomputer OCCAM [1] as platform.[10]

---

[9] As the variance between the runs for arithmetic aggregation was significantly high, data was aggregated with median instead of mean.
[10] The actual code experiment is available at https://bitbucket.org/gaudrito/experiment-optimal-collection.

4.1   Idempotent Aggregation

We tested collection for idempotent operators by setting $\oplus$ = min and values to be aggregated chosen to make the aggregation as difficult as possible, showcasing every possible source of error. In fact, a difficult idempotent aggregation problem requires both *obsolete* and *distant* values to be able to significantly contribute to the aggregation. If obsolete values have a negligible impact, multi-path collection is optimal as it does not need to react to environmental changes. If distant values have a negligible impact, single-path collection is optimal since even a small coverage of the network may be sufficient.

In order to maximise the impact of distant values, we selected a set X of devices at the opposite border of the circular area with respect to the active source. Devices in X transmit a changing value which will be the result of the aggregation, while devices outside X have a fixed high value (set to 400) which is never the minimum. In order to showcase the impact of obsolete data, the values transmitted in X were changing in time according to the following sinusoidal-like function (see Fig. 3 for a graphical depiction):

$$x(\epsilon) = \min(\max(A\cos(2\pi(\min(t(\epsilon), 300) + \phi)/T), -M), M)$$

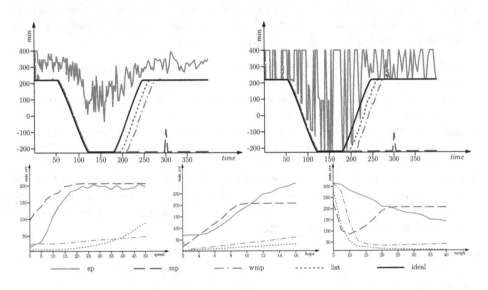

Fig. 3. Idempotent aggregation through different algorithms (sp=*single-path*, mp=*multi-path*, wmp=*weighted multi-path*, list=*lossless information speed thresholds*). Aggregation results are shown for a single run (top right) and averaged among 10 runs (top left) and *hops* = 10, *neigh* = 25, *speed* = 25. Aggregation error is shown for varying *speed*, *hops* and *neigh*, averaged among 10 runs and 400 simulated rounds (bottom).

where $t(\epsilon)$ is the time elapsed from the start of the simulation, $A = 300$ is the amplitude, $T = 250$ is the period, $\phi = -25$ is the phase, with values capped to stay within $\pm M = \pm 220$. Furthermore, at the time $t = 300$ of source switch, $x(\epsilon)$ becomes a constant equals to 220. This allows to see behaviour in all possible conditions: after a disruption, under steady inputs, and when input rises or drops.

Figure 3 summarises the evaluation results. Single-path proves to be unable to properly collect values from X in most situations except for some short time intervals, thus showing extreme variability in results, except when the number of hops is small, neighbourhood sizes are high and devices speeds are low. Multi-path produces very good results until $t = 200$, but is unable to recover when the input rises (not even after a source change), in fact behaving as a gossip algorithm, except for small networks with low density and speeds. Weighted multi-path performs quite well in all configurations, but is outperformed by *list* in all cases except for very high speeds ($>40\%$). At such high speeds, avoiding information losses forces *list* to choose a pessimistically low threshold, that could be significantly higher while keeping a low (but non-zero) probability of loss. Finally, notice that the source switch has a minimal impact on all algorithms for idempotent aggregations.

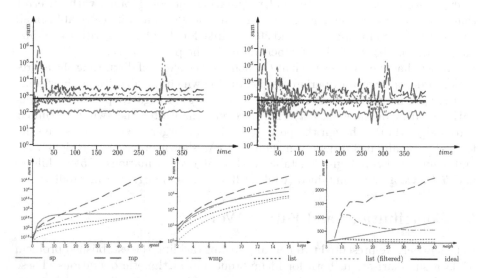

Fig. 4. Arithmetic aggregation through different algorithms (sp=*single-path*, mp=*multi-path*, wmp=*weighted multi-path*, list=*lossless information speed thresholds* with/without filter). Aggregation results are shown for a single run (top right) and averaged among 10 runs (top left) and *hops* = 10, *neigh* = 25, *speed* = 25. Aggregation error is shown for varying *speed*, *hops* and *neigh*, averaged among 10 runs and 400 simulated rounds (bottom).

4.2 Arithmetic Aggregation

We tested collection for arithmetic operators by setting $\oplus = +$ and values $x(\epsilon) = 1$ for each device. This choice amounts to *counting the total number of devices*, which is a commonly used routine and a paradigmatic example of arithmetic aggregation. We run 10 instances of each scenario and computed median results, as the relative standard errors between runs were significantly high: Fig. 4 summarises the evaluation results.

The single-path (*sp*) and multi-path (*mp*) algorithms score the worst results. Single-path underestimates the ideal value by a factor of 10 at all speeds above 5%, error that gets worse as the total number of devices increases (both by *hops* or *neigh*), showing the existence of an upper bound to the number of devices that are able to reach the source. Conversely, multi-path significantly overestimates the ideal value with errors that grow approximately linearly with the number of hops or neighbours, and exponentially with speed. Weighted multi-path, shows a behaviour similar to multi-path but with a lower error: in particular, unlike *mp*, the error decreases as the number of neighbours increases, showing better performance in high density scenarios. Finally, *list* scores the best performance in every scenario, only slightly underestimating the ideal value, with an error that tends to zero as the number of neighbors increases, and is reasonably small (below 10%) even for speeds around 30%. Unlike for the other algorithms, adding an exponential back-off filter further improves the performance.

Notice that the source switch at $t = 300$ has the effect of disrupting the aggregation process for a short period of time, during which the algorithms show some positive (for multi-path based algorithms *mp*, *wmp*) or negative peaks (for single-path based algorithms *sp*, *list*). The recovery time after the switch is similar across algorithm, although the positive peaks are larger in size (overestimating the value by about 3 orders of magnitude). As shown in Fig. 4 (top right), *mp* and *wmp* are always highly unstable, with peak overestimations of 5×; while *sp* and *list* have a more contained (while still significant) degree of instability.

5 Contributions and Future Work

In this paper, we presented two new algorithms tackling the established problem of data summarisation, both for idempotent and arithmetic operations. These algorithms are designed to maximise the speed of information flow (which translates into reactiveness to input changes) under the constraint of *no data loss*. We evaluated these algorithms in archetypal scenarios of maximal hardness, varying all fundamental (dimensionless) characteristics of a distributed network: diameter in hops, average number of neighbours, and node speed (relative to the ratio between communication radius and computation period). Overall, these algorithms significantly outperform the state-of-the-art, obtaining sound results even in scenarios with high mobility.

However, there is still some margin of future improvement. In very high mobility settings, the no-data-loss constraint forces our algorithms to an overly pessimistic behaviour, thus losing performance with respect to heuristic (lossy) techniques. In this case, future algorithms enforcing a relaxed constraint of a *maximum expected percentage* of data loss may allow for a more effective choice of the thresholds. Furthermore, our algorithms rely on a rough prediction of quantities (time and potential) across rounds: future work may directly address the prediction step, as more accurate predictions will directly translate into higher information speed thresholds, and thus reactiveness.

References

1. Aldinucci, M., Bagnasco, S., Lusso, S., Pasteris, P., Vallero, S., Rabellino, S.: The open computing cluster for advanced data manipulation (OCCAM). In: The 22nd International Conference on Computing in High Energy and Nuclear Physics (CHEP), San Francisco, USA (2016)
2. Audrito, G., Beal, J., Damiani, F., Pianini, D., Viroli, M.: The share operator for field-based coordination. In: Riis Nielson, H., Tuosto, E. (eds.) COORDINATION 2019. LNCS, vol. 11533, pp. 54–71. Springer, Cham (2019). https://doi.org/10. 1007/978-3-030-22397-7_4
3. Audrito, G., Beal, J., Damiani, F., Viroli, M.: Space-time universality of field calculus. In: Di Marzo Serugendo, G., Loreti, M. (eds.) Coordination Models and Languages. COORDINATION 2018. LNCS, vol 10852, pp. 1–20 Springer, Cham (2018). https://doi.org/10.1007/978-3-319-92408-3_1
4. Audrito, G., Bergamini, S.: Resilient blocks for summarising distributed data. In: 1st Workshop on Architectures, Languages and Paradigms for IoT (ALP4IoT), pp. 23–26 (2017). https://doi.org/10.4204/EPTCS.264.3
5. Audrito, G., Bergamini, S., Damiani, F., Viroli, M.: Effective collective summarisation of distributed data in mobile multi-agent systems. In: 18th International Conference on Autonomous Agents and MultiAgent Systems (AAMAS), pp. 1618–1626. IFAAMAS (2019). https://doi.org/10.5555/3306127.3331882
6. Audrito, G., Casadei, R., Damiani, F., Viroli, M.: Compositional blocks for optimal self-healing gradients. In: Self-Adaptive and Self-Organizing Systems (SASO), pp. 91–100. IEEE (2017). https://doi.org/10.1109/SASO.2017.18
7. Audrito, G., Damiani, F., Viroli, M.: Aggregate graph statistics. In: 1st Workshop on Architectures, Languages and Paradigms for IoT (ALP4IoT), pp. 18–22 (2017). https://doi.org/10.4204/EPTCS.264.2
8. Audrito, G., Damiani, F., Viroli, M.: Optimally-self-healing distributed gradient structures through bounded information speed. In: Jacquet, J.-M., Massink, M. (eds.) COORDINATION 2017. LNCS, vol. 10319, pp. 59–77. Springer, Cham (2017). https://doi.org/10.1007/978-3-319-59746-1_4
9. Audrito, G., Damiani, F., Viroli, M.: Optimal single-path information propagation in gradient-based algorithms. Sci. Comput. Program. **166**, 146–166 (2018). https:// doi.org/10.1016/j.scico.2018.06.002
10. Audrito, G., Damiani, F., Viroli, M., Bini, E.: Distributed real-time shortest-paths computations with the field calculus. In: IEEE Real-Time Systems Symposium (RTSS), pp. 23–34. IEEE Computer Society (2018). https://doi.org/10. 1109/RTSS.2018.00013
11. Audrito, G., Viroli, M., Damiani, F., Pianini, D., Beal, J.: A higher-order calculus of computational fields. ACM Trans. Comput. Log. **20**(1), 5:1–5:55 (2019). https:// doi.org/10.1145/3285956

12. Beal, J.: Flexible self-healing gradients. In: ACM Symposium on Applied Computing (SAC), pp. 1197–1201. SAC 2009. ACM (2009). https://doi.org/10.1145/1529282.1529550
13. Beal, J., Michel, O., Schultz, U.P.: Spatial computing: distributed systems that take advantage of our geometric world. ACM Trans. Auton. Adapt. Syst. 6(2), 11:1–11:3 (2011). https://doi.org/10.1145/1968513.1968514
14. Beal, J., Pianini, D., Viroli, M.: Aggregate programming for the Internet of Things. IEEE Comput. 48(9), 22–30 (2015). https://doi.org/10.1109/MC.2015.261
15. Beal, J., Usbeck, K., Loyall, J., Rowe, M., Metzler, J.: Adaptive opportunistic airborne sensor sharing. ACM Trans. Auton. Adapt. Syst. 13(1), 61–629 (2018). https://doi.org/10.1145/3179994
16. Bicocchi, N., Mamei, M., Zambonelli, F.: Self-organizing virtual macro sensors. ACM Trans. Auton. Adapt. Syst. 7(1), 21–228 (2012). https://doi.org/10.1145/2168260.2168262
17. Casadei, R., Pianini, D., Viroli, M., Natali, A.: Self-organising coordination regions: a pattern for edge computing. In: Riis Nielson, H., Tuosto, E. (eds.) COORDINATION 2019. LNCS, vol. 11533, pp. 182–199. Springer, Cham (2019). https://doi.org/10.1007/978-3-030-22397-7_11
18. Coutaz, J., Crowley, J.L., Dobson, S., Garlan, D.: Context is key. ACM Commun. 48(3), 49–53 (2005). https://doi.org/10.1145/1047671.1047703
19. Dean, J., Ghemawat, S.: MapReduce: simplified data processing on large clusters. ACM Commun. 51(1), 107–113 (2008). https://doi.org/10.1145/1327452.1327492
20. Jelasity, M., Montresor, A., Babaoglu, O.: Gossip-based aggregation in large dynamic networks. ACM Trans. Comput. Syst. 23(3), 219–252 (2005). https://doi.org/10.1145/1082469.1082470
21. Lamport, L.: Time, clocks, and the ordering of events in a distributed system. ACM Commun. 21(7), 558–565 (1978). https://doi.org/10.1145/359545.359563
22. Liu, Q., Pruteanu, A., Dulman, S.: Gradient-based distance estimation for spatial computers. Comput. J. 56(12), 1469–1499 (2013). https://doi.org/10.1093/comjnl/bxt124
23. Lluch-Lafuente, A., Loreti, M., Montanari, U.: Asynchronous distributed execution of fixpoint-based computational fields. Log. Methods Comput. Sci. 13(1) (2017). https://doi.org/10.23638/LMCS-13(1:13)2017
24. Mamei, M., Zambonelli, F., Leonardi, L.: Co-fields: a physically inspired approach to motion coordination. IEEE Pervasive Comput. 3(2), 52–61 (2004). https://doi.org/10.1109/MPRV.2004.1316820
25. Moustafa, H., Zhang, Y.: Vehicular Networks: Techniques, Standards, and Applications, 1st edn. Auerbach Publications, Boston (2009)
26. Nath, S., Gibbons, P.B., Seshan, S., Anderson, Z.R.: Synopsis diffusion for robust aggregation in sensor networks. TOSN 4(2), 71–740 (2008). https://doi.org/10.1145/1340771.1340773
27. Pianini, D., Montagna, S., Viroli, M.: Chemical-oriented simulation of computational systems with Alchemist. J. Simul. 7(3), 202–215 (2013). https://doi.org/10.1057/jos.2012.27
28. Pianini, D., Viroli, M., Beal, J.: Protelis: practical aggregate programming. In: ACM Symposium on Applied Computing (SAC), pp. 1846–1853 (2015). https://doi.org/10.1145/2695664.2695913
29. Talele, A.K., Patil, S.G., Chopade, N.B.: A survey on data routing and aggregation techniques for wireless sensor networks. In: International Conference on Pervasive Computing (ICPC), pp. 1–5. IEEE (2015)

30. Viroli, M., Audrito, G., Beal, J., Damiani, F., Pianini, D.: Engineering resilient collective adaptive systems by self-stabilisation. ACM Trans. Model. Comput. Simul. **28**(2), 16:1–16:28 (2018). https://doi.org/10.1145/3177774

31. Viroli, M., Beal, J., Damiani, F., Audrito, G., Casadei, R., Pianini, D.: From distributed coordination to field calculus and aggregate computing. J. Log. Algebraic Methods Program. **109**, 100486 (2019). https://doi.org/10.1016/j.jlamp.2019.100486

32. Viroli, M., Damiani, F.: A calculus of self-stabilising computational fields. In: Kühn, E., Pugliese, R. (eds.) COORDINATION 2014. LNCS, vol. 8459, pp. 163–178. Springer, Heidelberg (2014). https://doi.org/10.1007/978-3-662-43376-8_11

33. Viroli, M., Pianini, D., Ricci, A., Croatti, A.: Aggregate plans for multiagent systems. Int. J. Agent-Oriented Softw. Eng. **4**(5), 336–365 (2017). https://doi.org/10.1504/IJAOSE.2017.087638

34. Zhang, Y., Lin, X., Yuan, Y., Kitsuregawa, M., Zhou, X., Yu, J.X.: Duplicate-insensitive order statistics computation over data streams. IEEE Trans. Knowl. Data Eng. **22**(4), 493–507 (2010). https://doi.org/10.1109/TKDE.2009.68

35. Zhou, G., He, T., Krishnamurthy, S., Stankovic, J.A.: Impact of radio irregularity on wireless sensor networks. In: 2nd International Conference on Mobile Systems, Applications, and Services, MobiSys 2004, pp. 125–138. ACM, New York (2004). https://doi.org/10.1145/990064.990081

Refined Mean Field Analysis: The Gossip Shuffle Protocol Revisited

Nicolas Gast[1], Diego Latella[2], and Mieke Massink[2(✉)]

[1] INRIA, University Grenoble Alpes, Grenoble, France
[2] Consiglio Nazionale delle Ricerche, Istituto di Scienza e Tecnologie
dell'Informazione 'A. Faedo', CNR, Pisa, Italy
mieke.massink@isti.cnr.it

Abstract. Gossip protocols form the basis of many smart collective adaptive systems. They are a class of fully decentralised, simple but robust protocols for the distribution of information throughout large scale networks with hundreds or thousands of nodes. Mean field analysis methods have made it possible to approximate and analyse performance aspects of such large scale protocols in an efficient way that is *independent* of the number of nodes in the network. Taking the gossip shuffle protocol as a benchmark, we evaluate a recently developed *refined* mean field approach. We illustrate the gain in accuracy this can provide for the analysis of medium size models analysing two key performance measures: replication and coverage. We also show that refined mean field analysis requires special attention to correctly capture the coordination aspects of the gossip shuffle protocol.

Keywords: Mean field · Collective adaptive systems · Discrete time Markov chains · Gossip protocols · Self-organisation

1 Introduction and Related Work

Many collective adaptive systems rely on the decentralised distribution of information. Gossip protocols have been proposed as a paradigm that can provide a stable, scalable and reliable method for such decentralised spreading of information [2–4,6,8,9,16,21,22]. The basic mechanism of information spreading followed by a gossip shuffle protocol is that nodes exchange part of the data they keep in their cache with randomly selected peers in pairwise synchronous communications on a regular basis.

Interesting performance aspects of such gossip protocols are the replication of a newly inserted fresh data element in a network and the dynamics of network coverage. Replication of a data element occurs when nodes exchange the data element in pairwise communication. Network coverage concerns the fraction of

This research has been partially supported by the Italian MIUR project PRIN 2017FTXR7S "IT-MaTTerS" (Methods and Tools for Trustworthy Smart Systems).

© IFIP International Federation for Information Processing 2020
Published by Springer Nature Switzerland AG 2020
S. Bliudze and L. Bocchi (Eds.): COORDINATION 2020, LNCS 12134, pp. 230–239, 2020.
https://doi.org/10.1007/978-3-030-50029-0_15

the population of network nodes that have "seen" the data element since its introduction into the network, even if they may no longer have it in their cache due to further exchanges with other peers.

Traditionally, these performance measures have been studied based on simulation models. However, when large populations of nodes are involved, such simulations may be very resource consuming. Recently these protocols have been studied using classic mean field approximation techniques [1,2]. In that classic approach the full stochastic model of a gossip network, i.e. one in which each node is modelled individually, is replaced by a much simpler model in which the pairwise synchronous interactions between individual nodes are replaced by the average effect that all those interactions have on a single node and then the model of this single node is studied in the context of the overall average network behaviour. Of course, the average effects may change over time as nodes change their local states. This is taken into account in a mean field model by letting the probabilities of interactions depend on the fraction of nodes that are in a particular local state. Compared to traditional simulation methods, mean field approximation techniques scale very well to large populations because these techniques are *independent of the exact population size*[1] allowing analysis that is orders of magnitudes faster than discrete event simulation. This method of derivation of a mean field model from a large population of interacting objects relies on what is known as the assumption of "propagation of chaos" (also called "statistical independence" or "decoupling of joint probabilities") [7,10,17,19]. The assumption is based on the fact that when the number of interacting nodes becomes very large, their interactions tend to behave as if they were statistically independent.

In this paper we revisit an analysis of the gossip shuffle protocol by Bahkshi et al. in [1,2,4] by using a *refined* mean field approximation for *discrete time population models* that we developed in [12,13], and which was in turn inspired by an earlier result for continuous time population models presented in [11].

Contributions. The main contribution of this short paper (full version in [14]) is a novel benchmark (clock-synchronous) DTMC population model of the gossip shuffle protocol analysed using refined mean field analysis [12,13]. In particular:

- We show that, by using the refined mean field, a more accurate approximation can be obtained, compared to classical mean field approximation, for *medium size* populations for this gossip protocol, but that this requires a *novel model* that reflects the synchronisation effects of the pairwise interaction of the original protocol.
- The refined mean field results we obtained are very close both to those of independent Java based simulation from the literature in [2] (taken as "ground truth" for comparison with our results) and to those of the event simulation of the model itself, but several *orders of magnitude faster* and *independent* of the system size.

---

[1] As long as this size is large enough to obtain a sufficiently accurate approximation. The computational complexity of these techniques *do* depend on the number of local states of an object in a population.

Like classic mean field approaches, the refined approach is also highly scalable and computationally non-intensive. Therefore it is an interesting candidate for being integrated with other analysis approaches such as (on-the-fly) mean field model checking [18], which is planned in future work. The current study aims at providing further insight in the feasibility of applying the refined mean field approach, that implies the use of symbolic differentiation, on larger benchmark examples and in the possible complications of such an analysis that need to be taken into consideration.

2   Benchmark Gossip Shuffle Protocol

We consider the gossip shuffle protocol described in [1,2,15]. This particular version has been extensively studied by Bahkshi et al., leading to an analytical model of the gossip protocol [3], a classical mean field model [2] and a Java implementation[2] of a simulator for the protocol [1,2], which makes it a very suitable candidate of a real-world application that allows for the comparison of our results with those available in the literature. Figure 1 recalls the pseudo code of a generic shuffle protocol (adapted from [1]). Further details can be found in [1,2].

while true do	while true do
wait (Δt time units)	
B := randomPeer()	
s_A := itemsToSend(c_A);	
send s_A to B;	s_A := receive($\cdot$);
	s_B := itemsToSend(c_B);
	send s_B to sender(s_A);
s_B := receive($\cdot$);	c_B := itemKeep($c_B \setminus (s_B \setminus s_A), s_A \setminus c_B$);
c_A := itemKeep($c_A \setminus (s_A \setminus s_B), s_B \setminus c_A$);	
(a) An active node A	(b) A passive contacted node B

Fig. 1. Pseudo code of a generic shuffle protocol (adapted from [1]). c_A and s_A denote the cache and selection of active node A. Similarly, c_B and s_B denote those of passive node B. $\Delta t = G_{max}$. The operation 'itemsToSend(c_i)' selects the items to be sent from the cache c_i. The operation 'itemKeep(c, s)' in node A decides which items to keep in the cache (c) removing from the cache those selected for sending (s_A) except those that where received from B (s_B), and adding to those the elements from s_B that were not yet in the cache of A. Similarly for the operation in node B.

Two main key measures that are of interest for this protocol are the transient aspects of the *replication* of a newly introduced element in the network and that of the *coverage* of the network, i.e. the fraction of network nodes that have seen

---

[2] We thank Rena Bahkshi for sharing her Java simulator source code with us.

the new data element when time is passing. These measures depend on a number of characteristics of the network. In the following we use N to denote the size of the network, i.e. the number of gossiping nodes, n to denote the number of *different* data items in the network, c to denote the size of the cache and s to denote the size of the selected items from the cache to be exchanged with a neighbour. In the context of this work, and for comparison with the results presented in [1], the network is assumed to be *fully connected*. We consider a discrete time variant of the protocol with a maximal delay between two subsequent active data-exchanges of a node denoted by G_{max}.

3 Background

In the sequel we use theoretical results on discrete time mean field approximation [7,12,19]. We briefly recall the notation and main results in the following. We consider a population model of a system composed of $0 < N \in \mathbb{N}$ identical interacting objects, i.e. a (model of a) system of *size* N. We assume that the set $\{0, \ldots, n-1\}$ of local states of each object is finite; we refer to [12] for a discussion on how to deal with infinite dimensional models. Time is *discrete* and the behaviour of the system is characterised by a (time homogeneous) *discrete time Markov chain* (DTMC) $X^{(N)}(t) = (X_1^{(N)}(t), \ldots, X_N^{(N)}(t))$, where $X_i^{(N)}(t)$ is the state of object i at time t, for $i = 1, \ldots, N$.

The *occupancy measure vector* at time t of the model is the row-vector DTMC $M^{(N)}(t) = (M_0^{(N)}(t), \ldots, M_{n-1}^{(N)}(t))$ where, for $j = 0, \ldots, n-1$, the stochastic variable $M_j^{(N)}(t)$ denotes the *fraction* of objects in state j at time t, over the total population of N objects:

$$M_j^{(N)}(t) = \frac{1}{N} \sum_{i=1}^{N} 1_{\{X_i^{(N)}(t)=j\}}$$

and $1_{\{x=j\}}$ is equal to 1 if $x = j$ and 0 otherwise. At each time step $t \in \mathbb{N}$ each object performs a local transition, possibly changing its state. The transitions of any two objects are assumed to be independent from each other, while the transition probabilities of an object may depend also on $M(t)$, thus, for large N, the probabilistic behaviour of an object is characterised by the one-step transition probability $n \times n$ matrix $\mathbf{K}(m)$, where $\mathbf{K}_{ij}(m)$ is the probability for the object to jump from state i to state j when the occupancy measure vector is $m \in \mathcal{U}^n$, the unit simplex of $\mathbb{R}_{\geq 0}^n$, that is, $\mathcal{U}^n = \{m \in [0,1]^n \mid \sum_{i=1}^n m_i = 1\}$. In this paper, for simplicity, we assume $\mathbf{K}(m)$ to be a continuous function of m that does not depend on N. In the sequel, for reasons of presentation, we provide a graphical specification of the relevant models. The computation of matrix $\mathbf{K}(m)$ from such a model specification is straightforward.

3.1 Discrete Time Classical Mean Field Approximation

Below we recall Theorem 4.1 of [19] on classic mean field approximation, under the simplifying assumptions mentioned above:

Theorem 4.1 of [19] **(Convergence to Mean Field).** *Assume that the initial occupancy measure* $M^{(N)}(0)$ *converges almost surely to the deterministic limit* $\mu(0)$. *Define* $\mu(t)$ *iteratively by (for* $t \geq 0$*):*

$$\mu(t + 1) = \mu(t)\,\mathbf{K}(\mu(t)). \tag{1}$$

Then for any fixed time t*, almost surely,* $\lim_{N \to \infty} M^{(N)}(t) = \mu(t)$.

The above result thus allows one to use, for *large* N, a *deterministic* approximation μ of the average behaviour of a discrete population model.

3.2   Discrete Time Refined Mean Field Approximation

The following corollary illustrates the relationship between the refined mean field result and the classic convergence theorem:

Corollary 1(i) of [12] *Under the assumptions of* **Theorem 1 of** [12], *it holds that for any coordinate* i *and any time-step* $t \in \mathbb{N}$

$$\mathbb{E}\left[M_i^{(N)}(t)\right] = \mu_i(t) + \frac{V_i(t)}{N} + o\left(\frac{1}{N}\right).$$

In other words, the expected value of the fraction of the objects in local state i of the full stochastic model with population size N at time t, is equal to the classic limit mean field value $\mu_i(t)$ plus a factor $V_i(t)$, divided by the population size N plus a residual amount of order $o\left(\frac{1}{N}\right)$. $V_i(t)$ satisfies a linear recurrence relation that uses differentiation of functions and the covariance of $\mu(t)$, as shown in Theorem 1 of [12] (see also [14]), and can be implemented efficiently using symbolic differentiation software packages. It is easy to see that the larger is N the smaller this additional factor gets. Essentially, the refined mean field takes not only the first moment (the mean) but also the second moment (variance) into consideration in the approximation. In [12] we have applied this discrete time refined mean field approximation on a number of examples ranging from the well-known epidemic model SEIR to wireless networks. Here we investigate its application to a novel model of the more complex gossip shuffle protocol.

A proof-of-concept implementation of both the classical and the refined mean field techniques and a discrete event simulator has been developed by one of the authors of the present paper in F# using the DiffSharp package [5] for symbolic differentiation. The results in this paper have been obtained using this implementation which can be found at [20].

4   Refined Mean Field Approximation of the Gossip Shuffle Protocol

The classical mean field model of the gossip protocol in [1], and aggregated versions thereof in [14], are based on the principle of decoupling of joint probabilities [7,19] and on a careful study of the pairwise probabilities of the various possible outcomes of a shuffle between two gossip nodes. This model provides reasonable accuracy for systems with tens of thousands of nodes or more. However, discrete event simulation of this model for medium size systems shows that it does not respect important properties of the original gossip shuffle protocol, in particular the property that the new data element never gets lost from the system. We have found that this is caused by an inaccurate modelling of the *effects of coordination* between interacting nodes (see [14] for details).

We present a novel model in which (1) the system can never completely loose the inserted data element and (2) the model reflects the *effects* of the pairwise interaction between nodes satisfying basic properties of the original gossip shuffle protocol while still adhering to the principle of decoupling of joint probabilities. We distinguish the effects of a node getting a data element through *exchanging* it with another node–in which case the total number of replicas of the data element in the system remains the same–or through *replication*, i.e. the other node retains its copy of the data element and the global number of the data element in the system increases by one. With reference to Fig. 2, for what concerns point (1) above, we introduce the state PD to the model representing that there always is a gossip node in the network that possesses the data element.

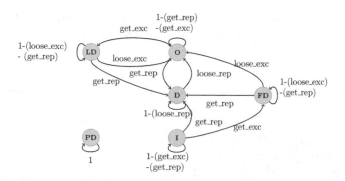

Fig. 2. Six-state model of an individual gossip node with rounds of length G_{max}.

To address point (2), we introduce states FD and LD to distinguish between the effect of interactions between gossip nodes. State FD represents the fact that the gossip node received the data element for the *first time* via an *exchange* of the data element with another node. State LD also represents the fact that the node received the data element via an *exchange*, but that it had already seen the data element in the past. Note that we can retrieve the total number of gossip nodes in the system that do *not* possess the data element as *the sum* of the nodes that are in states FD, LD, I and O because for each node in state FD (LD, resp.) there is a node in the network that just lost its data element in the synchronous shuffle with our current node. A gossip node can also get involved in an interaction in which the data element is replicated, i.e. a node gives it to another one but also retains a copy itself, and one in which two nodes, both possessing the data element, interact and one of them looses its copy. Note that in this model it is not possible that both nodes loose their copy in a single interaction. The conditional probabilities of pairs of interacting nodes obtaining or loosing the data element can be expressed in terms of n (number of different data elements), c (size of the cache) and s (number of selected elements for exchange), as follows[3]:

$$P(OD|DO) = P(DO|OD) = \frac{s}{c} * \frac{n-c}{n-s}$$
$$P(OD|OD) = P(DO|DO) = \frac{c-s}{c}$$
$$P(DD|OD) = P(DD|DO) = \frac{s}{c} * \frac{c-s}{n-s}$$
$$P(OD|DD) = P(DO|DD) = \frac{s}{c} * \frac{c-s}{c} * \frac{n-c}{n-s}$$
$$P(DD|DD) \qquad\qquad = 1.0 - 2.0 * \frac{s}{c} * \frac{c-s}{c} * \frac{n-c}{n-s}$$
$$P(OO|OO) \qquad\qquad = 1.0$$

The probability functions of the state transitions in the model below depend on m, i.e. the occupancy measure vector, the conditional probabilities, the 'no collision' probability noc, and G_{max} (see [14] for further details).

$$\mathsf{get\_exc}\,(m) \;= 2 * \frac{G_{max}}{(G_{max}+1)^2}(m_D + m_{PD})P(OD|DO)\mathsf{noc}$$
$$\mathsf{get\_rep}\,(m) \;= 2 * \frac{G_{max}}{(G_{max}+1)^2}(m_D + m_{PD})P(DD|DO)\mathsf{noc}$$

$$\mathsf{loose\_exc}\,(m) = 2 * \frac{G_{max}}{(G_{max}+1)^2}(m_O + m_I + m_{LD} + m_{FD})P(OD|DO)\mathsf{noc}$$
$$\mathsf{loose\_rep}\,(m) = 2 * \frac{G_{max}}{(G_{max}+1)^2}(m_D + m_{PD})P(DO|DD)\mathsf{noc}$$

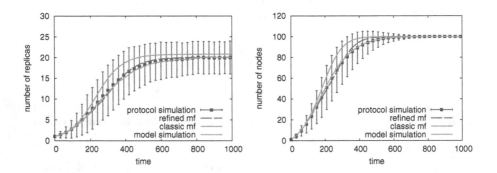

Fig. 3. Replication (left) and network coverage (right) of the data element in the network for $N = 100$ with initially 99 nodes in the I-state and 1 node in the PD-state for $G_{max} = 3$. Average of 500 simulation runs of both the model and Java simulations. Vertical bars show standard deviation for the Java simulation.

Figure 3 shows the replication as sum of the number of nodes in states D and PD and the coverage as the sum of the number of nodes in D, PD, FD, LD and O for a network with $N = 100$, $n = 500$, $c = 100$ and $s = 50$ with

---

[3] $P(A'B'|AB)$ is the conditional probability of the state of an active-passive pair AB to have state $A'B'$ after their interaction, where $A, B, A', B' \in \{O, D\}$, see [1,2].

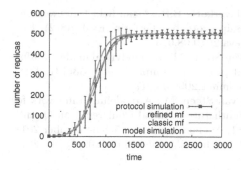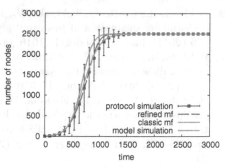

Fig. 4. Replication (left) and network coverage (right) of data element for $N = 2500$ with initially 2499 nodes in I and 1 in PD, for $G_{max} = 9$. Average of 500 simulation runs for both model and Java simulations. Vertical bars show standard deviation for the Java simulation.

initially one node in state PD and all the others in state I. Besides the classic and refined mean field approximations for the model in Fig. 2 and the Java simulation results of the actual shuffle protocol, Fig. 3 also shows the average of the model simulation. Note the good approximation of the simulation results by the refined mean field even in this very small network. Similarly good results have been found for a system with $N = 2,500$ shown in Fig. 4. A first comparison of the (non-optimised) performance of the implementation in F# of the analysis for $N = 2,500$, producing the results in Fig. 4, is: 0.5 s (classic mean field); 25.5 s (refined mean field[4]); 7 m 1.4 s (fast model simulation [19], 500 runs); 3 h 42 m 41.5 s (Java simulation, 500 runs) on a MacBook Pro, Intel i7, 16 GB.

5   Conclusions

We have developed a novel mean field model for the shuffle gossip protocol with which more accurate approximations for medium size gossip protocols can be obtained via refined mean field approximation techniques. This model respects key aspects of the protocol such as the effects of different kinds of interactions and the fact that a new data element cannot be lost by the system as a whole. Accurate approximation of medium size systems is important because many practical systems consist of many, but not a huge number of, components and simulation of such systems is still a resource consuming effort. A refined mean field approximation can provide very fast and accurate approximations.

References

1. Bakhshi, R.: Gossiping models - formal analysis of epidemic protocols. Ph.D. thesis, Vrije Universiteit Amsterdam, January 2011. http://www.cs.vu.nl/en/Images/ Gossiping_Models_van_Rena_Bakhshi_tcm210-256906.pdf

---

[4] Recall that the mean field analyses times are *independent* of the size of the system.

2. Bakhshi, R., Cloth, L., Fokkink, W., Haverkort, B.R.: Mean-field framework for performance evaluation of push-pull gossip protocols. Perform. Eval. **68**(2), 157–179 (2011). https://doi.org/10.1016/j.peva.2010.08.025

3. Bakhshi, R., Gavidia, D., Fokkink, W., van Steen, M.: An analytical model of information dissemination for a gossip-based protocol. Comput. Netw. **53**(13), 2288–2303 (2009). https://doi.org/10.1016/j.comnet.2009.03.017

4. Bakhshi, R., Gavidia, D., Fokkink, W., van Steen, M.: A modeling framework for gossip-based information spread. In: Eighth International Conference on Quantitative Evaluation of Systems, QEST 2011, Aachen, Germany, 5–8 September 2011, pp. 245–254. IEEE Computer Society (2011). https://doi.org/10.1109/QEST.2011.39

5. Baydin, A.G., Pearlmutter, B.A., Radul, A.A., Siskind, J.M.: Automatic differentiation in machine learning: a survey. J. Mach. Learn. Res. **18**, 153:1–153:43 (2018). http://jmlr.org/papers/v18/17-468.html

6. Birman, K.: The promise, and limitations, of gossip protocols. Oper. Syst. Rev. **41**(5), 8–13 (2007). https://doi.org/10.1145/1317379.1317382

7. Bortolussi, L., Hillston, J., Latella, D., Massink, M.: Continuous approximation of collective system behaviour: a tutorial. Perform. Eval. **70**(5), 317–349 (2013)

8. Frei, R., Serugendo, G.D.M.: Advances in complexity engineering. Int. J. Bio-Inspired Comput. **3**(4), 199–212 (2011). https://doi.org/10.1504/IJBIC.2011.041144

9. Frei, R., Serugendo, G.D.M.: Concepts in complexity engineering. Int. J. Bio-Inspired Comput. **3**(2), 123–139 (2011). https://doi.org/10.1504/IJBIC.2011.039911

10. Gast, N., Gaujal, B.: A mean field approach for optimization in discrete time. Discrete Event Dyn. Syst. **21**(1), 63–101 (2011). https://doi.org/10.1007/s10626-010-0094-3

11. Gast, N., Houdt, B.V.: A refined mean field approximation. Proc. ACM Meas. Anal. Comput. Syst. **1**(2), 33:1–33:28 (2017). https://doi.org/10.1145/3154491

12. Gast, N., Latella, D., Massink, M.: A refined mean field approximation of synchronous discrete-time population models. Perform. Eval. **126**, 1–21 (2018). https://doi.org/10.1016/j.peva.2018.05.002

13. Gast, N., Latella, D., Massink, M.: A refined mean field approximation for synchronous population processes. In: Workshop on Mathematical Performance Modeling and Analysis (MAMA 2018), pp. 30–32. ACM (2019). ACM SIGMETRICS Perform. Eval. Rev

14. Gast, N., Latella, D., Massink, M.: Refined mean field analysis of the gossip shuffle protocol - extended version - (2020). arXiv:2004.07519v1

15. Gavidia, D., Voulgaris, S., van Steen, M.: A gossip-based distributed news service for wireless mesh networks. In: Conference on Wireless On demand Network Systems and Services (WONS), pp. 59–67. IEEE Computer Society (2006)

16. Jelasity, M.: Gossip. In: Serugendo, G.D.M., Gleizes, M.P., Karageorgos, A. (eds.) Self-organising Software - From Natural to Artificial Adaptation. NCS, pp. 139–162. Springer, Heidelberg (2011). https://doi.org/10.1007/978-3-642-17348-6_7

17. Latella, D., Loreti, M., Massink, M.: On-the-fly PCTL fast mean-field approximated model-checking for self-organising coordination. Sci. Comput. Program. **110**, 23–50 (2015). https://doi.org/10.1016/j.scico.2015.06.009

18. Latella, D., Loreti, M., Massink, M.: FlyFast: a mean field model checker. In: Legay, A., Margaria, T. (eds.) TACAS 2017. LNCS, vol. 10206, pp. 303–309. Springer, Heidelberg (2017). https://doi.org/10.1007/978-3-662-54580-5_18

19. Le Boudec, J., McDonald, D.D., Mundinger, J.: A generic mean field convergence result for systems of interacting objects. In: Fourth International Conference on the Quantitative Evaluation of Systems (QEST 2007), Edinburgh, Scotland, UK, 17–19 September 2007, pp. 3–18. IEEE Computer Society (2007)
20. Massink, M.: Refined mean field F# implementation and gossip shuffle model. https://github.com/mimass/RefinedMF
21. Pianini, D., Beal, J., Viroli, M.: Improving gossip dynamics through overlapping replicates. In: Lluch Lafuente, A., Proença, J. (eds.) COORDINATION 2016. LNCS, vol. 9686, pp. 192–207. Springer, Cham (2016). https://doi.org/10.1007/978-3-319-39519-7_12
22. Voulgaris, S., Jelasity, M., van Steen, M.: A robust and scalable peer-to-peer gossiping protocol. In: Moro, G., Sartori, C., Singh, M.P. (eds.) AP2PC 2003. LNCS (LNAI), vol. 2872, pp. 47–58. Springer, Heidelberg (2004). https://doi.org/10.1007/978-3-540-25840-7_6

Smart Contracts

A True Concurrent Model of Smart Contracts Executions

Massimo Bartoletti[1]([✉]) [iD], Letterio Galletta[2] [iD], and Maurizio Murgia[3] [iD]

[1] University of Cagliari, Cagliari, Italy

[2] IMT School for Advanced Studies, Lucca, Italy

[3] University of Trento, Trento, Italy

Abstract. The development of blockchain technologies has enabled the trustless execution of so-called *smart contracts*, i.e. programs that regulate the exchange of assets (e.g., cryptocurrency) between users. In a decentralized blockchain, the state of smart contracts is collaboratively maintained by a peer-to-peer network of mutually untrusted nodes, which collect from users a set of *transactions* (representing the required actions on contracts), and execute them in some order. Once this sequence of transactions is appended to the blockchain, the other nodes validate it, re-executing the transactions in the same order. The serial execution of transactions does not take advantage of the multi-core architecture of modern processors, so contributing to limit the throughput. In this paper we propose a true concurrent model of smart contracts execution. Based on this, we show how static analysis of smart contracts can be exploited to parallelize the execution of transactions.

1 Introduction

Smart contracts [21] are computer programs that transfer digital assets between users without a trusted authority. Currently, smart contracts are supported by several blockchains, the first and most widespread one being Ethereum [9]. Users interact with a smart contract by sending *transactions*, which trigger state updates, and may possibly involve transfers of crypto-assets between the called contract and the users. The sequence of transactions on the blockchain determines the state of each contract, and the balance of each user.

The blockchain is maintained by a peer-to-peer network of nodes, which follow a consensus protocol to determine, at each turn, a new block of transactions to be added to the blockchain. This protocol guarantees the correct execution of contracts also in the presence of (a minority of) adversaries in the network, and ensures that all the nodes have the same view of their state. Nodes play the role of *miner* or that of *validator*. Miners gather from the network sets of transactions sent by users, and execute them *serially* to determine the new state. Once

© IFIP International Federation for Information Processing 2020
Published by Springer Nature Switzerland AG 2020
S. Bliudze and L. Bocchi (Eds.): COORDINATION 2020, LNCS 12134, pp. 243–260, 2020.
https://doi.org/10.1007/978-3-030-50029-0_16

a block is appended to the blockchain, validators re-execute all its transactions, to update their local view of the contracts state and of the users' balance. To do this, validators process the transactions exactly in the same order in which they occur in the block, since choosing a different order could potentially result in inconsistencies between the nodes (note that miners also act as validators, since they validate all the blocks received from the network).

Although executing transactions in a purely sequential fashion is quite effective to ensure the consistency of the blockchain state, in the age of multi-core processors it fails to properly exploit the computational capabilities of nodes. By enabling miners and validators to concurrently execute transactions, it would be possible to improve the efficiency and the throughput of the blockchain.

This paper exploits techniques from concurrency theory to provide a formal backbone for parallel executions of transactions. More specifically, our main contributions can be summarised as follows:

- As a first step, we formalise blockchains, giving their semantics as a function which maps each contract to its state, and each user to her balance. This semantics reflects the standard implementation of nodes, where transactions are evaluated in sequence, without any concurrency.
- We introduce two notions of *swappability* of transactions. The first is purely semantic: two adjacent transactions can be swapped if doing so preserves the semantics of the blockchain. The second notion, called *strong* swappability, is more syntactical: it checks a simple condition (inspired by Bernstein's conditions [7]) on static approximations of the variables read/written by the transactions. Theorem 2 shows that strong swappability is strictly included in the semantic relation. Further, if we transform a blockchain by repeatedly exchanging adjacent strongly swappable transactions, the resulting blockchain is observationally equivalent to the original one (Theorem 4).
- Building upon strong swappability, we devise a true concurrent model of transactions execution. To this purpose, we transform a block of transactions into an *occurrence net*, describing exactly the partial order induced by the swappability relation. We model the concurrent executions of a blockchain in terms of the *step firing sequences* (i.e. finite sequences of *sets* of transitions) of the associated occurrence net. Theorem 5 establishes that the concurrent executions and the serial one are semantically equivalent.
- We describe how miners and validators can use our results to concurrently execute transactions, exploiting the multi-core architecture available on their nodes. Remarkably, our technique is compatible with the current implementation of the Ethereum blockchain, while the other existing approaches to parallelize transactions execution would require a soft-fork.
- We apply our technique to ERC-721 tokens, one of the most common kinds of contracts in Ethereum, showing them to be suitable for parallelization.

Because of space constraints, all the proofs of our results are in [6].

2   Transactions and Blockchains

In this section we introduce a general model of transactions and blockchains, abstracting from the actual smart contracts language.

A smart contract is a finite set of functions, i.e. terms of the form $\mathtt{f}(\boldsymbol{x})\{S\}$, where $\mathtt{f}$ is a function name, $\boldsymbol{x}$ is the sequence of formal parameters (omitted when empty), and S is the function body. We postulate that the functions in a contract have distinct names. We abstract from the actual syntax of S, and we just assume that the semantics of function bodies is defined (see e.g. [5] for a concrete instance of syntax and semantics of function bodies).

Let **Val** be a set of *values*, ranged over by $v, v', \ldots$, let **Const** be a set of *constant names* $x, y, \ldots$, and let **Addr** be a set of *addresses* $\mathcal{X}, \mathcal{Y}, \ldots$, partitioned into *account addresses* $\mathcal{A}, \mathcal{B}, \ldots$ and *contract addresses* $\mathcal{C}, \mathcal{D}, \ldots$. We assume a mapping Γ from addresses to contracts.

We assume that each contract has a key-value store, which we render as a partial function **Val** $\rightharpoonup$ **Val** from keys $k \in$ **Val** to values. The state of the blockchain is a function $\sigma : $ **Addr** $\rightarrow$ (**Val** $\rightharpoonup$ **Val**) from addresses to key-value stores. We postulate that $\mathtt{balance} \in \operatorname{dom} \sigma \mathcal{X}$ for all $\mathcal{X}$. A *qualified key* is a term of the form $\mathcal{X}.k$. We write $\sigma(\mathcal{X}.k)$ for $\sigma \mathcal{X} k$; when $k \notin \operatorname{dom} \sigma \mathcal{X}$, we write $\sigma(\mathcal{X}.k) = \bot$. We use $p, q, \ldots$ to range over qualified keys, $P, Q, \ldots$ to range over sets of them, and $\mathbb{P}$ to denote the set of all qualified keys.

To have a uniform treatment of accounts and contracts, we assume that for all account addresses $\mathcal{A}$, $\operatorname{dom} \sigma \mathcal{A} = \{\mathtt{balance}\}$, and that the contract $\Gamma(\mathcal{A})$ has exactly one function, which just skips. In this way, the statement $\mathcal{A}.$ (n), which transfers n currency units to $\mathcal{A}$, can be rendered as a call to this function.

State updates define how values associated with qualified keys are modified.

Definition 1 (State update). *A state update* $\pi : $ **Addr** $\rightharpoonup$ (**Val** $\rightharpoonup$ **Val**) *is a function from qualified keys to values; we denote with* $\{v/\mathcal{X}.k\}$ *the state update which maps* $\mathcal{X}.k$ *to* v. *We define* keys(π) *as the set of qualified keys* $\mathcal{X}.k$ *such that* $\mathcal{X} \in \operatorname{dom} \pi$ *and* $k \in \operatorname{dom} \pi \mathcal{X}$. *We apply updates to states as follows:*

$$(\sigma \pi)\mathcal{X} = \delta_{\mathcal{X}} \quad where \quad \delta_{\mathcal{X}} k = \begin{cases} \pi \mathcal{X} k & if \ \mathcal{X}.k \in \operatorname{keys}(\pi) \\ \sigma \mathcal{X} k & otherwise \end{cases} \qquad \diamond$$

We denote with $[\![S]\!]_{\sigma,\rho}^{\mathcal{X}}$ the semantics of the statement S. This semantics is either a blockchain state σ', or it is undefined (denoted by $\bot$). The semantics is parameterised over a state σ, an address $\mathcal{X}$ (the contract wherein S is evaluated), and an *environment* $\rho : $ **Const** $\rightharpoonup$ **Val**, used to evaluate the formal parameters and the special names $\mathtt{sender}$ and $\mathtt{value}$. These names represent, respectively, the caller of the function, and the amount of currency transferred along with the call. We postulate that $\mathtt{sender}$ and $\mathtt{value}$ are not used as formal parameters.

We define the auxiliary operators $+$ and $-$ on states as follows:

$$\sigma \circ (\mathcal{X} : n) = \sigma\{(\sigma \mathcal{X} \mathtt{balance}) \circ n / \mathcal{X}.\mathtt{balance}\} \qquad (\circ \in \{+, -\})$$

i.e., $\sigma + \mathcal{X} : n$ updates σ by increasing the $\mathtt{balance}$ of $\mathcal{X}$ of n currency units.

A *transaction* T is a term of the form:

$$A \xrightarrow{n} \mathcal{C} : \mathtt{f}(\boldsymbol{v})$$

Intuitively, A is the address of the caller, $\mathcal{C}$ is the address of the called contract, $\mathtt{f}$ is the called function, n is the value transferred from A to $\mathcal{C}$, and $\boldsymbol{v}$ is the sequence of actual parameters. We denote the semantics of T in σ as $[\![T]\!]_\sigma$, where the function $[\![\cdot]\!]_\sigma$ is defined in Fig. 1, which we briefly comment.

$$\dfrac{\begin{array}{c}\mathtt{f}(\boldsymbol{x})\{S\} \in \varGamma(\mathcal{C}) \\ \sigma\, A\, \mathtt{balance} \geq n \\ [\![S]\!]^{\mathcal{C}}_{\sigma - A:n + \mathcal{C}:n,\, \{A/\mathtt{sender},\, n/\mathtt{value},\, v/\boldsymbol{x}\}} = \sigma'\end{array}}{[\![A \xrightarrow{n} \mathcal{C} : \mathtt{f}(v)]\!]_\sigma = \sigma'}\ {\scriptstyle[\text{Tx1}]} \qquad \dfrac{\begin{array}{c}\mathtt{f}(\boldsymbol{x})\{S\} \in \varGamma(\mathcal{C}) \\ \left(\begin{array}{cc}\sigma\, A\, \mathtt{balance} < n & \text{or} \\ [\![S]\!]^{\mathcal{C}}_{\sigma - A:n + \mathcal{C}:n,\, \{A/\mathtt{sender},\, n/\mathtt{value},\, v/\boldsymbol{x}\}} = \bot\end{array}\right)\end{array}}{[\![A \xrightarrow{n} \mathcal{C} : \mathtt{f}(v)]\!]_\sigma = \sigma}\ {\scriptstyle[\text{Tx2}]}$$

Fig. 1. Semantics of transactions.

The semantics of a transaction $T = A \xrightarrow{n} \mathcal{C} : \mathtt{f}(\boldsymbol{v})$, in a given blockchain state σ, is a new state σ'. Rule [Tx1] handles the case where the transaction is successful: this happens when A's balance is at least n, and the function call terminates in a non-error state. Note that n units of currency are transferred to $\mathcal{C}$ *before* starting to execute $\mathtt{f}$, and that the names sender and value are bound, respectively, to A and n. Rule [Tx2] applies either when A's balance is not enough, or the execution of $\mathtt{f}$ fails. In these cases, T does not alter the state.

A *blockchain* **B** is a finite sequence of transactions; we denote with ϵ the empty blockchain. The semantics of a blockchain is obtained by folding the semantics of its transactions, starting from a given state σ:

$$[\![\epsilon]\!]_\sigma = \sigma \qquad [\![T\mathbf{B}]\!]_\sigma = [\![\mathbf{B}]\!]_{[\![T]\!]_\sigma}$$

Note that erroneous transactions can occur within a blockchain, but they have no effect on its semantics (as rule [Tx2] makes them identities w.r.t. the append operation). We assume that in the initial state of the blockchain, denoted by $\sigma^\star$, each address $\mathcal{X}$ has a balance $n^\star_\mathcal{X} \geq 0$, while all the other keys are unbound.

We write $[\![\mathbf{B}]\!]$ for $[\![\mathbf{B}]\!]_{\sigma^\star}$, where $\sigma^\star \mathcal{X} = \{n^\star_\mathcal{X}/\mathtt{balance}\}$. We say that a state σ is *reachable* if $\sigma = [\![\mathbf{B}]\!]$ for some **B**.

Example 1. Consider the following functions of a contract at address $\mathcal{C}$:

$$\mathtt{f}_0()\{x := 1\} \qquad \mathtt{f}_1()\{\mathbf{if}\ x = 0\ \mathbf{then}\ \mathcal{B}. \qquad (1)\} \qquad \mathtt{f}_2()\{\mathcal{B}. \qquad (1)\}$$

Let σ be a state such that $\sigma A\, \mathtt{balance} \geq 2$, and let $\mathbf{B} = T_0 T_1 T_2$, where:

$$T_0 = A \xrightarrow{0} \mathcal{C} : \mathtt{f}_0() \qquad T_1 = A \xrightarrow{1} \mathcal{C} : \mathtt{f}_1() \qquad T_2 = A \xrightarrow{1} \mathcal{C} : \mathtt{f}_2()$$

By applying rule [Tx1] three times, we have that:

$$[\![T_0]\!]_\sigma = [\![x:=1]\!]^{\mathcal{C}}_{\sigma,\,\{^{\mathcal{A}}/\text{sender},\,0/\text{value}\}} = \sigma\{1/\mathcal{C}.x\} = \sigma'$$

$$[\![T_1]\!]_{\sigma'} = [\![\text{if } x = 0 \text{ then } \mathcal{B}. \qquad (1)]\!]^{\mathcal{C}}_{\sigma'-\mathcal{A}:1+\mathcal{C}:1,\,\{^{\mathcal{A}}/\text{sender},\,1/\text{value}\}}$$

$$= \sigma' - \mathcal{A} : 1 + \mathcal{C} : 1 = \sigma''$$

$$[\![T_2]\!]_{\sigma''} = [\![\mathcal{B}. \qquad (1)]\!]^{\mathcal{C}}_{\sigma''-\mathcal{A}:1+\mathcal{C}:1,\,\{^{\mathcal{A}}/\text{sender},\,1/\text{value}\}} = \sigma'' - \mathcal{A} : 1 + \mathcal{B} : 1$$

Summing up, $[\![\mathbf{B}]\!]_\sigma = \sigma\{1/\mathcal{C}.x\} - \mathcal{A} : 2 + \mathcal{B} : 1 + \mathcal{C} : 1$. ◇

3   Swapping Transactions

We define two blockchain states to be *observationally equivalent* when they agree on the values associated to all the qualified keys. Our formalisation is parameterised on a set of qualified keys P over which we require the agreement.

Definition 2 (Observational equivalence). *For all $P \subseteq \mathbb{P}$, we define $\sigma \sim_P \sigma'$ iff $\forall p \in P : \sigma p = \sigma' p$. We say that σ and σ' are observationally equivalent, in symbols $\sigma \sim \sigma'$, when $\sigma \sim_P \sigma'$ holds for all P.* ◇

Lemma 1. *For all $P, Q \subseteq \mathbb{P}$: (i) $\sim_P$ is an equivalence relation; (ii) if $\sigma \sim_P \sigma'$ and $Q \subseteq P$, then $\sigma \sim_Q \sigma'$; (iii) $\sim = \sim_{\mathbb{P}}$.* ◇

We extend the equivalence relations above to blockchains, by passing through their semantics. For all P, we define $\mathbf{B} \sim_P \mathbf{B}'$ iff $[\![\mathbf{B}]\!]_\sigma \sim_P [\![\mathbf{B}']\!]_\sigma$ holds for all reachable σ (note that all the definitions and results in this paper apply to reachable states, since the unreachable ones do not represent actual contract executions). We write $\mathbf{B} \sim \mathbf{B}'$ when $\mathbf{B} \sim_P \mathbf{B}'$ holds for all P. The relation $\sim$ is a *congruence* with respect to the append operation, i.e. if $\mathbf{B} \sim \mathbf{B}'$ then we can replace $\mathbf{B}$ with $\mathbf{B}'$ in a larger blockchain, preserving its semantics.

Lemma 2. $\mathbf{B} \sim \mathbf{B}' \implies \forall \mathbf{B}_0, \mathbf{B}_1 : \mathbf{B}_0 \mathbf{B} \mathbf{B}_1 \sim \mathbf{B}_0 \mathbf{B}' \mathbf{B}_1$. ◇

Two transactions are *swappable* when exchanging their order preserves observational equivalence.

Definition 3 (Swappability). *Two transactions $T \neq T'$ are swappable, in symbols $T \rightleftarrows T'$, when $TT' \sim T'T$.* ◇

Example 2. Recall the transactions in Example 1. We have that $T_0 \rightleftarrows T_2$ and $T_1 \rightleftarrows T_2$, but $T_0 \not\rightleftarrows T_1$ (see Fig. 5 in Appendix A of [6]). ◇

We shall use the theory of trace languages originated from Mazurkiewicz's works [17] to study observational equivalence under various swapping relations. Below, we fix the alphabet of trace languages as the set $\mathbf{Tx}$ of all transactions.

Definition 4 (Mazurkiewicz equivalence). *Let I be a symmetric and irreflexive relation on $\mathbf{Tx}$. The Mazurkiewicz equivalence $\simeq_I$ is the least congruence in the free monoid $\mathbf{Tx}^*$ such that: $\forall T, T' \in \mathbf{Tx}: T I T' \implies TT' \simeq_I T'T$.*

Theorem 1 below states that the Mazurkiewicz equivalence constructed on the swappability relation $\rightleftarrows$ is an observational equivalence. Therefore, we can transform a blockchain into an observationally equivalent one by a finite number of exchanges of adjacent swappable transactions.

Theorem 1. $\simeq_{\rightleftarrows} \subseteq \sim$.   ◇

Example 3. We can rearrange the transactions in Example 1 as $T_0 T_1 T_2 \sim T_0 T_2 T_1 \sim T_2 T_0 T_1$. Instead, $T_1 T_0 T_2 \not\sim T_2 T_0 T_1$ (e.g., starting from a state σ such that $\sigma \mathcal{A}\mathsf{balance} = 2$ and $\sigma \mathcal{C} x = 0$, see Fig. 6 in Appendix A of [6]).   ◇

Note that the converse of Theorem 1 does not hold: indeed, $\mathbf{B} \simeq_{\rightleftarrows} \mathbf{B}'$ requires that $\mathbf{B}$ and $\mathbf{B}'$ have the same length, while $\mathbf{B} \sim \mathbf{B}'$ may also hold for blockchains of different length (e.g., $\mathbf{B}' = \mathbf{B}T$, where T does not alter the state).

Safe Approximations of Read/Written Keys. Note that the relation $\rightleftarrows$ is undecidable whenever the contract language is Turing-equivalent. So, to detect swappable transactions we follow a static approach, consisting of two steps. First, we over-approximate the set of keys read and written by transactions, by statically analysing the code of the called functions. We then check a simple condition on these approximations (Definition 7), to detect if two transactions can be swapped. Since static analyses to over-approximate read and written variables are quite standard [18], here we just rely on such approximations, by only assuming their safety. In Definition 5 we state that a set P safely approximates the keys *written* by T, when T does not alter the state of the keys not in P. Defining set of *read* keys is a bit trickier: intuitively, we require that if we execute the transaction starting from two states that agree on the values of the keys in the read set, then these executions should be equivalent, in the sense that they do not introduce new differences between the resulting states (with respect to the difference already existing before).

Definition 5 (Safe approximation of read/written keys). *Given a set of qualified keys P and a transaction T, we define:*

$$P \models^w T \quad \textit{iff} \quad \forall Q : Q \cap P = \emptyset \implies T \sim_Q \epsilon$$
$$P \models^r T \quad \textit{iff} \quad \forall \mathbf{B}, \mathbf{B}', Q : \mathbf{B} \sim_P \mathbf{B}' \wedge \mathbf{B} \sim_Q \mathbf{B}' \implies \mathbf{B}T \sim_Q \mathbf{B}'T \qquad ◇$$

Example 4. Let $T = \mathcal{A} \xrightarrow{1} \mathcal{C} : \mathtt{f}()$, where $\mathtt{f}()\{\mathcal{B}. \qquad (1)\}$ is a function of $\mathcal{C}$. The execution of T affects the $\mathsf{balance}$ of $\mathcal{A}$, $\mathcal{B}$ and $\mathcal{C}$; however, $\mathcal{C}.\mathsf{balance}$ is first incremented and then decremented, and so its value remains unchanged. Then, $\{\mathcal{A}.\mathsf{balance}, \mathcal{B}.\mathsf{balance}\} \models^w T$, and it is the smallest safe approximation of the keys written by T. To prove that $P = \{\mathcal{A}.\mathsf{balance}\} \models^r T$, assume two blockchains $\mathbf{B}$ and $\mathbf{B}'$ and a set of keys Q such that $\mathbf{B} \sim_P \mathbf{B}'$ and $\mathbf{B} \sim_Q \mathbf{B}'$. If $[\![\mathbf{B}]\!]\mathcal{A}\mathsf{balance} < 1$, then by [Tx2] we have $[\![\mathbf{B}T]\!] = [\![\mathbf{B}]\!]$. Since $\mathbf{B} \sim_P \mathbf{B}'$, then also $[\![\mathbf{B}']\!]\mathcal{A}\mathsf{balance} < 1$, and so by [Tx2] we have $[\![\mathbf{B}'T]\!] = [\![\mathbf{B}']\!]$. Then, $\mathbf{B}T \sim_Q \mathbf{B}'T$. Otherwise, if $[\![\mathbf{B}]\!]\mathcal{A}\mathsf{balance} = n \geq 1$, then by [Tx1] the execution of T transfers one unit of currency from $\mathcal{A}$ to $\mathcal{B}$, so the execution of T affects exactly $\mathcal{A}$.balance and $\mathcal{B}$.balance. So, it is enough to show that $\mathbf{B} \sim_{\{q\}} \mathbf{B'}$ implies $\mathbf{BT} \sim_{\{q\}} \mathbf{B'T}$ for $q \in \{\mathcal{A}.\text{balance}, \mathcal{B}.\text{balance}\}$. For $q = \mathcal{A}.\text{balance}$, we have that $[\![\mathbf{B'T}]\!]\mathcal{A}\text{balance} = n - 1 = [\![\mathbf{BT}]\!]\mathcal{A}\text{balance}$. For $q = \mathcal{B}.\text{balance}$, we have that $[\![\mathbf{B'T}]\!]\mathcal{B}\text{balance} = [\![\mathbf{B'}]\!]\mathcal{B}\text{balance} + 1 = [\![\mathbf{B}]\!]\mathcal{B}\text{balance} + 1 = [\![\mathbf{BT}]\!]\mathcal{B}\text{balance}$. Therefore, we conclude that $P \models^r \mathsf{T}$.   ◇

Widening a safe approximation (either of read or written keys) preserves its safety; further, the intersection of two safe write approximations is still safe (see Lemma 6 in Appendix A of [6]). From this, it follows that there exists a *least* safe approximation of the keys written by a transaction.

Strong Swappability. We use safe approximations of the read/written keys to detect when two transactions are swappable. To achieve that, we check whether two transactions T and $\mathsf{T'}$ operate on disjoint portions of the blockchain state. More specifically, we recast in our setting Bernstein's conditions [7] for the parallel execution of processes: it suffices to check that the set of keys written by T is disjoint from those written or read by $\mathsf{T'}$, and vice versa. When this happens we say that the two transactions are *strongly swappable*.

Definition 6 (Strong swappability). *We say that two transactions $\mathsf{T} \neq \mathsf{T'}$ are strongly swappable, in symbols $\mathsf{T}\#\mathsf{T'}$, when there exist $W, W', R, R' \subseteq \mathbb{P}$ such that $W \models^w \mathsf{T}$, $W' \models^w \mathsf{T'}$, $R \models^r \mathsf{T}$, $R' \models^r \mathsf{T'}$, and:*

$$(R \cup W) \cap W' = \emptyset = (R' \cup W') \cap W \qquad ◇$$

Example 5. Let $\mathtt{f_1}()\{\mathtt{skip}\}$ and $\mathtt{f_2}(x)\{x.\qquad (\mathtt{value})\}$ be functions of the contracts $\mathcal{C}_1$ and $\mathcal{C}_2$, respectively, and consider the following transactions:

$$\mathsf{T}_1 = \mathcal{A} \xrightarrow{1} \mathcal{C}_1 : \mathtt{f_1}() \qquad\qquad \mathsf{T}_2 = \mathcal{B} \xrightarrow{1} \mathcal{C}_2 : \mathtt{f_2}(\mathcal{F})$$

where $\mathcal{A}$, $\mathcal{B}$, and $\mathcal{F}$ are account addresses. To prove that $\mathsf{T}_1\#\mathsf{T}_2$, consider the following safe approximations of the written/read keys of T_1 and T_2, respectively:

$$W_1 = \{\mathcal{A}.\text{balance}, \mathcal{C}_1.\text{balance}\} \models^w \mathsf{T}_1 \qquad R_1 = \{\mathcal{A}.\text{balance}\} \models^r \mathsf{T}_1$$
$$W_2 = \{\mathcal{B}.\text{balance}, \mathcal{F}.\text{balance}\} \models^w \mathsf{T}_2 \qquad R_2 = \{\mathcal{B}.\text{balance}\} \models^r \mathsf{T}_2$$

Since $(W_1 \cup R_1) \cap W_2 = \emptyset = (W_2 \cup R_2) \cap W_1$, the two transactions are strongly swappable. Now, let:

$$\mathsf{T}_3 = \mathcal{B} \xrightarrow{1} \mathcal{C}_2 : \mathtt{f_2}(\mathcal{A})$$

and consider the following safe approximations W_3 and R_3:

$$W_3 = \{\mathcal{B}.\text{balance}, \mathcal{A}.\text{balance}\} \models^w \mathsf{T}_3 \qquad R_3 = \{\mathcal{B}.\text{balance}\} \models^r \mathsf{T}_3$$

Since $W_1 \cap W_3 \neq \emptyset \neq W_2 \cap W_3$, then $\neg(\mathsf{T}_1\#\mathsf{T}_3)$ and $\neg(\mathsf{T}_2\#\mathsf{T}_3)$.   ◇

The following theorem ensures the soundness of our approximation, i.e. that if two transactions are strongly swappable, then they are also swappable. The converse implication does not hold, as witnessed by Example 6.

Theorem 2. $T \# T' \implies T \rightleftarrows T'$.   ◇

Example 6 (Swappable transactions, not strongly). Consider the following functions and transactions of a contract at address C:

$$f_1()\{\text{if sender} = A \quad k_1 = 0 \text{ then } k_1{:=}1 \text{ else throw}\} \quad T_1 = A \xrightarrow{1} C : f_1()$$

$$f_2()\{\text{if sender} = B \quad k_2 = 0 \text{ then } k_2{:=}1 \text{ else throw}\} \quad T_2 = B \xrightarrow{1} C : f_2()$$

We prove that $T_1 \rightleftarrows T_2$. First, consider a state σ such that $\sigma A \text{balance} > 1$, $\sigma B \text{balance} > 1$, $\sigma C \text{balance} = n$, $\sigma C k_1 = 0$ and $\sigma C k_2 = 0$. We have that:

$$[\![T_1 T_2]\!]_\sigma = \sigma\{1/C.k_1, 1/C.k_2, n+2/C.\text{balance}\} = [\![T_2 T_1]\!]_\sigma$$

In the second case, let σ be such that $\sigma A \text{balance} < 1$, or $\sigma B \text{balance} < 1$, or $\sigma C k_1 \neq 0$, or $\sigma C k_2 \neq 0$. It is not possible that the guards in f_1 and f_2 are both true, so T_1 or T_2 raise an exception, leaving the state unaffected. Then, also in this case we have that $[\![T_1 T_2]\!]_\sigma = [\![T_2 T_1]\!]_\sigma$, and so T_1 and T_2 are swappable. However, they are *not* strongly swappable if there exist reachable states σ, σ' such that $\sigma C k_1 = 0 = \sigma' C k_2$. To see why, let $W_1 = \{A.\text{balance}, C.\text{balance}, C.k_1\}$. From the code of f_0 we see that W_1 is the least safe over-approximation of the written keys of T_1 ($W_1 \models^w T_1$). This means that every safe approximation of T_1 must include the keys of W_1. Similarly, $W_2 = \{B.\text{balance}, C.\text{balance}, C.k_2\}$ is the least safe over-approximation of the written keys of T_2 ($W_2 \models^w T_2$). Since the least safe approximations of the keys written by T_1 and T_2 are not disjoint, $T_1 \# T_2$ does not hold.   ◇

Theorem 3 states that the Mazurkiewicz equivalence $\simeq_\#$ is stricter than $\simeq_\rightleftarrows$. Together with Theorem 1, if **B** is transformed into **B'** by exchanging adjacent strongly swappable transactions, then **B** and **B'** are observationally equivalent.

Theorem 3. $\simeq_\# \subseteq \simeq_\rightleftarrows$.   ◇

Note that if the contract language is Turing-equivalent, then finding approximations which satisfy the disjointness condition in Definition 6 is not computable, and so the relation $\#$ is undecidable.

Parameterised Strong Swappability. Strongly swappability abstracts from the actual static analysis used to obtain the safe approximations: it is sufficient that such an analysis exists. Definition 7 below parameterises strong swappability over a static analysis, which we represent as a function from transactions to sets of qualified keys, just requiring it to be a safe approximation. Formally, we say that W is a *static analysis of written keys* when $W(T) \models^w T$, for all T; similarly, R is a *static analysis of read keys* when $R(T) \models^r T$, for all T.

Definition 7 (Parameterised strong swappability). *Let W and R be static analyses of written/read keys. We say that T, T' are strongly swappable w.r.t. W and R, in symbols $T \#_R^W T'$, if:*

$$(R(T) \cup W(T)) \cap W(T') = \emptyset = (R(T') \cup W(T')) \cap W(T) \qquad ◇$$

Note that an effective procedure for computing W and R gives an effective procedure to determine whether two transactions are (strongly) swappable.

Lemma 3. *For all static analyses W and R: (i) $\#_R^W \subseteq \#$; (ii) if W and R are computable, then $\#_R^W$ is decidable.* ◇

From the inclusion in item (i) of Lemma 3 and from Theorem 3 we obtain:

Theorem 4. $\simeq_{\#_R^W} \subseteq \simeq_\# \subseteq \simeq_\rightleftarrows.$ ◇

4 True Concurrency for Blockchains

Given a swappability relation $\mathcal{R}$, we transform a sequence of transactions **B** into an *occurrence net* $N_\mathcal{R}(\mathbf{B})$, which describes the partial order induced by $\mathcal{R}$. Any concurrent execution of the transactions in **B** which respects this partial order is equivalent to the serial execution of **B** (Theorem 5).

From Blockchains to Occurrence Nets. We start by recapping the notion of Petri net [19]. A *Petri net* is a tuple $N = (P, Tr, F, m_0)$, where P is a set of *places*, Tr is a set of *transitions* (with $P \cap Tr = \emptyset$), and $F : (P \times Tr) \cup (Tr \times P) \to \mathbb{N}$ is a *weight function*. The state of a net is a *marking*, i.e. a multiset $m : P \to \mathbb{N}$ defining how many *tokens* are contained in each place; we denote with m_0 the initial marking. The behaviour of a Petri net is specified as a transition relation between markings: intuitively, a transition t is enabled at m when each place p has at least $F(p, t)$ tokens in m. When an enabled transition t is fired, it consumes $F(p, t)$ tokens from each p, and produces $F(t, p')$ tokens in each p'. Formally, given $x \in P \cup Tr$, we define the *preset* $^\bullet x$ and the *postset* $x^\bullet$ as multisets: $^\bullet x(y) = F(y, x)$, and $x^\bullet(y) = F(x, y)$. A transition t is *enabled* at m when $^\bullet t \subseteq m$. The transition relation between markings is defined as $m \xrightarrow{t} m - {}^\bullet t + t^\bullet$, where t is enabled. We say that $t_1 \cdots t_n$ is a *firing sequence from m to m'* when $m \xrightarrow{t_1} \cdots \xrightarrow{t_n} m'$, and in this case we say that m' is *reachable from* m. We say that m' is *reachable* when it is reachable from m_0.

An *occurrence net* [8] is a Petri net such that: (i) $|p^\bullet| \leq 1$ for all p; (ii) $|^\bullet p| = 1$ if $p \notin m_0$, and $|^\bullet p| = 0$ if $p \in m_0$; (iii) F is a relation, i.e. $F(x, y) \leq 1$ for all x, y; (iv) F^* is a acyclic, i.e. $\forall x, y \in P \cup Tr : (x, y) \in F^* \land (y, x) \in F^* \implies x = y$ (where F^* is the reflexive and transitive closure of F).

In Fig. 2 we transform a blockchain $\mathbf{B} = T_1 \cdots T_n$ into a Petri net $N_\mathcal{R}(\mathbf{B})$, where $\mathcal{R}$ is an arbitrary relation between transactions. Although any relation $\mathcal{R}$ ensures that $N_\mathcal{R}(\mathbf{B})$ is an occurrence net (Lemma 4 below), our main results hold when $\mathcal{R}$ is a strong swappability relation. The transformation works as follows: the i-th transaction in **B** is rendered as a transition (T_i, i) in $N_\mathcal{R}(\mathbf{B})$, and transactions related by $\mathcal{R}$ are transformed into concurrent transitions. Technically, this concurrency is specified as a relation $<$ between transitions, such that $(T_i, i) < (T_j, j)$ whenever $i < j$, but T_i and T_j are not related by $\mathcal{R}$. The places, the weight function, and the initial marking of $N_\mathcal{R}(\mathbf{B})$ are chosen to ensure that the firing ot transitions respects the relation $<$.

$\text{Tr} = \{(T_i, i) \mid 1 \le i \le n\}$

$P = \{(*, t) \mid t \in \text{Tr}\} \cup \{(t, *) \mid t \in \text{Tr}\} \cup \{(t, t') \mid t < t'\}$

    where $(T, i) < (T', j) \triangleq (i < j) \wedge \neg(T \mathcal{R} T')$

$$F(x, y) = \begin{cases} 1 & \text{if } y = t \text{ and } \big(x = (*, t) \text{ or } x = (t', t)\big) \\ 1 & \text{if } x = t \text{ and } \big(y = (t, *) \text{ or } y = (t, t')\big) \\ 0 & \text{otherwise} \end{cases} \qquad m_0(p) = \begin{cases} 1 & \text{if } p = (*, t) \\ 0 & \text{otherwise} \end{cases}$$

Fig. 2. Construction of a Petri net from a blockchain $\mathbf{B} = T_1 \cdots T_n$.

Example 7. Consider the following transactions and functions of a contract $\mathcal{C}$:

$$T_f = \mathcal{A} \xrightarrow{0} \mathcal{C} : f() \qquad f() \{\text{if } x = 0 \text{ then } y := 1 \text{ else throw}\}$$

$$T_g = \mathcal{A} \xrightarrow{0} \mathcal{C} : g() \qquad g() \{\text{if } y = 0 \text{ then } x := 1 \text{ else throw}\}$$

$$T_h = \mathcal{A} \xrightarrow{0} \mathcal{C} : h() \qquad h() \{z := 1\}$$

Let $P_f^w = P_g^r = \{\mathcal{C}.y\}, P_f^r = P_g^w = \{\mathcal{C}.x\}, P_h^w = \{\mathcal{C}.z\}, P_h^r = \emptyset$. It is easy to check that these sets are safe approximations of their transactions (e.g., P_f^w safely approximates the keys written by T_f). By Definition 6 we have that $T_f \# T_h$, $T_g \# T_h$, but $\neg(T_f \# T_g)$. We display $N_\#(T_f T_h T_g)$ in Fig. 3, where $t_f = (T_f, 1)$, $t_h = (T_h, 2)$, and $t_g = (T_g, 3)$. Note that t_g can only be fired after t_f, while t_h can be fired independently from t_f and t_g. This is coherent with the fact that T_h is swappable with both T_f and T_g, while T_f and T_g are not swappable. $\diamond$

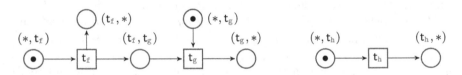

Fig. 3. Occurrence net for Example 7.

Lemma 4. $N_\mathcal{R}(\mathbf{B})$ *is an occurrence net, for all $\mathcal{R}$ and $\mathbf{B}$.*

Step Firing Sequences. Theorem 5 below establishes a correspondence between concurrent and serial execution of transactions. Since the semantics of serial executions is given in terms of blockchain states σ, to formalise this correspondence we use the same semantics domain also for concurrent executions. This is obtained in two steps. First, we define concurrent executions of $\mathbf{B}$ as the *step firing sequences* (i.e. finite sequences of *sets* of transitions) of $N_\#(\mathbf{B})$. Then, we give a semantics to step firing sequences, in terms of blockchain states.

We denote finite sets of transitions, called *steps*, as $U, U', \ldots$. Their preset and postset are defined as ${}^\bullet U = \sum_{p \in U} {}^\bullet p$ and $U^\bullet = \sum_{p \in U} p^\bullet$, respectively. We say that U is *enabled at* m when ${}^\bullet U \leq m$, and in this case firing U results in the move $m \xrightarrow{U} m - {}^\bullet U + U^\bullet$. Let $U = U_1 \cdots U_n$ be a finite sequence of steps. We say that U is a *step firing sequence from* m *to* m' if $m \xrightarrow{U_1} \cdots \xrightarrow{U_n} m'$, and in this case we write $m \xrightarrow{U} m'$.

Concurrent Execution of Transactions. We now define how to execute transactions in parallel. The idea is to execute transactions in *isolation*, and then merge their changes, whenever they are mutually disjoint. The state updated resulting from the execution of a transaction are formalised as in Definition 1.

An *update collector* is a function Π that, given a state σ and a transaction T, gives an update $\pi = \Pi(\sigma, T)$ which maps (at least) the updated qualified keys to their new values. In practice, update collectors can be obtained by instrumenting the run-time environment of smart contracts, so to record the state changes resulting from the execution of transactions. We formalise update collectors abstracting from the implementation details of such an instrumentation:

Definition 8 (Update collector). *We say that a function Π is an* update collector *when* $[\![T]\!]_\sigma = \sigma(\Pi(\sigma, T))$, *for all σ and T.*   ◇

There exists a natural ordering of collectors, which extends the ordering between state updates (i.e., set inclusion, when interpreting them as sets of substitutions): namely, $\Pi \sqsubseteq \Pi'$ holds when $\forall \sigma, T : \Pi(\sigma, T) \subseteq \Pi'(\sigma, T)$. The following lemma characterizes the least update collector w.r.t. this ordering.

Lemma 5 (Least update collector). *Let $\Pi^\star(\sigma, T) = [\![T]\!]_\sigma - \sigma$, where we define $\sigma' - \sigma$ as $\bigcup_{\sigma'p \neq \sigma p} \{\sigma'p/p\}$. Then, $\Pi^\star$ is the least update collector.*   ◇

The merge of two state updates is the union of the corresponding substitutions; to avoid collisions, we make the merge operator undefined when the domains of the two updates overlap.

Definition 9 (Merge of state updates). *Let π_0, π_1 be state updates. When* $\text{keys}(\pi_0) \cap \text{keys}(\pi_1) = \emptyset$, *we define $\pi_0 \oplus \pi_1$ as follows:*

$$(\pi_0 \oplus \pi_1)p = \begin{cases} \pi_0 p & \text{if } p \in \text{keys}(\pi_0) \\ \pi_1 p & \text{if } p \in \text{keys}(\pi_1) \\ \bot & \text{otherwise} \end{cases} \qquad ◇$$

The merge operator enjoys the commutative monoidal laws, and can therefore be extended to (finite) sets of state updates.

We now associate step firing sequences with state updates. The semantics of a step $U = \{(T_1, 1), \ldots, (T_n, n)\}$ in σ is obtained by applying to σ the merge of the updates $\Pi(\sigma, T_i)$, for all $i \in 1..n$—whenever the merge is defined. The semantics of a step firing sequence is then obtained by folding that of its steps.

Definition 10 (Semantics of step firing sequences). *We define the semantics of step firing sequences, given Π and σ, as:*

$$[\![\epsilon]\!]_\sigma^\Pi = \sigma \qquad [\![UU]\!]_\sigma^\Pi = [\![U]\!]_{\sigma'}^\Pi \quad \text{where } \sigma' = [\![U]\!]_\sigma^\Pi = \sigma \bigoplus_{(T,i)\in U} \Pi(\sigma, T) \qquad \diamond$$

Example 8. Let $t_f, t_g,$ and t_h be as in Example 7, and let $\sigma \mathcal{C} x = \sigma \mathcal{C} y = 0$. Since $\Pi^\star(\sigma, T_f) = \{1/\mathcal{C}.y\}$, $\Pi^\star(\sigma, T_g) = \{1/\mathcal{C}.x\}$, and $\Pi^\star(\sigma, T_h) = \{1/\mathcal{C}.z\}$, we have:

$$[\![\{t_f, t_h\}]\!]_\sigma^{\Pi^\star} = \sigma(\{1/\mathcal{C}.y\} \oplus \{1/\mathcal{C}.z\}) = \sigma\{1/\mathcal{C}.y, 1/\mathcal{C}.z\}$$

$$[\![\{t_g, t_h\}]\!]_\sigma^{\Pi^\star} = \sigma(\{1/\mathcal{C}.x\} \oplus \{1/\mathcal{C}.z\}) = \sigma\{1/\mathcal{C}.x, 1/\mathcal{C}.z\}$$

$$[\![\{t_f, t_g\}]\!]_\sigma^{\Pi^\star} = (\sigma\{1/\mathcal{C}.y\} \oplus \{1/\mathcal{C}.x\}) = \sigma\{1/\mathcal{C}.y, 1/\mathcal{C}.x\}$$

Note that, for all σ:

$$[\![T_f T_h]\!]_\sigma = [\![T_h T_f]\!]_\sigma = \sigma\{1/\mathcal{C}.y, 1/\mathcal{C}.z\} = [\![\{t_f, t_h\}]\!]_\sigma^{\Pi^\star}$$
$$[\![T_g T_h]\!]_\sigma = [\![T_h T_g]\!]_\sigma = \sigma\{1/\mathcal{C}.x, 1/\mathcal{C}.z\} = [\![\{t_g, t_h\}]\!]_\sigma^{\Pi^\star}$$

So, the serial execution of T_f and T_h (in both orders) is equal to their concurrent execution (similarly for T_g and T_h). Instead, for all σ such that $\sigma \mathcal{C} x = \sigma \mathcal{C} y = 0$:

$$[\![T_f T_g]\!]_\sigma = \sigma\{1/\mathcal{C}.y\} \qquad [\![T_g T_f]\!]_\sigma = \sigma\{1/\mathcal{C}.x\} \qquad [\![\{t_f, t_g\}]\!]_\sigma^{\Pi^\star} = \sigma\{1/\mathcal{C}.y, 1/\mathcal{C}.x\}$$

So, concurrent executions of T_f and T_g may differ from serial ones. This is coherent with the fact that, in Fig. 3, t_f and t_g are *not* concurrent. $\diamond$

Concurrent Execution of Blockchains. Theorem 5 relates serial executions of transactions to concurrent ones (which are rendered as step firing sequences). Item (a) establishes a confluence property: if two step firing sequences lead to the same marking, then they also lead to the same blockchain state. Item (b) ensures that the blockchain, interpreted as a sequence of transitions, is a step firing sequence, and it is *maximal* (i.e., there is a bijection between the transactions in the blockchain and the transitions of the corresponding net). Finally, item (c) ensures that executing maximal step firing sequences is equivalent to executing serially the blockchain.

Theorem 5. *Let $\mathbf{B} = T_1 \cdots T_n$. Then, in $N_\#(\mathbf{B})$:*

(a) if $m_0 \xrightarrow{U} m$ and $m_0 \xrightarrow{U'} m$, then $[\![U]\!]_\sigma^{\Pi^\star} = [\![U']\!]_\sigma^{\Pi^\star}$, for all reachable σ;
(b) $\{(T_1, 1)\} \cdots \{(T_n, n)\}$ is a maximal step firing sequence;
(c) for all maximal step firing sequences $\mathbf{U}$, for all reachable σ, $[\![U]\!]_\sigma^{\Pi^\star} = [\![\mathbf{B}]\!]_\sigma$.

Remarkably, the implications of Theorem 5 also apply to $N_{\#_R^W}(\mathbf{B})$.

Example 9. Recall $\mathbf{B} = T_f T_h T_g$ and $N_\#(\mathbf{B})$ from Example 7, let $\mathbf{U} = \{t_f, t_h\}\{t_g\}$, and let σ be such that $\sigma \mathcal{C} x = \sigma \mathcal{C} y = 0$. As predicted by item (c) of Theorem 5:

$$[\![\mathbf{B}]\!]_\sigma = \sigma\{1/\mathcal{C}.y\}\{1/\mathcal{C}.z\} = [\![\mathbf{U}]\!]_\sigma^{\Pi^\star}$$

Let $\mathbf{U}' = \{t_f\}\{t_g, t_h\}$. We have that $\mathbf{U}$ and $\mathbf{U}'$ lead to the same marking, where the places $(t_f, *)$, $(t_g, *)$ and $(t_h, *)$ contain one token each, while the other places have no tokens. By item (a) of Theorem 5 we conclude that $[\![\mathbf{U}]\!]_\sigma^{\Pi^*} = [\![\mathbf{U}']\!]_\sigma^{\Pi^*}$. Now, let $\mathbf{U}'' = \{t_h\}\{t_f, t_g\}$. Note that, although $\mathbf{U}''$ is maximal, it is not a step firing sequence, since the second step is not enabled (actually, t_f and t_g are not concurrent, as pointed out in Example 8). Therefore, the items of Theorem 5 do not apply to $\mathbf{U}''$, coherently with the fact that $\mathbf{U}''$ does not represent any sequential execution of $\mathbf{B}$. ◇

5   Case Study: ERC-721 Token

We now apply our theory to an archetypal Ethereum smart contract, which implements a "non-fungible token" following the standard ERC-721 interface [14, 15]. This contract defines the functions to transfer tokens between users, and to delegate their trade to other users. Currently, token transfers involve ∼50% of the transactions on the Ethereum blockchain [1], with larger peaks due to popular contracts like Cryptokitties [22].

We sketch below the implementation of the   contract, using Solidity, the main high-level smart contract language in Ethereum (see Appendix B of [6] for the full implementation).

The contract state is defined by the following mappings:

Each token is uniquely identified by an integer value (of type   ), while users are identified by an   . The mapping   maps tokens to their owners' addresses (the zero address is used to denote a dummy owner). The mapping   tells whether a token has been created or not, while gives the number of tokens owned by each user. The mapping allows a user to delegate the transfer of all her tokens to third parties.

The function   transfers a token from the owner to another user. The   assertion rules out some undesirable cases, e.g., if the token does not exist, or it is not owned by the   user, or the user attempts to transfer the token to himself. Once all these checks are passed, the transfer succeeds if the   of the transaction owns the token, or if he has been delegated by the owner. The mappings   and   are updated as expected.

The function   delegates the transfers of all the tokens of
the   to the   when the boolean   is true, otherwise it
revokes the delegation.

Assume that user $\mathcal{A}$ owns two tokens, identified by the integers 1 and 2, and consider the following transactions:

$$T_1 = \mathcal{A} \xrightarrow{0} \text{Token} : \texttt{transferFrom}(\mathcal{A}, \mathcal{P}, 1)$$

$$T_2 = \mathcal{A} \xrightarrow{0} \text{Token} : \texttt{setApprovalForAll}(\mathcal{B}, \textbf{true})$$

$$T_3 = \mathcal{B} \xrightarrow{0} \text{Token} : \texttt{transferFrom}(\mathcal{A}, \mathcal{Q}, 2)$$

$$T_4 = \mathcal{P} \xrightarrow{0} \text{Token} : \texttt{transferFrom}(\mathcal{P}, \mathcal{B}, 1)$$

We have that $T_1 \# T_2$, $T_2 \# T_4$, and $T_3 \# T_4$ (this can be proved e.g. by using the static approximations in Appendix B of [6]), while the other combinations are not swappable. Let $\textbf{B} = T_1 T_2 T_3 T_4$. The resulting occurrence net is displayed in Fig. 4. For instance, let $\textbf{U} = \{T_1, T_2\}\{T_3, T_4\}$, i.e. T_1 and T_2 are executed concurrently, as well as T_3 and T_4. From item (c) of Theorem 5 we have that this concurrent execution is equivalent to the serial one.

Although this example deals with the marginal case where the sender and the receiver of tokens overlap, in practice the large majority of transactions in a block either involves distinct users, or invokes distinct ERC-721 interfaces, making it possible to increase the degree of concurrency of   transactions.

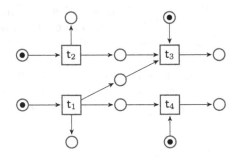

Fig. 4. Occurrence net for the blockchain $\textbf{B} = T_1 T_2 T_3 T_4$ of the ERC-721 token.

6   Related Work and Conclusions

We have proposed a static approach to improve the performance of blockchains by concurrently executing transactions. We have started by introducing a model of transactions and blockchains. We have defined two transactions to be *swappable* when inverting their order does not affect the blockchain state. We have then introduced a static approximation of swappability, based on a static analysis of the sets of keys read/written by transactions. We have rendered concurrent executions of a sequence of transactions as *step firing sequences* in the associated occurrence net. Our main technical result, Theorem 5, shows that these concurrent executions are semantically equivalent to the sequential one.

We can exploit our results in practice to improve the performances of miners and validators. Miners should perform the following steps to mine a block:

1. gather from the network a set of transactions, and put them in an arbitrary linear order **B**, which is the mined block;
2. compute the relation $\#^W_R$ on **B**, using a static analysis of read/written keys;
3. construct the occurrence net $N_{\#^W_R}(\mathbf{B})$;
4. execute transactions concurrently according to the occurrence net, exploiting the available parallelism.

The behaviour of validators is almost identical to that of miners, except that in step (1), rather than choosing the order of transactions, they should adhere to the ordering of the mined block **B**. Note that in the last step, validators can execute any maximal step firing sequence which is coherent with their degree of parallelism: item (c) of Theorem 5 ensures that the resulting state is equal to the state obtained by the miner. The experiments in [12] suggest that parallelization may lead to a significant improvement of the performance of nodes: the benchmarks on a selection of representative contracts show an overall speedup of 1.33× for miners and 1.69× for validators, using only three cores.

Note that malevolent users could attempt a denial-of-service attack by publishing contracts which are hard to statically analyse, and therefore are not suitable for parallelization. This kind of attacks can be mitigated by adopting a mining strategy that gives higher priority to parallelizable transactions.

Applying Our Approach to Ethereum. Applying our theory to Ethereum would require a static analysis of read/written keys at the level of EVM bytecode. As far as we know, the only tool implementing such an analysis is ES-ETH [16]. However, the current version of the tool has several limitations, like e.g. the compile-time approximation of dictionary keys and of values shorter than 32 bytes, which make ES-ETH not directly usable to the purposes of our work. In general, precise static analyses at the level of the Ethereum bytecode are difficult to achieve, since the language has features like dynamic dispatching and pointer aliasing which are notoriously a source of imprecision for static analysis. However, coarser approximations of read/written keys may be enough to speed-up the execution of transactions. For instance, in Ethereum, blocks typically contain many transactions which transfer tokens between participants, and many of them involve distinct senders and receivers. A relatively simple analysis of the code of token contracts (which is usually similar to that in Sect. 5) may be enough to detect that these transactions are swappable.

Aiming at minimality, our model does not include the *gas mechanism*, which is used in Ethereum to pay miners for executing contracts. The sender of a transaction deposits into it some crypto-currency, to be paid to the miner which appends the transaction to the blockchain. Each instruction executed by the miner consumes part of this deposit; when the deposit reaches zero, the miner stops executing the transaction. At this point, all the effects of the transaction (except the payment to the miner) are rolled back. Our transaction model could be easily extended with a gas mechanism, by associating a cost to statements and recording the gas consumption in the environment. Remarkably, adding gas does not invalidate approximations of read/written keys which are correct while neglecting gas. However, a gas-aware analysis may be more precise of a gas-oblivious one: for instance, in the statement if k then $f_{long}()$; $x:=1$ else $y:=1$ (where f_{long} is a function which exceeds the available gas) a gas-aware analysis would be able to detect that x is not written.

Related Work. A few works study how to optimize the execution of smart contracts on Ethereum, using dynamic techniques adopted from software transactional memory [4,12,13]. These works are focussed on empirical aspects (e.g., measuring the speedup obtained on a given benchmark), while we focus on the theoretical counterpart. In [12,13], miners execute a set of transactions speculatively in parallel, using abstract locks and inverse logs to dynamically discover conflicts and to recover from inconsistent states. The obtained execution is guaranteed to be equivalent to a serial execution of the same set of transactions. The work [4] proposes a conceptually similar technique, but based on optimistic software transactional memory. Since speculative execution is non-deterministic, in both approaches miners need to communicate the chosen schedule of transactions to validators, to allow them to correctly validate the block. This schedule must be embedded in the mined block: since Ethereum does not support this kind of block metadata, these approaches would require a "soft-fork" of the blockchain to be implemented in practice. Instead, our approach is compatible with the current Ethereum, since miners only need to append transactions to the blockchain. Compared to [4,12], where conflicts are detected dynamically, our approach relies on a static analysis to detect potential conflicts. Since software transactional memory introduces a run-time overhead, in principle a static technique could allow for faster executions, at the price of a preprocessing phase. Saraph and Herlihy [20] study the effectiveness of speculatively executing smart contracts in Ethereum. They sample past blocks of transactions (from July 2016 to December 2017), replay them by using a speculative execution engine, and measure the speedup obtained by parallel execution. Their results show that simple speculative strategies yield non-trivial speed-ups. Further, they note that many of the data conflicts (i.e. concurrent read/write accesses to the same state location) arise in periods of high traffic, and they are caused by a small number of popular contracts, like e.g. tokens.

In the permissioned setting, Hyperledger Fabric [3] follows the "execute first and then order" paradigm: transactions are executed speculatively, and then their ordering is checked for correctness [2]. In this paradigm, appending a transaction requires a few steps. First, a client proposes a transaction to a set of "endorsing" peers, which simulate the transaction without updating the blockchain. The output of the simulation includes the state updates of the transaction execution, and the sets of read/written keys. These sets are then signed by the endorsing peers, and returned to the client, which submits them to the "ordering" peers. These nodes order transactions in blocks, and send them to the "committing" peers, which validate them. A block $T_1 \cdots T_n$ is valid when, if a key k is read by transaction T_i, then k has not been written by a transaction T_j with $j < i$. Finally, validated blocks are appended to the blockchain. Our model is coherent with Ethereum, which does not support speculative execution.

Future Works. A relevant line of research is the design of domain-specific languages for smart contracts that are directly amenable to techniques that, like ours, increase the degree of concurrency of executions. For this purpose, the language should support static analyses of read/written keys, like the one we use to define the strong swappability relation. Although the literature describes various static analyses of smart contracts, most of them are focussed on finding security vulnerabilities, rather than enhancing concurrency.

Outside the realm of smart contracts, a few papers propose static analyses of read/written variables. The paper [11] describes an analysis based on separation logic, and applies it to resolve conflicts in the setting of *snapshot isolation* for transactional memory in Java. When a conflict is detected, the read/write sets are used to determine how the code can be modified to resolve it. The paper [10] presents a static analysis to infer read and write locations in a C-like language with atomic sections. The analysis is used to translate atomic sections into standard lock operations. The design of new smart contract languages could take advantage of these analyses.

Acknowledgements. Massimo Bartoletti is partially supported by Aut. Reg. Sardinia projects *"Smart collaborative engineering"* and *"Sardcoin"*. Letterio Galletta is partially supported by IMT Lucca project *"PAI VeriOSS"* and by MIUR project PRIN 2017FTXR7S *"Methods and Tools for Trustworthy Smart Systems"*. Maurizio Murgia is partially supported by MIUR PON *"Distributed Ledgers for Secure Open Communities"* and by Aut. Reg. Sardinia project *"Smart collaborative engineering"*.

References

1. Ethereum token dynanics. https://stat.bloxy.info/superset/dashboard/tokens
2. Hyperledger fabric: read-write set semantics. https://hyperledger-fabric.readthedocs.io/en/release-1.4/readwrite.html
3. Androulaki, E., et al.: Hyperledger fabric: a distributed operating system for permissioned blockchains. In: EuroSys, pp. 30:1–30:15 (2018). https://doi.org/10.1145/3190508.3190538

4. Anjana, P.S., Kumari, S., Peri, S., Rathor, S., Somani, A.: An efficient framework for optimistic concurrent execution of smart contracts. In: PDP, pp. 83–92 (2019). https://doi.org/10.1109/EMPDP.2019.8671637

5. Bartoletti, M., Galletta, L., Murgia, M.: A minimal core calculus for solidity contracts. In: Pérez-Solà, C., Navarro-Arribas, G., Biryukov, A., Garcia-Alfaro, J. (eds.) DPM/CBT -2019. LNCS, vol. 11737, pp. 233–243. Springer, Cham (2019). https://doi.org/10.1007/978-3-030-31500-9_15

6. Bartoletti, M., Galletta, L., Murgia, M.: A true concurrent model of smart contracts executions. CoRR abs/1905.04366 (2020). http://arxiv.org/abs/1905.04366

7. Bernstein, A.J.: Analysis of programs for parallel processing. IEEE Trans. Electron. Comput. **EC-15**(5), 757–763 (1966). https://doi.org/10.1109/PGEC.1966.264565

8. Best, E., Devillers, R.R.: Sequential and concurrent behaviour in Petri net theory. Theor. Comput. Sci. **55**(1), 87–136 (1987). https://doi.org/10.1016/0304-3975(87)90090-9

9. Buterin, V.: Ethereum: a next generation smart contract and decentralized application platform (2013). https://github.com/ethereum/wiki/wiki/White-Paper

10. Cherem, S., Chilimbi, T.M., Gulwani, S.: Inferring locks for atomic sections. In: ACM SIGPLAN PLDI, pp. 304–315 (2008). https://doi.org/10.1145/1375581.1375619

11. Dias, R.J., Lourenço, J.M., Preguiça, N.M.: Efficient and correct transactional memory programs combining snapshot isolation and static analysis. In: USENIX Conference on Hot Topics in Parallelism (HotPar) (2011)

12. Dickerson, T.D., Gazzillo, P., Herlihy, M., Koskinen, E.: Adding concurrency to smart contracts. In: ACM PODC, pp. 303–312 (2017). https://doi.org/10.1145/3087801.3087835

13. Dickerson, T., Gazzillo, P., Herlihy, M., Koskinen, E.: Adding concurrency to smart contracts. Distrib. Comput. **33**, 209–225 (2020). https://doi.org/10.1007/s00446-019-00357-z

14. Entriken, W., Shirley, D., Evans, J., Sachs, N.: EIP 721: ERC-721 non-fungible token standard. https://eips.ethereum.org/EIPS/eip-721

15. Fröwis, M., Fuchs, A., Böhme, R.: Detecting token systems on ethereum. In: Goldberg, I., Moore, T. (eds.) FC 2019. LNCS, vol. 11598, pp. 93–112. Springer, Cham (2019). https://doi.org/10.1007/978-3-030-32101-7_7

16. Marcia, D.: ES-ETH: ethereum state change examiner (2019). https://github.com/DiegoMarcia/ES-ETH

17. Mazurkiewicz, A.: Basic notions of trace theory. In: de Bakker, J.W., de Roever, W.-P., Rozenberg, G. (eds.) REX 1988. LNCS, vol. 354, pp. 285–363. Springer, Heidelberg (1989). https://doi.org/10.1007/BFb0013025

18. Nielson, F., Nielson, H.R., Hankin, C.: Principles of Program Analysis (1999). https://doi.org/10.1007/978-3-662-03811-6

19. Reisig, W.: Petri Nets: An Introduction. Monographs in Theoretical Computer Science: An EATCS Series, vol. 4. Springer, Heidelberg (1985). https://doi.org/10.1007/978-3-642-69968-9

20. Saraph, V., Herlihy, M.: An empirical study of speculative concurrency in Ethereum smart contracts. CoRR abs/1901.01376 (2019). http://arxiv.org/abs/1901.01376

21. Szabo, N.: Formalizing and securing relationships on public networks. First Monday **2**(9) (1997). http://firstmonday.org/htbin/cgiwrap/bin/ojs/index.php/fm/article/view/548

22. Young, J.: CryptoKitties sales hit $12 million, could be Ethereum's killer app after all (2017). https://cointelegraph.com/news/cryptokitties-sales-hit-12-million-could-be-ethereums-killer-app-after-all

Renegotiation and Recursion in Bitcoin Contracts

Massimo Bartoletti[1(✉)], Maurizio Murgia[2], and Roberto Zunino[2]

[1] University of Cagliari, Cagliari, Italy

[2] University of Trento, Trento, Italy

Abstract. BitML is a process calculus to express smart contracts that can be run on Bitcoin. One of its current limitations is that, once a contract has been stipulated, the participants cannot renegotiate its terms: this prevents expressing common financial contracts, where funds have to be added by participants at run-time. In this paper, we extend BitML with a new primitive for contract renegotiation. At the same time, the new primitive can be used to write recursive contracts, which was not possible in the original BitML. We show that, despite the increased expressiveness, it is still possible to execute BitML on standard Bitcoin, preserving the security guarantees of BitML.

1 Introduction

Smart contracts—computer protocols that regulate the exchange of assets in trustless environments—have become popular with the growth of interest in blockchain technologies. Mainstream blockchain platforms like Ethereum, Libra, and Cardano, feature expressive high-level languages for programming smart contracts. This flexibility has a drawback in that it may open the door to attacks that steal or tamper with the assets controlled by vulnerable contracts [4,22].

An alternative approach, pursued first by Bitcoin and more recently also by Algorand, is to sacrifice the expressiveness of smart contracts to reduce the attack surface. For instance, Bitcoin has a minimal language for transaction redeem scripts, containing only a limited set of logic, arithmetic, and cryptographic operations. Despite the limited expressiveness of these scripts, it is possible to encode a variety of smart contracts (like gambling games, escrow services, crowdfunding systems, etc.) by suitably chaining transactions [1–3,5,8,10,13,18–21,23]. The common trait of these works is that they render contracts as cryptographic protocols, where participants can exchange/sign messages, read the blockchain, and append transactions. Verifying the correctness of these protocols is hard, since it requires to reason in a computational model, where participants can manipulate arbitrary bitstrings, only being constrained to use PPTIME algorithms.

Departing from this approach, BitML [11] allows to write Bitcoin contracts in a high-level, process-algebraic language. BitML features a compiler that translates contracts into sets of standard Bitcoin transactions, and a sound and complete verification technique of relevant trace properties [12]. The computational

© IFIP International Federation for Information Processing 2020
Published by Springer Nature Switzerland AG 2020

S. Bliudze and L. Bocchi (Eds.): COORDINATION 2020, LNCS 12134, pp. 261–278, 2020.
https://doi.org/10.1007/978-3-030-50029-0_17

soundness of the compiler guarantees that the execution of the compiled contract is coherent with the semantics of the source BitML specification, even in the presence of adversaries. Although BitML can express many of the Bitcoin contracts presented in the literature, it is not "Bitcoin-complete", i.e. there exist contracts that can be executed on Bitcoin, but are not expressible in BitML [6].

For instance, consider a zero-coupon bond [17], where an investor A pays $1\dot{B}$ upfront to a bank B, and receives back $2\dot{B}$ after a maturity date (say, year 2030). We can express this contract in BitML as follows. First, as a precondition to the stipulation of the contract, we require both A and B to provide a deposit: A's deposit is $1\dot{B}$, while B's deposit is $2\dot{B}$. In BitML, we write this precondition as:

$$A:1\dot{B} \quad x_1 \mid B:2\dot{B} \quad x_2$$

where x_1 and x_2 are the identifiers of transactions containing the required amount of bitcoins ($\dot{B}$). Under this precondition, we can specify the zero-coupon bond contract ZCB as follows:

$$ZCB = \quad (1\dot{B} \to \quad B \mid 2\dot{B} \to \quad 2030: \quad A)$$

Upon stipulation, all the deposits required in the preconditions pass under the control of ZCB, and can no longer be spent by A and B. The contract splits these funds in two parts: $1\dot{B}$, that can be withdrawn by B at any moment, and $2\dot{B}$, that can be withdrawn by A after the maturity date.

Although ZCB correctly implements the functionality of zero-coupon bounds, it is quite impractical: for the whole period from the stipulation to the maturity date, $2\dot{B}$ are frozen within the contract, and cannot be used by the bank in any way. Although this is a desirable feature for the investor, since it guarantees that he will receive $2\dot{B}$ even if the bank fails, it is quite undesirable for the bank. In the real world, the bank would be free to use its own funds, together with those of investors, to make further financial transactions through which to repay the investments. The risk that the bank fails is mitigated by external mechanisms, like insurances or government intervention.

In this paper we propose an extension of BitML that overcomes this issue. The idea is to allow the contract participants to *renegotiate* it after stipulation, in a controlled way. Renegotiation makes it possible to inject in the contract new funds, that were not specified in the original precondition. We can use this feature to solve the issue with the ZCB contract. The new precondition is $A:1\dot{B} \quad x_1$, i.e. we only require A's deposit. The revised contract is:

$$ZCB2 = \quad (1\dot{B} \to \quad B \mid 0\dot{B} \to * : \quad \langle\rangle)$$
$$\langle\rangle = \{B:2\dot{B} \quad d\} \quad 2030: \quad A$$

As before, the bank can withdraw $1\dot{B}$ at any moment after stipulation. In the second part of the   , the participants renegotiate the contract: if they both agree, $0\dot{B}$ pass under the control of the contract $\langle\rangle$. The precondition of $\langle\rangle$ requires the bank to provide $2\dot{B}$ in a fresh deposit; upon renegotiation, A can withdraw $2\dot{B}$ after the maturity date. The crucial difference with ZCB is that the deposit variable d is instantiated at *renegotiation* time, unlike x, which must be fixed at *stipulation* time.

The revised contract $ZCB2$ solves the problem of ZCB, in that it no longer freezes 2Ƀ for the whole duration of the bond: the bank could choose to renegotiate the contract, paying 2Ƀ, just before the maturity date. This flexibility comes at a cost, since A loses the guarantee to eventually receive 2Ƀ. To address this issue we need to add, as in the real world, an external mechanism. More specifically, we assume an insurance company I that, for an annual premium of pɃ paid by the bank, covers a face amount of fɃ (with $2 > f > 10p$):

$$\text{A}:1Ƀ \quad x_1 \mid \text{B}:pƀ \quad x_2 \mid \text{I}:fƀ \quad x_3$$

We revise the bond contract as follows:

$$
\begin{aligned}
ZCB3 \;=\; & \left(1Ƀ \rightarrow \qquad\qquad \text{B} \right.\\
& \mid pƀ \rightarrow \qquad\qquad \text{I}\\
& \mid fƀ \rightarrow * : \qquad \langle 1 \rangle + \qquad 2021 : \qquad\qquad \text{A}\bigg)\\
\langle n \in 1..9 \rangle \;=\; & \{\text{B}:pƀ \quad d\}\\
& \left(pƀ \rightarrow \qquad\qquad \text{I}\right.\\
& \mid fƀ \rightarrow * : \qquad \langle n+1 \rangle + \qquad (2021+n) : \qquad \text{A}\bigg)\\
\langle 10 \rangle \;=\; & \{\text{B}:2Ƀ \quad d\}\\
& \left(fƀ \rightarrow \qquad\qquad \text{I}\right.\\
& \mid 2Ƀ \rightarrow \qquad 2030 : \qquad \text{A}\bigg)
\end{aligned}
$$

The contract starts by transferring 1Ƀ to the bank, and the first year of the premium to the insurer. The remaining fɃ are transferred to the renegotiated contract $\langle 1 \rangle$, or, if the renegotiation is not completed by 2021, to the investor.

We remark that the pattern $D + \qquad t:D'$, where D requires some authorizations but D' does not, is rather common in BitML, as it ensures that the contract can proceed even if the authorizations are not provided. Indeed, in such case an honest participant is enough to execute D' after time t. By suitably exploiting this pattern, it is possible to guarantee that a BitML contract enjoys liveness, by just assuming that at least one participant is honest.

The contracts $\langle n \rangle$, for $n \in 1..9$, allow the insurer to receive the annual premium until 2030: if the bank does not renegotiate the contract for the following year (paying the corresponding premium), then the investor can redeem the face amount of fɃ. Finally, the contract $\langle 10 \rangle$ can be triggered if the bank deposits the 2Ƀ: when this happens, the face amount is given back to the insurer, and the investor can redeem 2Ƀ after the maturity date.

Compared to $ZCB2$, the contract $ZCB3$ offers more protection to the investor. To see why, we must evaluate A's payoff for all the possible behaviours of the other participants. If B and I are both honest, then A will redeem 2Ƀ, as in the ideal contract ZCB. Instead, if either B or I do not accept to renegotiate some $\langle n \rangle$, then A can redeem fɃ as a partial compensation (unlike in $ZCB2$, where A just loses 1Ƀ). In the real world, A could use this compensation to cover the legal fee to sue the bank in court; also, I could e.g. increase the premium for future interactions with B. By further refining the contract, we could model these real-world mechanisms as oracles, which sanction dishonest participants according to the evidence collected in the blockchain and in messages broadcast by participants. For instance, if B and I accept the renegotiation $\langle n \rangle$ but A does not, then the oracle would be able to detect A's dishonesty by inspecting the authorizations broadcast in year $2021 + n$. The sanction could consist e.g. in blacklisting A, so to prevent her from buying other bonds from B.

Contributions. We summarise our main contributions as follows:

- We extend BitML with the renegotiation primitive $*$: $\qquad \langle \rangle$, suitably adapting the language syntax and semantics. The new primitive increases the expressiveness of BitML: besides allowing participants to provide new deposits and secrets at run-time, it also allows for *unbounded* recursion.
- We extend the BitML compiler to the new primitive, making it possible to execute renegotiations on Bitcoin. We accordingly extend the computational soundness result in [11], guaranteeing that the BitML semantics is coherent with the actual Bitcoin executions, also in the presence of adversaries.
- We exploit renegotiation to design a new gambling game where two players repeatedly flip coins, and whoever wins twice in a row takes the pot (a form of unbounded recursion). We prove the game to be fair.
- We introduce alternative renegotiation primitives, which allow participants to choose some parameters (e.g. the amounts to be deposited) at renegotiation time, and to change the set of participants involved in the renegotiated contract. We show that both primitives can be executed on Bitcoin *as is*. We also introduce a primitive that, at the price of minor Bitcoin extensions, supports *non-consensual* renegotiations, which are automatically triggered by the contract without requiring the participants' agreement.

Because of space constraints, we relegate part of the technicalities to [9].

2   BitML with Renegotiation and Recursion

We start by formalising contract preconditions. We use $A, B, \ldots$ to range over participants. We assume a set of *deposit names* $x, y, \ldots$, a set of deposit variables $d, e, \ldots$, and a set of *secret names* $a, b, \ldots$. We use $\chi, \chi', \ldots$ to range over deposit names and variables, and v, v' to range over non-negative values.

Definition 1 (Contract precondition). *Contract preconditions have the following syntax (the deposits χ in a contract precondition G must be distinct):*

$$
\begin{array}{llll}
G ::= & A{:}v \;\; \chi & & \text{deposit of } v\text{B put by } A \\
& | \;\; A{:} \qquad a & & \text{secret committed by } A \\
& | \;\; G \,|\, G & & \text{composition} \qquad\qquad \diamond
\end{array}
$$

The precondition A: v χ requires A to own $v\mathbb{B}$ in a deposit χ, and to spend it for stipulating the contract. The precondition A : a requires A to generate a secret a, and commit to it before the contract starts. After stipulation, A can choose whether to disclose the secret a, or not.

To define contracts, we assume a set of recursion variables, ranged over by , ,..., and a language of *static expressions* $\mathcal{E}, \mathcal{E}',\ldots$, formed by integer constants k, integer variables $\alpha, \beta, \ldots$, and the usual arithmetic operators. We omit to define the syntax and semantics of static expressions, since they are standard. We assume that a closed static expression evaluates to a 32-bit value. We use the bold notation for sequences, e.g. $\boldsymbol{x}$ denotes a finite sequence of deposit names.

Definition 2 (Contract). *Contracts are terms with the syntax in Fig. 1, where: (i) each recursion variable   has a unique defining equation $(\boldsymbol{\alpha}) = \{G\}C$; (ii) renegotiations* * : $\langle\mathcal{E}\rangle$ *have the correct number of arguments;(iii) the names* $\boldsymbol{a}$ *in* $\boldsymbol{a}$ p *are distinct, and they include those occurring in p; (iv) in a prefix* $\boldsymbol{v} \to C$, *the sequences* $\boldsymbol{v}$ *and* C *have the same length. We denote with* 0 *the empty sum. We assume that the order of decorations is immaterial, e.g.,* $\mathcal{E} : A : B : D$ *is equivalent to* B : A : $\mathcal{E} : D$. ◇

A contract C is a choice among guarded contracts D_i. A guarded contract $\boldsymbol{a}$ p. C' continues as C' once all the secrets $\boldsymbol{a}$ have been revealed and satisfy the predicate p. The guarded contract $(v_1 \to C_1 \mid \cdots \mid v_n \to C_n)$ divides the contract into n contracts C_i, each one with balance v_i. The sum of the v_i must coincide with the current balance. The action   A transfers the whole balance to A. When enabled, the above actions can be fired by anyone at anytime. To restrict *who* can execute a branch and *when*, one can use the decoration $A : D$, requiring to wait for A's authorization, and the decoration $\mathcal{E} : D$, requiring to wait until the time specified by the static expression $\mathcal{E}$. The action * : $\langle\mathcal{E}\rangle$ allows the participants involved in the contract to renegotiate it. Intuitively, if $(\boldsymbol{\alpha}) = \{G\}C$, then the contract continues as $C\{\mathcal{E}/\alpha\}$ if all the participants give their authorization, and satisfy the precondition G.

Definition 3 (Contract advertisement). *A contract advertisement is a term* $\{G\}C$ *such that: (i) each secret name in* C *occurs in* G; *(ii)* G *requires a deposit from each* A *in* $\{G\}C$; *(iii) each* * : $\langle\mathcal{E}\rangle$ *in* C *refers to a defining equation* $(\boldsymbol{\alpha}) = \{G'\}C'$ *where the participants in* G' *are the same as those in* G. ◇

The second condition is used to guarantee that the contract is stipulated only if *all* the involved participants give their authorizations. The last condition is only used to simplify the technical development. We outline in Sect. 5 how to relax it, by allowing renegotiations to exclude some participants, or to include new ones, which were not among those who originally stipulated the contract.

We now extend the reduction semantics of BitML [11], by focussing on the new renegotiation primitive. Because of space limitations, here we just provide the underlying intuition, relegating the full formalisation to [9]. We start by defining the configurations of the semantics.

$C ::= \sum_{i \in I} D_i$	contract	$p ::= true$	truth
$D ::=$	guarded contract	$\mid p \wedge p$	conjunction
$\textbf{reveal } a \textbf{ if } p.\, C$	reveal secrets (if p is true)	$\mid \neg p$	negation
$\mid \textbf{withdraw } A$	transfer the balance to A	$\mid E = E$	equality
$\mid \textbf{split } v \rightarrow C$	split the balance	$\mid E < E$	less than
$\mid A : D$	wait for A's authorization	$E ::= \mathcal{E}$	static expression
$\mid \textbf{after } \mathcal{E} : D$	wait until time $\mathcal{E}$	$\mid a$	secret
$\mid * : \textbf{rngt } X \langle \mathcal{E} \rangle$	renegotiate the contract	$\mid E + E$	addition
		$\mid E - E$	subtraction

Fig. 1. Syntax of BitML contracts.

Definition 4 (Configuration). *Configurations have the following syntax:*

$\Gamma ::= 0$	*empty*
$\mid \{G\}^x C$	*contract advertisement (name x is optional)*
$\mid \langle C, v \rangle_x$	*active contract containing $v \mathcal{B}$*
$\mid \langle A, v \rangle_x$	*deposit of $v \mathcal{B}$ redeemable by A*
$\mid A[\chi]$	*authorization of A to perform action χ*
$\mid \{A : a \# N\}$	*committed secret of A ($N \in \mathbb{N} \cup \{\bot\}$)*
$\mid A : a \# N$	*revealed secret of A ($N \in \mathbb{N}$)*
$\mid A : d \leftarrow x$	*A's deposit variable d assigned to deposit name x*
$\mid \Gamma \mid \Gamma'$	*parallel composition*

We denote with $\Gamma \mid t$ a timed configuration, where $t \in \mathbb{N}$ is a global time.   ◇

We illustrate configurations and their semantics through a series of examples.

Deposits. A deposit $\langle A, v \rangle_x$ can be subject to several operations, like e.g. split into two smaller deposits, join with another deposit, transfer to another participant, or destroy. In all cases A must authorise the operation. For instance, to authorize the join of two deposits, A can perform the following step:

$$\langle A, v \rangle_x \mid \langle A, v' \rangle_y \;\rightarrow\; \langle A, v \rangle_x \mid \langle A, v' \rangle_y \mid A[x, y \rhd \langle A, v + v' \rangle]$$

where $x, y \rhd \langle A, v + v' \rangle$ is the authorization of A to spend x. After A also provides the dual authorization to spend y, anyone can actually join the deposits:

$$\langle A, v \rangle_x \mid \langle A, v' \rangle_y \mid A[x, y \rhd \langle A, v + v' \rangle] \mid A[y, x \rhd \langle A, v + v' \rangle] \;\rightarrow\; \langle A, v + v' \rangle_z$$

Advertisement. Any participant can broadcast a new contract advertisement $\{G\}C$, provided that all the deposits mentioned in G exist in the current configuration, and that the names of the secrets declared in G are fresh.

Stipulation. To stipulate an advertised contract $\{G\}C$, all the participants mentioned in it must fulfill the preconditions, and authorise the stipulation. For instance, let $G = $ A:1 x | B:1 y | A : $\quad a$, and let C be an arbitrary contract involving only A and B. The stipulation starts from a configuration containing the advertisement and the participants' deposits:

$$\Gamma = \{G\}C \mid \langle A,1\rangle_x \mid \langle B,1\rangle_y$$

At this point the participants must commit to their secrets (in this case, only A has a secret). This is rendered as a sequence of steps:

$$\Gamma \to^* \Gamma \mid \{A : a\#N\} \mid A[\# \rhd \{G\}C] \mid B[\# \rhd \{G\}C] = \Gamma'$$

where $\{A : a\#N\}$ represents the fact that A has committed to the secret N, while $A[\# \rhd \{G\}C]$ and $B[\# \rhd \{G\}C]$ represent ending the commitment phase (these steps might seem redundant, but they are useful to obtain a step-by-step correspondence between BitML executions and Bitcoin executions).

After that, A and B must perform an additional sequence of steps to authorize the transfer of their deposits x, y to the contract:

$$\Gamma' \to^* \Gamma' \mid A[x \rhd \{G\}C] \mid B[y \rhd \{G\}C] = \Gamma''$$

where $A[x \rhd \{G\}C]$ and $B[y \rhd \{G\}C]$ are the authorizations to spend x and y.

At this point all the needed authorizations have been given, so the advertisement can be turned into an active contract. This step consumes the deposits and all the authorizations, and creates an active contract, with a fresh name z:

$$\Gamma'' \to \langle C,2\rangle_z \mid \{A : a\#N\}$$

Renegotiation. We illustrate the steps to renegotiate $\langle \alpha \rangle = \{G\}C$, where $G = $ A:1 d | B:1 e | A : $\quad a$, and C is an arbitrary contract involving only A and B, and possibly containing the integer variable α in static expressions. Here, G requires A and B to spend two 1₿ deposits, and A to commit to a secret. Unlike in the case of contract stipulation above, deposits names are unknown before renegotiation, so we use the deposit variables d, e to refer to them.

Consider a configuration $\langle * : \quad \langle k \rangle + C'', v\rangle_x \mid \Gamma$, where C'' contains the branches alternative to the renegotiation. A possible execution of the action $* : \quad \langle k \rangle$ starts as follows:

$$\langle * : \quad \langle k \rangle + C'', v\rangle_x \mid \Gamma \to \langle * : \quad \langle k \rangle + C'', v\rangle_x \mid \{G'\}^x C' \mid \Gamma = \Gamma'$$

where the advertisement $\{G'\}^x C'$ is obtained by transforming $\{G\}C$ as follows: (i) variables d, e are renamed into fresh ones d', e', and similarly the secret name a into a',(ii) the static expressions in C are evaluated, assuming $\alpha = k$, and replaced with their results.The superscript x in the advertisement is used to record that, when the renegotiation is concluded, the contract x must be reduced.

In the subsequent steps participants choose the actual deposit names, and A commits to her secret. If A owns in Γ a deposit $\langle A,1\rangle_y$, she can choose $d' = y$

to satisfy the precondition G. Similarly, B can choose $e' = z$ if he owns such a deposit in Γ. These choices are performed as follows:

$$\Gamma' \to^* \ \Gamma' \mid A : d' \leftarrow y \mid \{A : a' \# N\} \mid A[\# \rhd \{G'\}^x C']$$
$$\mid B : e' \leftarrow z \mid B[\# \rhd \{G'\}^x C'] \qquad = \Gamma''$$

At this point, participants must authorise spending their deposits and the balance of the contract at x. This is done through a series of steps:

$$\Gamma'' \to^* \ \Gamma'' \mid A[y \rhd \{G'\}^x C'] \mid A[x \rhd \{G'\}^x C']$$
$$\mid B[z \rhd \{G'\}^x C'] \mid B[x \rhd \{G'\}^x C'] \ = \ \Gamma'''$$

Finally, the new contract is stipulated. This closes the old contract, and transfers its balance to the newly generated one, with a fresh name x':

$$\Gamma''' \to \ \langle C', v + 2 \rangle_{x'} \mid \Gamma$$

Note that the branches in C'' are discarded only in the last step above, where we complete the renegotiation. Before this step, it would have been possible to take one of the branches in C'', aborting the renegotiation.

Withdraw. Executing   A transfers the whole contract balance to A:

$$\langle \qquad\quad A + C', v \rangle_x \ \to \ \langle A, v \rangle_y$$

After the execution, the alternative branch C' is discarded, and a fresh deposit of $v\Bbb{B}$ for A is created. Note that the active contract x is terminated.

Split. The   primitive divides the contract balance in n parts, each one controlled by its own contract. For instance, if $n = 2$:

$$\langle\langle \qquad v_1 \to C_1 \mid v_2 \to C_2) + C', v_1 + v_2 \rangle_x \ \to \ \langle C_1, v_1 \rangle_y \mid \langle C_2, v_2 \rangle_z$$

After this step, the new spawned contracts C_1 and C_2 are executed concurrently.

Reveal. The prefix a p can be fired if all the committed secrets a have been revealed, and satisfy the guard p. For instance, if $\Gamma = A : a \# N \mid B : b \# N$:

$$\langle\langle \qquad ab \quad a = b. \ C) + C', v \rangle_x \mid \Gamma \ \to \ \langle C, v \rangle_y \mid \Gamma$$

The terms $A : a \# N$ and $B : b \# N$ represent the fact that the secrets a and b have been revealed. Crucially, only the participant who performed the commitment can add the corresponding term to the configuration.

Authorizations. A branch decorated by $A : \cdots$ can be taken only if the participant A has provided her authorization. For instance:

$$\langle A : \qquad\quad B + C', v \rangle_x \mid A[x \rhd A : \qquad\quad B] \ \to \ \langle B, v \rangle_y$$

The leftmost configuration contains the term $A[x \rhd A : \qquad B]$, which represents A's authorization to take the branch   B. This enables the step to be taken. When multiple authorizations are required, the branch can be taken only after all of them occur in the configuration.

Time Constraints. We represent time in configurations as $\Gamma \mid t$, where Γ is the untimed part of the configuration and t is the current time. We always allow the time to advance through the rule $\Gamma \mid t \to \Gamma \mid t + \delta$, for all $\delta > 0$. A branch decorated with $\quad d$ can be taken only if time d has passed. For instance:

$$\langle \quad d : \quad\quad\quad \mathsf{B}, v\rangle_x \mid t \;\to\; \langle \mathsf{B}, v\rangle_y \mid t \quad\quad\quad \text{if } t \geq d$$

For the branches not guarded by $\quad$, we lift transitions from untimed to timed configurations: namely, for an untimed transition $\Gamma \to \Gamma'$, we also have the timed transition $\Gamma \mid t \to \Gamma' \mid t$. This reflects the assumption that participants can always meet deadlines, if they want to.

3   Executing BitML on Bitcoin

To execute a BitML contract, participants first compile it to a set of Bitcoin transactions, and then append these transactions to the blockchain, each following their own strategy. Participants' strategies can involve other actions besides appending transactions, like e.g. broadcasting signatures on given transactions (which corresponds, in BitML, to add an authorization to the configuration), revealing secrets, and waiting some time (see Definition 16 in [11]). The coherence between the BitML semantics and the execution on Bitcoin is guaranteed by a step-by-step correspondence between the transitions of the BitML semantics and the actions performed by participants on the Bitcoin network.

In this section we illustrate the compiler and the execution protocol through a couple of examples, focussing on the new renegotiation primitive. The needed background on Bitcoin will be introduced along with these examples. We relegate the formal definition of the compilation rules to [9].

Zero-Coupon Bond. Recall the *ZCB* contract from Sect. 1:

$$ZCB = \quad\quad (1 \to \quad\quad\quad \mathsf{B} \mid 2 \to \quad\quad 2030 : \quad\quad\quad \mathsf{A})$$

The precondition $\mathsf{A}:1 \quad x_1 \mid \mathsf{B}:2 \quad x_2$ requires A to deposit $1\math{B}$ in the contract, and B to deposit $2\math{B}$. In Bitcoin, this precondition corresponds to requiring two unspent transactions redeemable by A and B, and containing the required amounts. We represent these transactions as follows, using the notation in [7]:

T_{x_1}
in   : $\cdots$
wit : $\cdots$
out : $(\lambda x.\mathsf{versig}_{\mathbf{K}(\mathsf{A})}(x), 1\math{B})$

T_{x_2}
in   : $\cdots$
wit : $\cdots$
out : $(\lambda x.\mathsf{versig}_{\mathbf{K}(\mathsf{B})}(x), 2\math{B})$

The transaction T_{x_1} is a record with three fields (T_{x_2} is similar). The in field points to one or more previous transactions in the blockchain. The field out is a pair, whose first element is a boolean predicate (with parameter x), and the second element, $1\math{B}$, is the amount that a subsequent transaction satisfying the predicate can redeem from T_{x_1}. Here, the predicate $\mathsf{versig}_{\mathbf{K}(\mathsf{A})}(x)$ is true when x is a signature of A on the redeeming transaction (i.e., one having T_{x_1} as in).

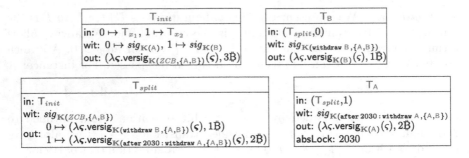

Fig. 2. Transactions obtained by compiling the ZCB contract.

The contract ZCB is compiled into the transactions in Fig. 2. The first one that can be appended to the blockchain is T_{init}. This requires a few conditions to be met: (i) T_{x_1} and T_{x_2} are *unspent* on the blockchain, i.e. no other transactions spend them; (ii) the amount specified in the out field of T_{init} does not exceed the sum of the amounts in T_{x_1} and T_{x_2};(iii) the predicates in the out fields of T_{x_1} and T_{x_2} are true, after replacing the formal parameters with the signatures $sig_{K(A)}$ and $sig_{K(B)}$, contained in the wit field of T_{init}. The contract ZCB becomes stipulated once T_{init} is on the blockchain.

After that, the   action can be performed by either A or B, by redeeming T_{init} with T_{split}. This transaction uses $\mathbf{K}(ZCB, \{A, B\})$, a set of two key pairs, each one owned by each participant. These keys are only used in this step, to ensure that no transaction but T_{split} can redeem T_{init}.

The transaction T_{split} creates two unspent outputs (indexed by 0 and 1), corresponding to the two parallel components of the   , each with its own balance. These outputs can be redeemed independently, by different transactions. The output at index 0 can only be redeemed by T_B (note that T_B's in field refers to the output 0 of T_{split}), transferring 1$\dot{\text{B}}$ to B. No other redemption is possible, since such output requires a signature with a specific key set, i.e. $\mathbf{K}($ $B, \{A, B\})$, which is not used for any other purpose. Further, the output of T_B can be redeemed with B's key, without A's one. Similarly, the output 1 of T_{split} can be redeemed by T_A, which in turns transfers 2$\dot{\text{B}}$ to A. The absLock field in T_A ensures that this may only happen after time 2030.

The stipulation protocol followed by participants requires that all the signatures needed to append the transactions in Fig. 2 are exchanged *before* T_{init} is appended. This is obtained by exchanging the signatures of T_{init} after all the other signatures. This ensures that, once the execution of ZCB starts, any honest participant can make it proceed, by appending a transaction that correspond to any of the enabled BitML actions.

In general, to guarantee that such liveness property holds, the contract must be suitably crafted, using the $D +$ $t : D'$ pattern discussed in Sect. 1. In Sect. 6 we discuss techniques to statically verify this property.

Zero-Coupon Bond with Renegotiation. Compiling $ZCB2$ yields the transactions:

T_{init}	T_{split}	T_B
in : T_{x_1} wit : $sig_{\mathbf{K}(A)}$ out : $(\lambda\varsigma.\mathsf{versig}_{\mathbf{K}(ZCB2,\{A,B\})}(\varsigma),$ $1\text{Ƀ})$	in : T_{init} wit : $sig_{\mathbf{K}(ZCB2,\{A,B\})}$ out : $0 \mapsto (\lambda\varsigma.\mathsf{versig}_{\mathbf{K}(\qquad B,\{A,B\})}(\varsigma),1\text{Ƀ})$ $1 \mapsto (\lambda\varsigma.\mathsf{versig}_{\mathbf{K}(*: \quad \langle\rangle,\{A,B\})}(\varsigma), 0\text{Ƀ})$	in : $(T_{split},0)$ wit : $sig_{\mathbf{K}(\qquad B,\{A,B\})}$ out : $(\lambda\varsigma.\mathsf{versig}_{\mathbf{K}(B)}(\varsigma),$ $1\text{Ƀ})$

Once these three transactions are on the blockchain, the only enabled action in the corresponding BitML contract is $*:\qquad \langle\rangle$, which asks 2Ƀ from B as a precondition. At the Bitcoin level, satisfying this precondition requires B to broadcast the identifier of a transaction T_y holding 2Ƀ and redeemable by himself. In BitML, this corresponds to choosing the deposit name y for the deposit variable d. Then, participants compile the contract advertisement $\{B:2 \quad d\}C$, where $C = \qquad 2030: \qquad A$, after replacing d with y. The compiler produces the following transactions:

$T_{init}^{\langle\rangle}$	T_A
in : $0 \mapsto (T_{split},1), 1 \mapsto T_y$ wit : $0 \mapsto sig_{\mathbf{K}(*: \quad \langle\rangle,\{A,B\})}$ $\quad\;\; 1 \mapsto sig_{\mathbf{K}(B)}$ out : $(\lambda\varsigma.\mathsf{versig}_{\mathbf{K}(C,\{A,B\})}(\varsigma), 2\text{Ƀ})$	in : $T_{init}^{\langle\rangle}$ wit : $sig_{\mathbf{K}(C,\{A,B\})}$ out : $(\lambda\varsigma.\mathsf{versig}_{\mathbf{K}(A)}(\varsigma), 2\text{Ƀ})$ absLock : 2030

The renegotiation succeeds once $T_{init}^{\langle\rangle}$ is on the blockchain. After that, any participant can perform the   A, by appending T_A to the blockchain.

As shown by this example, the compiler handles renegotiation as follows:

- at stipulation time, it does not produce transactions for any $*:\qquad \langle\rangle$;
- at renegotiation time, the participants broadcast the identifiers of their new deposits, and the commitments of their new secrets. Static expressions are then evaluated, and replaced by their value. Finally, the new contract is compiled as usual, with the exception that the new initial transaction has an extra input, which transfers the balance of the caller contract to the callee (in the $ZCB2$ example, this extra input is $(T_{split},1)$ within $T_{init}^{\langle\rangle}$).

Computational Soundness. The main result of [11] is computational soundness, which ensures that each execution trace at the Bitcoin level has a corresponding one in the semantics of BitML. This was achieved by formalizing the semantics of Bitcoin using a computational model, where participants can exchange bitstrings as messages, and append transactions to the blockchain. Then, a coherence relation was defined to relate symbolic runs to computational ones, essentially matching symbolic moves with their implementation in Bitcoin.

Our extension of BitML with renegotiation still enjoys computational soundness. The argument is similar, and requires extending the coherence relation to the new primitive. In particular, the reduction:

$$\{G\}^x C \mid \Gamma \;\to\; \{G\}^x C \mid \Gamma \mid \;\|_i \{A : a_i \# N_i\} \mid \;\|_j A : d_j \leftarrow x_j \mid A[\# \rhd \{G\}^x C]$$

corresponds, in Bitcoin, to A broadcasting a message which contains the hashes of her secrets and the transaction identifiers that she wishes to use as deposits.

Instead, the reduction:

$$\{G\}^x C \mid \Gamma \;\rightarrow\; \{G\}^x C \mid \Gamma \mid \mathsf{A}[x \triangleright \{G\}^x C]$$

corresponds to A signing all the transactions obtained by compiling the new contract, and broadcasting the signatures. A participant signs T_{init} only after receiving the signatures of the other transactions from all the other participants.

Computational soundness requires that each contract involves at least one participant, say A, who follows the Bitcoin implementation of BitML. In particular, A follows the stipulation and renegotiation protocols correctly, i.e. signing nothing but the protocol messages, and signing T_{init} last. We also make the usual assumptions on computational adversaries: they can only run PPTIME algorithms, and they can break the underlying cryptography with negligible probability, only. Consequently, we only consider computational runs of polynomial length (with respect to the security parameter). This is because in longer runs the adversary would be able to break the cryptography by brute force.

Below, we provide an intuitive statement of computational soundness. The formal statement is in [9].

Theorem 1 (Computational soundness). *Under the hypotheses above, each Bitcoin-level computational run has a corresponding coherent BitML run, with overwhelming probability.*

4   A Fair Recursive Coin Flipping Game

To illustrate recursion in our extended BitML, we introduce a simple game where two players repeatedly flip coins, and the one who wins two consecutive flips takes the pot. The precondition requires each player to deposit 3Ƀ and choose a secret:

$$\mathsf{A}{:}3 \; x \mid \mathsf{A}{:} \qquad a \mid \mathsf{B}{:}3 \; y \mid \mathsf{B}{:} \qquad b$$

The contract CFG (Fig. 3) asks B to reveal his secret first: if B waits too much, A can withdraw the contract funds after time 1. Then, it is A's turn to reveal (before time 2, otherwise B can withdraw the funds). The current flip winner is A if the secrets of A and B are equal, otherwise it is B. At this point, the contract can be renegotiated as $_\mathsf{A}\langle 1 \rangle$ or $_\mathsf{B}\langle 1 \rangle$, depending on the flip winner (the parameter 1 represents the round). If players do not agree on the renegotiation, then the funds are split fairly, according to the current expected win.

The contract $_\mathsf{A}\langle n \rangle$ requires A and B to generate fresh secrets for the n-th turn. If A wins again, she can withdraw the pot, otherwise the contract can be renegotiated as $_\mathsf{B}\langle n + 1 \rangle$. If the players do not agree on the renegotiation, the pot is split fairly between them. The contract $_\mathsf{B}$ is similar.

The following theorem states that our coin flipping game is fair. Fairness ensures that the expected payoff of a *rational* player is always non-negative, notwithstanding the behaviour of the other player. Rational players must choose random secrets in $\{0, 1\}$. Indeed, non uniformly distributed secrets can make

$CFG =$ **reveal** b **if** $0 \le b \le 1.($
 reveal ab **if** $a = b.$ ($*$: **rngt** $X_A \langle 1 \rangle$ + **after** $3 : Split_A$)
 + **reveal** ab **if** $a \ne b.$ ($*$: **rngt** $X_B \langle 1 \rangle$ + **after** $3 : Split_B$)
 + **after** $2 :$ **withdraw** B)
 + **after** $1 :$ **withdraw** A

$X_A \langle n \rangle = \{$A : **secret** a | B : **secret** $b\}$
 reveal b **if** $0 \le b \le 1.($
 reveal ab **if** $a = b.$ **withdraw** A
 + **reveal** ab **if** $a \ne b.$ ($*$: **rngt** $X_B \langle n + 1 \rangle$ + **after** $(3n + 3) : Split_B$)
 + **after** $(3n + 2) :$ **withdraw** B)
 + **after** $(3n + 1) :$ **withdraw** A

$X_B \langle n \rangle = \{$A : **secret** a | B : **secret** $b\}$
 reveal b **if** $0 \le b \le 1.($
 reveal ab **if** $a = b.$ ($*$: **rngt** $X_A \langle n + 1 \rangle$ + **after** $(3n + 3) : Split_A$)
 + **reveal** ab **if** $a \ne b.$ **withdraw** B
 + **after** $(3n + 2) :$ **withdraw** B)
 + **after** $(3n + 1) :$ **withdraw** A

$Split_A =$ **split** ($4 \to$ **withdraw** A | $2 \to$ **withdraw** B)

$Split_B =$ **split** ($4 \to$ **withdraw** B | $2 \to$ **withdraw** A)

Fig. 3. A recursive coin flipping game.

the adversary bias the coin flip in her favour. Further, choosing a secret different from 0 or 1 would decrease the player payoff. Indeed, B would be prevented from revealing his secrets (by the predicate in the b), and so A could win after the timeout. If A chooses a secret different from 0 or 1, she makes B win the round (since B wins when the secrets are different). Rationality also requires to reveal secrets in time (before the alternative   branch is enabled), and to take the *Split* branch if restipulation does not occur in time. This ensures that, when renegotiation happens, there is still time to reveal the round secrets. Indeed, a late renegotiation could enable the other player to win by timeout.

Theorem 2. *The expected payoff of a rational player is always non-negative.*

Proof (Sketch). First, we consider the case where renegotiation always happens. A rational player wins each coin flip with probability $1/2$, at least: so, the probability of winning the whole game is also $1/2$, at least. In the general case, the renegotiation at the end of each round may fail. When this happens, the rational player takes the *Split* branch, distributing the pot according to the expected payoff in the *current* game state, thus ensuring the fairness of the whole game. The player who won the last coin flip is expected to win $p\mbox{Ƀ}$, with $p = 1/2 \cdot 6 + 1/2 \cdot (1/2 \cdot p + 1/2 \cdot 0)$, giving $p = 4$. Accordingly, the *Split* contracts transfer $4\mbox{Ƀ}$ to the winner of the last flip and $(6 - 4)\mbox{Ƀ} = 2\mbox{Ƀ}$ to the other player.

5 More Expressive Renegotiation Primitives

The renegotiation primitive we have proposed for BitML is motivated by its simplicity, and by the possibility of compiling into standard Bitcoin transactions. By adding some degree of complexity, we can devise more general primitives, which could be useful in certain scenarios. We discuss below some alternatives.

Renegotiation-Time Parameters. The primitive $* : \quad \langle \mathcal{E} \rangle$ allows participants to choose at run-time only the deposit variables used in the renegotiated contracts, and to commit to new secrets. A possible extension is to allow participants to choose at run-time *arbitrary* values for the renegotiation parameters $\mathcal{E}$.

For instance, consider a mortgage payment, where a buyer A must pay 10Ḃ to a bank B in 10 installments. After A has paid the first five installments (of 1Ḃ each), the bank might propose to renegotiate the contract, varying the amount of the installment. Using the BitML renegotiation primitive presented in Sect. 2, we could not model this contract, since the new amount and the number of installments are unknown at the time of the original stipulation. Technically, the issue is that the primitive $* : \quad \langle \mathcal{E} \rangle$ only involves static expressions $\mathcal{E}$, the value of which is determined at stipulation time.

To cope with non-statically known values, we could extend guarded contracts with terms of the form $* : \quad \langle B : v \rangle$, declaring that the value v is to be chosen by B at renegotiation time. For instance, this would allow to model our installments payment plan as $\langle 1 \rangle$, with the following defining equations:

$$
\begin{aligned}
\langle \alpha < 5 \rangle &= \{A\!:\!1 \quad d\}(& 1 \to & & B \mid 0 \to * : & & \langle \alpha + 1 \rangle) \\
\langle 5 \rangle &= \{A\!:\!1 \quad d\}(& 1 \to & & B \mid 0 \to * : & & \langle B : k, B : v \rangle) \\
\langle \alpha \neq 1, \beta \rangle &= \{A\!:\!\beta \quad d\}(& \beta \to & & B \mid 0 \to * : & & \langle \alpha - 1, \beta \rangle) \\
\langle 1, \beta \rangle &= \{A\!:\!\beta \quad d\} & B & &
\end{aligned}
$$

where in $\langle 5 \rangle$, the bank chooses the number of installments k, as well as the amount v of each installment. Note that if A does not agree with these values, the renegotiation fails. A more refined version of the contract should take this possibility into account, by adding suitable compensation branches. Although adding the new primitive would moderately increase the complexity of the semantics and of the compiler, this extension can still be implemented on top of standard Bitcoin, preserving our computational soundness result.

Renegotiation with a Given set of Participants. As we have remarked in Sect. 2, a renegotiation can be performed only if *all* the participants of the contract agree. To generalise, we could require the agreement of a *given* set of participants (possibly, not among those who originally stipulated the contract).

For instance, consider an escrow service between a buyer A and a seller B for the purchase of an item worth 1Ḃ. The normal case is that the buyer authorizes the transfer of 1Ḃ after receiving the item, but it may happen that a dishonest seller never sends the item, or that a dishonest buyer never authorizes the payment. To cope with these cases, the participants can renegotiate the contract, including an escrow service M which mediates the dispute, as follows:

A :   B + B :   A + A : M : $_A\langle\rangle$ + B : M : $_B\langle\rangle$

P = {P : 0.1 d}   (0.1 →   M | 1 →   P)

where A : M : $_A\langle\rangle$ means that only A and M need to agree in order for the contract   A to be executed, resolving the dispute. In this case it is crucial that the renegotiation is possible even without the agreement between A and B. Indeed, if M decides to refund A (by authorizing   A), it is not to be expected that also B agrees. Similarly to the one discussed before, also this extension can be implemented on-top of Bitcoin. The computational soundness property is preserved, under the assumption that at least one participant in any renegotiation is *honest*, i.e. it follows the renegotiation protocol. Crucially, if a renegotiation only involves dishonest participants, the renegotiated contract could be anything, not necessarily that prescribed in the original contract.

Non-consensual Renegotiation. In the variants of ∗ :   discussed before, renegotiation requires one or more participants to agree. Hence, each use of ∗ :   must include suitable alternative branches, to be fired in case the renegotiation fails. In certain scenarios, we may want to renegotiate the contract without the participants having to agree. To this purpose, we can introduce a new primitive $\langle\rangle$, which continues as $\langle\rangle$ without requiring anyone to agree. For simplicity, we assume the defining equations of this primitive of the form $(\alpha) = \{v\}C$, where v represents the amount of ฿ added to the contract, by anyone.

We exemplify the new primitive to design a two-players game which starts with a bet of 1฿ from A, and a bet of 2฿ from B. Then, starting from A, players take turns adding 2฿ each to the pot. The first one who is not able to provide the additional 2฿ within a given time loses the game, allowing the other player to take the whole pot. The contract is as follows:

$$C = \{A : 1 \quad x \mid B : 2 \quad y\}(\qquad _A\langle 2\rangle + \qquad 1 : \qquad B)$$
$$_A\langle n\rangle = \{2\}(\qquad _B\langle n + 1\rangle + \qquad n : \qquad A)$$
$$_B\langle n\rangle = \{2\}(\qquad _A\langle n + 1\rangle + \qquad n : \qquad B)$$

Unlike ∗ :   , the action   can be fired without the authorizations of all the players: it just requires that the authorization to gather 2฿ is provided, by anyone. Even though the sender of these 2฿ is not specified in the contract, it is implicit in the game mechanism: for instance, when $_A\langle n\rangle$ calls $_B\langle n + 1\rangle$, only B is incentivized to add 2฿, since not doing so will make A win.

Implementing the   primitive on top of Bitcoin seems unfeasible: even if it were possible to use complex off-chain multiparty computation protocols [16], doing so might be impractical. Rather, we would like to extend Bitcoin as much as needed for the new primitive. In our implementation of BitML, we compile contracts to sets of transactions and make participants sign them. In standard BitML this is doable since, at stipulation time, we can finitely over-approximate the reducts of the original contract. Recursion can make this set infinite, e.g. $_A\langle 2\rangle$, $_A\langle 3\rangle$, ..., hence impossible to compile and sign statically. A way to cope with this is to extend Bitcoin with *malleable* signatures which only cover the part of the transaction not affected by the parameter n in $_B\langle n\rangle$. Further, signatures must not cover the in fields of transactions, since they change as recursion unfolds. In this way, the same signature can be reused for each call.

Adding malleability provides flexibility, but poses some risks. For instance, instead of redeeming the transaction corresponding to $_A\langle n\rangle$ with the transaction of $_B\langle n+1\rangle$ one could instead use the transaction of $_B\langle n+100\rangle$, since the two transactions have the same signature. To overcome this problem, we could add a new opcode to allow the output script of $_B\langle n\rangle$ to access the parameter in the redeeming transaction, so to verify that it is indeed $n+1$ as intended. Similarly, to check that we have 2Ƀ more in the new transaction, an opcode could provide the value of the new output. The same goal could be achieved by adapting the techniques used in [24,25] to realize *covenants*.

6 Conclusions

We have investigated linguistic primitives to renegotiate BitML contracts, and their implementation on standard Bitcoin. More expressive primitives could be devised by relaxing this constraint, e.g. assuming the extended UTXO model [14].

The existing verification technique for BitML [12] is based on a sound and complete abstraction of the state space of contracts. Since this abstraction is finite-state, it can be model-checked to verify the required properties. The same technique can be directly applied to BitML contracts featuring renegotiation (but without recursion), since the abstraction would remain finite. Instead, the same abstraction on recursive contracts would lead to infinitely many states. Even if we could exploit the fact that Bitcoin uses 32-bit integers to make the state space finite, it would still be too large for verification to be practical.

If we assume that integers are unbounded, and that participants always accept renegotiations, the extension of BitML presented in Sect. 2 can simulate a counter machine, so making BitML Turing-complete. Hence, verification cannot be sound and complete. Alternative techniques to model checking (e.g., type-based approaches [15]) could be used to analyse relevant contract properties.

Acknowledgements. Massimo Bartoletti is partially supported by Aut. Reg. of Sardinia projects *Sardcoin* and *Smart collaborative engineering*. Maurizio Murgia and Roberto Zunino are partially supported by MIUR PON *Distributed Ledgers for Secure Open Communities*.

References

1. Andrychowicz, M., Dziembowski, S., Malinowski, D., Mazurek, Ł.: Fair two-party computations via Bitcoin deposits. In: Böhme, R., Brenner, M., Moore, T., Smith, M. (eds.) FC 2014. LNCS, vol. 8438, pp. 105–121. Springer, Heidelberg (2014). https://doi.org/10.1007/978-3-662-44774-1_8
2. Andrychowicz, M., Dziembowski, S., Malinowski, D., Mazurek, L.: Secure multiparty computations on Bitcoin. In: IEEE S & P, pp. 443–458 (2014). https://doi.org/10.1109/SP.2014.35. first appeared on Cryptology ePrint Archive. http://eprint.iacr.org/2013/784
3. Andrychowicz, M., Dziembowski, S., Malinowski, D., Mazurek, L.: Secure multiparty computations on Bitcoin. Commun. ACM **59**(4), 76–84 (2016). https://doi.org/10.1145/2896386
4. Atzei, N., Bartoletti, M., Cimoli, T.: A survey of attacks on ethereum smart contracts (SoK). In: Maffei, M., Ryan, M. (eds.) POST 2017. LNCS, vol. 10204, pp. 164–186. Springer, Heidelberg (2017). https://doi.org/10.1007/978-3-662-54455-6_8
5. Atzei, N., Bartoletti, M., Cimoli, T., Lande, S., Zunino, R.: SoK: unraveling Bitcoin smart contracts. In: Bauer, L., Küsters, R. (eds.) POST 2018. LNCS, vol. 10804, pp. 217–242. Springer, Cham (2018). https://doi.org/10.1007/978-3-319-89722-6_9
6. Atzei, N., Bartoletti, M., Lande, S., Yoshida, N., Zunino, R.: Developing secure Bitcoin contracts with BitML. In: ESEC/FSE (2019). https://doi.org/10.1145/3338906.3341173
7. Atzei, N., Bartoletti, M., Lande, S., Zunino, R.: A formal model of Bitcoin transactions. In: Meiklejohn, S., Sako, K. (eds.) FC 2018. LNCS, vol. 10957, pp. 541–560. Springer, Heidelberg (2018). https://doi.org/10.1007/978-3-662-58387-6_29
8. Banasik, W., Dziembowski, S., Malinowski, D.: Efficient zero-knowledge contingent payments in cryptocurrencies without scripts. In: Askoxylakis, I., Ioannidis, S., Katsikas, S., Meadows, C. (eds.) ESORICS 2016. LNCS, vol. 9879, pp. 261–280. Springer, Cham (2016). https://doi.org/10.1007/978-3-319-45741-3_14
9. Bartoletti, M., Murgia, M., Zunino, R.: Renegotiation and recursion in Bitcoin contracts. CoRR abs/2003.00296 (2020)
10. Bartoletti, M., Zunino, R.: Constant-deposit multiparty lotteries on Bitcoin. In: Brenner, M., et al. (eds.) FC 2017. LNCS, vol. 10323, pp. 231–247. Springer, Cham (2017). https://doi.org/10.1007/978-3-319-70278-0_15
11. Bartoletti, M., Zunino, R.: BitML: a calculus for Bitcoin smart contracts. In: ACM CCS (2018). https://doi.org/10.1145/3243734.3243795
12. Bartoletti, M., Zunino, R.: Verifying liquidity of Bitcoin contracts. In: Nielson, F., Sands, D. (eds.) POST 2019. LNCS, vol. 11426, pp. 222–247. Springer, Cham (2019). https://doi.org/10.1007/978-3-030-17138-4_10
13. Bentov, I., Kumaresan, R.: How to use Bitcoin to design fair protocols. In: Garay, J.A., Gennaro, R. (eds.) CRYPTO 2014. LNCS, vol. 8617, pp. 421–439. Springer, Heidelberg (2014). https://doi.org/10.1007/978-3-662-44381-1_24
14. Chakravarty, M.M., Chapman, J., MacKenzie, K., Melkonian, O., Jones, M.P., Wadler, P.: The extended UTXO model. In: Workshop on Trusted Smart Contracts (2020)
15. Das, A., Balzer, S., Hoffmann, J., Pfenning, F.: Resource-aware session types for digital contracts. CoRR abs/1902.06056 (2019)
16. Gudgeon, L., Moreno-Sanchez, P., Roos, S., McCorry, P., Gervais, A.: Sok: Off the chain transactions. IACR Cryptology ePrint Archive 2019, 360 (2019)

17. Jones, S.L.P., Eber, J., Seward, J.: Composing contracts: an adventure in financial engineering, functional pearl. In: International Conference on Functional Programming (ICFP), pp. 280–292 (2000). https://doi.org/10.1145/351240.351267

18. Kumaresan, R., Bentov, I.: How to use Bitcoin to incentivize correct computations. In: ACM CCS, pp. 30–41 (2014). https://doi.org/10.1145/2660267.2660380

19. Kumaresan, R., Bentov, I.: Amortizing secure computation with penalties. In: ACM CCS, pp. 418–429 (2016). https://doi.org/10.1145/2976749.2978424

20. Kumaresan, R., Moran, T., Bentov, I.: How to use Bitcoin to play decentralized poker. In: ACM CCS, pp. 195–206 (2015). https://doi.org/10.1145/2810103.2813712

21. Kumaresan, R., Vaikuntanathan, V., Vasudevan, P.N.: Improvements to secure computation with penalties. In: ACM CCS, pp. 406–417 (2016). https://doi.org/10.1145/2976749.2978421

22. Luu, L., Chu, D.H., Olickel, H., Saxena, P., Hobor, A.: Making smart contracts smarter. In: ACM CCS, pp. 254–269 (2016). https://doi.org/10.1145/2976749.2978309

23. Miller, A., Bentov, I.: Zero-collateral lotteries in Bitcoin and Ethereum. In: Euro S&P Workshops, pp. 4–13 (2017). https://doi.org/10.1109/EuroSPW.2017.44

24. Möser, M., Eyal, I., Gün Sirer, E.: Bitcoin covenants. In: Clark, J., Meiklejohn, S., Ryan, P.Y.A., Wallach, D., Brenner, M., Rohloff, K. (eds.) FC 2016. LNCS, vol. 9604, pp. 126–141. Springer, Heidelberg (2016). https://doi.org/10.1007/978-3-662-53357-4_9

25. O'Connor, R., Piekarska, M.: Enhancing Bitcoin transactions with covenants. In: Brenner, M., et al. (eds.) FC 2017. LNCS, vol. 10323, pp. 191–198. Springer, Cham (2017). https://doi.org/10.1007/978-3-319-70278-0_12

Modelling

Architecture Modelling of Parametric Component-Based Systems

Maria Pittou and George Rahonis[✉]

Department of Mathematics, Aristotle University of Thessaloniki,
54124 Thessaloniki, Greece
{mpittou,grahonis}@math.auth.gr

Abstract. We study formal modelling of architectures applied on parametric component-based systems consisting of an unknown number of instances of each component. Architecture modelling is achieved by means of logics. We introduce an extended propositional interaction logic and investigate its first-order level which serves as a formal language for the interactions of parametric systems. Our logic effectively describes the execution order of interactions which is a main feature in several important architectures. We state the decidability of equivalence, satisfiability, and validity of first-order extended interaction logic formulas, and provide several examples of formulas describing well-known architectures.

Keywords: Architecture modelling · Parametric component-based systems · First-order extended interaction logic

1 Introduction

Developing well-founded modelling techniques is a challenging task for large and complex systems. Rigorous formalisms in systems engineering are mainly component-based that allow reconfigurability and validation [8]. Component-based design lies in constructing multiple components which coordinate in order to generate the global model for a system [8,20]. Therefore, defining the communication patterns of systems is one of the key aspects in modelling process. Coordination principles can be specified by means of architectures that characterize the permissible interactions and their implementation order as well as the topology, of the system's components [28,34]. Architectures have been proved important in systems modelling since they enforce design rules on the components, and hence ensure correctness by construction with respect to basic properties such as deadlock freedom and mutual exclusion [7,10,28].

M. Pittou—⊕ HFRI The research work was supported by the Hellenic Foundation for Research and Innovation (HFRI) under the HFRI PhD Fellowship grant (Fellowship Number: 1471).

© IFIP International Federation for Information Processing 2020
Published by Springer Nature Switzerland AG 2020

S. Bliudze and L. Bocchi (Eds.): COORDINATION 2020, LNCS 12134, pp. 281–300, 2020.
https://doi.org/10.1007/978-3-030-50029-0_18

In this paper we provide a formal framework for the architecture modelling of parametric component-based systems using a first-order logic. Parametric systems represent a wide class of component-based systems including communication protocols and concurrent and distributed algorithms [1,9,17]. Parametric systems are constructed by a finite number of component types each consisting of an unknown number of instances [4,9]. We address the problem of modelling the ordering restrictions for the components' connections, an important aspect of several parametric architectures, including Publish/Subscribe and Request/Response [15,38]. For instance, in a Request/Response architecture a service needs firstly to enroll in the service registry and then receives requests from the interested clients. On the other hand, several services fulfilling the same task, maybe be enrolled in the registry in any order. We model components with the standard formalism of labelled transitions systems (cf. [2,3,8,22]) where communication is performed by their set of labels, called ports, and is defined by interactions, i.e., sets of ports. Then, architectures are modelled by logic formulas encoding allowed interactions and their execution order. Briefly, the contributions of our work are the following:

(1) We introduce *Extended Propositional Interaction Logic* (EPIL for short) over a finite set of ports, which augments PIL from [28] with two operators namely the concatenation $*$ and the shuffle operator $\sqcup\!\sqcup$. In contrast to PIL, where the satisfaction relation is checked against interactions, EPIL formulas are interpreted over finite words whose letters are interactions. Intuitively, the semantics of concatenation and shuffle operator specifies the execution of consecutive and interleaving interactions, respectively. We apply EPIL formulas for formalizing *Blackboard* [14], *Request/Response* [15], and *Publish/Subscribe* [18] architectures.

(2) We introduce *First-Order Extended Interaction Logic* (FOEIL for short), as a modelling language for the architectures of parametric systems. The syntax of FOEIL is over typed variables and is equipped with the syntax of EPIL, the common existential and universal quantifiers, and four new quantifiers, namely existential and universal concatenation and shuffle quantifiers. The new quantifiers achieve to encode the partial and whole participation of component instances in sequential and interleaved interactions of parametric architectures.

(3) We show the expressiveness of FOEIL by examples for architectures of parametric component-based systems. Specifically, we consider the architectures *Blackboard, Request/Response,* and *Publish/Subscribe,* that impose orders on the implementation of their interactions.

(4) We state an effective translation of FOEIL formulas to finite automata and prove the decidability of equivalence, validity and satisfiability for FOEIL sentences.

The structure of the paper is as follows. In Sect. 2 we discuss related work and in Sect. 3 we recall the basic notions for component-based systems and interactions. Then, in Sect. 4 we introduce the syntax and semantics of EPIL and present three examples of architectures defined by EPIL formulas. In Sect. 5 we introduce the syntax and semantics of our FOEIL and provide examples of FOEIL sentences describing concrete parametric architectures. Section 6 deals with the decidability results for FOEIL sentences. Finally, in Conclusion, we present open problems and future work.

2   Related Work

In [28] the authors introduced a Propositional Configuration Logic (PCL) as a modelling language for the description of architectures. First- and second-order configuration logic was considered for parametric architectures (called styles of architectures in that paper). PCL which was interpreted over sets of interactions has a nice property: for every PCL formula an equivalent one in full normal form can be constructed. This implied the decidability of equivalence of PCL formulas in an automated way. Though PCL does not describe the order of interactions required by architectures as it is done by our logics, EPIL and FOEIL.

In [26] the first-order level of PIL, namely First-Order Interaction Logic (FOIL) was introduced to describe finitely many interactions, for parametric systems in BIP (cf. [8]). FOIL applied for modelling classical architectures (Star, Ring etc.) and contributed to model checking of parametric systems. Monadic Interaction Logic (MIL) was introduced in [10] as an alternative logic for the interactions of parametric systems. MIL was used for the description of parametric rendezvous and broadcast communication and applied for developing an automated method for detecting deadlocks. In the same line, in [11], an Interaction Logic with One Successor (IL1S) was developed for describing rendezvous and broadcast communications, and the architectures of parametric systems. IL1S was proved to be decidable and used for checking correctness of safety properties of parametric systems. FOIL, MIL, and IL1S, have been proved satisfactory for formalizing communication and architectures in parametric systems, though without capturing any order restrictions, as required by each architecture.

One of the main features in BIP framework is "priorities among interactions" (cf. [8]). A priority system is determined by a strict partial order $\prec$ among the set of permitted interactions. If $a \prec a'$ for two interactions a and a', then a' must be implemented before a since it has bigger priority. Clearly the set of strings of interactions satisfying an EPIL sentence containing a shuffle operator, cannot be obtained by any strict partial order among the set of interactions.

In [5] the authors established a strict framework for architectures composability. There, architectures were considered as operators enforcing properties to semantics of systems' components. Preservation of safety and liveness properties was also studied for composed architectures. The subsequent work in [7] investigated architectures of composed-based systems with data and conditions under which safety properties are preserved. In both works the required order of the interactions' execution in architectures has not been considered.

Hennessy and Milner introduced in 1985 (cf. [23]) a logic, called HML, as a calculus for the specification of concurrent programs and their properties.

In [19] the authors studied μHML, i.e., HML with least and greatest fixpoints and focused on a fragment of that logic that is monitored for runtime verification of programs' execution. μHML succeeded to describe simple client/server processes but it is far from describing complex architectures. Specifically our shuffle operator cannot be described in μHML.

In [20] the authors introduced the Components and Behaviors (CAB) process calculus which extended BIP with dynamic capabilities and showed the expressiveness of its priorities. The paper studied dynamic composition of subcomponents based on the calculus language which though does not cover the architecture of the compound system.

Distributed systems were investigated in the setup of pomsets in [21] (cf. also [36]) where the execution order of interactions was considered. Though, due to the imposed orders of pomsets, our shuffle operation cannot be sufficiently described in this framework. For instance, the subfomula $\varphi_1 \sqcup \varphi_2$ of the EPIL formula φ describing the Publish/Subscribe architecture (cf. Example 3) cannot be described by means of pomsets.

Multiparty session types described efficiently communication protocols and their interactions patterns (cf. for instance [24,25]). The relation among multiparty session types and communicating automata was studied in [16]. Parameterized multiparty session types were investigated in [13,17]. Nevertheless, the work of [17] did not study the implementation order of the parameterized interactions and the models of [13,16,24,25] did not consider the architectures of the systems.

Finally, an architectural design rewriting model for the development and reconfiguration of software architectures was introduced in [12]. Though, no order of interactions' execution was considered.

3   Preliminaries

For every natural number $n \geq 1$ we denote by $[n]$ the set $\{1,\ldots,n\}$. For every set S we denote by $\mathcal{P}(S)$ the powerset of S. Let A be an alphabet, i.e., a finite nonempty set. We denote by A^* the set of all finite words over A and we let $A^+ = A^* \setminus \{\varepsilon\}$ where ε denotes the empty word. Given $w, u \in A^*$, the shuffle product $w \sqcup u$ of w and u is a language over A defined by $w \sqcup u = \{w_1 u_1 \ldots w_m u_m \mid w_1,\ldots,u_m \in A^*$ and $w = w_1 \ldots w_m, u = u_1 \ldots u_m\}$.

A component-based system consists of a finite number of components of the same or different type. We define components by labelled transition systems (LTS for short) like in well-known component-based modelling frameworks including BIP [8], REO [3], X-MAN [22], and B [2].

Formally, an *atomic component* is an LTS $B = (Q, P, q_0, R)$ where Q is a finite set of *states*, P is a finite set of *ports*, q_0 is the *initial state* and $R \subseteq Q \times P \times Q$ is the set of *transitions*. We call an atomic component B a *component*, when we deal with several atomic components. For every set $\mathcal{B} = \{B(i) \mid i \in [n]\}$ with $B(i) = (Q(i), P(i), q_0(i), R(i))$, $i \in [n]$, we assume that $(Q(i) \cup P(i)) \cap (Q(i') \cup P(i')) = \emptyset$ for every $1 \leq i \neq i' \leq n$.

Here we focus only on the communication patterns of systems' components, using the terminology of BIP for the basic notions. Communication is achieved through components' interfaces. The interface of an LTS corresponds to its set of labels, called ports. Then, communications of components are defined by interactions, i.e., sets of ports, that can be represented by formulas of *propositional interaction logic* (PIL for short) [10,11,28]. Hence, firstly we need to recall PIL.

Let P be a nonempty finite set of *ports*. Then $I(P) = \mathcal{P}(P) \setminus \{\emptyset\}$ is the set of interactions over P. The syntax of PIL formulas ϕ over P is given by the grammar $\phi ::= \text{true} \mid p \mid \neg\phi \mid \phi \vee \phi$ where $p \in P$. We set false $= \neg$true and $\neg(\neg\phi) = \phi$, $\phi \wedge \phi' := \neg(\neg\phi \vee \neg\phi')$, $\phi \rightarrow \phi' := \neg\phi \vee \phi'$ for PIL formulas ϕ, ϕ' over P. PIL formulas are interpreted over interactions in $I(P)$. For every PIL formula ϕ and $a \in I(P)$ we define the satisfaction relation $a \models_{\text{PIL}} \phi$ by induction on the structure of ϕ as follows:

$a \models_{\text{PIL}} \text{true}$, $a \models_{\text{PIL}} \neg\phi$ iff $a \not\models_{\text{PIL}} \phi$,

$a \models_{\text{PIL}} p$ iff $p \in a$, $a \models_{\text{PIL}} \phi_1 \vee \phi_2$ iff $a \models_{\text{PIL}} \phi_1$ or $a \models_{\text{PIL}} \phi_2$.

Note that PIL differs from propositional logic, since it is interpreted over interactions, and thus the name "interaction" is assigned to it.

Two PIL formulas ϕ, ϕ' are called equivalent, denoted by $\phi \equiv \phi'$, when $a \models \phi$ iff $a \models \phi'$ for every $a \in I(P)$. For every $a = \{p_1, \ldots, p_l\} \in I(P)$ we consider the PIL formula $\phi_a = p_1 \wedge \ldots \wedge p_l$. Then, $a \models_{\text{PIL}} \phi_a$, and for every $a, a' \in I(P)$ we get $a = a'$ iff $\phi_a \equiv \phi_{a'}$. We can describe a set of interactions as a PIL formula. Specifically for $\gamma = \{a_1, \ldots, a_m\}$, the PIL formula ϕ_γ of γ is $\phi_\gamma = \phi_{a_1} \vee \ldots \vee \phi_{a_m}$.

Let $\mathcal{B} = \{B(i) \mid i \in [n]\}$ and set $P_\mathcal{B} = \bigcup_{i \in [n]} P(i)$. An *interaction of* $\mathcal{B}$ is an interaction $a \in I(P_\mathcal{B})$ such that $|a \cap P(i)| \leq 1$, for every $i \in [n]$. We denote by $I_\mathcal{B}$ the set of all interactions of B, i.e.,

$$I_\mathcal{B} = \{a \in I(P_\mathcal{B}) \mid |a \cap P(i)| \leq 1 \text{ for every } i \in [n]\}.$$

Definition 1. *A* component-based system *is a pair* $(\mathcal{B}, \gamma)$ *where* $\mathcal{B} = \{B(i) \mid i \in [n]\}$ *is a set of components, with* $B(i) = (Q(i), P(i), q_0(i), R(i))$ *for every* $i \in [n]$, *and* γ *is a set of interactions in* $I_\mathcal{B}$.

The set γ of interactions of $(\mathcal{B}, \gamma)$ specifies the architecture of the system. Obviously, we can replace γ by its corresponding PIL formula ϕ_γ, i.e., in a logical directed notation. Expression of software architectures by logics has been used in several works and gave nice results (cf. [10,11,28]).

4 Extended Propositional Interaction Logic

PIL describes nicely several architectures but its semantics does not capture the execution order of the interactions imposed by each architecture. Ordered interactions occur in common architectures, including Request/Response and Publish/Subscribe. In this section, we introduce a propositional logic that extends PIL with two operators, the concatenation $*$ and the shuffle operator $\sqcup\!\sqcup$, and we model architectures of component-based systems with order restrictions.

Definition 2. *Let P be a finite set of ports. The syntax of* extended propositional interaction logic *(EPIL for short) formulas φ over P is given by the
grammar*

$$\zeta ::= \phi \mid \zeta * \zeta$$
$$\varphi ::= \zeta \mid \neg\zeta \mid \varphi \vee \varphi \mid \varphi \wedge \varphi \mid \varphi * \varphi \mid \varphi \sqcup\!\sqcup \varphi$$

where ϕ is a PIL formula over P.

The binding strength, in decreasing order, of the EPIL operators is: negation,
shuffle, concatenation, conjunction, and disjunction. Negation is applied only
in PIL formulas and EPIL formulas of type ζ. The latter ensures exclusion of
erroneous interactions in architectures. The restricted use of negation allows
a reasonable complexity of translation of FOEIL formulas to finite automata.
This in turn implies the decidability of equivalence, satisfiability, and validity of
FOEIL sentences (cf. Sect. 6). Our assumption has no impact in expressiveness
of EPIL formulas, since they can efficiently model most known architectures.

EPIL formulas are interpreted over finite words $w \in I(P)^*$. Intuitively, a word
w encodes each of the distinct interactions within a system as a letter. Moreover,
the position of each letter in w depicts the order in which the corresponding
interaction is executed in the system, in case there is an order restriction.

Definition 3. *Let φ be an EPIL formula over P and $w \in I(P)^*$. If $w = \varepsilon$ and
$\varphi = \text{true}$, then we set $w \models \text{true}$. If $w \in I(P)^+$, then we define the satisfaction
relation $w \models \varphi$ by induction on the structure of φ as follows:*

- $w \models \phi$ *iff* $w \models_{\text{PIL}} \phi$,
- $w \models \zeta_1 * \zeta_2$ *iff*   *there exist* $w_1, w_2 \in I(P)^*$ *such that* $w = w_1 w_2$ *and* $w_i \models \zeta_i$
  for $i = 1, 2$,
- $w \models \neg\zeta$ *iff* $w \not\models \zeta$,
- $w \models \varphi_1 \vee \varphi_2$ *iff* $w \models \varphi_1$ *or* $w \models \varphi_2$,
- $w \models \varphi_1 \wedge \varphi_2$ *iff* $w \models \varphi_1$ *and* $w \models \varphi_2$,
- $w \models \varphi_1 * \varphi_2$ *iff*   *there exist* $w_1, w_2 \in I(P)^*$ *such that* $w = w_1 w_2$ *and* $w_i \models \varphi_i$
  for $i = 1, 2$,
- $w \models \varphi_1 \sqcup\!\sqcup \varphi_2$ *iff*   *there exist* $w_1, w_2 \in I(P)^*$ *such that* $w \in w_1 \sqcup\!\sqcup w_2$ *and*
  $w_i \models \varphi_i$ *for* $i = 1, 2$.

If $\varphi = \phi$ is a PIL formula, then $w \models \phi$ implies that w is a letter in $I(P)$. Two
EPIL formulas φ, φ' are called *equivalent*, denoted by $\varphi \equiv \varphi'$, when $w \models \varphi$ iff
$w \models \varphi'$ for every $w \in I(P)^*$. Now, we define an updated version of component-
based systems by replacing the PIL formula by an EPIL formula. Specifically, a
component-based system is a pair $(\mathcal{B}, \varphi)$ where $\mathcal{B} = \{B(i) \mid i \in [n]\}$ is a set of
components and φ is an EPIL formula over $P_{\mathcal{B}}$. The investigation of semantics
and verification of component-based systems is a part of future work.

Next we present three examples of component-based models $(\mathcal{B}, \varphi)$ whose
architectures have ordered interactions encoded by EPIL formulas satisfied by
words over $I_{\mathcal{B}}$. Clearly, there exist several variations of the following architectures

and their order restrictions, that EPIL formulas could also model sufficiently by applying relevant modifications. We need to define the following macro EPIL formula. Let $P = \{p_1, \ldots, p_n\}$ be a set of ports. Then, for $p_{i_1}, \ldots, p_{i_m} \in P$ with $m < n$ we let

$$\#(p_{i_1} \wedge \ldots \wedge p_{i_m}) ::= p_{i_1} \wedge \ldots \wedge p_{i_m} \wedge \bigwedge\nolimits_{p \in P \backslash \{p_{i_1}, \ldots, p_{i_m}\}} \neg p.$$

Example 1 (**Blackboard**). We consider a component-based system $(\mathcal{B}, \varphi)$ with the Blackboard architecture. The latter is applied in planning and scheduling [35] as well as in artificial intelligence [6]. Blackboard architecture involves a blackboard, a controller and the (knowledge) sources components [14, 29]. Blackboard presents the state of the problem to be solved and sources provide partial solutions without knowing about the existence of other sources. When there is enough information for a source to provide its partial solution, the source is triggered, i.e., is keen to write on the blackboard. Since multiple sources may be triggered, a controller component is used to resolve any conflicts.

We consider three knowledge sources components. Hence, $\mathcal{B} = \{B(i) \mid i \in [5]\}$ where $B(1), \ldots, B(5)$ refer to blackboard, controller and the sources components, respectively (Fig. 1). Blackboard has two ports p_d, p_a to declare the state of the problem and add the new data as obtained by a source, respectively. Sources have three ports $p_{n_k}, p_{t_k}, p_{w_k}$, for $k = 1, 2, 3$, for being notified about the existing data on the blackboard, the trigger of the source, and for writing on the blackboard, respectively. Controller has three ports, p_r used to record blackboard data, p_l for logging the triggered sources, and p_e for their execution to blackboard. Here we assume that all sources are triggered, i.e., that they participate in the architecture. The EPIL formula φ for Blackboard architecture is

$$\varphi = \#(p_d \wedge p_r) * \left(\#(p_d \wedge p_{n_1}) \sqcup \#(p_d \wedge p_{n_2}) \sqcup \#(p_d \wedge p_{n_3}) \right) *$$

$$\left(\varphi_1 \vee \varphi_2 \vee \varphi_3 \vee (\varphi_1 \sqcup \varphi_2) \vee (\varphi_1 \sqcup \varphi_3) \vee (\varphi_2 \sqcup \varphi_3) \vee (\varphi_1 \sqcup \varphi_2 \sqcup \varphi_3) \right)$$

where $\varphi_i = \#(p_l \wedge p_{t_i}) * \#(p_e \wedge p_{w_i} \wedge p_a)$ for $i = 1, 2, 3$.

The first PIL subformula encodes the connection among blackboard and controller. The EPIL subformula between the two $*$ operators represents the connections of knowledge sources to blackboard. The last part of φ captures the connection of some of knowledge sources with controller and blackboard. The use of $*$ operator in φ ensures that the controller is informed before the sources, and that sources are triggered before writing on blackboard. The shuffle operator in φ captures any possible order, among the sources, for connecting with controller and blackboard.

Before our second example we show the expressive difference among EPIL and PCL formulas of [28].

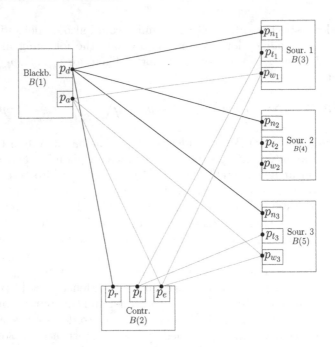

Fig. 1. Blackboard architecture. A possible execution for the interactions.

Remark 1. Consider the Blackboard architecture presented in the previous example. Then the corresponding PCL formula ρ (cf. [28]) describing that architecture is

$$\rho = \#(p_d \wedge p_r) + \#(p_d \wedge p_{n_1}) + \#(p_d \wedge p_{n_2}) + \#(p_d \wedge p_{n_3}) +$$
$$\big(\phi_1 \sqcup \phi_2 \sqcup \phi_3 \sqcup (\phi_1 + \phi_2) \sqcup (\phi_1 + \phi_3) \sqcup (\phi_2 + \phi_3) \sqcup (\phi_1 + \phi_2 + \phi_3)\big)$$

where $+$ denotes the coalescing operator, $\sqcup$ denotes the union operator, and
$$\phi_i = \#(p_l \wedge p_{t_i}) + \#(p_e \wedge p_{w_i} \wedge p_a)$$
for $i = 1, 2, 3$.

Then, the PCL formula ρ is interpreted over sets of interactions in $\mathcal{P}(I(P)) \backslash \{\emptyset\}$ which trivially cannot express the required order of the execution of the interactions. For instance the set of interactions $\big\{\{p_d, p_r\},$ $\{p_d, p_{n_1}\}, \{p_d, p_{n_2}\}, \{p_d, p_{n_3}\}, \{p_l, p_{t_2}\}, \{p_e, p_{w_2}, p_a\}\big\}$ satisfies ρ but represents no order of the interactions' execution.

Example 2 (**Request/Response**). Request/Response architectures refer to services and clients, and are classical interaction patterns widely used for web services [15]. Services become available to clients by enrolling in the so-called service registry. Then clients scan the registry and choose a service. Each client that is interested in a service sends a request and waits until the service's respond. Meanwhile no other client is connected to the service. To achieve this, in [28] a third component called coordinator was added for each service.

For our example we consider seven components, namely the service registry, two services with their coordinators, and two clients. (Fig. 2). Service registry has the ports p_e, p_u, and p_t, for the services' enrollment and for allowing a client to search and take the service's address, respectively. Services have the ports $p_{r_k}, p_{g_k}, p_{s_k}$, for $k = 1, 2$, for enrolling to service registry, and connecting to a client (via coordinator) for receiving a request and responding, respectively. Clients have the ports p_{l_k}, p_{o_k} for connecting with service registry to look up and obtain a service's address, while the ports p_{n_k}, p_{q_k} and p_{c_k} express the connection of the client to coordinator, to service (via coordinator) for sending the request and for collecting its response, respectively, for $k = 1, 2$. Coordinators have three ports, p_{m_k} for controlling that only one client is connected to a service, p_{a_k} for acknowledging that the connected client sends a request, and p_{d_k} that disconnects the client when the service responds to the request, for $k = 1, 2$. The EPIL formula φ for the Request/Response architecture equals to

$$\left(\#(p_e \wedge p_{r_1}) \sqcup \#(p_e \wedge p_{r_2})\right) * (\xi_1 \sqcup \xi_2) * \left(\left(\varphi_{11} \vee \varphi_{21} \vee (\varphi_{11} * \varphi_{21}) \vee (\varphi_{21} * \varphi_{11})\right) \vee\right.$$

$$\left(\varphi_{12} \vee \varphi_{22} \vee (\varphi_{12} * \varphi_{22}) \vee (\varphi_{22} * \varphi_{12})\right) \vee \left((\varphi_{11} \vee \varphi_{21} \vee (\varphi_{11} * \varphi_{21}) \vee (\varphi_{21} * \varphi_{11})) \sqcup\right.$$

$$\left.\left.\left(\varphi_{12} \vee \varphi_{22} \vee (\varphi_{12} * \varphi_{22}) \vee (\varphi_{22} * \varphi_{12})\right)\right)\right)$$

where $\xi_i = \#(p_{l_i} \wedge p_u) * \#(p_{o_i} \wedge p_t)$ for $i = 1, 2$, and
$\varphi_{ij} = \#(p_{n_i} \wedge p_{m_j}) * \#(p_{q_i} \wedge p_{a_j} \wedge p_{g_j}) * \#(p_{c_i} \wedge p_{d_j} \wedge p_{s_j})$ for $i = 1, 2$ (clients) and $j = 1, 2$ (services).

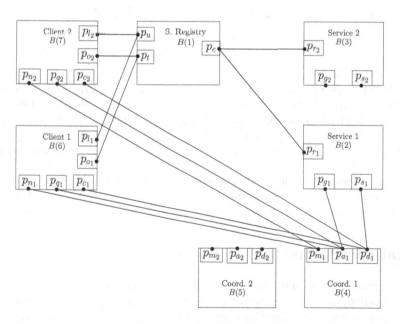

Fig. 2. Request/Response architecture. The omitted interactions are derived similarly.

The subformulas at the left of the first two concatenation operators encode the connections of the two services and the two clients with registry. Then, each of the three subformulas connected with the big disjunctions expresses that either one of the two clients or both of them (one at each time) are connected with the first service only, the second service only, or both of the services, respectively.

Example 3 (**Publish/Subscribe**). Publish/Subscribe architecture is used in IoT applications (cf. [30,31]), and recently in cloud systems [37] and robotics [27]. It involves publishers, subscribers, and topics components. Publishers advertise and transmit to topics the type of messages they produce. Then, subscribers are connected with topics they are interested in, and topics in turn transfer the messages from publishers to corresponding subscribers. Once a subscriber receives the requested message, it is disconnected from the relevant topic. Publishers cannot check the existence of subscribers and vice-versa [18].

We consider two publisher, two topic and three subscriber components (Fig. 3). Publishers have two ports, p_{a_k} and p_{t_k}, for $k = 1, 2$, for advertising and transferring their messages to topics, respectively. Topics are notified from the publishers and receive their messages through ports p_{n_k} and p_{r_k}, for $k = 1, 2$, respectively. Ports p_{c_k}, p_{s_k} and p_{f_k}, for $k = 1, 2$, are used from topics for the connection, the sending of a message, and disconnection with a subscriber, respectively. Subscribers use the ports $p_{e_m}, p_{g_m}, p_{d_m}$, for $m = 1, 2, 3$, for connecting with the topic (express interest), getting a message from the topic, and disconnecting from the topic, respectively. The EPIL formula for the Publish/Subscribe architecture is $\varphi = \varphi_1 \vee \varphi_2 \vee (\varphi_1 \sqcup\!\sqcup \varphi_2)$ with

$$\varphi_i = \Bigg(\big(\xi_i * \varphi_{i1}\big) \vee \big(\xi_i * \varphi_{i2}\big) \vee \big(\xi_i * \varphi_{i3}\big) \vee \big(\xi_i * (\varphi_{i1} \sqcup\!\sqcup \varphi_{i2})\big) \vee \big(\xi_i * (\varphi_{i1} \sqcup\!\sqcup \varphi_{i3})\big) \vee$$

$$\big(\xi_i * (\varphi_{i2} \sqcup\!\sqcup \varphi_{i3})\big) \vee \big(\xi_i * (\varphi_{i1} \sqcup\!\sqcup \varphi_{i2} \sqcup\!\sqcup \varphi_{i3})\big) \Bigg)$$

for $i \in \{1, 2\}$ (topics) and $\xi_1 = \xi_{11} \vee \xi_{12} \vee (\xi_{11} \sqcup\!\sqcup \xi_{12})$, $\xi_2 = \xi_{21} \vee \xi_{22} \vee (\xi_{21} \sqcup\!\sqcup \xi_{22})$ encode that each of the two topics connects with the first publisher, or the second one, or with both of them, where $\xi_{ij} = \#(p_{n_i} \wedge p_{a_j}) * \#(p_{r_i} \wedge p_{t_j})$ for $i, j \in \{1, 2\}$, and $\varphi_{ij} = \#(p_{c_i} \wedge p_{e_j}) * \#(p_{s_i} \wedge p_{g_j}) * \#(p_{f_i} \wedge p_{d_j})$ for $i \in \{1, 2\}$ and $j \in \{1, 2, 3\}$, describes the connections of the two topics with each of the three subscribers.

The presented examples demonstrate that EPIL formulas can encode the order restrictions within architectures and also specify all the different instantiations for the connections among the coordinated components in the system.

5   Parametric Component-Based Systems

In this section we deal with the parametric extension of component-based systems defined by a finite number of distinct *component types* whose number of *instances* is a parameter for the system. In real world applications we do not need an unbounded number of components. Though, the number of instances

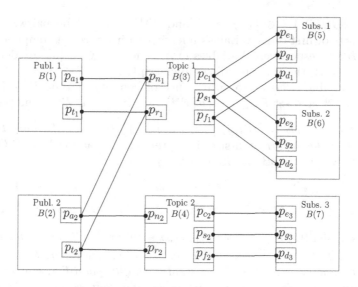

Fig. 3. Publish/Subscribe architecture. A possible execution for the interactions.

of every component type is unknown or it can be modified during a process. Next we consider parametric component-based systems, i.e., component-based systems with infinitely many instances of every component type.

Let $\mathcal{B} = \{B(i) \mid i \in [n]\}$ be a set of component types. For every $i \in [n]$ and $j \geq 1$ we consider a copy $B(i,j) = (Q(i,j), P(i,j), q_0(i,j), R(i,j))$ of $B(i)$, namely the j-*th instance* of $B(i)$. Hence, for every $i \in [n]$ and $j \geq 1$, the instance $B(i,j)$ is also a component and we call it a *parametric component* or a *component instance*. We assume that $(Q(i,j) \cup P(i,j)) \cap (Q(i',j') \cup P(i',j')) = \emptyset$ whenever $i \neq i'$ or $j \neq j'$ for every $i, i' \in [n]$ and $j, j' \geq 1$. This restriction permits us to use, without any confusion, the notation $P(i,j) = \{p(j) \mid p \in P(i)\}$ for every $i \in [n]$ and $j \geq 1$. We set $p\mathcal{B} = \{B(i,j) \mid i \in [n], j \geq 1\}$ and call it a set of *parametric components*, with $P_{p\mathcal{B}} = \bigcup_{i \in [n], j \geq 1} P(i,j)$.

Since parametric systems consist of an unknown number of component instances, we need a symbolic representation to describe their architectures. For this, we introduce the first-order extended interaction logic whose semantics describes the order of interactions implemented in a parametric architecture. Our logic is proved sufficient to model several complex architectures. This is important because parametric systems based on well-defined architectures satisfy most of their requirements [4,9].

5.1   First-Order Extended Interaction Logic

We introduce the first-order extended interaction logic as a modelling language for describing the interactions of parametric component-based systems. For this, we equip EPIL formulas with variables. Due to the nature of parametric systems we need to distinguish variables referring to different component types.

Let $pB = \{B(i,j) \mid i \in [n], j \geq 1\}$ and $\mathcal{X}^{(1)}, \ldots, \mathcal{X}^{(n)}$ be pairwise disjoint countable sets of first-order variables referring to instances of component types $B(1), \ldots, B(n)$, respectively. Variables in $\mathcal{X}^{(i)}$, for every $i \in [n]$, are denoted by small letters with the corresponding superscript, i.e., $x^{(i)} \in \mathcal{X}^{(i)}$, $i \in [n]$, is a first-order variable referring to an instance of component type $B(i)$. Let $\mathcal{X} = \mathcal{X}^{(1)} \cup \ldots \cup \mathcal{X}^{(n)}$ and set $P_{pB(\mathcal{X})} = \{p\left(x^{(i)}\right) \mid i \in [n], x^{(i)} \in \mathcal{X}^{(i)}, \text{ and } p \in P(i)\}$.

Definition 4. *Let $pB = \{B(i,j) \mid i \in [n], j \geq 1\}$ be a set of parametric components. Then the syntax of* first-order extended interaction logic *(FOEIL for short) formulas ψ over pB^1 is given by the grammar*

$$\psi ::= \varphi \mid x^{(i)} = y^{(i)} \mid \neg(x^{(i)} = y^{(i)}) \mid \psi \vee \psi \mid \psi \wedge \psi \mid \psi * \psi \mid \psi \sqcup \psi \mid$$
$$\exists x^{(i)}.\psi \mid \forall x^{(i)}.\psi \mid \exists^* x^{(i)}.\psi \mid \forall^* x^{(i)}.\psi \mid \exists^{\sqcup} x^{(i)}.\psi \mid \forall^{\sqcup} x^{(i)}.\psi$$

where φ is an EPIL formula over $P_{pB(\mathcal{X})}$, $i \in [n]$, $x^{(i)}, y^{(i)}$ are first-order variables in $\mathcal{X}^{(i)}$, $\exists^*$ denotes the existential concatenation quantifier, $\forall^*$ the universal concatenation quantifier, $\exists^{\sqcup}$ is the existential shuffle quantifier, and $\forall^{\sqcup}$ the universal shuffle quantifier. Furthermore, we assume that whenever ψ contains a subformula of the form $\exists^* x^{(i)}.\psi'$ or $\exists^{\sqcup} x^{(i)}.\psi'$, then the application of negation in ψ' is permitted only in PIL formulas and formulas of the form $x^{(j)} = y^{(j)}$.

Let ψ be a FOEIL formula over pB. We denote by free(ψ) the set of free variables of ψ. If ψ has no free variables, then it is a *sentence*. We consider a mapping $r : [n] \to \mathbb{N}$. The value $r(i)$, for every $i \in [n]$, represents the finite number of instances of the component type $B(i)$ in the parametric system. We let $pB(r) = \{B(i,j) \mid i \in [n], j \in [r(i)]\}$ and call it the *instantiation of pB w.r.t. r*. Also $P_{pB(r)} = \bigcup_{i \in [n], j \in [r(i)]} P(i,j)$ and $I_{pB(r)} = \{a \in I(P_{pB(r)}) \mid |a \cap P(i,j)| \leq 1 \text{ for every } i \in [n] \text{ and } j \in [r(i)]\}$.

Let $\mathcal{V} \subseteq \mathcal{X}$ be a finite set of first-order variables and set $P_{pB(\mathcal{V})} = \{p(x^{(i)}) \in P_{pB(\mathcal{X})} \mid x^{(i)} \in \mathcal{V}\}$. A $(\mathcal{V}, r)$-*assignment* is a mapping $\sigma : \mathcal{V} \to \mathbb{N}$ such that $\sigma(\mathcal{V} \cap \mathcal{X}^{(i)}) \subseteq [r(i)]$ for every $i \in [n]$, and $\sigma[x^{(i)} \to j]$ is the $(\mathcal{V} \cup \{x^{(i)}\}, r)$-assignment which acts as σ on $\mathcal{V} \setminus \{x^{(i)}\}$ and assigns j to $x^{(i)}$. If φ is an EPIL formula over $P_{pB(\mathcal{V})}$, then $\sigma(\varphi)$ is an EPIL formula over $P_{pB(r)}$ which is obtained by φ by replacing every port $p(x^{(i)})$ in φ by $p(\sigma(x^{(i)}))$.

We interpret FOEIL formulas ψ over triples consisting of a mapping $r : [n] \to \mathbb{N}$, a $(\mathcal{V}, r)$-assignment σ, and a word $w \in I_{pB(r)}^*$. The semantics of formulas of the form $\exists^* x^{(i)}.\psi$ and $\forall^* x^{(i)}.\psi$ (resp. $\exists^{\sqcup} x^{(i)}.\psi$ and $\forall^{\sqcup} x^{(i)}.\psi$) refer to satisfaction of ψ by subwords of w. The subwords correspond to component instances which are determined by the application of the assignment σ to $x^{(i)}$, and w results by the $*$ (resp. $\sqcup$) operator among the subwords.

Definition 5. *Let ψ be a FOEIL formula over a set $pB = \{B(i,j) \mid i \in [n], j \geq 1\}$ of parametric components and $\mathcal{V} \subseteq \mathcal{X}$ a finite set containing free(ψ). Then for*

---

[1] According to our terminology for EPIL formulas, a FOEIL formula should be defined over the set of ports of pB. Nevertheless, we prefer for simplicity to refer to the set pB of parametric components.

every $r : [n] \to \mathbb{N}$, $(\mathcal{V}, r)$-*assignment* σ, *and* $w \in I^*_{p\mathcal{B}(r)}$ *we define the satisfaction relation* $(r, \sigma, w) \models \psi$, *inductively on the structure of* ψ *as follows:*

- $(r, \sigma, w) \models \varphi$ *iff* $w \models \sigma(\varphi)$,
- $(r, \sigma, w) \models x^{(i)} = y^{(i)}$ *iff* $\sigma(x^{(i)}) = \sigma(y^{(i)})$,
- $(r, \sigma, w) \models \neg(x^{(i)} = y^{(i)})$ *iff* $(r, \sigma, w) \not\models x^{(i)} = y^{(i)}$,
- $(r, \sigma, w) \models \psi_1 \vee \psi_2$ *iff* $(r, \sigma, w) \models \psi_1$ *or* $(r, \sigma, w) \models \psi_2$,
- $(r, \sigma, w) \models \psi_1 \wedge \psi_2$ *iff* $(r, \sigma, w) \models \psi_1$ *and* $(r, \sigma, w) \models \psi_2$,
- $(r, \sigma, w) \models \psi_1 * \psi_2$ *iff there exist* $w_1, w_2 \in I^*_{p\mathcal{B}(r)}$ *such that* $w = w_1 w_2$ *and* $(r, \sigma, w_i) \models \psi_i$ *for* $i = 1, 2$,
- $(r, \sigma, w) \models \psi_1 \sqcup\!\sqcup \psi_2$ *iff there exist* $w_1, w_2 \in I^*_{p\mathcal{B}(r)}$ *such that* $w \in w_1 \sqcup\!\sqcup w_2$ *and* $(r, \sigma, w_i) \models \psi_i$ *for* $i = 1, 2$,
- $(r, \sigma, w) \models \exists x^{(i)}.\psi$ *iff there exists* $j \in [r(i)]$ *such that* $(r, \sigma[x^{(i)} \to j], w) \models \psi$,
- $(r, \sigma, w) \models \forall x^{(i)}.\psi$ *iff* $(r, \sigma[x^{(i)} \to j], w) \models \psi$ *for every* $j \in [r(i)]$,
- $(r, \sigma, w) \models \exists^* x^{(i)}.\psi$ *iff there exist* $w_{l_1}, \ldots, w_{l_k} \in I^*_{p\mathcal{B}(r)}$ *with* $1 \le l_1 < \ldots < l_k \le r(i)$ *such that* $w = w_{l_1} \ldots w_{l_k}$ *and* $(r, \sigma[x^{(i)} \to j], w_j) \models \psi$ *for every* $j = l_1, \ldots, l_k$,
- $(r, \sigma, w) \models \forall^* x^{(i)}.\psi$ *iff there exist* $w_1, \ldots, w_{r(i)} \in I^*_{p\mathcal{B}(r)}$ *such that* $w = w_1 \ldots w_{r(i)}$ *and* $(r, \sigma[x^{(i)} \to j], w_j) \models \psi$ *for every* $j \in [r(i)]$,
- $(r, \sigma, w) \models \exists^{\sqcup\!\sqcup} x^{(i)}.\psi$ *iff there exist* $w_{l_1}, \ldots, w_{l_k} \in I^*_{p\mathcal{B}(r)}$ *with* $1 \le l_1 < \ldots < l_k \le r(i)$ *such that* $w \in w_{l_1} \sqcup\!\sqcup \ldots \sqcup\!\sqcup w_{l_k}$ *and* $(r, \sigma[x^{(i)} \to j], w_j) \models \psi$ *for every* $j = l_1, \ldots, l_k$,
- $(r, \sigma, w) \models \forall^{\sqcup\!\sqcup} x^{(i)}.\psi$ *iff there exist* $w_1, \ldots, w_{r(i)} \in I^*_{p\mathcal{B}(r)}$ *such that* $w \in w_1 \sqcup\!\sqcup \ldots \sqcup\!\sqcup w_{r(i)}$ *and* $(r, \sigma[x^{(i)} \to j], w_j) \models \psi$ *for every* $j \in [r(i)]$.

By definition of parametric systems, all instances of each component type are identical, hence the order specified above in the semantics of $\exists^*, \forall^*, \exists^{\sqcup\!\sqcup}, \forall^{\sqcup\!\sqcup}$ quantifiers causes no restriction in the derived architecture.

If ψ is a FOEIL sentence over $p\mathcal{B}$, then we write $(r, w) \models \psi$. Let also ψ' be a FOEIL sentence over $p\mathcal{B}$. Then, ψ and ψ' are called *equivalent w.r.t.* r when $(r, w) \models \psi$ iff $(r, w) \models \psi'$, for every $w \in I^*_{p\mathcal{B}(r)}$.

In the sequel, we shall write also $x^{(i)} \neq y^{(i)}$ for $\neg(x^{(i)} = y^{(i)})$. Let β be a boolean combination of atomic formulas of the form $x^{(i)} = y^{(i)}$ and ψ a FOEIL formula over $p\mathcal{B}$. Then, we define $\beta \to \psi ::= \neg\beta \vee \psi$.

For simplicity we denote boolean combinations of formulas of the form $x^{(i)} = y^{(i)}$ as constraints. For instance we write $\exists x^{(i)} \forall y^{(i)} \exists x^{(j)} \forall y^{(j)} ((x^{(i)} \neq y^{(i)}) \wedge (x^{(j)} \neq y^{(j)})).\psi$ for $\exists x^{(i)} \forall y^{(i)} \exists x^{(j)} \forall y^{(j)}.(((x^{(i)} \neq y^{(i)}) \wedge (x^{(j)} \neq y^{(j)})) \to \psi)$.

Note that in [28] the authors considered a universe of component types and hence, excluded in their logic formulas the erroneous types for each architecture. Such a restriction is not needed in our setting since we consider a well-defined set $[n]$ of component types for each architecture.

Definition 6. *A* parametric component-based system *is a pair* $(p\mathcal{B}, \psi)$ *where* $p\mathcal{B} = \{B(i, j) \mid i \in [n], j \ge 1\}$ *is a set of parametric components and* ψ *is a* FOEIL *sentence over* $p\mathcal{B}$.

In the sequel, we refer to parametric component-based systems simply as parametric systems. We remind that in this paper we focus on the architectures of parametric systems. The study of parametric systems' behavior is left for investigation in subsequent work as a part of parametric verification.

For our examples in the next subsection, we shall need the following macro FOEIL formula. Let $p\mathcal{B} = \{B(i,j) \mid i \in [n], j \geq 1\}$ and $1 \leq i_1, \ldots, i_m \leq n$ be pairwise different indices. Then

$$\#\left(p_{i_1}(x^{(i_1)}) \wedge \ldots \wedge p_{i_m}(x^{(i_m)})\right) ::= \left(p_{i_1}(x^{(i_1)}) \wedge \ldots \wedge p_{i_m}(x^{(i_m)})\right) \wedge$$

$$\left(\bigwedge_{j=i_1,\ldots,i_m} \bigwedge_{p \in P(j) \setminus \{p_j\}} \neg p(x^{(j)})\right) \wedge \left(\bigwedge_{j=i_1,\ldots,i_m} \forall y^{(j)}(y^{(j)} \neq x^{(j)}). \bigwedge_{p \in P(j)} \neg p(y^{(j)})\right) \wedge$$

$$\left(\bigwedge_{k \in [n] \setminus \{i_1,\ldots,i_m\}} \bigwedge_{p \in P(k)} \forall x^{(k)}.\neg p(x^{(k)})\right).$$

The first $m - 1$ conjunctions express that the ports in the argument of $\#$ participate in the interaction. The double indexed conjunctions in the first pair of big parentheses disable all the other ports of the participating instances of components of type $i_1, \ldots, i_m$ described by $x^{(i_1)}, \ldots, x^{(i_m)}$, respectively; conjunctions in the second pair of parentheses disable all ports of remaining instances of component types $i_1, \ldots, i_m$. The last conjunct in the third line ensures that no ports in instances of remaining component types participate in the interaction.

5.2   Examples of FOEIL Sentences for Parametric Architectures

We present examples of FOEIL sentences describing parametric architectures, where the order of interactions is a main feature. We should note that FOEIL describes effectively as well, architectures with no order restrictions. Due to space limitations, we refer the reader to [32] for such examples.

Example 4 (**Blackboard**). The subsequent FOEIL sentence ψ encodes the interactions of Blackboard architecture, described in Example 1, in the parametric setting. We let $\mathcal{X}^{(1)}, \mathcal{X}^{(2)}, \mathcal{X}^{(3)}$ to be set of variables for blackboard, controller, and knowledge sources component instances, respectively.

$$\psi = \exists x^{(1)} \exists x^{(2)}. \left(\#(p_d(x^{(1)}) \wedge p_r(x^{(2)})) * \left(\forall^{\sqcup} x^{(3)}.\#(p_d(x^{(1)}) \wedge p_n(x^{(3)}))\right)\right) *$$

$$\left(\exists^{\sqcup} y^{(3)}. \left(\#(p_l(x^{(2)}) \wedge p_t(y^{(3)})) * \#(p_e(x^{(2)}) \wedge p_w(y^{(3)}) \wedge p_a(x^{(1)}))\right)\right).$$

Example 5 (**Request/Response**). We present a FOEIL sentence ψ for Request/Response architecture, described in Example 2, in the parametric setting. Let $\mathcal{X}^{(1)}, \mathcal{X}^{(2)}, \mathcal{X}^{(3)}$, and $\mathcal{X}^{(4)}$ refer to instances of service registry, service, client, and coordinator component, respectively. Then,

$$\psi = \left(\exists x^{(1)} . \left((\forall^{\sqcup} x^{(2)} . \#(p_e(x^{(1)}) \wedge p_r(x^{(2)}))) * \right. \right.$$

$$\left. \left. (\forall^{\sqcup} x^{(3)} . (\#(p_l(x^{(3)}) \wedge p_u(x^{(1)})) * \#(p_o(x^{(3)}) \wedge p_t(x^{(1)})))) \right) \right) *$$

$$\left(\exists^{\sqcup} y^{(2)} \exists x^{(4)} \exists^* y^{(3)} . \xi \wedge \left(\forall y^{(4)} \forall z^{(3)} \forall z^{(2)} . (\theta \vee (\forall t^{(3)} \forall t^{(2)} (z^{(2)} \neq t^{(2)}) . \theta')) \right) \right)$$

where the EPIL formulas ξ, θ, and θ' are given respectively, by:

$\xi = \#(p_n(y^{(3)}) \wedge p_m(x^{(4)})) * \#(p_q(y^{(3)}) \wedge p_a(x^{(4)}) \wedge p_g(y^{(2)})) * \#(p_c(y^{(3)}) \wedge p_d(x^{(4)}) \wedge p_s(y^{(2)}))$,

$\theta = \neg(\text{true} * \#(p_q(z^{(3)}) \wedge p_a(y^{(4)}) \wedge p_g(z^{(2)})) * \text{true})$,

and

$$\theta' = (\text{true} * \#(p_q(z^{(3)}) \wedge p_a(y^{(4)}) \wedge p_g(z^{(2)})) * \text{true}) \wedge$$
$$\neg(\text{true} * \#(p_q(t^{(3)}) \wedge p_a(y^{(4)}) \wedge p_g(t^{(2)})) * \text{true}).$$

The subformula $\forall y^{(4)} \forall z^{(3)} \forall z^{(2)} . (\theta \vee (\forall t^{(3)} \forall t^{(2)} (z^{(2)} \neq t^{(2)}) . \theta'))$ in ψ serves as a constraint to ensure that a unique coordinator is assigned to each service.

Example 6 (**Publish/Subscribe**). We consider Publish/Subscribe architecture, described in Example 3, in the parametric setting. In the subsequent FOEIL sentence ψ, we let variable sets $\mathcal{X}^{(1)}, \mathcal{X}^{(2)}, \mathcal{X}^{(3)}$ correspond to publisher, topic, and subscriber component instances, respectively.

$$\psi = \exists^{\sqcup} x^{(2)} . \left(\left(\exists^{\sqcup} x^{(1)} . (\#(p_a(x^{(1)}) \wedge p_n(x^{(2)})) * \#(p_t(x^{(1)}) \wedge p_r(x^{(2)}))) \right) * \right.$$

$$\left. \left(\exists^{\sqcup} x^{(3)} . (\#(p_e(x^{(3)}) \wedge p_c(x^{(2)})) * \#(p_g(x^{(3)}) \wedge p_s(x^{(2)})) * \#(p_d(x^{(3)}) \wedge p_f(x^{(2)}))) \right) \right).$$

In [28] a simpler version of Request/Response and Blackboard architectures is described where the resulting sets of interactions do not depict any order. Publish/Subscribe architecture has not been studied in [10, 26, 28].

Observe that in the presented examples, whenever is defined a unique instance for a component type we may also consider the corresponding set of variables as a singleton.

6 Decidability Results for FOEIL

In this section, we prove that the equivalence and validity problems for FOEIL sentences are decidable in doubly exponential time, whereas the satisfiability problem is decidable in exponential time. For this, we establish an effective translation of every FOEIL formula to an expressive equivalent finite automaton, and hence we take advantage of well-known computational results for finite automata. We refer the reader to [32] for detailed proofs of our results.

Theorem 1. *Let ψ be a FOEIL sentence over a set $p\mathcal{B} = \{B(i,j) \mid i \in [n], j \geq 1\}$ of parametric components and $r : [n] \to \mathbb{N}$. Then, we can effectively construct a finite automaton $\mathcal{A}_{\psi,r}$ over $I_{p\mathcal{B}(r)}$ such that $(r,w) \models \psi$ iff $w \in L(\mathcal{A}_{\psi,r})$ for every $w \in I^*_{p\mathcal{B}(r)}$. The worst case run time for the translation algorithm is exponential and the best case is polynomial.*

We prove Theorem 1 using the subsequent proposition. Let $\mathcal{V} \subseteq \mathcal{X}$ be a finite set of variables. For every $i \in [n]$ and $x^{(i)} \in \mathcal{V}$, we define the set $P(i)(x^{(i)}) = \{p(x^{(i)}) \mid p \in P(i) \text{ and } x^{(i)} \in \mathcal{V}\}$ and let $I_{p\mathcal{B}(\mathcal{V})} = \{a \in I(P_{p\mathcal{B}(\mathcal{V})}) \mid |a \cap P(i)(x^{(i)})| \leq 1 \text{ for every } i \in [n] \text{ and } x^{(i)} \in \mathcal{V}\}$. Next let σ be a $(\mathcal{V}, r)$-assignment and L a language over $I_{p\mathcal{B}(\mathcal{V})}$. We denote by $\sigma(L)$ the language over $I(P_{p\mathcal{B}(r)})^2$ which is obtained by L by replacing every variable $x \in \mathcal{V}$ by $\sigma(x)$.

Proposition 1. *Let ψ be a FOEIL formula over a set $p\mathcal{B} = \{B(i,j) \mid i \in [n], j \geq 1\}$ of parametric components. Let also $\mathcal{V} \subseteq \mathcal{X}$ be a finite set of variables containing free(ψ) and $r : [n] \to \mathbb{N}$. Then, we can effectively construct a finite automaton $\mathcal{A}_{\psi,r}$ over $I_{p\mathcal{B}(\mathcal{V})}$ such that for every $(\mathcal{V}, r)$-assignment σ and $w \in I^*_{p\mathcal{B}(r)}$ we have $(r, \sigma, w) \models \psi$ iff $w \in \sigma(L(\mathcal{A}_{\psi,r})) \cap I^*_{p\mathcal{B}(r)}$. The worst case run time for the translation algorithm is exponential and the best case is polynomial.*

Proof. We prove our claim by induction on the structure of the FOEIL formula ψ. The input of the translation algorithm is the FOEIL formula ψ and the complexity measure refers to the set of states of the derived finite automaton $\mathcal{A}_{\psi,r}$.

Proof (of Theorem 1). We apply Proposition 1. Since ψ is a sentence it contains no free variables. Hence, we get a finite automaton $\mathcal{A}_{\psi,r}$ over $I_{p\mathcal{B}(r)}$ such that $(r,w) \models \psi$ iff $w \in L(\mathcal{A}_{\psi,r})$ for every $w \in I^*_{p\mathcal{B}(r)}$, and this concludes our proof.

Theorem 2. *Let $p\mathcal{B} = \{B(i,j) \mid i \in [n], j \geq 1\}$ be a set of parametric components and $r : [n] \to \mathbb{N}$ a mapping. Then, the equivalence problem for FOEIL sentences over $p\mathcal{B}$ w.r.t. r is decidable in doubly exponential time.*

Next, we deal with the decidability of satisfiability and validity results for FOEIL sentences. For this, we recall firstly these notions. A FOEIL sentence ψ over $p\mathcal{B}$ is called *satisfiable w.r.t.* r whenever there exists a $w \in I^*_{p\mathcal{B}(r)}$ such that $(r,w) \models \psi$, and *valid w.r.t.* r whenever $(r,w) \models \psi$ for every $w \in I^*_{p\mathcal{B}(r)}$.

Theorem 3. *Let $p\mathcal{B} = \{B(i,j) \mid i \in [n], j \geq 1\}$ be a set of parametric components and $r : [n] \to \mathbb{N}$ a mapping. Then, the satisfiability problem for FOEIL sentences over $p\mathcal{B}$ w.r.t. r is decidable in exponential time.*

---

[2] $\sigma(L)$ is not always over $I_{p\mathcal{B}(r)}$. For instance, assume that $a \in L$ with $a \in I_{p\mathcal{B}(\mathcal{V})}$, $p(x^{(i)}), p'(y^{(i)}) \in a$ for some $i \in [n]$, $p, p' \in P(i)$, and $\sigma(x^{(i)}) = \sigma(y^{(i)})$. Then $\sigma(a) \notin I_{p\mathcal{B}(r)}$.

Proof. Let ψ be a FOEIL sentence over $p\mathcal{B}$. By Theorem 1 we construct, in exponential time, a finite automaton $\mathcal{A}_{\psi,r}$ such that $(r,w) \models \psi$ iff $w \in L(\mathcal{A}_{\psi,r})$ for every $w \in I^*_{p\mathcal{B}(r)}$. Then, ψ is satisfiable iff $L(\mathcal{A}_{\psi,r}) \neq \emptyset$ which is decidable in linear time [33], and thus satisfiability of FOEIL sentences over $p\mathcal{B}$ is decidable in exponential time.

Theorem 4. *Let $p\mathcal{B} = \{B(i,j) \mid i \in [n], j \geq 1\}$ be a set of parametric components and $r : [n] \to \mathbb{N}$ a mapping. Then, the validity problem for FOEIL sentences over $p\mathcal{B}$ w.r.t. r is decidable in doubly exponential time.*

Proof. Let ψ be a FOEIL sentence over $p\mathcal{B}$. By Theorem 1 we construct, in exponential time, a finite automaton $\mathcal{A}_{\psi,r}$ such that $(r,w) \models \psi$ iff $w \in L(\mathcal{A}_{\psi,r})$ for every $w \in I^*_{p\mathcal{B}(r)}$. Then, ψ is valid iff $L(\mathcal{A}_{\psi,r}) = I^*_{p\mathcal{B}(r)}$ which is decidable in exponential time [33]. Hence, we can decide whether ψ is valid or not in doubly exponential time.

7   Conclusion

In this paper we deal with the formal study of architectures for parametric component-based systems. We introduce a propositional logic, EPIL, which augments PIL from [28] with a concatenation and a shuffle operator, and interpret EPIL formulas over finite words of interactions. We also study FOEIL, the first-order level of EPIL, as a modelling language for the architectures of parametric systems. EPIL and FOEIL encode the permissible interactions and the order restrictions of complex architectures. Several examples are presented and we show the decidability of equivalence, satisfiability and validity of FOEIL sentences.

Ongoing work involves the verification of parametric systems against formal properties, and specifically the application of architectures modelled by FOEIL, for studying the behavior and proving properties (such as deadlock-freedom) of parametric systems. Several architectures, like Ring and Linear [28] cannot be formalized by FOEIL sentences. For this, the study of second-order level of EPIL is needed which is left as future work. Another direction is the extension of our framework for modelling architectures with data applied on parametric systems. Also, it would be interesting to investigate in our setting the architecture composition problem (cf. [5]). Finally, in a forthcoming paper we study parametric component-based systems and FOEIL in the weighted setup.

Acknowledgement. We are deeply grateful to Simon Bliudze for discussions on a previous version of the paper.

References

1. Abdulla, P.A., Delzanno, G.: Parameterized verification. Int. J. Softw. Tools Technol. Transf. **18**(5), 469–473 (2016). https://doi.org/10.1007/s10009-016-0424-3
2. Alagar, V.S., Periyasamy, K.: The B-Method. In: Specification of Software Systems. Texts in Computer Science. Springer, London (2011). https://doi.org/10.1007/978-0-85729-277-3_19
3. Amaro, S., Pimentel, E., Roldan, A.M.: REO based interaction model. Electron. Notes Theor. Comput. Sci. **160**, 3–14 (2006). https://doi.org/10.1016/j.entcs.2006.05.012
4. Aminof, B., Kotek, T., Rubin, S., Spegni, F., Veith, H.: Parameterized model checking of rendezvous systems. Distrib. Comput. **31**(3), 187–222 (2017). https://doi.org/10.1007/s00446-017-0302-6
5. Attie, P., Baranov, E., Bliudze, S., Jaber, M., Sifakis, J.: A general framework for architecture composability. Formal Aspects Comput. **28**(2), 207–231 (2016). https://doi.org/10.1007/s00165-015-0349-8
6. Barr, A., Cohen, P., Feigebaum, E.A. (eds.): Handbook of Artificial Intelligence. Addison-Wesley, Boston (1989)
7. Bliudze, S., Henrio, L., Madelaine, E.: Verification of concurrent design patterns with data. In: Riis Nielson, H., Tuosto, E. (eds.) COORDINATION 2019. LNCS, vol. 11533, pp. 161–181. Springer, Cham (2019). https://doi.org/10.1007/978-3-030-22397-7_10
8. Bliudze, S., Sifakis, J.: The algebra of connectors - structuring interaction in BIP. IEEE Trans. Comput. **57**(10), 1315–1330 (2008). https://doi.org/10.1109/TC.2008.2
9. Bloem, R., et al.: Decidability in parameterized verification. SIGACT News **47**(2), 53–64 (2016). https://doi.org/10.2200/S00658ED1V01Y201508DCT013
10. Bozga, M., Iosif, R., Sifakis, J.: Checking deadlock-freedom of parametric component-based systems. In: Vojnar, T., Zhang, L. (eds.) TACAS 2019. LNCS, vol. 11428, pp. 3–20. Springer, Cham (2019). https://doi.org/10.1007/978-3-030-17465-1_1
11. Bozga, M., Iosif, R., Sifakis, J.: Structural invariants for parametric verification of systems with almost linear architectures (2019). https://arxiv.org/pdf/1902.02696.pdf
12. Bruni, R., Lluch Lafuente, A., Montanari, U., Tuosto, E.: Service oriented architectural design. In: Barthe, G., Fournet, C. (eds.) TGC 2007. LNCS, vol. 4912, pp. 186–203. Springer, Heidelberg (2008). https://doi.org/10.1007/978-3-540-78663-4_14
13. Charalambides, M., Dinges, P., Agha, G.: Parameterized, concurrent session types for asynchronous multi-actor interactions. Sci. Comput. Program. **115–116**, 100–126 (2016). https://doi.org/10.1016/j.scico.2015.10.006
14. Corkill, D.D.: Blackboard systems. AI Expert **6**(9), 40–47 (1991)
15. Daigneau, R. (ed.): Service Design Patterns: Fundamental Design Solutions for SOAP/WSDL and RESTful web services. Addison-Wesley, Boston (2012). https://doi.org/10.1145/2237796.2237821
16. Deniélou, P.-M., Yoshida, N.: Multiparty session types meet communicating automata. In: Seidl, H. (ed.) ESOP 2012. LNCS, vol. 7211, pp. 194–213. Springer, Heidelberg (2012). https://doi.org/10.1007/978-3-642-28869-2_10
17. Deniélou, P.-M., Yoshida, N., Bejleri, A., Hu, R.: Parameterised multiparty session types. Log. Methods Comput. Sci. **8**(4:6), 1–46 (2012). https://doi.org/10.2168/LMCS-8(4:6)2012

18. Eugster, P., Felber, P., Guerraoui, R., Kermarrec, M.A.: The many faces of Publish/Subscribe. ACM Comput. Surv. **35**(2), 114–131 (2003). https://doi.org/10.1145/857076.857078

19. Francalanza, A., Aceto, L., Ingolfsdottir, A.: Monitorability for the Hennessy–Milner logic with recursion. Formal Methods Syst. Des. **51**(1), 87–116 (2017). https://doi.org/10.1007/s10703-017-0273-z

20. Giusto Di, C., Stefani, B.J.: Revising glue expressiveness in component-based systems. In: Meuter, W.D., Ronan, G.C. (eds.) COORDINATION 2011. LNCS, vol. 6721, pp. 16–30 (2011). https://doi.org/10.1007/978-3-642-21464-6_2

21. Guanciale, R., Tuosto, E.: Realisability of pomsets. J. Log. Algebr. Methods Program. **108**, 69–89 (2019). https://doi.org/10.1016/j.jlamp.2019.06.003

22. He, N., et al.: Component-based design and verification in X-MAN. In: ERTS² (2012). https://web1.see.asso.fr/erts2012/Site/0P2RUC89/1D-2.pdf

23. Hennessy, M., Milner, R.: Algebraic laws for nondeterminism and concurrency. J. ACM **32**(1), 137–161 (1985). https://doi.org/10.1145/2455.2460

24. Honda, K., Yoshida, N., Carbone, M.: Multiparty asynchronous session types. J. ACM **63**(1), 9:1–9:67 (2016). https://doi.org/10.1145/2827695

25. Hüttel, H., et al.: Foundations of session types and behavioural contracts. ACM Comput. Surv. **49**(1), 3:1–3:36 (2016). https://doi.org/10.1145/2873052

26. Konnov, I., Kotek, T., Wang, Q., Veith, H., Bliudze, S., Sifakis, J.: Parameterized systems in BIP: design and model checking. In: Desharnais, J., Jagadeesan, R. (eds.) CONCUR 2016. LIPIcs, vol. 59, pp. 30:1–30:16. Schloss Dagstuhl - Leibniz-Zentrum fuer Informatik (2016). https://doi.org/10.4230/LIPIcs.CONCUR.2016.30

27. Malavolta, I., Lewis, G., Schmerl, B., Lago, P., Garlan, D.: How do you architect your robots? State of the practice and guidelines for ROS-based systems. In: ICSE-CEIP 2020. ACM (2020). https://doi.org/10.1145/3377813.3381358

28. Mavridou, A., Baranov, E., Bliudze, S., Sifakis, J.: Configuration logics: modelling architecture styles. J. Log. Algebr. Methods Program. **86**, 2–29 (2016). https://doi.org/10.1016/j.jlamp.2016.05.002

29. Nii, H.: Blackboard Systems, chap. in [6]

30. Olivieri, A., Rizzo, G., Morand, F.: A publish-subscribe approach to IoT integration: the smart office use case. In: Baroli, L., Takizawa, M., Xhafa, F., Enokido, T., Park, J. (eds.) 29th International Conference on Advanced Information Networking and Applications Workshops, pp. 644–651. IEEE (2015). https://doi.org/10.1109/WAINA.2015.28

31. Patel, S., Jardosh, S., Makwana, A., Thakkar, A.: Publish/Subscribe mechanism for IoT: a survey of event matching algorithms and open research challenges. In: Modi, N., Verma, P., Trivedi, B. (eds.) Proceedings of International Conference on Communication and Networks. AISC, vol. 508, pp. 287–294. Springer, Singapore (2017). https://doi.org/10.1007/978-981-10-2750-5_30

32. Pittou, M., Rahonis, G.: Architecture modelling of parametric component-based systems (2020). http://arxiv.org/abs/1904.02222

33. Sakarovitch, J.: Elements of Automata Theory. Cambridge University Press, Cambridge (2009)

34. Sharmaa, A., Kumarb, M., Agarwalc, S.: A complete survey on software architectural styles and patterns. Procedia Comput. Sci. **70**, 16–28 (2015). https://doi.org/10.1016/j.procs.2015.10.019

35. Straub, J., Reza, H.: The use of the blackboard architecture for a decision making system for the control of craft with various actuator and movement capabilities. In: Latifi, S. (ed.) ITNG 2014. pp. 514–519. IEEE (2014)

36. Tuosto, E., Guanciale, R.: Semantics of global view of choreographies. J. Log. Algebr. Methods Program. **95**, 17–40 (2018). https://doi.org/10.1016/j.jlamp. 2017.11.002

37. Yang, K., Zhang, K., Jia, X., Hasan, M.A., Shen, X.: Privacy-preserving attribute-keyword based data publish-subscribe service on cloud platforms. Inform. Sci. **387**, 116–131 (2017). https://doi.org/10.1016/j.ins.2016.09.020

38. Zhang, K., Muthusamy, V., Jacobsen, A., H.: Total order in content-based Publish/Subscribe systems. In: 2012 32nd IEEE International Conference on Distributed Computing Systems, pp. 335–344. IEEE (2012). https://doi.org/10.1109/ICDCS.2012.17

Weighted PCL over Product Valuation Monoids

Vagia Karyoti and Paulina Paraponiari[(✉)]

Department of Mathematics, Aristotle University of Thessaloniki,
54124 Thessaloniki, Greece
{vagiakaryo,parapavl}@math.auth.gr

Abstract. We introduce a weighted propositional configuration logic over a product valuation monoid. Our logic is intended to serve as a specification language for software architectures with quantitative features such as the average of all interactions' costs of the architecture and the maximum cost among all costs occurring most frequently within a specific number of components in an architecture. We provide formulas of our logic which describe well-known architectures equipped with quantitative characteristics. Moreover, we prove an efficient construction of a full normal form which leads to decidability of equivalence of formulas in this logic.

Keywords: Software architectures · Configuration logics · Product valuation monoids · Weighted configuration logics · Quantitative features

1 Introduction

Architectures are a critical issue in design and development of complex software systems since they characterize coordination principles among the components of a system. Whenever the construction of a software system is based on a "good" architecture, then the system satisfies most of its functional and quality requirements. Well-defined architectures require a formal treatment in order to efficiently characterize their properties. A recent work towards this direction is [13], where the authors introduced propositional configuration logic (PCL for short) which was proved sufficient enough to describe architectures: the meaning of every PCL formula is a configuration set, which intuitively represents permissible component connections, and every architecture can be represented by a configuration set on the collection of its components. Furthermore, the authors of [13] studied the relation among architectures and architecture styles, i.e., architectures with the same types of components and topologies.

P. Paraponiari—ⓔ HFRI The research work was supported by the Hellenic Foundation for Research and Innovation (HFRI) under the HFRI PhD Fellowship grant (Fellowship Number: 1200).

ⓒ IFIP International Federation for Information Processing 2020
Published by Springer Nature Switzerland AG 2020
S. Bliudze and L. Bocchi (Eds.): COORDINATION 2020, LNCS 12134, pp. 301–319, 2020.
https://doi.org/10.1007/978-3-030-50029-0_19

PCL is a specification logic of software architectures which is able to describe their qualitative features. However, several practical applications require also quantitative characteristics of architectures such as the cost of the interactions among the components of an architecture, the time needed, or the probability of the implementation of a concrete interaction. For instance, several IoT and cloud applications, which are based on Publish/Subscribe architecture, require quantitative features [14, 18, 19]. Moreover, considering a set of components and an architecture style, there may occur several architectures where each of them has a specific amount of some resource (e.g. memory or energy consumption). In such a setting, the most suitable architecture must be chosen, depending on the available resources or the performance. Generally, quantitative properties are essential for performance related properties and for resource-constrained systems.

The authors in [17] introduced and investigated a weighted PCL (wPCL for short) over a commutative semiring $(K, \oplus, \otimes, 0, 1)$ which serves as a specification language for the study of software architectures with quantitative features such as the maximum cost of an architecture or the maximum priority of a component. Nevertheless, operations like average for response time or power consumption cannot be described within the algebraic structure of semirings. Such operations are important for practical applications and have been investigated for weighted automata in [4–6]. In [7, 8] the authors provided valuation monoids as a general algebraic framework, which describe several operations that cannot fit in the structure of semirings. More recently, in [15] nested weighted automata have been considered under probabilistic semantics for expressing properties such as "the long-run average resource consumption is below a threshold". Also, the authors in [6] presented algorithms which are designed specifically for computing the average response time on graphs, game graphs, and Markov chains.

However, the aforementioned works have not been developed for the setting of systems' architectures and therefore cannot express characteristics such as the average cost of an architecture or the maximum most frequent cost/priority that occurs in an architecture. In this paper, we tackle this problem by extending the work of [17]. Specifically, we introduce and investigate a weighted PCL over product valuation monoids (w_{pvm}PCL for short) which is proved sufficient to serve as a specification language for software architectures with important quantitative features that are not covered in [17].

The contributions of our work are the following. We introduce the syntax and semantics of w_{pvm}PCL. The semantics of w_{pvm}PCL formulas are polynomials with values in the product valuation monoid. Then, in our main result, we prove that for every w_{pvm}PCL formula over a set of ports and a product valuation monoid with specific properties, we can effectively construct an equivalent one in full normal form, which is unique up to the equivalence relation. The second main result is the decidability of equivalence of w_{pvm}PCL formulas. Lastly, we describe in a strict logical way several well-known software architectures with quantitative characteristics. We skip detailed proofs of our results which are similar to the corresponding ones of [17] and [16]. We refer the reader to the full version of our paper on arXiv [11].

2   Preliminaries

In this section, we recall valuation monoids and product valuation monoids [8]. A *valuation monoid* $(D, \oplus, \mathrm{val}, 0)$ consists of a commutative monoid $(D, \oplus, 0)$ and a valuation function $\mathrm{val} : D^+ \to D$, where D^+ denotes the set of nonempty finite words over D, with $\mathrm{val}(d) = d$ for all $d \in D$ and $\mathrm{val}(d_1, \ldots, d_n) = 0$ whenever $d_i = 0$ for some $i \in \{1, \ldots, n\}$.

$(D, \oplus, \mathrm{val}, \otimes, 0, 1)$ is a *product valuation monoid*, or *pv-monoid* for short if $(D, \oplus, \mathrm{val}, 0)$ is a valuation monoid, $\otimes : D^2 \to D$ is a binary operation, $1 \in D$ with $\mathrm{val}(1)_{1 \leq i \leq n} = 1$ for all $n \geq 1$ and $0 \otimes d = d \otimes 0 = 0$, $1 \otimes d = d \otimes 1 = d$ for all $d \in D$. The pv-monoid is denoted simply by D if the operations and the constant elements are understood. A pv-monoid D is *left-$\oplus$-distributive* if $d \otimes (d_1 \oplus d_2) = (d \otimes d_1) \oplus (d \otimes d_2)$ for any $d, d_1, d_2 \in D$. *Right-$\oplus$-distributivity* is defined analogously. If a pv-monoid D is both left- and right-$\oplus$-distributive, then it is $\oplus$-*distributive*. If $\otimes$ is associative, then D is called *associative*. We call D *left*-val-*distributive* if for all $n \geq 1$ and $d, d_i \in D$ with $i \in \{1, \ldots, n\}$, it holds $d \otimes \mathrm{val}(d_1, \ldots, d_n) = \mathrm{val}(d \otimes d_1, \ldots, d \otimes d_n)$. Moreover, the pv-monoid D is called (additively) idempotent if $d \oplus d = d$ for every $d \in D$.

In the following we recall some pv-monoids from [8]. The algebraic structures $(\mathbb{R} \cup \{-\infty\}, \max, \mathrm{avg}, +, -\infty, 0)$ and $(\mathbb{R} \cup \{+\infty\}, \min, \mathrm{avg}, +, +\infty, 0)$ with $\mathrm{avg}(d_1, \ldots, d_n) = \frac{1}{n} \sum_{i=1}^{n} d_i$ are pv-monoids. More precisely, they are left-val-distributive and $\oplus$-distributive pv-monoids. Also, the structure $(\mathbb{R} \cup \{-\infty, +\infty\}, \min, \mathrm{maj}, \max, +\infty, -\infty)$, where $\mathrm{maj}(d_1, \ldots, d_n)$ is the greatest value among all values that occur most frequently among $d_1, \ldots, d_n$, is a $\oplus$-distributive pv-monoid but not left-val-distributive. Both avg and maj are symmetric functions, i.e., the value of the function given n arguments is the same no matter the order of the arguments. Moreover, the pv-monoids mentioned before are idempotent.

Throughout the paper $(D, \oplus, \mathrm{val}, \otimes, 0, 1)$ will denote an idempotent pv-monoid where val *is symmetric.*

Let Q be a set. A *formal series* (or simply *series*) *over Q and D* is a mapping $s : Q \to D$. The *support of s* is the set $\mathrm{supp}(s) = \{q \in Q \mid s(q) \neq 0\}$. A series with finite support is called also a *polynomial*. We denote by $D \langle Q \rangle$ the class of all polynomials over Q and D.

3   Weighted Propositional Interaction Logic

In this section, we introduce the weighted propositional interaction logic over pv-monoids. Firstly, we recall from [13] the propositional interaction logic.

Let P be a nonempty finite set of *ports*. We let $I(P) = \mathcal{P}(P) \backslash \{\emptyset\}$, where $\mathcal{P}(P)$ denotes the power set of P. Every set $\alpha \in I(P)$ is called an *interaction*.

The syntax of *propositional interaction logic* (PIL for short) formulas over P is given by the grammar

$$\phi ::= true \mid p \mid \overline{\phi} \mid \phi \vee \phi$$

where $p \in P$. As usual, we set $\overline{\overline{\phi}} = \phi$ for every PIL formula ϕ and $false = \overline{true}$. Hence, the conjunction of two PIL formulas ϕ, ϕ' is defined by $\phi \wedge \phi' = \overline{(\overline{\phi} \vee \overline{\phi'})}$. A PIL formula of the form $p_1 \wedge \cdots \wedge p_n$ with $n > 0$, and $p_i \in P$ or $p_i = p_i'$ with $p_i' \in P$ for every $1 \leq i \leq n$, is called a *monomial*. For simplicity we denote a monomial $p_1 \wedge \cdots \wedge p_n$ by $p_1 \ldots p_n$. Monomials of the form $\bigwedge_{p \in P_+} p \wedge \bigwedge_{p \in P_-} \overline{p}$ with $P_+ \cup P_- = P$ and $P_+ \cap P_- = \emptyset$ are called *full monomials*.

Let ϕ be a PIL formula and α an interaction. We define the satisfaction relation $\alpha \models_i \phi$ by induction on the structure of ϕ as follows:

- $\alpha \models_i true$,
- $\alpha \models_i p$ iff $p \in \alpha$,

- $\alpha \models_i \overline{\phi}$ iff $\alpha \not\models_i \phi$,
- $\alpha \models_i \phi_1 \vee \phi_2$ iff $\alpha \models_i \phi_1$ or $\alpha \models_i \phi_2$.

For every $\alpha \in I(P)$ it holds $\alpha \not\models_i false$. Moreover, for every interaction $\alpha \in I(P)$ we define its characteristic monomial $m_\alpha = \bigwedge_{p \in \alpha} p \wedge \bigwedge_{p \not\in \alpha} \overline{p}$. A characteristic monomial m_α is actually a full monomial that formalises the interaction α. Then, for every $\alpha' \in I(P)$ we trivially get $\alpha' \models_i m_\alpha$ iff $\alpha' = \alpha$.

Throughout the paper P will denote a nonempty finite set of ports.

Definition 1. *Let D be a pv-monoid. Then, the syntax of formulas of weighted PIL (w$_{pvm}$PIL for short) over P and D is given by the grammar*

$$\varphi ::= d \mid \phi \mid \varphi \oplus \varphi \mid \varphi \otimes \varphi$$

where $d \in D$ and ϕ denotes a PIL formula over P.

We denote by $PIL(D, P)$ the set of all w$_{pvm}$PIL formulas over P and D. Next, we present the semantics of formulas $\varphi \in PIL(D, P)$ as polynomials $\|\varphi\| \in D\langle I(P) \rangle$. For the semantics of PIL formulas ϕ over P we use the satisfaction relation as defined above. Hence, the semantics of PIL formulas ϕ gets only the values 0 and 1.

Definition 2. *Let $\varphi \in PIL(D, P)$. The semantics of φ is a polynomial $\|\varphi\| \in D\langle I(P) \rangle$. For every $\alpha \in I(P)$ the value $\|\varphi\|(\alpha)$ is defined inductively on the structure of φ as follows:*

- $\|d\|(\alpha) = d$,
- $\|\phi\|(\alpha) = \begin{cases} 1 & \text{if } \alpha \models_i \phi \\ 0 & \text{otherwise} \end{cases}$,

- $\|\varphi_1 \oplus \varphi_2\|(\alpha) = \|\varphi_1\|(\alpha) \oplus \|\varphi_2\|(\alpha)$,
- $\|\varphi_1 \otimes \varphi_2\|(\alpha) = \|\varphi_1\|(\alpha) \otimes \|\varphi_2\|(\alpha)$.

4   Weighted Propositional Configuration Logic

In this section, we introduce and investigate the weighted propositional configuration logic over pv-monoids. But first, we recall the propositional configuration logic (PCL for short) from [13]. The syntax of PCL formulas over P is given by the grammar

$$f ::= true \mid \phi \mid \neg f \mid f \sqcup f \mid f + f$$

where ϕ denotes a PIL formula over P. The operators $\neg$, $\sqcup$, and $+$ are called *complementation*, *union*, and *coalescing*, respectively. The *intersection* $\sqcap$ is defined by $f_1 \sqcap f_2 := \neg(\neg f_1 \sqcup \neg f_2)$.

We let $C(P) = \mathcal{P}(I(P)) \setminus \{\emptyset\}$. For every PCL formula f and $\gamma \in C(P)$ the satisfaction relation $\gamma \models f$ is defined inductively on the structure of f as follows:

- $\gamma \models true$, $\quad$ - $\gamma \models \neg f$ iff $\gamma \not\models f$,
- $\gamma \models \phi$ iff $\alpha \models_i \phi$ for every $\alpha \in \gamma$, $\quad$ - $\gamma \models f_1 \sqcup f_2$ iff $\gamma \models f_1$ or $\gamma \models f_2$,
- $\gamma \models f_1 + f_2$ iff there exist $\gamma_1, \gamma_2 \in C(P)$ such that $\gamma = \gamma_1 \cup \gamma_2$,

$$\text{and } \gamma_1 \models f_1 \text{ and } \gamma_2 \models f_2.$$

We define the *closure* $\sim f$ of every PCL formula f by $\sim f := f + true$.

Two PCL formulas f, f' are called *equivalent*, and we denote it by $f \equiv f'$, whenever $\gamma \models f$ iff $\gamma \models f'$ for every $\gamma \in C(P)$. We refer the reader to [13] and [17] for properties of PCL formulas.

Next, we introduce our weighted PCL over pv-monoids.

Definition 3. *Let D be a pv-monoid. The syntax of formulas of the weighted PCL (*w_{pvm}PCL *for short) over P and D is given by the grammar*

$$\zeta ::= d \mid f \mid \zeta \oplus \zeta \mid \zeta \otimes \zeta \mid \zeta \uplus \zeta \mid {*}\zeta$$

where $d \in D$, f denotes a PCL formula over P, and $\uplus$ denotes the coalescing operator among w_{pvm}PCL *formulas. The operator $*$ is called valuation operator.*

We denote by $PCL(D,P)$ the set of all w_{pvm}PCL formulas over P and D. We present the semantics of formulas $\zeta \in PCL(D,P)$ as polynomials $\|\zeta\| \in D\langle C(P) \rangle$. For the semantics of PCL formulas we use the satisfaction relation as defined previously.

Definition 4. *Let $\zeta \in PCL(D, P)$. The semantics of ζ is a polynomial $\|\zeta\| \in D\langle C(P) \rangle$ where for every $\gamma \in C(P)$ the value $\|\zeta\|(\gamma)$ is defined inductively on the structure of ζ as follows:*

- $\|d\|(\gamma) = d$,
- $\|f\|(\gamma) = \begin{cases} 1 & \text{if } \gamma \models f \\ 0 & \text{otherwise} \end{cases}$,
- $\|\zeta_1 \oplus \zeta_2\|(\gamma) = \|\zeta_1\|(\gamma) \oplus \|\zeta_2\|(\gamma)$,
- $\|\zeta_1 \otimes \zeta_2\|(\gamma) = \|\zeta_1\|(\gamma) \otimes \|\zeta_2\|(\gamma)$,
- $\|\zeta_1 \uplus \zeta_2\|(\gamma) = \bigoplus_{\gamma_1 \cup \gamma_2 = \gamma} (\|\zeta_1\|(\gamma_1) \otimes \|\zeta_2\|(\gamma_2))$,
- $\|{*}\zeta\|(\gamma) = \bigoplus_{n>0} \bigoplus_{\bigcup_{i=1}^{n} \gamma_i = \gamma} \mathrm{val}(\|\zeta\|(\gamma_1), \ldots, \|\zeta\|(\gamma_n))$

where $\cup$ denotes that the sets $\gamma_1, \ldots, \gamma_n$ consist a partition of γ for every $n > 0$.

It is important to note here that since the semantics of every $w_{pvm}PCL$ formula is defined on $C(P)$, the sets γ_1 and γ_2 in $\|\zeta_1 \uplus \zeta_2\| (\gamma)$ and the sets $\gamma_1, \ldots, \gamma_n$ in $\|*\zeta\| (\gamma)$ are nonempty. Trivially in $\|*\zeta\| (\gamma)$, the maximum value of n is $|\gamma|$, i.e., the cardinality of γ. Hence,

$$\|*\zeta\| (\gamma) = \bigoplus_{n \in \{1, \ldots, |\gamma|\}} \bigoplus_{\bigcup_{i=1}^n \gamma_i = \gamma} \mathrm{val} \left(\|\zeta\| (\gamma_1), \ldots, \|\zeta\| (\gamma_n) \right).$$

Moreover, in $\|*\zeta\| (\gamma)$, let the sets $\gamma_i \in C(P)$ where $i \in \{1, \ldots, n\}$ and $\bigcup_{i=1}^n \gamma_i = \gamma$. Consider a permutation $(i_1, \ldots, i_n)$ of $(1, \ldots, n)$. Then

$$\mathrm{val}(\|\zeta\| (\gamma_1) \ldots, \|\zeta\| (\gamma_n)) = \mathrm{val}(\|\zeta\| (\gamma_{i_1}), \ldots, \|\zeta\| (\gamma_{i_n})).$$

Hence, $\mathrm{val}(\|\zeta\| (\gamma_1), \ldots, \|\zeta\| (\gamma_n)) \oplus \mathrm{val}(\|\zeta\| (\gamma_{i_1}), \ldots, \|\zeta\| (\gamma_{i_n})) = \mathrm{val}(\|\zeta\| (\gamma_1), \ldots, \|\zeta\| (\gamma_n))$ by the idempotency of D. Therefore, for every analysis of $\gamma = \bigcup_{i=1}^n \gamma_i$, the value $\mathrm{val} (\|\zeta\| (\gamma_1), \ldots, \|\zeta\| (\gamma_n))$ in $\|*\zeta\| (\gamma)$ is computed only once.

Two $w_{pvm}PCL$ formulas ζ_1, ζ_2 are called equivalent, and we write $\zeta_1 \equiv \zeta_2$, whenever $\|\zeta_1\| (\gamma) = \|\zeta_2\| (\gamma)$ for every $\gamma \in C(P)$. The *closure* $\sim \zeta$ of every $w_{pvm}PCL$ formula $\zeta \in PCL(D, P)$ is determined by:

$$- \sim \zeta := \zeta \oplus (\zeta \uplus 1).$$

Lemma 1. *Let $\zeta \in PCL(D, P)$. Then*

$$\|\sim\zeta\| (\gamma) = \bigoplus_{\gamma' \subseteq \gamma} \|\zeta\| (\gamma')$$

for every $\gamma \in C(P)$.

Next, we present several properties of our $w_{pvm}PCL$ formulas.

Proposition 1. *Let $\zeta, \zeta_1, \zeta_2, \zeta_3 \in PCL(D, P)$ and $d \in D$. Then*

(i) $\zeta \uplus 0 \equiv 0 \equiv 0 \uplus \zeta$.

If $\otimes$ is commutative, then

(ii) $\zeta_1 \uplus \zeta_2 \equiv \zeta_2 \uplus \zeta_1$.

If D is associative and $\oplus$-distributive, then

(iii) $(\zeta_1 \uplus \zeta_2) \uplus \zeta_3 \equiv \zeta_1 \uplus (\zeta_2 \uplus \zeta_3)$.

If D is left-$\oplus$-distributive, then

(iv) $\zeta \otimes (\zeta_1 \oplus \zeta_2) \equiv (\zeta \otimes \zeta_1) \oplus (\zeta \otimes \zeta_2)$.

If D is right-$\oplus$-distributive, then

(v) $(\zeta_1 \oplus \zeta_2) \otimes \zeta \equiv (\zeta_1 \otimes \zeta) \oplus (\zeta_2 \otimes \zeta)$.

Proposition 2. *Let $\zeta \in PCL(D, P)$ with $\zeta = d \in D$. If D is left-val-distributive, then*

$$*\zeta \equiv d.$$

Proof. For every $\gamma = \{a_1, \ldots, a_s\}$ where $s \in \mathbb{N}$, we have

$$\|*\zeta\|(\gamma) = \bigoplus_{n \in \{1, \ldots, s\}} \bigoplus_{\gamma_1 \uplus \ldots \uplus \gamma_n = \gamma} \mathrm{val}(\|\zeta\|(\gamma_1), \ldots, \|\zeta\|(\gamma_n))$$

$$= \mathrm{val}(d) \oplus \mathrm{val}(d, d) \oplus \ldots \oplus \mathrm{val}(\overbrace{d, \ldots, d}^{s \text{ times}})$$
$$= (d \otimes \mathrm{val}(1)) \oplus (d \otimes \mathrm{val}(1, 1)) \oplus \ldots \oplus (d \otimes \mathrm{val}(1, \ldots, 1))$$
$$= (d \otimes 1) \oplus (d \otimes 1) \oplus \ldots \oplus (d \otimes 1) = d \oplus \ldots \oplus d = d$$

where the second and the last equalities hold since D is idempotent, and the third one since D is left-val-distributive.

Moreover, D is called $\oplus$-preservative whenever $\mathrm{val}(d_1 \oplus d_2, d) = \mathrm{val}(d_1, d) \oplus \mathrm{val}(d_2, d)$ and $\mathrm{val}(d, d_1 \oplus d_2) = \mathrm{val}(d, d_1) \oplus \mathrm{val}(d, d_2)$ for every $d, d_1, d_2 \in D$. The pv-monoids $(\mathbb{R} \cup \{-\infty\}, \max, \mathrm{avg}, +, -\infty, 0)$ and $(\mathbb{R} \cup \{+\infty\}, \min, \mathrm{avg}, +, +\infty, 0)$, are $\oplus$-preservative.

By a straightforward calculation we can show the next proposition.

Proposition 3. *Let D be a valuation monoid. If val is $\oplus$-preservative, then*

$$\mathrm{val}\left(\bigoplus_{i \in I} d_i, \bigoplus_{j \in J} d'_j\right) = \bigoplus_{i \in I, j \in J} \mathrm{val}(d_i, d'_j)$$

where I, J are finite index sets and $d_i, d'_j \in D$ for every $i \in I$ and $j \in J$.

Proposition 4. *Let $\zeta \in PCL(D, P)$. If D is $\oplus$-preservative, then*

$$\sim(*\zeta) \equiv *(\sim \zeta).$$

Proof. Let $\gamma \in C(P)$. Then

$$\|*(\sim \zeta)\|(\gamma) = \bigoplus_{n > 0} \bigoplus_{\gamma_1 \uplus \ldots \uplus \gamma_n = \gamma} \mathrm{val}(\|\sim \zeta\|(\gamma_1), \ldots, \|\sim \zeta\|(\gamma_n))$$

$$= \bigoplus_{n > 0} \bigoplus_{\gamma_1 \uplus \ldots \uplus \gamma_n = \gamma} \mathrm{val}\left(\bigoplus_{\gamma'_1 \subseteq \gamma_1} \|\zeta\|(\gamma'_1), \ldots, \bigoplus_{\gamma'_n \subseteq \gamma_n} \|\zeta\|(\gamma'_n)\right)$$

$$= \bigoplus_{n > 0} \bigoplus_{\gamma_1 \uplus \ldots \uplus \gamma_n = \gamma} \bigoplus_{\gamma'_1 \subseteq \gamma_1} \cdots \bigoplus_{\gamma'_n \subseteq \gamma_n} \mathrm{val}(\|\zeta\|(\gamma'_1), \ldots, \|\zeta\|(\gamma'_n))$$

$$= \bigoplus_{\gamma' \subseteq \gamma} \bigoplus_{n > 0} \bigoplus_{\gamma_1 \uplus \ldots \uplus \gamma_n = \gamma'} \mathrm{val}(\|\zeta\|(\gamma_1), \ldots, \|\zeta\|(\gamma_n))$$

$$= \bigoplus_{\gamma' \subseteq \gamma} \|*\zeta\|(\gamma') = \|\sim(*\zeta)\|(\gamma)$$

where the third equality holds since D is $\oplus$-preservative and the next equalities due to the commutativity of $\oplus$.

Proposition 5. *Let* $\zeta, \zeta_1, \zeta_2 \in PCL(D, P)$. *If* D *is left-$\oplus$-distributive, then*

$$\zeta \uplus (\zeta_1 \oplus \zeta_2) \equiv (\zeta \uplus \zeta_1) \oplus (\zeta \uplus \zeta_2).$$

Next, we show a special case when $\otimes$ distributes over $\uplus$. In general $\otimes$ does not distribute over $\uplus$. For example, let $P = \{p, q\}$ and the $\mathrm{w_{pvm}}$PCL formulas ζ, ζ_1, ζ_2, where $\zeta = 2$ and $\zeta_1 = \zeta_2 = 1$. If we consider the set $\gamma = \{\{p\}, \{q\}\}$ and the pv-monoid $(\mathbb{R} \cup \{-\infty\}, \max, \mathrm{avg}, +, -\infty, 0)$, then it is easy to show that $\|\zeta \otimes (\zeta_1 \uplus \zeta_2)\| (\gamma) \neq \|(\zeta \otimes \zeta_1) \uplus (\zeta \otimes \zeta_2)\| (\gamma)$. Hence, $\zeta \otimes (\zeta_1 \uplus \zeta_2) \not\equiv (\zeta \otimes \zeta_1) \uplus (\zeta \otimes \zeta_2)$. However, this is not the case when ζ is a PIL formula and D is left-$\oplus$-distributive.

Proposition 6. *Let* ϕ *be a PIL formula over* P *and* $\zeta_1, \zeta_2 \in PCL(D, P)$. *If* D *is left-$\oplus$-distributive, then*

$$\phi \otimes (\zeta_1 \uplus \zeta_2) \equiv (\phi \otimes \zeta_1) \uplus (\phi \otimes \zeta_2).$$

5   Full Normal Form for $\mathrm{W_{pvm}}$PCL Formulas

In this section, we show that for every $\mathrm{w_{pvm}}$PCL formula $\zeta \in PCL(D, P)$, where D is a pv-monoid satisfying specific properties, we can effectively construct an equivalent formula of a special form which is called *full normal form*. For this, we will use corresponding results from [13] and [17]. More precisely, for every PCL formula f over P we can effectively construct a unique equivalent PCL formula of the form $true^1$ or $\bigsqcup_{i \in I} \sum_{j \in J_i} m_{i,j}$ (cf. Theorem 4.43 in [13]), and for every weighted PCL formula ζ over P and a commutative semiring $(K, \oplus, \otimes, 0, 1)$ we can construct a unique equivalent weighted PCL formula of the form k or $\bigoplus_{i \in I} \left(k_i \otimes \sum_{j \in J_i} m_{i,j} \right)$ (cf. Theorem 1 in [17] and Theorem 25 in [16]). The index sets I and J_i, for every $i \in I$, are finite, k and $k_i \in K$ and $m_{i,j}$'s are full monomials over P. We show that we can also effectively build a unique full normal form for every $\mathrm{w_{pvm}}$PCL formula over P and a pv-monoid D satisfying specific properties shown below. Uniqueness is up to the equivalence relation. Lastly, we show that the equivalence problem of $\mathrm{w_{pvm}}$PCL formulas is decidable.

Definition 5. *A* $\mathrm{w_{pvm}}$PCL *formula* $\zeta \in PCL(D, P)$ *is said to be in full normal form if either*

1. $\zeta = d$, *with* $d \in D$, *or*
2. *there are finite index sets* I *and* J_i *for every* $i \in I$, $d_i \in D$, *and full monomials* $m_{i,j}$ *for every* $i \in I$ *and* $j \in J_i$ *such that* $\zeta = \bigoplus_{i \in I} \left(d_i \otimes \sum_{j \in J_i} m_{i,j} \right)$.

---

[1] Following [16] we consider *true* as a full normal form.

Following [16], for every full normal form we can construct an equivalent one satisfying the subsequent statements:

(i) $j \neq j'$ implies $m_{i,j} \not\equiv m_{i,j'}$ for every $i \in I$, $j, j' \in J_i$, and
(ii) $i \neq i'$ implies $\sum_{j \in J_i} m_{i,j} \not\equiv \sum_{j \in J_{i'}} m_{i',j}$ for every $i, i' \in I$.

By Lemma 1 in [17], if $m_{i,j} \equiv m_{i,j'}$ for some $j \neq j'$, then we get $m_{i,j} + m_{i,j'} \equiv m_{i,j}$. So, we replace $m_{i,j} + m_{i,j'}$ by $m_{i,j}$. For the second case, let $\sum_{j \in J_i} m_{i,j} \equiv \sum_{j \in J_{i'}} m_{i',j}$ for some $i \neq i'$. Then, we replace $\left(d_i \otimes \sum_{j \in J_i} m_{i,j} \right) \oplus \left(d_{i'} \otimes \sum_{j \in J_{i'}} m_{i',j} \right)$ by its equivalent formula $(d_i \oplus d_{i'}) \otimes \sum_{j \in J_i} m_{i,j}$. In the sequel, we assume that every full normal form satisfies Statements (i) and (ii).

For the construction of the full normal form of every $\zeta \in PCL(D, P)$ we shall need the next results. Specifically, we omit the proofs of Lemmas 2, 3 and Proposition 7 which are similar to the corresponding ones in [16].

Lemma 2. *Let J be an index set and m_j full monomials for every $j \in J$. Then, there exists a unique $\overline{\gamma} \in C(P)$ such that for every $\gamma \in C(P)$ we have $\left\| \sum_{j \in J} m_j \right\| (\gamma) = 1$ if $\gamma = \overline{\gamma}$ and $\left\| \sum_{j \in J} m_j \right\| (\gamma) = 0$, otherwise.*

Proposition 7. *Let f be a PCL formula over P and D a pv-monoid. Then there exist finite index sets I and J_i for every $i \in I$, and full monomials $m_{i,j}$ for every $i \in I$ and $j \in J_i$ such that*

$$ f \equiv \bigoplus_{i \in I} \sum_{j \in J_i} m_{i,j} \equiv \bigoplus_{i \in I} \left(1 \otimes \sum_{j \in J_i} m_{i,j} \right). $$

Lemma 3. *Let m_i, m'_j be full monomials for every $i \in I$ and $j \in J$. Then,*

$$ \left(\sum_{i \in I} m_i \right) \otimes \left(\sum_{j \in J} m'_j \right) \equiv \begin{cases} \sum_{i \in I} m_i & \text{if } \sum_{i \in I} m_i \equiv \sum_{j \in J} m'_j, \\ 0 & \text{otherwise.} \end{cases} $$

Proposition 8. *Let $d_1, d_2 \in D$ and $\zeta_1, \zeta_2 \in PCL(D, P)$. If D is left-$\oplus$-distributive and $\otimes$ is commutative and associative, then*

$$ (d_1 \otimes \zeta_1) \uplus (d_2 \otimes \zeta_2) \equiv d_1 \otimes d_2 \otimes (\zeta_1 \uplus \zeta_2). $$

Proposition 9. *Let m_i, m'_j be full monomials for every $i \in I$ and $j \in J$. Then*

$$ \left(\sum_{i \in I} m_i \right) \uplus \left(\sum_{j \in J} m'_j \right) \equiv \begin{cases} \sum_{i \in I} m_i + \sum_{j \in J} m'_j & \text{if } m_i \not\equiv m'_j \text{ for every } i \in I \\ & \text{and } j \in J \\ 0 & \text{otherwise} \end{cases} $$

Proposition 10. *Let $\zeta \in PCL(D, P)$ which is in full normal form, i.e., $\zeta = \bigoplus_{i \in I} \left(d_i \otimes \sum_{j \in J_i} m_{i,j} \right)$. Then*

$i.$ $*\zeta \equiv \bigoplus_{I' \subseteq I} \left(\mathrm{val}(d_i)_{i \in I'} \otimes \left(\biguplus_{i \in I'} \sum_{j \in J_i} m_{i,j} \right) \right),$

$ii.$ $(*\zeta) \otimes \left(\biguplus_{i \in I} \sum_{j \in J_i} m_{i,j} \right) \equiv \mathrm{val}(d_1, \ldots, d_{|I|}) \otimes \left(\biguplus_{i \in I} \sum_{j \in J_i} m_{i,j} \right).$

Proof. i. Let $\gamma \in C(P)$. Then we get

$$\|*\zeta\|(\gamma) = \bigoplus_{n > 0} \bigoplus_{\bigcup_{i=1}^n \gamma_i = \gamma} \mathrm{val}\left(\|\zeta\|(\gamma_1), \ldots, \|\zeta\|(\gamma_n) \right).$$

By Lemma 2, for every $i \in I$ there exists a unique $\overline{\gamma_i} \in C(P)$ such that for every $\gamma \in C(P)$ we have $\left\| \sum_{i \in J_i} m_{i,j} \right\|(\gamma) = 1$ if $\gamma = \overline{\gamma_i}$ and $\left\| \sum_{i \in J_i} m_{i,j} \right\|(\gamma) = 0$, otherwise. Hence, $\mathrm{val}\left(\|\zeta\|(\gamma_1), \ldots, \|\zeta\|(\gamma_n) \right) \neq 0$ when for every $i \in \{1, \ldots, n\}$ there exists $j_i \in I$ such that $\gamma_i = \overline{\gamma_{j_i}}$ and, by definition of $\|*\zeta\|(\gamma)$, the sets $\gamma_1, \ldots, \gamma_n$ consist a partition of γ. Moreover,

$$\mathrm{val}\left(\|\zeta\|(\overline{\gamma_{j_1}}), \ldots, \|\zeta\|(\overline{\gamma_{j_n}}) \right) = \mathrm{val}\left(d_{j_1}, \ldots, d_{j_n} \right).$$

Since val is a symmetric function and D is idempotent, we get $\|*\zeta\|(\gamma) = \bigoplus_{I'' \subseteq I} \mathrm{val}(d_i)_{i \in I''}$ where for every $I'' \subseteq I$ it holds $\gamma = \bigcup_{i \in I''} \overline{\gamma_i}$ or equivalently $\left\| \biguplus_{i \in I''} \sum_{j \in J_i} m_{i,j} \right\|(\gamma) = 1$. For every other I''' subset of I it holds $\left\| \biguplus_{i \in I'''} \sum_{j \in J_i} m_{i,j} \right\|(\gamma) = 0$. So, we get the following $*\zeta \equiv \bigoplus_{I' \subseteq I} \left(\mathrm{val}(d_i)_{i \in I'} \otimes \left(\biguplus_{i \in I'} \sum_{j \in J_i} m_{i,j} \right) \right).$

ii. Let $\gamma \in C(P)$. Then we get

$$\left\| (*\zeta) \otimes \left(\biguplus_{i \in I} \sum_{j \in J_i} m_{i,j} \right) \right\|(\gamma) = \|*\zeta\|(\gamma) \otimes \left\| \biguplus_{i \in I} \sum_{j \in J_i} m_{i,j} \right\|(\gamma).$$

We can easily prove that $\left\| \biguplus_{i \in I} \sum_{j \in J_i} m_{i,j} \right\|(\gamma) = 1$ if $\gamma = \bigcup_{i \in I} \overline{\gamma_i}$ and $\left\| \biguplus_{i \in I} \sum_{j \in J_i} m_{i,j} \right\|(\gamma) = 0$ otherwise. If $\gamma = \bigcup_{i \in I} \overline{\gamma_i}$, then since D is idempotent we get $\|*\zeta\|(\gamma) = \mathrm{val}\left(d_1, \ldots, d_{|I|} \right).$ Hence,

$$\left\| (*\zeta) \otimes \left(\biguplus_{i \in I} \sum_{j \in J_i} m_{i,j} \right) \right\|(\gamma) = \begin{cases} \mathrm{val}(d_1, \ldots, d_{|I|}) & \text{if } \gamma = \bigcup_{i \in I} \overline{\gamma_i} \\ 0 & \text{otherwise.} \end{cases}$$

$$= \mathrm{val}(d_1, \ldots, d_{|I|}) \otimes \left\| \biguplus_{i \in I} \sum_{j \in J_i} m_{i,j} \right\|(\gamma)$$

$$= \left\| \mathrm{val}(d_1, \ldots, d_{|I|}) \otimes \left(\biguplus_{i \in I} \sum_{j \in J_i} m_{i,j} \right) \right\|(\gamma),$$

and we are done.

Theorem 1. *Let D be an associative, idempotent and $\oplus$-distributive pv-monoid, where $\otimes$ is commutative. Then, for every w_{pvm}PCL formula $\zeta \in PCL(D,P)$ we can effectively construct an equivalent w_{pvm}PCL formula $\zeta' \in PCL(D,P)$ in full normal form which is unique up to the equivalence relation.*

Proof. We prove our theorem by induction on the structure of w_{pvm}PCL formulas over P and D. Let $\zeta = f$ be a PCL formula. Then, we conclude our claim by Proposition 7. Next let $\zeta = d$ with $d \in D$, then we have nothing to prove.

In the sequel, assume that $\zeta_1, \zeta_2 \in PCL(D,P)$. In [11] we show how we can construct w_{pvm}PCL formulas $\zeta^{(1)}, \zeta^{(2)}$ and $\zeta^{(3)}$ in full normal form which are equivalent to $\zeta_1 \oplus \zeta_2$, $\zeta_1 \otimes \zeta_2$ and $\zeta_1 \uplus \zeta_2$, respectively.

Finally, let $\zeta = *\zeta_1$ and $\zeta_1' = \bigoplus_{i_1 \in I_1} \left(d_{i_1} \otimes \sum_{j_1 \in J_{i_1}} m_{i_1,j_1} \right)$ be its equivalent w_{pvm}PCL formula in full normal form. We consider the formula $\zeta' = *\zeta_1'$. By Proposition 10, ζ' can be equivalently written as follows

$$\zeta' \equiv \bigoplus_{I_1' \subseteq I_1} \left(\mathrm{val}(d_{i_1})_{i_1 \in I_1'} \otimes \left(\biguplus_{i_1 \in I_1'} \sum_{j_1 \in J_{i_1}} m_{i_1,j_1} \right) \right).$$

We consider the sets $I_1^{(1)}, \ldots, I_1^{(k)}$ with $k \in \mathbb{N}$ to be an enumeration of all I_1''s such that $\biguplus_{i_1 \in I_1'} \sum_{j_1 \in J_{i_1}} m_{i_1,j_1} \not\equiv 0$. Hence, by Proposition 9, $\biguplus_{i \in I_1^{(s)}} \sum_{j \in J_i} m_{i,j} \equiv \sum_{i \in I_1^{(s)}} \sum_{j \in J_i} m_{i,j}$ for every $s \in \{1, \ldots, k\}$. Moreover, for every $s \in \{1, \ldots, k\}$ we let $d_s' = \mathrm{val}(d_i)_{i \in I_1^{(s)}}$. So,

$$\zeta' \equiv \bigoplus_{s \in \{1, \ldots, k\}} \left(d_s' \otimes \left(\sum_{i \in I_1^{(s)}} \sum_{j \in J_i} m_{i,j} \right) \right).$$

Lastly, if $\sum_{i \in I_1^{(s)}} \sum_{j \in J_i} m_{i,j} \not\equiv \sum_{i \in I_1^{(s')}} \sum_{j \in J_i} m_{i,j}$ for every $s, s' \in \{1, \ldots, k\}$ with $s \neq s'$, then we are done. However, let $\sum_{i \in I_1^{(s)}} \sum_{j \in J_i} m_{i,j} \equiv \sum_{i \in I_1^{(s')}} \sum_{j \in J_i} m_{i,j}$ for some $s \neq s'$. Then, we replace $\left(d_s' \otimes \left(\sum_{i \in I_1^{(s)}} \sum_{j \in J_i} m_{i,j} \right) \right) \oplus \left(d_{s'}' \otimes \left(\sum_{i \in I_1^{(s')}} \sum_{j \in J_i} m_{i,j} \right) \right)$ by its equivalent formula $(d_s' \oplus d_{s'}') \otimes \sum_{i \in I_1^{(s)}} \sum_{j \in J_i} m_{i,j}$. We conclude to a full normal form which by construction, it is equivalent to ζ.

The uniqueness of $\zeta^{(1)}, \zeta^{(2)}, \zeta^{(3)}$ and ζ', up to equivalence, is derived in a straightforward way using Statements (i) and (ii).

In the sequel, we present an example where we compute the full normal form of a w_{pvm}PCL formula.

Example 1. Let P be the set of ports and D a pv-monoid which satisfies the properties of Theorem 1. We consider the w_{pvm}PCL formula

$$\zeta = ((d_1 \otimes m_1) \uplus (d_2 \otimes (m_2 \oplus m_3))) \oplus (d_3 \otimes (m_4 + m_5))$$

where $d_1, d_2, d_3 \in D$ and m_i is a full monomial over P for every $i \in \{1, \ldots, 5\}$. We will compute the full normal form of $\zeta' = *\zeta$. Firstly, we compute the full normal form of ζ.

$$\zeta \equiv ((d_1 \otimes d_2) \otimes (m_1 + m_2)) \oplus ((d_1 \otimes d_2) \otimes (m_1 + m_3)) \oplus (d_3 \otimes (m_4 + m_5)).$$

By Proposition 10 we get

$$\zeta' \equiv ((d_1 \otimes d_2) \otimes (m_1 + m_2)) \oplus ((d_1 \otimes d_2) \otimes (m_1 + m_3)) \oplus (d_3 \otimes (m_4 + m_5)) \oplus$$
$$(\mathrm{val}(d_1 \otimes d_2, d_3) \otimes (m_1 + m_2 + m_4 + m_5)) \oplus$$
$$(\mathrm{val}(d_1 \otimes d_2) \otimes (m_1 + m_3 + m_4 + m_5)))$$

which is in full normal form.

Theorem 2. *Let D be an associative, idempotent and $\oplus$-distributive pv-monoid, where $\otimes$ is commutative, and P a finite nonempty set of ports. Then for every $\zeta, \xi \in PCL(D, P)$ the equality $\|\zeta\| = \|\xi\|$ is decidable.*

Proof. We follow the proof of Theorem 26 in [16]. By Theorem 1 we can effectively construct $w_{\mathrm{pvm}}PCL$ formulas ζ', ξ' in full normal form such that $\|\zeta\| = \|\zeta'\|$ and $\|\xi\| = \|\xi'\|$. Let us assume that $\zeta' = \bigoplus_{i \in I} \left(d_i \otimes \sum_{j \in J_i} m_{i,j} \right)$ and $\xi' = \bigoplus_{l \in L} \left(d'_l \otimes \sum_{r \in M_l} m'_{l,r} \right)$ which moreover satisfy Statements (i) and (ii). Then, by Statement (ii) we get that $\|\zeta'\| = \|\xi'\|$ iff the following requirements (1)–(3) hold:

1) $\mathrm{card}(I) = \mathrm{card}(L)$,
2) $\{d_i \mid i \in I\} = \{d'_l \mid l \in L\}$, and
3) a) if $\mathrm{card}(I) = \mathrm{card}(\{d_i \mid i \in I\})$, then $\sum_{j \in J_i} m_{i,j} \equiv \sum_{r \in M_l} m'_{l,r}$ for every $i \in I$ and $l \in L$ such that $d_i = d'_l$,
    or
    b) if $\mathrm{card}(I) > \mathrm{card}(\{d_i \mid i \in I\})$, then we get
    $\zeta' \equiv \bigoplus_{i' \in I'} \left(d_{i'} \otimes \bigsqcup_{i \in R_{i'}} \sum_{j \in J_i} m_{i,j} \right)$ where $I' \subsetneq I$, $d_{i'}$'s $(i' \in I')$ are pairwise disjoint, and $R_{i'}$ $(i' \in I')$ is the set of all i in I such that $d_i = d_{i'}$. Similarly, we get $\xi' \equiv \bigoplus_{l' \in L'} \left(d'_{l'} \otimes \bigsqcup_{l \in S_{l'}} \sum_{r \in M_l} m'_{l,r} \right)$ where $L' \subsetneq L$, $d'_{l'}$'s $(l' \in L')$ are pairwise disjoint, and $S_{l'}$ $(l' \in L')$ is the set of all l in L such that $d'_l = d'_{l'}$. Then $\bigsqcup_{i \in R_{i'}} \sum_{j \in J_i} m_{i,j} \equiv \bigsqcup_{l \in S_{l'}} \sum_{r \in M_l} m'_{l,r}$ for every $i' \in I'$ and $l' \in L'$ such that $d_{i'} = d'_{l'}$.

By Lemma 2 the decidability of equivalences in (3a) is reduced to decidability of equality of sets of interactions corresponding to full monomials, whereas the decidability of equivalences in (3b) is reduced to the decidability of equality of sets whose elements are sets of interactions corresponding to full monomials.

6   Examples

In this section, we provide $\mathrm{w_{pvm}PCL}$ formulas which describe well-known architectures equipped with quantitative features. But first, we introduce a new symbol which we use in order to simplify the form of the formulas in our examples.

Let ζ be a $\mathrm{w_{pvm}PCL}$ formula. By Theorem 1, ζ can be written in full normal form, hence $\zeta \equiv \bigoplus_{i \in I} \left(d_i \otimes \sum_{j \in J_i} m_{i,j} \right)$. We define the *full valuation* $\circledast\zeta$ of ζ by:

- $\circledast\zeta := (\ast\zeta) \otimes \left(\biguplus_{i \in I} \sum_{j \in J_i} m_{i,j} \right)$.

Then, by Proposition 10 we get $\circledast\zeta \equiv \mathrm{val}(d_1, \ldots, d_{|I|}) \otimes \left(\biguplus_{i \in I} \sum_{j \in J_i} m_{i,j} \right)$.

Example 2. We recall from [13] the Master/Slave architecture for two masters M_1, M_2 and two slaves S_1, S_2 with ports m_1, m_2 and s_1, s_2, respectively. Masters can interact only with slaves, and vice versa, and each slave can interact with only one master. In the following we present four different $\mathrm{w_{pvm}PCL}$ formulas, which according to the underlying pv-monoid we get interesting results.

The monomial $\phi_{i,j} = m_{\{s_i,m_j\}}$ for every $i,j \in \{1,2\}$ represents the binary interaction between the ports s_i and m_j. For every $i,j \in \{1,2\}$ we consider a value $d_{i,j} \in D$ and the $\mathrm{w_{pvm}PIL}$ formula $\varphi_{i,j} = d_{i,j} \otimes \phi_{i,j}$. Hence, $d_{i,j}$ can be considered as the "cost" for the implementation of the interaction $\{s_i, m_j\}$. For our example we consider the configuration set $\gamma = \{\{s_1,m_1\}, \{s_1,m_2\}, \{s_2,m_1\}, \{s_2,m_2\}\}$ and the pv-monoid $(\mathbb{R} \cup \{-\infty\}, \max, \mathrm{avg}, +, -\infty, 0)$.

Let us assume that we want to compute the average cost of each of the possible architectures and then the maximum of those values. We consider the $\mathrm{w_{pvm}PCL}$ formula

$$\zeta =\sim \bigoplus_{i,j \in \{1,2\}} \circledast (\varphi_{1,i} \oplus \varphi_{2,j}).$$

Then, the value

$$\|\zeta\|(\gamma) = \left\| \sim \bigoplus_{i,j \in \{1,2\}} \circledast (\varphi_{1,i} \oplus \varphi_{2,j}) \right\|(\gamma)$$

$$= \max \{\mathrm{avg}(d_{1,1}, d_{2,1}), \mathrm{avg}(d_{1,1}, d_{2,2}), \mathrm{avg}(d_{1,2}, d_{2,1}), \mathrm{avg}(d_{1,2}, d_{2,2})\}$$

computes the average cost for each of the four possible instances and then the maximum of those values. It is interesting to note that $\|\zeta\|(\gamma) = \|\zeta\|(\gamma')$ for every $\gamma' \in C(P)$ with $\gamma \subseteq \gamma'$.

Moreover, let the following $\mathrm{w_{pvm}PCL}$ formula

$$\zeta = \bigotimes_{i,j \in \{1,2\}} \sim (\circledast (\varphi_{1,i} \oplus \varphi_{2,j})).$$

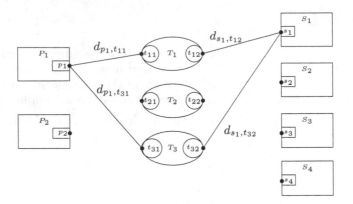

Fig. 1. Weighted Publish/Subscribe architecture.

Then, the value

$$\|\zeta\| (\gamma) = \mathrm{avg}(d_{1,1}, d_{2,1}) + \mathrm{avg}(d_{1,2}, d_{2,1}) + \mathrm{avg}(d_{1,1}, d_{2,2}) + \mathrm{avg}(d_{1,2}, d_{2,2})$$

is the sum of the average costs of all architecture schemes.

As a third case, we want to compute the slave which has the maximum average cost with the existing masters. Therefore, we consider the following $\mathrm{w_{pvm}PCL}$ formula:

$$\zeta = \sim \bigoplus_{i \in \{1,2\}} (\circledast (\varphi_{i,1} \oplus \varphi_{i,2})).$$

Then we get

$$\|\zeta\| (\gamma) = \left\| \sim \bigoplus_{i \in \{1,2\}} (\circledast (\varphi_{i,1} \oplus \varphi_{i,2})) \right\| (\gamma) = \max\{\mathrm{avg}(d_{1,1}, d_{1,2}), \mathrm{avg}(d_{2,1}, d_{2,2})\}$$

which is the wanted outcome.

Example 3. Publish/Subscribe is a software architecture used in development of applications in IoT [14], cloud computing [19] and robots' operating systems [12]. It has three types of components namely, publishers, topics, and subscribers denoted by the letters P, T, S, respectively (cf. [9,10,17]). Publishers send messages to subscribers but they do not have any information about subscribers and vice versa. So, in order to send messages, publishers characterize messages according to classes/topics. Subscribers, on the other hand, express their interest in one or more topics and receive all messages which have been published to the topics to which they subscribe (Fig. 1).

In our example we assign weights, describing priorities, to interactions among publishers and topics, and to interactions among topics and subscribers.

Component P has one port p, T has two ports t_1 and t_2, and S has the port s. We assume two publisher components P_1, P_2, four subscriber components S_1, S_2, S_3, S_4 and three topic components T_1, T_2, T_3. Hence, the set of ports is $P = \{p_1, p_2, s_1, s_2, s_3, s_4, t_{11}, t_{12}, t_{21}, t_{22}, t_{31}, t_{32}\}$. For every $i \in \{1, 2, 3, 4\}$, $j \in \{1, 2, 3\}$ and $k \in \{1, 2\}$ we denote by $d_{s_i, t_{j2}} \in D$ the weight of the interaction among S_i and T_j, i.e., the priority that the subscriber S_i assigns to the receivement of a message from T_j, and by $d_{p_k, t_{j1}} \in D$, the weight of the interaction among P_k and T_j, i.e., the priority that the topic T_j assigns to the receivement of a message from P_k.

In the sequel, we develop $\mathrm{w_{pvm}PCL}$ formulas whose semantics compute the maximum average priority with which a subscriber will receive a message and also the maximum most frequent priority of each topic. For every $i \in \{1, 2\}$ and $j \in \{1, 2, 3\}$, the $\mathrm{w_{pvm}PIL}$ formula $\varphi_{pt}(p_i, t_{j1}) = d_{p_i, t_{j1}} \otimes m_{\{p_i, t_{j1}\}}$ characterizes the interaction between a publisher P_i and a topic T_j with its corresponding weight. Moreover, for every $i \in \{1, 2, 3, 4\}$ and $j \in \{1, 2, 3\}$, the $\mathrm{w_{pvm}PIL}$ $\varphi_{st}(s_i, t_{j2}) = d_{s_i, t_{j2}} \otimes m_{\{s_i, t_{j2}\}}$ characterizes the interaction between a subscriber S_i and a topic T_j with its corresponding weight. Then, the $\mathrm{w_{pvm}PCL}$ formula

$$\zeta_{s_i} = \bigoplus_{j \in \{1,2,3\}} \bigoplus_{k \in \{1,2\}} \circledast \left(\varphi_{pt}(p_k, t_{j1}) \oplus \varphi_{st}(s_i, t_{j2}) \right)$$

describes the behavior of subscriber S_i with publishers P_1, P_2 and topics T_1, T_2, T_3. Let the configuration set $\gamma = \{\{p_i, t_{j1}\}, \{s_k, t_{j2}\} \mid i \in \{1, 2\}, j \in \{1, 2, 3\}, k \in \{1, 2, 3, 4\}\}$, and the pv-monoid $(\mathbb{R} \cup \{-\infty\}, \max, \mathrm{avg}, +, -\infty, 0)$. Then the value $\|\sim \zeta_{s_i}\|(\gamma)$ represents the maximum average priority with which the subscriber S_i will receive a message. Also, consider the $\mathrm{w_{pvm}PCL}$ formula $\zeta = \bigotimes_{i \in \{1,2,3,4\}} (\sim \zeta_{s_i})$. Then, the following value

$$\|\zeta\|(\gamma) = \sum_{i \in \{1,2,3,4\}} \left(\max_{j \in \{1,2,3\}} \left\{ \mathrm{avg}(d_{p_1, t_{j1}}, d_{s_i, t_{j2}}), \mathrm{avg}(d_{p_2, t_{j1}}, d_{s_i, t_{j2}}) \right\} \right)$$

is the sum of the values $\|\sim \zeta_{s_i}\|(\gamma)$ for $i \in \{1, 2, 3, 4\}$.

Moreover, let us assume that we want to erase one component of the architecture in case, for example, where the system is overloaded and needs to be 'lightened'. Consider the case where we choose to erase a topic which is not as popular as the others. A way to do this is to compute for every topic the most frequent priorities that the publishers and subscribers give to that component and then the maximum one of those. Hence, the topic that has the minimum most frequent priority among the other topics is the least popular topic and so it can be erased. The following $\mathrm{w_{pvm}PCL}$ formula

$$\zeta_{t_i} = \circledast \left(\bigoplus_{j \in \{1,2\}} \varphi_{pt}(p_j, t_{i1}) \oplus \bigoplus_{k \in \{1,2,3,4\}} \varphi_{st}(s_k, t_{i2}) \right)$$

for $i \in \{1, 2, 3\}$ describes the full valuation of the weighted interactions of the topic T_i with the publishers P_1, P_2 and the subscribers S_1, S_2, S_3 and S_4.

Consider the configuration γ given above and the pv-monoid $(\mathbb{R} \cup \{+\infty, -\infty\},$ $\min, \text{maj}, \max, +\infty, -\infty)$. Then,

$$\|\sim \zeta_{t_i}\| (\gamma) = \text{maj} \left(d_{p_1, t_{i1}}, d_{p_2, t_{i1}}, d_{s_1, t_{i2}}, d_{s_2, t_{i2}}, d_{s_3, t_{i2}}, d_{s_4, t_{i2}} \right)$$

for $i \in \{1, 2, 3\}$ is the maximum priority, among the most frequent ones, that the publishers and subscribers give to topic T_i. Lastly, if we consider the w_{pvm}PCL formula

$$\zeta' = \sim \left(\zeta_{t_1} \oplus \zeta_{t_2} \oplus \zeta_{t_3} \right),$$

then $\|\zeta'\| (\gamma) = \min_{i \in \{1,2,3\}} \{\text{maj} \left(d_{p_1, t_{i1}}, d_{p_2, t_{i1}}, d_{s_1, t_{i2}}, d_{s_2, t_{i2}}, d_{s_3, t_{i2}}, d_{s_4, t_{i2}} \right)\}$ and so we erase the topic with the minimum value.

Example 4. Consider the Star architecture [13]. Star architecture is a software architecture relating components of the same type. Given a set of components one of them is considered as the central one and is connected to every other component through a binary interaction. No other interactions are permitted.

In our example we consider five components. We assume that each component has a single port, hence the set of ports is $P = \{s_1, s_2, s_3, s_4, s_5\}$. We denote by $d_{i,j} \in D$ the weight of the binary interaction between s_i and s_j for every $i, j \in I = \{1, \ldots, 5\}$ with $i \neq j$, when s_i is considered as the central component. The w_{pvm}PIL formula characterizing this interaction, for every $i, j \in I$ with $i \neq j$, is given by $\varphi_{ij} = d_{i,j} \otimes m_{\{s_i, s_j\}}$. Therefore, the w_{pvm}PCL formula

$$\zeta_i = \circledast \left(\bigoplus_{j \in I \setminus \{i\}} \varphi_{ij} \right)$$

describes the full valuation of the binary interactions of the central component s_i with the rest of all other components. Next, consider the w_{pvm}PCL formula $\zeta = \sim$ $\left(\bigoplus_{i \in I} \zeta_i \right)$ which describes the five alternative versions of the Star architecture. Let $\gamma = \{\{s_i, s_j\}/ i, j \in I \text{ and } i \neq j\}$ and $(\mathbb{R} \cup \{+\infty\}, \min, \text{avg}, +, +\infty, 0)$. Then we get

$$\|\zeta\| (\gamma) = \min\{\text{avg}(d_{1,2}, d_{1,3}, d_{1,4}, d_{1,5}), \ldots, \text{avg}(d_{5,1}, d_{5,2}, d_{5,3}, d_{5,4})\}$$

which is the minimum value among the average costs of each component when it is considered as the central one.

7   Discussion

In our definition of w_{pvm}PIL and w_{pvm}PCL over P and D, we excluded, following [13], the empty interaction and the empty set of interactions. The empty interaction satisfies only the PIL formula *false*. If we consider the empty interaction, then several properties do not hold in PCL of [13]. For instance the equivalence $f + \text{false} \equiv \text{false}$ (Proposition 4.4 in [13]) for $f \not\equiv \text{false}$, which is used in the computation of the full normal form of a PCL formula (more specifically in proof of Proposition 4.19 and in turn in proof of Proposition 4.35 in [13]). Hence, it is clear that if we consider the empty interaction and the empty set of interactions, then we need to rebuilt not only our theory but also the theory of PCL. Moreover, the empty interaction adds no value in single interactions but it does in architectural composition (cf. for instance [2,3]), where it represents the case where two architectures cannot be composed. However, this is beyond the scope of this paper.

In our logic we consider the algebraic structure of product valuation monoids. The semantics of w_{pvm}PCL formulas are polynomials with values in the product valuation monoid. In Theorem 1 we prove that for every w_{pvm}PCL formula $\zeta \in PCL(D, P)$, where D satisfies specific properties, we can effectively construct an equivalent w_{pvm}PCL formula $\zeta' \in PCL(D, P)$ in full normal form. For this, we require D to be an associative, idempotent and $\oplus$-distributive pv-monoid, where $\otimes$ is commutative. We need to clarify that a pv-monoid D satisfying those properties is not a semiring since a pv-monoid contains a valuation function which can not be supported by the structure of semirings. For instance, let the pv-monoid $(\mathbb{R} \cup \{-\infty\}, \max, \text{avg}, +, -\infty, 0)$ which is associative, idempotent, $\oplus$-distributive and the operator $+$ is commutative. The valuation function avg can not be written using the operations max and $+$ of the semiring $(\mathbb{R} \cup \{-\infty\}, \max, +, -\infty, 0)$. Hence, the pv-monoids satisfying the above properties constitute a different structure than the one of semirings.

8 Conclusion

We introduced a weighted PCL over a set of ports and a pv-monoid, and investigated several properties of the class of polynomials obtained as semantics of this logic with the condition that our pv-monoid satisfies specific properties. We proved that for every w_{pvm}PCL formula ζ over a set of ports P and a pv-monoid D which is associative, $\oplus$-distributive, idempotent and $\otimes$ is commutative, we can effectively construct an equivalent one ζ' in full normal form. This result implied the decidability of the equivalence problem for w_{pvm}PCL formulas. Lastly, we provided examples describing well-known software architectures with quantitative characteristics such as the average cost of an architecture or the maximum most frequent priority of a component in the architecture. These are important properties which can not be represented by the framework of semirings in [17]. Future work includes the investigation of the complexity for the construction of full normal form for formulas in our logic and the time needed for that construction using the Maude rewriting system [1]. Furthermore, it would be interesting to study the first-order level of w_{pvm}PCL for the description of architecture styles with quantitative features.

References

1. http://maude.cs.illinois.edu/w/index.php/The_Maude_System
2. Attie, P., Baranov, E., Bliudze, S., Jaber, M., Sifakis, J.: A general framework for architecture composability. Formal Aspects Comput. **28**(2), 207–231 (2015). https://doi.org/10.1007/s00165-015-0349-8
3. Bozga, M., Iosif, R., Sifakis, J.: Local reasoning about parametric and reconfigurable component-based systems. hal-02267423 (2019)
4. Chatterjee, K., Doyen, L., Henzinger, T.: Expressiveness and closure properties for quantitative languages. In: 2009 24th Annual IEEE Symposium on Logic In Computer Science, pp. 199–208. IEEE (2009). https://doi.org/10.1109/LICS.2009.16
5. Chatterjee, K., Doyen, L., Henzinger, T.: Quantitative languages. ACM Trans. Comput. Log. **11**(4), 1–38 (2010). https://doi.org/10.1145/1805950.1805953
6. Chatterjee, K., Henzinger, T.A., Otop, J.: Computing average response time. In: Lohstroh, M., Derler, P., Sirjani, M. (eds.) Principles of Modeling. LNCS, vol. 10760, pp. 143–161. Springer, Cham (2018). https://doi.org/10.1007/978-3-319-95246-8_9
7. Droste, M., Meinecke, I.: Weighted automata and regular expressions over valuation monoids. Int. J. Found. Comput. Sci. **22**(08), 1829–1844 (2011). https://doi.org/10.1142/S0129054111009069
8. Droste, M., Meinecke, I.: Weighted automata and weighted MSO logics for average and long-time behaviors. Inf. Comput. **220**, 44–59 (2012). https://doi.org/10.1016/j.ic.2012.10.001
9. Eugster, P., Felber, P., Guerraoui, R., Kermarrec, A.M.: The many faces of publish/subscribe. ACM Comput. Surv. **35**(2), 114–131 (2003). https://doi.org/10.1145/857076.857078
10. Hasan, S., O'Riain, S., Curry, E.: Approximate semantic matching of heterogeneous events. In: Proceedings of the 6th ACM International Conference on Distributed Event-Based Systems, pp. 252–263 (2012). https://doi.org/10.1145/2335484.2335512
11. Karyoti, V., Paraponiari, P.: Weighted PCL over product valuation monoids. arXiv preprint https://arxiv.org/abs/2002.10973 (2020)
12. Malavolta, I., Lewis, G., Schmerl, B., Lago, P., Garlan, D.: How do you architect your robots? State of the practice and guidelines for ROS-based systems. In: Proceedings of ICSE-CEIP. ACM (2020). https://doi.org/10.1145/3377813.3381358
13. Mavridou, A., Baranov, E., Bliudze, S., Sifakis, J.: Configuration logics: modeling architecture styles. J. Log. Algebraic Methods Program. **86**(1), 2–29 (2017). https://doi.org/10.1016/j.jlamp.2016.05.002
14. Olivieri, A., Rizzo, G., Morand, F.: A publish-subscribe approach to IoT integration: the smart office use case. In: Proceedings of the 29th International Conference on Advanced Information Networking and Applications Workshops, pp. 644–651. IEEE (2015). https://doi.org/10.1109/WAINA.2015.28
15. Otop, J., Henzinger, T., Chatterjee, K.: Quantitative automata under probabilistic semantics. Log. Methods Comput. Sci. **15**(3) (2019). https://doi.org/10.23638/LMCS-15(3:16)2019
16. Paraponiari, P., Rahonis, G.: Weighted propositional configuration logics: a specification language for architectures with quantitative features. Inform. Comput. (accepted). https://arxiv.org/abs/1704.04969

17. Paraponiari, P., Rahonis, G.: On weighted configuration logics. In: Proença, J., Lumpe, M. (eds.) FACS 2017. LNCS, vol. 10487, pp. 98–116. Springer, Cham (2017). https://doi.org/10.1007/978-3-319-68034-7_6

18. Patel, S., Jardosh, S., Makwana, A., Thakkar, A.: Publish/subscribe mechanism for IoT: a survey of event matching algorithms and open research challenges. In: Modi, N., Verma, P., Trivedi, B. (eds.) Proceedings of International Conference on Communication and Networks. AISC, vol. 508, pp. 287–294. Springer, Singapore (2017). https://doi.org/10.1007/978-981-10-2750-5_30

19. Yang, K., Zhang, K., Jia, X., Hasan, M.A., Shen, X.: Privacy-preserving attribute-keyword based data publish-subscribe service on cloud platforms. Inf. Sci. **387**, 116–131 (2017). https://doi.org/10.1016/j.ins.2016.09.020

Operational Representation of Dependencies in Context-Dependent Event Structures

G. Michele Pinna[✉]

Dipartimento di Matematica e Informatica, Università di Cagliari, Cagliari, Italy
gmpinna@unica.it

Abstract. The execution of an event in a complex and distributed system where the dependencies vary during the evolution of the system can be represented in many ways, and one of them is to use Context-Dependent Event structures. Many kinds of event structures are related to various kind of Petri nets. The aim of this paper is to find the appropriate kind of Petri net that can be used to give an operational flavour to the dependencies represented in a Context/Dependent Event structure.

Keywords: Petri nets · Event structures · Operational semantics · Contextual nets

1 Introduction

Since the introduction of the notion of Event structure [21] and [28] the close relationship between this notion and suitable nets has been investigated. The ingredients of an event structure are, beside a set of events, a number of relations used to express which events can be part of a configuration (the snapshot of a concurrent system), modeling a consistency predicate, and how events can be added to reach another configuration, modeling the dependencies among the (sets of) events. On the nets side we have transitions, modeling the activities, and places, modeling resources the activities may need, consume or produces. These ingredients, together with some constraints on how places and transitions are related (via flow, inhibitor or read arcs satisfying suitable properties), can give also a more *operational* description of a concurrent and distributed system. Indeed the relationship between event structures and nets is grounded on the observation that also in (suitable) Petri nets the relations among events are representable, as it has been done in [14] for what concern the partial order and [21] for the partial order and conflict.

Since then several notions of event structures have been proposed. We recall just few of them: the classical *prime* event structures [28] where the dependency between events, called *causality*, is modeled by a partial order and the consistency is described by a symmetric *conflict* relation. Then *flow* event structures [6] drop

© IFIP International Federation for Information Processing 2020
Published by Springer Nature Switzerland AG 2020
S. Bliudze and L. Bocchi (Eds.): COORDINATION 2020, LNCS 12134, pp. 320–338, 2020.
https://doi.org/10.1007/978-3-030-50029-0_20

the requirement that the dependency should be a partial order on the whole set of events, *bundle* event structures [17] represent OR-causality by allowing each event to be caused by a unique member of a bundle of events (and this constraint may be relaxed). *Asymmetric* event structures [4], via notion of weak causality, model asymmetric conflicts, whereas *Inhibitor* event structures [3] are able to faithfully capture the dependencies among events which arise in the presence of read and inhibitor arcs in safe nets. In [5] a notion of event structures where the causality relation may be circular is investigated, and in [1] the notion of dynamic causality is considered. Finally, we mention the quite general approach presented in [13], where there is a unique relation, akin to a *deduction relation*. To each of the mentioned event structures a particular class of nets is related. Prime event structures have a correspondence in *occurrence nets*, flow event structures have flow nets whereas *unravel nets* [7] are related to bundle event structures. Continuing we have that asymmetric and inhibitor event structures have a correspondence with *contextual nets* [3,4], and event structures with circular causality with *lending nets* [5], finally to those with dynamic causality we have *inhibitor unravel nets* [9] and to the configuration structures presented in [13] we have the notion of *1-occurrence nets*. Most of the approaches relating nets with event structures are based on the equation "event = transition", even if many of the events represent the same *high level* activity. The idea that some of the transitions may be somehow identified as they represent the same activity is the one pursued in many works aiming at reducing the size of the net, like *merged processes* [16], *trellis processes* [11], *merging relation* approach [8] or *spread nets* [12] and [25], but these approaches are mostly unrelated with event structure of any kind.

In this paper we pursue the usual problem: given an event structure, find a net which may *correspond* to it. To find the kind of net that can be associated to *context-dependent* event structures [23] and [24] we first observe that in these event structures each event may happen in many different and often unrelated contexts, hence the same event cannot have (almost) the same *past* as it happens in many approaches. The second observation is that dependencies among transitions (events) in nets may be represented in different ways. Consider the case of a Petri net with inhibitor arcs [15] where the precondition of the transition e' inhibits the transition e (the net N). The latter to happens needs that the transition e' happens first, and the *observation* testifies that the activity e needs that e' has already happened, though resources are not exchanged between e' and e. On the contrary, in the net N without inhibitor arcs the token (resource) produced by e' is mandatory for e to happen.

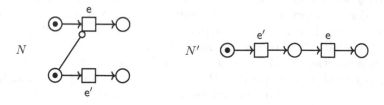

Both nets represent the same dependency: e' should happen before e. Following these two observations we argue that each of the context that are *allowing* an event to happen can be modeled with *inhibitor* and/or *read* arcs. It should be stressed that these kind of arcs have been introduced for different purposes, but never for nets which are meant to describe the behaviour of another one. The approach we pursue here is originated in the one we adopted for dynamic event structures in [9], though here also the *classical* dependencies among events (those called causal dependencies) are boiled down to the same machinery. Indeed we argued that the proper net corresponding to these kind of event structure are meant to give an *operational* representation of what *denotationally* can be characterized as a single event but operationally are rather different transitions. The approach is a conservative one: the dependencies represented in different kind on nets can be represented also in this approach and similarly to suitably characterized nets it is possible to associate the corresponding context-dependent event structure. It should be stressed that the conflicts between events in causal nets are explicitly represented and cannot be inferred otherwise.

Organization of the Paper. In the next section we recall the notions of contextual nets, occurrence net and prime event structure and also ho the two latter notions are related. In Sect. 3 we recall the notion of context-dependent event structure and in Sect. 4 we introduce the notion of *causal* net and we show also how occurrence nets can be seen as causal nets. We also give a direct translation from prime event structures to causal net and vice versa. In Sect. 5 we discuss how to associate a causal net to a context-dependent event structure and vice versa, showing that the notion of causal net is adequate. Some conclusions end the paper.

2   Preliminaries

We denote with $\mathbb{N}$ the set of natural numbers. Let A be a set, a *multiset* of A is a function $m : A \to \mathbb{N}$. The set of multisets of A is denoted by μA. We assume the usual operations on multisets such as union $+$ and difference $-$. We write $m \subseteq m'$ if $m(a) \leq m'(a)$ for all $a \in A$. For $m \in \mu A$, we denote with $[\![m]\!]$ the multiset defined as $[\![m]\!](a) = 1$ if $m(a) > 0$ and $[\![m]\!](a) = 0$ otherwise. When a multiset m of A is a set, *i.e.* $m = [\![m]\!]$, we write $a \in m$ to denote that $m(a) \neq 0$, and often confuse the multiset m with the set $\{a \in A \mid m(a) \neq 0\}$ or a subset $X \subseteq A$ with the multiset $X(a) = 1$ if $a \in A$ and $X(a) = 0$ otherwise. Furthermore we use the standard set operations like $\cap$, $\cup$ or $\setminus$.

Given a set A and a relation $< \subseteq A \times A$, we say that $<$ is an irreflexive partial order whenever it is irreflexive and transitive. We shall write $\leq$ for the reflexive closure of an irreflexive partial order $<$. Given an irreflexive relation $\prec \subseteq A \times A$, with $\prec^+$ we denote its transitive closure.

Given a function $f : A \to B$, $dom(f) = \{a \in A \mid \exists b \in B.\ f(a) = b\}$ is the domain of f, and $codom(f) = \{b \in B \mid \exists a \in A.\ f(a) = b\}$ is the codomain of f.

Given a set A, a sequence of elements in A is a partial mapping $\rho : \mathbb{N} \rightharpoonup A$ such that, given any $n \in \mathbb{N}$, if $\rho(n)$ is defined and equal to $a \in A$ then $\forall i \leq n$

also $\rho(i)$ is defined. A sequence is finite if $|dom(\rho)|$ is finite, and the length of a sequence ρ, denoted with $len(\rho)$, is the cardinality of $dom(\rho)$. A sequence ρ is often written as $a_1 a_2 \cdots$ where $a_i = \rho(i)$. With $\overline{\rho}$ we denote the codomain of ρ. Requiring that a sequence ρ has distinct elements accounts to stipulate that ρ is injective on $dom(\rho)$.

2.1   Contextual Petri Nets

We review the notion of labeled Petri net with contextual arcs along with some auxiliary notions [20] and [3]. We recall that a *net* is the 4-tuple $N = \langle S, T, F, \mathsf{m} \rangle$ where S is a set of *places* (usually depicted with circles) and T is a set of *transitions* (usually depicted as squares) and $S \cap T = \emptyset$, $F \subseteq (S \times T) \cup (T \times S)$ is the *flow* relation and $\mathsf{m} \in \mu S$ is called the *initial marking*. We assume to have a set L of labels.

Definition 1. *A* contextual Petri net *is the tuple* $N = \langle S, T, F, I, R, \mathsf{m}, \ell \rangle$, *where* $\langle S, T, F, \mathsf{m} \rangle$ *is a net,* $I \subseteq S \times T$ *are the* inhibitor *arcs,* $R \subseteq S \times T$ *are the* read *arcs, and* $\ell : T \to \mathsf{L}$ *is the labeling mapping, and* ℓ *is a total function.*

Inhibitor arcs depicted as lines with a circle on one end, and read arcs as plain lines. We sometimes omit the ℓ mapping when L is T and ℓ is the identity. We will often call a contextual Petri net as Petri net or simply net.

Given a net $N = \langle S, T, F, I, R, \mathsf{m} \rangle$ and $x \in S \cup T$, we define the following (multi)sets: $^{\bullet}x = \{y \mid (y, x) \in F\}$ and $x^{\bullet} = \{y \mid (x, y) \in F\}$. If $x \in S$ then $^{\bullet}x \in \mu T$ and $x^{\bullet} \in \mu T$; analogously, if $x \in T$ then $^{\bullet}x \in \mu S$ and $x^{\bullet} \in \mu S$. Given a transition t, with $^{\circ}t$ we denote the (multi)set $\{s \mid (s, t) \in I\}$ and with $\underline{t}$ the (multi)set $\{s \mid (s, t) \in R\}$.

A transitions $t \in T$ is enabled at a marking $m \in \mu S$, denoted by $m\,[t\rangle$, whenever $^{\bullet}t + \underline{t} \subseteq m$ and $\forall s \in [\![\,^{\circ}t]\!]$. $m(s) = 0$. Observe that no token must be present in a place connected to a transition with an inhibitor arc. A transition t enabled at a marking m can *fire* and its firing produces the marking $m' = m - {}^{\bullet}t + t^{\bullet}$. The firing of t at a marking m is denoted by $m\,[t\rangle\,m'$. We assume that each transition t of a net N is such that $^{\bullet}t \neq \emptyset$, meaning that no transition may fire *spontaneously*. Given a generic marking m (not necessarily the initial one), the *firing sequence* (shortened as fs) of $N = \langle S, T, F, I, R, \mathsf{m} \rangle$ starting at m is defined as:

- m is a firing sequence (of length 0), and
- if $m\,[t_1\rangle\,m_1 \cdots m_{n-1}\,[t_n\rangle\,m_n$ is a firing sequence and $m_n\,[t\rangle\,m'$, then also $m\,[t_1\rangle\,m_1 \cdots m_{n-1}\,[t_n\rangle\,m_n\,[t\rangle\,m'$ is a firing sequence.

The set of firing sequences of a net N starting at a marking m is denoted by $\mathcal{R}_m^N$ and it is ranged over by σ. Given a fs $\sigma = m\,[t_1\rangle\,\sigma'\,[t_n\rangle\,m_n$, we denote with $start(\sigma)$ the marking m and with $lead(\sigma)$ the marking m_n. $tail(\sigma)$ denotes the fs $\sigma'\,[t_n\rangle\,m_n$, provided that σ is not of length 0, otherwise it is not defined. Given a net N, a marking m is *reachable* iff there exists a fs $\sigma \in \mathcal{R}_m^N$ such that $lead(\sigma)$ is m. The set of reachable markings of N is $\mathcal{M}_N = \bigcup_{\sigma \in \mathcal{R}_m^N} lead(\sigma)$. Given a fs $\sigma = m\,[t_1\rangle\,m_1\cdots m_{n-1}\,[t_n\rangle\,m'$, we write $X_\sigma = \sum_{i=1}^n \{t_i\}$ for the multiset of transitions associated to fs. We call X_σ a *state* of the net and write $\mathsf{St}(N) = \{X_\sigma \in \mu T \mid \sigma \in \mathcal{R}_{\mathsf{m}}^N\}$ for the set of states of the net N. The configurations of a net are the sets of labels of the executed transitions. Hence $\mathsf{Conf}_{net}(N)$, is the set $\{\ell(X) \mid X \in \mathsf{St}(N)\}$.

Example 1. The following net is a simple contextual Petri net. At the initial marking t_2 and t_3 are enabled whereas t_1 is not. After the execution of t_2 no other transition is enabled. After the firing of t_3 the transition t_1 is enabled, as no token is present in the place s_2 and a token is present in the place s_6, the former being connected to transition t_1 with an inhibitor arc and the latter being connected to transition t_1 with a read arc.

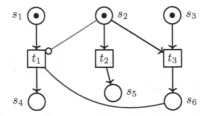

The following definitions characterize nets from a *semantical* point of view.

Definition 2. *A net* $N = \langle S, T, F, I, R, \mathsf{m}, \ell \rangle$ *is said to be* safe *if each marking* $m \in \mathcal{M}_N$ *is such that* $m = [\![m]\!]$.

In this paper we will consider safe nets, where each place contains at most one token. The following definitions outline nets with respect to states and configurations.

Definition 3. *A net* $N = \langle S, T, F, I, R, \mathsf{m}, \ell \rangle$ *is said to be a* single execution *net if each state* $X \in \mathsf{St}(N)$ *is such that* $X = [\![X]\!]$.

In a single execution net a transition t in a firing sequence may be fired just once, as the net in Example 1. In [26] and [13] these nets (without inhibitor and read arcs) are called *1-occurrence* net.

Definition 4. *A net* $N = \langle S, T, F, I, R, \mathsf{m}, \ell \rangle$ *is said to be an* unfolding *if each configuration* $C \in \mathsf{Conf}_{net}(N)$ *is such that* $C = [\![C]\!]$.

Clearly each unfolding is also a single execution one, but the vice versa does not hold. When the labeling of the net is an injective mapping we have that to each state a configuration corresponds and vice versa.

Remark 1. In literature *unfolding* is often used to denote not only a net with suitable characteristic (among them the fact that each transition is fired just once in each execution), but also how this net is related to another one (the one to be unfolded). Here we use it to stress that each configuration is a set.

The following definition characterizes when two transitions never happen together in any execution (conflicting transitions).

Definition 5. *Let* $N = \langle S, T, F, I, R, \mathsf{m}, \ell \rangle$ *be a net and let* $t, t' \in T$ *such that* $\forall X \in \mathsf{St}(N)$ *it holds that* $\{t, t'\} \not\subseteq [\![X]\!]$. *Then* N *is* conflict saturated *with respect to* t, t' *if* $^\bullet t \cap\, ^\bullet t' \neq \emptyset$.

Each net can be transformed into an equivalent one conflict saturated.

Proposition 1. *Let* $N = \langle S, T, F, I, R, \mathsf{m}, \ell \rangle$ *be a net and let* $t, t' \in T$ *such that* $\forall X \in \mathsf{St}(N)$ *it holds that* $\{t, t'\} \not\subseteq [\![X]\!]$, *then the net* $N^\# = \langle S \cup \{s_{t,t'}\}, T, F \cup \{(s_{t,t'}, t), (s_{t,t'}, t')\}, I, R, \mathsf{m} \cup \{s_{t,t'}\}, \ell \rangle$ *is conflict saturated with respect to* t, t' *and* $\mathsf{St}(N) = \mathsf{St}(N^\#)$.

Iterating this we can always construct a net which is conflict saturated with respect to all the possible conflicting transitions.

2.2 Occurrence Nets and Prime Event Structure

We recall the notion of *occurrence* net, and as it has no inhibitor or read arc nor a labeling, we omit I, R and ℓ in the following, assuming that $I = \emptyset = R$ and ℓ being the identity on transitions. Given a net $N = \langle S, T, F, \mathsf{m} \rangle$, we write $<_N$ for transitive closure of F. We say N is *acyclic* if $\leq_N$ is a partial order. For occurrence nets, we adopt the usual convention: places and transitions are called as *conditions* and *events*, and use B and E for the sets of conditions and events. We may confuse conditions with places and events with transitions. The initial marking is denoted with c.

Definition 6. *An* occurrence net *(on)* $O = \langle B, E, F, \mathsf{c} \rangle$ *is an acyclic, safe net satisfying the following restrictions:*

- $\forall b \in B.$ $^\bullet b$ *is either empty or a singleton, and* $\forall b \in \mathsf{c}.$ $^\bullet b = \emptyset$,
- $\forall b \in B.$ $\exists b' \in \mathsf{c}$ *such that* $b' \leq_O b$,
- *for all* $e \in E$ *the set* $\lfloor e \rfloor = \{e' \in E \mid e' \leq_O e\}$ *is finite, and*
- $\#$ *is an irreflexive and symmetric relation defined as follows:*
  - $e \#_0 e'$ *iff* $e, e' \in E$, $e \neq e'$ *and* $^\bullet e \cap\, ^\bullet e' \neq \emptyset$,
  - $x \# x'$ *iff* $\exists y, y' \in E$ *such that* $y \#_0 y'$ *and* $y \leq_O x$ *and* $y' \leq_O x'$.

The intuition behind occurrence nets is the following: each condition b represents the occurrence of a token, which is produced by the *unique* event in $^\bullet b$, unless b belongs to the initial marking, and it is used by only one transition (hence if $e, e' \in b^\bullet$, then $e \# e'$). On an occurrence net O it is natural to define a notion of *causality* among elements of the net: we say that x is *causally dependent* on y iff $y \leq_O x$. Occurrence nets are often the result of the *unfolding* of a (safe) net. In this perspective an occurrence net is meant to describe precisely the nonsequential semantics of a net, and each reachable marking of the occurrence net corresponds to a reachable marking in the net to be unfolded. Here we focus purely on occurrence nets and not on the nets they are the unfolding of.

Proposition 2. *Let $O = \langle B, E, F, \mathsf{c} \rangle$ be an occurrence net. Then O is a single execution net and it is an unfolding.*

Occurrence nets are relevant as they are tightly related to *prime event structures,* which we briefly recall here [28].

Definition 7. *A prime event structure (PES) is a triple $\mathsf{P} = (E, <, \#)$, where*

- *E is a countable set of events,*
- *$< \subseteq E \times E$ is an irreflexive partial order called the causality relation, such that $\forall e \in E. \{e' \in E \mid e' < e\}$ is finite, and*
- *$\# \subseteq E \times E$ is a conflict relation, which is irreflexive, symmetric and heredi-tary relation with respect to $<$: if $e \# e' < e''$ then $e \# e''$ for all $e, e', e'' \in E$.*

Given an event $e \in E$, $\lfloor e \rfloor$ denotes the set $\{e' \in E \mid e' \leq e\}$. A subset of events $X \subseteq E$ is left-closed if $\forall e \in X. \lfloor e \rfloor \subseteq X$. Given a subset $X \subseteq E$ of events, X is *conflict free* iff for all $e, e' \in X$ it holds that $e \neq e' \Rightarrow \neg(e \# e')$, and we denote it with $\mathsf{CF}(X)$. Given $X \subseteq E$ such that $\mathsf{CF}(X)$ and $Y \subseteq X$, then also $\mathsf{CF}(Y)$.

Definition 8. *Let $\mathsf{P} = (E, <, \#)$ be a PES. Then $X \subseteq E$ is a configuration if $\mathsf{CF}(X)$ and $\forall e \in X. \lfloor e \rfloor \subseteq X$. The set of configurations of the PES P is denoted by $\mathsf{Conf}_{PES}(\mathsf{P})$.*

Configurations are definable also in occurrence nets.

Definition 9. *Let $O = \langle B, E, F, \mathsf{c} \rangle$ be an on and $X \subseteq E$ be a subset of events. Then X is a configuration of O whenever $\mathsf{CF}(X)$ and $\forall e \in X. \lfloor e \rfloor \subseteq X$. The set of configurations of the on O is denoted by $\mathsf{Conf}_{on}(O)$.*

Given an on $O = \langle B, E, F, \mathsf{c} \rangle$ and a state $X \in \mathsf{St}(O)$, it is easy to see that it is *conflict free,* i.e. $\forall e, e' \in X. e \neq e' \Rightarrow \neg(e \# e')$, and *left closed,* i.e. $\forall e \in X. \{e' \in E \mid e' \leq_O e\} \subseteq X$.

Proposition 3. *Let $O = \langle B, E, F, \mathsf{c} \rangle$ be an occurrence net and $X \in \mathsf{St}(O)$. Then $X \in \mathsf{Conf}_{on}(O)$.*

Occurrence nets and prime event structures are connected as follows [28].

Proposition 4. *Let $O = \langle B, E, F, \mathsf{c} \rangle$ be an on, and define $\mathcal{P}(O)$ as the triple $(E, <_C, \#)$ where $<_C$ is the irreflexive and transitive relation obtained by F restricting to $E \times E$ and $\#$ is the irreflexive and symmetric relation associated to O. Then $\mathcal{P}(O)$ is a PES, and $\mathsf{Conf}_{on}(O) = \mathsf{Conf}_{PES}(\mathcal{P}(O))$.*

Also the vice versa is possible, namely given a prime event structure one can associate to it an occurrence net. The construction is indeed quite standard (see [5,28] among many others).

Definition 10. *Let $\mathsf{P} = (E, \leq, \#)$ be a PES. Define $\mathcal{E}(\mathsf{P})$ ad the net $\langle B, E, F, \mathsf{c} \rangle$ where*

- $B = \{(*, e) \mid e \in E\} \cup \{(e, *) \mid e \in E\} \cup \{(e, e', <) \mid e < e'\} \cup \{(\{e, e'\}, \#) \mid e \# e'\}$,

- $F = \{(e, b) \mid b = (e, *)\} \cup \{(e, b) \mid b = (e, e', <)\} \cup \{(b, e) \mid b = (*, e)\} \cup \{(b, e) \mid b = (e', e, <)\} \cup \{(b, e) \mid b = (Z, \#) \land e \in Z\}$, and
- $\mathsf{c} = \{(*, e) \mid e \in E\} \cup \{(\{e, e'\}, \#) \mid e \# e'\}$.

Proposition 5. *Let* $\mathsf{P} = (E, \leq, \#)$ *be a* PES. *Then* $\mathcal{E}(\mathsf{P}) = \langle B, E, F, \mathsf{c} \rangle$ *as defined in Definition 10 is an occurrence net.*

In essence an occurrence net is fully characterized by the partial order relation and the *saturated* conflict relation. This observation, together with the fact that an immediate conflict in a safe net is represented by a common place in the preset of the conflicting events, suggests that conflicts may be modeled directly, which is the meaning of the following proposition and that will be handy in rest of the paper.

Proposition 6. *Let* $O = \langle B, E, F, \mathsf{c} \rangle$ *be an* on *and let* $\#$ *be the associated conflict relation. Then* $O^\# = \langle B \cup B^\#, E, F \cup F^\#, \mathsf{c} \cup B^\# \rangle$ *where* $B^\# = \{\{e, e'\} \mid e \# e'\}$ *and* $F^\# = \{(A, e) \mid A \in B^\# \land e \in A\}$, *is an* on *such that* $\mathsf{Conf}_{on}(O) = \mathsf{Conf}_{on}(C^\#)$.

3   Context-Dependent Event Structure

We recall the notion of *Context-Dependent* event structure introduced in [23] and further studied in [24]. The idea is that the happening of an event depends on a set of modifiers (the *context*) and on a set of *real* dependencies, which are activated by the set of modifiers.

Definition 11. *A* context-dependent event structure *(*CDES*) is a triple* $\mathsf{E} = (E, \#, \gg)$ *where*

- E *is a set of* events,
- $\# \subseteq E \times E$ *is an irreflexive and symmetric relation, called* conflict relation, *and*
- $\gg \subseteq 2^{\mathsf{A}} \times E$, *where* $\mathsf{A} \subseteq 2^E_{fin} \times 2^E_{fin}$, *is a relation, called the* context-dependency *relation (*CD-relation*), which is such that for each* $Z \gg e$ *it holds that*
  - $Z \neq \emptyset$,
  - *for each* $(X, Y) \in Z$ *it holds that* $\mathsf{CF}(X)$ *and* $\mathsf{CF}(Y)$, *and*
  - *for each* $(X, Y), (X', Y') \in Z$ *if* $X = X'$ *then* $Y = Y'$.

The CD-relation models, for each event, which are the possible contexts in which the event may happen (the first component of each pair) and for each context which are the events that have to be occurred (the second component). We stipulate that dependencies and contexts are formed by non conflicting events. We recall the notion of enabling of an event. We have to determine, for each $Z \gg e$, which of the contexts X_i should be considered. To do so we define the *context* associated to each entry of the CD-relation. Given $Z \gg e$, where $Z = \{(X_1, Y_1), \ldots, (X_n, Y_n)\}$, with $\mathsf{CxT}(Z)$ we denote the set of events $\bigcup_{i=1}^{|Z|} X_i$, and this is the one regarding $Z \gg e$.

Definition 12. *Let* $\mathsf{E} = (E, \#, \gg)$ *be a* CDES *and* $C \subseteq E$ *be a subset of events. Then the event* $e \notin C$ *is* enabled *at* C, *denoted with* $C[e\rangle$, *if for each* $\mathsf{Z} \gg e$, *with* $\mathsf{Z} = \{(X_1, Y_1), \ldots, (X_n, Y_n)\}$, *there is a pair* $(X_i, Y_i) \in \mathsf{Z}$ *such that* $\mathrm{CXT}(\mathsf{Z}) \cap C = X_i$ *and* $Y_i \subseteq C$.

Observe that requiring the non emptiness of the set Z in $\mathsf{Z} \gg e$ guarantees that an event e may be enabled at some subset of events.

Definition 13. *Let* $\mathsf{E} = (E, \#, \gg)$ *be a* CDES. *Let* C *be a subset of* E. *We say that* C *is a* configuration *of the* CDES E *iff there exists a sequence of distinct events* $\rho = e_1 e_2 \cdots$ *over* E *such that*

- $\overline{\rho} = C$,
- $\overline{\rho}$ *is conflict-free, and*
- $\forall 1 \leq i \leq len(\rho). \ \overline{\rho}_{i-1}[e_i\rangle.$

With $\mathrm{Conf}_{\mathrm{CDES}}(\mathsf{E})$ *we denote the set of configurations of the* CDES E.

We illustrate this kind of event structure with some examples, mainly taken from [23] and [24].

Example 2. Consider three events a, b and c. All the events are singularly enabled but a and b are in conflict unless c has not happened (we will see later that this are called *resolvable* conflicts). Hence for the event a we stipulate

$$\{(\emptyset, \emptyset), (\{\mathsf{c}\}, \emptyset), (\{\mathsf{b}\}, \{\mathsf{c}\})\} \gg \mathsf{a}$$

that should be interpreted as follows: if the context is $\emptyset$ or $\{\mathsf{c}\}$ then a is enabled without any further condition (the Y are the empty set), if the context is $\{\mathsf{b}\}$ then also $\{\mathsf{c}\}$ should be present. The set $\mathrm{CXT}(\{(\emptyset, \emptyset), (\{\mathsf{c}\}, \emptyset), (\{\mathsf{b}\}, \{\mathsf{c}\})\})$ is $\{\mathsf{b}, \mathsf{c}\}$. Similarly, for the event b we stipulate

$$\{(\emptyset, \emptyset), (\{\mathsf{c}\}, \emptyset), (\{\mathsf{a}\}, \{\mathsf{c}\})\} \gg \mathsf{b}$$

which is justified as above and finally for the event c we stipulate

$$\{(\emptyset, \emptyset), (\{\mathsf{a}\}, \emptyset), (\{\mathsf{b}\}, \emptyset)\} \gg \mathsf{c}$$

namely any context allows to add the event.

Example 3. Consider three events a, b and c, and assume that c depends on a unless the event b has occurred, and in this case this dependency is removed. Thus there is a classic causality between a and c, but it can dropped if b occurs. Clearly a and b are always enabled. The CD-relation is $\{(\emptyset, \emptyset)\} \gg \mathsf{a}$, $\{(\emptyset, \emptyset)\} \gg \mathsf{b}$ and $\{(\emptyset, \{\mathsf{a}\}), (\{\mathsf{b}\}, \emptyset)\} \gg \mathsf{c}$.

Example 4. Consider three events a, b and c, and assume that c depends on a just when the event b has occurred, and in this case this dependency is added, otherwise it may happen without. Thus classic causality relation between a and c is added if b occurs. Again a and b are always enabled. The CD-relation is $\{(\emptyset, \emptyset)\} \gg \mathsf{a}$, $\{(\emptyset, \emptyset)\} \gg \mathsf{b}$ and $\{(\emptyset, \emptyset), (\{\mathsf{b}\}, \{\mathsf{a}\})\} \gg \mathsf{c}$.

These examples should clarify how the CD-relation is used and also that each event may be *implemented* by a different pair (X, Y) of modifiers and dependencies.

In [23] and [24] we have shown that many event structures can be seen as a CDES, and this is obtained taking the configurations of an event structure and from these synthesizing the conflict and the $\gg$ relations. The CDES obtained in this way have the same set of configurations of the event structure one started with, and furthermore for each event e there is just one entry $Z \gg e$.

Definition 14. *Let* $\mathsf{E} = (E, \#, \gg)$ *be a* CDES. *We say that* E *is* simple *if* $\forall e \in E$ *there is just one entry* $Z \gg e$.

Proposition 7. *Let* $\mathsf{E} = (E, \#, \gg)$ *be a* CDES. *Then there exists a simple* CDES $\mathsf{E}' = (E, \#', \gg')$ *such that* $\mathsf{Conf}_{\mathrm{CDES}}(\mathsf{E}) = \mathsf{Conf}_{\mathrm{CDES}}(\mathsf{E}')$.

4   Causal Nets

We introduce a notion that will play the same role of occurrence net when related to context-dependent event structure.

Given a contextual Petri net $N = \langle S, T, F, I, R, \mathsf{m}, \ell \rangle$, we can associate to it a relation on transitions, denoted with $\prec_N$ and defined as $t \prec_N t'$ when ${}^\bullet t \cap {}^\circ t' \neq \emptyset$ or $t^\bullet \cap \underline{t'} \neq \emptyset$, with the aim of establishing the dependencies among transitions related by inhibitor or read arcs. Similarly we can introduce a conflict relation among transitions, which is a *semantic* one. For this is enough to stipulate that two transitions $t, t' \in T$ are in conflict, denoted with $t \#_N t'$ if $\forall X \in \mathsf{St}(N)$. $\{t, t'\} \not\subseteq [\![X]\!]$. With the aid of these relations we can introduce the notion of *causal* net.

Definition 15. *Let* $U = \langle S, T, F, I, R, \mathsf{m}, \ell \rangle$ *be a labeled Petri net over the set of label* L. *Then* U *is a* causal *net* (cn net) *if the following further conditions are satisfied:*

1. $<_U \cap \ (T \times T) = \emptyset$, $\forall t \in T$. ${}^\bullet t \cap {}^\circ t = \emptyset$ *and* $t^\bullet \cap \underline{t} = \emptyset$,
2. $\forall t \in T. \ \forall s \in {}^\circ t. \ |\ell(s^\bullet)| = 1$,
3. $\forall t, t' \in T, \ t \prec_U t' \ \Rightarrow t' \not\prec_U t$,
4. $\forall t \in T$ *the set* ${}^\circ t \cup \underline{t}$ *is finite,*
5. $\forall t, t' \in T. \ t \#_U t' \ \Rightarrow \ {}^\bullet t \cap {}^\bullet t' \neq \emptyset$,
6. $\forall X \in \mathsf{St}(U) \prec_U^*$ *is a partial order on* X, *and*
7. $\forall C \in \mathsf{Conf}_{cn}(U). \ C = [\![C]\!]$

The first requirement implies that $\forall t, t' \in T$ we have that $t^\bullet \cap {}^\bullet t' = \emptyset$, hence in this kind of net the dependencies do not arise from the flow relation, furthermore inhibitor and read arcs do not interfere with the flow relation. The second condition implies that if a token in a place inhibits the happening of a transition, then all the transitions removing this token have the same label, the third is meant to avoid cycles between transitions arising from inhibitor and read arcs, the fourth one implies that for each transition t the set $\{t' \in T \mid t' \prec_U t\}$ is finite, the fifth one stipulates that two conflicting transitions (which never appear together in any execution of the net) are conflicting as they consume the same token from a place. Finally the last two conditions guarantee that the transitions in each execution can be totally ordered with respect the dependency relation associated to the net and that two transitions with the same label do not happen in the same computation. In particular the last condition implies that a causal net is also an unfolding.

It should be clear that the conditions posed on a causal net are meant to mimic some of the conditions posed on an occurrence net or on similar one, like for instance *unravel* nets [7,22] or [9] or flow nets [6], and they should assure that it is comprehensible what a computation in such a net can be looking at labels, as the main intuition is that for the same activity (label) there may be several incarnations.

Example 5. The following one is a causal net:

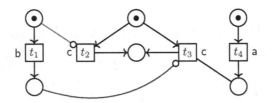

All the conditions of Definition 15 are fulfilled. The two transitions bearing the same label (t_2 and t_3) are conflicting ones, namely they never appear together in any computation though the activity realized by these two transitions (c) appears in all maximal computations.

The first observation we make on causal nets is that they are good candidates to be seen as a *semantic* net, namely a net meant to represent the behaviour of a system properly modeling dependencies and conflicts of any kind.

Proposition 8. *Let* $U = \langle S, T, F, I, R, \mathsf{m}, \ell \rangle$ *be a causal net. Then* U *is an unfolding.*

To give further evidence that this notion could be the appropriate one, we show that each occurrence net can be turned into a causal one, thus this is a conservative extension of this notion. The idea behind the construction is simple: to each event of the occurrence net a transition in the causal net is associated, the places in the preset of all transitions are initially marked and they are not in the postset of any other transition. The dependencies between events are modeled using inhibitor arcs. All the conflicts are modeled like in a conflict saturated net (with suitable marked places).

Proposition 9. *Let* $O = \langle B, E, F, \mathsf{c} \rangle$ *be an occurrence net. The net* $\mathcal{O}(O) = \langle S, E, F', I, \emptyset, \mathsf{m}, \ell \rangle$ *where*

- $S = \{(*,e) \mid e \in E\} \cup \{(e,*) \mid e \in E\} \cup \{\{e,e'\} \mid e \,\#\, e'\}$,
- $F' = \{(s,e) \mid s = (*,e)\} \cup \{(s,e) \mid e \in s\} \cup \{(e,s) \mid s = (e,*)\}$,
- $I = \{(s,e) \mid s = (*,e') \wedge e' <_C e\}$,
- $\mathsf{m} : S \to \mathbb{N}$ *is such that* $\mathsf{m}(s) = 0$ *if* $s = (e,*)$ *and* $\mathsf{m}(s) = 1$ *otherwise, and*
- ℓ *is the identity,*

is a causal net over the set of label E, *and* $\mathsf{Conf}_{on}(O) = \mathsf{Conf}_{cn}(\mathcal{O}(O))$.

Below we depict a simple occurrence net (on the left) and the associated causal one.

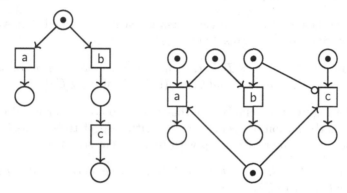

Proposition 10. *Let* O *be an occurrence net and* $\mathcal{O}(O)$ *be the associated causal net. Then* $\mathcal{O}(O)$ *is conflict saturated.*

In the causal net the dependencies are much more complicated to understand with respect to an occurrence net. However the Proposition 9, together with the connection among PES and on (Definition 10 and Proposition 5), suggests that a relation between PES and cn can be established. Here the intuition is to use the same construction hinted in Proposition 9.

Definition 16. *Let* $\mathsf{P} = (E,<,\#)$ *be a* PES. *Define* $\mathcal{A}(\mathsf{P})$ *as the causal Petri net* $\langle S,E,F,I,\emptyset,\mathsf{m},\ell\rangle$ *where*

- $S = \{(*,e) \mid e \in E\} \cup \{(e,*) \mid e \in E\} \cup \{(\{e,e'\},\#) \mid e \,\#\, e'\}$,
- $F = \{(e,s) \mid s = (e,*)\} \cup \{(s,e) \mid s = (*,e) \vee (s = (W,\#) \wedge e \in W)\}$,
- $I = \{(s,e) \mid s = (*,e') \wedge e' < e\}$,
- $\mathsf{m} = \{(*,e) \mid e \in E\} \cup \{(\{e,e'\},\#) \mid e \,\#\, e'\}$, *and*
- ℓ *is the identity.*

Proposition 11. *Let* P *be a* PES, *and* $\mathcal{A}(\mathsf{P})$ *be the associated Petri net. Then* $\mathcal{A}(\mathsf{P})$ *is a causal net and* $\mathsf{Conf}_{\text{PES}}(\mathsf{P}) = \mathsf{Conf}_{cn}(\mathcal{A}(\mathsf{P}))$.

Proposition 12. *Let* P *be a* PES, *and* $\mathcal{A}(\mathsf{P})$ *be the associated causal net. Then* $\mathcal{A}(\mathsf{P})$ *is conflict saturated.*

The vice versa is a bit more tricky as we have to require that the dependency relation $\prec$ and the conflict relation have a particular shape.

Definition 17. *Let $U = \langle S, T, F, I, R, \mathsf{m}, \ell \rangle$ be a causal net. U is said to be an occurrence causal* net *whenever $R = \emptyset$, $\prec_U^*$ is a partial order over T, and if $t \mathrel{\#_U} t' \prec_U^* t''$ then $t \mathrel{\#_U} t''$.*

The above definition simply guarantees that the dependencies give a partial order and that the conflict relation is inherited along the reflexive and transitive closure of the dependency relation.

Proposition 13. *Let P be a* PES, *and $\mathcal{A}(\mathsf{P})$ be the associated Petri net. Then $\mathcal{A}(\mathsf{P})$ is an occurrence causal net.*

Finally we show that also the vice versa is feasible provided that we restrict our attention to occurrence causal net.

Proposition 14. *Let $U = \langle S, T, F, I, R, \mathsf{m}, \ell \rangle$ be an occurrence causal net. Then $\mathcal{Q}(U) = (T, \prec_U^+, \#_U)$ is a* PES, *and $\mathsf{Conf}_{cn}(U) = \mathsf{Conf}_{\mathrm{PES}}(\mathcal{Q}(U))$.*

The following two theorems assure that the notion of (occurrence) causal net is adequate as the notion of occurrence net with respect to the classical notion of occurrence net in the relationship with prime event structure.

Theorem 1. *Let $U = \langle S, T, F, I, R, \mathsf{m}, \ell \rangle$ be an occurrence causal net such that $R = \emptyset$. Then $U = \mathcal{A}(\mathcal{Q}(U))$.*

Theorem 2. *Let P be a* PES. *Then $\mathsf{P} = \mathcal{P}(\mathcal{A}(\mathsf{P}))$.*

We end this section observing that if the causal net is injectively labeled, then the *event* labeling the transition happens just once.

5   Context-Dependent Event Structures and Causal Nets

We are now ready to relate Context-dependent event structures and causal nets. We recall that in a Context-dependent event structure each event may happen in different context and thus each happening has a different operational meaning. Therefore we model each happening with a different transition and all the transitions representing the same happening bear the same label. Dependencies are inferred using inhibitor and read arcs, as it will be clear.

Definition 18. *Let $\mathsf{E} = (E, \#, \gg)$ be a simple* CDES *such that $\forall Z \gg e$. $\mathrm{CXT}(Z \gg e)$ is finite. Define $\mathcal{B}(\mathsf{E})$ as the net $\langle S, T, F, I, R, \mathsf{m}, \ell \rangle$ where*

- $S = \{(*, e) \mid e \in E\} \cup \{(e, *) \mid e \in E\} \cup \{(\{e, e'\}, \#) \mid e \mathrel{\#} e'\}$,
- $T = \{(e, X, Y) \mid (X, Y) \in Z \wedge Z \gg e\}$,
- $F = \{(s, (e, X, Y)) \mid s = (*, e) \vee (s = (W, \#) \wedge e \in W)\} \cup$
    $\{((e, X, Y), s) \mid s = (e, *)\}$,
- $I = \{(s, (e, X, Y)) \mid s = (e', *) \wedge e' \in \mathrm{CXT}(Z \gg e) \backslash (X \cup Y)\} \cup$
    $\{(s, (e, X, Y)) \mid s = (*, e') \wedge e' \in X\}$,
- $R = \{(s, (e, X, Y)) \mid s = (e', *) \wedge e' \in Y\}$,

- $m = \{(*, e) \mid e \in E\} \cup \{(\{e, e'\}, \#) \mid e \# e'\}$, and
- $\ell : T \to E$ is defined as $\ell((e, X, Y)) = e$.

We introduce a transition (e, X, Y) for each pair (X, Y) of the entry associated to the event e, and all these transitions are labeled with the same event e. All these transitions consume the token present in the place $(*, e)$ and put a token in the place $(e, *)$, thus just one transition labeled with e can be fired in each execution of the net. Recall that the event e is enabled at a configuration C (here signaled by the places $(e', *)$ marked) if, for some $(X, Y) \in Z$, it holds that $\text{CxT}(Z \gg e) \cap C = X$ and $Y \subseteq C$. The inhibitor arcs assure that some of the events in $\text{CxT}(Z \gg e)$ have actually happened (namely the one in X) but the others (the ones in $\text{CxT}(Z \gg e) \backslash (X \cup Y)$) have not, and the Y are other events that must have happened and this is signaled by read arcs. We cannot require $\text{CxT}(Z \gg e) \backslash X$ as some of the events there may be present in Y.

Example 6. Consider the CDES in Example 3, the corresponding causal net is the one depicted in Example 5. The event c has two incarnations as the entry $\{(\emptyset, \{a\}), (\{b\}, \emptyset)\} \gg c$ has two elements: $(\emptyset, \{a\})$ and $(\{b\}, \emptyset)$.

Example 7. Consider the CDES of Example 4, the event c has two incarnations as the entry $\{(\emptyset, \emptyset), (\{b\}, \{a\})\} \gg c$ has two elements, whereas a and b have one. The associated causal net is

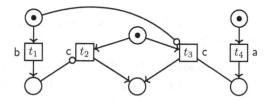

Example 8. Consider now the CDES in Example 2 (modeling the resolvable conflict of [27]).

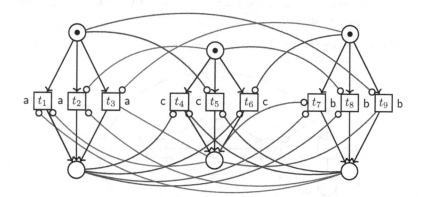

the actual implementation of this CDES into the causal net depicted before, where each event has three incarnations. The inhibitor and read arcs are colored depending on event they are related to.

The net obtained from a CDES using Definition 18 is indeed a causal net, and furthermore it is also conflict saturated.

Proposition 15. *Let* E *be a* CDES, *and* $\mathcal{B}(\mathsf{E})$ *be the associated contextual Petri net. Then* $\mathcal{B}(\mathsf{E})$ *is a causal net and* $\mathsf{Conf}_{\mathrm{CDES}}(\mathsf{E}) = \mathsf{Conf}_{cn}(\mathcal{B}(\mathsf{E}))$.

Proposition 16. *Let* E *be a* CDES, *and* $\mathcal{B}(\mathsf{E})$ *be the associated contextual Petri net. Then* $\mathcal{B}(\mathsf{E})$ *is conflict saturated.*

For the vice versa we do need to make a further assumption on the causal net. The intuition is that equally labeled transitions are different incarnation of the same activity, happening in different contexts. Henceforth one has to make sure that the equally labeled transitions indeed represent the same *event* and each incarnation of an event should have the same *environment*, meaning with environment the events related to it (which in the CDES is calculated with CXT). Given a causal net $U = \langle S, T, F, I, R, \mathsf{m}, \ell \rangle$ on a set of label L and a transition $t \in T$, with $\overrightarrow{°t}$ we denote the set of labels $\{a \in \mathsf{L} \mid s \in °t \wedge \ell(s^\bullet) = a\}$, with $\overleftarrow{°t}$ the set of labels $\{a \in \mathsf{L} \mid s \in °t \wedge \ell(^\bullet s) = a\}$, and with $\widetilde{\underline{t}}$ the set of labels $\{a \in \mathsf{L} \mid s \in \underline{t} \wedge \ell(^\bullet s) = a\}$.

Definition 19. *Let* $U = \langle S, T, F, I, R, \mathsf{m}, \ell \rangle$ *be a causal net labeled over* L, *we say that* U *is* well behaved *if*

1. $\forall a \in \mathsf{L}.\ \forall t, t' \in \ell^{-1}(a)$ *it holds that* $^\bullet t \cup {}^\bullet t' = \{s\}$ *and* $t^\bullet \cup t'^\bullet = \{s'\}$, *and*
2. $\forall a \in \mathsf{L}.\ \forall t, t' \in \ell^{-1}(a)$ *it holds that* $\overrightarrow{°t} \cup \widetilde{\underline{t}} \cup \overleftarrow{°t} = \overrightarrow{°t'} \cup \widetilde{\underline{t'}} \cup \overleftarrow{°t'}$.

In a well behaved causal net all the transitions sharing equally labeled have a common input place and also a common output place (condition 1). The equally labeled transitions in the causal net are the various incarnation of the *event* they represent, thus they have the same context, though the various kind of involved arcs are different (condition 2).

Example 9. Consider the net below:

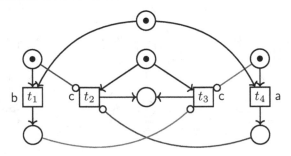

The transitions labeled with c have the same environment, namely the set of labels $\{a, b\}$.

It is worth to observe that when associating a causal net to a CDES we obtain a well behaved one.

Proposition 17. *Let* E *be a* CDES, *and* $\mathcal{B}(E)$ *be the associated contextual Petri net. Then* $\mathcal{B}(E)$ *is a well behaved causal net.*

To a causal net we can associate a triple where the relations will turn out to be, under some further requirements, those of a CDES. Here the events are the labels of the transitions, conflicts between events are inferred using the presets of the transitions and the entries are calculated using inhibitor and read arcs.

Definition 20. *Let* $U = \langle S, T, F, I, R, \mathsf{m}, \ell \rangle$ *be a causal net labeled over* $\mathsf{L} = E$. *Define* $\mathcal{R}(U) = (E, \gg, \#)$ *as the triple where*

- $E = \ell(T)$,
- $\forall e \in E.\ \mathsf{Z} \gg e$ *where* $\mathsf{Z} = \{(X, Y) \mid t \in T.\ \ell(t) = e \wedge X = {}^{\circ}\vec{t} \wedge Y = \widetilde{\underline{t}}\}$, *and*
- $\forall e, e' \in E.\ e \# e$ *is there exists* $t, t' \in T.\ \ell(t) \neq \ell(t')$ *and* ${}^{\bullet}t \cap {}^{\bullet}t' \neq \emptyset$.

The construction above gives the proper CDES, provided that the cn is well behaved.

Proposition 18. *Let* $U = \langle S, T, F, I, R, \mathsf{m}, \ell \rangle$ *be a well behaved causal net and* $\mathcal{R}(U) = (E, \gg, \#)$ *the associated triple, then* $\mathcal{R}(U)$ *is a* CDES *and* $\mathsf{Conf}_{cn}(U) = \mathsf{Conf}_{\text{CDES}}(\mathcal{R}(U))$.

The following two theorems assure that the notion of (well behaved) causal net is adequate in the relationship with context-dependent event structure.

Theorem 3. *Let* $U = \langle S, T, F, I, R, \mathsf{m}, \ell \rangle$ *be a well behaved causal net. Then* $U = \mathcal{B}(\mathcal{R}(U))$.

Theorem 4. *Let* E *be a* CDES. *Then* $E = \mathcal{P}(\mathcal{B}(E))$.

6   Conclusions and Future Works

In this paper we have proposed the notion of causal net as the net counterpart of the context-dependent event structure, and shown that the notion is adequate. Like context-dependent event structure subsumes other kinds of event structures, also the new notion comprises other kinds of nets, and we have given a direct translation of occurrence nets into causal one, and also the usual constructions associating event structures to nets can be rewritten in this setting. Like context-dependent event structures, also causal nets have a similar drawback, namely the difficulty in understanding easily the dependencies among events, which in some of the event structures is much more immediate.

We have focussed on the objects and not on the relations among them, hence we have not investigated the categorical part of the new kind of net, which we intend to pursue in the future. Furthermore we have given a net counterpart without attempting to reduce its size, meaning that *equivalent* incarnations of an event are never identified, and finding appropriate equivalence to reduce the size would be quite useful.

Recently a notion of unfolding representing reversibility has been pointed out [19] and the issue of how find the appropriate notion of net relating *reversible* event structure has been tackled [18] and solved for a subclass of reversible event structure. The notion of causal net can be a basis for obtaining the more general result.

It should also be mentioned that *persistent* nets have been connected to event structures [10] and [2], and in these nets events may happen in different contexts, hence it would be interesting to compare these approaches to the one pursued here.

Acknowledgements. The author wish to thank the anonymous reviewers for their useful suggestions and criticisms.

References

1. Arbach, Y., Karcher, D.S., Peters, K., Nestmann, U.: Dynamic causality in event structures. Log. Methods Comput. Sci. **14**(1) (2018). https://doi.org/10.23638/LMCS-14(1:17)2018
2. Baldan, P., Bruni, R., Corradini, A., Gadducci, F., Melgratti, H.C., Montanari, U.: Event structures for petri nets with persistence. Log. Methods Comput. Sci. **14**(3) (2018). https://doi.org/10.23638/LMCS-14(3:25)2018
3. Baldan, P., Busi, N., Corradini, A., Pinna, G.M.: Domain and event structure semantics for Petri nets with read and inhibitor arcs. Theor. Comput. Sci. **323**(1–3), 129–189 (2004)
4. Baldan, P., Corradini, A., Montanari, U.: Contextual Petri nets, asymmetric event structures and processes. Inf. Comput. **171**(1), 1–49 (2001)
5. Bartoletti, M., Cimoli, T., Pinna, G.M.: Lending Petri nets. Sci. Comput. Program. **112**, 75–101 (2015). https://doi.org/10.1016/j.scico.2015.05.006
6. Boudol, G.: Flow event structures and flow nets. In: Guessarian, I. (ed.) LITP 1990. LNCS, vol. 469, pp. 62–95. Springer, Heidelberg (1990). https://doi.org/10.1007/3-540-53479-2_4
7. Casu, G., Pinna, G.M.: Flow unfolding of multi-clock nets. In: Ciardo, G., Kindler, E. (eds.) PETRI NETS 2014. LNCS, vol. 8489, pp. 170–189. Springer, Cham (2014). https://doi.org/10.1007/978-3-319-07734-5_10
8. Casu, G., Pinna, G.M.: Merging relations: a way to compact Petri nets' behaviors uniformly. In: Drewes, F., Martín-Vide, C., Truthe, B. (eds.) LATA 2017. LNCS, vol. 10168, pp. 325–337. Springer, Cham (2017). https://doi.org/10.1007/978-3-319-53733-7_24
9. Casu, G., Pinna, G.M.: Petri nets and dynamic causality for service-oriented computations. In: Seffah, A., Penzenstadler, B., Alves, C., Peng, X. (eds.) Proceedings of SAC 2017, pp. 1326–1333. ACM (2017). https://doi.org/10.1145/3019612.3019806

10. Crazzolara, F., Winskel, G.: Petri nets with persistence. Electron. Notes Theor. Comput. Sci. **121**, 143–155 (2005). https://doi.org/10.1016/j.entcs.2004.10.012

11. Fabre, E.: Trellis processes: a compact representation for runs of concurrent systems. Discrete Event Dyn. Syst. **17**(3), 267–306 (2007). https://doi.org/10.1007/s10626-006-0001-0

12. Fabre, E., Pinna, G.M.: Toward a uniform approach to the unfolding of nets. In: Bartoletti, M., Knight, S. (eds.) ICE 2018 Conference Proceedings. EPTCS, vol. 279, pp. 21–36 (2018). https://doi.org/10.4204/EPTCS.279.5

13. van Glabbeek, R.J., Plotkin, G.D.: Configuration structures, event structures and Petri nets. Theor. Comput. Sci. **410**(41), 4111–4159 (2009). https://doi.org/10.1016/j.tcs.2009.06.014

14. Goltz, U., Reisig, W.: The non-sequential behavior of Petri nets. Inf. Control **57**(2/3), 125–147 (1983). https://doi.org/10.1016/S0019-9958(83)80040-0

15. Janicki, R., Koutny, M.: Semantics of inhibitor nets. Inf. Comput. **123**, 1–16 (1995). https://doi.org/10.1006/inco.1995.1153

16. Khomenko, V., Kondratyev, A., Koutny, M., Vogler, W.: Merged processes: a new condensed representation of Petri net behaviour. Acta Informatica **43**(5), 307–330 (2006). https://doi.org/10.1007/s00236-006-0023-y

17. Langerak, R.: Bundle event structures: a non-interleaving semantics for LOTOS. In: Diaz, M., Groz, R. (eds.) FORTE 1992 Conference Proceedings. IFIP Transactions, vol. C-10, pp. 331–346. North-Holland (1993)

18. Melgratti, H.C., Mezzina, C.A., Philipps, I., Pinna, G.M., Ulidowski, I.: Reversible occurrence nets and causal reversible prime event structures. In: Lanese, I., Rawski, M. (eds.) RC 2020 Conference Proceedings. LNCS, vol. 11533. Springer, Cham (2020, to appear)

19. Melgratti, H., Mezzina, C.A., Ulidowski, I.: Reversing P/T nets. In: Riis Nielson, H., Tuosto, E. (eds.) COORDINATION 2019. LNCS, vol. 11533, pp. 19–36. Springer, Cham (2019). https://doi.org/10.1007/978-3-030-22397-7_2

20. Montanari, U., Rossi, F.: Contextual nets. Acta Informatica **32**(6) (1995). https://doi.org/10.1007/BF01178907

21. Nielsen, M., Plotkin, G., Winskel, G.: Petri nets, event structures and domains, part 1. Theor. Comput. Sci. **13**, 85–108 (1981). https://doi.org/10.1016/0304-3975(81)90112-2

22. Pinna, G.M.: How much is worth to remember? A taxonomy based on Petri nets unfoldings. In: Kristensen, L.M., Petrucci, L. (eds.) PETRI NETS 2011. LNCS, vol. 6709, pp. 109–128. Springer, Heidelberg (2011). https://doi.org/10.1007/978-3-642-21834-7_7

23. Pinna, G.M.: Representing dependencies in event structures. In: Riis Nielson, H., Tuosto, E. (eds.) COORDINATION 2019. LNCS, vol. 11533, pp. 3–18. Springer, Cham (2019). https://doi.org/10.1007/978-3-030-22397-7_1

24. Pinna, G.M.: Representing dependencies in event structures. Log. Methods Comput. Sci. (2020, to appear)

25. Pinna, G.M., Fabre, E.: Spreading nets: a uniform approach to unfoldings. J. Log. Algebraic Methods Program. **112**, 100526 (2020). http://www.sciencedirect.com/science/article/pii/S2352220820300110

26. van Glabbeek, R.J., Plotkin, G.: Configuration structures. In: LICS 1995, pp. 199–209. IEEE Computer Society Press, June 1995. https://doi.org/10.1109/LICS.1995.523257

27. van Glabbeek, R., Plotkin, G.: Event structures for resolvable conflict. In: Fiala, J., Koubek, V., Kratochvíl, J. (eds.) MFCS 2004. LNCS, vol. 3153, pp. 550–561. Springer, Heidelberg (2004). https://doi.org/10.1007/978-3-540-28629-5_42

28. Winskel, G.: Event structures. In: Brauer, W., Reisig, W., Rozenberg, G. (eds.) ACPN 1986. LNCS, vol. 255, pp. 325–392. Springer, Heidelberg (1987). https://doi.org/10.1007/3-540-17906-2_31

Verification and Analysis

Towards a Formally Verified EVM
in Production Environment

Xiyue Zhang[1], Yi Li[1], and Meng Sun[1,2(✉)]

[1] School of Mathematical Sciences, Peking University, Beijing 100871, China
{zhangxiyue,liyi_math,sunm}@pku.edu.cn
[2] Center for Quantum Computing, Peng Cheng Laboratory, Shenzhen 518055, China

Abstract. Among dozens of decentralized computing platforms, Ethereum attracts widespread attention for its native support of smart contracts by means of a virtual machine called Ethereum Virtual Machine (EVM). Programs can be developed in various front-end languages. For example, Solidity can be deployed to the blockchain in the form of compiled EVM opcodes. However, such flexibility leads to critical safety challenges. In this paper, we formally define the behavior of EVM in Why3, a platform for deductive program verification, which facilitates the verification of different properties. The extracted implementation in OCaml can be directly integrated into the production environment and tested against the standard test suite. The combination of proofs and testing in our framework serves as a powerful analysis basis for EVM and smart contracts.

Keywords: EVM · Why3 · Verification · Testing

1 Introduction

Ever since the inception of the Bitcoin blockchain system [12], cryptocurrencies have become a well-known global revolutionary phenomenon. Meanwhile, the decentralized blockchain system with no server or central authority, which emerges as a side product of Bitcoin and provides a continuously growing ledger of transactions being represented as a chained list of blocks distributed and maintained over a peer-to-peer network [17], shows great potential in carrying out secure online transactions. From then on, there have been a lot of changes and growth on the blockchain technology. Ethereum [5] extends Bitcoin's design, which can process not only transactions but also complex programs and *smart contracts*. Smart contracts running on the blockchain make it possible to use blockchain techniques in many other application domains besides cryptocurrencies, and have attracted a lot of attention from government, finance, health, entertainment and industry. This feature makes Ethereum a popular ecosystem for building blockchain-applications, which gains much more interest to innovate the options to utilize blockchain.

Smart contracts are often written in a Turing-complete programming language called *Solidity* [14] and then compiled into EVM bytecode, which can be

© IFIP International Federation for Information Processing 2020
Published by Springer Nature Switzerland AG 2020
S. Bliudze and L. Bocchi (Eds.): COORDINATION 2020, LNCS 12134, pp. 341–349, 2020.
https://doi.org/10.1007/978-3-030-50029-0_21

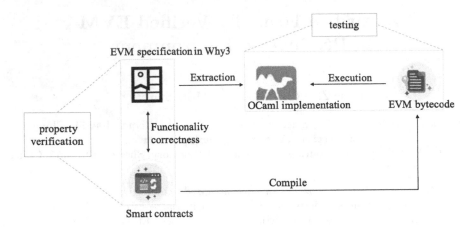

Fig. 1. The framework of generating verified EVM for production environment

mapped into a list of machine instructions (*opcodes*). EVM is a quasi-Turing complete machine. It provides a runtime environment for smart contracts to be executed. Given a sequence of bytecode instructions, which are compiled from smart contracts by an EVM compiler, and the environment data, this execution model specifies how the blockchain transits from one state to another.

However, EVM and smart contracts are faced with several security vulnerabilities. A taxonomy of vulnerabilities and related attacks against Solidity, the EVM, and the blockchain is presented in [1]. To deal with the security challenges against EVM, we propose a formal framework of generating verified EVM for production environment in this paper. The contributions of this work are:

- A formal definition of EVM specified in WhyML, the programming and specification language used in Why3 [7].
- An implementation of EVM in OCaml generated through an extraction mechanism based on a series of customized drivers.
- The verification of sample properties and testing of the OCaml implementation for EVM against a standard test suite for Ethereum.

This paper is organized as follows: We outline the framework for formalizing, property verifying and testing of EVM in Sect. 2. Section 3 presents some related work. Finally, we summarize this paper in Sect. 4.

2 The Framework of Generating Verified EVM for Production Environment

In this section, we present the framework of generating verified EVM for production environment in detail. The framework is as shown in Fig. 1 and the main idea is to combine verification and testing techniques towards developing more secure EVM implementations. It also provides a platform to verify the functionality properties of smart contracts. This framework is mainly comprised of two parts: (1) EVM specification and property verification in Why3; (2) experimental testing based on OCaml extraction and Rust connection. This approach leverages formal methods and engineering approaches, allowing us to perform both rigorous verification and efficient testing for EVM implementations and smart contracts.

2.1   EVM in Why3

The first phase of the framework is to define a formal specification of EVM in Why3 and provide a platform for rigorous verification. We develop the EVM specification, following the Ethereum project yellow paper [16]. More specifically, the EVM implementation is translated into WhyML, the programming and specification language of Why3. Verification conditions can be further generated based on the pre- and post-condition specification. Generated verification goals are solved directly through the supported solvers or go through a sequence of transformations first. In cases when the automatic SMT solvers cannot deal with, users can resort to interactive theorem provers for the remaining unsolved proof goals.

EVM is essentially a stack-based machine. The memory model of EVM is a word-addressed byte array and the storage model is a word-addressed word array. These three components form the infrastructure of EVM. Based on the formalization of the infrastructure, the most important aspect in this framework is to capture the execution result of the EVM instructions. The perspective from which we deal with the execution process of a sequence of opcodes (instructions) is as a state transition process. This process starts with an initial state and leads to a series of changes in the stack, memory etc. The formalization of base infrastructure and the instruction set are specified through *Type Definition* and *Instruction Definition*, respectively. The main function *Interpreter* provides the specification of transition results for the instructions.

Type Definition. To formalize the infrastructure of EVM, we need to first provide the formalization of commonly-used types in EVM, such as the types of machine words and the addresses in the EVM. Hence, we developed a series of type modules such as `UInt256` and `UInt160` to ease the representation of corresponding types in EVM. Type alias supported by Why3 are also used to make the basic formalization more readable and consistent with the original definition.

To this end, the components of the base infrastructure can be specified. Stack is defined as a list of elements whose type is `uint256`, aliased by `machine word`. Memory is defined as a function that maps `machine word` to an option type `option memory_content`. Similarly, storage is defined as a function that maps `machine word` to `machine word`. To reflect the implicit change of the machine state, we defined more miscellaneous types. For example, we use `vmstatus`, `error` and `return_type` to capture the virtual machine status, the operation error, and the view of the returned result. Furthermore, the record type `machine_state` is defined to represent the overall machine state which consists of stack, memory, storage, program counter, vmstatus, the instruction list, etc.

Instruction Definition. The infrastructure has been built above to specify the state of the virtual machine. Inspired by the instruction formalization in Lem [9], the instruction set is defined in multiple groups, such as *arithmetic operations* and *stack operations*, then these groups are integrated into a summarized type definition `instruction`. Different subsets of instructions are wrapped up to form the complete specification in the definition of `instruction`.

The organization of the instruction category is a bit different from the yellow paper [16]. The information related instructions including environmental and block information are defined in type `info_inst`, except CALL and CODE instructions, such as CALLDATACOPY, CODECOPY and CALLDATALOAD. These instructions are more closely related to memory and stack status. Therefore, they are added to the memory and stack instruction groups. In case when some illegal command occurs, the instruction Invalid is included in the `instruction` definition. The specification of the remaining instruction groups are basically the same as the corresponding instruction subsets in [16].

Interpreter Definition. The specification of `interpreter` formalizes the state transition result of different instructions. For a specific instruction, the interpreter determines the result machine state developing from the current state. Some auxiliary functions are defined to make the definition of the interpreter more concise and compact.

```
let interpreter (m: machine_state): machine_state =
let inst = get_inst m in
match inst with
  | Some (Arith ADD) -> let (st', a) = (pop_stack (m.mac_stack)) in
    let (st'', b) = (pop_stack st') in ...
    {m with mac_stack = push_stack st'' (a' + b'); ...}
```

In the above code snippet, `get_inst` is used to obtain the next instruction to be executed. It is obtained from the instruction list following the program counter. In the case of `Arith ADD` instruction, the numbers to perform the add operation on are popped out of the stack first and the result is pushed into the stack after the calculation. As a result, the stack state is updated as a component of the machine state. In this process, functions `push_stack` and `pop_stack` are defined to control the push and pop manipulations for the state transition of stack. With the support of pre-defined auxiliary functions, the definition of the interpreter function is essentially comprised of machine state update with regard to the instructions.

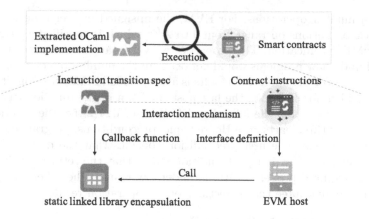

Fig. 2. Running EVM in production environment

2.2 Running EVM in Production Environment

Figure 2 shows the second phase of the framework: deploy the extracted OCaml implementation from Why3 in production environments. The deployment is essentially based on a co-compilation framework between OCaml and Rust.

OCaml is a functional programming language that shares a highly identical language definition and formal semantics with Why3. Through the official OCaml code generator equipped with Why3, we extract the verified specification of EVM into an executable OCaml module. A JSON-based protocol is developed as a bridge between the OCaml implementation and the EVM host in Rust.

Rust is a multi-paradigm system programming language which is designed to provide better memory safety while maintaining high performance [10]. The framework provides the interaction mechanism between Rust and Why3. By gluing them together, verified models can be directly executed in production environments for further testing. The coupling between Rust and extracted OCaml implementation enables us to perform VM tests to test the basic workings of the verified VM. Information of the overarching environment is obtained through the interface of Rust implementation, and the test can be performed on the execution of the OCaml implementations to check the operations in different transactions.

2.3 Examples of Property Verification and Tests

We now show some examples of property verification towards smart contracts and tests against Ethereum test suites. Specifically, we present the specification and verification of *SafeMath* library and *SimpleAuction* contract. For the tests, we perform the testing of arithmetic operations against the Ethereum test suite.

Overflow/Underflow Property Verification. We first take the example of *SafeMath* from Solidity library. Overflow/Underflow problems often occur when we deal with number operations. For EVM, the unsigned integer type we perform arithmatic operations on range from 0 to 2^{256}, which is specified as uint256 in the WhyML specification. The properties we verify are to guarantee that overflow and underflow problems would not occur in the number operations. Besides, the correctness of the operation results is also specified in the postconditions and further verified, for example, the last postcondition in the function div_safe.

As can be seen from the following definition of div_safe, the function body is comprised of three parts, as a Hoare triple, preconditions, program expressions and postconditions. The first precondition specifies that the divisor should be greater than zero. The first postcondition states that the returned value should satisfy the required property with no underflow issues. The other two postconditions are to guarantee the correctness of the operation result.

```
let div_safe (a:uint256) (b:uint256): uint256
requires {to_int b > 0}
ensures {to_int result >= 0}
ensures {to_int a = 0 -> to_int result = 0}
ensures {to_int a <> 0 ->
to_int a = (to_int result) * (to_int b) + mod (to_int a) (to_int b)}
= a / b
```

We now proceed to the verification of the properties. The verification conditions can be obtained through running why3 prove on the WhyML file. The proving goals for div_safe are derived as follows:

```
goal VC div_safe :
forall a:uint256, b:uint256.
  to_int b > 0 -> (not b = 0 && in_bounds (div a b)) /\
  (forall result:uint256. result = div a b -> to_int result >= 0 &&
  (to_int a = 0 -> to_int result = 0) &&
  (not to_int a = 0 ->
  to_int a = (to_int result * to_int b + mod (to_int a) (to_int b))))
```

To prove the goals, we first apply the split VC transformation and then call theorem provers *alt-ergo* and *cvc4* to prove the subgoals automatically. The proof session state will be stored in an XML file, which includes the proved WhyML file, the applied transformations, the used provers and the proof results. Complete proving goals derived from the functions and proof sessions can be found at [6].

Open Auction Contract Verification. The open auction contract is mainly comprised of three functions: (1) Everyone can send their bids through the bid function when the bidding period is not finished. When the bid sent by one bidder exceeds the current recorded highest bid, the auction state including the highestBidder and highestBid would be updated. Then the withdrawal amount of the previous highest bidder should be increased by the previous highest bid. (2) When one bid is beaten by another higher raised bid, the previous bid should be returned back to the corresponding bidder. Bidders can call the withdraw function to get the money/Ether back. (3) The auction is ended by the `auctionEnd` function. If current time is already greater than the auctionEnd-Time, then the auction `end_state` should be set to True. As the bidding ended, the beneficiary would receive the final highest Bid.

In the WhyML specification, `auction_status` records the current state of the auction including the current highest bidder, the highest bid and the auction ended state. `auction_constant` records the beneficiary and the auctionEndTime and `auction_ended` records the final bidder, bid and the beneficiary claimed money/Ether amount. The properties to be verified are to guarantee the correctness of the functionality. For example, in the `auctionEnd` definition, the postcondition specifies the constraints of auction ended state and beneficiary claimed amount that the returned result should satisfy. Complete specification of the functions can be found at [6]. The generated verification conditions can be discharged through *alt-ergo* and *cvc4* automatically.

```
let auctionEnd (current_time: uint) (auc_st: auction_status)
(auc_const: auction_constant) (auc_end: auction_ended):
(auction_status, auction_ended)
... ensures {let (_auc_st, _auc_end) = result in
_auc_st.end_state = True
&& _auc_end.finalBidder = auc_st.highestBidder
&& _auc_end.finalBid = auc_st.highestBid
&& _auc_end.bene_amount.benefici = auc_const.beneficiary
&& _auc_end.bene_amount.benefit_amount = _auc_end.finalBid} = ...
```

Testing of Arithmatic Operations. CITA-VM [3] is a Rust implementation of the EVM developed by the CITAHub team. In a forked version of CITA-VM, we patched the EVM interpreter by redirecting it to the OCaml implementation. From the official EVM Consensus Tests [4], we select the *vmArithmeticTest* set and run the test cases. The OCaml EVM implementation passes all the selected test cases and proves its capability in the production environment. A guide of reproducing the test result can be found at [6].

3   Related Work

Research interest of blockchain technology has exploded since the inception of Bitcoin. As the popularity of the second generation of blockchain, Ethereum, grows, a series of vulnerabilities have also appeared. Since EVM and smart contracts deal directly with the transactions of valuable cryptocurrency units among multiple parties, the safety of smart contracts and EVM implementations is of paramount importance. To address these challenges, researchers resorted to the techniques of formal methods and program analysis.

Specification and Verification. An executable formal semantics of EVM has been created in the K framework by Everett et al. [8]. Compared with KEVM with the support of matching logic for verification, we use Hoare logic, which serves as a good framework for verification condition specification, to avoid the complex definitions of the operational semantics. A framework to analyze and verify the safety and the correctness of Solidity smart contracts in F* was presented in [2]. Hirai [9] proposed an EVM implementation in Lem, a language that can be compiled for a few interactive theorem provers. Then, safety properties of smart contracts can be proved in proof assistants like Isabelle/HOL. While in our work, we use WhyML for specification and programming, which supports both logical theories and programming data structures. Moreover, both automated and interactive external theorem provers can be relied on to discharge verification conditions.

Testing and Debugging. The hevm project [15] is implemented in Haskell for unit testing and debugging of smart contracts. Sergey et al. [13] provided a new perspective between smart contracts and concurrent objects, based on which existing tools for understanding and debugging concurrent objects can be used on smart contract behaviors. In [11], several new security problems were pointed out and a way to enhance the operational semantics of Ethereum was proposed to make smart contracts less vulnerable. Due to the difficulty of correcting the semantics of Ethereum, Luu et al. [11] also implemented a symbolic execution tool OYENTE to find security bugs. While in our work, executable OCaml programs can be directly extracted from WhyML programs for further tests with the support of customized drivers and extraction mechanism.

4   Conclusion

We propose a framework to enable formal specification, verification and testing towards EVM. In this framework, the formalization of EVM is specified in WhyML, based on which, automatic SMT solvers and interactive theorem provers can be employed for verification. The OCaml implementation of EVM is extracted from the WhyML specification and then glued with Rust implementation based on the coupling framework. The coupling framework provides the interaction mechanism between OCaml and Rust, which allows us to perform tests on the new implementation without additional interface implementation.

Acknowledgement. This work has been supported by the National Natural Science Foundation of China under grant no. 61772038 and 61532019, and the Guangdong Science and Technology Department (Grant no. 2018B010107004). Thanks to members of Cryptape, especially Jan and Zhiwei, for the helpful discussions during the development of this framework.

References

1. Atzei, N., Bartoletti, M., Cimoli, T.: A survey of attacks on Ethereum smart contracts. IACR Cryptology ePrint Archive 2016, 1007 (2016)
2. Bhargavan, K., et al.: Formal verification of smart contracts: short paper. In: Proceedings of PLAS@CCS 2016, pp. 91–96. ACM (2016)
3. CITA-VM. https://github.com/citahub/cita-vm

4. Common tests for all Ethereum implementations. https://github.com/ethereum/tests
5. Ethereum. https://github.com/ethereum. Accessed 2 Apr 2019
6. Examples. https://github.com/Xiyue-Selina/coordination20
7. Filliâtre, J.-C., Paskevich, A.: Why3—where programs meet provers. In: Felleisen, M., Gardner, P. (eds.) ESOP 2013. LNCS, vol. 7792, pp. 125–128. Springer, Heidelberg (2013). https://doi.org/10.1007/978-3-642-37036-6_8
8. Hildenbrandt, E., et al.: KEVM: a complete formal semantics of the Ethereum virtual machine. In: 31st IEEE Computer Security Foundations Symposium, CSF 2018, Oxford, United Kingdom, 9–12 July 2018, pp. 204–217. IEEE Computer Society (2018)
9. Hirai, Y.: Defining the Ethereum virtual machine for interactive theorem provers. In: Brenner, M., et al. (eds.) FC 2017. LNCS, vol. 10323, pp. 520–535. Springer, Cham (2017). https://doi.org/10.1007/978-3-319-70278-0_33
10. Lin, Y., Blackburn, S.M., Hosking, A.L., Norrish, M.: Rust as a language for high performance GC implementation. In: Proceedings of the 2016 ACM SIGPLAN International Symposium on Memory Management, Santa Barbara, CA, USA, 14 June 2016, pp. 89–98. ACM (2016)
11. Luu, L., Chu, D.H., Olickel, H., Saxena, P., Hobor, A.: Making smart contracts smarter. In: Proceedings of the 2016 ACM SIGSAC Conference on Computer and Communications Security, pp. 254–269. ACM (2016)
12. Nakamoto, S., et al.: Bitcoin: a peer-to-peer electronic cash system (2008)
13. Sergey, I., Hobor, A.: A concurrent perspective on smart contracts. In: Brenner, M., et al. (eds.) FC 2017. LNCS, vol. 10323, pp. 478–493. Springer, Cham (2017). https://doi.org/10.1007/978-3-319-70278-0_30
14. Solidity Documentation. https://solidity.readthedocs.io/en/v0.5.6/. Accessed 2 Apr 2019
15. The Hevm Project. https://github.com/dapphub/dapptools/tree/master/src/hevm. Accessed 2 Apr 2019
16. Wood, G.: Ethereum: a secure decentralised generalised transaction ledger. Ethereum project yellow paper 151, pp. 1–32 (2014)
17. Zheng, Z., Xie, S., Dai, H., Chen, X., Wang, H.: Blockchain challenges and opportunities: a survey. Int. J. Web Grid Serv. **14**(4), 352–375 (2018)

On Implementing Symbolic Controllability

Adrian Francalanza$^{(\boxtimes)}$ (iD) and Jasmine Xuereb$^{(\boxtimes)}$ (iD)

University of Malta, Msida, Malta
{adrian.francalanza,jasmine.xuereb.15}@um.edu.mt

Abstract. Runtime Monitors observe the execution of a system with the aim of reaching a verdict about it. One property that is expected of monitors is consistent verdict detections; this property was characterised in prior work via a symbolic analysis called symbolic controllability. This paper explores whether the proposed symbolic analysis lends itself well to the construction of a tool that checks monitors for this deterministic behaviour. We implement a prototype that automates this symbolic analysis, and establish complexity upper bounds for the algorithm used. We also consider a number of optimisations for the implemented prototype, and assess the potential gains against benchmark monitors.

Keywords: Deterministic monitors · Symbolic analysis · Runtime verification

1 Introduction

Monitors are computational entities that are *instrumented* to execute alongside a *program* of interest. This paper focusses on a specific class of monitors called execution monitors [34], also termed sequence recognisers [25] or partial-identity monitors [21]. Execution monitors observe a *sequence of events* exhibited by the running program with the aim of reaching an *irrevocable verdict*. Conceptually, these monitors may be described as suffix-closed sets of traces of events that lead to the respective verdicts [5,11,36]. Operationally, however, they are best conceived as a branching structure whereby a sequence of events may lead a monitor to reach *a number of possible states* [2,16,20,22]. This better captures the potential monitor behaviour in concurrent/distributed settings [7–9,15,19,23,26], or the behaviour encountered in practical implementations that may occasionally (and unexpectedly) operate erratically [12,13,32]. Put differently, monitors themselves may, either by necessity or inadvertently, behave *non-deterministically*.

This research was supported by project BehAPI, funded by the EU H2020 RISE programme under the Marie Skłodowska-Curie grant (No: 778233).

© IFIP International Federation for Information Processing 2020
Published by Springer Nature Switzerland AG 2020
S. Bliudze and L. Bocchi (Eds.): COORDINATION 2020, LNCS 12134, pp. 350–369, 2020.
https://doi.org/10.1007/978-3-030-50029-0_22

In spite of this potential behaviour, deterministic monitor operation for the verdicts reached is still a desirable quality and is often a prerequisite for monitor correctness [6]. In prior work [17, Def. 6], we proposed an observational definition for a *consistently-detecting* monitor. Intuitively, fixed a trace exhibited by the program it is instrumented with, such a monitor is required to always reach the *same* verdict for *that* trace. Crucially, consistent detection allows such a monitor to pass through *different intermediate states* during the course of its verdict-reaching trace analysis (since these states are not observable from a consistently-detecting sense). An alternative characterisation called *monitor controllability* [17, Def. 11] is also proposed in this work, with the aim of providing a more tractable method for assessing deterministic monitor behaviour. This characterisation improves on reasoning about monitor consistent detection in two ways: (*i*) *avoids universal quantifications* over the programs that a monitor can be instrumented with (*i.e.*, contexts); (*ii*) it is *coinductive*, permitting reasoning about an infinite number of traces in a finite manner (for certain monitor cases). Monitor controllability is also shown to be both sound and complete w.r.t. consistent detection.

There is one further complication when reasoning about monitor behaviour. In most practical settings, events carry a *payload* from some infinite data domain. A refinement to the coinductive definition, called *symbolic (monitor) controllability*, is thus developed in [17] to assist with abstracting over universal quantifications on payload data and data-dependent monitor states. This work also claims that the resulting *symbolic analysis* mandated by the new definition lends itself well to the construction of a tool that analyses monitors for their capacity to perform deterministic detections. The goal of our paper is to verify this claim. The contributions are twofold:

1. In Sect. 3, we build a prototype that automates the analysis for symbolic controllability, demonstrating the *implementability* of the approach proposed in [17]; we also provide *complexity bounds* for the algorithm implemented.
2. In Sect. 4, we identify implementation bottlenecks that limit the *scalability* of the tool in practice. Subsequently, in Sect. 5, we empirically evaluate a number of proposed solutions using a series of pathological monitor descriptions devised in Sect. 4.

2   Preliminaries

We assume the existence of an expression language, $e, d \in \text{EXP}$ and a boolean expression language $b, c \in \text{BEXP}$. Expressions are defined in terms of a denumerable set of *expression variables*, $x, y \in \text{VARS}$, and a value domain, $v, u \in \text{VAL}$; for expository purposes, we assume the value domain to be infinite. Boolean expressions are defined over the expression language EXP, and include the standard constructs for the basic values true and false, conjunctions $b \wedge c$, expression equality $e = d$, and negation $\neg b$. The meta-function $\mathbf{fv}(e)$ and $\mathbf{fv}(b)$ computes the *free variables* in the respective expressions e and b. (Boolean) expressions

Monitors

$w, o \in$ VERD $::=$ $\top$ (accept) $\mid \bot$ (reject)

           $\mid \mathbf{0}$ (inconclusive)

$m, n \in$ MON $::=$ w (verdict) $\mid$ let $x = e$ in m (evaluate)

           $\mid l\langle e \rangle.m$ (expression guard) $\mid l(x).m$ (quantified guard)

           $\mid m + n$ (choice) $\mid$ if b then m else n (conditional)

           $\mid$ rec $X.m$ (recursion) $\mid X$ (monitor variable)

Symbolic Transitions

sVER

$$w \xrightarrow[\text{true}]{\theta} w$$

sIFT

$$\text{if } b \text{ then } m \text{ else } n \xrightarrow[b]{\tau} m$$

sIFF

$$\text{if } b \text{ then } m \text{ else } n \xrightarrow[\neg b]{\tau} n$$

sREC

$$\text{rec } X.m \xrightarrow[\text{true}]{\tau} m[\text{rec } X.m/X]$$

sCHL

$$\dfrac{m \xrightarrow[b]{\mu} m'}{m + n \xrightarrow[b]{\mu} m'}$$

sGRE

$$l\langle e \rangle.m \xrightarrow[e=x]{l\langle x \rangle} m$$

sGRQ

$$l(y).m \xrightarrow[\text{true}]{l\langle x \rangle} m[x/y]$$

sLET

$$\text{let } x = e \text{ in } m \xrightarrow[\text{true}]{\tau} m[e/x]$$

Weak Symbolic Transitions and Reductions

sWTR1

$$\dfrac{m \xrightarrow[b]{\theta} m'}{m \overset{\theta}{\underset{b}{\Longrightarrow}} m'}$$

sWTR2

$$\dfrac{m \xrightarrow[b]{\tau} m' \qquad m' \overset{\theta}{\underset{c}{\Longrightarrow}} m''}{m \overset{\theta}{\underset{b \wedge c}{\Longrightarrow}} m''}$$

sWRD1

$$\dfrac{}{m \underset{\text{true}}{\Longrightarrow} m}$$

sWTR2

$$\dfrac{m \xrightarrow[b]{\tau} m' \qquad m' \underset{c}{\Longrightarrow} m''}{m \underset{b \wedge c}{\Longrightarrow} m''}$$

Fig. 1. A symbolic semantics for monitors

without any free variables are said to be *closed*, and *open* otherwise. *Substitutions*, denoted by $[\vec{e}/\vec{x}]$, are partial maps from VARS to EXP, with the term $d[\vec{e}/\vec{x}]$ signifying that every *free* occurrence of $x_i \in \vec{x}$ in d is substituted by the corresponding expression $e_i \in \vec{e}$. As is standard, open terms are interpreted over *valuations*, $\rho \in$ VARS $\to$ VAL, *i.e.*, complete maps instantiating free variables to concrete values. (Open) expressions and boolean expressions come equipped with partial evaluation functions taking a valuation and returning the respective values, $\llbracket e\rho \rrbracket = v$ and $\llbracket b\rho \rrbracket \in \{\text{true}, \text{false}\}$; the terms $e\rho$ and $b\rho$ denote the instantiation of the free variables in e and b respectively by the corresponding values mapped to in ρ. A boolean expression b is *satisfiable* if there exists some valuation ρ that maps b to true, *i.e.*, $\mathsf{sat}(b) = \exists \rho . \llbracket b\rho \rrbracket = \text{true}$.

Programs are seen as entities that generate *events* of the form $l\langle v \rangle$ where $l, k \in$ LAB is the *event label* and v is the *payload* from the value domain. A sequence of events, *i.e.*, a *trace*, thus represents a program execution that is analysed by the instrumented monitor.[1] For our study, monitors are modelled

---

[1] Operationally, a program p is instrumented with a monitor m as $m \lhd p$ where p drives the execution and m passively reacts by analysing observable events generated by p [4,16,18]. In the case of controllability, the results in [17] show how this instrumentation can be abstracted as a monitor reacting to an event trace.

as Labelled Transition Systems (LTSs), described by the syntax in Fig. 1. They consist of two *conclusive verdicts* (namely *acceptance*, $\top$, and *rejection*, $\bot$) and an *inconclusive verdict*, $\mathbf{0}$, to describe the state a monitor transitions to when it is asked to analyse an event it is not expecting. The syntax defines two guards describing event analysis. Expression guards, $l\langle e\rangle.m$, require the monitor to first analyse an event $l\langle v\rangle$ where the payload v is equal to (the evaluation of) the expression e, and then to proceed as the continuation m. Quantified guards, $l(x).m$, require the monitor to dynamically learn the payload v from an analysed event $l\langle v\rangle$ with a matching label l, and then bind the learnt payload value v to the variable x in the continuation m; we use the suggestive notation $l(\_).m$ when the binding variable is not used in m. The remaining constructs are standard.

Example 1. A program operating a thermostat is initialised to a starting temperature i via the event $\mathsf{init}\langle i\rangle$ $(i \in \mathbb{N})$. After this, it can either terminate reporting $\mathsf{end}\langle j\rangle$ with the error code $j \in \mathbb{N}$, or repeatedly read the current temperature value i, $\mathsf{get}\langle i\rangle$, and adjust the temperature i, $\mathsf{set}\langle i\rangle$, for some value i.

$$m_1 = \mathsf{init}\langle 0\rangle.\mathsf{end}(\_).\bot$$

$$m_2 = \mathsf{init}\langle 50\rangle.\mathsf{rec}\,X.\mathsf{get}(y).\mathsf{if}\;y > 50\,\mathsf{then}\,\mathsf{set}(\_).\bot\,\mathsf{else}\,\mathsf{set}\langle y+1\rangle.X$$

$$m_3 = \mathsf{init}(x).\mathsf{let}\;lim = e_{calc}\;\mathsf{in}\;\big(\mathsf{if}\;x < lim\,\mathsf{then}\,\mathsf{end}(\_).\bot\,\mathsf{else}$$
$$\mathsf{rec}\,X.\mathsf{get}(y).\mathsf{if}\;y \geq lim\,\mathsf{then}\,\mathsf{set}\langle y+1\rangle.\top\,\mathsf{else}\,\mathsf{set}(\_).X\big)$$

Monitors m_1, m_2 and m_3 check for three different specifications. Monitor m_1 rejects executions that terminate after the thermostat is initialised to 0. When the thermostat is initialised to 50, monitor m_2 repeatedly checks that it is *not* set if the temperature read is greater than the initialisation value. Monitor m_3 checks whether the initialised value (learnt at runtime) is less than some predetermined value calculated via some complex calculation e_{calc}: if so, it rejects terminations and accepts executions where the thermostat is set to the temperature just read increased by one, where the former is higher than the predetermined value. The monitor instrumentation assumed (used extensively in other settings [1,4,16,18]) preempts the monitor execution to the inconclusive state, $\mathbf{0}$, whenever the monitor is presented with an event this not specified by its description. For instance, if the monitor m_1 is presented with the event $\mathsf{set}\langle 42\rangle$ (or event $\mathsf{init}\langle 42\rangle$ for that matter), the instrumentation aborts the runtime analysis by reducing the monitor to $\mathbf{0}$.   ∎

Following [17], the monitor semantics is given in Fig. 1 in terms of a *symbolic* LTS $\langle \text{Mon}, \text{BExp}, \text{Act}, \longrightarrow\rangle$ where Act is a set containing symbol actions, $\theta \in \text{SEvt}$, and the silent action $\tau \notin \text{SEvt}$. Symbolic actions, $l\langle x\rangle$, *abstract* over concrete trace events by carrying variables x instead of values; we let $\mu \in \text{SEvt} \cup \{\tau\}$. The transition relation $\longrightarrow \subseteq (\text{Mon} \times \text{Act} \times \text{BExp} \times \text{Mon})$ is denoted as $m \xrightarrow[b]{\mu} n$; it models the transition from a monitor state m to a new monitor state n via the symbolic action μ where the predicate b constrains the free variables in the action μ and the monitor states m and n. It is defined as the least relation satisfying the rules in Fig. 1 (we elide the symmetric rule sChR).

Rule SVER states that a verdict w can analyse any symbolic action θ under any circumstance, *i.e.*, true, and transition to itself, modelling *verdict irrevocability*. A conditional monitor if b then m else n can (silently) τ-transition to either m under the pretext that b holds (rule SIFT), or to n if the converse, $\neg b$, holds (rule SIFF). The other key rules are SGRE and SGRQ for expression and quantified guards respectively: whereas the latter rule transitions with the symbolic event $l\langle x \rangle$ without constraining x, the former rule requires that x is equivalent to the guard expression e, *i.e.*, $e = x$. The remaining rules are fairly straightforward; see [17] for details. Figure 1 also defines derivation rules for *weak symbolic transitions* (without trailing silent actions), $m \overset{\theta}{\underset{b}{\Longrightarrow}} n$, and *reductions*, $m \underset{b}{\Longrightarrow} n$. The predicate $m \overset{\theta}{\underset{b}{\Longrightarrow}}$ is used as a shorthand notation for the requirement $\exists n \cdot m \overset{\theta}{\underset{b}{\Longrightarrow}} n$.

The symbolic transitions in Fig. 1 are defined over general terms that are potentially open. They are used to abstract over concrete transitions—defined over closed monitor terms—in our symbolic analysis. The pair $\langle b, m \rangle$ is used to represent the set of concrete terms $\{\, m\rho \mid [\![b\rho]\!] = \text{true}\,\}$. Typically, a symbolic analysis starts off from a concrete term m, denoted by the pair $\langle \text{true}, m \rangle$ where m is closed. General constraining conditions b in a pair $\langle b, m \rangle$ are accrued from prior transitions as follows. The symbolic transition relation $m \overset{\mu}{\underset{c}{\longrightarrow}} n$ is used to abstractly calculate the set of concrete transitions $m\rho \overset{\mu\rho}{\longrightarrow} n\rho$ from the pair $\langle b, m \rangle$ for any ρ satisfying b, *i.e.*, $[\![b\rho]\!] = \text{true}$, *whenever* ρ *also* satisfies c. In order to record this fact, the resulting set of monitor states is encoded as $\langle b \wedge c, n \rangle$.

Our symbolic analysis rests on another important technical machinery. Since it is concerned with abstracting over internal non-determinism (as long as it does not manifest itself in terms of the verdicts reached) we need to (symbolically) reason with respect to *sets* of (open) monitor terms, $M \subseteq \text{MON}$, denoting the set of possible monitor states that we could have reached thus far. Concretely, the symbolic analysis works on *constrained monitor-sets*, $\langle b, M \rangle$, where the boolean condition b constrains the free variables present in *every* monitor $m \in M$, *i.e.*, $[\![\langle b, M \rangle]\!] \overset{\text{def}}{=} \{\, m\rho \mid m \in M \text{ and } [\![b\rho]\!] = \text{true}\,\}$. The meta-function $\mathbf{fv}(-)$ is lifted to constrained monitor-sets in the obvious manner *i.e.*, $\mathbf{fv}(\langle b, \{m_1, \ldots, m_n\}\rangle) = \mathbf{fv}(b) \cup \mathbf{fv}(m_1) \cup \ldots \cup \mathbf{fv}(m_n)$. In the sequel, we also use the notation $\wedge B$ for some set of boolean conditions $B = \{c_1, \ldots, c_n\}$ to denote the syntactic conjunction of all the conditions in B. The helper function $\mathbf{frsh}(V)$ is also used to generate the next fresh variable x which is *not* in the variable set $V \subseteq \text{VARS}$.

Symbolic controllability employs two predicates on constrained monitor-sets. The predicate $\mathbf{spr}(\langle b, M \rangle, w)$ holds if some monitor $m \in M$ that can symbolically reach a verdict after a finite sequence of silent actions along some condition c where $b \wedge c$ is satisfiable. The predicate $\mathbf{spa}(\langle b, M \rangle, \theta, c)$ holds if some monitor $m \in M$ can weakly analyse the event θ with condition c with a satisfiable $b \wedge c$.

Definition 1 (Symbolic Predicates [17]). *A constrained monitor-set* $\langle b, M \rangle$

1. *symbolically potentially reaches a verdict* w, *denoted as* $\mathbf{spr}(\langle b, M \rangle, w)$, *whenever* $\exists c \in \text{BEXP}, \exists m \in M$ *such that* $m \underset{c}{\Longrightarrow} w$ *and* $\mathbf{sat}(b \wedge c)$.

2. symbolically potentially analyses *an event θ along condition c, denoted as* $spa(\langle b, M \rangle, \theta, c)$, *whenever* $\exists m \in M$ *where* $m \overset{\theta}{\underset{c}{\Rightarrow}}$ *and* $sat(b \wedge c)$. ∎

Example 2. Recall monitor m_2 from Example 1. Consider the constrained monitor-set $\langle b, M \rangle$ where b is $y < 20$, $M = \{$if $y > 50$ then $set(\_).\bot$ else $set\langle y+1 \rangle$. $m_2'\}$, and

$$m_2' = \operatorname{rec} X.\mathsf{get}(y).\mathsf{if}\ y > 50\ \mathsf{then}\ \mathsf{set}(\_).\bot\ \mathsf{else}\ \mathsf{set}\langle y + 1 \rangle.X.$$

This constrained monitor-set *cannot* potentially reach a verdict, $\neg spr(\langle b, M \rangle, w)$. In fact, via (symbolic) τ-transitions it can only reach the monitor states $set(\_).\bot$ and $set\langle y+1 \rangle.m_2'$. When observing the (symbolic) event $set\langle z \rangle$, the monitor-set M can weakly transition to two potential monitor states: one, $\bot$, along condition $c_1 = (y > 50)$ and the other, m_2', along $c_2 = (y \leq 50) \wedge (y' = y + 1)$. However, since the condition $b \wedge c_1$ is *not* satisfiable, only the second branch corresponds to an actual transition in the concrete semantics (*i.e.,* there is a valuation ρ that satisfies $(y < 20) \wedge (y \leq 50) \wedge (z = y + 1)$). In fact, we can say that the constrained monitor-set can potentially analyse the event $set\langle z \rangle$ along c_2, *i.e.,* predicate $spa(\langle b, M \rangle, set\langle z \rangle, c_2)$ from Definition 1. ∎

From a specific set of potential states in a monitor computation, say $\langle b, M \rangle$, the symbolic analysis needs to calculate the possible next set of (symbolic) events the potential states can analyse. This does not only depend on the ability to symbolically transition with an event θ, but also the *conditions* required for this transition to be performed. The function $rc(M, \theta)$ defined below computes the *set of all possible conditions* along which event θ may occur; it also accounts for the computation sequences that lead a monitor to deadlock and not be able to (weak-) symbolically transition with event θ. Once this set of *relevant* conditions for event θ is calculated, $\{c_1, \ldots, c_n\}$, the analysis needs to calculate which of these are realisable when paired with b from $\langle b, M \rangle$. Since each of these conditions can either be satisfied or violated at runtime, $sc(b, \{c_1, \ldots, c_n\})$ returns the set of all the *possible ways* $\{b, c_1', \ldots, c_n'\}$ can be combined together where c_i' is either equal to c_i or its negation; the resulting combinations partition the valuations satisfying b, with some of the them being possibly *empty*. This then allows the symbolic analysis to calculate $saft(\langle b, M \rangle, \theta, c)$, the reachable (symbolic) monitor states from $\langle b, M \rangle$ after analysing event θ with condition c. Note also how $saft(\langle b, M \rangle, \theta, c)$ accounts for the possibility that an execution branch of $\langle b, M \rangle$ is unable to analyse a symbolic event θ along c: when this is the case, it introduces the inconclusive verdict, 0, in the set of reachable monitors to model monitor analysis preemption.

Definition 2 (Symbolic Reachability Analysis [17]). *The* relevant *conditions for a monitor-set M w.r.t. the symbolic event θ is given by:*

$$rc(M, \theta) \overset{def}{=} \{ c \mid \exists m \in M \cdot (m \overset{\theta}{\underset{c}{\Rightarrow}}\ or\ \exists n \cdot (m \underset{c}{\Longrightarrow} n\ and\ n \overset{\tau}{\nRightarrow}\ and\ n \overset{\theta}{\nRightarrow})) \}$$

The satisfiability combinations *w.r.t.* b *for set* $\{c_1, \ldots, c_n\}$ *is given by:*

$$sc(b, \{c_1, \ldots, c_n\}) \stackrel{def}{=} \{\, \{b, c'_1, \ldots, c'_n\} \mid \forall i \in 1..n \cdot (c'_i = c_i \text{ or } c'_i = \neg c_i)\,\}$$

The reachable constrained monitor-sets *from* $\langle b, M \rangle$ *after* θ *along* c *are:*

$$saft(\langle b, M \rangle, \theta, c) \stackrel{def}{=} \{\, \langle \wedge B, saft(M, B, \theta) \rangle \mid B \in sc(b \wedge c, rc(M, \theta)) \text{ and } sat(\wedge B) \,\}$$

$$saft(M, B, \theta) \stackrel{def}{=} \left\{\, n \,\middle|\, \begin{array}{l} \exists m \in M, c \cdot sat((\wedge B) \wedge c) \text{ and } (m \overset{\theta}{\underset{c}{\Longrightarrow}} n \\ \text{or } (\exists n' \cdot m \underset{c}{\Longrightarrow} n' \overset{\tau}{\nrightarrow} \text{ and } n' \overset{\theta}{\nrightarrow} \text{ and } n = \mathbf{0})) \end{array} \right\} \quad \blacksquare$$

Equipped with this set of machinery, we can define Symbolic Monitor Controllability. It requires that:

1. whenever a set of potential states can (autonomously) reach a conclusive verdict, they must all do so and must do it immediately (without requiring further τ-transitions, since this can be interfered with when the instrumented process diverges to create a form of spinlock);
2. whenever a set of potential states can analyse an event, the reachable set of monitor states after carrying out that event is also included in the relation (*i.e.*, the relation is closed).

The interested reader is invited to consult [17] for further details.

Definition 3 (Symbolic Monitor Controllability [17]**).** *A relation over constrained monitor-sets* $\mathcal{S} \subseteq (\text{BEXP} \times \mathcal{P}(\text{MON}))$ *is said to be* symbolically controllable *iff for all* $\langle b, M \rangle \in \mathcal{S}$*, the following two conditions are satisfied:*

1. $spr(\langle b, M \rangle, w)$ *and* $w \in \{\top, \bot\}$ *implies* $M = \{w\}$;
2. $spa(\langle b, M \rangle, l\langle x \rangle, c)$ *where* $frsh(fv(\langle b, M \rangle)) = x$ *implies* $saft(\langle b, M \rangle, l\langle x \rangle, c) \subseteq \mathcal{S}$.

For a monitor m *to be symbolically controllable, there must exist some symbolically controllable relation* $\mathcal{S}$ *s.t.* $\langle true, \{m\} \rangle \in \mathcal{S}$. $\quad \blacksquare$

Since symbolic controllability is both *sound* and *complete* w.r.t. consistent monitor detection, it can also be used to determine violations to the latter definition (recall that consistent detection is defined in terms of concrete events).

Example 3. It is tempting to monitor for the consolidated specifications denoted by m_2 and m_3 from Example 1, via the monitor $m_4 = m_2 + m_3$. Upon observing the (concrete) event $\text{init}\langle 50 \rangle$, m_4 may reach either of two monitor states, m'_2 (from Example 2) and m'_3 (described below); this is permitted by symbolic controllability (and by consistent detection), as long as both states reach the same verdict.

$m'_3 =$ let $lim = e_{calc}$ in $\big($if $x < lim$ then end$(\_).\bot$ else

$\qquad\qquad\qquad\qquad$ rec $X.\text{get}(y).$if $y \geq lim$ then set$\langle y + 1 \rangle.\top$ else set$(\_).X\big)$

But consider a trace of events such as $\mathsf{init}\langle 50\rangle \cdot \mathsf{get}\langle 60\rangle \cdot \mathsf{set}\langle 61\rangle$. If the monitor transitions to the first monitor state, m_2', the execution will *always* be rejected, whereas if the monitor transitions to the second monitor state, $m_3'[50/x]$, two further cases must be considered. If the predetermined value lim is larger than 50, a conclusive verdict will *never* be reached. Otherwise, the execution is accepted. The aforementioned trace thus proves that m_4 is *not* consistently detecting.

According to our symbolic analysis of Definition 3, for m_4 to be symbolically controllable, there *must* exists some relation $\mathcal{S}$ that contains $\langle \mathsf{true}, \{m_4\}\rangle$. By Definition 3.2, $\mathcal{S}$ must also contain $\langle \mathsf{true} \wedge x = 50, \{m_2', m_3'\}\rangle$. If we assume that lim greater than 50 (the converse case is similar), $\mathcal{S}$ must also contain $\langle \mathsf{true} \wedge (x = 50) \wedge \mathsf{true}, \{\mathsf{if}\ y > 50\ \mathsf{then}\ \mathsf{set}(\_).\bot\ \mathsf{else}\ \mathsf{set}\langle y + 1\rangle.m_2', \mathsf{end}(\_).\bot\}\rangle$ and, in turn (after considering the symbolic event $\mathsf{set}\langle z\rangle$ with condition $y > 50$), it must also contain $\langle \mathsf{true} \wedge (x = 50) \wedge \mathsf{true} \wedge (y > 50), \{\bot, \mathbf{0}\}\rangle$. But, clearly, the latter constrained monitor-set violates Definition 3.1. Thus, no such symbolically controllable relation exists.   ∎

The reachability closure requirement of Definition 3.2, defined using the (symbolic after) $\mathbf{saft}(\langle b, M\rangle, \theta, c)$ function of Definition 2, keeps on aggregating the conditions of the transitions to the constraining condition b in a constrained set $\langle b, M\rangle$. This complicates the formulation of a finite symbolic relation (whenever this exists). To overcome this, the work in [17] defines a sound method for consolidating constraining boolean conditions, thus garbage collecting redundant constraints that bear no effect on the meaning of the (open) monitor-set M.

Definition 4 (Optimised Symb. Controllability [17]**).** *The consolidation of a boolean expression b w.r.t. variable-set V, denoted $\mathbf{cns}(b, V)$, is defined as:*

$$\mathbf{cns}(b, V) \stackrel{\text{def}}{=} b_1 \text{ whenever } \mathbf{prt}(b, V) = \langle b_1, b_2\rangle \text{ for some } b_2$$

where the boolean expression partitioning operation $\mathbf{prt}(b, V)$ is defined as:

$$\mathbf{prt}(b, V) \stackrel{\text{def}}{=} \begin{cases} \langle b_1, b_2\rangle & \text{if } \mathbf{sat}(b) \text{ and } b = b_1 \wedge b_2 \text{ and } \mathbf{fv}(b_1) \subseteq V \text{ and } V \cap \mathbf{fv}(b_2) = \emptyset \\ \langle b, \mathbf{true}\rangle & \text{otherwise} \end{cases}$$

Let optimised symbolic reachability from $\langle b, M\rangle$ for θ and c, $\mathbf{osaft}(\langle b, M\rangle, \theta, c)$, be defined as:

$$\mathbf{osaft}(\langle b, M\rangle, \theta, c) \stackrel{\text{def}}{=} \left\{ \langle \mathbf{cns}(\wedge B, V), \mathbf{saft}(M, B, \theta)\rangle \,\middle|\, \begin{array}{l} B \in \mathbf{sc}(b \wedge c, \mathbf{rc}(M, \theta)) \\ \text{and } \mathbf{sat}(\wedge B) \text{ and} \\ V = \mathbf{fv}(\mathbf{saft}(M, B, \theta)) \end{array} \right\}$$

A relation $\mathcal{S} \subseteq (\mathrm{BEXP} \times \mathcal{P}(\mathrm{MON}))$ is called optimised symbolically-controllable *iff for all $\langle b, M\rangle \in \mathcal{S}$:*

1. $\mathbf{spr}(\langle b, M\rangle, w)$ *and* $w \in \{\top, \bot\}$ *implies* $M = \{w\}$;
2. $\mathbf{spa}(\langle b, M\rangle, l\langle x\rangle, c)$ *s.t.*
   $\mathbf{frsh}(\mathbf{fv}(\langle b, M\rangle)) = x$ *implies* $\mathbf{osaft}(\langle b, M\rangle, l\langle x\rangle, c) \subseteq \mathcal{S}$.

The largest *optimised symbolically-controllable relation is denoted by* $\mathcal{C}^{opt}$, *and contains all optimised symbolically-controllable relations. We say that a monitor m is optimised symbolically-controllable iff there exists an optimised symbolically-controllable relation* $\mathcal{S}$ *such that* $\langle true, \{m\}\rangle \in \mathcal{S}$. ∎

Example 4. Although monitoring for a different combined specification involving m_1 and m_3 from Example 1, *i.e.*, monitor $m_1 + m_3$, may reach different internal states, it can be shown to be symbolically controllable via the relation $\mathcal{S}$ defined below:

$$\mathcal{S} = \left\{ \begin{array}{l} \langle true, \{m_1 + m_3\}\rangle,\ \langle x{=}0, \{end(\_).\bot, m_3''\}\rangle,\ \langle true, \{\bot\}\rangle,\ \langle x{\neq}0, \{m_3''\}\rangle, \\ \langle true, \{m_3'''\}\rangle,\ \langle true, \{get(y).if\ y \geq e_{calc}\ then\ set\langle y{+}1\rangle.\bot\ else\ set(\_).m_3'''\}\rangle \end{array} \right\}$$

where

$$m_3'' = \left\{ \begin{array}{l} let\ lim{=}e_{calc}\ in\ if\ x < lim\ then\ end(\_).\bot\ else \\ \qquad rec\ X.get(y).if\ y \geq lim\ then\ set\langle y{+}1\rangle.\bot\ else\ set(\_).X \end{array} \right.$$

$$m_3''' = rec\ X.get(y).if\ y \geq e_{calc}\ then\ set\langle y{+}1\rangle.\bot\ else\ set(\_).X$$

Definition 4 allows us to discard redundant boolean conditions in the constrained monitor-sets of $\mathcal{S}$, collapsing semantically equivalent entries into the same syntactic representation. For instance, the entry $\langle true, \{m_1 + m_3\}\rangle$ can potentially analyse the event $init\langle x\rangle$ with the relevant conditions $\{true, x = 0\}$. The satisfiability combinations, $sc(true, \{true, x = 0\})$, are given by $\{true \wedge x = 0, true \wedge \neg(x = 0)\}$. The reachable monitor-set obtained by $saft(\langle true, \{m_1{+}m_3\}\rangle, init\langle x\rangle, true \wedge x = 0)$ is $\langle true \wedge x = 0, \{end(\_).\bot, m_3''\}\rangle$, and that obtained by the symbolic calculation $saft(\langle true, \{m_1 + m_3\}\rangle, init\langle x\rangle, true \wedge x \neq 0)$ is $\langle true \wedge x{\neq}0, \{m_3''\}\rangle$. The respective conditions are consolidated as $x = 0$ and $x{\neq}0$.

Similarly, the entry $\langle x = 0, \{end(\_).\bot, m_3''\}\rangle$ can potentially analyse the event $end\langle x'\rangle$ with the relevant conditions $\{true, x < e_{calc} \wedge true\}$. The monitor-set obtained by $saft(\langle true, \{end(\_).\bot, m_3''\}\rangle, end\langle x'\rangle, (x = 0) \wedge (x < e_{calc}) \wedge true)$ is given by $\langle (x = 0) \wedge (x < e_{calc}) \wedge true, \{\bot\}\rangle$; importantly, the conditions are consolidated as $true$ since none of them impose any constraint on monitor-set $\{\bot\}$. ∎

3   Preliminary Implementation

Symbolic Controllability, Definitions 3 and 4, is declarative in nature: to show that a monitor m is symbolically controllable, it suffices to provide a symbolically controllable relation $\mathcal{S}$ containing the constrained monitor-set $\langle true, \{m\}\rangle$. However, this does *not* provide any indication on how this relation can be obtained.

Our preliminary attempt devising this algorithm is described in Agorithm 1. Intuitively, the procedure starts from the initial constrained monitor-set $\langle true, \{m\}\rangle$, checks for clause Definition 3.1 and then generates new monitor-sets to analyse using clause Definition 3.2. Constrained monitor-sets are represented as a pair containing a list of conditions (*i.e.*, conjuncted constraining conditions) and a list of monitors (*i.e.*, the monitor-set); the base condition $true$ is represented by the empty list. The algorithm uses a list of pairs, $\mathcal{S}$, and a queue, $\mathcal{Q}$.

```
 1  def COMPSYMREL(S, Q)               19  def COMPREACH(sevts,⟨b, M⟩,Q,S)
 2  if Q.empty then                    20   for s in sevts do
 3     return true                     21    c ← rc(M, s)
 4  else                               22    satComb ← sc(b, c)
 5    # unseen constrained monitor-set 23    for scomb in satCombs do
 6    ⟨b, M⟩ ← Q.remove                24     if spa ⟨b, M⟩ s scomb then
 7    S ← ⟨b, M⟩                        25      cms ← saft(⟨b, M⟩, s, scomb)
 8    # condition (1) true             26      for cm in cms do
 9    if spr ⟨b, M⟩ then               27       if cm ∉ S then
10      # generate a fresh variable    28        S ← ⟨b, M⟩
11      x ← frsh(fv⟨b, M⟩)             29        Q.append cm # add to queue
12      sevts ← GENSYMEVENTS(M, x)     30   return Q
13      # generate the reachable cms
14      Q ← COMPREACH(sevts,⟨b, M⟩,Q,S) 31  def ISSYMCONTROLLABLE(M)
15      COMPSYMREL (S, Q)              32   b ← [ ] # [ ] represents true
16    else                            33   cm ← ⟨b, M⟩
17      # condition (1) false         34   Q ← cm # init a queue
18      return false                  35   COMPSYMREL([ ], Q)
```

Alg. 1: Pseudocode for the Algorithm automating Symbolic Controllability

The list of pairs (initialised to empty) stores the constrained monitor-sets that will make up the relation we are trying to construct; the queue, initialised to the singleton element $\langle \text{true}, \{m\} \rangle$, is used to store the constrained monitor-sets that have not been analysed yet. Lists are convenient for reading and adding data; however, queues perform better when data needs to be removed since they have a time complexity of $O(n)$ and $O(1)$ respectively. The list S observes two key invariants, namely that (i) all the pairs in S satisfy Definition 3.1 and (ii) all reachable constrained monitor-sets from these pairs, obtained via saft(-), are either in S itself or in Q, waiting to be analysed. When Q becomes empty, a fixpoint is reached: all reachable constrained monitor-sets from S must be in S itself, satisfying Definition 3.2, and the resulting S is closed.

Function COMSYMREL( ) in Algorithm 1 is the main function. If Q is empty, there are no further constrained monitor-sets to analyse and $true$ is returned (line 3). Otherwise, a constrained monitor-set is removed from Q. Condition Definition 3.1 is checked (line 9) and the analysis terminates with $false$ if violated. Line 12 obtains all symbolic events that can be observed by the current constrained monitor-set using function GENSYMEVENTS( ), which is then used to get the reachable constrained monitor-sets using function COMPREACH( ). This function follows closely Definition 1 and Definition 2, but function SC( ) on line 22 returns only the combinations that are satisfiable; this removes the need to compute $\mathbf{sc}(b \wedge c)$ in spa(-) and $\mathbf{sc}(\wedge B)$ in saft(-). The reachable constrained monitor-sets are generated on line 25, and those that have not been analysed yet are pushed to Q on line 29. Alg. 29 is implemented in straightforward fashion using OCaml [27].

Interfacing with the SAT Solver. Generating the set of satisfiability combinations w.r.t. a set of relevant conditions (line 22) requires the invocation of an external satisfiability solver to determine reachable paths. We used the *Z3* [28] theorem prover for this; its numerous APIs allow a seamless integration with our tool. Z3 relies on hand-crafted heuristics [30] to determine whether a set of formulas, also known as *assertions*, is satisfiable. Instead of opting to use the default solver, we used a custom strategy based on the built-in tactics **ctx-solver-simplify( )** and **propagate-ineqs( )**, performing simplification and inequality propagation respectively. We used another important feature of Z3: instead of returning a boolean verdict, the function invoking the SAT solver, SAT( ), returns the simplified formula together with the verdict. This increases the number of discarded conditions during boolean consolidation and makes future satisfiability checks that refine this condition *less* expensive.

Complexity Bounds. The complexity of Algorithm 1 depends on two parameters:

1. The terms reachable from the initial monitor m via the symbolic semantics of Fig. 1, denoted here as the set **reach**(m). Since our monitors are expressed using a regular grammar, we can show that this set is finite for any monitor $m \in$ MON, i.e., **size**(**reach**(m)) $= i$ for some $i \in \mathbb{N}$; see [4] for a similar proof of this fact. As our controllability analysis relies on *sets* of reachable monitors, the standard complexity for the power set construction is $O(2^i)$.
2. The satisfiability checks of the boolean constraints b generated by the symbolic analysis. In general, Algorithm 1 needs to check the satisfiability of the boolean condition of *every* monitor set from the previous point. Satisfiability is usually a function of the number of free variables, $j \in \mathbb{N}$, in the boolean condition b. Although the standard boolean satisfiability would be $O(2^j)$, the boolean conditions in Algorithm 1 involve variables for integers with operators, i.e., integer programming. Since we are agnostic of the expression language used, this is not decidable for general integer expressions [29] (e.g., expressions with both addition and multiplication). Limiting expressions to Presburger arithmetic would recover decidability [10], yielding a complexity that can be safely approximated to $2^{O(j)}$.

When decidable, the complexity of Algorithm 1 can be safely approximated to $2^{O(i+j)}$.

4   Evaluating Efficiency

Although Sect. 3 demonstrates that controllability analysis can be implemented, albeit with high worst-case complexity bound, it is unclear whether the implementation scales well in practice. In this section we devise an evaluation strategy for our tool that attempts to capture typical use-cases; whenever performance bottlenecks are detected, alternative implementation methods are studied in Sect. 5 and compared to our baseline implementation.

Table 1. Parametrisable monitor descriptions

$$\mathrm{M_{rec}}(n) \;=\; \mathrm{rec}\,X. \sum_{i=1}^{n+1}\big(k\langle i\rangle.(l\langle i\rangle.X) + (q\langle i\rangle.\top)\big)$$

$$\mathrm{M_{cnd}}(n) \;=\; \begin{aligned} &l(x).(\text{if } x{=}4 \text{ then } k\langle x\rangle.\bot \text{ else } k\langle x\rangle.\top) \qquad\qquad\quad \overbrace{}^{i=2..n}\\ &\quad + \textstyle\sum_{i=2}^{n}\big(\text{if } x \bmod 2{=}0 \text{ then } \text{if } x{<}2(n{-}i{+}3) \text{ then}\ldots \text{if } x{<}2(n{-}i{+}3) \text{ then}\\ &\qquad\qquad\qquad \underbrace{\text{if } x{>}2 \text{ then } k\langle x\rangle.\bot \text{else } k\langle x\rangle.\top \ldots \text{else } k\langle x\rangle.\top)}_{i=2..n+1} \end{aligned}$$

$$\mathrm{M_{brc}}(n) \;=\; \begin{aligned} &l(x).\big(\text{if } x{=}4 \text{ then } k\langle x\rangle.\bot \text{ else } k\langle x\rangle. \textstyle\sum_{j=1}^{3n}(k\langle j\rangle.\top)\big) \quad \overbrace{}^{i=2..n}\\ &\quad + \textstyle\sum_{i=2}^{n}\big(\text{if } x \bmod 2 = 0 \text{ then } \text{if } x{<}2(n{-}i{+}3) \text{ then}\ldots \text{if } x{<}2(n{-}i{+}3) \text{ then}\\ &\qquad\qquad \text{if } x{>}2 \text{ then } k\langle x\rangle. \textstyle\sum_{j=1}^{3n}(k\langle j\rangle.\bot)\\ &\qquad\qquad\quad \underbrace{\text{else } k\langle x\rangle.\sum_{j=1}^{3n}(k\langle j\rangle.\top) \ldots \text{else } k\langle x\rangle.\sum_{j=1}^{3n}(k\langle j\rangle.\top))}_{i=2..n+1} \end{aligned}$$

A Benchmark for Assessing Deterministic Monitor Analysis. A major obstacle for assessing the scalability of Algorithm 1 is the absence of a proper benchmark. To this end, we use the monitor modelling syntax of Fig. 1 to design a suite of pathological monitor template descriptions that are parametrisable in size and complexity, allowing us to carry out our evaluation in a systematic manner; see Table 1. Each template targets a specific feature of a symbolic analysis for non-deterministic behaviour. Concretely, $\mathrm{M_{rec}}(n)$ is a monitor template that generates monitor instances that can transition to multiple sub-monitors, some of which lead to a verdict while others recurse to induce further iterations in the monitor analysis loop; this pathological behaviour induces large relation sizes $\mathcal{S}$ in the analysis of Algorithm 1. In $\mathrm{M_{cnd}}(n)$, (symbolic) events may be observed along various boolean conditions with the intention of increasing the number of constraints b in the corresponding constrained monitor-set $\langle b, M\rangle$ analysed in Algorithm 1. The monitor instances generated by $\mathrm{M_{cnd}}(n)$ also have a high branching factor, which induces larger monitor-sets M. The final monitor template $\mathrm{M_{brc}}(n)$ generates monitors with nested branching that alternates with event analysis; this impacts the number of relevant conditions that need to be considered when calculating the reachable constrained monitor-sets in Algorithm 1.

Preliminary Results. We evaluated the mean running time (over 3 repeated runs) of our preliminary (*Naive*) implementation for the three monitor templates of Table 1, instantiated by an ascending parameter n. All experiments were conducted on a Quad-Core Intel Core i5 64-bit machine with 16 GB memory, running OCaml version 4.08.0 on OSX Catalina. They can be *reproduced* using the sources provided at https://github.com/jasmine97xuereb/sym-cont, whereby the *master* branch contains the preliminary implementation and the other branches the individual optimisations.

The plotted time results (in blue) are reported in Fig. 2 on a *logarithmic* scale; missing plot-points mean that the (controllability) analysis did not terminate

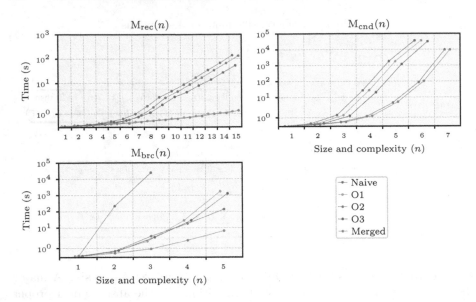

Fig. 2. Mean running time for different monitors (Color figure online)

within a stipulated time threshold (over 10 h). The results confirm that the preliminary implementation does not scale well; although it has a low response time for low values of n, its performance degrades quickly as n increases (the worst behaviour measured was that for the pathological cases of $M_{brc}(n)$, where we immediately witnessed a sharp spike at $n = 3$). A closer inspection into the working of the algorithm reveals that the invocations to the Z3 solver are expensive operations, incurring a cost that is magnitudes higher than any other aspect of the analysis. In turn, the number of invocations is dependent on the number of relevant conditions: in the preliminary implementation of Algorithm 1, the algorithm considers all 2^i possible combinations for a given number i of relevant conditions, each of which needs to be checked for satisfiability. This insight gave us a focus of attack for improving the tool's scalability.

5   Optimisation Techniques

Upon closer inspection, we notice that a substantial number of conjuncted conditions generated by SC( ) of Algorithm 1 are (trivially) unsatisfiable. Ideally, these cases should *not* result in invocations to the satisfiability solver.

Optimisation Technique O1. The first optimisation technique relies on the notion of (easily identifiable) *mutual exclusion*, whereby the satisfaction of one boolean condition necessarily violates that of the other.

Example 5. Recall the constrained monitor-set $\langle b, \{m_1 + m_2\} \rangle$ from Example 1. The relevant conditions w.r.t. event init$\langle x \rangle$ are $\{b_1, b_2\}$, where b_1 is $x = 0$

```
 1  def SC(b,cs)
 2    result ← [ ]
 3    (X,Y) ← partition cs # X contains var assignments and Y all others
 4    for x ∈ VAR(X) do # cluster expressions in X by their variable name
 5      X_x ← {(y = v) ∈ X | x = y}
 6      first_x ← X_x ++ [∧(negate all c in X_x)]
 7    second ← all possible combinations for Y
 8    combinations ← (X_{x∈VAR(X)} first_x) × second # cartesian product of first and second
 9    for c in combinations do
10      t ← SAT ( [b, c] ) # t:(bool, exp list)
11      if FST(t) then
12        result ← result ++ SND(t)
```

Alg. 2: Pseudocode for first optimised function $\mathbf{sc}(b, \{c_1, ..., c_n\})$

and b_2 is $x = 50$. Accordingly, the satisfiability combinations generated for $\mathbf{sc}(\text{true}, \{b_1, b_2\})$ are $b_1 \wedge b_2$, $\neg b_1 \wedge b_2$, $b_1 \wedge \neg b_2$, and $\neg b_1 \wedge \neg b_2$. Since x cannot be equal to values 0 and 50 simultaneously, conditions b_1 and b_2 are mutually exclusive. ∎

A close inspection of the transition rules in Fig. 1 reveals that the constraints introduced tend to be of the form $x = e$; whenever $e = v$, it is easy to syntactically determine mutually exclusive conditions as in Example 5. The pseudocode in Algorithm 2 first partitions the set of boolean conditions into two (line 3): the first partition, X, consists solely of variable assignments *i.e.*, expressions of the form $x = n$ for $n \in \mathbb{N}$, whereas the second partition, Y, contains the remaining conditions. For partition Y, all the possible combinations are generated as in Algorithm 1 (line 7). As for partition X, we first cluster them according to the constrained variable (line 6); for each cluster, either one condition is *true*, or all of them are *false* (since they are necessarily mutually exclusive). The resulting combinations are merged by computing their *Cartesian Product* (line 8).

Example 6. Consider the *open* monitor term $m_5 = \text{init}\langle y \rangle.\top$ and constrained monitor-set $\langle b, M \rangle$ where $M = \{m_1 + m_2 + m_5\}$ with m_1 and m_2 from Example 1. The relevant conditions for M along event $\text{init}\langle x \rangle$, $\mathbf{rc}(M, \text{init}\langle x \rangle)$ are $c = \{b_1, b_2, b_3\}$, where b_1 is $x = 0$, b_2 is $x = 50$, and b_3 is $x = y$. When calculating $\mathbf{sc}(\text{true}, c)$ using Algorithm 2, condition-set c is partitioned into $X = \{b_1, b_2\}$ and $Y = \{b_3\}$. All the conditions in the X are mutually exclusive. Thus, the possible ways the conditions in X can be combined are given by the condition-set $\{b_1, b_2, \neg b_1 \wedge \neg b_2\}$. The possible combinations of the conditions in Y are generated as before, and are given by $\{b_3, \neg b_3\}$ on line 7. These two resulting sets are merged as: $\{b_1, b_3\}$, $\{b_1, \neg b_3\}$, $\{b_2, b_3\}$, $\{b_2, \neg b_3\}$, $\{\neg b_1 \wedge \neg b_2, b_3\}$, and $\{\neg b_1 \wedge \neg b_2, \neg b_3\}$. Note that whereas Algorithm 1 generates 8 combinations (and SAT solver invocations), this is now reduced to 6. Moreover, the latter combinations of logical formulas are less complex. ∎

In general, given a set of relevant conditions of length k, a set of clusters $X_{x \in \text{VAR}(X)}$ and Y where $|X_{x \in \text{VAR}(X)}| = n_x$, $|Y| = m$, and $k = m + \sum_{x \in \text{VAR}(X)} n_x$, the number of times the SAT solver is invoked is reduced from $2^k = 2^m \prod_{x \in \text{VAR}(X)} 2^{n_x}$ to $2^m \prod_{x \in \text{VAR}(X)} (n_x + 1)$. Hence, the larger the first partition is, $i.e.$, $|X|$, the more effective the optimisation. When we evaluate the optimised implementation against the benchmark in Table 1, depicted by the plot labelled $O1$ in Fig. 2, we noticed that even though the running time for monitors $M_{\text{rec}}(n)$ and $M_{\text{brc}}(n)$ decreased substantially, that of monitors $M_{\text{cnd}}(n)$ was unaffected.

Optimisation Technique 2. Storing the aggregated boolean conditions as a *flat structure* loses information regarding the monitor branching structure.

Example 7. Consider m_6, a slight modification of monitor m_2 from Example 1.

$m_6 = \text{init}\langle 50 \rangle.\text{let } lim = e_{calc} \text{ in } m_6'$

$m_6' = \text{rec } X.\text{get}(y).\text{if } y \geq 50 \text{ then set}(\_).\bot \text{ else if } y < lim \text{ then set}\langle y+1 \rangle.X \text{ else set}(\_).\bot$

Upon observing event $\text{init}\langle 50 \rangle$, followed by event $\text{get}\langle y \rangle$, both along the boolean condition true, the reachable monitor-set for $\langle \text{true}, \{m_6\} \rangle$ is given by $\langle \text{true}, \{m_6''\} \rangle$, where $m_6'' = \text{if } y \geq 50 \text{ then set}(\_).\bot \text{ else if } y < e_{calc} \text{ then set}\langle y+1 \rangle.m_6' \text{ else set}(\_).\bot$.

Monitor-set $\{m_6''\}$ analyses event $\text{set}\langle x \rangle$ with relevant conditions c_1, c_2, and c_3, where c_1 is $(y > 50) \wedge (y < e_{calc}) \wedge (x = y+1)$, c_2 is $(y > 50) \wedge \neg (y < e_{calc})$, and c_3 is $\neg (y > 50)$. Computing the set of satisfiable combinations, $\text{sc}(\text{true}, \{c_1, c_2, c_3\})$, in a naive manner entails the invocation of the SAT solver $2^3 = 8$ times. However, there are multiple combinations that cannot hold. For instance, $c_1 \wedge c_2$ is not satisfiable because condition c_2 occurs along an *if true* branch, whereas condition b_1 occurs along the *else* branch of the *same* monitor. ∎

We consider a hierarchic representation of expressions, $i.e.$, expression trees represented as tuples $e = \langle e', [e''], [e'''] \rangle$ with e' as the root. For convenience, we use the suggestive dot notation (.) to access specific elements. The condition of expression tree, e', is accessed via the field $e.\text{cond}$. Expression trees have a list of left and a list of right expressions. The left expressions, $[e'']$, can only be reached if $\text{sat}(e')$ and are accessed via the field $e.\text{true}$. Similarly, the right expressions, $[e''']$, can only be reached if $\neg \text{sat}(e')$ and are accessed via $e.\text{false}$. Since $[e'']$ and $[e''']$ can be reached when e' is true or false respectively, the expressions along the left and the right paths are mutually exclusive. Condition true is still represented by an empty list; expressions e'' and e''' may be expression trees themselves.

Example 8. Recall monitor-set $\{m_6''\}$ from Example 7. If we recompute the relevant conditions for this monitor-set w.r.t. event $\text{set}\langle x \rangle$, $\text{rc}(\{m_6''\}, \text{set}\langle x \rangle)$, using the new representation we obtain $b = \langle y \geq 50, [\langle y < e_{calc}, [x = y+1], [\,] \rangle], [\,] \rangle$. ∎

1 **def** TRAV(e: exp)	18 **def** SC(b,cs)
2 **def** GETPATHS(e': exp list)	19 $paths \leftarrow [\,]$, $result \leftarrow [\,]$
3 $paths \leftarrow [\,]$	20 # X *contains only expression trees*
4 **if** e' not empty **then**	21 $(X, Y) \leftarrow$ partition cs
5 **for** x in e' **do**	22 **for** x in X **do**
6 $paths \leftarrow paths$ ++ TRAV(x)	23 $paths \leftarrow paths$ ++ TRAV(x)
7 # *cartesian product of all p in paths*	24 # *cartesian product of all p in paths*
8 **return** $\mathsf{X}_{i=1}^{n}\ paths_i$	25 $k \leftarrow \mathsf{X}_{i=1}^{n}\ paths_i$
9 **if** e is an expression tree **then**	26 $first \leftarrow X$ ++ [$\wedge$(negate all x in k)]
10 $branchT \leftarrow$ GETPATHS(e.true)	27 $second \leftarrow$ all combinations for Y
11 $branchF \leftarrow$ GETPATHS(e.false)	28 # *cartesian prod of first and second*
12 # *add e.cond to each p in branchT*	29 $combinations \leftarrow first \times second$
13 $x \leftarrow e.\text{cond} \wedge p_i \cdot \forall p_i \in branchT$	30 #*filter out unsatisfiable conditions*
14 $y \leftarrow \neg\, e.\text{cond} \wedge p_i \cdot \forall p_i \in branchF$	31 **for** c in $combinations$ **do**
15 **return** x ++ y	32 $t \leftarrow$ SAT ($[b, c]$)
16 **else**	33 **if** FST(t) **then**
17 **return** e	34 $result \leftarrow result$ ++ SND(t)

Alg. 3: Pseudocode for second optimised function **sc**($b, \{c_1, ..., c_n\}$)

The pseudocode for the second optimisation in Algorithm 3 relies on the function TRAV( ). It traverses expression tree e passed as parameter and returns a list of mutually exclusive conditions. This function recursively computes all the paths along the *true* and *false* branches on lines 10 and 11 respectively. Once all the possible combinations along the *true* branch of the initial condition e.cond are generated, each combination is conjuncted with the corresponding initial condition, e.cond, on line 13. Similarly, those along the *false* branch are conjuncted with its negation, $\neg e$.cond, on line 14.

The function computing the satisfiability combinations, SC( ) in Algorithm 3, works by first partitioning the set of boolean conditions into two, X, and Y, such that X contains only expression trees. The set of possible combinations of the conditions in X is obtained via function TRAV( ), which returns a list of condition-sets, $\{c_1, \cdots, c_n\}$, where each condition-set consists of mutually exclusive conditions. The cartesian product of these condition-sets is then computed, $c_1 \times \cdots \times c_n$, denoted by the generalised cartesian product $\mathsf{X}_{i=1}^{n}\ c_i$ (line 8). The possible combinations relative to the conditions in Y are generated as before. These two lists of combinations are then joined through their cartesian product (line 29).

Example 9. Recall boolean condition $b = \langle b_1, [\langle b_2, [b_3], [\,]\rangle], [\,]\rangle$ from Example 8, where b_1 is $(y \geq 50)$, b_2 is $(y < e_{calc})$, and b_3 is $(x = y+1)$. We illustrate how the set of combinations deducible from expression tree b are obtained. Calling TRAV( ) on expression b generates the set of all possible combinations by traversing its left and right sub-branches recursively (lines 10, 11) to produce two lists of mutually exclusive conditions, $[b_2 \wedge b_3, \neg b_2]$ and $[\,]$. The conditions in $[b_2 \wedge b_3, \neg b_2]$ are conjuncted with b_1 (line 14), resulting in

$c_1 = b_1 \wedge b_2 \wedge b_3$ and $c_2 = b_1 \wedge \neg b_2$. Similarly, $[\,]$ is conjuncted with $\neg b_1$, resulting in $c_3 = \neg b_1$. TRAV( ) then returns $[c_1, c_2, c_3]$. Generating the satisfiability combinations, $\mathsf{sc}(\mathsf{true}, \{c_1, c_2, c_3\})$ in Example 7 decreases the number of possible combinations from 8 to 3. ∎

It is worth noting that the effectiveness of this optimisation depends on both the depth and the number of expression trees, *i.e.*, size of partition X. Evaluating it against the benchmark in Table 1, we obtain the plot labelled *O2* in Fig. 2. The resulting graph confirms that the tool performs better for $M_{cnd}(n)$.

Optimisation Technique 3. Despite the merits afforded by the preceding optimisations, multiple instances where the satisfiability solver must be invoked still prevail. We attempt to circumvent this overhead by batching the satisfiability checks. If all two-pairs are simultaneously satisfiable, the satisfiability of the entire list is checked, otherwise, if one pair is unsatisfiable, then it immediately follows that the list of conditions is unsatisfiable. This results in the mean running times shown by the plot labelled *O3* in Fig. 2 (recall that the values on the y-axis are in logarithmic form). This technique yields a substantial gain as well. For instance, comparing the mean running time against that of the preliminary version for monitor $M_{cnd}(5)$ from Table 1 there is a percentage decrease of 35%. Even better, for monitor $M_{brc}(3)$, there is a percentage decrease of 99.99%. However, the other two optimisation techniques depicted by the plots labelled *O1* and *O2* in Fig. 2 generally give improvements with better orders of magnitude.

Merged Optimisations. Merging all the optimisation techniques, an improvement in the mean running time is immediately noticeable, especially for monitors $M_{brc}(n)$ from Table 1. For instance, comparing the mean running time for $n = 3$ using the preliminary and the final optimised version, there is a percentage decrease of 99.996%. In fact, the plot labelled *Merged* in Fig. 2, acts as a lower bound for all other versions.

6   Conclusion

This paper investigates the implementability aspects of monitor controllability [17]. We discuss the realisability of a prototype that directed us towards the execution bottlenecks of the monitor analysis; we devised a number of solutions to these bottlenecks, implemented them, and studied which ones are the most effective. Our implementation remains closely faithful to the original definition of symbolic controllability, reassuring us of the correctness of our analysis.

Future Work. We plan to build translator tools that generate model descriptions of monitors in terms of the syntax discussed in Sect. 2, as is done in tools such as Soter [14]. This allows us to analyse a wider range of real-world monitor implementations using our tool. We also plan to investigate further optimisations to symbolic controllability that continue to improve the utility of our tool.

Related Work. An alternative approach to analysing for monitor deterministic behaviour is that of converting the monitor description itself into a deterministic one. This approach was investigated extensively in [2,3] for a variety of methods and concludes that any conversion typically incurs a triple exponential blow-up. The closest work to ours is [24], which uses SMT-based model checking to prove invariants about monitors. One illustrative invariant they consider is the analysis of a combined execution of two monitors (akin to our monitor sets) using k-induction (*i.e.*, bounded model checking); by contrast we consider the entire (possibly infinite) run through coinduction. Similar work on verifying dynamic programming monitors for LTL that uses the *Isabelle/HOL* proof assistant [33] is also limited to *finite* traces. *Isabelle/HOL* is used in [35] to extract certifiably-correct monitoring code from specifications expressed in Metric First-Order Temporal Logic (MFOTL). Although MFOTL uses quantifications over event data (similar to ours), the analysis in [35] is limited to formulas that are satisfied by *finitely-many* valuations; our techniques do not have this restriction. Further afield, the work in [31] uses symbolic analysis and SMT solvers to reason about the runtime monitoring of contracts. Their symbolic analysis is however concerned with shifting monitoring computation to the pre-deployment phase, which is different from our aim.

Acknowledgements. The authors thank Antonis Achilleos, Duncan Paul Attard, Stefania Damato, Clément Fauconnet and John Parnis for their help, and the anonymous reviewers for their comments and suggestions for improvement.

References

1. Aceto, L., Achilleos, A., Francalanza, A., Ingólfsdóttir, A.: A framework for parameterized monitorability. In: Baier, C., Dal Lago, U. (eds.) FoSSaCS 2018. LNCS, vol. 10803, pp. 203–220. Springer, Cham (2018). https://doi.org/10.1007/978-3-319-89366-2_11
2. Aceto, L., Achilleos, A., Francalanza, A., Ingólfsdóttir, A., Kjartansson, S.Ö.: On the complexity of determinizing monitors. In: Carayol, A., Nicaud, C. (eds.) CIAA 2017. LNCS, vol. 10329, pp. 1–13. Springer, Cham (2017). https://doi.org/10.1007/978-3-319-60134-2_1
3. Aceto, L., Achilleos, A., Francalanza, A., Ingólfsdóttir, A.,Kjartansson, S.Ö.: Determinizing monitors for HML with recursion. JLAMP **111** (2020).https://doi.org/10.1016/j.jlamp.2019.100515
4. Aceto, L., Achilleos, A., Francalanza, A., Ingólfsdóttir, A., Lehtinen, K.: Adventures in monitorability: from branching to linear time and back again. PACMPL, **3**(POPL) (2019). https://doi.org/10.1145/3290365
5. Aceto, L., Achilleos, A., Francalanza, A., Ingólfsdóttir, A., Lehtinen, K.: An operational guide to monitorability. In: Ölveczky, P.C., Salaün, G. (eds.) SEFM 2019. LNCS, vol. 11724, pp. 433–453. Springer, Cham (2019). https://doi.org/10.1007/978-3-030-30446-1_23
6. Bartocci, E., Falcone, Y., Francalanza, A., Reger, G.: Introduction to runtime verification. In: Bartocci, E., Falcone, Y. (eds.) Lectures on Runtime Verification. LNCS, vol. 10457, pp. 1–33. Springer, Cham (2018). https://doi.org/10.1007/978-3-319-75632-5_1

7. Berkovich, S., Bonakdarpour, B., Fischmeister, S.: Runtime verification with minimal intrusion through parallelism. Form. Methods Syst. Des. **46**(3), 317–348 (2015). https://doi.org/10.1007/s10703-015-0226-3

8. Bocchi, L., Chen, T., Demangeon, R., Honda, K., Yoshida, N.: Monitoring networks through multiparty session types. TCS **669** (2017).https://doi.org/10.1016/j.tcs.2017.02.009

9. Bonakdarpour, B., Fraigniaud, P., Rajsbaum, S., Rosenblueth, D.A., Travers, C.: Decentralized asynchronous crash-resilient runtime verification. In: CONCUR. LIPIcs, vol. 59 (2016). https://doi.org/10.4230/LIPIcs.CONCUR.2016.16

10. Büchi, J.R.: Weak second-order arithmetic and finite automata. Math. Logic Q. **6**(1–6) (1960). https://doi.org/10.1002/malq.19600060105

11. d'Amorim, M., Roşu, G.: Efficient monitoring of ω-languages. In: Etessami, K., Rajamani, S.K. (eds.) CAV 2005. LNCS, vol. 3576, pp. 364–378. Springer, Heidelberg (2005). https://doi.org/10.1007/11513988_36

12. Debois, S., Hildebrandt, T., Slaats, T.: Safety, liveness and run-time refinement for modular process-aware information systems with dynamic sub processes. In: Bjørner, N., de Boer, F. (eds.) FM 2015. LNCS, vol. 9109, pp. 143–160. Springer, Cham (2015). https://doi.org/10.1007/978-3-319-19249-9_10

13. Demangeon, R., Honda, K., Hu, R., Neykova, R., Yoshida, N.: Practical interruptible conversations: distributed dynamic verification with multiparty session types and Python. Form. Methods Syst. Des. **46**(3), 197–225 (2014). https://doi.org/10.1007/s10703-014-0218-8

14. D'Osualdo, E., Kochems, J., Ong, C.-H.L.: Automatic verification of erlang-style concurrency. In: Logozzo, F., Fähndrich, M. (eds.) SAS 2013. LNCS, vol. 7935, pp. 454–476. Springer, Heidelberg (2013). https://doi.org/10.1007/978-3-642-38856-9_24

15. Fraigniaud, P., Rajsbaum, S., Travers, C.: On the number of opinions needed for fault-tolerant run-time monitoring in distributed systems. In: Bonakdarpour, B., Smolka, S.A. (eds.) RV 2014. LNCS, vol. 8734, pp. 92–107. Springer, Cham (2014). https://doi.org/10.1007/978-3-319-11164-3_9

16. Francalanza, A.: A theory of monitors. In: Jacobs, B., Löding, C. (eds.) FoSSaCS 2016. LNCS, vol. 9634, pp. 145–161. Springer, Heidelberg (2016). https://doi.org/10.1007/978-3-662-49630-5_9

17. Francalanza, A.: Consistently-detecting monitors. In: CONCUR. LIPIcs, vol. 85 (2017). https://doi.org/10.4230/LIPIcs.CONCUR.2017.8

18. Francalanza, A., Aceto, L., Ingolfsdottir, A.: Monitorability for the Hennessy–Milner logic with recursion. Form. Methods Syst. Des. **51**(1), 87–116 (2017). https://doi.org/10.1007/s10703-017-0273-z

19. Francalanza, A., Mezzina, C.A., Tuosto, E.: Reversible choreographies via monitoring in erlang. In: Bonomi, S., Rivière, E. (eds.) DAIS 2018. LNCS, vol. 10853, pp. 75–92. Springer, Cham (2018). https://doi.org/10.1007/978-3-319-93767-0_6

20. Francalanza, A., Seychell, A.: Synthesising correct concurrent runtime monitors. Form. Methods Syst. Des. **46**(3), 226–261 (2014). https://doi.org/10.1007/s10703-014-0217-9

21. Gommerstadt, H., Jia, L., Pfenning, F.: Session-typed concurrent contracts. In: Ahmed, A. (ed.) ESOP 2018. LNCS, vol. 10801, pp. 771–798. Springer, Cham (2018). https://doi.org/10.1007/978-3-319-89884-1_27

22. Grigore, R., Distefano, D., Petersen, R.L., Tzevelekos, N.: Runtime verification based on register automata. In: Piterman, N., Smolka, S.A. (eds.) TACAS 2013. LNCS, vol. 7795, pp. 260–276. Springer, Heidelberg (2013). https://doi.org/10.1007/978-3-642-36742-7_19

23. Jia, L., Gommerstadt, H., Pfenning, F.: Monitors and blame assignment for higher-order session types. In: POPL (2016). https://doi.org/10.1145/2837614.2837662
24. Laurent, J., Goodloe, A., Pike, L.: Assuring the guardians. In: Bartocci, E., Majumdar, R. (eds.) RV 2015. LNCS, vol. 9333, pp. 87–101. Springer, Cham (2015). https://doi.org/10.1007/978-3-319-23820-3_6
25. Ligatti, J., Bauer, L., Walker, D.: Edit automata: enforcement mechanisms for run-time security policies. Int. J. Inf. Secur. 4(1), 2–16 (2004). https://doi.org/10.1007/s10207-004-0046-8
26. Luo, Q., Roşu, G.: EnforceMOP: a runtime property enforcement system for multithreaded programs. In: ISSTA. ACM (2013). https://doi.org/10.1145/2483760.2483766
27. Minsky, Y., Madhavapeddy, A., Hickey, J.: Real World OCaml - Functional Programming for the Masses (2013)
28. de Moura, L., Bjørner, N.: Z3: an efficient SMT solver. In: Ramakrishnan, C.R., Rehof, J. (eds.) TACAS 2008. LNCS, vol. 4963, pp. 337–340. Springer, Heidelberg (2008). https://doi.org/10.1007/978-3-540-78800-3_24
29. de Moura, L., Bjørner, N.: Satisfiability modulo theories: introduction and applications. CACM 54(9), 69–77 (2011). https://doi.org/10.1145/1995376.1995394
30. de Moura, L., Passmore, G.O.: The strategy challenge in SMT solving. In: Bonacina, M.P., Stickel, M.E. (eds.) Automated Reasoning and Mathematics. LNCS (LNAI), vol. 7788, pp. 15–44. Springer, Heidelberg (2013). https://doi.org/10.1007/978-3-642-36675-8_2
31. Nguyen, P.C., Tobin-Hochstadt, S., Horn, D.V.: Higher order symbolic execution for contract verification and refutation. JFP 27(2017).https://doi.org/10.1017/S0956796816000216
32. Reger, G., Cruz, H.C., Rydeheard, D.: MARQ: monitoring at runtime with QEA. In: Baier, C., Tinelli, C. (eds.) TACAS 2015. LNCS, vol. 9035, pp. 596–610. Springer, Heidelberg (2015). https://doi.org/10.1007/978-3-662-46681-0_55
33. Rizaldi, A., et al.: Formalising and monitoring traffic rules for autonomous vehicles in Isabelle/HOL. In: Polikarpova, N., Schneider, S. (eds.) IFM 2017. LNCS, vol. 10510, pp. 50–66. Springer, Cham (2017). https://doi.org/10.1007/978-3-319-66845-1_4
34. Schneider, F.B.: Enforceable security policies. ACM Trans. Inf. Syst. Secur. 3(1), 30–50 (2000). https://doi.org/10.1145/353323.353382
35. Schneider, J., Basin, D., Krstić, S., Traytel, D.: A formally verified monitor for metric first-order temporal logic. In: Finkbeiner, B., Mariani, L. (eds.) RV 2019. LNCS, vol. 11757, pp. 310–328. Springer, Cham (2019). https://doi.org/10.1007/978-3-030-32079-9_18
36. Vardi, M.Y., Wolper, P.: Reasoning about infinite computations. Inf. Comput. 115(1), 1–37 (1994). https://doi.org/10.1006/inco.1994.1092

Combining SLiVER with CADP
to Analyze Multi-agent Systems

Luca Di Stefano[1,2(✉)] (iD), Frédéric Lang[3], and Wendelin Serwe[3]

[1] Gran Sasso Science Institute (GSSI), L'Aquila, Italy
luca.distefano@gssi.it
[2] IMT School of Advanced Studies, Lucca, Italy
[3] Univ. Grenoble Alpes, Inria, CNRS,
Grenoble INP (Institute of Engineering Univ. Grenoble Alpes), LIG,
38000 Grenoble, France

Abstract. We present an automated workflow for the analysis of multi-agent systems described in a simple specification language. The procedure is based on a structural encoding of the input system and the property of interest into an LNT program, and relies on the CADP software toolbox to either verify the given property or simulate the encoded system. Counterexamples to properties under verification, as well as simulation traces, are translated into a syntax similar to that of the input language: therefore, no knowledge of CADP is required. The workflow is implemented as a module of the verification tool SLiVER. We present the input specification language, describe the analysis workflow, and show how to invoke SLiVER to verify or simulate two example systems. Then, we provide details on the LNT encoding and the verification procedure.

1 Introduction

Multi-agent systems are composed of standalone computational units, the agents, that interact with each other and with an external environment. Computation within each agent may be a composition of multiple interleaving processes. The agents may also interleave their executions and interact with each other, possibly through asynchronous interaction patterns. As a consequence, multi-agent systems typically feature extremely large state spaces, which makes them hard to design and reason about.

Therefore, there is a need for languages that allow to specify these systems in a concise and intuitive fashion, as well as tools that can certify or increase confidence in the correctness of such specifications. This need is felt far beyond the multi-agent community, as agent-based models are gaining popularity in economics [13,29], social sciences [3,4], and many other research fields. However, the development of tools for such new languages may be a daunting task, as it

Work partially funded by MIUR project PRIN 2017FTXR7S *IT MATTERS* (Methods and Tools for Trustworthy Smart Systems).

© IFIP International Federation for Information Processing 2020
Published by Springer Nature Switzerland AG 2020

S. Bliudze and L. Bocchi (Eds.): COORDINATION 2020, LNCS 12134, pp. 370–385, 2020.
https://doi.org/10.1007/978-3-030-50029-0_23

must keep pace with both the evolution of the language and the state of the art in formal analysis of systems.

An alternative solution is to encode a system specification into an existing language, and reuse mature tools for that language to analyze the encoded system. An example of this approach is given by SLiVER, a prototype tool for the automated verification of multi-agent systems that are described in the simple specification language LAbS [10].[1] The tool is highly modular: it exploits the formal semantics of LAbS to encode the input system into an *emulation program* in a given language, through a structural translation procedure, and verifies the emulation program with off-the-shelf tools for that language to reach a verdict on the correctness of the input system. Previously [10], SLiVER only generated sequential C programs and verified them through bounded model checking [5], by using tools such as 2LS [8], CBMC [9], and ESBMC [14] as back ends.

In this paper, instead, we present a new analysis workflow based on process-algebraic tools. Namely, we choose the process calculus LNT [17] as the target language, and CADP [16] as the back end analysis tool.[2] The workflow is implemented as a SLiVER module and can verify both *invariance* properties (i.e., all reachable states satisfy a given formula) and *inevitable reachability* ones (i.e., all executions lead to a state where the given formula is satisfied), over the full state space of the input system. Furthermore, we can use the same workflow to *simulate* the evolution of the system and return a set of execution traces. This is the first SLiVER module that supports simulation. These two approaches may complement each other: even though simulation can rarely lead to strong conclusions about the correctness of a system [31], it is a valuable design aid and can provide quick feedback even on very large systems.

The rest of the paper is organized as follows. Section 2 briefly describes the specification language LAbS supported by SLiVER through an example, and contains an overview of LNT and CADP. Section 3 introduces the analysis workflow and its implementation as a SLiVER module, and provides usage examples. In Sect. 4 we describe in further detail how the tool generates emulation programs, and in Sect. 5 we explain how it performs property verification through model checking of such programs. Finally, we discuss related work in Sect. 6 and provide concluding remarks in Sect. 7.

2   Background

System Specifications. LAbS [10] is a domain-specific language to describe the *behavior* of agents in a multi-agent system. A behavior is made of basic *actions*, which tell the agent to assign a value to a variable. There are three kinds of assignments: to an internal variable, denoted by $x \leftarrow E$ (where x is a variable identifier and E a value expression); to a shared variable, denoted by $x \leftarrow\!-\!- E$; and to a *stigmergic* variable, denoted by $x \leftsquigarrow E$. Stigmergic variables are a distinguishing feature of LAbS. Their value is bound to a timestamp and stored

---

[1] A Linux release of SLiVER is available at https://git.io/sliver-tool.

[2] CADP is available at http://cadp.inria.fr.

on a decentralized data structure, allowing agents to share their knowledge with the rest of the system by exchanging asynchronous messages [26]. In brief, agents send *propagation* messages after updating a stigmergic variable. A propagation message contains the name of this variable, its new value, and its associated timestamp. An agent that receives a message checks whether its timestamp is newer than the local one for the same variable. If this is the case, the local value and timestamp are overwritten by the received ones; furthermore, the receiver will in turn propagate this new value to others. Otherwise, the message is simply discarded. Agents also send *confirmation* messages after reading the value of a stigmergic variable (i.e., by using it as part of a value expression). The contents of a confirmation message are the same as those of a propagation message. However, a receiver of a confirmation message that stores a value with a higher timestamp will react by propagating its own value. This mechanism facilitates the spread of up-to-date values through the system.

A single action may specify multiple assignments to variables of the same kind: for instance, an assignment to multiple internal variables is denoted by $x_1, \ldots, x_n \leftarrow E_1, \ldots, E_n$. Multiple assignments to variables of different kinds (e.g., an internal one and a shared one) are not allowed. Actions may be composed with traditional process-algebraic operators: sequential composition (;), nondeterministic choice (+), interleaving (|), and calls to other behaviors (possibly including recursive calls). Furthermore, a behavior B may be guarded by a condition g (denoted as $g \rightarrow B$), meaning that the agent may start behaving as B only if g holds.

SLiVER takes as input a system specification in a machine-readable version of LAbS, which is extended with constructs to specify the property of interest and the initial state of the system through (possibly nondeterministic) variable initialization expressions. Furthermore, the input format allows to parameterize systems in one or more external variables.

Figure 1a shows an example specification describing the well-known *dining philosophers* scenario. The system is parameterized in the number _n of agents (line 2), and features an array `forks`, which is shared by all the agents and whose elements are all initialized to 0 (line 3: the set of shared variables within a system is called its *environment*). Each element of the array models a fork: a value 0 means that the fork is available, while a value 1 means that it is currently held by one of the agents. The (recursive) behavior of the agents is specified at lines 10–21. Each agent repeatedly tries to acquire two forks, by checking and updating the elements `id` and `(id+1)%_n` of the array `forks`. The special variable `id` has a different value for each agent, and % denotes the modulo operator. After acquiring both forks, the agent releases them and starts over. Each agent maintains an internal variable `status`, initially set to 0, which describes its current situation (line 8: the set of internal variables of an agent is called its *interface*). When `status` is set to either 0, 1, or 2, it denotes the number of forks currently held by the agent. When `status` is set to 3, it means that the agent has just released one fork and is going to release the other one during its next action. Lastly,

```
1   system {
2     extern = _n
3     environment = fork[_n]: 0
4     spawn = Phil: _n
5   }
6
7   agent Phil {
8     interface = status: 0
9
10    Behavior =
11      fork[id] = 0 ->
12        fork[id] <-- 1;
13        status <- 1;
14        fork[(id+1) % _n] = 0 ->
15          fork[(id+1) % _n] <-- 1;
16          status <- 2;
17          fork[(id+1) % _n] <-- 0;
18          status <- 3;
19          fork[id] <-- 0;
20          status <- 0;
21          Behavior
22  }
23
24  check {
25    NoDeadlock =
26      always exists Phil p,
27        status of p != 1
28  }
```

```
1   system {
2     extern = _n
3     spawn = Node: _n
4   }
5
6   stigmergy Election {
7     link = true
8     leader: _n
9   }
10
11  agent Node {
12    stigmergies = Election
13    Behavior =
14      leader > id ->
15        leader <~ id;
16        Behavior
17  }
18
19  check {
20    LeaderIs0 =
21      eventually forall Node a,
22        leader of a = 0
23  }
```

(a) Dining philosophers.   (b) Leader election.

Fig. 1. Two example systems in LAbS.

invariant NoDeadlock (lines 25–27) states that the system should never reach a state where all agents are waiting for the second fork.

Figure 1b contains a simple *leader election* system, which we will use to illustrate stigmergic variables. Lines 6–9 define a stigmergy Election containing a single variable leader. The link predicate is, in general, a Boolean expression over the state of two agents: an agent may only send a stigmergic message to another one if they satisfy this predicate. In this case, the predicate is simply true, so any two agents may communicate at any time. The stigmergic variable leader is initially set to the value of external parameter _n. The definition of Node agents states that they can access the Election stigmergy (line 12). Their behavior (lines 13–16) simply tells them to repeatedly update the variable leader to their own id as long as it contains a greater value. Finally, property LeaderIs0 (lines 20–22) specifies that the system should eventually reach a state where all Node agents agree on a value of 0 for variable leader.

Supported Properties. SLiVER currently supports invariants and inevitable reachability properties. A property is expressed by a modality keyword (always for invariants, eventually for inevitability properties), followed by a predicate over the state of agents. The predicate may contain existential (exists) or universal (forall) quantifiers. Alternation of existential and universal quantifiers in the same property is not supported yet.

LNT and CADP. LNT is a formally defined language for the description of asynchronous concurrent systems [17]. A system is modeled as a process, generally composed of several, possibly concurrent processes, which may perform communication actions on gates and exchange information by multiway (value-passing) rendezvous, in the style of the Theoretical CSP [19] and LOTOS [20] process algebras. The syntax of LNT is inspired from both imperative languages (assignments, sequential composition, loops) and functional languages (pattern matching, recursion), with many static checks, such as binding, typing, and dataflow analysis ensuring the proper definition of variables and function results.

CADP [16] is a software toolbox for the analysis of asynchronous concurrent systems, in particular systems described in LNT. It contains a wide range of tools for simulation, test generation, verification (model checking and equivalence checking), performance evaluation, etc. We briefly describe two CADP tools named Evaluator and Executor. Evaluator is a model checker that can evaluate properties expressed in the language MCL [25], a temporal logic based on the modal μ-calculus [21] extended with regular action formulas and value-passing constructs.[3] Executor, on the other hand, performs a bounded random exploration of the state space of a given program. Starting from the initial state, it repeatedly enumerates and then randomly chooses one of the transitions going out of the current state, until it has generated a sequence of the requested length. Explorations can be made reproducible by manually providing a seed for the internal pseudo-random number generator.[4]

3   Overview of SLiVER

Workflow. The analysis workflow is shown in Fig. 2. First, a front end parses the input file and substitutes external parameters with the values provided in the command line, to obtain a system specification $\mathbb{S}$ and a property of interest φ. After that, we perform a two-step encoding procedure. The first step is independent of the target language and builds a structural symbolic representation $\mathbb{T}$ of the behaviors of the agents within $\mathbb{S}$. This representation is used in the second step to encode $\mathbb{S}$ and φ into an LNT program $\mathbb{P}$. At this point, a wrapper invokes a specific program from the CADP toolbox, depending on the analysis task requested by the user. In verification mode, the tool invokes Evaluator to model-check $\mathbb{P}$. If a counterexample is found, a translation module converts it to a LAbS-like syntax and shows it to the user; otherwise, the user is notified that φ holds in $\mathbb{S}$. In simulation mode, instead, we call Executor to obtain one or more random traces of $\mathbb{P}$. Each trace is then translated and shown to the user. Simulation traces will also display a message whenever an invariant is violated or an **eventually** property is satisfied.

---

[3] See http://cadp.inria.fr/man/evaluator.html and http://cadp.inria.fr/man/mcl.html.

[4] See http://cadp.inria.fr/man/executor.html.

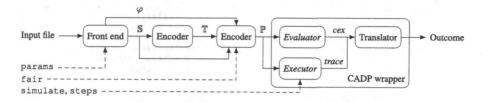

Fig. 2. Workflow of SLiVER with the CADP back end.

Implementation Details and Availability. The front end and encoder are implemented in about 2500 lines of F#, and rely on LNT templates amounting to 450 additional lines. The rest of SLiVER consists of roughly 1000 lines of Python. All Python source code for SLiVER, along with licensing information, is available at https://git.io/sliver-tool. A demonstration video is available at https://drive. google.com/file/d/12kvZXbUiVHRZiXINvOm81D941CYaTeBL.

Usage. This command invokes SLiVER with CADP as the analysis back end:

```
sliver.py <specfile> [params] --backend cadp --fair
          [--simulate <n> --steps <s>]
```

where `specfile` is the name of the input specification file. If the input system is parameterized, the user must provide a sequence `params` in the form `param=val` to assign a value to each parameter. Argument `--backend cadp` is needed to force SLiVER to use the CADP analysis module. As an example, if we invoke SLiVER on the system of Fig. 1a with the command

```
sliver.py philosophers.labs n=5 --backend cadp
```

we obtain the counterexample of Fig. 3a, disproving property `NoDeadlock`.

By default, the tool assumes that there are no constraints on the interleaving of agents. However, in some cases it might be convenient to restrict the analysis to traces where interleaving is restricted according to some policy. Currently, SLiVER allows to enforce round-robin execution of agents through the optional `--fair` flag.

If the optional arguments `--simulate <n> --steps <s>` are omitted, the tool attempts to verify the input property on the given system. Otherwise, it returns `n` execution traces, each one containing at most `s` transitions. As an example, Fig. 3b contains part of a simulation trace for the *leader election* system of Fig. 1b, with three agents[5]. This trace shows the asynchronous nature of stigmergic messages. Notice that all stigmergic assignments within the trace show both the value and its attached timestamp. In the first steps, nodes 0 and 2 update `leader` to their respective ids. Then, node 0 sends a confirmation message for `leader`. It does so because it had to compute the guard `leader >`

---

[5] The full command used to obtain this trace is `sliver.py leader.labs n=3 --backend cadp --simulate 1 --steps 100`.

```
1   <initialization>
2                fork[0] <-- 0
3                fork[1] <-- 0
4                fork[2] <-- 0
5                fork[3] <-- 0
6                fork[4] <-- 0
7   Phil 0: status <- 0
8   Phil 1: status <- 0
9   Phil 2: status <- 0
10  Phil 3: status <- 0
11  Phil 4: status <- 0
12  <end initialization>
13  Phil 0: fork[0] <-- 1
14  Phil 4: fork[4] <-- 1
15  Phil 4: status <- 1
16  Phil 3: fork[3] <-- 1
17  Phil 3: status <- 1
18  Phil 2: fork[2] <-- 1
19  Phil 2: status <- 1
20  Phil 1: fork[1] <-- 1
21  Phil 1: status <- 1
22  Phil 0: status <- 1
23  <property violated>
```

```
1   <initialization>
2   Node 0: leader <~ 3,0
3   Node 1: leader <~ 3,1
4   Node 2: leader <~ 3,2
5   <end initialization>
6   Node 0: leader <~ 0,3
7   Node 2: leader <~ 2,4
8   <Node 0: confirm 'leader'>
9   Node 1: leader <~ 0,3
10  <Node 0: end confirm 'leader'>
11  <Node 1: propagate 'leader'>
12  <Node 1: end propagate 'leader'>
13  <Node 0: propagate 'leader'>
14  <Node 0: end propagate 'leader'>
15  <Node 2: confirm 'leader'>
16  Node 0: leader <~ 2,4
17  Node 1: leader <~ 2,4
18  <Node 2: end confirm 'leader'>
19  <Node 0: propagate 'leader'>
20  <Node 0: end propagate 'leader'>
21  Node 0: leader <~ 0,8
22  <Node 0: propagate 'leader'>
23  Node 1: leader <~ 0,8
24  Node 2: leader <~ 0,8
25  <Node 0: end propagate 'leader'>
26  <property satisfied>
```

(a) A counterexample trace for property NoDeadlock of Listing 1a.

(b) A simulation of the *leader election* system (Listing 1b).

Fig. 3. Example of SLiVER outputs.

id. Node 1 picks up the message and updates its value of `leader` accordingly (lines 8–10). On the other hand, node 2 ignores the message, since its own value of `leader` has a higher timestamp. After a sequence of messaging rounds, during which node 0 sets `leader` to 2 (line 16), the same node updates yet again `leader` to 0 (line 21). Then, a propagation messages from node 0 forces the other nodes to accept that value for `leader`, and property `LeaderIs0` becomes satisfied (line 26).

The tool supports other flags, not shown above. If an invocation is enriched with `--verbose`, SLiVER will print the full output from the back end. The `--debug` flag enables the output of additional messages for diagnostic purposes. Finally, the `--show` flag forces SLiVER to print the emulation program and quit without performing any analysis.

4   Program Generation

In this section we describe how we encode a LAbS system $\mathbb{S}$ and a property φ into an LNT *emulation program* $\mathbb{P}$ by using the intermediate representation $\mathbb{T}$.

We illustrate our description with simplified excerpts of LNT code generated from the tool.[6]

Intermediate Representation. The intermediate representation of an agent behavior B contains one record for each basic action within B. Each record is decorated with an *entry condition* and an *exit condition*. An entry condition is a predicate over a set of symbolic variables, which we call the *program counter* of the agent. Intuitively, the program counter tracks the actions which the agent can perform at any given time. An exit condition, on the other hand, is a (possibly nondeterministic) assignment to the program counter. Exit conditions are constructed so as to preserve the control-flow of B. We use multiple variables for the program counter to compactly represent parallel compositions of LAbS processes within a single behavior.

Program Stub. Once the intermediate representation $\mathbb{T}$ is obtained, the generation of the emulation program $\mathbb{P}$ starts from a stub, containing a type definition Sys that encodes the full state of $\mathbb{S}$. A system is composed of a collection of agents, an environment env, and a global clock time (Listing 1, lines 1–3). The latter is needed to model the semantics of stigmergic variables. Throughout Listing 1, the with "get", "set" construct implements standard functions for accessing and updating elements (for array types) or fields (for record types). The LNT type Agent models a LAbS agent: each agent has an identifier id, a program counter pc, two stores I and L respectively used for local and stigmergic variables, two stores Zprop and Zconf to keep track of pending propagation and confirmation messages, and an init field that tracks whether the agent has been initialized (lines 4–8). Agents, Env, PC, Iface, Lstig, and Pending are all implemented as arrays (lines 10–12).

Their sizes are determined by SLiVER through static analysis of the input specifications. $\#spawn$ is the total number of agents within the system, as specified in the spawn section (e.g., at line 4 in Fig. 1a). $\#\mathcal{I}$, $\#\mathcal{L}$, and $\#\mathcal{E}$ respectively denote the number of internal, stigmergic, and shared variables within the behavioral specifications. $\#\mathcal{P}$ is the number of program counter variables, which is computed during the construction of $\mathbb{T}$. Finally, type ID is a natural number strictly less than the number of agents in the system (line 16). The stub also contains LNT functions and processes that implement the semantics of LAbS, and thus never change (see Sect. 4.1 for an example of such a process). Notice that SLiVER is able to alter this stub according to the features of $\mathbb{S}$. For instance, if the system does not feature any stigmergic variables, the emulation program will not contain Lstig, Pending, nor the functions that implement stigmergic messaging, and the Sys type will not have a time field.

---

[6] The full LNT programs for the *dining philosophers* system (with $n = 5$) and the *leader election* one (with $n = 3$) can be found at https://git.io/philosophers-lnt and https://git.io/leader-lnt, respectively.

```
1   type Sys is
2     sys(agents: Agents, env: Env, time: Nat) with "get", "set"
3   end type
4   type Agent is
5     agent(id: ID, I: Iface, pc:PC,
6       L: Lstig, Zprop:Pending, Zconf: Pending, init: Bool)
7     with "get", "set"
8   end type
9
10  type Agents is array [ 0 .. #spawn−1 ] of Agent with "get", "set" end type
11  type Env is array [ 0 .. #E − 1 ] of Int with "get", "set" end type
12  type PC is array [ 0 .. #P − 1 ] of Nat with "get", "set" end type
13  type Iface is array [ 0 .. #I − 1 ] of Int with "get", "set" end type
14  type Lstig is array [ 0 .. #L − 1 ] of Int with "get", "set" end type
15  type Pending is array [ 0 .. #L − 1 ] of Bool with "get", "set" end type
16  type ID is X:Nat where X < #spawn end type
```

Listing 1: Type definitions.

Emulation Functions. We populate the stub by encoding each record within $\mathbb{T}$ as a separate LNT process. We call these processes *emulation functions*. An emulation function for a given record alters the state of the system according to the semantic rule of its action, and then updates the program counter of the selected agent according to its exit condition. For instance, Listing 2 emulates action

fork[id] = 0 -> fork[id] <-- 1

from the *dining philosophers* example (lines 11–12 of Fig. 1a). The guard is encoded by the only if ... then ... end if construct, while the assignment to fork[id] is represented by the update of the corresponding element of array E (lines 20–21). We refer the reader to Sect. 4.2 for additional examples of emulation functions.

The main section of the program (Listing 3) implements a *scheduler*, that repeatedly selects an agent and calls an emulation function. Agent selection happens by assigning a value to a variable id. If the tool is invoked with the --fair flag, the variable is simply incremented modulo the number of agents; otherwise, a nondeterministic assignment is performed (lines 34–37). Listing 4 shows the LNT process implementing an iteration of the scheduler. Notice that an emulation function may only be called if the program counter of the selected agent satisfies its corresponding entry condition (see e.g. lines 48–50). This prevents spurious executions. At each iteration, instead of calling an emulation function, the scheduler may call one of several system functions implementing other semantic rules of the language, e.g., communication between agents (line 39).

```
17  process action_0_9
18  (in out a:Agent, in out E:Env)
19  is
20    only if (E[a.id]) == 0) then
21      E[a.id] := 1;
22      var p: PC in
23        p := a.pc; p[0] := 8;
24        agent := a.{pc => p}
25      end var
26    end if
27  end process
```

Listing 2: An emulation function.

```
28  process MAIN [m:Any] is
29    -- initialize sys and id
30    loop
31      monitor[m](sys.agents);
32      select
33        step(?!sys, id);
34        -- if-fair flag was used
35        id := (id + 1) mod #spawn
36        -- otherwise
37        id := any ID
38      []
39        -- system functions
40      end select
41    end loop
42  end process
```

Listing 3: Main section of ℙ.

Property Instrumentation. The generated program is then instrumented for the verification of φ. First, we obtain a propositional formula φ' from φ by quantifier elimination. Then, we add a *monitor* process to ℙ, which is executed before each iteration of the scheduler (Line 23 of Listing 3). A stub of the monitor process is shown in Listing 5. If φ is an invariant and φ' is violated, the monitor emits a *false* value over a gate m (line 63). On the other hand, if φ is an inevitable reachability property and φ' holds, a *true* value will be emitted over m (line 68). In any case, when the monitor emits a value, it also terminates ℙ by means of a stop instruction, since there is no need to further explore the evolution of ℙ. This instruction is only added to the program when in verification mode: in simulation mode, the program will keep running until it reaches either a deadlocked state or the user-provided bound.

```
43  process step (in out sys:Sys, i:ID)
44  is
45    ...
46    agent := sys.agents[i]; E := sys.env;
47    select
48      only if (agent.pc[0] == 9) then
49        action_0_9(!?agent, !?E)
50      end if
51    []
52      ...
53    end select;
54    agents[i] := agent;
55    sys := sys.{agents => agents, env => E,
56      time => sys.time + 1}
57  end process
```

Listing 4: A scheduler iteration.

```
58  process monitor [m: Any]
59  (sys:Sys)
60  is
61    -- invariants
62    if not(φ') then
63      m(false);
64      stop
65    end if
66    -- inevitability
67    if φ' then
68      m(true);
69      stop
70    end if
```

Listing 5: Property encoding.

Size of Emulation Programs. The behavior of multiple identical agents is only encoded once, by parameterizing all emulation functions in the *id* of the agent. Therefore, the number of lines of code in ℙ scales well with the number of agents in the input system. To show that, we consider the systems of Fig. 1a–1b, as well as the *boids* and *majority* systems introduced in [10]. For each one, we build a 10-agent and a 100-agent emulation program, and compare their sizes. Table 1 shows the size of the input specification and of the two programs. *Dining philosophers* is the only system where the size of ℙ increases, roughly by a factor of 1.5. This is due to initialization code for array **forks**, whose length depends on the number of agents. The other systems have a fixed-size state, and thus their encodings have the same size, regardless of the number of agents. The growth of the *dining philosophers* program may be avoided by improving the LNT code generator, e.g., by initializing LAbS arrays within a loop. We plan to implement improvements of this kind in a future release of SLiVER.

Table 1. Size of LNT emulation programs with respect to the number n of agents.

Input system		LNT size	
Name	Size	$n = 10$	$n = 100$
Boids	55	530	530
Dining philosophers	28	332	512
Leader election	26	344	344
Majority	57	584	584

```
1  process propagate (in out sys: Sys) is
2    var senderId:ID, key: Nat, sender:Agent, agents:Agents,
3    j, k: Nat, L: Lstig, a:Agent in
4    senderId := any ID where not(empty(sys.agents[senderId].Zprop));
5    agents := sys.agents; sender := agents[senderId];
6    key := any Nat where member(key, sender.Zprop);
7      for j := 0 while j < #spawn by j := j + 1 loop
8      a := agents[j];
9      if (a.id != sender.id) and link(sender, a, key) and
10     (a.L[key].tstamp < sender.L[key].tstamp) then
11       L := a.L;
12       for k := key while k <= TUPLEEND(key) by k := k + 1 loop
13         L[k] := sender.L[k];
14       end loop;
15       agents[j] := a.{
16         L => L, Zprop => insert(key, a.Zprop),
17         Zconf => remove(key, a.Zconf) }
18     end if
19     end loop;
20     agents[senderId] := sender.{Zprop => remove(key, sender.Zprop)};
21     sys := sys.{agents => agents}
22   end var
23 end process
```

Listing 6: Propagation of stigmergic variables in LNT.

4.1 Example: A System Function

Listing 6 contains an LNT process that implements LAbS propagation messages. This process may be called at each iteration of the scheduler of the emulation program (line 39 of Listing 3). A similar function, not shown here, implements confirmation messages.

The process first selects an agent with at least one pending message, i.e., with a non-empty `Zprop` field. The selection happens via a nondeterministic assignment of an agent identifier to a variable `senderId` (line 4). Once a suitable sender is found, an element of `Zprop` is nondeterministically selected and stored in the `key` variable (line 6). This value is the index of the stigmergic variable that will be propagated. The process then finds all potential receivers of the message: sender and receiver must be different agents, and they have to satisfy the `link` predicate for the stigmergic variable that is being sent (line 9).

If an agent satisfies all the above requirements, it can receive the message. Furthermore, if its own timestamp for `key` is less than the one of the sender (line 10), it will update its value and timestamp for `key` with the ones from the message (otherwise, it will just discard it). Notice that multiple stigmergic variables may actually be updated (lines 12–14). This is because LAbS allows the user to put multiple stigmergic variables together in a *tuple*, and its semantics guarantee that variables within a tuple are always propagated together [10]. The loop in the LNT process enforces these guarantees. In lines 15–17, the state of the receiver is updated, and `key` is added to its set of pending propagation messages. Additionally, `key` is removed from its pending *confirmation* messages: intuitively, the agent needs no further confirmation for that variable, since it has just received a newer value. Finally, the value `key` is removed from the pending propagation messages of the sender (line 20).

4.2 Example: Emulation Functions

Listing 7 contains all LNT emulation functions for the *dining philosophers* example. The name of each emulation function is constructed from its entry condition. For instance, function `action_0_2` has entry condition `pc[0] == 2`. A comment within each process reports its corresponding LAbS action. Updates to local and shared variables are implemented through the *attr* and *env* processes, respectively. Notice how the assignments to the program counter at the end of each function preserve the control flow of the input specification.

5   Property Verification

In this section we explain how we determine whether a system $\mathbb{S}$ satisfies a property φ by model-checking the emulation program generated from $(\mathbb{S}, \varphi)$. We use the Evaluator tool to verify the values emitted by the `monitor` process (Listing 5). If φ is an invariant, we check that the program never emits a *false* value over m. This property is encoded as the MCL query

```
[ true * . "M !FALSE"]false
```

```
process action_0_2
(in out a: Agent, in out E: Env) is
−−status <− 0
  attr(!?a, 0, 0);
  var p: PC in
    p := a.pc; p[0] := 9;
    a := a.{pc => p}
  end var
end process

process action_0_3
(in out a: Agent, in out E: Env) is
−−fork[id] <−− 0
  env(!?E, 0 + (a.id), 0);
  var p: PC in
    p := a.pc; p[0] := 2;
    a := a.{pc => p}
  end var
end process

process action_0_4
(in out a: Agent, in out E: Env) is
−−status <− 3
  attr(!?a, 0, 3);
  var p: PC in
    p := a.pc; p[0] := 3;
    a := a.{pc => p}
  end var
end process

process action_0_5
(in out a: Agent, in out E: Env) is
−−fork[id + 1 % 5] <−− 0
  env(!?E, 0 + (a.id + 1) mod 5, 0);
  var p: PC in
    p := a.pc; p[0] := 4;
    a := a.{pc => p}
  end var
end process

process action_0_6
(in out a: Agent, in out E: Env) is
−−status <− 2
```

```
  attr(!?a, 0, 2);
  var p: PC in
    p := a.pc; p[0] := 5;
    a := a.{pc => p}
  end var
end process

process action_0_7
(in out a: Agent, in out E: Env) is
−−(fork[id + 1 % 5]) == (0)−>
−−fork[id + 1 % 5] <−− 1
  only if (E[(a.id + 1) mod 5]) == 0)
    then
    env(!?E, 0 + (a.id + 1) mod 5, 1);
    var p: PC in
      p := a.pc; p[0] := 6;
      a := a.{pc => p}
    end var
  end if
end process

process action_0_8
(in out a: Agent, in out E: Env) is
−−status <− 1
  attr(!?a, 0, 1);
  var p: PC in
    p := a.pc; p[0] := 7;
    a := a.{pc => p}
  end var
end process

process action_0_9
(in out a: Agent, in out E: Env) is
−−(fork[id]) == (0)−>fork[id] <−− 1
  only if (E[a.id]) == 0) then
    env(!?E, 0 + (a.id), 1);
    var p: PC in
      p := a.pc; p[0] := 8;
      a := a.{pc => p}
    end var
  end if
end process
```

Listing 7: Emulation functions for the dining philosophers system.

When φ is an inevitability property, instead, we check that all *fair executions* [27] of $\mathbb{P}$ emit a value of *true* over m at some point. To do that, we use the following MCL query:

$$[(not ("M !TRUE"))*]<true * . "M !TRUE">true$$

To trust that the outcome of the model checker is also a verdict on the original problem (namely, whether φ holds in $\mathbb{S}$), we need to prove that intermediate representation $\mathbb{T}$ preserves all traces of each behavior in the system, and also that the emulation program $\mathbb{P}$ correctly interleaves these traces with calls to system functions, without introducing spurious executions. We cannot include a detailed proof for reasons of space, but this procedure adapts a previous structure-aware encoding [11] (which was tied to explicit-state model checking) to the semantics of LAbS, and makes it independent of the verification technique. Thus, our argument for correctness closely follows the one for that encoding.

6   Related Work

There are several specialized tools for the formal analysis of multi-agent systems. MCMAS [24] verifies multi-agent systems of unbounded size with synchronous communication. Its language lacks value-passing actions, so it is not clear whether their technique could be applied to LAbS. AJPF [7] can perform explicit-state model-checking on a variety of agent-oriented languages. Differently from AJPF, SLiVER is modular with respect to the analysis back end, and may support explicit-state techniques as well as symbolic ones, such as SAT-based bounded model checking [10]. Peregrine [6] can verify and simulate *population protocols*, i.e. collections of identical mobile agents [2]. It can check that a population of unbounded size inevitably ends up satisfying a given predicate over its initial state. SLiVER cannot reason over unbounded-size systems, but it allows for the verification of invariants in addition to inevitable reachability properties.

The concept of verifying domain-specific languages by means of a structural translation into more amenable formalisms is not new. For instance, in [18] hardware specifications are translated into LOTOS and verified with CADP, while [11] shows a translation from an attribute-based process algebra [1] to UMC [30].

7   Conclusion

We have presented an automated analysis workflow for multi-agent systems based on CADP and implemented as part of the SLiVER tool. Through an LNT encoding, the workflow allows to formally verify the input system via model checking, as well as generate random execution traces. The end user does not need to be familiar with either LNT or CADP: knowledge of the input language LAbS is the only requirement.

Future work may improve the presented workflow at several levels. We currently represent the whole system as a *sequential* LNT program: one might instead represent agents as parallel processes and apply compositional verification [15,22,23] to improve model checking performance. We could verify much more expressive properties than the current ones, by devising a translation into MCL queries with data variables [25] to be passed to the model checker. This would require an extension of the property language currently understood by the tool, as well as a correct encoding of this (state-based) language into MCL, which is action-based [12]. Finally, we could use the new trace generation capability to implement simulation-based analysis techniques, such as statistical model checking [28].

References

1. Abd Alrahman, Y., De Nicola, R., Loreti, M.: A calculus for collective-adaptive systems and its behavioural theory. Inf. Comput. **268** (2019). https://doi.org/10.1016/j.ic.2019.104457

2. Aspnes, J., Ruppert, E.: An introduction to population protocols. In: Garbinato, B., Miranda, H., Rodrigues, L. (eds.) Middleware for Network Eccentric and Mobile Applications, pp. 97–120. Springer, Heidelberg (2009). https://doi.org/10.1007/978-3-540-89707-1_5

3. Axtell, R.L., et al.: Population growth and collapse in a multiagent model of the Kayenta Anasazi in Long House Valley. Proc. Natl. Acad. Sci. 99(suppl 3), 7275–7279 (2002). https://doi.org/10.1073/pnas.092080799

4. Baeza, A., Janssen, M.A.: Modeling the decline of labor-sharing in the semi-desert region of Chile. Reg. Environ. Change 18(4), 1161–1172 (2017). https://doi.org/10.1007/s10113-017-1243-0

5. Biere, A., Cimatti, A., Clarke, E.M., Zhu, Y.: Symbolic model checking without BDDs. In: Cleaveland, W.R. (ed.) 5th International Conference on Tools and Algorithms for Construction and Analysis of Systems (TACAS). LNCS, vol. 1579, pp. 193–207. Springer, Heidelberg (1999). https://doi.org/10.1007/3-540-49059-0_14

6. Blondin, M., Esparza, J., Jaax, S.: PEREGRINE: a tool for the analysis of population protocols. In: Chockler, H., Weissenbacher, G. (eds.) CAV 2018. LNCS, vol. 10981, pp. 604–611. Springer, Cham (2018). https://doi.org/10.1007/978-3-319-96145-3_34

7. Bordini, R.H., Dennis, L.A., Farwer, B., Fisher, M.: Automated verification of multi-agent programs. In: 23rd International Conference on Automated Software Engineering (ASE), pp. 69–78. IEEE (2008). https://doi.org/10.1109/ASE.2008.17

8. Chen, H.Y., David, C., Kroening, D., Schrammel, P., Wachter, B.: Synthesising interprocedural bit-precise termination proofs. In: 30th International Conference on Automated Software Engineering (ASE), pp. 53–64. IEEE (2015). https://doi.org/10.1109/ASE.2015.10

9. Clarke, E., Kroening, D., Lerda, F.: A tool for checking ANSI-C programs. In: Jensen, K., Podelski, A. (eds.) TACAS 2004. LNCS, vol. 2988, pp. 168–176. Springer, Heidelberg (2004). https://doi.org/10.1007/978-3-540-24730-2_15

10. De Nicola, R., Di Stefano, L., Inverso, O.: Multi-agent systems with virtual stigmergy. Sci. Comput. Program. 187 (2020). https://doi.org/10.1016/j.scico.2019.102345

11. De Nicola, R., Duong, T., Inverso, O., Mazzanti, F.: Verifying properties of systems relying on attribute-based communication. In: Katoen, J.-P., Langerak, R., Rensink, A. (eds.) ModelEd, TestEd, TrustEd. LNCS, vol. 10500, pp. 169–190. Springer, Cham (2017). https://doi.org/10.1007/978-3-319-68270-9_9

12. De Nicola, R., Vaandrager, F.: Action versus state based logics for transition systems. In: Guessarian, I. (ed.) LITP 1990. LNCS, vol. 469, pp. 407–419. Springer, Heidelberg (1990). https://doi.org/10.1007/3-540-53479-2_17

13. Farmer, J.D., Foley, D.: The economy needs agent-based modelling. Nature 460(7256), 685–686 (2009). https://doi.org/10.1038/460685a

14. Gadelha, M.Y.R., Monteiro, F.R., Morse, J., Cordeiro, L.C., Fischer, B., Nicole, D.A.: ESBMC 5.0: an industrial-strength C model checker. In: 33rd International Conference on Automated Software Engineering (ASE), pp. 888–891. ACM (2018). https://doi.org/10.1145/3238147.3240481

15. Garavel, H., Lang, F., Mateescu, R.: Compositional verification of asynchronous concurrent systems using CADP. Acta Informatica 52(4–5), 337–392 (2015). https://doi.org/10.1007/s00236-015-0226-1

16. Garavel, H., Lang, F., Mateescu, R., Serwe, W.: CADP 2011: a toolbox for the construction and analysis of distributed processes. Softw. Tools Technol. Transf. 15(2), 89–107 (2013). https://doi.org/10.1007/s10009-012-0244-z

17. Garavel, H., Lang, F., Serwe, W.: From LOTOS to LNT. In: Katoen, J.-P., Langerak, R., Rensink, A. (eds.) ModelEd, TestEd, TrustEd. LNCS, vol. 10500, pp. 3–26. Springer, Cham (2017). https://doi.org/10.1007/978-3-319-68270-9_1
18. Garavel, H., Salaün, G., Serwe, W.: On the semantics of communicating hardware processes and their translation into LOTOS for the verification of asynchronous circuits with CADP. Sci. Comput. Program. **74**(3), 100–127 (2009). https://doi.org/10.1016/j.scico.2008.09.011
19. Hoare, C.A.R.: Communicating Sequential Processes. Prentice-Hall, Upper Saddle River (1985)
20. ISO/IEC: LOTOS – A formal description technique based on the temporal ordering of observational behaviour. International Standard 8807 (1989)
21. Kozen, D.: Results on the propositional μ-Calculus. Theoret. Comput. Sci. **27**, 333–354 (1983). https://doi.org/10.1016/0304-3975(82)90125-6
22. Lang, F., Mateescu, R., Mazzanti, F.: Compositional verification of concurrent systems by combining bisimulations. In: ter Beek, M.H., McIver, A., Oliveira, J.N. (eds.) FM 2019. LNCS, vol. 11800, pp. 196–213. Springer, Cham (2019). https://doi.org/10.1007/978-3-030-30942-8_13
23. Lang, F., Mateescu, R., Mazzanti, F.: Sharp congruences adequate with temporal logics combining weak and strong modalities. TACAS 2020. LNCS, vol. 12079, pp. 57–76. Springer, Cham (2020). https://doi.org/10.1007/978-3-030-45237-7_4
24. Lomuscio, A., Qu, H., Raimondi, F.: MCMAS: an open-source model checker for the verification of multi-agent systems. Int. J. Softw. Tools Technol. Transf. **19**(1), 9–30 (2015). https://doi.org/10.1007/s10009-015-0378-x
25. Mateescu, R., Thivolle, D.: A model checking language for concurrent value-passing systems. In: Cuellar, J., Maibaum, T., Sere, K. (eds.) FM 2008. LNCS, vol. 5014, pp. 148–164. Springer, Heidelberg (2008). https://doi.org/10.1007/978-3-540-68237-0_12
26. Pinciroli, C., Lee-Brown, A., Beltrame, G.: A tuple space for data sharing in robot swarms. In: 9th International Conference on Bio-inspired Information and Communications Technologies (BICT), pp. 287–294. ICST/ACM (2015). https://doi.org/10.4108/eai.3-12-2015.2262503
27. Queille, J.P., Sifakis, J.: Fairness and related properties in transition systems - a temporal logic to deal with fairness. Acta Informatica **19**, 195–220 (1983). https://doi.org/10.1007/BF00265555
28. Sen, K., Viswanathan, M., Agha, G.: Statistical model checking of black-box probabilistic systems. In: Alur, R., Peled, D.A. (eds.) CAV 2004. LNCS, vol. 3114, pp. 202–215. Springer, Heidelberg (2004). https://doi.org/10.1007/978-3-540-27813-9_16
29. Stiglitz, J.E., Gallegati, M.: Heterogeneous interacting agent models for understanding monetary economies. Eastern Econ. J. **37**(1), 6–12 (2011). https://doi.org/10.1057/eej.2010.33
30. ter Beek, M.H., Fantechi, A., Gnesi, S., Mazzanti, F.: A state/event-based model-checking approach for the analysis of abstract system properties. Sci. Comput. Program. **76**(2), 119–135 (2011). https://doi.org/10.1016/j.scico.2010.07.002
31. Winikoff, M.: Assurance of agent systems: what role should formal verification play? In: Dastani, M., Hindriks, K., Meyer, J.J. (eds.) Specification and Verification of Multi-Agent Systems, pp. 353–383. Springer, Heidelberg (2010). https://doi.org/10.1007/978-1-4419-6984-2_12

Formal Modeling and Analysis of Medical Systems

Mahsa Zarneshan[1], Fatemeh Ghassemi[1(✉)], and Marjan Sirjani[2]

[1] School of Electrical and Computer Engineering, University of Tehran, Tehran, Iran
{m.zarneshan,fghassemi}@ut.ac.ir
[2] School of Innovation, Design and Engineering,
Mälardalen University, Västerås, Sweden
marjan.sirjani@mdh.se

Abstract. Medical systems are composed of medical devices and apps which are developed independently by different vendors. A set of communication patterns, based on asynchronous message-passing, has been proposed to loosely integrate medical devices and apps. These patterns guarantee the point-to-point quality of communication service (QoS) by local inspection of messages at its constituent components. These local mechanisms inspect the property of messages to enforce a set of parametrized local QoS properties. Adjusting these parameters to achieve the required point-to-point QoS is non-trivial and depends on the involved components and the underlying network. We use Timed Rebeca, an actor-based formal modeling language, to model such systems and asses their QoS properties by model checking. We model the components of communication patterns as distinct actors. A composite medical system using several instances of patterns is subject to state-space explosion. We propose a reduction technique preserving QoS properties. We prove that our technique is sound and show the applicability of our approach in reducing the state space by modeling a clinical scenario made of several instances of patterns.

Keywords: Communication patterns · Actor · Message passing · Reduction

1 Introduction

Medical systems are composed of medical devices and apps which are developed independently by different vendors. The ASTM F2761 standard [4] proposes an architecture for integrated clinical environments (ICE) that enable a component-based approach to medical systems. The AAMI-UL JC 2800 standards completes F2671 by defining safety/security requirements for both the ICE architecture and its development process. A set of communication requirements that enables dynamic composition of devices and apps has been identified [16]. As a solution, a set of communication patterns has been proposed in [9] that can serve as the

© IFIP International Federation for Information Processing 2020
Published by Springer Nature Switzerland AG 2020
S. Bliudze and L. Bocchi (Eds.): COORDINATION 2020, LNCS 12134, pp. 386–402, 2020.
https://doi.org/10.1007/978-3-030-50029-0_24

schema to describe the communication needs of devices/apps. These communication patterns, based on asynchronous message-passing, facilitate development and forensic analysis of clinical scenarios. The use of message passing as the basic communication model is quite common in Internet of Things applications. While the individual components can be very different and operate independently, their interactions typically expose and deliver important emergent properties [2].

These communication patterns consist of a set of components which are responsible to check a set of quality of service (QoS) properties locally. The combination of these quality of service properties should guarantee point-to-point communication requirements. These local QoS properties are parametrized by a set of thresholds on timing behavior of messages like the interval time between consequent messages, the lifetime of messages, etc. A medical system may use several instances of such patterns among its constituent devices and apps. Adjusting these parameters is non-trivial and depends not only to the architecture of the system but also the underlying network. Communication failures in medical systems may result in loss of life. For example, the X-ray machine should stop after two seconds, otherwise it causes harmful prolonged exposure. We can exploit formal methods to verify that the configuration of parameters results the point-to-point communication requirements of medical systems at design time. We use the actor-based formal modeling language of Rebeca [11,15] to verify medical systems. Actor model is a computational model for event-based distributed systems in which actors communicate by asynchronous message-passing. The computation model of Rebeca helps to model the communication patterns with minimal effort and mistake. We exploit the timed extension of Rebeca to address local QoS properties defined in terms of the timing behavior of messages. Timed Rebeca [10,13] is supported by the Afra tool which efficiently verifies timed properties by model checking. Timed Rebeca supports inheritance among actors which facilitates modeling of communication patterns that their components communicate with the shared network entity.

In this paper we model and analyze communication patterns in Timed Rebeca using the implementation architecture proposed for the communication patterns [9]. The components of patterns are modeled by distinct actors. Since the timing behavior network have effect on satisfying QoS properties of pattern, we also model network as a separate entity from actors. As the number of devices increases in a medical systems, the resulting semantic model may explode which prohibits application of the model checking technique. To tackle the problem, we propose a partial reduction technique for merging states such that the QoS properties of communication patterns are preserved. We prove the correctness of our reduction. We have implemented the reduction technique in a tool in Java which automatically reduces the semantic model generated by Afra. We illustrate the applicability of our reduction technique through a case study on a clinical scenario made of several instances of patterns. Our experimental result shows that our reduction technique can minimize the number of states almost to 30%.

2   Preliminaries

As we model communication patterns by Rebeca, first we provide an outline of patterns and then explain timed Rebeca.

2.1   Communication Patterns

Devices and apps involved in a communication pattern are known as components that communicate with each other via a *communication substrate*, e.g., networking system calls or a middleware. Each pattern is composed of a set of roles accomplished by components. We remark that a component may participate in several patterns with different roles simultaneously. Patterns are parametrized by a set of local QoS properties that their violation can lead to a failure. In addition, each pattern has a point-to-point QoS requirement that should be guaranteed by communication substrate. There are four communication patterns:

- **Publisher-Subscriber:** a publisher role broadcasts data about a topic and every devices/apps that need it can subscribe to data. Publisher does not wait for any acknowledge or response from subscribers.
- **Requester-Responder:** a requester role requests data from a specific responder and waits for data from the responder.
- **Sender-Receiver:** a sender role sends data to a specific receiver and waits until either data is accepted or rejected.
- **Initiator-Executor:** an initiator role requests a specific executor to perform an action and waits for action completion or its failure.

As the communication patterns of Sender-Receiver and Initiator-Executor patterns resemble the Requester-Responder pattern, we only focus on Publisher-Subscriber and Requester-Responder patterns in this paper.

2.1.1   Publisher-Subscriber

In this pattern, the component with the publisher role sends a *publish* message to those components that have subscribed previously. This pattern is parameterized with the following local QoS properties:

- MinimumSeparation (N_{pub}): if the interval between two consecutive *publish* messages from the publisher is less than N_{pub}, then the second one is dropped by announcing a *fast Publication* failure.
- MaximumLatency (L_{pub}): if the communication substrate fails to accept *publish* message within L_{pub} time units, it informs the publisher of *timeout*.
- MinimumRemainingLifeTime (R_{pub}): if the data arrive at the subscriber late, i.e., after R_{pub} time units since publication, the subscriber is notified by a *stale data* failure.
- MinimumSeparation (N_{sub}): if the interval between arrival of two consecutive messages at the subscriber is less than N_{sub}, then the second one is dropped.

- MaximumSeparation (X_{sub}): if the interval between arrival of two consecutive messages at the subscriber is greater than X_{sub} then the subscriber is notified by a *slow publication* failure.
- MaximumLatency (L_{sub}): if the subscriber fails to consume a message within L_{sub} time units, then it is notified by a *slow consumption* failure.
- MinimumRemainingLifeTime (R_{sub}): if the remaining life time of the *publish* message is less than R_{sub}, then the subscriber is notified by a *stale data* failure.

Each communication pattern owns a point-to-point *QoS Requirement* that should be guaranteed by the communication substrate. In this pattern the requirement is "the data to be delivered with lifetime of at least R_{sub}, communication substrate should ensure maximum message delivery latency (Lm) does not exceed $R_{pub} - R_{sub} - L_{pub} \geq L_m$".

For example assume a pulse oximeter device which publishes pulse rate data of the patient. A patient monitor application can subscribe to this data to get the patients pulse rate. In other words, the application communicates with the device using the Publisher-Subscriber pattern.

2.1.2 Requester-Responder

In this pattern, the component with the role requester, sends a *request* message to the component with the role responder. The responder should replies within a time limit as specified by its local QoS properties. This pattern is parameterized with the following local QoS properties:

- MinimumSeparation (N_{req}): if interval between two consecutive *request* messages is less than N_{req}, then the second one is dropped with a *fast Request* failure.
- MaximumLatency (L_{req}): if the *response* message does not arrive within L_{req} time units, then the request is ended by a *timeout* failure.
- MinimumRemainingLifeTime (R_{req}): if the *response* message arrives at the requester with a remaining lifetime less than R_{req}, then the requester is notified by a *stale data* failure.
- MinimumSeparation (N_{res}): if the duration between the arrival of two consecutive *request* messages is less than N_{res}, then the request is dropped while announcing a *excess load* failure.
- MaximumLatency (L_{res}): if the *response* message is not provided within the L_{res} time units, the request is ended by a *timeout* failure.
- MinimumRemainingLifeTime (R_{res}): if the *request* message with the promised minimum remaining lifetime cannot be responded by the responder, then request is ended by a *data unavailable* failure.

The point-to-point *QoS Requirement* defined for this pattern concerns the delivery of response with lifetime of at least R_{req}. So the communication substrate should ensure that "the sum of maximum latencies to deliver the request to the responder (L_m) and the resulting response to the requester (L'_m) does not exceed $L_{req} + R_{req} - L_{res} - R_{req} \geq L_m + L'_m$".

For example assume a patient monitor application that communicates with a blood pressure (BP) monitor using the Requester-Responder pattern. The application requests blood pressure measurement from the BP which periodically measures the blood pressure of the patient.

2.2   Timed Rebeca and Actor Model

Actor model [1,3] is a concurrent model based on computational objects, called actors, that communicate asynchronously with each other. Actors are encapsulated modules with no shared variables. Each actor has a unique address and mailbox. Messages sent to an actor are stored in its mailbox. Each actor is defined through a set of message handlers to specify the actor behavior upon processing of each message.

Rebeca [11,15] is an actor model language with a Java-like syntax which aims to bridge the gap between formal verification techniques and the real-world software engineering of concurrent and distributed applications. Rebeca is supported by a robust model checking tool, named Afra[1]. Timed Rebeca is an extension of Rebeca for modeling and verification of concurrent and distributed systems with timing constraints. As all QoS properties in communication patterns are based on time, we use Timed Rebeca for modeling and formal analysis of patterns by Afra. Hereafter, we use Rebeca as short for Timed Rebeca in the paper.

The syntax of Timed Rebeca [10,13] is given in Fig. 1. Each Rebeca model contains *reactive classes* definition and *main* part. Main part contains instances of reactive classes. These instances are actors that are called rebecs. Reactive classes have three parts: *known rebecs*, *state variables* and *message servers*. Each rebec can communicate with its known rebecs or itself. Local state of a rebec is indicated by its state variables and received messages which are in the rebec's mailbox. Rebecs are reactive, there is no explicit receive and the messages trigger the execution of the message servers when they are taken from the message mailbox. The timing features are *computation time*, *message delivery time* and *message expiration*. These three primitives are supported by the statements *delay*, *after* and *deadline*.

2.3   State-Space of Rebeca Models

The state-space of Rebeca models are generated as a state transition system to show the behavior in a formal way. The global states change due to the handling of messages by rebecs. Each rebec takes a message from its mailbox, modeled by a bag, and execute its message server, and hence, the value of state variables may update. Due to the encapsulation of rebec variables, intermediate values of each rebec during execution of message servers are not observable to other rebecs. Thus, semantics of Rebeca models are defined coarsely; each state transition shows the effect of handling of a message by a rebec. Floating Time Transition System (FTTS), a variation of state transition systems introduced in [7], gives a

---

[1] http://www.rebeca-lang.org/alltools/Afra.

$$
\begin{aligned}
\text{Model} &::= \langle Class \rangle^{+} \text{ Main} \\
\text{Main} &::= \textsf{main } \{\text{InstanceDcl}^{*}\} \\
\text{InstanceDcl} &::= \textsf{C } \textsf{r } (\langle \textsf{r} \rangle^{*}) : (\langle \textsf{c} \rangle^{*}) \\
\text{Class} &::= \textsf{reactiveclass } \textsf{C } \{\textsf{KnownRebecs Vars MsgSrv}^{*}\} \\
\text{KnowRebecs} &::= \textsf{knownrebecs } \{\text{VarDcl}\} \\
\text{Vars} &::= \textsf{statevars } \{\text{VarDcl}\} \\
\text{VarDcl} &::= \langle \text{T } \text{v} \rangle^{*}; \\
\text{MesgSrv} &::= \textsf{msgsrv } \textsf{m } (\text{VarDcl}) \{\text{Stmt}^{*}\} \\
\text{Stmt} &::= \textsf{v} = e; \mid \text{Call}; \mid \textsf{if}(e) \text{ MSt } [\textsf{else } \text{MSt}] \mid \textsf{delay}(\textsf{t}); \\
\text{Call} &::= \textsf{r.m}(\langle e \rangle^{*})[\textsf{deadline } e][\textsf{after } e] \\
\text{MSt} &::= \{\text{Stmt}^{*}\} \mid \text{Stmt}
\end{aligned}
$$

Fig. 1. Abstract syntax of Timed Rebeca. Angle brackets $\langle \rangle$ denotes meta parenthesis, superscripts $+$ and $*$ respectively are used for repetition of one or more and repetition of zero or more times. Combination of $\langle \rangle$ with repetition is used for comma separated list. Brackets $[\,]$ are used for optional syntax. Identifiers C, T, m, v, c, e, and r respectively denote class, type, method name, variable, constant, expressions, and rebec name, respectively.

natural event-based semantics for timed actors, providing a significant amount of reduction in the state space. For efficient analysis of Rebeca models, different approaches are proposed for generating the semantic models [5,12,14]. FTTS uses isolation of actors, i.e., no coupling among the actors [14]. The states of FTTS are defined by the local states of rebecs. The local states of rebecs are defined by the triple $\langle v, q, t \rangle$, where v defines the value of state variables, q the message bag, and t the local time. In each state, different actors do not necessarily have the same local time and the time *floats* across the actors in the state space [7]. Note that at the level of Timed Rebeca models, actors have synchronized local clocks (as opposed to the semantic level) which gives the modeler a notion of global time.

Let *ID* denote the set of Rebeca identifiers, and S the set of global states. Each global state $s \in S$ is a mapping from the Rebeca identifier to its local state. Assume *Var*, *Value*, and *Msg* be the set of variables, values, and messages, respectively. We use the notation $bag(Msg)$ to represent the bag of messages and $\mathbb{N}$ to denote the local time of actors. So, the set of global states is defined by mapping each rebec identifier to its local state, $S = ID \rightarrow (Var \rightarrow Value) \times bag(Msg) \times \mathbb{N}$. Each message $m \in Msg$ constituted of three parts, namely $m = (msgsig, arrival, deadline)$, where *msgsig* is the message content, *arrival* is the arrival time of the message, and *deadline* is the deadline of the message. We use $msgsig(m)$, $arrival(m)$, and $deadline(m)$ to indicate the corresponding part. The message content constitutes of the name of message and its parameter values. We use $Type(msgsig(m))$ to show the name of the message content. Let *statevars*$(s(x))$, *bag*$(s(x))$, and *now*$(s(x))$ denote the state variable valuation, message bag, and the local time of the rebec with the identifier $x \in ID$. The reduction introduced by FTTS merges the states s and s' that the local time of their rebecs has a fixed delay with each other, called shift equivalent.

Definition 1 (shift-equivalent). *Two states s and s' are called* shift equivalent, *denoted by $s \simeq_\delta s'$, if for all the rebecs with identifier $x \in ID$ there exists δ such that:*

1. *Condition on state variables: statevars$(s(x))$ = statevars$(s'(x))$,*
2. *Condition on local time: now$(s(x))$ = now$(s'(x))$ + δ,*
3. *Condition on bag content:*

$$\forall m \in bag(s(x)) \Leftrightarrow (msgsig(m), arrival(m) + \delta, deadline(m) + \delta) \in bag(s'(x)).$$

Intuitively, the local time of rebecs in s' has the fixed shift value δ with respect to the local time of rebecs in s. In other words, it can be considered s' as a state occurred in future of s, but with the same behavior. We remark that the first and third conditions force the state variables of rebecs and the message contents (including message parameters) of corresponding rebecs in the two states be equivalent [6].

The *bounded floating-time transition systems* (BFTTS) $\langle S_f, s_{0_f}, \hookrightarrow \rangle$ of a rebeca model is achieved by merging those states of its FTTS $\langle S, s_0, \to \rangle$ that are shift equivalent. Formally speaking, if $(s, m, s') \in \hookrightarrow$ in BFTTS as a consequence of processing the message m, then there exists $s'' \in S$ such that $(s, m, s'') \in \to$ and $s' \simeq_\delta s''$ for some δ. BFTTS preserve the timed properties of FTTS specified by weak modal μ-calculus where the actions are taking messages from the bag [7].

3   Modeling Patterns in Rebeca

We use the architecture proposed in [9] for implementing communication patterns. We will explain the main components of publisher-subscriber pattern as the others are almost the same. This architecture specifies two interfaces between its constituent roles, e.g., publisher and subscriber, and the communication substrate. These interfaces encapsulate details of patterns from low-level details of various substrate layers. As illustrated in Fig. 2, the client and service are devices/apps which aim to communicate with each other. The components *PublisherRequester* and *SubscriberInvoker* are interfaces that check the local QoS properties related to the client or service side, respectively, and the *communication substrate* component is responsible for transmitting data.

We model each component of this architecture as a distinct actor or rebec in Rebeca. We explain the model of the Publisher-Subscriber pattern in detail. Other patterns are modeled with the same discussion.

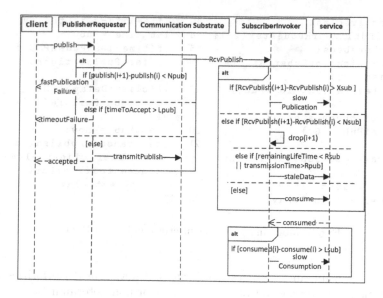

Fig. 2. Publisher-subscriber pattern sequence diagram

Figure 3 illustrates *PublisherRequester* reactive class, which is an interface between the client (device/app) and the communication substrate. As we see in lines 3 and 4, it has two known rebecs. The instances of this reactive class can send messages to them. We define the state variable *lastPub* in line 5 for saving the time of last publication message. We use this time for computing the interval between two consecutive messages. This rebec has a message server named *publish*. We pass *Lm* and *life* parameters through all message servers in the model to compute the delivery time and remaining lifetime of each message. To model the communication delay between the interface and the communication substrate, we define the variable *clientDelay* (in line 11) with non-deterministic values. The parameters of *Lm* and *life* are updated in lines 12 and 13 regarding to *clientDelay*. This interface is responsible for checking N_{pub} and L_{pub} properties as specified in lines 15–23. To check N_{pub}, the interval between two consecutive *publish* messages should be computed by subtracting the current local time of rebec from *lastPub*. The reserved word *now* represents the local time of the rebec. As this reserved word can not be used directly in expressions, we first assign it to the local variable *time* in line 14. If both properties are satisfied, it sends a *transmitPublish* message to the communication substrate and an *accepted* message to the client. These messages are delivered to their respective receivers with a non-deterministic delay, modeled by *clientDelay*, using the statement *after*. It means that the message is delivered to the client after passing this time. In case that the N_{pub} property is violated, it sends a message *fastPublicationFailure* to the client. If the L_{pub} property is violated, it sends a message *timeOutFailure*.

Communication substrate abstracts a network like Ethernet, wireless networks, Controller Area Network (CAN) bus [8] by specifying the effects of the

```
1   reactiveclass                      13    life=life-clientDelay;
        PublisherRequester(20){       14    int time = now;
2   knownrebecs{                       15    if(time-lastPub<NPUB){
3   CommunicationSubstrate cs;         16      c.fastPublicationFailure()
4   Client c;}                                  ;}
5   statevars {int lastPub;}           17    if(clientDelay>LPUB){
6                                      18      c.timeOutFailure();}
7   PublishRequester(){                19    else{
8     lastPub = 0;}                    20      lastPub = now;
9                                      21      cs.transmitPublish(Lm,life)
10  msgsrv publish(int Lm,int                     after(clientDelay);
        life){                         22      c.accepted() after(
11    int clientDelay=?(1,2);                     clientDelay);
12    Lm=Lm+clientDelay;               23  }}}
```

Fig. 3. Modeling publisher interface in Timed Rebeca

network on transmitting messages. To this aim, it may consider priorities among received messages to transmit or assign specific or non-deterministic latency for sending messages. A specification of *communication substrate* reactive class is shown in Fig. 4. It handles *transmitPublish* messages by sending a *RcvPublish* message to its known rebec, a rebec of *SubscriberInvoker* class in line 11. It considers a non-deterministic communication delay for each message, modeled by the local variable *netDelay* in line 8. We remark that this rebec updates the parameters *Lm* and *lifetime* based on *netDelay* before sending *RcvPublish* in lines 9 and 10.

```
1   reactiveclass                      7    msgsrv transmitPublish(int
2       CommunicationSubstrate(20)           Lm,int life){
3   {                                   8    int netDelay=?(1,2);
4     knownrebecs{                      9    Lm=Lm+netDelay;
          SubscriberInvoker si;}       10    life=life-netDelay;
5     statevars{}                      11    si.RcvPublish(Lm,life)
6     CommunicationSubstrate(){}              after(netDelay);}}
```

Fig. 4. Modeling communication substrate in Timed Rebeca

The *SubscriberInvoker* reactive class, given in Fig. 5, is an interface between the communication substrate and the service (device/app). It has only one known rebec that is the destination for the messages of its instances. We define a state variable *lastPub* in line 5 to save the time of the last publication message that arrived in this rebec. This reactive class is responsible for checking N_{sub}, X_{sub}, R_{pub}, R_{sub}, and L_{pub} properties (see Subsect. 2.1). Message servers in this rebec are *RcvPublish* and *consume*. It checks N_{sub}, X_{sub}, R_{pub}, and R_{sub} properties in the message server *RcvPublish*. To model the communication delay between the interface and the service, we define the variable *serviceDelay* (in line 11) with non-deterministic values. It computes the interval between two consecutive *RcvPublish* messages in line 13 to inspect N_{sub} in line 14 and X_{sub} in line 16. It checks R_{sub} and R_{pub} properties using *life* and *Lm* parameters in line 19. Any violation of these properties will result in sending a failure message to the service or dropping the message. With satisfying the properties, it saves the local time of the actor in *lastPub* and sends a *consume* message to the service using *after* statement. The message server *consumed* checks L_{sub} property in line 31 and sends a failure to the service.

```
1  reactiveclass                     19  if (life<RSUB||Lm>RPUB){
       SubscriberInvoker(20){        20   s.staleData(Lm)
2  knownrebecs{                      21   after(serviceDelay);
3  Service s;}                       22  }
4                                    23  else{
5  statevars{int lastPub;}           24   lastPub = now;
6                                    25   s.consume(Lm+serviceDelay)
7  SubscribeInvoker(){                        after(serviceDelay);
8  lastPub = 0;}                     26  }
9                                    27  }
10 msgsrv RcvPublish(int Lm,int      28  msgsrv consumed(int Lm){
       life){                        29   int time = now;
11  int serviceDelay=?(1,2);         30   int serviceDelay=?(1,2);
12  int time = now;                  31   if (time-lastPub>LSUB){
13  int interval=time-lastPub;       32    s.slowConsumption(Lm+
14  if (interval<NSUB){                       serviceDelay)
15   self.drop(Lm);}                 33    after(serviceDelay);
16  if (interval>XSUB){              34  }}
17   s.slowPublication(Lm)           35  msgsrv drop(int Lm){...}}
18    after(serviceDelay);}
```

Fig. 5. Modeling subscriber interface in Timed Rebeca

4   State-Space Reduction

A medical system is composed of several devices/apps that communicate with each other by using any of communication patterns. With the aim of verifying the QoS requirements of medical systems at the early stage of development, we use model checking technique by using Rebeca framework. As we explained in Sect. 3, each communication pattern is at least modeled by five rebecs. It is well-known that as the number of rebecs increases in a model, the state space grows exponentially. For a simple medical system composed of two devices that communicate with an app, there exist nine rebecs (as communication substrate in common) in the model. In a more complex system, adding more devices may result in state-space explosion, and model checking cannot be applied. We propose a partial reduction technique at the semantic level FTTS which merges those states with regard to the local QoS properties of communication patterns.

In other words, such states not only satisfy the same local QoS properties but also preserve the same class of timed properties specified by weak modal μ-calculus where the actions are taking messages from the bag [7].

We relax those conditions of shift-equivalent relation that are applied on state variables and the message contents in the bags. We consider those state variables that are used for measuring the interval between two consecutive messages like *lastPub*. Such variables grow as the local time of rebecs proceeds. However, always $now - lastPub$ are used to check local QoS properties like N_{sub}, N_{pub}, and X_{sub} and the value of *lastPub* is not used anymore. Intuitively, two semantic states are shift-equivalent if their instances of *PubliserRequester* have the same value for all state variables except *lastPub*. As the behaviors of such instances depend on $now - lastPub$, the value of their *lastPub* variable can be shift-equivalent similar to their local time (see Sect. 2.3). This idea can be generalized for such variables (measuring interval) in other types of classes.

Assume two states with an instance of *SubscriberInvoker*. This instance has a *RcvPublish* message in its bag. The value of its *life* parameter is used by its message server to check the local QoS property R_{sub}. This variable is not used anymore and hence, the value of this variable has no effect on the future behavior of the rebec. Intuitively, if the value of this parameter in the message in these assumed states leads to the same satisfaction of R_{sub}, these messages can be considered equivalent.

Definition 2 (relaxed shift-equivalent). *Two semantic states s and s', denoted by $s \sim_\delta s'$, are relaxed shift-equivalent if for all the rebecs with identifier $x \in ID$ there exists δ such that:*

1. *Condition on state variables:*

$$\forall v \in Var \setminus \{lastPub, lastReq\} \cdot statevars(s(x))(v) = statevars(s'(x))(v),$$
$$lastPub \in Dom(s(x)) \Rightarrow statevars(s(x))(lastPub) = statevars(s'(x))(lastPub) + \delta,$$
$$lastReq \in Dom(s(x)) \Rightarrow statevars(s(x))(lastReq) = statevars(s'(x))(lastReq) + \delta.$$

2. *Condition on local time:* $now(s(x)) = now(s'(x)) + \delta.$
3. *Condition on bag content:*

$$\forall m \in bag(s(x)) \wedge Type(msgsig(m)) \notin \{RcvPublish, RcvResponse\} \Leftrightarrow$$
$$(msgsig(m), arrival(m) + \delta, deadline(m) + \delta) \in bag(s'(x)),$$
$$\forall (RcvPublish(Lm_1, life_1), t, d) \in bag(s(x)) \Leftrightarrow$$
$$(RcvPublish(Lm_2, life_2), t + \delta, d + \delta) \in bag(s'(x)) \wedge$$
$$Lm_1 = Lm_2 \wedge (life_1 > R_{sub} \Leftrightarrow life_2 > R_{sub}),$$
$$\forall (RcvResponse(Lm_1, life_1), t, d) \in bag(s(x)) \Leftrightarrow$$
$$(RcvResponse(Lm_2, life_2), t + \delta, d + \delta) \in bag(s'(x)) \wedge$$
$$(Lm_1 = Lm_2 \wedge life_1 > R_{res} \Leftrightarrow life_2 > R_{res}).$$

We merge states that are relaxed shift-equivalent. The following theorem shows that the FTTS modulo relaxed shift equivalency preserves the properties of the original one.

Theorem 1. *For the given FTTS* $\langle S, s_0, \rightarrow \rangle$, *assume the states* $s, s' \in S$ *such that* $s \sim_\delta s'$. *If* $(s, m, s^*) \in \rightarrow$, *then there exists* s^{**} *such that* $(s', m, s^{**}) \in \rightarrow$ *and* $s^* \sim_\delta s^{**}$.

Proof. Assume that $(s, m, s^*) \in \rightarrow$ by handling the message m by the rebec i. Regarding the third condition of Definition 2, there is also a message m' such that $Type(msgsig(m')) = Type(msgsig(m))$ in the bag of Rebec i in the state s'. Assume s^{**} is the resulting state as the consequence of handling m' in the state s'. We show that $s^* \sim_\delta s^{**}$. Regarding $Type(msgsig(m))$, three cases can be distinguished:

- $Type(msgsig(m)) \notin \{RcvPublish, RcvResponse\}$: The message m' handled by the rebec i is $(msgsig(m), arrival(m) + \delta, deadline(m) + \delta) \in bag(s'(x))$. The assumption $s \sim_\delta s'$ implies that all the variables except $\{lastPub, lastReq\}$ have the same values while the value of variables $\{lastPub, lastReq\}$ have δ-difference. We remark that all variables except $\{lastPub, lastReq\}$ may be accessed/updated during execution of the message handler. So, all variables except $\{lastPub, lastReq\}$ are updated by the message handler m and m' similarly. As rebec i has only access to its own variables, the variables of other rebecs do not change. Thus the state s^{**} and s^* satisfy the first condition. Furthermore, the local time of rebec i in the both states s^* and s^{**} are progressed by the message handler m and m' similarly and hence, their local timers have still δ-difference. So, the second condition is satisfied. The messages sent to other rebecs during handling m and m' are sent at the same point. As their local timers have δ-difference, the arrival and deadline of sent messages have δ-difference. So, the third condition is also satisfied.
- $Type(msgsig(m)) = RcvPublish$ and $m \equiv (RcvPublish(Lm_1, life_1), t, d)$: By the third condition, the message $m' \equiv (RcvPublish(Lm_2, life_2), t + \delta, d + \delta)$. As $Lm_1 = Lm_2 \wedge (life_1 > R_{sub} \Leftrightarrow life_2 > R_{sub})$ holds, the same statements, as shown in Fig. 5, are executed by the rebec i during handling m and m'. We remark that the value of $interval$ is the same for both as $statevars(s(x))(lastPub) = statevars(s'(x))(lastPub) + \delta$. As no variable is updated, the states s^* and s^{**} satisfy the first condition. As no delay statement is executed, still the second condition holds for s^* and s^{**}. The messages sent by handling m and m' are all parametrized by Lm_1 and Lm_2 which are equal. So, the third condition is also satisfied.
- $Type(msgsig(m)) = RcvResponse$: This case is discussed in the same way of the previous case.

The relaxed shift equivalency preserves the conditions of shift equivalency on all variables except the variables defined for checking local QoS properties, i.e., $\{lastPub, lastReq\}$. Furthermore, it preserves the conditions of shift equivalency on all message content in the bag except for messages of type $\{RcvPublish, RcvResponse\}$. But the relaxed condition of the value of $life$ ensures that the same statements will be executed. Therefore, by Theorem 1 FTTS modulo relaxed shift equivalency not only preserve the local QoS properties of the original one but also preserves the Timed properties defined on events (taking messages from the bag).

5   Case Study

Reduction technique is more applicable when using several patterns and devices in a medical system. For recovering a patient from an operation, he is controlled by a fixed dose of analgesia connected to an infusion pump. In addition, he is hooked up to a pulse oximeter to measure his pulse rate and oxygen saturation (SPO2) and to a capnometer to measure the concentration of carbon dioxide in his respiratory gases (end-tidal co2[ETCO2]) and respiratory rate. A monitoring application is composed of the pulse oximeter, capnometer, and infusion pump as shown in Fig. 6 to control the activation of the infusion pump based on the measurements of the devices. If the application detects any deterioration in the patient's condition, it will deactivate the infusion pump and alert the nurses.

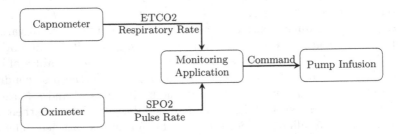

Fig. 6. Communication between entities in the clinical scenario.

Capnometer and oximeter publish data through the publisher-subscriber pattern, and monitoring application detects if data stray outside of the valid range and sends the appropriate command to pump infusion. There are two instances of the publisher-subscriber pattern and one of the requester-responder pattern in the resulting Timed Rebeca model of the application. To avoid modeling some components like communication substrate that is common in the patterns, we use the inheritance concept in Rebeca. We implement a base reactive class for the *communication substrate* of patterns as shown in Fig. 7 named *Base* inspired by the approach of [17].

```
1  reactiveclass Base(20){
2    statevars {int id;}
3    Base find(int _id) {
4      ArrayList<ReactiveClass> allActors = getAllActors();
5      for(int i = 0 ; i < allActors.size(); i++){
6        Base actor = (Base) allActors.get(i);
7        if (actor.id == _id) {return actor;}
8    }}}
```

Fig. 7. Base reactive class

We define the state variable *id* in line 2 to uniquely identify rebecs. This class has a method named find to get the rebec with the given identifier. In this method we define an array of reactive classes and initiate it with all actors specified in the model (in line 4) then we get ids of all actors that are derived from the *Base* (in line 6) actor and search through them for finding the specified one (line 7).

The *communication substrate* reactive class *extends Base* class. As illustrated in Fig. 8, this class has a parameter *id* in its constructor for assigning the *id* variable of the parent class (in line 2). This class has no known rebecs as opposed to the one specified at Fig. 4. Instead, rebecs append their identifier to their messages during their communication with the substrate. The communication substrate uses the *find* method for finding the rebec that wants to send data based on their ids (lines 6 and 11). As the *communication substrate* class is commonly used by the components of publisher-subscriber and requester-responder patterns, it has two message handlers *transmitPublish* and *transmitRequest* to transmit their messages, respectively.

```
1   reactiveclass CommunicationSubstrate extends Base(20){
2       CommunicationSubstrate(int _id){id = _id;}
3       msgsrv trasmitPublish(boolean data,int topic,int Lm,
4           int life,int subscriberId){
5         int csDelay = ?(1, 2);
6         SubscribeInvoker si=(SubscribeInvoker) find(subscriberId
            );
7         si.publish(data,topic,Lm+csDelay,life-csDelay)
8             after(csDelay);}
9       msgsrv transmitRequest(boolean data,int Lm,int
            responderInvokerId){
10        int cs1Delay = ?(1, 2);
11        ResponderInvoker ri=(ResponderInvoker) find(
            responderInvokerId);
12        ri.request(data,Lm + cs1Delay) after(cs1Delay);}
13      msgsrv transmitResponse(boolean data, int Lm, int life,
            int requesterId) {
14        int cs2Delay = ?(1, 2);
15        RequestRequester rr = (RequestRequester) find(
            requesterId);
16        rr.response( data, (Lm + cs2Delay), (life-cs2Delay))
            after(cs2Delay);
17        }
18        . . .
19  }
```

Fig. 8. Modeling communication substrate using inheritance in Rebeca

All interfaces that communicate through *communication substrate* should extend the *Base* class. As two devices (capnometer and oximeter) send data by using the publisher-subscriber pattern, we define two instances of PublisherRequester and SubscriberInvoker interfaces in *main*, as shown in Fig. 9. The instance of CommunicationSubstrate, called *cs*, is used by all the components which send message to Communication Substrate in the patterns.

```
 1  main{
 2     Capnometer c(pr_c):(0);
 3     PublishRequester pr_c(cs):(1, 0, 2);
 4     SubscribeInvoker si_c():(2, 10);
 5     Oximeter o(pr_o):(5);
 6     PublishRequester pr_o(cs):(6, 5, 7);
 7     SubscribeInvoker si_o():(7, 10);
 8     CommunicationSubstrate cs():(12);
 9     MonitoringApp ma(si_c, si_o, rr):(10);
10     RequestRequester rr(cs):(11,10,13);
11     ResponderInvoker ri(cs):(13, 14, 11);
12     Pump p(ri):(14);
13  }
```

Fig. 9. Main part of medical system model in Timed Rebeca

5.1 Experiment Results

We applied our reduction technique on the three cases we have modeled in Timed Rebeca. We developed a code in Java which automatically reduces the resulting FTTSs of these models generated by Afra[2]. We got 23% and 32% reduction in the model of requester-responder and publisher-subscriber patterns, respectively. In the clinical scenario which is a medical system using several patterns as explained in Sect. 5 we have 29% reduction in the state space (Table 1).

Table 1. Reduction in patterns and their composition

Model	No. states before reduction	No. states after reduction	Reduction
Requester-responder	205	157	23%
Publisher-subscriber	235	159	32%
Case study	1058492	753456	29%

6   Conclusion and Future Work

In this paper, we formally modeled the four communication patterns proposed for interconnecting medical devices in Timed Rebeca modeling language and then

---

[2] The Rebeca models and the Java code for the reduction of semantic models are available at fghassemi.adhoc.ir/shared/MedicalCodes.zip.

analyzed the configuration of their parameters separately by Afra tool using the model checking technique. Since modeling many devices using several patterns resulted in state-space explosion, we proposed a reduction technique by extending FTTS merging technique with regard to the local QoS properties. We inspected a medical system which used three devices and one app communicating by two patterns and we applied our reduction technique on this system. We used inheritance concept in Rebeca for modeling this system in order to have a common communication substrate between patterns. Our results show that there are possible reductions regarding the behavior of message handlers.

Elaborating our approach on more case studies or non-trivial orchestration patterns of communication [9] are among of our future work. We aim to generalize this approach by automatically deriving constraints on state variables like the one for *lastPub* or message contents to relax shift-equivalence relation in other domains. To this aim, we can use the techniques of static analysis.

Acknowledgment. We would like to thank Ehsan Khamespanh for his kind supports in resolving the problems in using Afra tool. The research of the third author is partially supported by the KKS Synergy project, SACSys, the SSF project Serendipity, and the KKS Profile project DPAC.

References

1. Agha, G.: ACTORS - A Model of Concurrent Computation in Distributed Systems. MIT Press, Cambridge (1990)
2. Hatcliff, J., et al.: Rationale and architecture principles for medical application platforms. In: Proceedings of the IEEE/ACM Third International Conference on Cyber-Physical Systems, pp. 3–12. IEEE Computer Society (2012)
3. Hewitt, C.: Viewing control structures as patterns of passing messages. Artif. Intell. **8**(3), 323–364 (1977)
4. ASTM International: ASTM F2761 - medical devices and medical systems - essential safety requirements for equipment comprising the patient-centric integrated clinical environment (ICE) (2009)
5. Jaghoori, M., Sirjani, M., Mousavi, M.R., Khamespanah, E., Movaghar, A.: Symmetry and partial order reduction techniques in model checking rebeca. Acta Informatica **47**(1), 33–66 (2010). https://doi.org/10.1007/s00236-009-0111-x
6. Khamespanah, E., Sirjani, M., Sabahi-Kaviani, Z., Khosravi, R., Izadi, M.: Timed Rebeca schedulability and deadlock freedom analysis using bounded floating time transition system. Sci. Comput. Program. **98**, 184–204 (2015)
7. Khamespanah, E., Sirjani, M., Viswanathan, M., Khosravi, R.: Floating time transition system: more efficient analysis of timed actors. In: Braga, C., Ölveczky, P.C. (eds.) FACS 2015. LNCS, vol. 9539, pp. 237–255. Springer, Cham (2016). https://doi.org/10.1007/978-3-319-28934-2_13
8. Pfeiffer, O., Ayre, A., Keydel, C.: Embedded Networking with CAN and CANopen, 1st edn. Copperhill Media Corporation, Greenfield (2008)
9. Ranganath, V., Kim, Y.J., Hatcliff, J., Robby: Communication patterns for interconnecting and composing medical systems (extended version). Technical report, Kansas State University (2016)

10. Reynisson, A., et al.: Modelling and simulation of asynchronous real-time systems using Timed Rebeca. Sci. Comput. Program. **89**, 41–68 (2014)
11. Sirjani, M.: Rebeca: theory, applications, and tools. In: de Boer, F.S., Bonsangue, M.M., Graf, S., de Roever, W.-P. (eds.) FMCO 2006. LNCS, vol. 4709, pp. 102–126. Springer, Heidelberg (2007). https://doi.org/10.1007/978-3-540-74792-5_5
12. Sirjani, M., Jaghoori, M.M.: Ten years of analyzing actors: rebeca experience. In: Agha, G., Danvy, O., Meseguer, J. (eds.) Formal Modeling: Actors, Open Systems, Biological Systems. LNCS, vol. 7000, pp. 20–56. Springer, Heidelberg (2011). https://doi.org/10.1007/978-3-642-24933-4_3
13. Sirjani, M., Khamespanah, E.: On time actors. In: Ábrahám, E., Bonsangue, M., Johnsen, E.B. (eds.) Theory and Practice of Formal Methods. LNCS, vol. 9660, pp. 373–392. Springer, Cham (2016). https://doi.org/10.1007/978-3-319-30734-3_25
14. Sirjani, M., Khamespanah, E., Ghassemi, F.: Reactive actors: isolation for efficient analysis of distributed systems. In: Proceedings of the 23rd IEEE/ACM International Symposium on Distributed Simulation and Real Time Applications, pp. 1–10 (2019)
15. Sirjani, M., Movaghar, A., Shali, A., de Boer, F.S.: Modeling and verification of reactive systems using Rebeca. Fundam. Informaticae **63**(4), 385–410 (2004)
16. Ranganath, V., Robby, Kim, Y., Hatcliff, J., Weininger, S.: Integrated clinical environment device model: stakeholders and high level requirements. In: Proceedings of the Medical Cyber Physical Systems Workshop (2015)
17. Yousefi, F., Khamespanah, E., Gharib, M., Sirjani, M., Movaghar, A.: VeriVANca: an actor-based framework for formal verification of warning message dissemination schemes in VANETs. In: Biondi, F., Given-Wilson, T., Legay, A. (eds.) SPIN 2019. LNCS, vol. 11636, pp. 244–259. Springer, Cham (2019). https://doi.org/10.1007/978-3-030-30923-7_14

Author Index

Printed in the United States
By Bookmasters

Printed in the United States
By Bookmasters